The poetry of Mildmay Fane, second Earl of Westmorland

Mildmay Fane in 1662. Peter Williamson engraving after ?Hendrick Bloemart

THE POETRY OF MILDMAY FANE, SECOND EARL OF WESTMORLAND

from the Fulbeck, Harvard and Westmorland Manuscripts

edited by Tom Cain

Manchester University Press
Manchester and New York

distributed exclusively in the USA by Palgrave

Copyright © P. G. Maxwell-Stuart 2000

The right of P. G. Maxwell-Stuart to be identified as the editor of this work has been asserted by him in accordance with the Copyright, Designs and Patents Act 1988.

Published by Manchester University Press
Oxford Road, Manchester M13 9NR, UK
and Room 400, 175 Fifth Avenue, New York, NY 10010, USA
www.manchesteruniversitypress.co.uk

Distributed exclusively in the USA by
Palgrave, 175 Fifth Avenue, New York NY 10010, USA

Distributed exclusively in Canada by
UBC Press, University of British Columbia, 2029 West Mall, Vancouver, BC, Canada V6T 1Z2

British Library Cataloguing-in-Publication Data
A catalogue record for this book is available from the British Library

Library of Congress Cataloging-in-Publication Data
A catalog record for this book is available from the Library of Congress

ISBN 13: 978 0 7190 8065 4

First published in hardback 2000 by Manchester University Press

This paperback edition first published 2009

Printed by Lightning Source

In memory of Mary Fane

CONTENTS

List of plates	*page* viii
Acknowledgements	ix
Abbreviations	x
Introduction	1
Provenance and descriptions	27
Editorial conventions	32
Vita Authoris	37
FULBECK HALL MS 1. POEMS, 1621–35	57
PUBLIC RECORD OFFICE: S.P. 16: 437.60	67
FULBECK HALL MS 2. POEMS, 1623–50	69
MS WESTMORLAND (A) 6.VI.1. POEMS, 1643–51	195
HOUGHTON LIBRARY, HARVARD: FMS ENG. 645. POEMS, 1637–61	205
FULBECK HALL MS 3. POEMS, 1649–65	297
MS WESTMORLAND (A) 6.VI.3/26	357
YALE CENTER FOR BRITISH ART: SAXTON'S ATLAS	361
Appendix 1 *A doubtful poem and summary list of English poems by other authors*	363
Appendix 2 *Calendar of Latin, French and Italian poems and prose*	367
Notes to the poems	377
Textual commentary	449
Index of titles and first lines	455

LIST OF PLATES

Mildmay Fane in 1662. Peter Williamson engraving after ?Hendrick Bloemart. (By Courtesy of the National Portrait Gallery, London)   *frontispiece*

1 Fulbeck Hall MS 1, f. 49r: *An Invitation to R.H.*	*page* 4
2 Fulbeck Hall MS 1, f. 58r: *She is sick*	5
3 Fulbeck Hall MS 2, p. 18: *Emblemata*	6
4 Fulbeck Hall MS 2, p. 38: *Cloris Complaint*	7
5 Fulbeck Hall MS 2, p. 124: illustrated acrostics	8
6 Fulbeck Hall MS 3, p. 92: *Post Tenebras Lux*	9

ACKNOWLEDGEMENTS

The discovery of a large body of manuscript poetry such as Fane's is a rare experience, the excitement and interest of which have carried me through most of the longeurs of editing and annotating over the past few years. I first realised that Fane had written more poetry than was then known while I was studying Herrick's circle of friends and patrons, but it is Simon Houfe whom I must thank for first alerting me to some manuscripts belonging to a branch of the Fane family at Fulbeck Hall, Lincolnshire, manuscripts which turned out to contain the main body of Fane's unpublished poetry. It is a great sadness that their owner, Mary Fane, died only a short time before this edition was published: her attitude of bemused wonder that anybody would want to read her ancestor's verse was I think at least partly affected. I owe her a geat debt of gratitude for her hospitality at Fulbeck over the years, and for her generosity in lending me the manuscripts for a considerable time. I must also thank and remember here Jeremy Maule, who was originally to have published this edition, and whose sudden and equally untimely death was an enormous loss to the study of Renaissance and early modern literature. My thanks also go to Manchester University Press for taking on the project so enthusiastically when Jeremy died. More formally, I must acknowledge permission from Mrs Mary Fane Fry, the Houghton Library, Harvard University, the Yale Center for British Art, Northamptonshire County Record Office, and the Earl of Westmorland Apethorpe Settlement, to publish poems from the manuscripts in their collections. Newcastle University's Research Committee aided the project with grants towards travel. Amongst the many others whom I would like to thank for their help in various ways over the years, my greatest obligations are due to Tom Wayman, Claire Chambers, James Reeson, Jeremy Paterson, Kelsey Thornton, Dennis Flynn, Lucy Ambrose, Gavin Hardy, Martin Wheeler, Jonathan Powell, Elisabeth Fairman and Warren Chernaik. Many others, though, have helped with isolated pieces of advice or information: although I have always welcomed their help and usually taken their advice, any errors (and there are probably many) are my responsibility. Finally, I would like to thank my children, Camilla, Miriam and Tom, and most of all my wife Lynn, who, despite considerable provocation from Mildmay Fane over many years, has been lovingly supportive throughout.

T.C.
Newcastle-upon-Tyne

ABBREVIATIONS

Fane manuscripts

F1   Fulbeck Hall MS 1. Poems, 1621–35.
F2   Fulbeck Hall MS 2. Poems, 1623–50.
F3   Fulbeck Hall MS 3. Poems, 1649–65.
H   Houghton Library, Harvard: fMS Eng 645. Poems, 1637–61.
N   Northamptonshire Record Office: MS Westmorland (A) 6.vi.1. Poems and prose, 1643–51.

The other Westmorland papers in Northamptonshire Record Office (NRO) are abbreviated as W(A) followed by number, and Fane's letters to Lord Brudenell in the NRO Brudenell papers as 'Brudenell I. x.' followed by their individual number.

Other abbreviations

Place of publication is London unless stated otherwise. References to Shakespeare are to the *Riverside* edition, ed. G. Blakemore Evans *et al.* (Boston MA, 1974); titles of Shakespeare's plays are abbreviated as in Onions, *Shakespeare Glossary*, p. x. Biblical quotations are from the King James Bible, Latin from the Loeb Classical Library, unless otherwise stated.

à Kempis   Thomas à Kempis, *Of the Imitation of Christ and The Valley of Lillies* (People's Library edn, 1956).
Aubrey   John Aubrey, *'Brief Lives,' chiefly of Contemporaries*, ed. Andrew Clark (Oxford, 1898).
Baker   Anne Elizabeth Baker, *Glossary of Northamptonshire Words and Phrases* (1854).
Barron   Oswald Barron, *Northamptonshire Families* (1906).
Bradbrook   M. C. Bradbrook, 'Marvell and the Poetry of Rural Solitude', *Review of English Studies* 17 (1941), 37–46.
Brand   John Brand, *Observations on Popular Antiquities*, ed. Sir Henry Ellis (1841).
Briquet   C.-M. Briquet, *Les filigranes: dictionnaire historique des marques du papier dès leur apparition vers 1282 jusqu'en 1600*, ed. Allan Stevenson (Amsterdam, 1968).
Browne, *Works*   *The Works of Sir Thomas Browne*, ed. Geoffrey Keynes (1964).
Cain, 'A sad Intestine warr'   Tom Cain, '"A sad Intestine warr": Mildmay Fane and the Poetry of Civil Strife', in *The English Civil Wars in the Literary Imagination* ed. Claude J. Summers and Ted-Larry Pebworth (Columbia MO, 1999), pp. 27–51.
Cain, *Christmas Carol*   Tom Cain, 'Herrick's "Christmas Carol": A New Poem and its Implications for Patronage', *ELR* 29 (1999), 131–53.
Cain, 'Robert Herrick'   Tom Cain, 'Robert Herrick, Mildmay Fane and Sir Simeon Stewart', *ELR* 15 (1985), 312–17.
Calamy   Edmund Calamy, *An Abridgement of Mr. Baxter's History of his Life and Times. With an Account of many others of those Worthy Ministers who were Ejected, after the Restauration of King Charles the Second* (1702).
Catalogue   'A Catalogue of the Books of Apthorpe Liberary', British Library Add. MS 34,220, ff. 25v–24r (*c.* 1690).
CCAM   *Calendar of the Proceedings of the Committee for Advance of Money, 1642–56*, ed. M. A. E. Green (1888).
CCC   *Calendar of the Proceedings of the Committee for Compounding &c., 1643–60*, ed. M. A. E. Green (1889).
Clarendon, *History*   Edward [Hyde], Earl of Clarendon, *The History of the Rebellion and the Civil Wars in England*, ed. W. Dunn Macray (Oxford, 1888).

Chamberlain, *Letters*   The Letters of John Chamberlain, ed. Norman Egbert McClure (Philadelphia PA, 1939).
Cleveland, *Poems*   The Poems of John Cleveland, ed. Brian Morris and Eleanor Withington (Oxford, 1967).
Commons' Journals   The Journals of the House of Commons (1803).
Cotgrave   Randle Cotgrave, *A Dictionarie of the French and English Tongues* (1611).
Country Houses   John Heward and Robert Taylor, *The Country Houses of Northamptonshire* (RCHME, Swindon, 1996).
Cowley, *Works*   The Works of Mr. Abraham Cowley, ed. A. R. Waller (Cambridge, 1905–06).
Croft-Murray   Edward Croft-Murray, *Decorative Painting in England* (1962).
CSPD   Calendar of State Papers, Domestic Series.
Crum, *Index*   Margaret Crum, *First-Line Index of English Poetry 1500–1800 in the Manuscripts of the Bodleian Library Oxford* (Oxford, 1969).
Denham, *Works*   The Poetical Works of Sir John Denham, ed. T. H. Banks (New Haven CT, 1928).
D'Ewes   *The Autobiography and Correspondence of Sir Simonds D'Ewes, Bart.*, ed. J. O. Halliwell (1845).
DNB   Dictionary of National Biography, ed. Leslie Stephen and Sidney Lee (1908–09).
Donne   *The Oxford Authors: John Donne*, ed. John Carey (Oxford, 1990).
Evelyn   *The Diary of John Evelyn*, ed. E. S. De Beer (Oxford, 1955).
Everitt   Alan Everitt, *The Community of Kent and the Great Rebellion 1640–60* (Leicester, 1966).
Fowler   Alastair Fowler, *The Country House Poem: A Cabinet of Seventeenth-Century Estate Poems and Related Items* (Edinburgh, 1994).
Friedman   Donald M. Friedman, *Marvell's Pastoral Art* (1970).
Fuller, *Worthies*   Thomas Fuller, *The History of the Worthies of England* (1662), ed. John Nichols (1811).
Hasted   Edward Hasted, *The History and Topographical Survey of the County of Kent* (Wakefield, 1972, reprint of 1797–1801 ed.).
Heawood   Edward Heawood, *Watermarks mainly of the 17th and 18th Centuries* (Hilversum, 1950).
Herbert, *Works*   The Works of George Herbert, ed. F. E. Hutchinson (Oxford, 1941).
Herrick   *The Poetical Works of Robert Herrick*, ed. L. C. Martin (Oxford, 1956).
HMC   Royal Commission on Historical Manuscripts.
Hollar   Richard T. Godfrey, *Wenceslaus Hollar: A Bohemian Artist in England* (New Haven CT, 1994).
Hore   J. P. Hore, *The History of Newmarket and the Annals of the Turf* (1886).
Hutchins, *Dorset*   John Hutchins, *The History and Antiquities of the County of Dorset*, third edn, ed. W. Shipp and J. W. Hodson (1861–74).
Jonson, *Poems   Ben Jonson: The Complete Poems*, ed. George Parfitt (Harmondsworth, 1975).
King, *Poems*   The Poems of Henry King, ed. Margaret Crum (Oxford, 1965).
Leech   *Mildmay Fane's Raguaillo D'Oceano 1640 and Candy Restored 1641*, ed. Clifford Leech (Louvain, 1938).
Leishman   J. B. Leishman, *The Art of Marvell's Poetry* (1966).
Loxley   James Loxley, *Royalism and Poetry in the English Civil Wars* (1997).
Lords' Journals   Journals of the House of Lords (1846).
Marvell   *The Oxford Authors: Andrew Marvell*, ed. Frank Kermode and Keith Walker (Oxford, 1990).
Masson   David Masson, *The Life of John Milton: Narrated in Connexion with the Political, Ecclesiastical, and Literary History of his Time* (1881–96).
Matthews, *Walker*   A. G. Matthews, *Walker Revised: being a Revision of John Walker's 'Sufferings of the Clergy during the Grand Rebellion 1642–60'* (Oxford, 1948).
Minsheu   John Minsheu, *Ductor in Linguas: The Guide into Tongues* (1617).
Morton   Gerald W. Morton, *A Biography of Mildmay Fane, Second Earl of Westmorland 1601–66: The Unknown Cavalier* (Lewiston/Queenston/Lampeter, 1991).
Norbrook   David Norbrook, *Writing the English Republic: Poetry, Rhetoric and Politics, 1627–60* (Cambridge, 1999).
OED   *The Oxford English Dictionary: Second Edition on Compact Disc* (Oxford, 1994).

OS   *Otia Sacra (1648), by Mildmay Fane, Second Earl of Westmorland*, Facsimile Reproduction with an Introduction by Donald M. Friedman (New York, 1975).
Partridge   Eric Partridge, *A Dictionary of Slang and Unconventional English* (5th edn, 1961).
Peerage   G. E. C., *The Complete Peerage of England Scotland Ireland Great Britain and the United Kingdom Extant Extinct or Dormant*, new edition revised, ed. Hon. Vicary Gibbs *et al.* (1910–59).
Pepys   *The Diary of Samuel Pepys*, ed. Robert Latham and William Matthews (1970).
Røstvig   Maren-Sofie Røstvig, *The Happy Man* (Oslo, 1954).
Rushworth   John Rushworth, *Historical Collections of Private Passages of State* (1659–91).
Schama   Simon Schama, *The Embarrassment of Riches: An Interpretation of Dutch Culture in the Golden Age* (1987).
Smith   Nigel Smith, *Literature and Revolution in England 1640–60* (New Haven CT and London, 1994).
Sotheby's, 1887   *Catalogue of a Portion of the Valuable Library of Rare Books and Important Manuscripts of a Nobleman.* Sotheby's sale catalogue, 13–15 July 1887. The annotated catalogue is in the British Library, SCS 934.
Stone, *Crisis*   Lawrence Stone, *The Crisis of the Aristocracy 1558–1641* (Oxford, 1965).
Survey   *The Survey of London* (1900–).
Thorn-Drury, *A Little Ark*   G. Thorn-Drury, *A Little Ark Containing Seventeenth-Century Verse* (1921).
Tilley   Morris Palmer Tilley, *A Dictionary of the Proverbs in England in the Sixteenth and Seventeenth Centuries* (Ann Arbor MI, 1950).
Turner   James Turner, *The Politics of Landscape: Rural Scenery and Society in English Poetry 1630–60* (Cambridge MA, 1979)
Venn   John Venn and J. A. Venn, *Alumni Cantabrigienses* (Cambridge, 1922).
Vilvain, *Enchiridion*   Robert Vilvain, *Enchiridion Epigrammatum Latino-Anglicum* (1654).
Waller, *Poems*   *The Poems of Edmund Waller*, ed. G. Thorn-Drury (1893).
Withington, 'Fugitive Poetry'   Eleanor Withington, 'The "Fugitive Poetry" of Mildmay Fane', *Harvard Library Bulletin* 9 (1955), 61–78
Withington, 'Political Satire'   Eleanor Withington, 'Mildmay Fane's Political Satire', *Harvard Library Bulletin* 11 (1957), 40–64.

INTRODUCTION

The discovery of a substantial body of hitherto unknown poetry by an early modern writer is an event whose resonances reach beyond the range of specialist scholarship, modifying our received picture of an earlier and pivotal century, changing, however slightly, the contours of the cultural and political map which we have inherited from the 1600s. The discovery in 1903 of Traherne's unpublished poetry is the nearest analogy to the publication, a century later, of this edition of the 500 or so English poems left in manuscript by Mildmay Fane, second Earl of Westmorland. Though Fane's is a less original voice than Traherne's, the importance of his manuscript poetry is that it presents a largely 'new' writer who was forced to confront one of the most climactic and influential sequences of events in early modern European history: the personal rule, the Great Rebellion of the 1640s, the execution of the King, the establishment of a republic and, with its failure, the restoration of the monarchy. Any new voice seeking to come to terms with these events as they unfolded would be of interest: that of a man who had so high a stake in the world that was turned upside down and back again, for whom the King had stood as godfather to his eldest son, and whose brother-in-law commanded the revolutionary army, is especially compelling.

Fane's is not a wholly new voice: he is already known to a very specialist scholarly audience as a minor poet, dramatist and patron, studied, if at all, for his possible influence on Marvell or his patronage of Herrick. One of his unheralded distinctions is that he was the first English peer to publish his own poetry, in *Otia Sacra* (1648).[1] That, however, contained only 137 English poems, compared with just over 500 in this edition. It was, moreover, published at a date and in circumstances which enforced circumspection: primarily devotional, its piety and restraint make his voice seem more etiolated, and less varied, than do these manuscripts. That Fane had written more poetry than was contained in *Otia Sacra*, together with plays and entertainments, had been known since the HMC report on the Earl of Westmorland's manuscripts in 1885. That report, however, described only one of the five manuscript volumes of Fane's poetry then at Apethorpe, a 'Volume entitled "Fugitive Poetry"'.[2] Soon after, most of the Apethorpe papers and books were dispersed in two major sales of the Westmorland library (see p. 27). Most of Fane's plays were bought by the British Museum, but while the book of 'Fugitive Poetry' found its way eventually to Harvard, the other four collections of his poetry disappeared from scholarly view for almost a century. Three of them, it transpires, were bought at the sales of the Westmorland library, along with a number of books which had also belonged to the second Earl, by a member of the Fane family, William Dashwood Fane. Since then they have been at his home, Fulbeck Hall, Lincolnshire, which had once been the home of Mildmay Fane's brother Francis, and which is, appropriately enough, the subject of a graceful country house poem in one of the manuscripts (p. 333). The fifth manuscript book, begun while Fane was under house arrest in the 1640s, was found among the unsold Westmorland papers that were deposited at Northamptonshire Record Office in the 1950s. As well as the English poems printed here, these five manuscript books contain over 370 Latin poems and acrostics, and a small amount of prose. All but a tiny handful of this material is by Fane himself, and all of it except for part of the Harvard manuscript was transcribed by him. There must have been at least one more such manuscript book, since forty-two of the English poems in *Otia Sacra* are not found in any of the five surviving books,[3] but it now seems unlikely that any more substantial collections of Fane's poetry will be found.

As the sheer number of his poems shows, poetry was a serious occupation for Fane. Thirty years after his death an anonymous family servant, trying to persuade his grandson, the fifth Earl, that he should devote time to his inheritance, wrote that 'Ld Milemey was a scoler & a good naturd man but to much gon away with divershons' (W(A) Misc. 15, f. 149v, 'Some Observashon of this familey & Estate. 1695'). In 1654 his nephew Francis (himself a playwright) had sent him an elaborately illustrated Italian manuscript treatise on the bridling of horses, with a Latin poem warning against spending too much time in his library:

> So when, learned Earl, seduced by love of the Muses,
> You wear a cheek more pale than your pages
> This book may warn you to control your steeds,
> Or in some other way rein in your studies.[4]

Clearly his family at least saw his intellectual life as something unusual. Although such characterisations of the 'doctus Comes' can be taken too seriously, a total output of around 900 poems in English and Latin, plus eight surviving plays and entertainments, does bear witness to considerable commitment, even if when spread over a writing life of more than forty years it need not represent an obsession that comes before all else. Despite his output, and despite the radical gesture of publishing *Otia Sacra*, Fane does not seem to have been greatly interested in establishing his name as a poet. Indeed, his poetry outside *Otia Sacra* (and perhaps much of that within it) seems little concerned with any audience wider than a small circle of family and friends. Only two of his poems have been found in a manuscript collection other than his own: one, *Upon the Scotch Sermon* (p. 68), was sent to Secretary Windebanke with a view to the King reading it, the other is a short Latin poem sent to a friend.[5] As a young man of seventeen Fane contributed three short Latin poems to the *Lacrymæ Cantabrigienses* on the death of Anne of Denmark, and in 1649 his poem *Upon the death of the most hopeful young Lord, The Lord Hastings: A Remembrance from a Kinsman* (cf. p. 203) led the elegies on Hastings in *Lacrymæ Musarum*,[6] but he did not otherwise look for public recognition as a poet, and when in 1646 Thomas Philpott dedicated his own *Poems* to Fane, it was because he was 'knowne to be the publike Assertor of Letters' (sig. A2r) rather than because he was a fellow poet, a fact of which Philpott seems to have been unaware.

Such considerations reinforce the argument that the decision to publish *Otia Sacra* in 1648 was a political one, the radical break with social convention being a way of justifying *otium* and patience as an honourable response, and even as a form of resistance.[7] That publication was encouraged by a much greater poet than Philpott, Robert Herrick, whose own collection, *Hesperides*, came out in the same year. Herrick, who had been on friendly terms with Fane since the 1620s, clearly knew the latter's poetry well: indeed, he had been the recipient of two poems from him in the 1620s, and another in the 1640s (see pp. 58, 61, 202). Herrick's *To the right Honourable Mildmay, Earle of Westmorland* (172.3)[8] addresses Fane with admiration as

> a Lord, an earle, nay more, a Man,
> Who writes sweet Numbers well as any can:
> If so, why then are not These Verses hurld,
> Like *Sybels* Leaves, throughout the ample world?

This poem is undated: it may be that Herrick was biased in the sense that he received financial support from Fane in the years between 1647 and 1660, when he was deprived of his living, but the poem is nevertheless revealing in its characterisation of Fane as primarily a 'Man, Who writes'. Similarly strong endorsement of Fane the poet came from John Cleveland, whose letter in reply to Fane's poem of strong admiration (p. 256) told him he was 'the Favourite of the Muses. Your Strain is so happy and hath the Reputation for so Matchless, as if you had a double Key to the Temple of Honour.'[9] Fane himself is engagingly modest about his poetry: sending some poems to Cleveland in response to this letter, he refuses, in *To Him again in return for a letter he wrot upon the former* (p. 256–7), to believe this fulsome praise. His response is

> Not like the bird whose bewteous train
> Being praisd is more displayd again
> Nor of the Academick witt
> Is raysd by Humms to cherish it.   (ll. 1–4)

Similarly, in *My Dedicatory at the end of Beaumont and fletchers playes now sett out 1646* (p. 240), he insists on the appropriateness of his inscribing his poem at the back of his copy of the folio:

> For my poore vaine which never could produce
> Of that Inspireing fountaines Nectar Juce
> Nor yet entitle to that power or skill
> To Crop a spell branch from parnassus hill
> Is far to meane, unless some Reader lookes
> Upon this as the Carrier of their bookes
> After them not in Print but wrot with quill
> And soe the last Page may not deem them ill.   (ll. 13–20)

Most twentieth-century critics would have agreed with this self-evaluation. Fane's published poetry has usually been dismissed as pedestrian at best: Bradbrook's 'Fane cannot be said to be a good poet' (p. 41) belongs to a realm of robust but typical value judgements whose confident simplicity few would now endorse (cf. Røstvig's equally crude 'little distinctive esthetic merit', p. 207), but it is true that there is an earnest flatness about much of *Otia Sacra*. In the manuscripts Fane is a more uneven poet, but even at his most apparently banal he is nearly always interesting because of the context in which he is writing, and the immediacy with which he reflects that context. Because of his modesty, his poetry is largely occasional, arising in one way or another like a journal out of his immediate experience. Even his religious poetry is, in its holograph form, often tied to a specific date or occasion: Christmas, Easter, a sermon, a birthday, a morning in Newcastle on the way to war against the Scots (p. 144). Despite his strong Presbyterian background and the dynastic, political alliances it brought, he does not attempt the kind of ambitious 'Heroick Poem', philosophical or historical, that might have been expected, and which his Cambridge and Lincoln's Inn contemporary Edward Benlowes did try, with mixed results, in *Theophila*.[10] Nor does he feel the need to universalise his experience, except in so far as he tries to understand it, where appropriate, in terms of Christian or classical history. Given the intrinsic interest for the modern reader of much of his experience, it is as well that he was thus modest in terms of both subject and audience. The fact that he was writing sometimes for himself alone, sometimes for a single other reader, at most for a small coterie, does, however, present problems: he feels no need to help the reader by providing punctuation (though his printer did in *Otia Sacra*), and he is allusive in the usual early modern way not just to classical and biblical discourse but to contemporary people, places and events that are now difficult, sometimes impossible, to recover. This means that the poems have had to be more heavily annotated than most such editions of seventeenth-century writers. Such copious allusion, however, has strong compensating factors. Whatever the quality of the poetry, it almost always takes the modern reader further into the *mentalité* of the mid-seventeenth century, into contact with the contingent detail of everyday experience, than does that of more ambitious writers. And this is so even though the everyday experience is scarcely that of a typical member of society: it is the everyday experience of an earl, the meditations and celebrations of a man who owned huge tracts of land in seven counties, had a household at Apethorpe alone of fifty-nine or more servants and attendants (there were two other major houses, at Mereworth, Kent, and St Bartholomew's, London) and whose annual income of £6,000–£7,000 compared favourably with the £30 he paid his chaplains or steward, let alone the £3–£5 a year paid to more middling servants. Perhaps because he was 'a scoler & a good naturd man', perhaps because his religion convinced him of his smallness in the sight of God, relatively little of this grandeur is made obvious in the poetry, so that as we see him experiencing travel, courtship, friendship, the births and illnesses of children, the deaths of friends, a visit to a brothel, his *persona* seems less remote than might be expected. This remains true even when the subject matter—imprisonment in the Tower, sequestration of estates, displeasure at the expense caused by a visit from Buckingham and his wife—is clearly a function of his status. The voice might often be that of a middling country gentleman, not a senior peer, and only occasionally does this become an obvious affectation, as when in *Dum Spiro Spero*, a poem written on his birthday (and therefore explicitly autobiographical), Apethorpe Hall, one of the great Jacobean houses, becomes a 'Lowly Cell' (p. 339).

Much of the contingent detail that makes the poems live is added straightforwardly by Fane in the titles, or in notes which themselves form part of the poem. Such particularity makes the poems more immediate, and also underlines the way all such poetry, not just that dealing with obviously public events, is embedded in the social and cultural matrix which shaped it: there is, for example, a considerable difference in the reader's response to a poem printed in *Otia Sacra* as *Upon the birth of a child*, and the same poem in *F2* under the title *Upon the Berth of my Sonn Henry the 13th of August at 11 a clock at night—1646*. The universalising title in *Otia Sacra*, intended to make the experience more available, in fact does the opposite. The specificity of the manuscript title is rare in published early modern poetry, but frequent in these poems. Where it is not supplied as part of the poem's title or marginalia, the circumstances of a poem's composition, or the probable addressee, can often be deduced from other sources, in particular from Fane's monthly accounts, which survive for the years from 1644 until the entry for his 'last account' made by his steward in 1666: 'Mildmay Earle of Westmorland died the 12th of feb: 1665 [1666] at 8 in the Morning' (W(A) Misc. 15, f. 107r). Though they are far from being a diary, the accounts provide information on where Fane was and with whom he was in contact at any given time, information of a kind that is rare if not unique for a seventeenth-century English poet. We can, for instance, tell that *My Cuntry Audit* (p. 171), dated here '*April. 25. 1647*', a poem that clearly owes much to Herbert's *Redemption* in its use of tenant–landlord imagery, must have been written not at Apethorpe or Mereworth, his main estates, but in Wiltshire, where he owned land at Lacock. On 22 April 1647 he recorded: 'Taken with me into Wiltshire . . . 50.0.0' (W(A) Misc. 7, f. 46r). The accounts do not record meetings with tenants, but the main purpose of the visit would have been to check on the management of his land in the area, most of it let to tenant farmers. It is probable that that spring following the end of the first Civil War was Fane's first chance for several years to make such a journey. There had been much fighting in the area in 1643, when Waller's Parliamentary army was almost completely destroyed in the bloody battle of Roundway Down, only five miles from Lacock. Farms would have been heavily plundered, and crops destroyed (the battle took place in July). It is not too fanciful to conjecture a link, conscious or not, between Fane's own exercise of the role of landlord in the difficult circumstances following the war, his memories of Herbert's poem and the reflections of ll. 9–16:

> Thus like that Tenant who behind-hand cast
> Intreats soe ofte forbearance til at last

1 Fulbeck Hall MS 1, f. 49r: *An Invitation to R.H.*

                    She is sick   1625
Well you wound, & sick you kill
                wch ill
Attends those who you adore
        & more
For ye first's a languishing
          dying
And ye second thought by death
            Leaues breath
To bemone ones desperate
          estate
Leaue to be ye other th'one
          is none
Wound me not in health of vowes
          to you
Your afflictions meaner shall
          my fall
Ingender, but I shall smile
        ye while
You weepe, when you laugh I'le morne
          in scorne
Of yr contempts, & for end
     yr   r
To yt self shall please y frend.

2 Fulbeck Hall MS 1, f. 58r: *She is sick*

18

In Pueros Bethlehemiticos quos Herodes morte trucidari fecit. Mat. 2. 16.

Innocuos Necuet, Faces dum incesta minatur
Infanda Infantum Laurea Pæna dabat.

In obit. Amicissimi Thō. Rii. filii Georgii Cancell.

Tramite nil metuat recta qui incedere vellet
Capreolus, casus dura rupis habet.

Ad Gallicantum.

Fur mea nocturnos pellat vigilantia somnos
Nuntius Auroræ immemori Gallus adest.

3 Fulbeck Hall MS 2, p. 18: *Emblemata*

Cloris Complaint — July 25. 1644.

Doe not ye Planets (how-som ere
They wander) stil retain a proper Sphere?
And Seasons serue ye Year to bless?
Although ye stormes & tempests are noe less?
Are not becalmed Seas more faier
Than if th'^d had neuer been irregular
And shall fond Man alone be sard
To be of all thinges else unpacefied.
  Lions to Lions kinde, & Bears
Frendly to such, soe wolues partake o'th' fears
  With their pursued kin, ye fell
Eft Tyger can wth his Asotiats dwell
  And yet (as if un-humand) we
By noe means wth each other can agree
  Soe (if wee may Degenerate
From Natures mandate) all our passion's state
All And w^here a Mischief may befall
  Dispositians turn'd to prodigall
  Nor is ther for Compassion
Left any room (now 'tis out of fashion).

  Befrend me wind, tide tyre ye waue
Though some ther be must sink, yet some 3 may saue
  My Calendar yet markes out Spring
Disgust may shake, not blast ye Blossoming
  And therfore though t'row'd astray
Tis reconciling truth points now ye way
  In wch I would be thought as farr
From variation as y^e Fixed'st Starr
  But wth a Constant Shining thence
Serue King & Cuntry by my Influence.

Translat.

Wth looks he gets whoere prefers
The Gentle kiss of his sweetest . . .

4 Fulbeck Hall MS 2, p. 38: *Cloris Complaint*

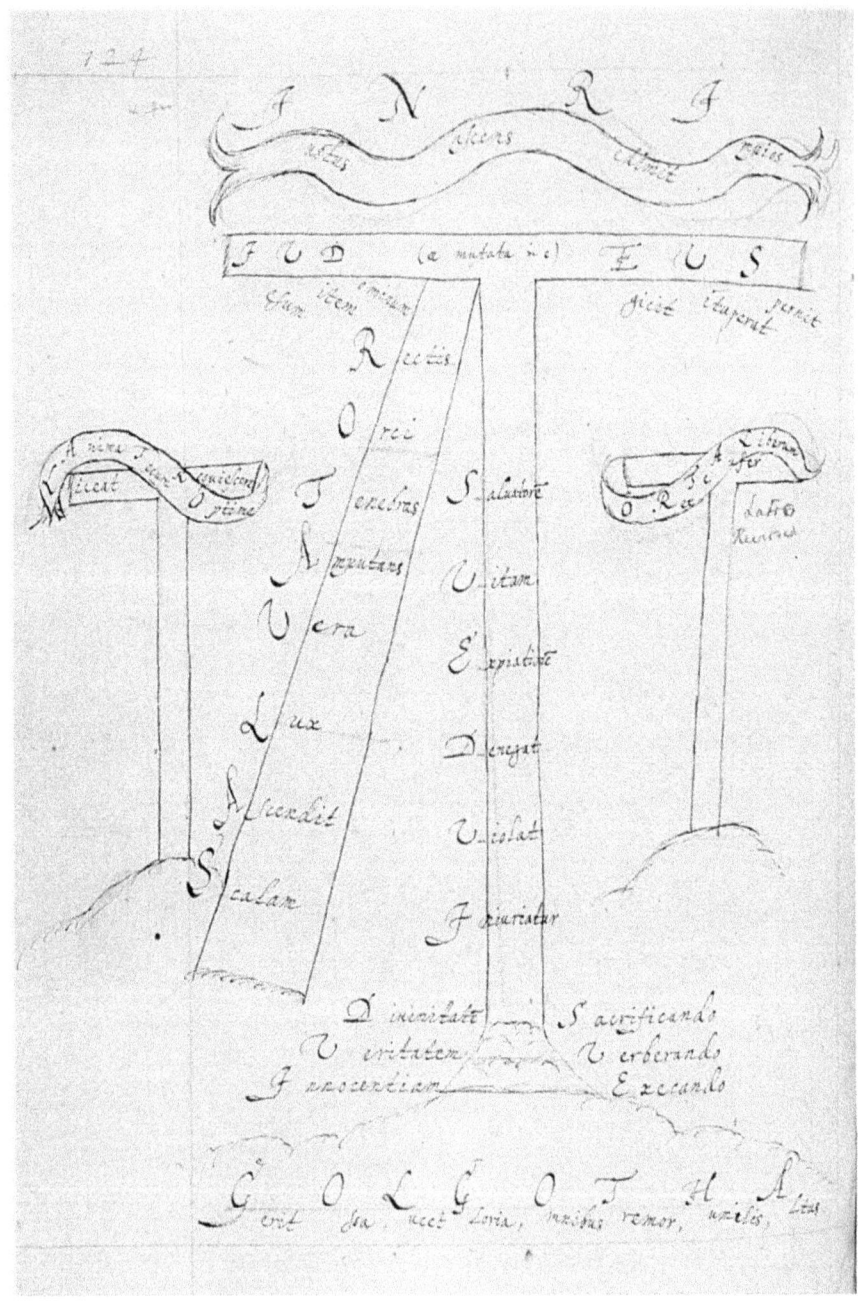

5 Fulbeck Hall MS 2, p. 124: illustrated acrostics

Post Tenebras Lux:
Apres La Pluïe Le Beau Temps:
After a Darke & Dismall night
The Sun arising in his Might
So Dissipates Those Clouds of Tears
     For His Decease
As Clarefies again our Spheres
     wth hopes of Peace
After a sad Intestine warr
Restoring His Succeeding Star

It was no slight Dew or small Raine
Showrd for ye Loss of Soueraign
But a whol Cataract to destroy
     At once our Joy
And sinke our Darkes, til now at last
     The Tempest past
We may enioy again faier weather
When Clouds pack all away together   *Knaues

Scenes haue their Changes, Moon Her Wayne
Those Vary, She fills vp again
So after Suffring Darknes, light
     Appeers more bright
And now our Charles from's Wayne doth rise
     He far out vies
All other Orbs changing this Land
From Egipt to a Canaan

His Presence, & His Peoples Loue
Those Black Nights & These Storms remoue
We stud winkt had so long lien Vnder
     That Calm & Cleer
A work wrought by ye God of wonder
     All might appeer
At His returne whose faier Aspect may guide
To Each His due t' Himself Prerogatiue.

6 Fulbeck Hall MS 3, p. 92: *Post Tenebras Lux*

> The summ surmounts his hopes and then noe more
> Expects but mercy to strike ofe the skoar
> Soe heer Me thinkes I see the Land Lords Grace
> Full of Compassion to my drooping Case
> Bidding me be of Comfort and not greevd
> My Rent His Sonn should pay if I beleevd

Sometimes the accounts give essential contextualising information of a more immediate kind: thus a poem addressed to *To Fran[k] Coortup* (p. 235) which refers to Cæsar's exploits at Alexandria as described in Lucan's *Pharsalia*, but mixes them cryptically with references to hunting, can be fully understood only through an entry in December 1646 which reads: 'To Cap Coortops man brought me Cesar a hound & Bewty a beagle 0-5-0.' Without this information the poem would be largely unintelligible, confirming that it was indeed written simply for Courthope (who knew the key) rather than with any other audience in view.[11] *Pharsalia* was much in vogue at the time as an epic which showed how one might deal with civil war: Courthope, a 'Captain' whose energies were now confined to hunting, would have been in a good position to note the ironies inherent in invoking Lucan just three months after the end of the first Civil War with reference to the hunting field, not the field of battle,

Fane can transmute such quotidian detail as the gift or purchase of a hound into such ironically complex poetry partly because he is very self-aware about poetry's role, in particular about the extent to which he is consciously using it as a way of dealing with the massive social and political upheaval around him. Occasionally that self-awareness combines with the passionate nature of his rejection of that disturbed world to produce a poetry of unusual originality and vision. In *Upon the Castle in the Ayer and Bower of Bliss* (p. 268) he challenges both the routine dismissal of castles in the air as escapist whimsies and more explicitly Spenser's puritan view of the Bower of Bliss as a place of disreputable *otium*. By actively welcoming the inner life of fantasy and daydream, Fane and his friends can create a world 'Without a whirlwind of controwle' in which

> harmless merth
> Skearce known on Earth
> Is dealt from evry whiter sowle
> And mutuall Love
> Doth gently move
> Without a whirlwind of controwle (ll. 13–18)

The 'harmless merth' of Fane's Bower of Bliss differentiates it from Spenser's intemperate one. 'Severd by waters from the shore' of civil war, he and his circle can find an honourable *otium* in which they 'Shun Discords Jarr / Soe build their Castles in the ayre':

> Fill me a glass
> Then let it pass
>   Til evry Lip hath done the same
> In silent stelth
> Of frends and helth
>   Performd alike and without name
>
> This done we'l part
> Though not in hart
>   Stil placing hopes above despaier
> And will be well
> And we may dwell
>   In Bowres and Castles in the Ayre (ll. 31–42)

This particular role for poetry was not obvious when Fane began to write in the 1620s, but his earliest poetry is already social, concerned most of all with friendship and courtship. The influence of

Jonson and Herrick is clearest in these early poems, two of which are in fact addressed to Herrick, then in his thirties and already ordained, but apparently living in London. Fane, then Lord le Despenser, is enthusiastically friendly:

> Robin sithence I saw thee last
> I cannot call't a weeke thats past
> But't seems a month, a year, an age
> (*An Invitation to R.H.*, ll. 1–3)

in eandem, probably written in 1633, is worthy of Jonson or Herrick, an urbane, graceful poem made more complex than it seems at first sight by the ambiguities of the woman's 'lightness'. It closes on a tender thigh, which it reaches by way of an equally tender image of near-weightlessness:

> The loosnes of her cariage shines
> As she were caried by the winds
> Her love to one sort makes all those
> Are trod scearce feel her as she goes
> She is soe nimbly stirring that
> Yould think to wear her in your hat
> But soft, sheel sooner let you try
> Your waight upon her tender thygh   (ll. 9–16)

Among these early poems is a group addressed to Fane's future wife, Grace Thornhurst, whom he married on 6 July 1626. Fifteen in all (see note to *In praise of my Fidelia*, p. 92), they constitute a rare, perhaps unique, example of the role played by love poetry in the preparation for a dynastic marriage, giving, rightly or wrongly, the impression of young lovers impatiently awaiting a union delayed by the negotiations of their elders, who are 'sticking' over the dowry. It may be that the poetry itself was, in effect, a ritual part of the proceedings of an arranged marriage, but, if Fane is merely playing the suitor's part expected of him, he effectively disguises the fact, as he does also in his *Vita*: 'Next I endured no small share of the ills which love calls pains, while our parents spun out insupportable delays: for love ill bears with delays. But the wedding completed, the pains disappeared and in the breast of each the warmest happiness shone forth.'

From the same year, 1626, comes the first of many poems in which male friendship and field sports are jointly celebrated. *An ode To N.B. an angler* (p. 59) is one of six poems sent between 1626 and 1648 to Ned Beecher, a minor Bedfordshire gentleman with whom Fane shared a love of fishing. As often in later poems, friendship and what is here called the 'innocent delight / Of Clubbing, morn and night' are as important as the sport itself. Here too is first seen an attractive and idiosyncratic development of his Presbyterian background: if it is mildly surprising to find the angling imagery being used to remind Beecher that he too will be hooked by death, it is still more so to realise that Fane's point is that, when Beecher does face his final audit, fishing and hospitality will both be important factors in the credit column:

> Nor thy affections Cloyster soe
>   By making them forgoe
> That innocent delight
>   Of Clubbing, morn and night
> But let quaint Olives purle thy plate
> When as thou heerst my Lord's at gate
>
> Then let thy sellers treasure opened be
>   For jollety
> Which sending forth rayes like the sun
>   Canary run
> Or the bright flaming Sherries fire
>   The fancy to inspire   (ll. 25–36)

While Puritan stereotypes have been sufficiently questioned recently for dourness and godliness not to be seen as inevitable companions, jollity, canary and 'flaming Sherries fire' still have stronger associations with Toby Belch than with Fane's Mildmay ancestors, or his Vere and Harley relatives. Such images of the country life have their Horatian and Virgilian counterparts, and their Roman ideals of hospitality and wine-fuelled 'jollety' may have been mediated for Fane by Herrick's undated poems combining wine and the country life, but some at least of these—for example, *The Hock-Cart, or Harvest Home To the Right Honourable, Mildmay, Earle of Westmorland*—are probably written later than this poem to Beecher. Certainly Fane's particular celebration of field sports, in which Herrick and Jonson show little or no interest, is recognisably new in the 1620s, and anticipates ways in which twenty years later for him, as for Walton, Cotton, Lovelace and other defeated Royalists, such country pastimes became a political issue.[12]

Although Fane's pastoral and urban landscapes are, like Jonson's or Herrick's, equally English outside the poems of field sports, classical literature and its myths are, as also in Jonson or Herrick, always infiltrating that contemporary world, so that, for instance, the short walk across the Strand from his house in the Savoy to Grace Thornhurst's lodging in Exeter House is like crossing the Hellespont, the relative scale of the two dwellings 'Like Sestos to Abydos' (*The Savoy—Excetter house 1626*, p. 60, ll. 1–3). Contemporary politics also provides him with terms of reference even before the Civil Wars make it a central theme: thus Gustavus Adolphus's winter camp on the Rhine is used to enforce the truth that 'The little winged Captain's all the year / In armes'. It is characteristic of Fane, however, that the analogy here should move from the great modern general back to Hannibal, with Cupid melting the frozen heart just as Hannibal shattered the Alpine rocks with vinegar (*La resverie or Loves Winter Seege*, p. 65, ll. 17–22).

Although he copies many of the poems found in *F1* into *F2*, the latter manuscript signals a change of emotional and intellectual climate with its first English poem, *Brook House Bay trees* (p. 70). A note to another version of the poem records that it was 'Comp[osed during] interm[en]t &c Lon[don] / Decem. 13. 1643'.[13] *F2* was begun before that date, as the differing inks and pens with which he writes his *Vita*, which opens the manuscript, indicate: the first four pages were written between his son Charles's birth in 1635 and his first wife's death in 1636. But the bulk of the poetry in *F2* was composed and transcribed during and after Fane's forced inactivity in the early years of the first Civil War, when, having raised a troop of horse for the King, he was captured at Northampton, just after the battle of Edgehill (October 1642: see below, pp. 43, 53). Imprisonment and house arrest meant that the usual business of life—managing his estates, hunting and fishing, local and national government—was suspended for nearly two years, so that the studies which were later to worry his nephew Francis must have come to fill a larger part of his life, both in terms of time and in terms of their significance, than they had before. Though many poems are undated, it seems likely that, of the 500 English poems in this edition, only about 100 were written in the years before his arrest in 1642, at which time he was forty. Even after the sequestration of his estates was lifted, in September 1644, Fane took no part in public life, even as a JP, until the Restoration. It is likely that poetry celebrating irenic retirement as an honourable role was one product of this part-enforced, part-chosen *otium*, as was poetry that lamented the state of the nation, and satire that attacked those who had brought it about. The activity of writing became a form of *negotium*, the only action available.

Fane began his large new manuscript book with some care: *Brook House Bay trees* is a late addition to a group of fourteen Latin and English *Emblemata*, poems preceded by a drawing on which they comment in some way (Plate 3). Fane is no draughtsman, and the drawings are sometimes unintentionally comic, but such home-made emblems are highly unusual, as are the more ambitious drawings found later in *F2*, in which the text, usually acrostic, becomes part of the emblem (Plate 5). These have something in common with the more abstract woodcuts in the emblem books, but an almost equally close analogy in their mixture of text and pattern is found in Apollinaire's *Calligrammmes* (1925). Were it not for the fact that they are all in Latin, Fane would have a claim to be the first English concrete poet.

The poems in the opening pages of *F2* give a good indication of Fane's range: emblems, Herrickian meditations on time and death, classical *imitatio* and translation, and epigrammatic observations on his fortunes in the Civil War, often tied closely to specific occasions and persons. *To Sir Jhon Wentworth upon his Curioseties and Curteous entertainments at Summerly in Lovingland* (p. 79), the first long poem in the manuscript, introduces new themes. Written in 1644, this is one of several country house poems (in this case, a garden or estate poem) by Fane. Like his poems on hunting, fishing or racing, they celebrate a rich and privileged version of English country life in the 1640s, and also an escapist one. Here, in the midst of war, and immediately following the lifting of his house arrest, he is concentrating understandably on the 'Civility' of Wentworth's elaborate gardens in a place whose names are silently modified from Somerlyton in Lothing Land (the latter only too appropriate in 1644) to emphasise a sunny amity that was markedly lacking in the country beyond Wentworth's estate. On the day this poem was written, 'April-24. 1644 . . . that night at Ipswich', Fane's brother-in-law Fairfax (who was himself to visit 'Lovingland' in 1648) was beginning his siege of York, having just stormed Selby, while Fane's brother Francis had just taken command of the Royalist garrison at Lincoln, recently captured along with Newark, Sleaford and Gainsborough by Rupert's army. No doubt the very richness of Fane's descriptions of the 'pleasures on pleasures hunge' is itself a response to these events, but no reader could deduce them from the poem alone, let alone realise that 'Lovingland' was strategically important, and in 1648 was 'rumoured to be the chosen site for a royalist bridgehead' (Loxley, p. 226). Only in the simile of trees which 'Like the Lifeguards upon the Hall attend' (l. 49), or in the contrasting orderliness of this micro-commonwealth in which

> The useful Ash and sturdy Oak are set
> At distance and obey, the Brambles mett
> Embrace and twine in t'arbours to conceal
> And harbour such as stock this Commonweal   (ll. 37–40)

is there a reminder of the country at war outside Lovingland.[14]

This is not to say that Fane avoids the war or the constitutional questions it raised. Nine months earlier in another long poem, *The Times Steerage* (p. 82), 'wrot in July 1643', when he was still under house arrest, he had explored the origins of the war in meandering, often tortuous detail. This is clearly a poem in which he is working out his ideas. Starting evenhandedly with two sides who both 'pretend They fight / . . . that Religion and the Lawes have right', he sees the war as driven by 'factions' (a favourite theme in his political prose in *N*), with the King as a victim, but a weak, culpable one. Charles is blamed for listening to the Queen and her coterie, but Parliament is blamed still more for driving the King away when 'they left t'express / The Counselers parts, and with Commanding pride / Petitiond humbly not to be denide'. Parliament as 'Council' was important to Fane: it is easy to forget that peers of his generation had had little or no experience of the House of Lords, which did not sit between March 1629 (the month Fane succeeded to his title) and April 1640. Until he attended the Lords for the first time in February 1641 (his mother's death having prevented attendance at the Short Parliament), Fane's parliamentary experience was as a young and apparently silent MP in the four parliaments of the 1620s. Circumstantial evidence, such as his friendship with Sir William Armine, an ally of Sir John Eliot, and himself imprisoned in 1627 for refusing the forced loan, suggests that Fane's sympathies were then probably with moderate oppositionists.[15] Now, in 1643, the two Houses in which he believes as the legal and traditional council to which the King must listen have become 'like Dictators that perpetuall are / Sole moderators . . . of Peace and warr'. The King has been cast as a contractual monarch, set

> But over them as Chevalier du guet
> He was at first but trusted from and for
> The Commonwealth as His Superior
> And now They'l make him know it   (ll. 138–41)

The old laws have been destroyed by the extremists on both sides. These moderate views, which do not place him at a great distance from Essex or Fairfax, express themselves predictably enough in a poetry which is rooted in a deep desire for peace, and a return to an idealised version of the old *status quo*. The King has failed but will, having learnt his lesson, 'rule anew', advised by his loyal counsellors in the two Houses.

Fane was realistic enough to recognise that such a return journey was going to be a very difficult one, and would indeed involve some acceptance of a new order, as *Cloris Complaint* (p. 87) shows. This poem has been assumed to be in the voice of Henrietta Maria (Loxley, p. 239), but it is dated '*July 25. 1644*', the day before the Goldsmiths' Hall Committee recommended Fane's estates be freed from sequestration on payment of the last part of his £3,000 fine (*CCC*, p. 832), and it is surely Fane, not the Queen (not known for her attachment to reconciliation), who decides to 'try the wave' of history:

> Befrend me wind, Ile trye the wave
> Though some ther be must sink, yet some't may save
> My Calender yet markes out Spring
> Dis-Gust may shake, not blast the Blossoming
> And therfore though I rov'd astray
> 'Tis reconciling Truth points now the way
> In which I would be thought as farr
> From Variation, as the Fixed'st starr
> But with a Constant shining thence
> Serve King and Cuntry by my Influence.   (ll. 21–30)

Such a conclusion points not to the relatively simple withdrawal from public affairs 'to apply a Horatian therapy to their mental wounds' that Røstvig (p. 60) assumes, but to the use at least of 'influence', partly but not exclusively poetic, to reconcile the two sides. It may not be accidental that this poem with its acceptance that the old order has indeed broken down is followed by *Over the Chimny in the great Chamber at Merworth*, inserted later, which emphasises individual 'merits' over inherited status:

> What doth He gett whoe're preferrs
> The scuttchions of His Ancesters
> This Chimni-peece of Gould or Brass
> That Coat of Armes blazond in glass
> When those with time and age have end
> Thy Prowess must thy self commend.   (ll. 1–6)

Despite the commitment to reconciliation and individual merit in action ('Prowess'), when Fane became one of the first Royalist peers to sign the Covenant, in February 1644, the choice he made was effectively for *otium* over *negotium*. He did not, like his friend and brother-in-law John Holles, Earl of Clare, change sides, but remained in uneasy neutrality. This was not a wholly new position. Fane had already found himself at odds with the Crown in the 1630s. For a major landowner, a senior peer, and a highly intelligent one at that, his political and courtly activities (in so far as they can be separated) were very limited. The suspension of Parliament in the 1630s was resented as much by those peers not in Charles's inner circle as by erstwhile members of the Commons, as Fane's play *Candy Restored* (1641) demonstrates. Although a poem *Upon his Majesties late jorny into Scotland and salf return* in 1633 (p. 106) is conventionally flattering in ascribing numinous, climate-enhancing qualities to the royal presence, this is the routine material of Caroline courtly poetry. There is not much evidence to suggest a warm relationship between the King and the new Earl of Westmorland: whereas James I had stayed often at Apethorpe, where the hunting in Rockingham Forest was good, and had even helped pay for improvements, Charles is only recorded as having made one visit, and that when he was hurrying back to London after the humiliating conclusion to the Bishops' War. And while the King had stood as godfather to Fane's heir in 1635, he may have done so by proxy. There is nothing to suggest that Fane spent much time at court in the 1630s, and the evidence outside the poems suggests a certain distance from the King and his advisers.[16] As Deputy Lieutenant and a JP he complained of the assessment for Ship Money in Northamptonshire in 1634, but that must have paled as a source of antipathy to the King and his advisers beside his personal assessment in 1637 for the enormous fine of £19,000 under the revived Forest Laws, one of the most dubious of the extraparliamentary devices used by Charles to raise revenue. Though eventually reduced to £2,500, it was not a move calculated to keep, or regain, loyalty. It is thus not surprising to find that Fane and his mother were both critical of the plans for military action against the Scots in 1639 (see *Upon the Scotsh business—1638*, p. 230), though they would in any case have had sympathy with the Presbyterian Scots. Fane at first responded to the summons sent out to peers by pleading illness. Although he did join the King in Newcastle in May (as did Fairfax), it is perhaps significant to find him and the Earl of Northampton dining with the Scottish general, Leslie, in his camp at Duns just before the treaty was signed.[17] The following year he wrote angrily to his cousin, Sir Henry Vane Snr, still a trusted servant of the King, complaining that Charles had awarded the gift of a disputed clerical living to Lord Coventry, son of Charles's Lord Keeper. The letter ends with what, in 1640, was a fairly clear threat:

My house has ever been obedient without dispute to his Majesty's commands and unwilling to contend with him; yet when we have any request to him, we find no more favour than his absolute opposers do. God send that way of his to work him no inconvenience. (*CSPD*, 1639–40, pp. 597–8; 30 March 1640)

One wonders in the light of this history just what kind of loss was involved in Fane's *My Farwell to the Court* (p. 127) in 1644. Certainly it is not surprising to find that in the 1630s the praises of the country life are already being sung at some length: the larger political responsibilities denied defeated Royalists in the later period had already been denied, if much less painfully, to men like Fane during the years of personal rule, one of the secondary aims of which was to encourage the nobility and gentry to stay in the country managing their estates, administering local justice and promoting the economies of their local communities, rather than hanging around London and the court, or, as Fane would have seen it, meeting to advise the King 'in that greatest council of Parliament' (*Vita*, p. 47). In the 1630s as well as the next two decades, Fane celebrates that life in a series of poems that deal with hunting and fishing, friendship and family. Sea-fishing in his own yacht was an unusual variation on the normal round of country sports: *A Fishing Sea-Voyage from Lin to Boston* (p. 103) took him and his two brothers-in-law 'the Lords Gerrard and Cope' across the Wash in 1633, and later, in 1645, a week's fishing prompted a religious meditation on the ocean, the port of 'true happines' and 'Our Hopes sheat Ancor of Salvation' (*After a weekes sea voyage for pleasure*, p. 163). More conventional sporting life is covered in such 1630s poems as *A Buck-hunting Jorny to Belvoyr* (p. 108), with its elaborate conceit of the hunters of the night sky, or *My Foxhuntinge* ('Apthorp 1632', p. 105).

Along with such poems go those on the hunters, animal and human. An elegy on a horse, *A Dierge For Hasty Ginny* (p. 109) is only partly playful, even if the mare's corpse does end up being fed to the hounds. Fane says in his *Vita* that 'of all the accomplishments of War and the Court ... I always held that of horsemanship the first' (p. 37), and in 1656 'that horse which Justly beats the Ground' still provides 'th'Elixir of Delight and Pleasure' (*To my Sonn Charles in prayse of Horsemanship*, p. 349). *A Dierge For Hasty Ginny* has echoes of both Herrick's *The Funerall Rites of the Rose* and the interpolated flower passage in *Lycidas* as Fane summons Ginny's fellow horses by name (the flowers are also the names of horses) to mourn her early death:

> O let not such invitement have
> To wayt upon my Ginny to her grave
>   But if ther be yet leaft a race
> Of Coursers, Jennetts, or Barbes to embrace
>   This service, lett such sacrefize
> Some tears heer at their Kindreds Obsequies
>   Let Peg-a briggs be calld to mourn
> And send into the North for Pepper corn
>   Lett Bess-a Brackley weep for Her
> And little Robin with th'red stomacher
>   And if ther be of Puppy kind
> Yett leaft, let them not leav a tear behind
>   Lett Marigould white and Red-Rose power
> Forth siths for her: Lett Primrose, Gilliflower

>   And Tulipe amidst that Dewe
>   Her herse with their Enameld leavs bestrew   (ll. 17–32)

Usually, however, it is human friends who are addressed: poems written to Ned Beecher, Phil Wood or John Mun use hunting or similar activities to celebrate friendship itself, while Fane's stepson, Horatio Townshend, is especially connected with racing. More sober Presbyterians such as Edward and Robert Harley or Sir Edward Armine are usually approached with more pious reflections (though Fane can always turn hunting or fishing into an occasion for meditating on God's justice and mercy). Often, male friendship becomes itself an explicit refuge from war and 'Fortunes', as in *Ode—To a frend in Imitation of these 1648*

>   Ned—might I sit
>   In a black Chimny Corner closs by Thee
>   With comfortable Ale and Tost
>   Brown as the Berry Nutt, or Rost
>   Presented in a Bowle Resembling it
>   With what Content, with what Securety
>   Would I imbalme my quiet and Conclude
>   All Fortunes else to be but Interlude   (ll. 1–8)

This poem is written '*in Imitation of* ' two Martial epigrams, translated immediately before it in *N*, which set the simple life against ambition and insecurity, and it is to such classical invocations of honourable rural *otium* and friendship that Fane turns habitually to place his response to the turmoil of (in this case) the second Civil War of 1648. Such local friendships as these, however, as well as friendly if less intimate contact with such powerful neighbours as the Manners family at Belvoir and the Cecils at Burleigh, are a staple subject of his poetry throughout the 1630s as well as during those later years in which 'Content' and 'Securety' were under threat as never before.

Other poems of the 1630s mark out important family events: Fane wrote four poems on the death of his first Countess, Grace Thornhurst, who died in 1636.[18] The first two are followed in *F2* by fair copies of eleven of the courtship poems he had written to her in 1626, a gesture that is deflated considerably by his decision to recycle the last of them, originally called '*An allay in love upon sticking at portian*', as a love poem to his second wife, Mary Vere, by the simple expedient of retitling it *Upon the Lady of my second adventure Verania* (p. 97). Fane's habit of returning to use the blank space left on a page also disturbs the sequence as it appears in *F2*, with *To the County of Kent upon its condition*, written in 1644, added sometime after the group prompted by Grace's death. A poem on the double wedding in 1632 of two of his sisters in Westminster Abbey, *Epithal[amium] in Nup[ti]as Sororu[m]*, and a group of poems which deal with the marriage in 1636 of his brother Francis to Elizabeth West, the eligible widow of Lord Darcy, follow those on his wives.

Most criticism of Fane has concentrated on his influence on a younger poet, Andrew Marvell, tutor from 1651 to 1652 to Fane's niece, Mary Fairfax, and it seems clear that the poetry Marvell wrote while at Appleton House did indeed reflect his reading of Fane, probably in the printed form of *Otia Sacra*.[19] Fane himself may have been influenced in the later 1620s through an analogous appointment to Marvell's with Fairfax, that of John Donne's friend Rowland Woodward as secretary to Fane's father, Francis. Woodward brought with him to Apethorpe one of the best collections of Donne's as yet unpublished poetry, the manuscript which has become known as the Westmoreland MS, and which, along with a number of Woodward's books, became Fane's property.[20] The influence of Donne (rather than Cleveland, whom he seems to have begun to read in manuscript in the late 1630s) is evident in the 'strong lines' which begin to replace the Herrickian grace of the earlier poems. The genuinely witty, self-deprecating poem on his second marriage, for example, which must date from 1637–1638, is written by a man who has been reading Donne's *Satires* and *Elegies* as well as the *Songs and Sonnets*:

>   Why did not some when first I undertook
>   This task of Love again, guive me my book
>   The crime is not soe hainous to deprive

> Me of my clergy, though again I wive:
> My years alow it, and those cannot stay
> But each reprive's as bad as cast away
> I did confess at first, soe hoapt to find
> A salm of mercy but the Judg unkind
> Turnd me to such a leaf and line in Her
> That the Caldayck is a caracter
> Of more facilety and th'Arab scrall
> When pointed (by much) more methodicall
> Nay, wher the berth of printing first began
> I'le sooner read th'obscurest Chinian. . . .
> (*My tryall and araignment at loves second barr*, p. 111, ll. 1–14)

During the 1630s Fane also becomes more at ease with the relatively long poem, writing the social comedy of *A Jorney into Norfolk* (p. 116), a poem of 145 lines which mixes mock heroic with satire 'Under the name of Smith' (l. 138). This too anticipates his marriage to Mary Vere, widow of Sir Roger Townshend: their eighty-nine-page marriage settlement (W(A) I. 10) is considerably less interesting, and certainly less lighthearted, but brought Fane land in Norfolk, as well as two stepsons.

His two longest poems, both of 208 lines (a coincidence that does not seem significant), belong to the darkest part of Fane's life, the early 1640s. One, *The Times Steerage*, has already been mentioned. Interesting for its political attitudes, it is a flawed, deeply troubled and meandering poem. Much more accomplished is the *By-Ward to some Cittisens entring the Tower* (p. 121), written towards the end of his imprisonment. This is still reminiscent of Donne's *Satires*, but its rhythms, imagery and structure now owe more to John Cleveland. Like *A Jorney into Norfolk*, *By-Ward* mixes social comedy and satire, but adds understandably darker reflections on the predicament of the various inmates:

> One righteous Judge Three Knights condemned are
> A Brace of Aldermen, Bishops a paire
> Two Earles, Three Kiernes and all to this sad fate
> The Times distraction Heer to Celebrat
> In much retirdness: neither heard nor tride
> They linger out a life as if they dide.
>   A sad condition: when nor foe, nor frend
>   Will help to Triall, that might put an end
>   Unto this living Death, or dead reprive
>   Wherin they only can but be, not live   (ll. 81–90)

This discursive and satirical voice is found more and more often in the poetry Fane wrote during the 1640s, and it is certainly the dominant note in the opening pages of *H*, the manuscript now in Harvard. Clearly by this time Fane had read such Cleveland satires as *The Mixt Assembly* and *Smectymnuus*. Although *H* opens with a comically critical account of his brother-in-law Fairfax's journey to London by public coach in 1653, most of the satire belongs to the 1640s, and much of it is aimed at Independents and radicals, several of whom had been contemporaries of his at Emmanuel. *Upon New Lights* (p. 215) is built around a series of puns on the names of such men, obscure enough now, but appearing in London in the early 1640s as potentially powerful revolutionary voices, 'mad inspird' priests sent by the Devil to question the truths of scripture and the sacraments:

> The Divells Raign is in declineing yeares
> And there upon he bends more rageing skill
> To Bring more proselites in sak's to's Mill
> Wher he may Grind all good in Tonle free and
> Sever the Apostle Peter's flower from Bran
> Syms-sonn Confute and call His Prophets nye

> With Coale man to make warme his Forgery
> Corne well may here begrownd and Brighter made
> By Grinding too a Cousning shefeld Blade
> Blacke well befits this story and the night
> A favorer to every newer Light.... (ll. 24–34)

The model for this was probably Cleveland's *Mixt Assembly*, which must belong to much the same date; there, however, Cleveland's play with names is simpler and more direct than Fane's puns on Grindal, Simpson, Nye and the rest. Fane differs too in that his satire is in general directed at the Independents and their allies, whereas in both *Smectymnuus* and *The Mixt Assembly* Cleveland is attacking Presbyterians like Edmund Calamy the elder, a man whom, like the Scots Presbyterian Alexander Henderson, Fane seems to have admired (see *Upon Master Alexander Henderson's Death and the Preaching Coachman*, p. 217, and *Ascensus Gratiarum descensus Gratiarum*, p. 154). Such allegiances as these, however, clearly did nothing to disturb his recent admiration for the anti-puritan Anglican Royalism of Cleveland, or his continued admiration for Herrick.

Such tolerance of differing religious and political ideologies was no doubt partly a function of being 'a good naturd man'. In fact the Presbyterianism which Fane inherited from the Mildmay family, and which was reinforced by his marriage to Mary Vere, rarely emerges unequivocally in his work. A pattern of alliances with the Vere, Harley, Fairfax and Holles families, and his enduring friendship with Independent Presbyterians like Armine, may seem to place his religious allegiances clearly enough, regardless of his apparently equally strong friendship with his Catholic neighbour Lord Brudenell, later the first Earl of Cardigan. But, though meditative religious verse is spread throughout his manuscripts, it is not doctrinally specific. The earliest indications of his religious attitudes are in fact not in his poems, but in the account of his foreign travels in the *Vita*. The Presbyterian climate in which he left for this journey is indicated by the fact that his passport forbids a visit to Rome, a requirement presumably inserted at the request of his family. (Such embarrassments as the conversion of Toby Matthew, son of the Archbishop of York, were fresh in the memory.) During his second year in France he is conventional enough in deploring the corruptions of papal Avignon (Jews and prostitutes) and noting the contrast with neighbouring Orange, which principality 'rejoices in its closeness to the truth as held by Calvin'. When he does get to Geneva, however, his Presbyterian sensibilities are shocked: its 'divergence from the trumpet sound of Fame is deep and wide, for within are found harlotries and a thousand evils'. Such knowledge may well have made him question the certainties of English Presbyterianism enough to be tolerant within the limits of Anglicanism, 'the true Catholic Church' as he calls it later in the *Vita* (p. 45). He is very clear in *Upon the Scotsh business—1638* (p. 230) that he has no desire to fight to impose bishops on the Scots:

> Soe were my counsailes heard I should perswade
> Not with the Drum and Trumpet him t'invade
> But with Cope, Ephod Rochet, hood, and all
> Tippet and Cap, and Robe Cannonnicall
> And Miter too soe should he not be free
> But straight submit unto our Litregy
> Else stand suspended: to performe this may
> Our Bishops all be sent, our people stay (ll. 7–14)

It is not so clear, however, that Fane extended this lack of sympathy with bishops to English Church government. He is scathing about Presbyterians by 1651 (despite his friendship with the Harleys at that date), when he claims that he and his wife named their eighth and last child (his fourteenth in all) Susanna 'so that she was safe from the Presbyterians and elders of the people' (p. 45). In April 1660 *Upon the little parler Garden at Mereworth* (p. 323) is again mockingly insulting:

> My Parler window doth descry
> The malice of Presbitery
> For wher of Owld Houshoulders sate

> To watch the entry of the Gate
> The stinking Elders rayse their head (ll. 1–5)

It is not therefore surprising to find that the emphases of his religious poetry are broadly Protestant rather than strictly Calvinist, the weight falling on original sin, the loss of Eden, and redemption through Christ, rather than on the priesthood of the elect or a strict insistence on salvation through grace alone. Most of the religious poetry written before 1647 was included in *Otia Sacra*, and Donald Friedman rightly points to doctrinal as well as aesthetic affinities with George Herbert in the first part of that book. One of the poems cited by Friedman, *Occationd upon the Communion when it was a snowe*, shows the similarities and the differences. Written in January 1646 (when Royalist fortunes were low, and Fairfax, taking advantage of the frozen roads that accompanied the snow, was marching into the West Country), it recalls *Love III* 'both in the situation they treat and in their insistence on finding how a "worthy guest" should be "drest"' (*OS*, p. viii). It is like much of *The Temple* also in its stanzas of varied line length. Where it differs most obviously is in its lack of the narrative drama of *Love III* and of the related complications of erotic and tender love that go along with the avowed unworthiness to 'sit and eat'. Fane's emphasis on his unworthiness is similar to Herbert's, but he describes the predicament rather than enacting it, except in those moments where his imagination does make new the sacrifice, as in the original and quite complex conceit in which the 'Naked and wounded' sinner is rescued by the 'True Samaritan' and bandaged in the cloths from Jesus's tomb, which are linked by a strong verbal echo of John 11. 26 to the 'graveclothes' which bound the resurrected Lazarus:

> Thus now upon recovery again
> Bound up in His Grave-Cloaths, brought to our Inn
> And earnest left, to prove
> His high Compassion, and Love: (ll. 25–8)

Fane is also closer to Herbert's Protestantism than to that of most of his Presbyterian friends in his enthusiasm for Christmas, the celebration of which was abolished by the Presbyterian-dominated Westminster Assembly in 1645 (though Presbyterians like Sir Symonds D'Ewes, another friend of Fane's, still hankered after it, and non-Presbyterians like Donne, had he been alive, would have been glad to see it go). Whether Fane wrote a Christmas poem every year is not clear, but twelve survive in these manuscripts, the earliest dated 1634, the latest 1656 (p. 301). At times he seems hesitant about this, as if trying to persuade reluctant co-religionists to

> Keep A Berth day for him through fayth
> For ther's noe more that scripture sayth
> And wher that finger silent is
> If man attempt he steers amiss
> For nothing fit to be reveald
> Must be presumd is ther conceald.
> (*In Natalem—1649*, p. 153, ll. 19–24)

But at others he is more aggressive, arguing in 1656 that it is arrogant 'Unbeleef' and 'neglect', 'Contempt' and 'scorn' that deny the celebration of Christmas:

> Noe place on earth, noe time be thought amiss
> To celebrate our Great Redeemers fall
>   To rayse us up again [who] were lost and gon
>   Without the Power of such Redemption:
>
> Wherfore if Parcht through Unbeleef we lie
> And in Contempt seem to neglect and scorn
>   The Memory of This Nativety
>   Noe Dew Distilled from the fragrant Morn

> Will add refreshment to that Grass and Hay
> Tramples upon soe Great an Holy day:
> (*Carroll—1656*, ll. 21-30)

Fane would no doubt have shared some of Herrick's motives for enjoying the celebration of Christmas: the growing awareness that it was related historically to the Roman Saturnalia; that, like other ancient calendar customs, it underpinned the old social hierarchies; that (as he had pointed out to Ned Beecher in 1626) festive hospitality was a virtue; and, more immediately, that it was a notable site of conflict between the old and the new in English society. All this emerges from the interchange between him and Herrick in 1647 or 1648 (see pp. 202-3). But the emphasis in many of Fane's carols is on the low-born child redeemer, 'a Lambe thats yeand, a Child thats borne / Noe spectacle of glory, but of scorne' (*A Christmass Karroll sung—an—1634*, p. 136), and of the saving sacrifice that birth anticipates:

> But let the Lambes blood wash away the staines
> And Characters were written in thy vaines
> By thy first Parents, and which sithence thou hast
> By thy endeavours into Volumes cast.
> Throw doun thy self for Him, who meekly came
> (Into the world for thee) a Child a Lambe
> Born to be slain for thee, yet slain before
> To make the victory or the conquest more (ll. 41-8)

Despite the emphasis on Original Sin, Fane is clear that Christ died for all, not just for the elect, as another Carol, this time from 1640, indicates with a degree of 'jollity', a word as unexpected in this devotional context as it was in *An ode To N.B. an angler*:

> And shall my frozen hart
> Not thaugh and bear its part
> In jollety for this
> Wherby not I alone
> But each beleeving one
> May promise to himself eternall bliss
> For such can nere be could
> Who have this berth-day in their harts enrould
> (*My Charroll—1640*, p. 143, ll. 17-24)

'Jollity' here means both inner happiness and the festivities which, for the reasons explained in the lines that immediately follow, are appropriate to Christmas, and to which Fane often contributed an entertainment to be performed in the elaborate theatre he had constructed at Apethorpe.[21]

Despite such allegiances, however, his religious verse retains a strong sense of his unworthiness in the sight of God, a spiritual humility that would have been recognised approvingly by his Mildmay ancestors. This has an important alleviating effect on the greatness of his social and economic status, a status which in any case he seems naturally disinclined to stress. The belief that without God's mercy

> Heer, am I lost
> Soe small,
> Yet soe much cost
> (*My Reformation*, p. 149, ll. 31-3)

perhaps led him to some of the modest characterisations of himself in the secular poems, in which *The contempt of this world raises the esteem of the other* (p. 169). These characterisations should be set against David Norbrook's assertion that Fane 'had a high sense of aristocratic honour' unbecoming in a man 'whose father had bought his title from Buckingham' (p. 253). He does indeed display hauteur at times, usually in the face of the overturning of the whole social order by the war, or (as in the case of the government of Geneva, p. 39) when tradesmen take over the reins of government. But, as has been said, he rarely draws attention to his position, and a number of poems sound uneasy about the moral status of wealth, *Upon Dives and Lazarus* (p. 168) being the most explicit. Here the anonymous rich man 'died and on that sleepy skoar / Was buried and noe more— '. Fane was forced to borrow so often, despite his huge income, and was so chivvied by creditors, in particular by husbands demanding the balance of their marriage portions, that he must at times have felt that the closing lines—'He who by hard Fate was heer opprest / In Abrams Bosom finds an Interest'—applied to him; but it also seems likely that his religion did indeed prompt some anxiety about the gulf between his position and that of, for example, the 'foule wench', lowest of the fifty-nine servants listed in his household at Apethorpe in 1650 (W(A) 15, f. 80r).

Fane's religious faith was inevitably pressed into service as a way of understanding the Civil Wars and their aftermath.[22] In the early stages, the King's weakness is that of Adam, seduced by his advisers, especially by Henrietta Maria:

> Our Gratious King
> Good in Himself, but ther's an other thing
> He is a Man, may not's affections cleav
> To be seduc't? Had not an Adam Eve?
> (*The Times Steerage*, ll. 19–22)

In this respect, all the participants are driven on by the old Adam, victims of original sin, and all are at fault. A Christmas poem, *In Natalem—1643* (written therefore in the Tower), prays that 'This Season' may

> alay the Fury stint the Rage
> And Madnes doth predominise this Age?
> When for to ransome Man (whose least Offence
> Was Characterd in Disobedience)
> He who knew noe sin came, that, to fullfill
> The mercy statute of His Fathers Will:
> Thus He Forguave, and Guave, to let us know
> What to our very Enemies we owe
> By His Example; and decrees this Fate
> To the posterety unfortunate
> Of too-beleeving-Adam, that They must
> Guive Themselves over to noe Other Trust
> Than what His word assures   (p. 152, ll. 3–15).

The horrified sense of animal fury that is the product of unredeemed Adam is still there at the end of the Protectorate, when it shapes Fane's response to the danger of civil war breaking out again in 1659:

> Whither O wicked Brood do'yea run
> Is't not enough what was begun
> In a mad Fury but do'yea still
> Invent new Fewds and how to kill
> (*To the People of England—June-5-1659*, p. 328, ll. 1–4)

The 'wicked Brood' are '*the People of England*', to whom the poem is addressed, and in whose wickedness he implicates himself as one of those whose 'Sin soe great' has caused the wars:

> Are we more fell than Beasts? doth Power
> And Force incite us to devower
> Each Other? is not Fury blind
> To Cause us t'rush on our owne kind?

> Or is our Sin soe great; noe Fate
> 'Save This may serve to Expiate   (ll. 19-24)

What has changed the picture decisively between 1643 and 1659, however, is the execution of the King. As has been seen, Fane had at best a limited respect for Charles before his death. But the *Vita* describes his death as that of a priest-king killed by the ungodly. He is no longer a weak Adam but a type of the persecuted Christ:

Who in telling, writing, or even thinking about such things can refrain from tears! But thus it was: we saw our King, so long holy and peace loving, fall by the blow of the axe at the hands of the impious and utterly profane soldiery. Immense grief now imposed silence as much on our thoughts as on our pens and words. Let it suffice that wickedness so great be recorded in heaven that it may eventually be punished. (p. 44)

Poems of the 1650s thus begin to present Charles I as, in Felltham's words, 'CHRIST the second'.[23] Just as mankind could be saved only by Christ's sacrifice, so England was so far gone in sin that it could have been redeemed (with hindsight) only by the sacrifice of its king:

> Once This a Glorious Kingdom when a King
>   Endude with Vertues All Times mought admire
> Governd the Scepter and such Peace did bring
>   To Church and State as None could more desire
>   But too Good for such people Heavns decreed
>   As just reward for Their sinns He should bleed
> (*Preces et Lachrimæ Sanctorum Oblationes*, p. 306, ll. 7-12)

If there are therefore times, especially later in the 1650s, when Fane looks forward to the return of the son, Charles II, as to a Second Coming, there are also times when he makes Cromwell a satanic figure, notably in a group of Latin poems in *H*, Horatian imitations most of which appear to have been written in the years between the execution of Charles I in January 1649 and the defeat of Charles II at Worcester in September 1651 (*H*, pp. 63-84, 90-7). But it is not true to say, as Norbrook does in discussing these poems, that 'Fane would grant no kind of dignity, even a negative one, to the republic's leaders' (p. 254). He certainly welcomes Cromwell's death, at which point he sees him as Goliath (*Nec Sicca morte Tyranni*, p. 332) and Romulus (*Le Monde Renversè*, p. 330), but in January 1654 he is willing to come to terms with the new Protector, whom he sees as the only man now capable of restoring peace. The terms are very clearly conditional, but do allow Cromwell much achieved, and yet more potential, dignity:

> Brave Captain though thine honor gaind increase
> By war let all concluded be in peace
> 'Tis commendable after Pallas spear
> Had brandisht been Her Olive branch to wear
> For being Protector and anoynted thence
> All suppling lenatives He should dispence
> Unto the People; make the sword to bend
> Into a sickle, th'Helmet to defend
> Hive like the laboring Bee; if this He'l doe
> I'le say He shall be my Protector too.
>   (*Ad Protectorem—January-30-1653*)

An anonymous Latin poem which Fane translates as *An Epigram upon His Highnes entertainment in the City translated* (p. 273) goes further than this in its surprising willingness to contemplate a republic of 'Cittizens':

> He who soe many Crowns despisd, seeks you
> The harts of men, nothing of stage or shew
> He brings his own bayes, broaken scepters yeild

> That Liberty He guave might take the feild
> Now are yea first made Cittizens, time past
> Were servants unto Kings; learn this at last
> To yeild to th'reigne of those whose power who skans
> Shall find them but your fellow Cittizens   (ll. 17–24)

It seems clear that Fane did for a while try to 'learn . . . To yeild to th'reigne' of fellow citizens, for the essentially Hobbesian reason that the new regime could deliver peace and stability, but that his attitude changed in the later 1650s when it became more and more clear that this was not so, that the Leviathan was not delivering its side of the contract (see e.g. *Upon taking up of Severall Persons of Honer and quallety by the Maior and souldiery and securing them at Northampton the 14th of Aprill-1658*, p. 337).

More personal factors probably governed his similarly fluctuating attitude to his brother-in-law, Fairfax. The complexity of their relationship is symbolised by the fact that in June 1642, when Fane had joined the King at York to prepare for the inevitable war, his wife Mary, accompanying him, stayed two nights with her sister at Appleton House. This visit took place a week after Charles had tried to ride over Fairfax as the latter presented him with a petition urging reconciliation with Parliament.[24] In March 1646 *Upon Sir Thomas Fayer-Fax whose vertues make Him shine a bright star in our Horizon* (p. 200) compares Fairfax favourably, with perhaps a touch of family pride, to Alexander and Cæsar, but in the undated *To Sir Thomas Fairfax* (p. 221) he is 'Black Tom . . . who prict with fame / Embroylst thy native country in a flame', and even in retirement in the 1650s he is mocked as '*Prince Tomaso ali: Black Tom*' when he travels (possibly staying overnight at Apethorpe) to London by public coach (*Upon the Strange adventure and memorable voyage of Prince Tomaso*, p. 206). The tone of such mockery is difficult to place: it may not be unequivocally hostile, but this is not so of *Upon the Generall the Lord Fairfaxes resigning up his Commissions to Oliver Crumwell* (p. 247, 1650), where Fairfax's principled resignation is seen as a falling out among thieves, and

> Rowland changd to Oliver
> Signefies that ther doth remain
> Nothing saving the same again
> When we ought drive a greater skoap
> On Pounds and Crownes to fix our hoap
> Whilst swords make plowgh shears, let Hemp R—
> (ll. 18–23)

Fane's changing attitudes throughout the wars and their aftermath are explained in part by the moderate position from which he started, and by the irenic disposition which makes him temperamentally ready to embrace Hobbesian ideas, ideas which also helped to justify retrospectively his early composition with Parliament. But the un-Hobbesian concept of Providence also plays a large part in his resigned acceptance of events, with even the execution of the King being left to 'be recorded in heaven that it may eventually be punished'. Patience is one of the main themes of *Otia Sacra*, and of many of the poems in the later manuscripts. More and more, however, in the poetry of the 1650s in *F3* Fane sees the Restoration as the event which will return England to the order in which he had such a huge stake, and which, almost from the day he succeeded to the earldom, had been in the process of being turned upside down, first by Charles, Laud and Strafford, then by Parliament. *Wrot at Raynam June-23-1659* (p. 305) looks forward, following Richard Cromwell's abdication in May, to the Restoration as a Providential event, and as a healing one:

> Lord in whose hand it is
> To make a Metamorphosis
>   And whose sole will creats
> A change in Kingdoms, Powers, and States
>   Smile on This sinfull Land
> Nor let Oppression bear Command
>   But Now in these Our Times

>   Cancell the Guilt of all our Crimes
>   Let not the Conquering Sword
>   Prevaile, but Sunshine of Thy word   (ll. 1–10)

Fane continued to write almost up to his death in February 1666. He describes the Restoration with great enthusiasm in his *Vita*, and added a triumphant postscript to a Latin poem of 1650 (*H*, p. 95) recording Charles's return on 29 May and his liberation 'of his people from a most iniquitous servitude'. He took his seat in the Lords again in May: his accounts of that and the following month describe a return to London in style, with 'Trumpeters'. He buys two new suits, two pairs of gloves, has his sword mended, and orders 'Riband'. On 20 June he pays 'To Blackwell for a Coronet 08.18.06' (W(A) Misc 8, ff. 5r–6r). Predictably, poems taking a positive view of public affairs increase slightly at the Restoration and the years immediately following it: Monck is praised as the George who has killed the dragon Rump (*Upon George Munks routing the Rump &c*, p. 327), and later poems celebrate naval victories against the Dutch (*To Sir F.F: neer Darby Shire upon Prince Rupert the Duke of Cumberlands Voyage to Ginny set out in Octobr. 64*, p. 309). But, in the relatively few poems that can be dated after 1660, the mixture of more personal religious and social subject matter continues much as before. Perhaps because of health and age, perhaps because he is disillusioned with the new court, as with the old, he rejects an offer from his friend Lord Brudenell, now the Earl of Cardigan:

> The Glory now preparing is not in Excelsis Which my Age & infirmities make me more look after The distibution of Ho[nou]rs hath brought on Contempt I were Spanish Breeches so need noe Garters & for the Bath I have been in Friers weeds & a Knight aldredy. . . . For Claymes I renounce all but to be able to serve my God, my King, my Cuntry, & my Frend (as your Lordship) which I will ever be most ambitious of . . .

He politely rejects a place

> in yoak with my noble Lord of Shrewsbury in your service which I heer is to be the twentieth of this month: I thank you most humbly but cannot Conster the broad brimmd hatt & Ausmonere I want a key for that I rejoice at our Princesses Nuptialls but shall over rjoyce to see our Master soe be it to his Content & the best of his subjects let it fall wher it will all Circumstances must be left to those governe in the spheres for *Quae supra nos nihil ad nos*.   (Brudenell I. x. 17, 8 April [?1661])

Despite the world-weariness of this, Fane did accept an appointment as joint Lord-lieutenant of Northamptonshire, and as such probably took a certain pleasure in destroying the fortifications around Northampton, the town where twenty years earlier he had been captured. He did not write about this (unless very obliquely in *Upon Jack Prick at North[ampton]*, p 324, but evidently asked for it to be commemorated in the vignettes which accompany his portrait of 1662 (*frontispiece*). Intelligent and self-aware as he was, he may well have seen that this inconsequential but irenic act formed a satisfyingly symbolic end to his public career.

Notes

1 For this claim, and for an account of the circumstances and motives for publication, see Cain, 'A sad Intestine warr', pp. 27–32, and Loxley, pp. 201–2, 223–8. *OS* was reprinted by Grosart (1879) and in facsimile with an introduction by Donald M. Friedman (see Abbreviations, *OS*). Of the poetry left in manuscript, two poems from *H* were published in Thorn-Drury, *A Little Ark*, pp. 16–18, and extracts from *H* were published in Withington, 'Fugitive Poetry' and 'Political Satire'. Three poems from *F1* were published in Cain, 'Robert Herrick', where the rediscovery of the Fulbeck Hall MSS was first noted; eleven poems from the Fulbeck Hall MSS were

subsequently transcribed by Morton, pp. 117–29; and another eleven, in modernised text with notes, by Fowler, pp. 208–55. Two poems from *N*, by Herrick and Fane, were published in Cain, *Christmas Carol*. Recently, Fane has received critical attention from Norbrook and Smith, and earlier from Turner, William A. McClung, *The Country House in English Renaissance Poetry* (Berkeley CA, 1977), Røstvig, pp. 206–23, and Bradbrook. For Fane's biography, see his *Vita* (pp. 36–55), *DNB*, Morton, Leech, pp. 9–21, and Cain, 'A sad Intestine warr'. For his influence on Marvell, see n. 19 below.

2 *Tenth Report*, Appendix, pt. IV, pp. 1–59. 'Fugitive Poetry' (*H* in this edition) is described on pp. 44–7. There is a brief and misleading mention of *F2* as 'Memoir of Mildmay, Earl of Westmorland, and collections of verse (Latin, a few folio pp.), 1601, &c.' (p. 58), but the other manuscripts are not noticed.

3 These include the two poems that first attracted the attention of Bradbrook and Røstvig, *To Retiredness* and *My Happy Life*.

4 *Modo da tenersi per imbrigliare I Cavalle*, f. 1v: 'Ergo ubi, (docte Comes) Mus<ae> deceptus amore / Ora geras chartis pallidiora tuis / Te moneat liber iste tuos domistare caballos, / Aut alio studijs addere frænæ modo,' ll. 7–10, signed 'F.F: iid' (Fulbeck Hall).

5 Five lines on the arrival of Catherine of Braganza, *Votum in Adventum Regina*, Portland MS PwV 217, University of Nottingham Library. For Cambridge University Library MS Add. 4189(E), a Latin version by William Wake of Fane's *My Happy Life, to a Friend* (*OS*, p. 134), see below, p. 31. Norbrook suggests 'an elite circle of alienated royalists' as readers of at least the Horatian anti-republican poems in *H* (Norbrook, p. 254): Herrick and Cleveland would be among possible recipients. The Portland MS, probably sent to one of the Harley, Cavendish or Holles family (John Holles, Earl of Clare, was a brother-in-law and friend), and the translation of the Earl of Derby's verses (*Charles Darbyes Coppy taught English*, p. 358) suggest the membership of such a group ten years later.

6 *Lacrymæ Cantabrigienses* (1619), pp. 28–9; *Lacrymæ Musarum: the Tears of the Muses* (1649), pp. 1–2.

7 Cf. Loxley, pp. 223–8; Cain, 'A sad Intestine warr', pp. 27–32. *OS* is always assumed, probably correctly, to have been printed for private circulation, though the absence of a bookseller's name on the title-page is the only evidence I know of for this assumption.

8 References to Herrick follow L. C. Martin's practice in his edition of giving the page number followed by the number of the poem on the page: Martin's pagination is identical with that of F. W. Moorman's 1915 edition.

9 For Fane's financial support of Herrick, see Cain, *Christmas Carol*, pp. 149–50. For Cleveland's letter, *Clievelandi Vindiciæ; or, Clieveland's Poems, Orations, Epistles; &c.*, 1677 edition, pp. 151–2.

10 Benlowes presented Fane with an inscribed copy of *Theophila*, now in the Widener Library at Harvard: see Harold Jenkins, *Edward Benlowes (1602–1676): Biography of a Minor Poet* (1952), pp. 232–3. For the role of epic during the Civil Wars, and the difficulties it presented, see Smith, chapter 7.

11 Smith (p. 204) nevertheless quotes ll. 15–24 as if 'this new Pharsalian field' refers straightforwardly to war. They can be read thus only if isolated from the rest of the poem.

12 Cf. Turner, p. 189, for 'a politics of landscape' in 'Milton or Mildmay Fane'.

13 My reading differs from that of Fowler, p. 233, who takes it to mean 'composed in term and London'.

14 For readings of *To Sir Jhon Wentworth*, which have largely seen it as a precursor of *Upon Appleton House*, see Kitty Scoular, *Natural Magic: Studies in the Presentation of Nature in English Poetry from Spenser to Marvell* (Oxford, 1965), p. 163; William A. McClung, *The Country House in English Renaissance Poetry* (Berkeley CA, 1977), pp. 152–3.

15 Cf. his favourable mention of 'the Petition of Right', passed in 1628, in *Song or Ode Upon the speakers of either houses leveing their charges and runing away to the Army* (p. 209, l. 26). For Armine, see *An Ode sent into Scotland to a frend* (p. 119).

16 For peers and the court, see Stone, *Crisis*, chapter VIII, esp. pp. 398–403.

17 Phillip A. J. Pettit, *The Royal Forests of Northamptonshire*, Northamptonshire Record Society 23 (Gateshead, 1968), pp. 87–8, 92. *CSPD 1639–40*, pp. 123–4 (Dowager Countess's letter, 6 May). *The Journal of John Aston, 1639*, Surtees Society CXVIII [1910], p. 28.

18 *Upon the Death of My Fidelia a farewell to wine, Upon the Death of My Fidelia, My Penthouse against the storm of greif* and *My Hand-kerchef to dry my eyes*.
19 I have found relatively few anticipations of Marvell in the poems not published in *OS*. Bradbrook and Røstvig both established the influence of *To Retiredness* (*OS*, pp. 172–4) on *The Garden* and *Upon Appleton House*; Friedman added further convincing parallels (see e.g. pp. 146, 155, 250–1), and Leishman pointed to an echo of *Anglia Hortus* (p. 126) in *Appleton House* (pp. 283–4).
20 The Westmoreland MS is now in the New York Public Library; six of Woodward's books are at Fulbeck Hall, with Fane's name and library motto added after Woodward's signature. Woodward died in 1636, and is buried in Apethorpe (monument in the church). He may well have continued to act as Fane's secretary up to his death. Fane borrowed money from a 'Ms Woodward', perhaps Rowland's widow, in 1644 (W(A) Misc. 7, ff. 14v–15r).
21 For the plays and entertainments, see Leech; *A Critical Edition of Mildmay Fane's Vertues Triumph (1644)*, ed. Gerald William Morton (New York, 1988); and Martin Butler, *Theatre and Crisis 1632–1642* (Cambridge, 1984), p. 123. For the dates of the performances, see Cain, *Christmas Carol*, p. 145.
22 For a fuller discussion of Fane's treatment of the wars and of his political views, see Cain, 'A sad Intestine warr'.
23 *An Epitaph to the Eternal Memory of Charles I*, in *The Poems of Owen Felltham*, ed. Ted-Larry Pebworth and Claude J. Summers (University Park PA, 1973), pp. 65–6.
24 *Memorials of the Civil War . . . Forming the Concluding Volumes of the Fairfax Correspondence*, ed. Robert Bell (1849), I, p. 14.

PROVENANCE AND DESCRIPTIONS

Provenance

The great majority of all seven manuscripts are in Fane's italic and, occasionally, secretary hands, and almost all the work they contain is of his authorship. They must, with the exception of the single poem sent to Windebanke, have remained among the Westmorland family papers at Apethorpe Hall from Fane's death in 1666 until the series of sales from 1887 to 1893 described below. Two are traceable in the rather unsatisfactory descriptions of the HMC report on the Apethorpe MSS (see p. 25). This report may have prompted the twelfth Earl (d. 1891) to sell: certainly the Westmorland papers were dispersed soon after in three sales, the first and largest of which was at Sotheby's, 13–15 July 1887 (1,062 lots). The thirteenth Earl continued with sales at Christie's, 16 July 1892 (lots 411–62), and (mainly nineteenth-century material) Puttick & Simpson's, 27 July 1893 (lots 243–620). Two of the Fulbeck Hall MSS, *F1* and *F3*, were bought at the first Sotheby's sale by a cousin, William Dashwood Fane, who in the same year also bought Fulbeck Hall back into the family from the creditors of Colonel Henry Fane's son. W. D. Fane bought *F2* five years later at Christie's 16 July sale, and all three manuscripts have been in the library at Fulbeck ever since. For the passage of *H* from Sotheby's to the Houghton Library, and of Saxton's *Atlas* to the Mellon Center for British Art, see below. *N* was never sold, and is among the Westmorland papers at Northamptonshire County Record Office, as is the single sheet containing *Charles Darbyes Coppy taught English*. The other single poem, *Upon the Scotch Sermon that compared the Kirke to a horsse*, must have been among the State Papers, since it was received by Secretary Windebanke in 1637–38. Among related Fane manuscripts, British Library MSS Add. 34,220 (containing the continuation of Fane's *Vita Authoris*), Add. 34,221 (containing six plays and entertainments), Add. 34,222 (Fane's correspondence 1660–65 as joint Lord-lieutenant of Northamptonshire), Add. 34,217 (containing two Latin poems), and Add. 34,251 (a translation by 'MW' of Fulvius Pacianus' *Of the Art of Well governing A people*) were all bought at the Christie's sale, as was another manuscript containing two plays (a second copy of *Candy Restored* and *Don Phoebo's Triumph*) which is now Huntington Library MS 770. *Ladrones or the Robbers' Iland, an Opera in a Romansike Way*, said to be in Fane's hand, and to feature Drake, 'Candish', Magellan et al., was lot 1,054 in the 1887 Sotheby's sale. It was bought by Toovey for £3 3s, but has since vanished.

Descriptions

Fulbeck Hall MS. Poems, 1621–35 (F1), is a small book of eighty-one unnumbered leaves, each now measuring 167 mm × 107 mm. Only the very top or bottom fragment of the watermark[1] is visible throughout, always at the top of pages on which it occurs. Chainmarks are identical throughout, but the fact that the text is very tight in the guttering, while the sewing is apparently original, indicates that Fane transcribed these poems on flatter sheets than the book now provides, before having it bound. The pages have been trimmed, apparently with scissors, going very close to the text but losing very little of it. This history explains both the loss of the watermarks, which are found at the top edge of pages which have been cut right down to the beginning of the text, and the now meaningless numbering of a few pages in Fane's hand: thus f. 11r is numbered *4*, 16r *2*, and 17r *12*. The book is bound in sections of sixteen leaves, which the vestigial watermarks suggest were octavo, and was rebound around 1900, probably for W. D. Fane after the 1887 sale, in maroon cloth binding, with a maroon label reading simply '*MANUSCRIPTS*'. Entirely in Fane's italic hand, it contains dated poems and prose written between 1621 and 1635. The earliest dated poem is *Navis in tempestate* (f. 15r), annotated by Fane in darker ink '*upon the sea—1621*', and the latest *Insula*

Britannica In Classem Navalem 1635 Mense Maij Littora solventem (f. 80r). The earlier-dated poems are on the whole in a neat italic hand, the later ones more often in a larger, sprawling version of the same, and in a darker ink, apparently the same ink Fane used to go through the book, probably sometime in the 1630s, adding date and place of composition to most of the poems. There is some crossing out and revision, especially in the later-dated poems, giving the book a more untidy appearance than his other manuscripts, an impression compounded by its small size and closely cropped, tight-sewn pages. Despite appearances, though, it is unlikely that many of the poems are first drafts. They are likely to be copies made (and occasionally revised) with a view to keeping a record of work that was otherwise scattered on loose sheets or, as in the case of the two poems addressed to Herrick (ff. 42r, 54r), sent to the addressee. It follows that Fane did not necessarily take the book on his French tour of 1622–25, but that papers from that trip were copied or bound up later. There is no way of knowing whether at this stage he already planned the more ambitious recording of his poetry which begins with the very much more grand *F2*. (The latter includes fair copies of many of the poems in *F1*, but was not started until 1635–36.) *F1* must have remained at Apethorpe until the first Sotheby's sale of 13–14 July 1887, where it is identifiable as lot 843, 'Westmoreland (Mildmay Earl of), Fugitive Poetry, Autograph Manuscript Paris, 1623–35'. It was bought for 14*s* by William Dashwood Fane, and has been at Fulbeck Hall since 1887.

Public Record Office, S.P. 16: 437.60. Upon the Scotch Sermon that compared the Kirke to a horsse
Addressed 'For his Majesties speciall affaires to Mr. Secretarie Windebanke'. A single sheet, folded once to form a page size of 296 mm × 192 mm, and folded subsequently for delivery as a letter. The watermark is a pair of posts or pillars, close to Heaward 3487-8. Addressed on the outer leaf 'For his Majesties speciall affaires to Mr. Secretarie Windebanke', and bearing the Earl of Westmorland's seal. Address and poem are in the italic hand used to copy the Waller poem in *N*, and the first half of Fane's *Vita Authoris* in the version in BL Add. 34,220. It mixes italic with some secretary forms, but has enough letter forms in common with Fane's usual italic to identify it tentatively as his. The poem is undated, but the subject matter implies 1637–38, since which date it must have been among the State Papers.

Fulbeck Hall MS. Poems, 1623–50 (*F2*), is a large, handsome volume with pages measuring 280 × 413 mm, all with ruled margins in the same red ink as *F3*, giving a writing area of 203 × 337 mm. There are 119 leaves, paginated 1-236, the numbering beginning on f. 2r (f. 1r is blank, and f. 1v has a map drawn by Fane of his tour of France and Switzerland). It contains 194 English and 130 Latin poems, together with Fane's Latin *Vita Authoris* up to 1650 (pp. 1–9), a Latin oration given by him in Emmanuel College in 1619 to take his MA *fil. nob.* (pp. 9–10), a map (on different paper, glued in on p. 94) of the disposition of the King's army at Berwick in 1639, and an English prose account of Sir Walter Mildmay (p. 215). It is sewn (on alum-treated pigskin thongs) in gatherings of six large sheets folded once. The paper is the same throughout, with the watermark of Nicolas Lebé of Troyes (a B in a shield with a crown above, and the letters 'NICOLASLEBE' below).[2] The fact that the map was glued in strongly suggests that the book was bought ready bound, or at least that Fane began to make his entries after having it bound. The binding is full calf, with a centred gilt ornament on front and back and a gilt tooled line between two blind lines, with Oxford corners, around the edges of the boards. The boards are original, and have holes for laces. They have been slightly damaged by heat, presumably in a fire. The spine was repaired, probably in the late eighteenth or early nineteenth century, in the style of the same binder who repaired *F3*, when a label 'Memoir of Mildmay, E. of Westmorland, 1601 &c.' was probably added. Early gatherings were repaired, and the spine was cleaned and reglued, in 1999. In pencil inside the front board is inscribed '£4 4/- W. D. Fane July 1892', confirming it was bought at Christie's, 16 July 1892, where it was lot 414, described as 'Memoir of Mildmay, Earl of Westmorland, by himself (in Latin) and a collection of verses, folio, *old calf* 1601'. The book begins (1635–36) with a careful, calligraphic style of italic, and was obviously undertaken then with much care. This care lapses gradually, and most poems post-1640 are copied in Fane's usual italic hand. Near the end of the manuscript the scatological *A letter to C. B. from Epsam Wells* by John Mennes (MS pp. 218–20: see Appendix 1) and *Upon a Coyne Stamp't at Newarke* (MS p. 230) are copied in a far less legible secretary hand which is probably, but not certainly, Fane's own. Though the stages of composition of the *Vita* suggest he began copying just before his wife died in 1636, most of the book is copied during 1643–50, starting from his time in the Tower and subsequent house arrest (1642–44). Although its earliest dated poem was written in 1623 (*In Piscatoris Genevensis*, p. 14) and its last in 1650 (*Upon occa[sion] of Mr Sharpes text in Great St Bartholmes / 20:-2-1649*), the great majority of dated poems, and therefore probably the majority of undated ones also, belong to the years 1640–47. A number of poems, however, are inserted in spaces at the foot of pages, or in space at the end of the manuscript: though most belong to the late 1640s, the dates of their copying cannot be determined with any certainty.

Northamptonshire Record Office: MS Westmorland (A) 6.vi.1. Poems and Prose, 1643–51 (N) A small (193 mm × 290 mm) folio of forty-four leaves, plus blank endpapers. Sewn in one gathering, with original cover of coarse, brown paper. Horn and crozier watermark with PLAMY below (corresponding exactly to Heawood 1220, an example from Lancashire, 1643). Not paginated. Except where indicated below, the manuscript is all in Fane's italic hand, and contains fourteen poems and several pages of political prose by him. Much of the latter was written in 1643–44 when he was under house arrest in London; most of the poems, on the other hand, belong to the years 1645–51. Folios 1r–8v have family mottoes, Latin verse, Latin, French and English prose, prayers and aphorisms, and a poem *Upon the K. Murthered* by 'Cap: Jackson.' Folios 9r–13r have Latin and English poems by or attributed to (among others) Ben Jonson, Falkland, George Herbert and Rowland Woodward. Fane's own poems are found between ff. 10v and 30r, and are interspersed with his prose and others' poems. One of the latter is an otherwise unknown poem by Robert Herrick (*A Christmas Carroll to the Earle of Westmoreland*, f. 23v) which, together with Fane's response on the facing page, is in the same secretary hand as the two poems transcribed in secretary hand in *F2* (see Cain, *Christmas Carol*). Folios 27v–28r, a copy of Waller's *To my Lady Morton on new years daye 1650*, is in what I believe to be his variant italic hand, also found in *H*. The manuscript is reversed from f. 31r to f. 44v with prose relating to Fane's predicament early in the Civil War: ff. 44v–40v contain a draft, in a hand which mixes secretary and italic forms, and which Fane says is his own ('Nor intrust this secrett to any quill but mine owne'), of a letter and memorandum to the King dated 1 November 1643 'from my Prison', urging Charles to return to London and settle with the Parliament; 40r is blank; 39v is a 'Query' deeply critical of the King's conduct; 39r, 'Questiones Politicae' Latin questions and answers on the King's position; 38v–36v, 'Riddles' and 'Responses' of a political nature, all highly critical of the King and his advisers; 36r is blank; f. 35v, draft of a second letter to the King (undated, in the same secretary hand as ff. 44v–40v) reminding him of his previous letter; 34v–35r are blank; 34r is a draft of his petition to the Lords for his sequestration to be lifted (January 1643/44); f. 33v is a draft of a supporting petition to the Lords from the Countess of Westmorland, dated February 1643/44; f. 33r is blank; f. 32v–f. 31v is a series of meditations justifying covenants, dated 14 February 1643/44; f. 31r is a draft of his petition to the Lords to take the Covenant and have his liberty and estates restored (cf. *Lords' Journal*, VI, p. 427a, 14 February 1644, when the petition was brought to the Lords by the Earl of Essex). The manuscript was deposited by the fifteenth Earl along with other Apethorpe papers at Northamptonshire Record Office in 1950–52.

Houghton Library, Harvard: fMS Eng. 645. Poems, 1637–61 (H) A small folio of ninety-seven leaves (195 mm × 295 mm), bound in six gatherings, and still in its original vellum binding, with a label, 'Fugitive Poetry', on the spine, probably of the same date as the labels on *F2* and *F3*. Pagination begins with '1' on f. 3r, and runs consecutively to '189' on f. 97r. Folios 1–2 are not paginated, and f. 3v (p. 2) is blank. Folio 97r (p. 189) and f. 97v (no pagination) are both blank. The watermark is a pot, similar to Heawood 3579 and following, Briquet 12731 and following. *H* is the only one of the four main manuscript collections of Fane's poetry that is not entirely in his own hand: the first two leaves are in his usual italic, and Latin prose on pp. 2–7 is in his secretary hand. Thereafter, most of pp. 7–59 are in an italic hand identifiable as that of William Wake.[3] Wake's hand is succeeded by Fane's variant, more carefully executed, italic hand on pp. 60–9. This is the same hand he uses to copy the Waller poem in *N*, and to transcribe the first half of his *Vita Authoris* in the version in BL Add. 34,220. It mixes italic with some secretary forms, but has enough letter forms in common with Fane's usual italic to identify it tentatively as his. Throughout the pages copied by Wake Fane has made corrections and annotations, and has added whole poems in his own hand, often but not always in the space left at the foot of a page. The rest of the manuscript (pp. 67–188) is entirely in his usual italic hand, with the exception of a Latin poem on pp.

92–3, which is in his variant italic. Although the earliest dated entry is the prose fantasy *My Dream the 8 of 7ʳ 1637*, copying probably began after October 1653, the date of the first poem in the manuscript. The largest number of dated poems, thirty-three in all, belong to the years 1651–55, and the latest is dated 1661 (*To my Lord of Portland for a nights Lodging*, p. 277). *H* was still among the Westmorland papers at Apethorpe in 1855 (HMC *Tenth Report*), where it was already entitled 'Fugitive Poetry'. It was sold at Sotheby's July 1887 sale as lot 1,052, 'Fugitive Poetry, Autograph Manuscript 1648–60'. Bought by Leighton's for £11, it had passed by the early 1920s to G. Thorn-Drury, who published the two poems addressed to Cleveland in *A Little Ark*. The fact that it had been described in detail in the HMC report explains the relatively high price, which may in turn explain why W. D. Fane did not buy it (he bought the next lot, *F3*, a manuscript of similar size and scope, for only £2 10s). *H* probably reached Harvard via one of Sotheby's sales of Thorn Drury's library in 1931, bought by Edgar H. Wells for the Lionel de Jersey memorial collection. It was presented to Harvard College Library in 1932.[4]

Fulbeck Hall MS. Poems, 1649–65 (*F3*), is a small folio (190 mm × 288 mm) bound in seven gatherings, but with the first two and last three leaves missing (seventy-nine leaves in all). The watermark is a one-handled pot with initials RDP, not in Briquet or Heawood, but similar in design to Heawood 3635–8 (all of which Heawood saw in London or Oxford books of the period 1655–74).[5] Pages are ruled vertically in fine red lines, apparently in the same ink as *F2*, to give three narrow columns to the left of each page and one to the right, leaving a central area for text 135 mm wide. The watermark runs in regular sequence throughout, indicating that like *F2* it was almost certainly bought as a book, rather than as loose papers bound later, as was the case with *F1*. It still has its original sewing, but was rebound, probably at the same time as *F2*, and certainly before the eleventh Earl of Westmorland's bookplate of 1856 was pasted on the inside front. It is a limp binding, quarter-leather with blue marbled paper sides cut flush and turned in, and with a label, 'Poems, 1655', on the spine. Pages have been cropped (but with no loss of text), and edges sprinkled red at the time of rebinding. *F3* was one of the manuscripts sold at Sotheby's, 13–14 July 1887, where it was lot 1,053, 'Poems in English and Latin Autograph Manuscript 1655–65'. It was bought by W. D. Fane for £2 10s. ('1/–1888', inscribed in pencil in the latter's hand on what is now the front endpaper, must have been the price of an engraved portrait of Fane which has been tipped in, presumably just after the sale.) *F3* is written throughout in a readily legible, fairly uniform version of Fane's italic hand. Folio 1r has his library inscription, 'Solus Deus protector Meus,' on the top right-hand corner; below it, centred, are two more mottoes: 'Nulla Dies sine Linea' and 'A Jove Principio', followed by a table of contents covering ff. 2–19. Folio 1v is blank, and pages are thereafter numbered in Fane's hand from f. 2r (which is '1') to f. 19r ('33'). This sequence culminates in *A Voyage to Heavnly Canaan*; p. 34 (f. 19v) is blank, but p. 35 (f. 20r) has *Sturbridg Fayer* in the same ink as the previous entries. Pages 36–51 (ff. 20v–28r) are blank, and entries begin again with *Coritanum Regio Vel Comitatus et Agris Darbiensis Descriptio* on f. 28v (p. 52). Thereafter only nine of the remaining 101 pages are left blank. Pagination from p. 35 on is in pencil, in W. D. Fane's hand, but on recto leaves only (i.e. ascending in twos). There are 187 English and Latin poems in the manuscript. The layout of poems in the earlier part of the manuscript suggests Fane began copying after August 1657 (the date of a Latin version of Psalm 23 on p. 12), while *On Good-friday—1659* (p. 30) gives a slightly later date for this first section (two post-1661 poems in the opening pages are both entered on the bottom part of the page, and were probably added after the first section had been copied). Poems that can be dated 1664 or later occur in greater numbers after the space left between pp. 36 and 51. The position and hand of *To Docter Brown a Phisitian maried to Ms. South widdow at Cliff the 9:th of May-1665* (p. 78) suggest that most of this book was in fact copied less than a year before Fane's death in February 1666, but the hand is clear and even, and shows no sign of illness.

Northamptonshire Record Office: MS Westmorland (A) 6.vi.3/26. Charles Darbyes Coppy taught English This poem, in Fane's hand, is on a loose sheet water-damaged and torn, but with little loss of text. It has been laid down on modern paper, making the watermark indistinguishable. Its subject (the arrival of Catharine of Braganza) dates it to soon after May 1662. Like *N*, it was deposited at Northamptonshire Record Office with other Westmorland papers.

Yale Center for British Art, Paul Mellon Collection: Christopher Saxton, Atlas of the Counties of England and Wales (1579), contains three holograph poems by Fane and a number of drawings which may also be his. The atlas was sold at Sotheby's 13–14 July, 1887, lot 1006. It was bought by Quaritch for £15. 10s., and was then sold (October, 1887) to Yates Thompson. It has the bookplate of a subsequent owner, Hermann Marx. It was one of two Saxton atlases bought by Paul Mellon in 1965 and 1966. The first two poems are written on the recto and verso of the blank leaf inserted following the Index, which itself follows the frontispiece. A version of *Coritanum Regio Vel Comitatus et Agris Darbiensis Descriptio* (see p. 309) is on the blank leaf, numbered *41* in ink, following the map of *Derbia*.

Notes

1 5–10 mm, unidentifiable, but seemingly grapes with the maker's initials or similar below or to the side; cf. Heawood nos. 2189, 2199.
2 Briquet nos. 8077–81, closest to 8077, dated 1566, but these sheets of 560 mm × 413 mm are considerably larger than any described by Briquet.
3 Identified by his holograph poem presented to Fane, a Latin version of Fane's *My Happy Life, to a Friend* (*OS*, p. 134), now Cambridge UL MS Add. 4189(E). Wake was a contemporary at Emmanuel (adm. 1 December 1617; BA 1621–22, MA Trinity Hall 1625), and became Rector of Holy Trinity, Wareham, Dorset, 1625–61, buried there 8 May 1661. His son became Archbishop of Canterbury. Like Fane, Wake contributed Latin verses to *Lacrymæ Cantabrigiensis* (1619) on the death of Queen Anne. A note in the Cambridge MS says he 'was Chaplain to the Earl of Westmoreland, and afterwards Rector of the churches of Holy Trinity and St Michael at Wareham, Dorsetshire'. He could have been chaplain to Fane's father from 1622 (his ordination) to his presentation to Wareham in 1625. Fane was abroad throughout this period, however, and since the dates of the poems in *H* in Wake's hand suggest he was copying them during the 1650s, that seems a more likely period for any appointment. But only two chaplains are mentioned in Fane's accounts, Foster (1650) and Harsard (1666), and since Wake was '19 times a prisoner in the time of the rebellion', mainly for preaching Anglicanism, but also for more militant activity, he would not have had much time to spare in those years, unless the copying went on in prison. Rushworth describes him leading a rising in Dorset in 1648. Fane twice records that he 'Sent W: Wake a token' of £1, in September 1653 and September 1654 (W(A) Misc. 4). One of these was accompanied by a Latin poem *To W.W. with a token I had promised but not performed* (*H*, p. 182). See Rushworth, IV. 2, pp. 1037–8; Hutchins, *Dorset*, I, pp. 119–21; Matthews, *Walker*, p. 138; Norman Sykes, *William Wake, Archbishop of Canterbury* (Cambridge, 1957), p. 8.
4 See also Withington, 'Fugitive Poetry' and 'Political Satire'.
5 Though Heawood elsewhere records similar marks in sixteenth-century paper. See 'Sources of English Paper-Supply II. The Sixteenth Century', *The Library*, fourth series, 10 (1930), 427–54.

EDITORIAL CONVENTIONS

Spelling and punctuation

I have throughout followed most of Fane's 'accidentals', even though the lightness of his punctuation, combined with his elliptical style and (to modern eyes) eccentric spelling causes problems of interpretation. Like many copyists at this date, he considers the line ending itself to be an indication of a pause. More unusually, he often leaves a slightly exaggerated space between words within a line for the same purpose; this practice, however, is not consistent enough to justify an editor inserting punctuation whenever there seems to be such a space. There is no doubt that Fane would often look a much better poet in a fully modernised text, and that when a selection of his poems was printed in *Otia Sacra* he, or more likely his printer Richard Coates, did punctuate more fully (and 'modernised' spelling by standardising it). But to modernise punctuation alone among his accidentals would be to impose readings on the holograph which, in a scholarly edition, are better left to the reader to negotiate. Thus to punctuate a line like 'Who thorough Prowess store and Might' (*Upon George Munks routing the Rump*, p. 327, l. 5) would mean choosing between 'Who thorough Prowess, store and Might' and 'Who thorough Prowess'[s] store and Might', and, by prioritising one reading, excluding the other.[1] Fane's spelling, which may reflect Northamptonshire (or Kentish?) pronunciation, just as Raleigh's reflected his 'broad Devonshire', is slightly more distracting than that of most other poets of the period, but forms like *cunterfet* for *counterfeit* (p. 348) or *Medsinall* for *medicinal* (p. 355), should only cause a momentary pause. Such more eccentric formulations as *A sigth the Nitingall* (from the same poem), or *falce illutians fier* ('false illusion's fire', p. 131) present bigger obstacles, and where they are so far from modern orthography as to be unrecognisable I have added an explanatory note. I have adopted the usage, already employed by Coates and other printers in the period, which distinguishes *i* and *u* as vowels, *j* and *v* as consonants. This distinction began to be made by printers from about 1625, but did not become common in manuscripts until the later seventeenth and early eighteenth centuries (the use of consonant *i* in handwriting survived well into the nineteenth century). Fane is typical in his manuscripts in using the traditional medieval and early modern system, in which the *i longa* (*j*) is used only as the second of two *i*-s, which usage is retained here for Latin *ii* but not for English, where *yi* is substituted, as it was by contemporary printers, and as Fane himself began to do in *F3*, the latest of the manuscripts. He also uses *V/v* as an initial letter only, with *u* elsewhere. Had these poems been printed during the period in which Fane was compiling these manuscripts they would have been set in the more modern form, and to retain the manuscript form seems like pointless obfuscation.[2] For the same reason I have replaced *Ff* and *ff* by *F* (as, again, did *OS*). Unlike Coates, however, I have also silently substituted the modern *s* for Fane's long *s*.

Changes to the holograph text

This is an edition of Fane's poetry, rather than a simple transcription of the manuscripts. Any move to print in any case dictates a major departure from the appearance of the manuscript copy, so that even the most faithful transcription represents a partial 'modernisation'. (See, for example, the list of manuscript symbols, including such basic features as versions of the long *s*, which have *not* been represented in Ernest W. Sullivan's fine 'facsimile edition' of the Dalhousie MSS.)[3] Once such concessions to type have been made, it is inconsistent to remain in the half-way house which tries to reproduce some conventions of handwriting and not others. Scanning or photocopying the manuscripts would avoid such problems, but at the expense of clarity, ease of reading, and the numerous interpretive decisions which are the business of the editor. The following changes, which are not noted individually in the apparatus, are made throughout this edition. They are based on contemporaneous typographical conventions, especially those employed by Coates in printing *OS* from copy which, it is reasonable to suppose, was very similar to these manuscripts.

Italics As in *OS*, I have adopted italics for the titles of all poems, and regularised the use of capitals at the beginning of lines (the latter is Fane's normal practice in the manuscripts). I have also used italics where Fane has underlined for emphasis, or to relate a passage to a marginal note, but not where he has underlined to mark a revision, unless both words are retained. Following Coates, I have italicised Latin words or phrases which appear in the English text.

Apostrophes I have silently moved Fane's apostrophes, which he habitually inserted before or after their due place (e.g. *i'st* for *is't*, *t'would* for *'twould*, *'th* for *th'*). He relied heavily on elision to drag his scansion into an often grudging obedience, and there are large numbers of such apostrophes. Often one apostrophe does the work of two, in structures such as *wi'th* and *fro'th*; sometimes the apostrophe is omitted entirely. I have normally emended silently.[4] Coates seems to have done the same silent correction in *OS*. I have also removed superfluous apostrophes in, e.g., *wer't* for *wert*, but have not corrected *It's* (or sometimes *I'ts*) for possessive *Its*. Fane also uses a Jonsonian 'metrical apostrophe', where no letters are missing, to indicate metrical elision of three syllables into two, as in *only' are* (*By-Ward to some Cittisens entring the Tower*, p. 124, l. 141).

Standard abbreviations These have been expanded, with the exception of *Mr, Mrs* (both already becoming distinct from *Master* and *Mistress*, and therefore not capable of being expanded), *Dr* used as a title, and *St* as a title or part of a surname.[5] Ampersands are replaced with *and* or *et* (except in *&c* for *etcetera*), and such dates as *7 br, 9 br* are expanded to *September, November*. Coates also expanded ampersands in English poems, though he retained them in Latin; there are two examples in *OS* where a date has probably been expanded: *The Fift of November* (*OS*, p. 132) was probably *5t of 9r* in the copy, and '*November, 1641*' (*OS*, p. 147) was probably *9 br 1641*. Non-standard abbreviations which occur frequently, such as *Ap:* or *Apth:* for *Apthorpe* (Fane's usual spelling), *Epig:* for *Epigram*, have also been silently expanded, but for infrequently used words the extension is enclosed in square brackets (e.g. *Kitt*[*chen*] p. 210), *Buck*[*ingham*] p. 271). The most common expansions made silently are: y^e / *the*, y^t / *that*, w^{ch} / *which*, y / *your*, w^{th} / *with*, *p* for *pro, per* etc. (as in *pcede* for *procede*), *Lo:* / *Lord, La:* / *Lady, S^r* / *Sir, Matie* for *Majestie*, and a nunnation mark ('tittle') above a letter to represent a missing *m* or *n*. Superscripts not covered by these changes have normally been lowered.

Capitals As frequently happens in manuscripts of this period, majuscule and miniscule (especially here *s, c, w, m* and *o*) are often impossible to differentiate when used as initial letters. A peculiarity of Fane's most cursive italic is that he often uses a capital *T* or *L* (and to a lesser extent *H, C* and *F*) as initial letter, and sometimes even as a medial one, where the context demands lower-case: Coates seems to have faced similar problems with his copy for *OS* (indicating that it was probably, as one would expect from his practice in these manuscripts, in Fane's hand).[6] Coates probably corrected to lower-case in such words as *then, to, let, lie, his, for* etc., but set upper case when the context allowed that Fane might have intended a capital for emphasis or symmetry. I have not followed this practice, partly because it involves a number of arbitrary decisions where Fane's intentions are not clear, but mainly because he is so liberal in his use of other initial capitals that to single out *T* and *L* for a 'correction' to lower-case which would in any case be uncertain would distort the distribution of majuscule and miniscule in the text in the opposite direction.

Corrections and marginalia Where a correction or alteration has been made by Fane, whether above the line or in the margin, I have transcribed it as part of the text, ignoring the deleted version, and not noting the latter unless it is of particular interest. Fane's marginal notes have, however, been transcribed in their original site wherever possible. Casual markings and underlinings (such as those indicating a space in a cramped entry) have been omitted. The occasional use of a flourish, or a colon and dash at the end of a poem, has been replaced by a full stop.

Drawings A striking feature of the early pages of *F2* in particular is the presence of drawings, of varying degrees of competence, placed at the head of poems. Since they are often of very poor quality, and since a scan of the drawings does not sit easily with a printed text, the drawings are not reproduced, but their presence is noted in the commentary. Plate 3 gives an idea of their appearance.

Catchwords (Rarely used by Fane.) These have been omitted.

Dates Old-style dating for days between 1 January and 24 March has naturally been retained in Fane's text, but has been modernised, usually silently, in the Introduction and notes. Substantial changes to the text have been kept to a minimum. Although he is copying his own poems, Fane does occasionally make apparent mistakes, and where it is probable that he has done so I have corrected the text, but always noted the original reading in the textual notes.

Latin poems

There are over 370 Latin poems and prose pieces in the five main manuscripts from which this edition is derived, some of them short epigrams, but many considerably longer. Texts of the Latin poems are not given here, but titles or first lines of all Latin poems and prose (and of the occasional item in Italian or French) are given in Appendix 2. In the case of the large number of poems which exist in both Latin and English versions, with the Latin providing a common title, I have given that title in the body of the text, followed by the English version of the poem.

Revision and duplication

Forty English poems occur in two versions in the manuscripts, most duplication being between *F1* and *F2*. In almost all these cases it is clear that *F2* provides Fane's revised fair copies, and I have transcribed these, but noted all variants of any significance (not minor variants of spelling or capitalisation). Seven poems are found in both *F2* and *H*. Though the latter is, in general, copied later, all seven poems it shares with *F2* are in the hand of William Wake, and include such errors as the transposition of lines. Nor are they necessarily copied later than the versions in *F2*, since all the poems *F2* shares with *H* are inserted in spaces in the manuscript at a date or dates that cannot be determined. Since they are all in Fane's own hand, and some include marginalia omitted in *H*, I have transcribed the versions in *F2*. I have also preferred *F2*'s texts in the case of the two poems it shares with *F3*. Though much of *F3* was copied late in Fane's life, these two poems occur in the opening pages, which were probably copied in the late 1650s. Since the versions in *F2* are added to that manuscript, and are found near its end, they cannot be dated securely; but since they include in one case the deletion of a word found in the *F3* version (*Mundus Vanitas*, l. 3), it seems that they are revisions of those versions. There are in any case few significant variants, and all are recorded in the textual notes. Ninety-three poems (nearly all in *F2*) are duplicated in *OS*: variants in the latter's text are also recorded in the textual notes.

Notes

1 Fane's spare punctuation is not unusual, especially at the end of lines. See Ted-Larry Pebworth, 'Manuscript Transmission and the Selection of Copy-Text in Renaissance Coterie Poetry', *Text*, 7 (1994), 243–61, p. 250.
2 *OED* s.v. *J* suggests that 'during the decade which followed 1625, J, j, *J, j*, appear to have been gradually added to all founts of type, and the present usage of restricting I i to the vowel, J j to the consonant appears to have been generally established soon after 1630'. Johnson, however, still treats I and J as one letter in his *Dictionary*, 'his first word *I* being followed by *Jabber, Jam* by *Iambick*, and this by *Jangle*'.
3 *The First and Second Dalhousie Manuscripts Poems and Prose by John Donne and Others*, ed. Ernest W. Sullivan, II (Columbia MO, 1988).
4 The exception is for the many occasions in *H* where no apostrophe is used at all in such constructions as *o' th'*. One of the most eccentric misplacings is *Neath'* for *'Neath* in *To David Earle of Exeter after the death of William Ruin-house* (p. 115, l. 5). For Fane's *T'were* etc, cf. Donne's

holograph verse letter to Lady Carey and Mrs Essex Rich: in l. 2, Donne's *T'were* was corrected by the *1633* printer to '*Twere*.
5 Fane uses *St.* rather than the *S.* favoured by Coates and most other English printers; it is silently expanded here when used generically.
6 Most of the poems in *F2* which were printed in *OS* are marked in the margin with a cross and 'Imp.', but the condition of the manuscript suggests that it could not have been used as printer's copy. It is not clear whether 'Imp.' is an instruction to a copyist (*imprime*) or a record of a poem having been printed (*impressus est* etc.).

VITA AUTHORIS

Since Fane wrote his own autobiography it seems appropriate to allow him to offer his own account here to accompany his poems, which themselves constitute, with the notes, a fuller if more fragmentary *Vita*. Since Fane leaves a great deal out, however, a large number of notes have been added to try to round out his version. There are two copies of the Latin *Vita*: the earlier is in *F2*, pp. 1–9, and is preceded by a full-page map, drawn by Fane, of France and the area around Geneva, illustrating his 'Tour' in the early 1620s. The *F2* version, written in at least fourteen separate stages, breaks off in mid-sentence because of lack of space while describing events of 1650. Fane then copied all of the *Vita* from *F2* into another book, now BL Add. 34,220, and carried on his account down to 1662. This translation is based on the full version in Add. 34,220. I have changed Fane's Cæsarean third person to first person and his present historic to past throughout (the first sentence would begin 'He is born at Badsell . . .'). His rather formal Latin has otherwise been followed closely, save where literal translation would be impossibly stilted. Dates have been adjusted to new-style.

I was born on 24 January 1602, in the reign of Elizabeth, at Badsell in the Weald of England's most unconquerable county.[1] I was descended from most noble stock, of the Neville family, but, as was fitting, I took my name from the Fanes.[2] In my third year I moved about a hundred miles north, where growing from infancy to boyhood, while I played at odd-and-even and rode on a hobbyhorse, imbued with a certain amount of learning I began at the same time to follow the Muses and to serve Diana.[3] After twelve years spent in play I was sent to grammar school, and handed over to Pythagoras. Then after finally completing the fourth winter with no few beatings I was set free, having got only this for an answer: 'The Master said so.'[4] I entered the Cambridge Athens[5] and there, applying myself to studies rather more diligently than before, towards the end of the fourth congregation I was awarded the degree of Master of Arts by special grace. Then putting off that gown (in the reign of James), I was ordered by my parents to assume another, namely that of a man and a senator, and was compelled to disguise my youth, until then dedicated to merriment and jest, in the sternness of a Cato and a seriousness altogether unsuited to my years.[6] Being awakened from that sleep, I changed my surroundings, but not my spirit, by hasting across the sea,[7] and passed a lively time in France in the pursuit of all the accomplishments of war and the court, among which I always held that of horsemanship the first.

During the seven months of winter I secluded myself at Orléans, a town situated on the nearer bank of the Loire, to acquire the language. At the end of that time, when

> the snows departed and the fields resumed
> their green and trees their brown[8]

enamoured as it were by their beauty, I travelled away to visit La Rochelle, that place which was afterwards the cause of so much honour to our nation and so much disastrous loss of men.[9] On my journey back the States of Poitiers and Anjou opened their gates to me, and the miniature garden of all France, Tours, which rivals that of Alcinous and is nearest to Paradise, a cornucopia of delights, invited me to stay for a considerable time. At length, after sufficient enjoyment of these, I was received into Paris, adding a drop so that the flow and ebb in the succession of men might not be wanting. The season of frost being passed once more, I grew anxious to visit more distant parts. On my way to Bordeaux I crossed the chestnut district of Limousin and, amply filled with the dainties of Tityrus, I came to the river Gironde, following the course of which I was carried in a kind of skiff to the city [Bordeaux] washed by the further waters of the stream, and extinguished the thirst of my curiosity in the wine born in its sandy ground (so dear to Londoners), drinking it, as it were, from its very cradle in its parent soil. Without leaving the guidance of the river I passed through traces of war and entered Montauban, which was surrounded by earthworks, and I praised the constancy and caution of the reformers. From here I went without much enthusiasm [*non corde*] to nearby Toulouse, where, being admitted (as was the custom) into the number of the students, I left a small gift, as a memorial of my grateful sense of so much munificence.

Then, as I had planned, I turned my steps towards Narbonne. There, looking towards the neighbouring kingdom, and separated from it only by snowy mountains, at first I supposed the whiteness came from a large snowy flock grazing there, and I was minded to describe the fertility of Spain with much admiration. But afterwards perceiving it was only snow and sterility, I wrote:

> When you are at Narbonne, look at the Pyrenees Mountains
> Thus indeed did we see the Western Land, and against our will
> Nor was it wrong that we saw it: he who has seen the waters of Styx
> Is made more cautious in what he looks at again.

Making a willing departure, I saw the Mediterranean glittering like a mirror in the rising sun. My journey lay through innumerable olive groves and thyme-covered plains scented with rosemary, greatly gratifying to the senses. At length I entered Montpellier ('The Mount of Girls' as Syncerus[10] calls it), a town not long before brought into obedience to its prince, and therefore subject to military government.[11] Not many miles distant is the little town of Aigues Mortes, noteworthy for the narrowness of its approach: indeed, scarce three men shoulder to shoulder can enter it together. From there my curiosity led me to Nimes, a town famous for its Arena and other Roman remains, and the next day I went on to visit the Pont du Gard, and turning in my mind Beza's Latin lines upon it, I translated them.[12]

Bidding farewell to this marvellous structure, I was soon a witness to the swiftness of the Rhone, and passing across it arrived safely at Arles, whose eastern bank is adorned with splendid buildings. For the next day's excursion I intended to visit La Crau,[13] the southern boundary of which the Tuscan Sea washes without ebb and flow. The sandy shores there, however, offered themselves to be walked on, and by them I went on to Marseilles. There, enchanted with rare beauties, I was lost in the contemplation of the city and the surrounding country. The one, with its fine marble buildings rising high into the air, worked a kind of fascination on my eyes; the other, deserving the name of gardens rather than of fields, and abounding with golden, russet and purple apples, almost stole away my senses altogether. However, bewitched by I know not what Siren song, I was enticed to the harbour, where I boarded a little boat which spread its sails in a favourable wind and made the voyage to the castle, built on a rock, I being eager for the delights of Neptune as well as Ceres. On my return, I went on to try the thermal baths at Aix-en-Provence (where the waters do indeed burst out hot from the ground). From there I came to Avignon, where (just as at Rome) everything is for sale.[14] Even sins with Thaises[15] are permitted, as is consorting with Jews, and for a price the papal pardon is readily granted both to the one and to the other, seeing that they bring in a good profit. As contraries placed near each other shine out more brightly, next to this country lies the charming principality of Orange, so very fertile in grain and fruit. Orange rejoices in its closeness to the truth as held by Calvin, Avignon in the meretricious teachings of Rome. Both of them are free from the sceptre of France.

I crossed the Rhone once more by the beautiful bridge of St Spiritus, and (looking at the course of the river backwards) retraced it as far as Lyons, where it seems to marry the Saone. So while in bed there I wrote a poem in the style of Martial:

> And the little bed watches more than one stream:
> Who sees the Rhone on this side, may see the Saone on the other.[16]

When the Moon's horns had met in full orb, I was seized by a wish to visit holy Geneva, and—the way that leads to the Saints is said to be arduous. Believe me, whoever climbs such a mountain (which I believe they call Mount Bressus)[17] whose top is among the stars, and which breaks the clouds with its middle slopes, will find it so, his head pouring moisture on to his feet in a clear sky. Nor other [than arduous] can be thought that way by which, after passing over the mountain, we travelled through many hills and many a difficulty. Nor was the way any less arduous which was nearest to the house[18] which Nature did not yet want to be marked out by better stones, but rather, that the stranger should shudder, she made the whole route one of hateful rockeries. These were not, however, so placed that they avoided being hit by the swift wave of the river: while they attempted in vain to check its course, and strove vainly with all their might, they howled with a sharp groan and beat the air as if with words. But now the Key and Eagle was here, now the other part was seen, and, fleeing from the shadows, we would be restored to the light.[19] But as the sun, coming forth in the shining east, reveals itself to the opening day and promises a clear sky, but afterwards puts on Aurora's wings painted with changeful red, then, driven by some evil wind, clouds appear, the earth becomes wet with tears and the day is darkened. So here Piety was marked only by its pretty colours, and Religion glittered. The divergence from the trumpet sound of Fame was deep and wide, for within were found harlotries and a thousand evils, so that

> Who has not seen you will perhaps call you Holy
> But he who has seen you can only tell the truth.

For a very large number there, while they imitated the Curii, lived like Bacchanals. There indeed it was most emphatically 'Let's drink!' but 'Let's tread a measure freely' must be only in secrecy.[20]

This town opens into two nearly equal parts (divided by the river Rhone) which are joined only by a bridge. Lake Leman is untroubled by the river's swiftness, and seems to wage as it were a war with its floods against the north, while the huge mountains surround it and

> The scaly fish with trembling tails leap through
> The limpid pools, and bigger trout perform
> Gentle games beneath the glassy sea

At about three o'clock on Sundays a public market is held for the people in the vicinity, and they devote the church of St Peter to the nourishment of their bodies as well as their souls. In the northern part of it you may see a place entirely closed to divine service and wholly dedicated instead to Ceres, perhaps with the motive of destroying the figure of the Cross inside, which they could not do outside without very great inconvenience, choosing rather to have this den of thieves in the house of prayer than the similitude of Him through whom all Christians triumph over death itself, showing themselves to be Jews in this matter as well as in that of practising usury. That their forces may not be wanting when enemies are to be resisted, they do violence to the Lord's day itself, and dedicate the afternoon to both Mars and Jove.[21]

Here the government is not in the hands of a Romulus or a Caesar, a single dictator or emperor, nor two Consuls for the year, nor a Decemvirate or Triumvirate, but a Quatrumvirate (if I may so say) called by the name of Syndics; to whose rule the last day of the year puts an end, and four others fresh from their workshops mount upon the throne to carry on the business of the Commonwealth. Not for nothing do they dispense justice as well as merchandise.[22] Here there is no episcopacy, but two of the Ministers are always called into the Senate, and they have the chief authority in all matters of voting.

After two months I left Geneva and by a journey of a mile betook myself to the country or canton of the Swiss Bears.[23] Following the shore of Lake Leman, I entered Lausanne, a university which differs greatly from the old rule: for while other universities aim at equality, nowhere did I find a greater inequality than here as regards the streets; the buildings are not placed together in rows, but it is an ascent or descent through the whole town.

Going on past the point where the Rhone flows into the lake, where you will perceive that there is a mighty conflict in one and the same element, I arrived at the mouth of the Valais, and although I was hungry I was forced to support fasting inasmuch as I could not buy fish at any price and it was unlawful to eat flesh there. That night I devoted to the Savoyards: I slept at Thonon, and on the next day finished this journey where I had begun it.

At length I had a mind to return, and by the windings of the Loire I hastened back to Orléans in a skiff, and passed the third winter at Paris. At a time when Venus's son was lighting his torch, and the Roses and Lilies were being prepared for a marriage,[24] I wrote of each of them after the manner of the classical poets:

> Why sing of the beauties of Ganymede and Jove's fire?
> For Cupid himself can make even the gods blind;
> Why praise Helen? For indeed her perfection of form is unique
> Since Lilies have been married with Roses.

Afterwards, while the year was still young, I planted myself in my native clime (the sea being favourable) with my domestic gods, and—to render life happier—while possessing a property acquired not by work but by inheritance,[25] I formed my mind to quietness and the greatest aversion to dispute. But my compatriots could not ignore the Parliament that had then been recalled.[26] Thereupon, that I might afford some proof of an exultant and joyful mind at the coronation of our most serene Lord King Charles, while still diligently applying myself to my office, I was inducted into the order of the Knights of the Bath, and girt with a sword.

Next I endured no small share of the ills which love calls pains, while our parents spun out insupportable delays: for love ill bears with delays. But, the wedding completed,[27] the pains disappeared and in the breast of each the warmest happiness shone forth, from whose heat I was enriched with sweet children adorned with the sex of the Graces, and with their number, after as many years. Of these the two younger fell asleep[28] and in their place another two were given by God ever gracious.[29] And in the eighth year after marriage not for Pollio but for myself 'a new progeny from heaven descends.'[30] On the same day of the new year on which we celebrate the Epiphany of the Magi, to this child Charles our most august Augustus deigned to grant his sponsorship and so was pleased of his extraordinary goodness and favour to dignify the little boy with his own name.[31] But when ten years from the marriage had passed in the greatest happiness and in the interchange of tender affections with a delicate wife, in a new confinement (as if to that born) she too fell asleep, and left me, who had been her most fortunate husband, a disconsolate widower.[32]

Touching her lineage, if you look to the better side you may find her sprung from the noblest, and the title of its Viscount commemorates the place of the victory of Kinegils over the Britons;[33] if you look to the other side, you may know her to be the daughter of a knight. She had received a gracious first name from the Graces, and you would have found her to be endowed as much with pleasantness and gentleness of manner as with beauty of figure and appearance, to such an extent that you would think the choir of the Graces had descended from heaven and made its nest in that human breast. She gave her entire faith to the Word of God: she rested her hope of pardon solely on the merits of the Son of God, and, inspired by the Spirit of Love, she gave herself up completely to tenderness and love of her children and her friends (in effect for everyone, for she could in no wise nourish any enmity). Although in its prow her maiden name had a thorny sound, yet both the soundness of her conversation and the gentleness of her virtues were such that I, whom God had vouchsafed to be so happy during ten years, gathered roses from these thorns. When six more months had passed my younger daughter Isabella, after being afflicted with various infirmities of body and weaknesses of mind, followed her mother to the grave.

After two years of sterile widowhood, I chose a widow for my second marriage,[34] on account of both her fertility and her qualities [*propter partus quam partes*]. She was truly [*vere*] gifted with very great fecundity, children, beauty and virtues, and you may take her, if you look at her name, to have been enriched also with no false endowments or honours, as is wont to be the case with too many widows. Her descent indicated that she was noble, her excellence that she was truly a Vere [*virtus vero Veram denotat*]: both of these showed again how fortunate I was to have found this jewel. By this second marriage I first had a daughter, and I ordered that she should be called Mary, after her mother's name.[35]

In the year 1639 a disturbance arose among the Scots over ecclesiastical authority and the regulation of discipline. In order to make peace, I was dragged away under arms, along with King Charles, in himself most peaceful, into those northern parts, hateful for both their miscreants and their mists [*tam nebulonibus quam nebulis*]; and there, having followed soldiering for the space of a month while a pseudo-war was waged, I witnessed the peace.[36] With the concession of those laws (although sacred as they say to antiquity), that armed state gave way to peace; and while the desired policy was Episcopacy, the Scots would contemplate only Presbyterianism. They wished only to restore the latter, and to extirpate the former as a thing held by them to be most odious (and thus it was granted to those particular bishops to say with more truth than usual for those times the two little words 'Nolo episcopari').[37] Whether this deed should be attributed more to the greatness of spirit of the people (endowed with obstinacy) or to the innate clemency of the King, this I will avow, the former reached the height of audacity, the latter of goodness. When that business was done (the relation of which appears as an argument for making peace rather than war) and while the Prince was contemplating his return, he condescended to honour the house of his servant with his sacred presence for the space of one night and to accept most contentedly whatever I could prepare in so short a time for so august a sovereign, who completed his servant's happiness by bringing with him his nephew, the Palatine.[38]

In the following year, the Scots having entered England and taken Gateshead without resistance,[39] I was once more summoned by the sovereign, with other magnates, prelates and peers, to the conference to be held at York.[40] There of his special grace and mere affection it pleased our most excellent Lord the King to inform all those persons of his intention to summon a parliament again and (to use his own words) he desired to be so bound to his people in love that he would never be willing to do anything in the future except what he was himself convinced would plainly tend to their benefit, so that he might in future govern this kingdom committed to him in the greatest peace and tranquillity; and to endeavour to do this with all care and vigilance would always be his intention.[41] This he has hitherto most faithfully performed, even to sacrificing for the sake of the Commonwealth those whom he had recently had closest to himself for office as well as for counsel.[42] This was from hearsay only, for I was prevented from being present in Parliament by a severe attack of smallpox. At this time of nativity, however, my little son was born whom I caused to receive my own name: thus sweets are given after the bitter has been tasted.[43]

Afterwards, when it was given to me to enjoy greater mental vigour, I set out to the parliament, and there by I know not what Remora of delays having been countenanced, while Parliament was proceeding to the defence of the Commonwealth at a pace all too slow, on the third day of May both Houses were surrounded by many thousands of citizens calling for justice, nor was any resistance to be made to that monster of many heads. So that, scarce five more days having passed, he whom the populace had previously judged was condemned by the votes of the peers, and on the twelfth day of the same month he was publicly beheaded.[44]

I have deemed that date worthy of special note, because this deed was done to him almost at the same moment, if you look to the month, day and hour (namely that nearest in the morning to noon) at which only one year previously he had advised his master to dissolve the Houses of Parliament,[45] so that he who had striven by means of a dissolution himself at last underwent dissolution, and with him all that host of crimes of monopoly although hitherto reserved for proper penalties.[46] When this had been transacted, and while the English Parliament applied itself to other matters with a view to a state of preparation, the Father of our Country, in its truest sense, went to his native country in order not to appear wanting in care or vigilance for those with whom he had first watched in the very cradle.[47] And there, the Scottish Parliament being also in session, he (it was said) so attracted and animated the hearts of all by rays of justice and pious attachment that all that had been reduced to squalor by the woes of frost and Northern discord could be seen most evidently to be in a state of restoration, and the remains of the laws to be so softened by the light of his prudence and the dew of his clemency that their harvest as well as this of ours seemed as if it would be crowned not merely with a happiness springing up afresh, but also with the mature fruit of peace. Upon this the Scots retired satisfied, being again closely united by a compact of fraternal affection. At the same time the English were overjoyed because the two nations could now appear to future times as serving the same God, and both of them always most dutiful and faithful to the same prince: and they become most truly a spectacle not of pity but of envy to all surrounding countries. In memory of which event and in thankfulness for the bounty of the Almighty let that seventh day of September 1641 be designated a Solemn Feast.

In November the Prince returned homeward from Scotland, once again his own, having left all things there in perfect tranquillity, and hastened with much rapidity to visit the Londoners and the English (always his own) now again assembled newly in Parliament. They came to meet him, some for business, others on the road and in the streets: both manifested their joy, the former by assistance, the latter by coming together and accompanying him.

Zeal in the affairs of the State possessed the former, folly in the shadow of honour or gain possessed the latter too much—too much, I say—since neither by these nor by those was sufficient moderation shown. Moreover, even the Prince's safety was in some degree endangered by those lawless mariners[48] and by the scum of the citizens. Further, his Ireland was also near disaster by reason of the unsuitable and lengthened delays which were contrived.[49] And while the business of, as it were, changing the monarchy into an aristocracy or rather (as was too evident) into a democracy was in train, I feared lest changing the sovereign in that region [Ireland] as well might, by reason of the delay in granting a subsidy to assist him, not only be proposed, but be hastened, and while a new scheme of government was under consideration for that island and ancient dominion annexed to this Crown, the reins of government might be altogether loosened.

That the rashness of the people might rage more and more, nothing was held to be more odious than the dignity of the clergy and the authority of the bishops.[50] This being admitted, no one was to be regarded as more worthy than the draper or more qualified than the bucklemaker as a workman for praying or preaching. So that henceforth there should be no value in the proverb 'Let the cobbler stick to his last', now it was 'Let everyone do as he pleases'.

On the thirteenth day of January this year my sweetest consort had another child, adding to her own sex Elizabeth,[51] the sister of Mary. Also on the twenty-fourth day of the same month in the year 1642 I could truly be called a 'quadragenerian'.[52] After a while, by order of the Parliament, I travelled to Dover to deliver to the King some proposals relating to Ireland, where I witnessed the departure not of Æneas from Dido but of Dido from Æneas.[53] She went with her daughter to Holland, while he took himself to York with his sons. In their absence S.P.Q.L.[54] willed with supreme authority that their ordinances should be obeyed as Laws so that they seemed to have left nothing to the King but the name;[55] and yet these great ones asserted loudly that our Charles was made greater by their operations. Why then the refusal of access to him to the Councillors and great Officers of the order of the Garter, although bound by their oaths that they would attend his service at that time? Why the removal of his military stores,

altogether without his concurrence? Finally, why was he wholly excluded from his fortified town and harbour which earlier rejoiced in being Royal in name?[56] Why, save that what had long before been the apprehension of all may be said to have duly come: the beginning of a Perpetual Parliament, the end of the reign of Charles the First. Yet that God might avert this I, the unfortunate witness of these things, most humbly prayed. Nevertheless the Prince, at once most clement and religious, persevered in softening so as gradually to exhaust Parliament with propositions plainly manifesting his desire of peace. But in vain. By a general resolution (so far as the votes tell the number) they chose a general for themselves.[57] Out of groundless fear and senseless alarm they called for a war that was not merely defensive but also for attacking enemies (as they wished them to be called) by every illegal method, as if they were panic-stricken. Yet they could find no enemies.

And so they attacked him, whom shortly before the common people themselves had driven away with their mobs because he could not assent to their insolent desires, amounting to wickedness. As before they had attacked him over his sacred privileges, so now they attacked him in his very person and his children, although again and again it was declared that he was most desirous that a scheme of accommodation should be brought forward.

How long will ye abuse that patience[58] in him whose peace-loving mind is so disposed that he himself should suffer, rather than his subjects? However, for his own defence and that of his friends he at length provided himself with a company of troops at York, of which number—not to be unmindful of the motto of my ancestors which runs thus 'Always prepared for any event in the cause of country and at the prince's command'[59]— I accepted the commission of a commander of cavalry,[60] and not to be without a device I caused this badge to be assumed:[61]

Thereafter, so that I might all the less denounce the varied fortunes of war, I was captured by a party of the enemy rejoicing in the name of dragoons,[62] about thirty in number, before the battle had its successful outcome, and was hauled off to the Parliament which was left and consigned to the security of the Tower.⁶³

When I had endured some months there in a hard enough condition I was released, but only on these terms, that I should be confined to my own house in that city by the obligation of my word and honour.⁶⁴ That this small particle of liberty might not be without a redeeming circumstance a little daughter was born then to this Laban, and she was named Rachel.⁶⁵ Thereafter, that this erring human being should be treated with greater humanity, I was permitted for the sake of my health to make excursions up to a distance of five miles about the City.⁶⁶

At length, when I had meditated long and seriously over that state of discord, and had more truly compared the first seeds of those unhappy disputations with the harvest of desolation and ruin in which so much horrible slaughter without any end was being committed; and also because proposals for peace hitherto remained as promises only, while everything was produced not from the quiver of the Principal Council but of a more secret one,⁶⁷ from which very sure destruction was threatened to the State and also to the Prince, so long as too great licence was given to savage factions, I was easily brought to change my mind. Therefore I yielded myself to join the Solemn League and Covenant, not being unmindful of the foreboding sounds of the blinking raven or of the wretchedness of the Germans⁶⁸ and being thus by reasoning led back into an obedience as much private and innate as a public duty, whatever measure of days or years was left to me I piously and willingly gave up and consecrated for the future to the public good of my prince and my country, that is, to the Parliament.⁶⁹

No long time having elapsed, when February numbered its thirteenth day and the year 1645, my very prolific wife was confined anew, and I received, in another son, the gift of an ever gracious God, truly [*vere*] a triple happiness for my House, and therefore I caused him to be named Vere (than which nothing is more true [*verius*]). That he might closely imitate the virtues of his grandfather was the earnest wish of his father. In remembrance of it, I was pleased to commemorate the birthday in some verses, as you will find.⁷⁰ Seventeen months having passed, there was added to this Vere and the rest, Henry, upon whose birth I again made verses as in fol. 186.⁷¹ My fruitful wife bore again, but a dead child, and in the following year yet another, both rejoicing in the female sex.

The populace, merely for the sake of liberty, rejected in great measure the calmness of peace by which our unique island may justly be said to have been victorious over all regions of the earth; and it no longer kept in use the bonds of peace and concord (that is, the established laws), which you may conclude had been so violated that it became very apparent that those arms had imposed silence upon them. So that it may now be said not unjustly of that sixth day of December 1648 on which we saw brutes or their soldiers invade the Councils of Parliament, the beginning of this perpetual war has put an end to a free Parliament.⁷²

Our Charles, once so dear to all and even now to not a few, while under the power of the army was seized by them (alas! the unspeakable wickedness), that the Almighty may no longer afford him protection, and having been thus carried off will perish.⁷³ Who in telling, writing, or even thinking about such things can refrain from tears!⁷⁴ But thus it was: we saw⁷⁵ our King, so long holy and peace-loving, fall by the blow of the axe at the hands of the impious and utterly profane soldiery. Immense grief now imposed silence as much on our thoughts as on our pens and words. Let it suffice that wickedness so great be recorded in heaven that it may eventually be punished.

The Almighty again responded to the prayer of my consort, eloquent as regards fruitfulness, so that on the fifteenth day of February she bore another daughter, whom, that she might be more fitly devoted to the wheel and the spindle, the works of Penelope, her parents caused to be named Katherine.[76]

The August Father of his Country having been put to death (though he will always be remembered by us), it was not to be doubted that the Almighty would at length turn the sun of his blessing on his children, so that out of the ashes of the paternal pyre, as it were, the son who had now become the eldest, being gifted with every virtue and talent out of the perfumed nest of the paternal clemency and piety, might be revived as another Phoenix to the wonder of the world. And though for some space of time he may have been thrown about on land and sea and may have tasted fully enough the benevolence and kindliness of the former, although a foreign one, and the rage and madness of the fierceness of the other, he made his way to his Scots, where being received and acknowledged with honours he was robed with the purple of a king and (as it was said) with the royal crown and sceptre.[77] Here, while he took his Northern subjects under his government and protection, he was both consulted and protected by them (now at last exulting in fidelity) until[78] by some poison or other of the Fates, or by the tireless work of the Devil, evil was again sought and won by force of arms; and so the people itself, whose loyalty and obedience had fed only on grass and not on suitable fodder, gave way to those brothers of Megaera, those friends of Cerberus.[79]

On 21 February 1651, between eleven p.m. and midnight, my most delightful wife gave birth to a daughter, whom we named Susanna,[80] dedicated to the Chaste Goddess at this time so that she was safe from the Presbyterians and elders of the people. Not many months later, while the war was being waged no less with cunning than with acts of bravery (or, to quote the proverb, 'What do you want in an enemy—cunning or bravery?'), when the English soldiers had again been carried into that part of Scotland which they call the peninsula of Fife, and when the virgin rejoicing in the name Edinburgh Castle had been won back, by trickery and not by force (as some people think) and by the strength of a golden bridge,[81] Charles conceived the idea of returning to England, now followed as the King of Scotland. While he was waiting for the auxiliary forces of his compatriot subjects (for the English crown was also rightly his by birth) to make up the greatest part of the army (the Scots were now almost defeated in Scotland), he resisted in a wonderful fashion. After he had given battle for several hours on 3 September,[82] and when he had shown himself ably skilled at fighting bravely and with real spirit, and had led his men with no simple fortune through the battle lines of the enemy, he appeared safe, sound and divinely protected in Paris. Before doing so, he went undiscovered through the midst of some soldiers of the seventh regiment not only in England but even in London, the capital of the island, until, with even the wind on his side, and with Neptune not frowning upon him, with good fortune he crossed over to France in a small boat.[83] He was received by the French (so it was said) with pomp and generosity. And he effected this escape on the advice of the most loyal Lord Wilmot.[84] Indeed, when there was no hope of victory left he hid in the hollow of a certain tree,[85] and was hidden by the good will of the night. Afterwards, making contact with a nearby house, he found so great a pattern of affection and so great a fruit of obedience there that straight away the mistress of that house (whose name was Mrs Lane) prepared a horse (she left her household behind) and mounted it with him; and, so well disguised as a servant with his mistress that he was believed to be such by passers-by, with much luck this dear Charles of ours reached the seashore.

But, alas, the faithlessness and fickle nature of the French, and their forgetfulness of their ancestry! For not many years later they were joined in some pact or other with the English people, and this most Christian prince, whose title they usurped, was expelled most cruelly from that country of his ancestors, along with his brothers, James, Duke of

York and Henry of Gloucester.[86] The reason for this temerity became apparent, of course, when religion made its demands. They earnestly asked him to show himself a Roman Catholic. He, the son of the true Catholic Church and the most upright patron of this English Church, rejected and despised the edicts of Rome. They utterly extinguished the light of grace and favour that exists in a mother for her sons, and the spark of charity that exists in a cardinal for his priests. Even if the mother was a queen, and a magnificent offspring of Henry the great king of France, imbued with faith and doctrine, she was nevertheless very easily trained in this same evil along with a Cardinal of the same ilk. As a result, neither the Cardinal's generosity nor the Queen's natural affection was of avail in deterring or keeping away envy from them. And so these princes, the most true heirs of their father's virtue as well as of these islands, found themselves in a second exile while they rightly and justly awaited help from their kinsmen.

Meanwhile, while the clouds of such enormity surrounded these most serene young men, they thought upon the inscription of the most serene Queen Elizabeth that is found on pennies, which reads 'I have made God my helper' and on the reverse 'God protects her'.[87] Thus provided, they placed their hope of armies in God alone, not fearing what evil men and demons wished for, or were able to do, out of their long-standing hatred of the human race. But they knew that God would, in his own time, free his servants from exile and from being slaves to men, and so awaited His will for all with great spirit and manly patience. And this Charles of ours did not eagerly seek peace through war (as we have recently seen embossed on some coins of another person), even if he was second to none for righteousness.[88] But, since he was the most true grandson [*filiolus*] of King James the peacemaker, he sought his undisputed patrimony and his usurped kingdom with every peaceable means and with peaceful hard work.

While this was the situation, he patiently awaited the decision of his Divine Majesty and retreated to the princes of Spain, who were of course endowed with far greater constancy. Neither that Frenchman Mazarin nor our own English Masaniello[89] was without so great, so treacherous, so monstrous a plot that, before this most noble Prince could be restored to his own goods and titles, neither expense nor blood should be spared. They advanced the Church Militant while the tall stem of the True Church waved to and fro. But freedom (albeit late in the day) might at last pay attention to him in his doldrums [*Inertem*], inasmuch as he was one for whom serving the Almighty increased the sure perfection of freedom.

But now, to heap up more certain hatred and ruin for these princes, their enemies waged war as vigorously as possible abroad or outside the kingdom. These allies invaded Spain and its maritime provinces; and, after the Fort of Mardyke had been captured they besieged Dunkirk,[90] while at home they incited countless intrigues and Trapans[91] (a type of traitor previously unheard of), in order to rid the world of both citizens and others greatly devoted to faithfulness by means of that most lofty pretext, justice. But, in the end, the Protector Oliver could find no protector to protect himself from the power of death, and he who had stirred up in this kingdom such a great plague of civil war was himself finished off by illness and was laid to rest by a better fate than he deserved, inasmuch as it was natural and peaceful, to the extent that he kept his body and did not die under the blade of the axe, or with the honour afforded to the evil cross. This was the reward to suit such great wickedness: for of course this was the man, rejoicing only in a name—Oliver—and not in a title, who had brought about exile from their homeland for those delightful roses and beautiful lilies. He had done this in order to promote his own foul offspring to be princes and princesses. But the bust of Mercury cannot be made from any old wood;[92] for, with the regicide dead, his elder son—that is, Richard—eagerly took the helm, but not for long. For each of the public enemies, contemplating their own merits, tried to throw him from his office now that he had acquired it, and along with him the whole race of his family, and the Parliament recently assembled by him, in order that the earlier Parliament should be restored, as they wished. Since even the army did not find him suitable, he was at once removed, so that it may more rightly be said that, amidst arms, law is silent—to such an extent that all authority was at once void, except, that is, for military authority and whatever was granted to each individual.[93] Thus Astraea left the earth[94]—that is to say, our barbarous isles—and we plunged headlong into confusion, rather as the poet says took place in the Trojan war:

> Mulciber stood against peace, Apollo for it;
> Venus was favourable to the Britons, Pallas unfavourable.[95]

But now, since a cowl does not make a monk, our Monk booed off the stage all those bewitched cuckoos of religion, enemies of peace and justice, in order that righteousness, a united Church, fraternal love, unanimity among the people and correct government through the laws should be brought back together for all men.[96]

Meanwhile, while affairs at home were in this changeable state, overseas France sought to be united with Spain in a mutual and conjugal pact, to such an extent that, once our Charles had been accepted into the pact, there was no doubt that with their advice and help he might in a short time be restored with honour to his patrimony, especially since his subjects would be divided as the Lord should command. In a short time and with favourable fortune it turned out immediately that the Foul Arse—that is, that arsehole council, the Rump—was ruptured.[97] As the proverb puts it, 'Whoever is ruptured bursts with envy.'[98] Then, with outstanding prudence and moderation (thanks to the wonderful grace of God), that Monk, most worthy of eternal commemoration, controlled the reins so cleverly (and yet so carefully) that not only were ancient and native rights and privileges returned to the magnates and nobles, but also that true Father of his Fatherland was restored to his patrimony, exalted by many and with the general consensus of the people. And just as he had excited his subjects to the obedience due to him by means of an almost divine clemency and by his love towards them, so were those subjects freed from their previous madness, and confessed the disgrace of their irreverence towards the King (whom they had inhumanely killed) and towards his stock. They poured out such great expressions of joy for the restoration of the former and happier times that it was doubtful which filled the air more—the shouts of the people or the noise of the bells.

The reintroduction and restoration of a prince so truly dutiful and most truly our own was unanimously announced on the first of May [1660], publicly by the Lords and Commons in that greatest council of Parliament,[99] and also by every type of citizen and much of the soldiery. And so, ten days later, six nobles and twelve others were sent to Holland, with replies to the kind and gracious letters and declaration of the King, in most humble hands, and requested the presence of the most serene King and his brothers with him, inviting him to his parental throne, his native soil and his rightful patrimony. I judge it not unfair to give here the names of these men, since posterity will wish to record those to whom the glory of so honourable a business was granted. Among the first was the Earl of Oxford, a man as truly distinguished by his antiquity as by his blood. The Earl of Warwick was nominated, but succumbing to a certain gouty weariness he clung to the shore and did not set out any further in this foreign visit; the Earl of Middlesex; Viscount Hereford; that distinguished man who is endowed with the title Baron Berkeley; and Lord Brooke. From the other House, that is, the lower House: Baron Fairfax of Cameron in Scotland; Lord Bruce; Lord Falkland; Lord Castleton; Lord

Herbert; Lord Mandeville; the baronets Horatio Townshend,[100] Anthony Ashley Cooper and George Booth; Denzil Holles Esq.; and the knights, John Holland and Henry Chambly [Cholmley]. From the City of London were sent twenty Aldermen and notable citizens. While opinion was so well disposed, what remained but a general expectation of seeing a King in this our England once more, and of the revival of a people who had for a long time been deprived of their ancient inheritance and laws? We must thank this west wind for this second royal favour, as magnificent as munificent; and we owe both to the Moderator of all things, that is, to Almighty God.

Meanwhile things were done in proper order in the Houses of both great Councils, in a way for which (for the most part) we rendered to God, as far as we were able, the thanks due to so marvellous a liberation and about-turn in public affairs; and we received the Prince restored to what was most rightly his with every honour and obedience, and went to meet him. That most faithful General of the army, although he bore the name Monk, yet he quickly set out to the seashore at Dover with much soldiery and with as many nobles as possible, to reinvest the Prince, now so long in exile, in his own Penates and in the Lares of his own home. With this done, this new arrival from foreign parts was given a warm welcome along with his brothers, and made the journey expeditiously to his Troy or Teucer-Novant,[101] and on his birthday—that is, on 29 May—he entered the city that had before this time been torn apart by much strife and left in a shabby state, but which now (thanks to the Grace of God) was in accord and full of glory. There our most gracious Prince both ratified and revived that greatest Council of the King, that is to say, the Parliament, while by his own order each House summoned its members to Whitehall to welcome him and his brothers in style. There (albeit individually and separately) reciprocal congratulations were expressed in speeches. But on the next day this gracious Prince proceeded to his Parliament with his brothers, and there presented himself in a short speech, to both Houses and also to his subjects, and was so gracious that he incited the maximum amount of joy possible in everyone. He thus rendered the Convention, a body set up only out of necessity and therefore up till now illegal (for necessity has no laws), legal, with this suitable utterance in French, 'Le Roy le veult'; and he revived laws that were near their last gasp. He asked modestly for money from the whole people to pay the wages of the military, in order to take away from the legions that had been formed the neccessity of living on freequarter.[102] Finally he distributed everything so readily and in so dutiful a fashion that neither the least procedure of the Church nor of the State was overlooked, checking the extravagances of the sinful and favourably rewarding the deserts of the virtuous with rewards and honours.

He thus eagerly showed himself to be, as much by his teachings as by his example, a promoter of righteousness, and keenly proved himself a cultivator of wisdom. He summoned advisers to his Privy Council, choosing them from those outstanding in righteousness and endowed with morals. It was granted to a certain man, who had once been opposed as much to his father's restoration as to his own, to appear among them nevertheless, because of pure emotion and outstanding grace, since he bestowed gifts on his whole people.[103] He did not deny them even his own person. Thus did he take a truly Caesarian model, and acquired such great glory that, among the most glorious kings and princes of the world, he deservedly comes out in the first rank. He appointed the brother closest to him in age—that is, James Duke of York—according to the national custom, to the traditional office of Lord High Admiral, so that he might extend his health-bringing rule as much over the sea as over the land. Thus did he take care that military power was shared out among individual court factions, to certain colleagues, and to some Lords who held posts, in order to avoid in future any fear of suspicion of an invasion from outside, of insurrection from within, or of any rebellion.

He was not, however, immediately free from the greatest cares: he went into council not only with that greatest royal Senate, but also with the leaders of the Privy Council, in order to wed pity happily to justice and to pay the soldiers' wages immediately, since, under his sceptre, all things were being brought back to a state of peace and concord. Nevertheless, we and those belonging to us owe a debt to death, who 'Knocks with equal foot at poor men's taverns and the towers of kings'.[104] Not long afterwards, his brother Henry, Duke of Gloucester, a young man of great promise, was snatched away from the bitterness of disease. On his death our most righteous and most prudent King, most full of majesty, stated, amid tears, that he had lost not only a dearly loved brother and a true and faithful friend, but also a prudent and most stout adviser.[105] A little later his sister, that august Princess who was crowned with the title of Orange,[106] endowed with outstanding gifts, both mental and physical, met her end in her own native land. Who in telling of such things can refrain from tears? But afterwards, when all those clouds of sadness had dispersed before the true standard of righteousness and the divine decree of providence, a bright light succeeded the darkness. That is to say, the coronation ceremony, at which he eagerly considered how those, very many of great condition, serving in the order of the Garter, were placed in position, as were also, from the lower orders, the Knights of the Bath.[107] This most powerful monarch was solemnly crowned under the name Charles II in April 1661 in Westminster Abbey (as is the custom). And then for the first time (because of the question of the succession) he thought about taking a wife; but lest he should accept one unworthy of so august a lineage, he sought and gained a progeny of foreign stock—that is, from Portugal.[108] Lest there were lacking for her most longed-for arrival as many gifts as possible I, the very least of his servants, acquainted with both languages, celebrated in English the sea-going wood that was to transport her,[109] and in Latin, in verse, the Prince of the sea, as humbly as I could:

A gift for the arrival of the Queen, sister of the King of Portugal.[110]

So let the progeny of Portugal ever shine,
And let flourish, flourish the Viburnum[111] of Braganzean stock;
And let Catherine sparkle (first and foremost) among the
New stars of this clime; and may her chariot be spun along
By a now favourable Neptune; and may she straight away
Come safe and sound to these our shores.
This is my earnest prayer.
W:

What now but the wishes that still remain: that from these mutual loves, joined so happily by a marriage contract, a most happy agreement will arise in these Islands, and a most mightily desired offspring, which the Almighty will accomplish in his own time.

Notes

1 For his date of birth, cf. the notes on end paper of *Terentius Christianus, sive Comoediae Terentiano stylo conscriptae* by Cornelius Schonaeus (Robert Robinson, 1595: British Library shelfmark: 11712.a.16). 'mr mildmay fane was borne att Badsell the 24th day of Januarie beinge a Sunday att v of the clocke in the morning in the year 1601' [i.e. 1602].

2 His grandmother Mary, who married (1574) Sir Thomas Fane of Badsell, was only daughter and heir of Henry Nevill, sixth Lord Bergavenny. The Nevills had held the title of Earl of Westmorland until the attainder of 1571. Mary Nevill's direct descent from the first Earl of the first creation was thus of some importance in confirming the legitimacy of the title granted *de novo* to Mildmay's father Francis in 1624 (with a substantial payment to Buckingham). The

Nevills still claimed the title in Mildmay's time: Edmund Neville, Lord Latimer (d. c. 1630–35), was contentiously styled 'Earle of Westmerland... and the 7th Earle... of the name of Nevills' on his monument in 1647 (*Peerage* XII, pt 2, pp. 564–6).
3 Hunting, for which he retained a lifelong enthusiasm.
4 Echoing Cicero on the Pythagoreans, *De Natura Deorum* I. 5. 10: ' "Ipse dixit." "Ipse" autem erat Pythagoras.'
5 Twelve years of play plus four winters of Pythagoras would place him at Cambridge in 1618, aged sixteen; Venn says he matriculated at Emmanuel as a fellow commoner at Michaelmas 1618, and graduated MA, *fil. nob.*, 1619 (see p. 28). The 'fourth congregation' (*quatuor fere peractis Comitiis*) therefore refers to termly assemblies. The date 1616, given in a marginal annotation in the version of the *Vita* in BL Add. MS 34,220, p. 6, is probably wrong.
6 Fane was MP for Peterborough 1620–22, 1626 and 1628–29, and for Kent 1625. In the 1625 election, backed by his father and the Earl of Montgomery, he stood successfully against Sir Edwyn Sandys, Buckingham's candidate. See John. K. Gruenfelder, *Influence in Early Stuart Elections* (Columbus OH, 1981), pp. 143–4.
7 Quoting Horace, *Epistles* I. 11, l. 27. The dates for this tour are confused by the marginal notes (apparently Fane's) to the later version of the *Vita* in Add. MS 34,220, which suggest it began in 1620 (p. 6). This clashes with dated epigrams in *F1*, which suggest that he left England in autumn 1622 and returned in spring 1625. These dates are supported by his admission to Lincoln's Inn (7 August 1622), and the issue on 9 September 1622 of a pass 'to travaile for three yeares with a tutor and twoe servants, with provisoe not to go to Rome' (*Acts of Privy Council*, 1621–23, p. 323). The tutor may have been his Cambridge tutor, Elias Travers, who resigned his fellowship in 1621 to become Rector of Thursacton: see *To my Tutors Ghost Doctor Travers* p. 322 and note; Parliament had been dissolved in January 1622, and Fane did not sit in the Parliament of 1624–25. Fane's subsequent dating of poems in *F1* is not wholly reliable: they place him in Orléans in 1622–23, in Geneva in 1623 (this should be 1624) and in Paris in the winters of 1623 (when he was in Orléans), 1624 and 1625. He was at Boulogne ('Bollin') when he heard of James I's death, which took place on 27 March 1625 (*F1*, f. 34r), but back at Mereworth by the 30th: 'My Lord Burghersh wth his company came To Merworth upon Wednesday: march 30th 1625' (W(A) Misc. 15, *A Howshold Booke*, f. 2v).
8 'Diffugere nives, rediere et gramina campis / Arboribusque comae' (adapting Horace, *Odes* IV. 7, ll. 1–2).
9 Buckingham's expeditionary force to relieve the besieged Protestants of La Rochelle in 1629, on which Robert Herrick went as a chaplain, was defeated with serious losses and not a great deal of honour.
10 Latin name of Just Zinderling (c. 1590–c. 1620), German philologist. His *Itinerarium Galliæ et finitimarum regionum* (Lyons, 1612) would have been an up-to-date travel guide for Fane.
11 Previously held by the Huguenots, it had fallen to Royal Catholic forces in September 1622.
12 See *TheoD Bezæ—Epigramma*, p. 63.
13 Campus Lapideus, the area bordering the Camargue between Arles and Istres.
14 Echoing Juvenal III. 183: 'Everything has its price in Rome.'
15 Prostitutes: Thais was an Athenian courtesan.
16 From Presqu'Ile, a narrow isthmus in the centre of Lyons, bounded by the two rivers. The following passage, down to 'So here Piety', is also in loose and sometimes obscure hexameters which do not lend themselves to verse translation.
17 Fane's map in *F2* suggests this is the Jura range: if he followed the Rhone from Lyons, he may have climbed the southern end of the range rather than taking the pass through Défilé de l'Ecluse.
18 *Proxima villæ*, perhaps meaning Geneva itself.
19 The arms of Geneva were described by Evelyn as 'a demie *Eagle*, & a *Crosse* between the *Crosse Keys*' over the motto '[*Nox Diem sequitur*,] *Post Tenebras, Lux*' (*Diary* II, p. 525). This is not quite the same as those recorded by A. C. Fox-Davies, *A Book of Public Arms* (1915), p. 306, as de Beer notes.
20 Adapting both Juvenal II. 3, 'qui Curios simulant et Bacchanalia vivunt', and Horace, *Odes*, I. 37, ll. 1–2: 'Nunc est bibendum, nunc pede libero / pulsanda tellus'.

21 *Tam Marti quam Jovi*, varying the usual '*Tam Marti quam Mercurio*' or '*quam Minerva*'.
22 *Judicium aeque ac merces*, punning on 'Justice and Mercy'.
23 *Ursorumque*, 'of the Bears', presumably for Berne; Latin for the Canton of Berne is *Bernensis Pagus*.
24 Negotiations for the marriage of Prince Charles to Henrietta Maria lasted throughout 1624, the treaty being signed in November. The following poem is dated 1624 in *FI* (f. 23r), and places Fane in Paris for the winter of 1624–25. Cf. *A Valentine for my Lord Savage*, p. 70, and Herrick, *Upon one Lillie, who marryed with a maid call'd Rose* (44.1). Fane met a Henry Martin, very probably the future regicide, in Paris in 1625, and addressed four friendly Latin epigrams to him.
25 This sounds as if Fane, now aged twenty-three, set up a separate establishment on his return, perhaps at Badsell.
26 See note 6.
27 On 6 July 1626, to Grace, daughter of Sir William Thornhurst of Agnes Court, Romney Marsh, Kent, and Winfrith Newburgh, Dorset.
28 '*Obdormierunt*'; ecclesiastical Latin, implying 'in the Lord', as in the death of Stephen (Vulgate, Acts 7. 59–60).
29 Diana b. 21 July 1627, m. 1 (1645) Edward Pelham, of Brocklesbury, Lincolnshire; 2 John Bill of Kenwood (*To my sonn Bill upon his Entertainment at Cane-wood*, p. 351); Mary (1629–32); Grace (1630–34); Frances (b. 1632, m. Sir Erasmus Harby of Aldenham); and Isabel (1633–36/37).
30 Quoting Virgil, *Eclogue* IV. 7.
31 Charles, third Earl, b. 6 January 1635, d. 1691. See *A Dedication to my Sonn Charles to Him that made him*, p. 135.
32 Grace died 29 June 1636 (*Peerage* XII, pt 2, p. 569, the year confirmed by this passage); she is buried at Apethorpe.
33 Her maternal grandfather was Thomas, Viscount Howard of Bindon. Cynegils or Kinegils (d. 643), king of the West Saxons, defeated the Britons in 614 at Beandûn, possibly the modern Bampton, Oxfordshire.
34 21 June 1638, at Hackney, to Mary, widow of Sir Roger Townshend (who d. 1 January 1637), second daughter and co-heir of Horatio, Baron Vere of Tilbury. Mary Vere brought Fane two stepsons, Sir Roger (d. *c*. 1648) and Horatio, b. 1630, MP Norfolk 1656–60, one of the twelve commissioners deputed to invite Charles II to return, 1660 (see p. 47). With the Earl of Clare he was supervisor of Fairfax's will, dated 1667. Mary Vere died at Mereworth, September 1669.
35 Mary, 1639–81, m. 1 Francis Palmes of Ashwell, Rutland (d. 1667), 2 (1670) John, fourth Earl of Exeter.
36 The first Bishops' War, which ended with humiliation for the King by the Pacification of Berwick, June 1639. Lacking funds from Parliament, which he still refused to call, the King was dependent on loans and on the mainly unenthusiastic feudal obligation of his peers to provide troops to quell the Scots' rebellion against the imposition of a Laudian prayer book and orders of service. Fane was critical of the use of arms in what he regarded as a war precipitated by the pride of the bishops (*Upon the Scotsh business—1638*, p. 230) and he pleaded illness at first (*CSPD*, 1638–39, February 1639, p. 467). On 6 May his mother wrote a powerful letter to Secretary Windebank urging the King to seek peace with the Scots (*CSPD*, 1639, pp. 123–4), but Fane had joined the King in Newcastle by late May (*My reveille-Matin—to my wife*, p. 144), and went with the army to Berwick soon after (*Writ at the Campe at Birkes*, p. 231). On 3–4 June at Berwick 'the Earl of Westmorland's brother being in bed had his bedtent and curtains shot through twice by his own unruly soldiers' (*CSPD*). On 19 June, just before the treaty was signed, Fane and the Earl of Northampton dined with the Scottish general, Leslie, in his camp at Duns (*The Journal of John Aston, 1639*, Surtees Society CXVIII [1910], p. 28).
37 'I do not want to be made a Bishop,' the customary modest response to the royal offer of a bishopric. Only two refusals were required: the third would be accepted.
38 'Apthorp,' Fane's marginal note. The King left Berwick for London at the end of July 1639.

Charles Louis, the Elector Palatine, had come to England in July seeking Charles's support, joining him at Durham.

39 The Scots crossed the Tyne at Newburn, west of Newcastle, took Gateshead on the south bank of the Tyne, and were amazed to find that Newcastle itself had been hurriedly abandoned. Leslie entered the city on 30 August 1640.

40 The 'Great Council' of peers met 24 September 1640.

41 The King had in fact been unwilling to call another parliament, and this was a late and grudging concession to the peers at York, whom he was setting out to placate. The terms in which Fane describes the event suggest his own moderate position at this time.

42 Charles affected to have abandoned Strafford, who was attacked at the Council.

43 Mildmay, 1640–55. 'That so great a blessing may not appear to have passed over in silence, see p. 145' (Fane's marginal note, referring to '*A morning Fancy upon the Berth of my Sonn Mildmay the 3d of Decembr-1640. And the hopes of My owne recovery of the smallpox*', p. 146). Because of smallpox, Fane missed the opening sessions of the Long Parliament (3 November 1640); on 16 November he sent a proxy (*Lords' Journals* IV, p. 92a), and is not recorded as present until 19 February 1641 (*Lords' Journals* IV, pp. 167b–168a).

44 This implies Fane was present at the trial of Strafford by the peers in March and April. On 4 May 1641 he was present to read and sign the 'Protestation' sent up by the Commons, but did not attend for the vote on the Bill of Attainder against Strafford on 8 May. The day after the execution (13 May) he was put on a committee for a Bill concerning the draining of the fens, but was recorded as absent without leave or proxy in a list of 14 May (*Lords' Journals* IV, p. 249b).

45 The dissolution of the Short Parliament had taken place on 5 May 1640, and Strafford had in fact been in a minority in the Council in arguing against a dissolution.

46 'For his Elogium also an Epigram of the Court of Accusation pray see in folio 99' (Fane's marginal note). The *Elogium* (Latin verse here in prose translation) presents Strafford as an overreacher but regrets the lack of legality in his sentence: 'As intrepid Strafford climbs the altar of death, he is a welcome gift sacrificed to a cruel people. Of course, what he wishes in his soul is taken to be sufficient danger, while the spirit of the populace attacks, and it does not regret having feared him whom it used to think merited it (nobody will be hated undeservedly). Everything is turned about and rushes on, while he boasts that his counsel is raised above everything, and while it does violence. Hence comes the people's fear, hence he seems to have accumulated his deserts. He was allowed at the same time to wish, and thus to be, badly empowered. As a young man he shone brightly from the beginning, but consider his end: he is strong in the morning, but in the evening the young men hold all. He reached adolescence as an outstanding individual; he became a renowned adult, but alas how quickly the day fell off to the bringers of clouds. The evil one may do evil for a long time: however, that evil one, of whom such great evils shortly became known, has become shorter.' [Marginal note reads 'by the head'] (*F2*, p. 99).

47 Charles left for Scotland, where he had been born, 10 August 1641, hoping to enlist support against his increasingly strong English opposition. He was shadowed by a group of parliamentary commissioners which included Fane's friend William Armine: see *An Ode sent into Scotland to a frend*, p. 119.

48 There were always a large number of mariners and lightermen in the Port of London: in January 1642 they rose in favour of Parliament, encouraged by the Earl of Warwick and Sir Harry Vane Jr.

49 The Irish revolt of October 1641 prompted a confrontation between King and Parliament over the King's right to control an army. The Grand Remonstrance, roundly condemning Charles's policies and showing his unfitness to be trusted with an army, was passed in November, while Charles was on his way back from Scotland.

50 On 14 February 1642 Charles had given assent to a Bill for excluding bishops from Parliament. Fane must have given this at least tacit support, since only three bishops voted against it on 5 February (Masson, II, pp. 349–53).

51 Died June 1643.

52 *Quadragenarius*, used thus by Seneca, *Epistles* 25. 1.

53 Fane delivered the 'Propositions concerning the Adventure for Ireland' to the King and reported his answer to the Lords (*Lords' Journals* IV, pp. 595b–596a, 607b–608a; 18–24 February 1642). Henrietta Maria left Dover with Princess Mary on 23 February.
54 'Senate and People of London', ironically adapting the Roman SPQR, *Senatus Populusque Romanus*.
55 See *The Times Steerage*, p. 82, ll. 40–5 n.
56 Kingston-upon-Hull, where Governor Hotham refused the King entry in April 1642.
57 The Earl of Essex, appointed July 1642. The sticking point for Fane seems to have come earlier, with the Commons' Declaration of Grievances and Remedies (a forerunner of the Nineteen Propositions): he asked for his dissent to be recorded before the motion was put that it should be supported by the Lords (5 April). He was still present on 15 April, but is listed as absent on 21 April (*Lords' Journals* IV, pp. 693, 719a; V, p. 8b).
58 Quoting Cicero, Cat. I. 1: 'Quosque tandem abutere, Catilina, patientia nostra?'
59 *Patriæ Causa et Principis iussu semper in utrumque paratus*.
60 Fane was one of thirty-six peers listed as having 'absented themselves from the Parliament, and are now with his Majestie' at York; he is also one of those listed as having 'subscribed to levie horse to assist his Majestie': in his case, twenty horses. See *A Catalogue of the Names of the Dukes, Marquesses, Earles and Lords that have absented themselves etc.* (1642), reprint ed. Edward Peacock (1863).
61 Fane's drawing is in the margin at this point.
62 There were five troops of 'dragooneers' in the Parliamentary army in 1642, each of about 100 men. One was commanded by a relatively near neighbour, Sir Anthony Irby, of Whaplode, Lincolnshire, and of Emmanuel (1620). He was later chairman of the Goldsmiths' Hall Committee which released Fane from sequestration.
63 'As Hydra's overcome by Hercules / So Patience Conquers like affronts as these.' Fane's (English) addition on facing page in BL Add. MS 34,220. The first 'successful' battle of the war almost certainly means Edgehill, on 23 October 1642, claimed as a Royalist victory. Fane was, however, reported captured 'at Northampton', twenty-six miles from Edgehill, the news reaching the writer of a Parliamentary newsletter on 27 October: see *Speciall Newes from the Army at Warwick since the Fight* (Henry Overton, 29 October 1642), A3r (Thomason Tracts, E124.33). He was taken before a parliamentary committee on 26 October, and committed to the Tower the next day. Cf. *By-Ward to some Cittisens entring the Tower*, p. 121.
64 1 April 1643: 'ORDERED, That the earl of *Westmerland*, a Prisoner in *The tower*, shall be delivered to the gentleman Usher of this House, to be first carried to the *earl of Manchester*, who is to promise upon his Honour unto the said Earl of *Manchester*, that he will be a true Prisoner in his House at *St. Bartholomew's*, and to return to *The Tower of London* when this House shall direct.' (*Lords' Journals* V, p. 686a).
65 2 March 1643, pass issued 'to bring a Waggon laden with Goods to *London*, belonging to the Countess of *Westm'land*, against her lying in' (*Lords' Journals* V, p. 629b). Rachel m. 1668 Gregory Hascard DD, who became Dean of Windsor 1684. She died after 1693.
66 18 August 1643: 'ORDERED, That the Earl of *Westmerland*, giving his Word upon his Honour to remain in safe Custody, shall have Leave to ride out, and take the Air, within Five Miles Distance from *London*, for his Health Sake' (*Lords' Journals* VI, p. 185).
67 That is, of the King's inner circle of advisers, towards whom Fane is highly critical in the prose 'Riddles' in *N*, ff. 38v–36v.
68 Presumably referring to the lessons the Thirty Years' War offered a country embroiled in the first years of a civil war.
69 Fane first petitioned the Lords for his sequestration to be lifted in October 1643 and then, in language similar to this, in January 1644 (draft in *N*, f. 34r). He wrote a series of prose meditations justifying covenants, dated 14 February 1644 (*N*, ff. 32v–31v), and on that day again petitioned the Lords (f. 31r), saying 'he was formerly seduced. Is now resolved to sacrifice life and fortunes to the real service of King and Parliament, for which he was born. To this end begs to take the Covenant, and be restored to his liberty, and to such part of his fortune as to their wisdom seems fit.' The petition was presented by the Earl of Essex: 'The Lord General acquainted this House That the Earl of *Westm* came to him, and desired him to deliver a Peti-

tion to this House . . . Hereupon this House ORDERED, That the Earl of *Westm.* shall first have the Covenant tendered to him, and then this House will take the rest of his desires into further Consideration. And the House appointed the Earls of *Rutland* and *Stamford* to tender the Covenant to him presently; and accordingly they went forth; and the Earl of *Westm'land* took and subscribed the Covenant.' (*Lords' Journals* VI, p. 427a, 14 February 1644.) He thus became one of the first Royalist peers to subscribe, and was at Mereworth by 11 March (*For Mr Conyers Darcy*, p. 159). An ordinance freeing his estate was finally read on 13 September 1644, Fane having paid the last part of a fine of £3,000. He did not attend the House of Lords again until 14 May 1660 (*Commons' Journals* III, p. 401). See Cain, 'A sad Intestine warr', pp. 38–41. He seems not to have returned to Apethorp until May 1646: see *In adventum meum ad antiquos Lares Abthorpienses*, p. 78.

70 Vere (1645–93) was named after his maternal grandfather, Lord Vere of Tilbury. Fane does not give a cross-reference for the verses, and omits this sentence in BL Add. MS 34,220, suggesting the poem was lost or never written. Two years later he wrote the *Ode Occationed upon my sonn Veres sicknes*, p. 166.

71 *Upon the Berth of my Sonn Henry*, p. 169. Henry was still alive in 1666, since he is in Fane's will, but seems to have died soon after.

72 'Pride's Purge' of nearly 100 'contrary-minded' MPs on 6 December cleared the way for the Commons to set up a court to try the King for treason.

73 Charles had first been 'seized' (*rapitur*) from Holdenby House by Cornet Joyce in June 1647, but the chronology here suggests Fane is thinking of his removal from Carisbrooke to Hurst Castle in November 1648, condemned as illegal by the unpurged Commons, a move which began the sequence of events leading up to his trial and execution in January 1649.

74 Quoting Virgil, *Aeneid* II. 6–8. Used again (p. 49) for the deaths of the Duke of Gloucester and Princess of Orange.

75 It is not clear whether Fane saw the execution. His accounts record 'A Jorney to London' in January, and three days after the execution 'At Eltham [near Greenwich] dinner wth a frend' (MS W(A) Misc. 7).

76 Katharine Fane, 1650–83. She married (1682) William Nelson, former page to her sister Mary, Countess of Exeter, he then aged nineteen but 'a tall handsome young man'. She was dead within the year.

77 In 1650: see *Ad Geo: Fane: in commemorationem natalitii Reg. Car: 2^{di}*, p. 248.

78 The version of the *Vita* in *F2* ends here; the continuation in BL Add. MS 34,220 is taken up in Fane's most relaxed italic hand, he having copied out the previous pages from *F2* in a more careful italic.

79 Megaera ('the envying one') was one of the Furies; Cerberus the three-headed dog that guarded the entrance to Hades.

80 Susanna Fane, 1651–78, died unmarried and was buried at Mereworth. The jibe against Presbyterians is significant: Fane's wife came from a strongly Presbyterian family, and the Mildmays had been leading puritans.

81 Edinburgh Castle, known as the 'Virgin Castle' because unconquered, fell relatively easily to Cromwell in December 1650, though not by 'trickery'. The 'golden bridge' was presumably an alleged bribe.

82 The battle of Worcester, 1651.

83 Charles did mingle with Commonwealth troops in Bridport, Dorset (perhaps of the seventh regiment), disguised as a servant; but though he originally planned to escape via London, he did not go there. He sailed from Shoreham.

84 Henry Wilmot, Earl of Rochester.

85 See *Upon a chip of the Royall Oak*, p. 316, for Fane's souvenir of Charles's escape.

86 Mazarin gave Charles and his followers only ten days to leave in summer 1653. The Anglo-French treaty was signed in 1657.

87 *Posui deum adiutorem meum* and *Aliter deus protegit ipsam*, found on several Elizabethan denominations.

88 The reverse of Cromwell's 'Protectoral Medal' of 1653 is inscribed 'Pax quæritur bello', 'Peace is sought in war'.

89 Cromwell: Masaniello (Tomaso Anniello), a fisherman, led the Neapolitan revolt against Spanish occupation in 1647. His excesses led to him being killed within a month by his followers.
90 By the Treaty of 1657 England allied with France to fight in Spanish Flanders, capturing the coastal fortresses of Mardyck and Dunkirk for England. Charles and his brother James fought on the Spanish side.
91 *Trapannos.* 'Trapans' were criminals or agents who trapped others into positions or actions leading to the victim's ruin or loss (*OED*, s.v. *trepan sb2*; first quotation, 1641).
92 Latin proverb, also used in *Sturbridg Fayer*, p. 308, l. 21.
93 See *To the People of England—June-5-1659*, p. 328, and notes.
94 Astraea, goddess of Justice, was the last of the immortals to abandon the earth in its decline after the Golden Age.
95 This summarises Homer's account, *Iliad* 21, but is not a quotation.
96 For Monck's part in the Restoration, see *Sonnet Feb: 1659*, p. 245 and note.
97 'Ars-e fœœtidus vel Podicis Consilii Rumpus Rumpitur,' exploiting the potential for puns in 'Rump': *podex* plays with the sense, *rumpitur* with the form of the word.
98 From Martial IX. 97.12. Fane may have remembered it as a 'proverb' from Jonson, who quotes it without attribution at the close of *Poetaster*.
99 Fane may not have been present: he is not recorded as such until 12 May 1660 (*Lords' Journals* XI, p. 25b).
100 Fane's stepson.
101 Teucer was the first king of Troy. For London as 'Troy-Novant', see *Upon the Strange adventure and memorable voyage*, p. 206, l. 6 n.
102 *Ut liberas vivendi.* For 'freequarter', billeting on the populace without compensation, cf. *To the County of Kent*, p. 97, l. 2 n.
103 Probably Anthony Ashley-Cooper, a member of Cromwell's Council of State from 1653, who became Chancellor of the Exchequer at the Restoration. Cooper had 'opposed his father's restoration' in the sense that he had gone over to Parliament in 1644.
104 Quoting Horace, *Odes* I. 4, ll. 13–14.
105 Henry died of smallpox, September 1660.
106 Mary Stuart, Princess of Orange, d. December 1660, also of smallpox.
107 Fane was one of the latter, but in an undated letter to the Earl of Cardigan he appears to reject the ceremony (see p. 24).
108 Catharine of Braganza arrived in England in May 1662.
109 See *To the Royall Fleet sent out of the Downes*, p. 320.
110 A shorter version of this Latin poem, in Fane's hand, is in University of Nottingham, Portland MS PwV 217, endorsed in a different seventeenth-century hand 'verses from the Earle of westmorland'. Another version is in *F3*. Latin and English versions of *Queen Katherin Landed at Portsmouth* (see p. 320) follow this poem in the *Vita*.
111 ?For the Portugal Laurel.

FULBECK HALL MS I
POEMS, 1621-35

To his Mistress

All night it raynes, but in the morn
Bright Phœbus that with it is born
Or begets it drives mists away
And in exchange of night bringes day
Whose life by his death's shortened   5
And night again raignes in its stead
The Gods these changes did decree
That soe they might part stakes with thee
And as the night is theirs; soe may
Be thine the Empire of the day   10

1626

Me nive cadente petijt mea Julia, rebar
Igne carere nivem nix tamen ignis erat

Snow falling Julia some at me did throw
When I thought fier could not have lodgd in snow
Yet found it did and those by nature foes
This way made friends: soe musick doth compose
Her concord out of discords, 't hath been seen   5
That tragique warr the cause of peace hath been
Soe they seem relatives, yet either die
In th'others birth, or its prosperity
And in these Elements ther's found this fate
The one the other, doth exasperate   10
Or lend themselves t'each other and wher one
Rules as predominant the other's none
For if once fire be kindled in the hart
The snow turnes then to fire and beares its part
Alike if snow prevaile to quench the fire   15
It turnes to snow affection and desire
But 'twas the nobler Element did command
In this snow-ball sent from her snow-whited hand
Me to consume: when my brest covered
With snow soon had that fire extinguished   20
And soe their natures int'each others turnd
Fire waxt in snow could, snow in fier burnd.

An Invitation to R. H.   at London 1626

Robin sithence I saw thee last
I cannot call't a weeke thats past

But't seems a month, a year, an age
Yet this long absence may presage
That our next meeting shall be 5
Crowned with a Jubile
After this day meet me then
Tell me where the Scene, what men
Shall actors be, and if I miss
Be assur'd I wrot not this. 10

An ode To N. B. an angler

Thou that dost cast into the silver brook
    Thy worm fed hooke
  The greedier fishes for to cheat
    Whilst they would eat
      Remember that times wheel will bring 5
  Thy deeds to censuring
    And then as thou through wile
    Those creatures didst beguile
Soe caught thou'lt be for thy deceipt
And made the food for thin own bayt. 10

Let this suffize to cause thee t'steer aright
    Both day and night
  That skilfully avoyding this
    That shelf thou miss
      For 'tis not all for to repent 15
  Thy youthfull dayes misspent
    But care must now be had
    The future be not bad
And as thy audite waxeth neer
  Soe thy accompts make perfecter. 20

Yet with that freedom stil and honest care
    May not impare
  Thy mind by causing it to fly
    Society
  Nor thy affections Cloyster soe 25
    By making them forgoe
    That innocent delight
    Of Clubbing, morn and night
But let quaint Olives purle thy plate
When as thou heerst my Lord's at gate 30

Then let thy sellers treasure opened be
    For jollety
  Which sending forth rayes like the sun
    Canary run
  Or the bright flaming Sherries fire 35
    The fancy to inspire
    Whilst that the duller call

  For some of Tom. Blotts alle
And thus beguiling time, at last
Our cares revive, cause it is past   40
   Ex Scotia missa   1626

The Savoy—Excetter house 1626

Like Sestos to Abydos wher my faire
Intoombed is, those neighbour turretts are
To this small roofe: an Hellespont the street
Yet not denying voice nor eyes to meet
Soe strait and favorable is it: not soe
As that which to Leanders praires sayd noe   5
Nor'st like it pav'd with terror but guives way
With too much ease to my fatall doomes-day
Soe that I with him have noe hopes to crye
Lett me goe scott free, in returning dye
For both are deadly and doe kill, the one   10
And gentler death is contemplation
Of her rich vertue-cloathing bewty rare
Beyond the reach of terreine wights compare
The other is returne or bannishment
From the fruishion of joy and content   15
Which though I suffer patience tells me 'tis
To add to th'second going greater bliss
Mine eyes shall fast cause once they did deprive
Me of all sence: ofte dying makes one live
The actiom saith, if soe i'le not dispaire   20
To live and dye with her whom I coumpt faire.

She is sick   1626

Well you wound, and sick you Kill
  Which ill
Attends those who you adore
  And more
For the first's a languishing
  dying   5
And the the second though't be death
  Leaves breath
To bemone onse desperate
  estate
Leave to be the other th'one   10
  is none
Wound me not in health I vowe
  to you
Your afflictions neaver shall
  my fall   15
Ingender, but I shall smile
  the while

You weepe, when you laugh I'le morne
    in scorne   20
Of your contempts, and soe end
As your self shall please your frend.

at Mereworth   *Mine eyes Ember weekes fast—1626*

If Papist for their Ember fastinges merrit
    Hope to inherrit
A Paradice, dispaire shall not dwell in me
    Of enjoying thee
Whom I accompt noe less, whilst mine eyes which were   5
    Fed from thy bright sphear
Now had fasted; graunt them againe a fullness
    Of thine true brightness
Thei'le shine more cleer, soe have I delia seen
    When as she hath been   10
Denide awhile her borrowd light grow more faire
    Her Brothers haire
More oriant when it had line plaighted under
    a clowde of thunder
Day would not be soe welcome did not the night   15
    Shut in all his light.

at Mereworth   *To R. H. with some Venison*   1626

I tooke for compagnion
Downe with me your Obberon
Wher he hunted and had sport
Which though it did come farr short
Of your soft welcomes he's content   5
To pass it o're in merriment
And what fortune for him slewe
Heer he sends some on't to you
That it is noe fatter know
Frute-trees bear not now, but blow   10
He leaves rareness to commend
It wholly and heer doth end.

'If one but anoint the sword'

If one but anoint the sword
That doth hurt it will afford
Reliefe unto the wound: why
Shall I not seeke remedy
When 'tis soe cheap? I can guive   5
To Phisitians to live
And not think how ofte I dye
Whilst I live in misery
Lif's but a being unless

Crouned with true happiness 10
Stranger to suspition, cares
And Free both from hopes and fears
Which sejourn with me, and call
Each hours thoughts my funerall
Then to'th'end I might repaire 15
My hopes wounded by despaire
Guive me leave for to apply
My balme to your cruelty
Vowes, which if they can appease
Your fury I may have ease 20
If not I shall begg youl'd make
The wound mortall for my sake

at apthorp *An owld man married a yong lass*
—1626

December once to May was married
What was the issue? When they were a bed
She doth expect some showres to procreat
He tells her's Aprills past and 'twas too late
But what his season, than her springtide later 5
Did promise strait he throwes two snowballs at her
Yett neither Julias, to requite which scorn
By Venus blest May crownes him with the horn.

'He who such strong lines wont compose'

He who such strong lines wont compose
Hath his cut ofe by Atropos
For underneath this marble ston
Sleepes now intoombd Sir Simion
His other name 'thout Treason he 5
Bore from the branch of Soveranty
Thus fates conspired to beguile
Of Eloquence our Ely Ile.

1627 *A tinder-box for Ned: Beech[er] chafing at play*

Thou soon takst fier poor Ned; and why?
Because thou art like tinder dry
And hard as flint; if fortunes wheel
Turn thee to leese, that serves for steel

1627 *Upon an Escheater a Knave that bought the place*

Cheaters thy true name, cousnedg christend thee
Yett buying es, thoul't now escheater be
What hast thou gott by that, i'st not as ill
For Es translated's, thou art; Cheater still.

Paris—1625	*TheoD Bezæ—Epigramma—In pontem Gardi.*

    Greece sung of Hills on Hills that heaped were
    Of Pyramids rude Memphis bosted her;
    But's more thou seest; two Mountaines made to joigne,
    Whome th'Arches of a trebble Bridge combine
    And'ts more than that t'have made a stream to run   5
    Over a streame (of Nature so t'have won)
    Again it's more, that he who did this frame,
    Contemning praise should here suppress his name.
    Though what's done admiration doth require
    Yett what's left undone I doe more admire.   10

    'Goe to the signe o'th'Hen and Cock'

Apth-/ 1633   Goe to the signe o'th'Hen and Cock
    Thear is a dore with out a lock
    Which entred thou shalt find a flore
    With in which is all Rushen ore
    Whence if thou chance repulct to be   5
    Know 'twas cause Worth went not with thee
    Yet still goe on for they'le account
    Th'an Ass if thou not seek To mount
    Which once attempted thou willt find
    She like a Nabir will prove kind   10
    Then thou mayst Dally with her heres
    Or steal some riban that she weres
    But if she guive thee' an I: the rest
    Of her name backward makes her husbands crest

    in eandem

    If it be a feathers praise
    To be light and shake all wayes
    If it make a pumise rare
    Cause all stons else heavy are
    If the thin and subtlest ayre   5
    Makes a day by much more fayre
    If than all these she be more light
    Why should not I her praises write
    The loosnes of her cariage shines
    As she were caried by the winds   10
    Her love to one sort makes all those
    Are trod scearce feel her as she goes
    She is soe nimbly stirring that
    Yould think to wear her in your hat
    But soft, sheel sooner let you try   15
    Your waight upon her tender thygh

A lecture to be mild in love

Whilst that in bleating flocks of snow
The Dounes are clad the meads below
With various heards all covered be
When from the yoak their necks are free

And all the fields by Ceres blest 5
Are turnd to ears that never rest
Each naked wood anew receives
A fresh light canopy of leavs

Under whose secret brainches quires
Of winged singers stirr up fires 10
Of action whilst the purling spring
Quenches not, but adds fuelling

The kisses wanton Zephirs threw
O'th'Corn, o'th'leavs o'th'morning dew
Shew that with soft attempts we may 15
Best to loves ends procure a way

'Tis by degrees not all at one
Time water workes concaves in ston
Soe if but frendly sparkes appeer
'Thin the bowres harmonious sphear 20

That ayre will blow them up to rise
And in flaming Sympothise
Which great prerogative's alone
Proper to loves pavillion

Whence under too we may discover 25
Each Champion like to a lover
Fand by Cupitts winges and made
To Kiss as well in ear as blade

The breath-perfuming new milcht kie
Bespicing th'medowy tapisry 30
    And from the hills above
We have a lecture to be mild in love

La resverie or Loves Winter Seege

The Martiall Swed, with Lap, and Finland joyne
To break the ice, and winter on the Rhine
    Which Season ne're was wont
    T'receive such an Affront
But when it's single Couler't did display 5
    All quitt the Field and run away
        The Drum could beat
      Nothing save a retreat
        And evry-one
    Did follow into Garrison 10

But sithence ore-come by Armes
Lett noe man doubt but that ther may be Charmes
    To thaugh It's frozen beard; the God
Of warr was whipt sometimes with Myrtle rod
        And Julia flinges   15
          In Snow her Stinges
The little winged Captain's all the year
In armes, nor is the Springes peculier
    And though he meet with frost-bound Harts
        His fiery darts   20
Can melt them, and make passage for His warr
As Haniball through th'Alpes, with Vinegar.

    Sharp weather is a spurr to make
    All slothful lovers to forsake
Their drowsy homes and to this leaguer run   25
Wher whilst they seek to conquer they are won
        For as the breach unguarded lies
Guiving invitement to their enterprise
So doe th'beseeged under it contrive
A mine to play and blow them up alive.   30

PUBLIC RECORD OFFICE:
S.P. 16: 437.60

Upon the Scotch Sermon that compared the Kirke to a horsse

    The kirk's a horse, the preacher sayd
    Forsooth and sea say I
    A foule unruly mistaught Jade
    A Cope carle certainly
    For her best riders she hath cast
    And Lay'd them all beside her   5
    So that ther none dare now at Last
    But dolefull Jockies ride her

    Her paces all are tint and gane
    The feind a Strack she'l gang   10
    But e'ne as please her selfe alone
    Gude faith my bird all's wrang
    And yet for all she has forgott
    Mount we once mare I vow
    Wee'l teach her, her owne pace and trott   15
    And Canterbury too.

FULBECK HALL MS 2
POEMS, 1623-50

Emblemata

Brook House Bay trees.

Noe Thunder Blasts Joves Plant, nor can
Misfortune warpe an Honest-Man
Shaken He may be by some one
Or other Gust, Unleavd by none
Though Tribulation's sharp and Keen   5
His Resolutions keep Green
And whilst Integrety's His wall
His year's all Spring and hath noe Fall.

In Davidem Lapideum
or Upon the Chimny peece in the Gallery at Apthorp

The Princely Prophet statued heer doth stand
   Like unto a musitian
And with deaf art his stil notes would present
   To the behoulders wonderment
But let not stones deceive the Gasers will   5
They cannot daunce because the harp stands still.

Upon the Clock going too fast

The Swifter lying wheel ore-runs the day
Would make it seem as guilty of delay
And the wingd hower out stretch as conquered
In swiftnes by the Plummets waight of lead
   The fallacy is easy for admitt   5
   That wayght were ofe, then time would out fly it
O let my flitting dayes soe numbred be
   By a wise hart they prove of waight to me
     Soe may I life dispose that in the end
     By setting bright it may a cleer day send.   10

A Valentine for my Lord Savage.

If that this Rose had blown alone
'T had shortend admiration
But wher the Rose and Lilly meet
   Both Fair and Sweet

  The Sences are held Captives to unfowld 5
  The Emblem they behowld
Which being Crownd too seemes t'imply
 A Sovranty
 And soe it doth; for this
  The Lenox Lilly is 10
The Richmond Rose the Other; both combine
To stile you happy in a Valentine.

A Hart Enamelld white to Nel. G.

Like Lillies when untoucht they grow
Or like the falling Flakes of snow
Like pollisht Ivory before
Defild, and in a pocket wore
Like new milk from all motes thats straind 5
Or like Mayes blossoming unstaind
Like to the kirnell of a nutt
Stript out of all wherin 'twas shutt
Like to the silver of a stream
Or like to Swanny-featherd cream 10
 Soe spottless is this Hart doth tell
 The Valentine to me befell.

Upon a small occation of 10000£s disburcementraptim

Two Daughters' Portians gon, and spent,
Th'one on the King T'other on the Parlement
Howses and Goods Confiscat: Woods hould out
Least I become at length a bankerout
 Yet whilst Integrety 'thout shuffling's delt 5
 Douries and Patrimonies Loss' less felt

De Imperatorum Julianorum lineæ ultimo
Et Sulpitij sive Electorum primo

That the unhappy Nero might be said
To fall like to a Tyrant not in bed
Vindex in France raisd armes and seekes therby
To vindicate the wronges of Italy
The Fates were just to him that frighted Roome 5
Making at last fear Master of His doome.
Soe Bald-pate-Galba to the Throne did rise
Whom strait the Common people 'gan despise
Crying, why wouldst Thou Cesars name put on
When all the hayer grew on thy head was gon 10
If he the Empires Bark anew would rigg
He should have brought with Him a Perewigg.

The Tragecomedy of Mans Life

Heer one is born, and thear an other dies
   Nativety and Obsequies
   Enter at one; what then is all
   This worlds pompe, but Theatricall
For to come out, and to goe in   5
   Hath evermore the custome been
   And will be; till the Latter Scene
   Summon us all at once again
Then shall the left-hand file in misery
Shut up the story of their Tragedy   10
   Whilst in a Chorus the right winge
The Bridegroomes Epithalamy doe singe
   Both guiving a Catastrophe
   Unto this Tragick Commedy.

Vita Humana quid?

Our Life's a span; the Emblem ont's a Flowre
   Sprung Lately from an April showre
     To add one to the nosegay
       Of Enameled May
         Which past, its bewty   5
         Fades and growes dry
         Short livd's that
           We rate
           High
What allthough Lachesis to seem more kind   10
   Lengthen thy thred out to thy mind
     Yett ere long thou'lt wish t'have dyde
       When as thy Youth and pride
         Of dayes bequeath thee
           To th'misery   15
         Of More years
         Wher cares
           Lye.
Then like a Taper turned upside down
   Which in'ts own tears its light doth drown   20
     Thou liv'st still dying and fain
       Woulst end Life, to end pain
         Which ere long graunted
         Thats out, thou'rt dead
          And timely   25
           Bury-
           Ed.

Translations:

Horace: Ode: 10: Lib 2
A Mediocrity to be observed in both Fortunes.

    Thou may'st live happy, if thy minde
    Neither aspire too high, nor grind
    Upon the shelf of baseness lowe,
But in the mid'st 'twixt both delight to goe.

    The golden Mediocrity   5
    Whoe loves is safe, for Poverty
    Is base, and too great Sumptuousness
Procureth Envy, Cares, and wretchednes.

    For oft the higher towers, and Pines
    Have greater falls, when struck with windes,   10
    And those high mountaines, which aspire
E'en to the Skies, are soonest struck with fire.

    A well form'd minde in miserie
    Hopes that good Fortune will him free,
    And in felicity doth feare   15
Least Fortune cast him downe, whoe him did reare.

    Jove causeth winters frozen showres
    For to deface the Summer flowers
    He is the cause of both, ne still
Doth Fortune stand, but turnes from good to ill.   20

    When as hard Fortune frownes, then be
    The more couragious and free;
    But when she smiles, be wise; strike Saile,
Least thou beêst sunk with too too fayre a gale.

Horace: Ode: 38: Lib: 1:

    I hate the princely Sumptuousness
    Of Persian banquetts, and the dress
    Of Rosie garlands: Pass not where
    Those Roses growe; but voyd of care
    Nothing but Myrtle doe prepare.   5

    (The Myrtle usefull is to mend
    The vapours, which from wine ascend)
    Neither disgrace will't be to thee
    It to provide; nor yett to mee,
    Drinking 'neath Bacchus shady tree.   10

Horace: Ode: 13: Lib: 3

    O sacred Fountaine, clearer farre
        Than purest Cristalls are.
    Worthy, like to a Pow'r divine,

    A Sacrifice of Wine:
And to be deckt about thy brinke   5
    With Violett, and Pinke:
Tomorrow I doe promise Thee
    To offer up a hee-
Kidd butted, for a Sacrafice
    Whose blood (like to the Skies   10
When Phebus setts) sprinkled shall be
    In honour of thy Purity.

Thee nor the scorching Dogdaies heat,
    Nor cann the Sun-beams beat
Through those same shades, which o're thee grow,   15
    First sprung from thy overflow;
But thou art coolest then, when heat
    Causeth the Flock to bleat
For water.—

Thou shalt hereafter counted be   20
    'Mongst the nobility
Of Fountaines; and thy purling spring
    In pibbles make a murmuring.

Vina bibant homines, animantia cætera fontes Englished:

Let Men drink wine; for other living things
    Let them rest satisfy'd with water-springs.

Horace: Ode: 7: Lib: 4

Snowes now are fled, and fields are deckt with flowers,
    With new leaves the naked bowers;
The time o'th'yeare is chang'd, and flouds that were,
    Now againe but Riv'letts are.
The Nymphs and Graces nak'd their daunces lead   5
    Through each pleasant flowry mead.
The yeare would teach by's mutability
Not t'hope for their lifes immortality

The Springs compagnion Zephirus doth charme
    The winters cold, and now'ts warme.   10
The Summer's next, whose heat consumes the pride,
    And glory of the Spring-tide.
Next followes Autumne loaden with rich wines,
    Corne, and fruit of divers kindes.
Then clumsy Winter comes, who wrags up all   15
Those beauteous mixtures in a frozen ball.

Time in a swift course wastes, and after waine
    Phœbe renews her light againe.

But if our light goe out, we shine no more,
No borrow'd Sunshine can our Life restore.   20

'S Æneas dead? could not his Piety
   Sheild him gainst mortality?
Tellus and Ancus too? Could they not buy
   For wealth Eternity?
Noe, we are all like shadowes; sprung from dust,   25
   And to dust returne we must.
Who knowes to day, whither his life shall be
Prolong'd till 'morrow by the Gods decree?

Be therefore libêrall whilst thou mayest, and give
   Thy self thine whilst thou do'st live.   30
For bêing once dead, and Minoes sentence past
   On thee, th'art for ever fast.
Nor cann thy nobleness of blood reprive
   Thee againe not long to live.
Nor (though thy beauty rare) cann it prevaile   35
Nor piety when death doth thee assaile.

For neither could Diana's power deny
   Her chaste Hyppolitus to dye:
Not yet could Theseus loose Perithoes bands,
Allthough in freindshipp linkt; Deaths sentence stands.   40

Horace: Ode: 9: Lib: 1:

Dos't thou not see how in one night
The fields grow aged, and turn white?
The ofspring of the Forrest now
Putts on a night-capp, and doth bow.
The sharper frost lays an arrest   5
Upon faire Avons Liquid brest.

Why should we shiv'ring turne with these to ice,
When an increase of fire, with Ale and spice
May thaugh us througly? double then thy pains
Thou blinking Ned; lett Leonard fill our vaines   10
With the Sunns last-years Nectar, better farre
Than the Diota, or Sabinian starre.

Putt we the rest to God; who makes
A warr at Sea with windes, yet shakes
Neither the Ash, nor Cypress tree;   15
Leave to Curiosity
What shall the morrow-work be, and
The Guifts of Fortune lett's command.

Nor whilst the rising sapp proclaimes us young,
And free from crooked Ages peivish toung   20
Lett us refuse to sport, to daunce or sing,

Sheltered under Cupids golden wing:
  Now on the Plaines with Hound, or Hawke
  Wee'll spend the day; at Even the walk

Shall our retreat be, where we may discover
The whisp'ring repetitions of some Lover?
Or heare the inward pretty giglings, beene
From a wench in a corner, and not seene?
Or see one runn away half madd for joy
He'd gott a Ring from's Mistress, or some toy?

  Thus, though both woods and fields seeme olde,
  And Avon's frozen up with colde,
  Whilst there is fire in Venus court
  We shall not want for heat and sport.

Martial: Lib: 5: Epigram: 18

That in December, when guifts fly
From this to that freind mutually
I nought but bookes sent, thou'lt judge thus
Perhaps; I'm avaricious.
Noe, know I hate those ill deceipts,
And crafts in Guifts, are like to baites
On hookes, wheron a flye would cheat
The greedier fish when it would eat:
And whilst a Poore man giveth not at all
Unto's rich frend, he proveth liberall.

Martial: Lib: 10: Epigram: 47

That which creates a happy life,
Are riches left, not gott with strife,
A fertile, and a thankfull Molde.
A Chimney, that is never colde,
Never to be the Client, nor
But seldome times the Counsellor,
A minde content with what is fitt,
Whose strength doth most consist in witt;
A body, that's not prone to be
Sick, a prudent simplicity;
Such freinds as of ones owne ranke are,
Homely fare not sought from farr,
The table without Arts help spred,
A night in wine not sepulchred,
Yett drowning Cares; a bed that's blest
With true joy, Chastety, and rest,
Such short sweet Slumber as may give
Less time to dye in't, more to live,
Thine owne estate whatsoêre commend,
And wish not for, nor feare thine End.

Pastor fido:

'They are true kisses'

They are true kisses, where with mutuall gaine
One gives and takes, one takes and gives againe:

'Fayre Mistress, lett's rejoyce and sing'

Fayre Mistress, lett's rejoyce and sing,
Time flyes away, and though the Spring
May recompence the winters cold,
Making the yeare seeme young, 'lookt old;
Yet if our youth beginne to waine   5
It never will growe greene againe,
And to an unleav'd branch may well returne
Fire to consume itself, not others burne.

Martiall. Lib. Epig:

Whilst Nature doubts which sex thou'rt best to wear
Faire Boy: Thou'rt allmost made a wench I swear.

'All present good seemes smal'

All present good seemes smal; our hopes they deeme
Things great, as lights far distant greater seeme.

Martiall Lib—7. Epigram—38

Whilst Celius can noe longer hear
The newes-transporting-Babbeler
Nor yet enduer a morning spent
In entertaining Complement
For this or that Great person: He   5
Faineth a gout-infirmety
And better truth for to disguise
His sounder feet with bands he ties
And seems to goe in pain, as far
As art may prove a Cripeler   10
Til she to nature turns at last
And soe in earnest Celius's fast.

'Fallere fallentem non est Operosa Puellam'

'Tis noe hard Task to cheat a Cosning Lass
Who taught thee first what to dissemble was.

In nasutum

Erect thy nose, gape, shew thy teeth and this
If the sun shine may tel what hower it is

In eundem Euro sufflante

Peep but abroad when as the East wind's bowld
Then sure thy mouth may well be fill'd with could.

Ben Jhonson Drunk

Stand foot stand my foot, least slipping thou'rt misled
Stand fast or else these stones may prove thy bed.

Horace Epod. 2.

Thrice happy he who voyd of Care
  As our Forefathers wear
Can with unborrowed Oxen till
  That ground his Fathers will
Bequeth'd him, and from dept is free   5
  Nor feeles the misery
Of warrfare nor through fears cast down
  Whilst th'angry Sea doth frown
And Law sutes shuns, nor haunts the gates
  Of Great ones for their Cates   10
But rather's more delighted far
  When to the poppler
The tender ofspring of the vine
  He doth unite and joyne
Whilst from the branch his pruning bill   15
  The useles cutts and ill.
That in their roomes he might insert
  Others of more desert
Or in a frutefull vale doth spie
  His scatterd heard of kie   20

In adventum meum ad antiquos Lares Abthorpienses.
May-20: 1646. Englisht thus

The Spring tide thus doth Earth repaier
The wood thus putts on leavy hayer
Of more acceptance soe's a spark
Of day after it hath been dark
The rivers soe express desire   5
Hastening to find their proper sier
  As all this my return implies
  To my owld houshould Deities.

Ad Scoto Brittannum cui Carolus noster novum operaturus
Opus se subtraxit—May-5: 1646
Englisht thus

What wonder ist the King to th'Scots is fled
When by the English He was borrowed

Soe now's restored: that all their debts pay thus
I'de wish our Brethren send him back to us.

To Sir Jhon Wentworth upon his Curioseties
and Curteous entertainments at Summerly in Lovingland.

April-24.
1644 wrot that
night at
Ipswich

When thou the choise of natures welth hast scand
And brought it to compare with Lovingland
Know that thou maist as well make wonder less
By fanceing of two timbering Phenixes
At the same time: and dream two Suns to rise 5
At once to cast fier midst those Spiceries.
   Pregnant she is, yet that must not deny
The purest gould to come from Barbery
Diamonds and Pearl fro'th'Indies to conferr
On every Clime some thing peculier 10
For soe she hath; and like a Summ to all
That Curious is, seems heer most liberall
Affording in Epitome at least
What ere the world can bost of, or call best
Now as contracted vertue doth excell 15
In power and force this seems a miracle
Wherin all Travailers may truely say
They never saw soe much in little way
And thence conclude their folly that did steer
To seek for that abroad, at home was neer 20
In more perfection; wouldst thou Phebe meet?
Apollo or the Muses? not in Creet
And Greece, but heer at Sommerly those are
Removd to dwell, under a Patrons care
Who can as much Civilety express 25
As Candy Lies, or Gretia Barbrousnes:
   Wouldst thou be sheltred under Daphne's groves
Or chuse to live in Tempe, or make Loves
To any place wher Shepards wont to Lie
Upon the Hills, piping securety 30
Unto their Flocks, heer the sweet park contains
More evenness than the Arcadian plaines
Nor yet enchaunted by those shadowed ringes
Some say the Faires print with revelings
But's all in one die clad, and doth appeer 35
Like the Springes Favorite throughout the year
   The useful Ash and sturdy Oak are set
At distance and obey, the Brambles mett
Embrace and twine in t'arbours to conceal
And harbour such as stock this Commonweal 40
Until their Master pleas they should delight
His or his frends desire and appetite
   All tales of Satyrs banisht are from hence
And fabled Goblins that delude the sence

'Tis reall Venison, and abroad, in past 45
Alike may satesfy both eye and tast:
   The nobler Plants as Firr-deal and the Pine
Weeping out Rozan, bleeding Turpentine
Like the Life-guards upon the Hall attend
At neerer distance: wher the Gods descend 50
To keep their Courts, and either Glob's devisd
To grasp the Elements Epitomizd;
   The Sun-beams steddy Fier, with the Ayer
Of the unconstant winds Endialled are
Soe whilst the one the hower would inferr 55
The Other points a rule for th'Mariner:
Earth heer's embroidred into walkes, Some strait
Others Meander-like or wormes to bayt
Occasions hook til every humor come
And feed ther fatt as in Elisium. 60
Nor is ther Water wanting in the wood
Cleer as if running, Calme as if it stood
And soe contrivd by Natures helper Art
Ther's noe appeerance from the whol or part
That any sullen Sluce to malice bent 65
Can open to impair that Element
Nor yet th'Ambition of a Springes ore-flow
Cause it t'exceed or limits overthrow.
   Thus like a gould Chain linkt, or bracelet strung
From Carkanet, pleasures on pleasures hunge 70
And such delightfull objects did descry
Pursuing of each other that the eye
Astonisht at such wonder did crave rest
For fear of forfeting its interest
In soe great bliss, for over dazeld 'twas 75
And dimm of sight made by that Looking-glas
Soe ther's a parle graunted, and some space
To guather strenght 'twixt this and t'other place
But very short, not half a mile at most
We landed were again, and made a Coast 80
Wher if all antient Poets were to write
They'd need noe other fountain to indite
Story of all kinds with, but dip their pen
Then swear the Muses were not nine but ten
For heer dwelt one whose magick could infuse 85
A Fluency beyond all other Muse
And Court the Soyle with soe much art applide
Til all the world seems barberous beside
Heer Fish and Foule inhabit with such state
As Lords and Ladies wont when servd in Plate 90
Rich Arras and the like, Bill, Breed, and Swimm
In all delightfull Sollace to the brimm
Decoyd by soe much rapture on we pass
Unto a Castle that enchanted was

By th'Magick spell of musick, til ther set 95
We found a Cod like to Euterpes nett
To catch all passengers, the Lesbian Lute
Ore come with harmony became ther mute
Whilst as for table to the song bookes servd
The Cristall Fountain: Soe have I observd 100
When walking neer a stream the heavens to be
Beneath my feet to ease Astronomy
Ther tell the Gammuth of the Stars and Crack
Of all their motians even with Tickebrack
 The Fablers of Owld I guess might find 105
 Some objects to help invention but the mind
 Was sure Prophetick, for what ever is
 Describ'd for rare by Them, 'twas meant of this
And yet this falls short too, when He to whom
The Cost and Care owes Tribute's thear to summ 110
Up all with such Humanety and press
Of Crowded Favours and heap't Curtises
As Frendship were a Jeweller the while
His welcome seemd the Diamond Those the foyle.

   De sene Veronense— Claud—pag-231
   Of an owld man of—

Happy is He who on his own fields stage
(And noe wher else) hath acted ore his Age
He Whom his own house (had it eyes and tongue
Might say it sees him Owld; and saw him yonge
Now trusting to his staff He treads those sands 5
He formerly had crept on with his hands
Soe reckons up the long descent and (dotage
Thorough decays) of that his lonely Cottage.
 He ne're was drawn with fortunes Train to hast
 Nor did he flatter forraign springs with tast 10
 He was noe Merchant that might fear the straits
 Nor soldad fancying Military Baytes
 He never Pleaded: that the Court seemd horse
 'Twas not His fault: Who knew nor strife nor force:
But as uncapable of Busnes: Free: 15
Cannot declare what the next Town should be
Yet doth enjoy a prospect (may controwle
All others) of the Freer Ayre and Pole
 Nor casts He up the year by Consulls nowe
 But as the Frute-Trees to their Seasons bowe 20
 By Apples Autumn, Spring, by flowers befalls him
 One field hides Phebus face, the same recalls him
 And thus this Cuntry-swaynes observing way
 Measures within his Orbe the Course of day.
He did remember Yon Great Oake when't stood 25
But for a sappling: soe's grown owld with's wood

And Judging that same Ile (with less witt's blest
More Barbarisme) to be th'Indies east
He doth conclude the Red-Sea to be neer
Behoulding Standground-Farcet and the meer   30
And yet through strength unconquered he may guather
Comfort the third Age sees him Grandfather
   Let Others wander to the fard'st of Spaine
   The way is only Theirs; but Life his guaine.

*Epigram: Upon one Beal a minister that took the
Covenant thinking therby to save and hould his living
but being discoverd lost it and soe was deceived*

Beal coming wher the Covenant was a guiving
Swallows it, rather than He'd loose his living
But when 'twas known upon what tearms he took it
They bid him for his living goe look it
Whoso playes fast and loose with God's not fit   5
T'partake of Benefice or benefit.

    The Times Steerage   wrot in July 1643

Like Ships by th'same wind favourd, yet can stear
A severall Course; soe now the Cavallier
And the Bowle-Noddled-Crue pretend They fight
Both that Religion and the Lawes have right
For Liberty tis doubtless thats their own   5
Wherby all Property and safety's gon
Then mark how They performe this: Lawes did wind
In favour heer to This, to That unkind
(According as interpreters) now, They
Draw them right out their factions to obey: 10
And for the Gospell, whilst They'd weed out one
Heresy They'l admitt Confusion
To mould the forme anew, not as't was writt
But as Each brain-sick Patist fancies it
Or Statist frend to Liberty: what's worce   15
They cheat the Vulger, whilst this severall course
They run: Who look to th'wind, enquier by sence
Not what is aymd at reall, but pretence.
And soe or Judg or wish: Our Gratious King
Good in Himself, but ther's an other thing   20
He is a Man, may not's affections cleav
To be seduc't? Had not an Adam Eve?
   Discerting of His Counsailes Great and Wise
   Through Feares and Jealouzies workes them t'surmise
   Some dangerous consequence, some Plott to spin   25
   Out all our owld woffe, bring new Customs in
   To Church and State, and as ther some before
   Had Bodies Could speak French, now teach't all ore

The Land, instruct both Kirk and Camp thus after
T'pray to the Lady but Challenge fro'the Daughter 30
Free quarter at the least. What wast do y'guess
Taught Him to leav them; Cause they left t'express
The Counslers parts, and with Commanding pride
Petitiond humbly not to be denide.
To teach Him to be prodigally bent 35
Making such partners in His government
As all posest with Cesars Gost and Theirs
Who in their Regencies admitt noe Peers
But like Dictators that perpetuall are
Sole moderators grow, of Peace and warr 40
A large prerogative: yet not too high
For Those assume infallebilety
In all They order, or Ordain, decree,
Voat, Pass, and Repass: Say 'tis Soveranty
When th'Soveran's away to guive consent 45
And not to be soe Costively up pent
In Ceremony, 'tis Abomination
To make Le Roy Le veut Rudder th'whol Nation
And noe Coast made but when the Pylotts heer it
Fro'th'Masters mouth Soy't faict comme ils desirent. 50
 Printed, and Publisht to maintain, advance,
 The Course what ere, and tiers of Ordinance
 To weary all the Presses, batter down
 That antique Superstition of the town
 It's Loyalty; and bannish quite from hence 55
 Forth with Ston Crosses, soft Obedience
 Workes this effect on all: the Gentler read
 But Henry Elsing and it's made Theyr Creed.
 The Others Stupid, like a Cross of wood
 Or ston, if Brown be thear conclude it good 60
 They should be ruind: Neither making doubt
 But that the new Kakt world will bring about
 Some new promotians to restore to haight
 The low condition of each suffring wight
 And make Them all Free-States: which though they shun 65
 In will (that might after Arminious run),
 All arbitrary Power would defye
 They seek t'have all things left at Liberty
 Cause all were made for man: (To use it's true
 Not to abuse) that savours of some new 70
 State-Brain whose Empty pan like yours or mine
 Never leavs tinkling to reform, refine,
 Cobble, or what you'll call it under-sett
 Lay-Prop the Churches and States Architect
 Till with a Sampsons strength they bear up all 75
 Shake the foundation, soe cause that to fall
 They soe profest to shore up; ruines are
 Sent from those hands that should be Tutelar

  Oft times to shew, that He who made all will
   Have them rely on His, not their own skill   80
Wher sticks the Reformation? God began
With His Vicegerent and our sovraign
Moord all his Ship-mony, to lanch noe more
Because it seemd t'oppress the subject sore:
Layd low the High Commission, Broak the Arches   85
Soe He that will be wanton swimms, not marches
In lewdnes now and in that posture fears
Nor Chancler, Procter, nor their Paraters
Such as were scurgd out of the Temple once
Take now the freedom ther to vent 'thout bones   90
Or interuptian what somere they pleas
To aggravate the sore; add to th'disease
Less hope of Cuer, Corrode, and make the skarr
Than any galld-horse-back more odious farr
And rather than an article or soe   95
(Though not repeald) should rule, they'l each one goe
A severall way, not meeting 'less in this
To judg all Fasts and Feastings lawfull is
When s'ere th'Elect shall chuse, noe time or place
What so'ere they doe must turn it to disgrace   100
For they'r inspird, and Frantick heer with all
Take sisters up that Antechrist may fall
Leaving noe lewd Prophanenes one can speak on
Untride to Master Him at his own weapon.
  How doe these err from holy writ to raise   105
  Divells 'gainst divells, lay trees 'thwart the waies
  (Cross were prophane) for tender Contienc't folk
  To stumble at; and all but to provoak
  The Commons to aspire to this degree
  To prize Rebellion above Loyalty   110
  They know ther is noe question now to bring
  To censure, but who are you for? the King
  Or Parlement? as if a body'and head
  Could severd be yet not the party dead
Indeed the Courts of Justice shut up shop   115
Now this exchange is open—Trees that drop
Soe on the shrubbs hinder the spring to rise
This writ's a supersedious to th'assise
And that the Table might more Counsail keep
All causes wont be wakt Ther now may sleep   120
  And though all Patents Damd that did oppress
  The People 'tis apparent They'r noe less
  If not much more undone by such as be
  Not Ope but Closs shut up in Committe
And all Affaires contracted 'thin that fist   125
Whose Throat had Swallowed the monopolist
That Art near dies; but though a starr may set
The influence may stil remain as great

Summon upon light information, send
To prison ther to lie world without end 130
Nor once Examined, why ist do y'think
The Proverb tels a T. thats stird will—
All This is nothing 'tis not through yet
Though Charles lay all down, They'd rise, His power guet
To make Him Glorious, Ships to rule the Sea 135
Strong Forts and Towns the Land, and heer's Their Plea
Those are the Kingdoms, and the King is set
But over them as Chevalier du guet
He was at first but trusted from and for
The Commonwealth as His Superior 140
And now They'l make him know it, and derive
All from the body representative
Themselvs They mean (In good time) when 'tis sayd
That needs must be a Monster hath noe head
Such Monsterous Reformers who can hope 145
T'see other change in than from Skarf to—
Sithence all the kingdome's taught by them to storm,
Plunder itself, Obey noe Law, nor Form
Of Government; but what their wisedom's reach
Contracted in the number now doth teach 150
   Soe have I read in Kimistry from whence
   They had it (questionless) the quintessence
   Of anything extracted proves of main
   Authorety: neer'st kin to soverain
If fower or five performe what more should doe 155
(Could doe noe more two Cyfers added to
I'st to be Blam'd? when 'tis in vaine t' conceive
Suffitiency needs any more receive
These make a house 'tis true, but all they act
If with one figures absence you substract 160
I fear the rest are Cyfers whose degree
Is to but fill up place; th'authorety
Of Somms being lodgd in th'other which Content
With Counsail and th'additionall supplement
To raise the numbers doth not though without it 165
Consent a Cyfer carries ought about it
Soe He that strikes a tally on this Skoar
May become rich in fancy else but poor
And yet These Gulls must not be thought to err
Whilst Publike Faith's made their Lord Treasurer 170
Yeil—all th'Exchequer Chamber wher they bring
The Bodkin, Thimble and the wedding-Ring
Now to be abrogated for a kind
Of Relike Papistry had left behind
All these the mincing Citty Dames present 175
As offerings to the Cause: from others went
Store of more massy Plate to fill the room
And shew the Empty sculls from whence they come

Then to the mint this goes wher coygnd and payd
To hier the Tradesmen from his Lawfull trade.   180
And Cause Him t'arme against his Lawfull Prince
The Guarland's won: noe reason can convince
These Animalls, of any less dessign
Than whilst their shops they ransack, spring this mine
Their Generalls advance should be posest   185
Of th'King, the Cavaleers and all the rest
Oppose and are opposd: see how they'r wip't
Of all those hopes, Smoak thats tobacco-pip't
Vapours not sooner into nothing, than
They heer his Excellencies forces can   190
By noe means march unless a fresh supply
Of men and mony be sent instantly
  But like a restif jade whose sides enurd
  To whip and spurr proves senceless, nor is curd
  Unless some other way, soe Dun i'th'mire   195
  At Brick-Hill's fast nor satisfies desire
Thus seing their substance all is coynd and spent
Expecting of the like from Parlement
For the Religion whilst noe stamp it bears
Noe wonder though't raise Jealouzies and Fears   200
And make them Dream of Daingers Fancy treason
  Because they saw not right nor would heer reason
  But the King in, and of Himself's soe good
  He will by them, and all be understood
  To have his thoughts bent forward, not reflect   205
  On By-past faults either in state, or Sect
    And that amendment may from all ensue
    Intends wherin He faild to Rule anew.

Upon the King and Queens happy meeting again after an absence (wherin She had changd clime) neer edge hill the 13th of July-1643.

The wellcome Showers of Aprills morning dew
Distilld upon the Bosome of the Earth
Begett a May: whose livery anew
Cloaths fields and woods, and ther creates such merth
  Amids the winged Quier; that Eccho tels   5
  It ore again from Natures Minsterells

The Spicy Gumms that soe perfume the East
To bid the Sun good morrow, are not more
Esteemd for that than is the Goulden West
But that of Treasures Both have hidden store   10
  Is manifest: noe perills can deterr
  The forward hopes of the Adventurer

Noe world, noe Season, Spring, Summer nor Fall
In Frute in Flowres, Treasures Could ere present
Such sweet and wealthy Joyes Harmoniall   15

From Cuntry, Season, or from Element
   As when our Gratious King and his bright Queen
   Did after 12. months absence interveen.

Cloris Complaint—July-25.-1644.

Doe not the Planets (how-somere
They wander) stil retain a proper Sphere?
   And Seasons serve the year to bless?
Although the stormes and tempests are noe less?
   Are not becalmed Seas more faier   5
Than if th'had never been Irregular
   And shall Fond Man alone be sayd
To be of all thinges else Unpacefied.
   Lions to Lions kinde, and Bears
Frendly to Such, soe Wolves partake o'th'Fears   10
   With their pursued kin, the Fell-
Est Tyger can with his Assotiats dwell
   And yet (as if Un-human'd) We
By noe means with each other can agree
   Soe, (that we may Degenerate   15
From Nature's mandate), all our Passion's Hate
   And wher a Mischief may befall
All Dispositian's turnd to Prodigall
   Nor is ther for Compassion
Left any room (now'ts out of fashion).   20

      Befrend me wind, Ile trye the wave
         Though some ther be must sink, yet some't may save
      My Calender yet markes out Spring
   Dis-Gust may shake, not blast the Blossoming
      And therfore though I rov'd astray   25
   'Tis reconciling Truth points now the way
      In which I would be thought as farr
   From Variation, as the Fixed'st starr
      But with a Constant shining thence
   Serve King and Cuntry by my Influence.   30

Over the Chimny in the great Chamber at Merworth.
Oxford Translat.

   What doth He gett whoe're preferrs
   The scuttchions of His Ancesters
   This Chimni-peece of Gould or Brass
   That Coat of Armes blazond in glass
   When those with time and age have end   5
   Thy Prowess must thy self commend.
      The smooty shadows of some one
      Or others Trophes carvd in ston
      Defac't are things to whet, not trye
      Thine owne Heroicisme by   10

For Cast how much thy merits skoar
Falls short of those went thee before
By soe much art thou in arear
And stainst Gentillety I fear
True Noblenes doth those alone engage 15
Who can add Vertues to their Parentage.

An Epitaph for Wimarke

Nature lent time, soe He grew owld
And prodigall at once, in this:
Setting it all at stake 'gainst Gould
Wherof He made his chiefest bliss 5
But when she saw he tooke of all-
Men interest yet payd Her none
She calls for in the principall
And layes it up under this ston.

In Histrionem quendam

Thou that soe oft in jest wast wont to die
Art now tain at thy word, and heer dost lye
Thine Acts had many Scenes, Deaths had but one
His entry was thine Exit, bad be gon:
Thou art a King noe more, no that's layd by 5
Nor Anie's Parasite in flattery
Thou hast put ofe the Clownes slops, now, nor art
Wrapt with the furies of a Lovers part
But sute'st thy self in one, wherin all must
Thy Fellow-Actors be: to sleep in dust. 10

In Obitum Ben: Jhons[on]

He who began from brick and lime
   The Muses Hill to clime
And whilom busied in laying ston
   Thirsted to drink of Helicon
   Changing his trowell for a pen 5
Wrote strayt the temper not of dirt, but men.

Now Sithence that He is turnd to clay and gon
   Let those remaine of th'occupation
He honeurd once, square him a toombe may say
   His craft exceeded far a Dawbers way
   Yet write upon't He could noe longer tarry 10
But was returnd again unto the Quarry.

He is not dead yet: but Dull.

Did I proclaime thee dead before the time
   Parden my forward rime

That tooke it up of Fame who's sayd to lie
Yet so't became the truer Poetry
Which though brought forth in hast's not blind but sees   5
   Sithence on the lees
The better part thy witt runns, and noe spirit
Retaines but what the times past did inherit
Soe that thy play is done; the people may
     Expecting of a farcey stay   10
  And cry he comes again: but if that loome
  Be spunn out too, thoul't find noe sanctuary
   But in the Tiering-roome.

A Letter sent to E. B. from Apthorpe to Howb[ury].

Did that Chast Grecian Dame soe long to see
Her Lords return from Ilioms Desteny
And shall not I wish Bedfordshire on fire
That keeps me widowed thus from my desier
Thy conversation: Yes, Let Hector fall   5
And brave Achilles triumph on the wall
Soe that my Ned Æneas-like may scape
I shall a worse revenge wish for this Rape
And if ther be a Priamus yet left
That dares avow the Justnes of this theft   10
I bid defiance to him and proclaime
Not Greece but I shall question him the same
And let him know: that Loss seems greater farr
Which doth concern any particuler
  They wrapt their quarrell in such generall pett   15
  As did noe less than ten years seige begett
  Yet were constraind to use a stratagem
  'Fore ever They had Power to Conquer them
     I will not borrow Agamemnon's sheild
     Nor Ajax Sword was brandisht in that field   20
     For my revenge false Simoes rhetorick
     Shall not be usd to Cause your Comming quick
But what sweet Thorp affords, whose bankes begin
To put themselves forth to Enameling
Whilst that the Gentle Stream would gladly trie   25
The vertue of your hookes Phlebottomy
And Fishes such securety doth sway
That 'bove their Element they Sport and Play
    You need noe Plumming Lead, nor quill to float
    To wellcome you They'l Leap into your boat   30
    To kiss your hands; and with Ambition swell
    Each Perch t'a Yard, each Pickrell to an Ell
Such was (the sea excepted) Formia's shore
For Fragrancy noe guarden can have more
In pleasure prospective it yeilds to none   35
But what are in the middle Region

Not doth the Roman Tibur; Paris Scene
Or Viens Danuby excell the Neen
If judgd aright and by the slower course
A river be thought better and not worse 40
Or if Imprisond waters, channelld lie
Twixt bankes that kiss can Challenge soveranty
Heer are noe more Calm-breaking-blasts then make
It's waters differ from a standing Lake
And add unto it's Creatures appetite 45
Wherby they soon betray themselves and bite
(Such like the Gale did seem when heat began
I saw a Virgin Once send from her Fann.)
Nor shall the Trowling Kemp, or silken Fly
Nor sand-scour'd worme longe claime attentive eye 50
Sithence from your hand the Line's noe sooner sent
But it drawes Tribut from that Element
Which if awak't by'ts Course-controwling-wind
At may time, you ready sport may find
In Sewlhey Poole, wher Carpes and other fish 55
Exchange their silver waters for a dish
The Tyrant Pike through many years grown great
At Last's ore come and proveth dainty meat
 Doth Howbery afford this? or canst say
 The year's not shortned to thee every day 60
 Thou'st Lost Ther from those bounties are prepard
 For thy content, yet are by others shard?
  Tis true a Brother and a Sister are
  Thinges of Content, yet not soe singuler
  Posessors of the whole, but that the Hart 65
  Composd of Angles should alott one part
  Or Corner to a Frend, whose hart againe
 Requiting Thine, both circuler remaine
 And in a True Proportion never jarr
 But howld one and the same Diameter 70
  Love being the Center Perioding those Lines
  Our Actions draw out and our Faith Confines.

1632   *A woollen night cap sent to the same pour Les estresnes*

That in Observance of the new-born year
I doe present you with noe hand-kacher
Noe guilded Paper, wax-book, or such Thinges
As were th'Owld Saturnalian Gossopings
Know my Love's greater than to be exprest 5
In pocket sheets like Plumms snatcht from a feast
Nor ist the guilded Quier that can shew
Unles by th'spottlesnes my Faith to you
The Virgin Book with Royall Heraldry
Might emblem out Loves Prodigallety 10
But being a Light consumes, and soe can not

    Define the thing that never wasts a jott
        Which though it have like heat as Damons had
        Towards his Pythias, yet I send it clad
        In season for the time; knowing each die 5
        Receives more Luster from its contrary
        And soe pretend Could to beget this flame
        In a preventing way yet still the same
            Le vostre &c:

    ### Upon the Death of My Fidelia
    ### a farewell to wine

St Peter—1636   Farewell Deer ofspring of the lusty vine
        Thou art too sprightfull for my care
        For as the month began its signe*   *Aquarius
        Soe my thoughts drownd in sorrowes are
        Now they reflect upon that loss of mine 5

    And as the radiant skorching beams draw nigh
        To kiss the fish that backward swimms
        I doe command thee from me t'fly
        And fill all others glasses brimms
    Whilst I alone think back and weep, and die 10

    Which though denide a while by Fates reprive
        Until some longer time be spent
        I shall importune th'next* to guive   *July
        Me Doggs for to pursue the sent
    And from my pallat in full chase thee t'drive 15

    That soe I may not cross to what I owe
        My self deceased, cease to be
        Under that sadnes overflow
        Should make me quite shake hands with thee
    And cause me from thy stock to Cypres t'grow 20

    Alone'ts the Plant with this time suteth best
        To emblem to the world my grief
        That robd of that wherin most blest
        I judgd my self all might releef
    Add whilst they seem to share i'th'interest 25

    Thus casting ofe my tender mirtle wreath
        And Rosy chaplet I put on
        That luckles guarland and bequeath
        Whats left unto devotion
    Till sights afloat sink all joyes underneath 30

    I mean vaporiall: for I deem noe less
        Of those thy magick art can raise
        Who though the glory of the press
        Lend'st but some thunder blasted bayes
    To crown my fancy soe disturb my rest 35

She's past thy reach for whom my troubled mind
    Thus workes like to the raging sea
    Tempt me noe more am left behind
    But graunt admittance to my plea
Nor in a blush but in a frown prove kind.   40

Upon my Fidelias Toomb

Pass not bye but read and see
    Wher all the Graces three
    Comprised are in an Epittome

For what of Love affection claimd in her
    Was my Peculier   5
    Nor did she that on any else conferr

The charitable part on all
    From Her free hand did fall
    Soe generously Generall

Ore th'Good soe far as Emulation led   10
    Her Ambitious Envy, spread
      The Ill she through compassion pittied

Soe Low a pitch Her Thoughts suffisd that they
    To Heavn knew noe other way
    But to beleev and pray   15

And for Her Faith to Husband, Frend
    Nay all the world Let Fame commend
    Crownd was Her Life by th'end

Ther was noe wave of Fortune heer
    Could toss her in soe great Fear   20
    (Though'er Sexes weaknes) but through hope She'd stear

    Faith was Her mast
      And Love the Sayles
        Assurance th'Anker that she cast
          Soe Thornes, whips, nails,   25
          Like winds convaighd Her, to her port at last

In praise of my Fidelia

    Get thee a Ship weel riggd and tight
    With ordnance store and mand for fight
    Snugg in Her timbers-mould for th'seas
    Yet Large in howld for Merchandes
    Spread forth Her Cloth and Ancors waygh   5
    And let her on the curld waves play
    Till Fortune-towde she chaunce to meet
    Th'Hesperian-home-bound western Fleet
    Then lett her bord'um and for prize

Take Gould-oar suger-canes and spice 10
   And when all these sh'hath brought ashore
     In my Fidelia I'le find more.

Her Lading

Her lips to me are far more pretious
Than were those frutes kept to Alcinous
Her Aromattick breath might serve to bring
Perfumes unto the Phenix timbering
Her hart's a mine whose treasure doth afford 5
More Gould than Midaes wishes to his bord
   Her Hart, Her Breath, Her Lip, faire, sweet, rich joygn
   To make Her of a Mortall seeme Divine.

My Fidelia with whom I had been cross the Street at Devotion opening her window finds me reading in on opposite and begins.

Fid: What at your prayrs again? B: It is most true
     I was when you
  My Goddes freely did vouchsalf the grace
     To shew your face
  My window turnd into an Altar was 5
     Of burning glass
  When yours first opened like a box wherin
     Fair Diamonds been
  Or like Clowds seavering 'tween which we descry
     Heavns brightest eye 10
  Yet dare not look on it too long: Least we
     Leese Liberty
  Of seing: soe enforc't I oft denide
     Mine eyes their pride
  Least me of them this Object should deprive 15
     Yet let me live
  But how? Like one thats blind, by others sight
     Taught which wayes right
  Oh How I envi'de Jove heer in his Shape
     When he the rape 20
  In Ida made; that soe I mought behowld
     The Rayes of Gould
  Phebus or you cast on me, yet goe on
     In Adoration
  To both your Deities, till I obtain 25
     The Faithfulls gaine
    Heaven in Your presence, which once graunted I
    Shall in your service ever Live and Dye.

Amor non patitur Moras. Sonnet

  Sithence on Earth it is a Fate
    That Time should ruinate

>   All things in It: wisely say
>   I will noe longer stay
>   Least He lay rude hands on you 5
>   And snatch from thence the true
>   Couler of the Lillies Snowe
>   Wheron faire Roses blowe
>   For those bud, blowe, and decay
>   In one and the same day 10
>   And snow fall'n on to ground's defilde
>   Soe must your bewty, yeild
>   Fade, decay, without recall
>   Hasten to its Funerall.

Sonnet Comparing Fid[elia] to the 4: Seasons—and the 4: times of the Day

Ha'st th'e're markt the joyfull Spring
  All clad in faire perfum'd array
    Or heard her Phylomele sing
      Or seen the dawning of a Day
        In Sumer e're the Sun had tann'd its bewty away 20

Ha'st th'observ'd how th'Evening Skies
  In Automn purple-mantled are
    When each bird homewards chirping flies
      Or Winters single couler rare
        When snow had dight the ground, and Frost had purg'd the Ayre. 25

Now would'st thou fain both see and heer
  At once all these conjoynd in one
    Contending whither seeme more cleer
      Whilst they cause a Perfection
        In Her whom Vertue, and wisedome cleap their Compagnion. 30

Sonnet: She is Fair and Verteous

>   Why is sleaved Silk soe hard
>   Or Jett smutch't or Ivory
>   But because they are compard
>   To Her Hayre, her browe, her eye,
>   And on her lipps Currall doth leese its die 5
>
>   Why should Snow be grown soe black
>   Roses soe pale but to see
>   That they those perfections lack
>   Which on her cheakes mingled be
>   Her Brests make wallnutts wear their tiffany 10
>
>   Why is Delia in one year
>   Twelve times fatt and lean? to show
>   That inconstancy bides thear
>   And it's contrary below
>   For wher She is thear will perfections flow. 15

Having suffered an absence from my Fidelia I am returnd—

Thus have I seen the Earth when the rude plowgh
Did shear it up in little fowlds to throw
It self into it self, like to those bands
Which Frends return'd to meet make with their hands

Soe have I Neptune seen when cutt in twain 5
Return soft kisses with more force again
Joves Consorts Kingdom smile after it had
Frownd in a Cloud, and than before more glad

And the Ambitious Element of Fier
When't hath been severed on earth aspier 10
To make's flames meet (noe more to part) i'th' Skies
Let imitation be the Sacrefize

To expiat what's past, and lett's returne
T'Embrace, to Kiss, to Smile, and more to burn.

Upon Fidelia only to be admired not drawn.

Did I not deem't presumption in the haight
To seek to draw Apelles' line more strait
Or t'add a touch where Nature had Limmd one
And In't a singuler perfection
My Fethred Pencill should be wett and bring 5
The Choisest Coulers from the Thespian spring
To paint Thy Vertues Features; but soe far
Sithence they beyond all imitation are
I'le but admire them, silence shall express
How much all Art than Natures Lawes is less 10
A piece of Rubines may as soone be thine
In coppy who canst only paint a Signe
Whilst to th'originall thou comest as neer
As writing over head what 'tis can steer
Such gross abuses are: went I about 15
To draw th'at Life, many thear are might doubt
By my faint coulers that 'twas made for thee
When thou had'st payd thy last to desteny
And soe I should noe Picture but a grave
Make for those praises which noe limmets have. 20

Sonnet

The Heavens countles twinkling Eyes
Contemplat Phebe's borrowed light
Until her Brothers Carr arise
Which drives both Her and Them to flight
Soe lesser bewties strive to shun 5
The greater by whose force their won

This Bowld Triumpher cast a raye
As He thought peerles for it's grace
Into the chamber wher She Laye

        Who could not brook such a disgrace 5
          But walking forth it made Him know
          His was but borrowed from below.

Fidelias Title to the Empire of the World

When Phebus quitts his watry Bed
    And his faint steeds refreshed has
The ground with sylver dewe bespred
    Which Pearle-like hanges upon each gras
        Searveth him for a looking-glass. 5

Wherat he kembs his Amber head
    And guives each goulden hair it's place
Until at length it vanished
    At the bright Splendor of His face
        As needless wher thear was such grace 10

Yett that noe sooner melted; Earth
    To welcom him did soone prepare
(As she could well) a suddain bearth
    Of divers sorts of Flowres most rare
        Sweet, and Fair beyond compare 15

The Rose that in both doth excell
    Rich Tulipes to please his sight
The Violet which for sweet smell
    Damsells place in their bosoms white
        With Lyllies store thus was She dight. 20

The Larke from that sweet bed, with sweet
    Notes mounts up to the crystall Skyes
Striving in vain Him for to meet
    Midd-way; whilst she tyr'd as she flies
        Doth rise and fall, doth fall and rise 25

With that the Tall-treed-wood sends forth
    From neath his thick-Curld-head all green
Melodious harmony whose worth
    Doth more excell in this I ween
        In being heard only, noe quier seen 30

Then Zephirus being charm'd by this
    Descends in mildest breath and makes
Each backward branch to daunce and kiss
    And in their gestures pastime takes
        Whilst he them kisses but, not shakes 35

These did invite my fayr abroad
    That soe she mought with Phebus share
But the Damaske wheron she troad
    Towld her that His titles all wear
        Cancelled in Her being thear. 40

To the County of Kent upon its condition at present—June-1-1644

Unconquered Coast: whilst all thy neighbours be
Nor Plunder, Billet, nor Freequarter free
How above such is thy Condition blest
That Labourst not, when Those can take noe rest
But by a Providentiall Care put on 5
Cherishest warr abroad which is Welldon
For soe thy Peace at home more fixed lies
Foundationd on thy frends, (not Enemies
As Soldads allwayes seem) and what Exise
Thy Purse draines, tis thy neighbours Compremise 10
Not Left to them who allwayes hungry press
To be th'r own Carvers of thy Substances
Heer in Thy Care excells and though't remaine
Some judg it hard the bye should shrink the maine
Yet be assurd the main and all relie 15
Soe much on this securing Polecy
That should but privat discontent ore flowe
The bankes of reason, it might overthrowe
Thee and thy force, yet sithence for ground thou'st layd
To Conquer first thyself, be not afrayd 20
For't speaks more power, nor can Plot rise T'unbridg
Thy Rivers Passes, People o'th Priviledg
Of free born subjects armd with this intent
To stand for God, the King, and's Parlement
As the renowned Yeomandry of Kent. 25

Upon the Lady of my second adventure Verania

What doe we call those silent Howers which
    Into Dead transes us bewitch
And such as would presage our destenny
    That Living Heer we ofte must dye
But Morpheus Charmes, under the name of Night 5
    When darknes drives away the light
And if at all Heaven bless us then'ts noe more
    Than if the Jewell which She wore
Were only now presented to My view
    Herself the Paragon and true 10
Sun of my thoughts denide to Shine me on
    By Earth's interposition
But my hopes tell me, as the Sun doth sett
    Soe must He rise and turne the Jett
Into pure Amber, Death to Life again 15
    Mourning to Joy with His bright Wayn
And with one Smile dispell the mists which sent
    Him into that short Bannishment
      Soe let a Gratious Smile from Her imply
      At my returne She loves: my crosses fly. 20

Upon the fairest Webb that Nature ever Spun. Sonnet

  Lett not Arachnes Loome be namd
  Wher Natures Curious hand hath framd
   A Webb soe Fair and fine
    A one
   That Pallas though Divine   5
  Enters not heer into Comparison

  'Twer Folly for to represent
  Jove on the Liquid Element
   When he Europa's Rape
    Procurd   10
  Sithence that Her heavnly shape

  Who've only seen, a greater rape endurd
  Or should the Goddes new compose
  Her Rock and in her Nett inclose
   Twelve Gods at once in vain   15
    'Twould be
   When the Celestiall Train
  On Her brest sitt in greater Majesty

  If for this bowld attempted peese
  Nature should be judgd to leese   20
   Or change her forme: Lett' be
    That I
   Through Metamorphosy
  Who am allready caught, hang thear a Flye.

Upon a fall which Mistress F: C: had from her horse
    hunting in my park

     Prologue

  Call in your balletts all yea that reherse
  With confidence soe many lies in verse
  Of Daphne's Fate, or how Acteon fell
  Of Prognes, and her sister Phylomell
  'Tis not a Fable that I goe to show   5
  Truth setts it forth cum privilegio

  In Cynthias Revells as I bare a part
  Last night a Nimph of Hers did wound my hart
  Till, in pursute least I should over-take her
  She beggd the Godds that They a Tree would make her 10
  Which They as soon did graunt; for instantly
  She's Metamorphisd by Philosophy
  Which proves revertion in our shapes to be
  The truest Emblem of a growing Tree
  The roote's our Heads wheron the haire doth growe 15
  The trunke's, our Bodies, and each Legg's a bowe
   Amazd at this strange site I stood, in doubt

Whither some fatall Doome would find me out
For the presumption, but thear followd none
'Save a sence rapture, th'admiration   20
Of Her faire skin begott, which had it been
Enlawnd within some Cristall Spring, then seen
I dare avowe't had servd for to have sworn
Ruine to all the Brothers of the horne
The fleesy down of Ledas Silver Swan   25
Snow whilst 'tis falling, or what ever can
Be thought more spottles; Lillies undefil'd
By touch of hand, a brighter Bason fild
With Moteles Milk, white sleaved Silk, thes all
But Coppies are to her Originall   30

Epilogue

Should I say all could heer be sayd I might
Not only sing all day, but sing all night
With' Daughter of Pandion and complain
The dainger She was like for to sustain

    Lett this suffice; the place wher she did stand   35
    Thus Tree-like, let't be calld the Terean Land.

Epithal[amium] in Nup[ti]as Sororu[m] uno eodemque tempore celebratas Westmon[asteri]æ

Sithence 'tis the time when all alive
Their Soules unto each other guive
And evry things inspird by thee
Cupid: and seekes an unety
    O let sweet Hymen thus-   5
    Far, seeme propitious
Noe longer now for to despise
    These Lares offering
But in a double sacrifize
    A full requitall't bring.   10

'Tis done, 'tis done; see wher they pass
Each others eye's a looking glass
Wherin, this rarety is wrought
That Turtles two, and two, are brought
    At once before thy Shrine,   15
    Great Bishop Valentine.
Wher having payd their vowes, and praires;
    The business is don.
And, though they thither, came in paires,
    Each Couple's, turnd to one.   20

The like in Medly for F.F.

Minime dum parcant; Parcæ
    Took away the owld Lord Darce

Filius Veneris Cupido
    Shot again Frank for the widow
Hymen O Hymenæe Hymen   5
    What theron's discoursed by men
Laertesque senex; Telemachusque puer
    She was content, but now's more pleasd I'm suer.

A Posy upon a weeks absence from her

What breath the dampe
    Of soe great absence doth allowe
        I heer instampe
    And signe it from my hart a vowe
It is short-winded, yet I long for you   5

Χαλεπα τα καλα ἐστιυ
To F.F.

But just it is, Nature should coynes use
    In setting higher price
      Upon Her Fairest Marchandise
    Thus Mortalls to abuse
Whilst they for Bewty, not for vertue chuse.   5

Far 'thin the bowells of the Earth doth lie
    The pretious Adamant
    (Which for our Pride we cannot want)
    Whilst with neglect thrown bye
The Pibbles are and Flints promiscuously.   10

If Gould like Corn as Corn like Gould
    Did grow above the ground
    Then would't not be of such renoun
    For I have heard it towld
How Easy thinges at easy rates are sowld   15

'Tis not the Holly, or the Misseltoe
    'Cause allwayes green disclose
    The spring tides treasure; I suppose
    If but a Rose should blow
'Twould more invite my fancy to think soe   20

Doe we not hide the Myrtles tender sett
    Both from the Could and Heat
    That it may neither freeze nor sweat
    But Fragrancy begett
Which may proclaime all savours counterfett   25

And can we think wher soe great Vertues run
    In soe great Bewty too
    To win at first before we woe
    That never can be don
Fair Troy endurd a seege before't was wonn.   30

The North-West Passage

Are not the Spicy Indies whence all store
        Of treasures come, soe far
    From us as in Diameter
        Unless we can a shore
Or North-West Bay, find out, which may yeild more   5

Though Davis broak the Ice without success
        And many sithence have tride
    To wayt with hopes upon that tide
        And soe have done noe less
Making Adventure cheefest happines   10

Yet if in Hudsons or in Buttons Bay
        We Winter till the Spring
    Open the stream for Steeraging
        And then can find noe way
For our designes; what shall we further say   15

    But that is presumption t'goe about
By the North-West to seek th'East Indies out.

Upon the names of her various sutors

How-art disposd of Widdow say
Wilt thou in a fond heathen Temple pray
Or for a point reserve thy bed
I kNow-well thou'lt at last be conquered
Yet not by Him (though Keepers trye   5
And Wall-Her in) |walls cannot love deny|
What though a Fairer-seat she shun
For ankerage and on a hausar run
And spring a Leak; if soe she ride
Out stoutly This And T'other, the third tide   10
May bear Her ofe which that it doe
Cause hopes 'thout prayers are Vain for Fane Ile wooe.

The Western Skye

What doth the red and doughtfull sett portend
  The Morrow to prove Foe or Frend
    By the Suns Shine
  Or rather that some wind
  Raise cloudes to shade its face   5
  And make it lowre in rain
  Noe, noe 'tis for a grace
The West hath borrowed from its Kindred stain

'Tis on Her Lip, 'tis on her cheek
Whatsoere all Curious eyes can seek   10
    And yet noe doubt, nor fear
Since that two bright Sunns doe controwle that Sphear

Her lovely eyes which with one ray
Dazel presumption away
    Doe with an other gleam invite 15
Th'obscurest vapour to turn light

Her Soule and Body howld
The same proportion well
    And as the Case or Mowld 20
Is exquisite, soe doth th'inclosd excell

Now through each others Influence of good
    What may be understood
Save by a Propagating power
        A Shower 25
Not to destroy but to increase
    Fullnes of Joy and Peace

That when all Almanacks through prescript lie
Mine may speake truth upon this Western Skye.

A Caracter of Newmarket and of The Company and Sports thear

Newmarket is the scene wher evry on
    Acts a perpetuall motion
And whilst they this and that way flurting ride
    Like ebbs and flowings in a tide
    Youl'd judg't a Sea of folly when they troope 5
And wagers lay which horse comes first to th'stoope

For as the waves unconstancy; the crack
Shifts from the Bay to th'Rhone, fro'th'white to th'Black
Dutton will winn of Crickett some suppose
Others that Bevis cariest from White-rose 10
Brandling had run with Talbot too some say
But that the forfaiture they chose to pay
Thus like that scumm or froths upon
    The briny Ocean
Soe if Their Goddess raise her windes 15
She workes up Bubbles in their mindes
    But if Her Calmes Misfortunes raine
    'T may be they'l know themselves and you again.

Upon Ms. B West Widdow to the Lord Darceay requiring more land with F.F. for 2d husband

Madam, if to your name you'ld add more land
    Take West-moreland
But if with fortune you will crowne an other
    Let't be at least his Brother
My modest pen can praise nor t'on nor t'other 5

Though you resolve not t'change your deer Lords name
I Dare-say U'L B happy, F. the same.

A Fishing Sea-Voyage from Lin to Boston

Nights Curtain ope; the Prologue to the day
On's Eastern stage his coulers 'gan display
And with a smile dark vapours did disperse
Casting a brightnes o're the universe
When Nereus charmd by Phebes power forbore 5
To print more kisses on the smooth-lipt shore
Who with a gale South-west accompanide
In greater hast back to the Ocean hied
These did invite our wandring thoughts to crave
A passage o're this self-conducting wave 10
Which we obtain, and having seen the main
Both Tide and wind brought us ashore againe
  Only from out blew Tritons Cabinett
  Some rareties we purchasd with a nett

Wher to their greater shame were open layd 15
The lusty Crab with nimble stirring Mayd
The threvy Scate, the purple-spotted Place
The dainty Sole the Butt-fish did embrace
The Mouse lay Creeping on the Damsells brest
The Hedghogg palizadoed salf did rest 20
The Crayfish of the Sea enthrond did dwell
Within the Laberinthian Winkle-shell
The headless Starr-fish too could crawle upon
The belly of his she Compagnion
  Each did express (though Prisners) They were free 25
  Wher Nature had commanded sympothy
  And whilst half breath-less, choakt with Ayre they lye
  They seeme to kiss each other; and soe die.
What could more pitty move? We can lament
When we a Frend lees in their Element 30
And shall we not soe much affection spare
Theirs that survive, in grief as t'have a share?
They'l noe deniall; strait we might discerne
The sable Porpus wallowing at our sterne
Attended by a Tempest Black as Clowdes 35
Could make, which soon had shadowed our Shroudes
Which casting perfect mourning on the deep
Burst forth in Tears and causd our decks to weep.
Neptune who earst was Halcedonian
To foam and swell int'billowes now began 40
The Surges gainst our Beak-head rise, and fall
Again like Tears shed at some funerall
Yett ere the glass ran out our skipper cries
Heer is an end of these solemnities
And makes a Coast, wher landing from the Storme 45
The last Obsequiall duties we performe
Intoombing Them: and to bedew their Herse
Make them to swimm in clarett, and this verse.

My adventure, or a new discovery under the Bear
Of an Evil thing which erected my Pole Artick.
July 12 1641

Fill me an Astrolabe with radiant sack
Then may I drink a health to Tickhobrack
And soe contract each motion of a starr
Till I become a rare Astronomer
Nor yet in Cygnas brest alone descry 5
Some new-born Orbe, but a whol Galexy
Of brighter flames to pave my fancies way
Until it turn a midnight to noon day
   Castor and Pollox both at once appeer
   To be my navigations fartherer 10
   And Argo lends a bark to waft me ore
   As it did Jason to the goulden shore
   The bank-side of delight, the Climat wher
   For Pole starr of direction's *fixt* the Bear   *shines*
Yet soe bedimmd with Aspects of more light 15
That seemd: I lost my self and found 'twas night
But such a one as when the fates conspire
To represent Solemnety in fier
Of sparkling Diamonds might serve to show
A richer starry Firmament below 20
   Yet was that darkned too: as I surmise
   (For I'le tell truth) I should see nought for eyes:
   Like as near peept out of Tyndarian race
   Shot from the features of a hevenly face
   Such killing gleams, I had been quite undon 25
   As are the Lesser Plannetts by the Sun
Had not the subtil thinner Cloud of lawne
Obeyd my humble wish and strait withdrawne
Wherby I did a milky path discover
Leads to that place for which the Gods might love her 30
   Thus shipwrackt at the bridg my thoughts (strook dead
   With what they wisht t'enjoy) sent me to bed.

The Peake. ode

   How dull are They
That can consume day after Day
In furrowing up of dirt and Clay

   Whilst in the Peak a wimbles bore
   May bring them up such ore 5
As that Theyl need not t'think of wanting more

   Yet ther are some more stupid sure
   Who will a tedious chase enduer
Or rend their throats after a kite to luer

When as the Phenix of the Sharper Hill 10
All with those rareties can fill
That may deprive them of all other will

Awake my Mun and let us not be stilde
(Because within a forrest) wilde
The woods as Hills have Conies Tame and milde 15

If such be Thear let us again goe on
For else the Season will be past and gon
Now'ts fit that each male Deer his head Had-on.

My Fox-huntinge

Not at those Groves chast Cynthias worshipt in
Nor 'mongst Her Brothers Laurells have I been
As far as Delphos soe I might have gon
Or don in Candy my devotion
But Fortune with a smile conducted to 5
A Coppice wher I sacrefize might doe
Yet save that jorney: Vowes performd at home
Accepted are, soe they in season come.

It was the last chime that the Cock did ring
And first of time all other birds gan sing 10
When overcom with drink the red fac't Sun
To issue forth his Bed-chamber begun
Who on a suddain cast the Eastern Skie
Into soe perfect a Vermillion dye
That ravisht with such splendor, out of bed 15
I leapt to win Aurora's maydenhead
Which I obtaind: and ere her bewty drew
Towards a wayne, my Hounds Volpone slew

He was a Rebel, and the Law alotts
To him that bringes in's head a dozen potts 20
He Tyrannisd on cunnies in the night
And in Lamb-time the snowy flocks wont fright
Great was his guile, strong were his forts: yet all
Searvd not t'prevent his destind Funerall
If we observe the place, that comfort lends 25
This Fox did end his dayes, midst all his frends
Laxon had mournd for him but that she knew
Ther were those leaft, would keep her Ale still new
And Finsett not dispaires, though he be dead
To see an other Fox ther canvassed 30
Whilst Hogen-Mogen lasts, or whilst the game
Of Ducks and Cunnies thear remain the same

Heer we performd the Obsequies, and were
As sad as (men a-hungry) with good cheer

    Whilst Phoebus (night-capt first after he riss 35
    Now all inmaskt) soe freely gan to piss
    That 'fore we could each to his Lares creep
    Our garments all were mourning, and did weep
        What double now remaines in all this chase?
        Save, ore the pantry dore to hange ups case. 40

Upon his Majesties late jorny into Scottland and salf return—Ann:-1633-Jun.

The Planets whilst they move in sevrall Sphears
Cutt out our time, in weekes, in months, in years
In night and Day, whose revolutions bring
The Day, Night, Week, Month, Year into a ring
What doe our Princes less when they are forth 5
A progress West or East, or South or North
Is not the first step that they forward sett
The Suns, when he his goulden locks doth wett
In Thetis lap to all that stay behinde
Is not the world Eclipst to them and blinde? 10
Doe not all minutes stretch themselves and growe
Each to an hower to such as thinke them soe?
Doe not our crost yet longing hopes present
Each hower a month or year in bannishment?
They doe: and 'twas not long sithence we were they 15
Who stood in exile from our Starr of day
Whilst visiting those parts whence He did rise
He casts a generall splendor through those skies
Leaving us only Cynthia and her train
To guive us hopes He would returne again 20
  Our Clime with Troppicks changed, and the same
  Season of day, now length of night doth claime
  Those only who by Elevation
  Before enjoyd a lucid Horizon
  Once yearly, now with more perfection shine 25
  A whol month, Phebus suffring noe decline
    Did I but call't a month; They deemd it less
    If they could apprehend their happines
    And we I'me sure had reason t'thinke it more
    Than many Ages counted o're and o're 30
For as the Suns withdrawing leaves one skye
A pray to cruell winters Tyranny
Whilst it doth bless an other; soe 'twas thus
In Scottland June but February with us.
Till His returne: which changd the Season quite 35
Then ours with Corn, with Snow their Hills were white
The night that was resignes, and dayes begun
With us allready by our Gratious Sunn
  Lett them pass Envy-free who boast them may
  In the possession of this month or day 40

For time wrapt up in swiftnes doth appeer
When past; as if an Age were but a year
A year a month, a month a week, and that
An hower or minute; whilst we consolate
Our selves may in this bliss; that future time 45
Seemes all wayes slower-winged in it's clime
 Thier Jubile was short and quickly gon
 Ours under Charles is a perpetuall on.

The Basse

Far North if Fables lie not thear's a land
Wher those whom we call Pigmeis doe command
Who yearly 'gainst the Cranes doe wage a warr
And sometimes beat, yet sometimes conquered are
And though they be not past a Cubit high 5
Their Army not consists in Infantry
But each is mounted if the tale say true
Upon the husband to the bleating ewe
Lanciers at least for soe provides the Soyle
Them Bullrushes wherwith their Foes to foyle 10
 Whither an Ile or Continent this be
 The Poets fictions doe not well agree
 Only by circomstance it most appeers
 These nations both of them are Ilanders
 For were they other they could not remain 15
 But be by Greater neighbouring powers tain.
It was my fortune lately to have been
In Caledonias Lowden, whence is seen
With ease neer to the steep Tantallon shore
A Rock i'th'Sea: you'ld judg it t'be noe more 20
Though't provd an Iland when my curious mind
Meeting with opportunety and wind
Had brought me thither, and the self same on
Wherof I formerly made mention
 For thear beseegd by Foules of evry sort 25
 Who seemd to me stil scaling of the fort
 A Lord within I found (one passage free)
 Who seemd the giant of the land to be
 For He two Cubits had attaind in haight
 And booted was ready to ride to faight 30
 Upon the summet were his Steeds at grass
 And this the place which now men call the Bass
 The Cranes are changd to Sollen-Geese and bear
 Noe Fewd, but proffit to Him evry year
 See what Time bringes to pass: Now Heer He bides 35
 Securer than he could elsewher besides
 And (more than Alexander) is content
 T'intoombe Himself alive, in's monument
 Proportiond to His pitch: for Fortune found

He was too little for soe great a ground 40
   As formerly'he possest, and plac't Him thear
   Amongst the Geese as in His propper Sphear.

A Buck-hunting Jorny to Belvoyr

Astronomers for to be easd
In their Distinctions are pleasd
To guive Heavns constellations
Their severall nominations
From Creatures on the Earth, i'th'Water 5
Or th'Aire, for the Fier'ts their Matter
   Now from the Heavns again I'le call
   These Creatures Astronomicall
   To meet in a Celestiall Sphere
   (On Earth) their proper shapes to were 10
Artophalax did drive his wayne
Thither wher Junoes Bird did raigne
And in it carried the Great-
Eye in the Bulls head: with the wheat-
Eare in the Virgins hand the Lyon 15
With's sword-guirting-belt Orion
And the kind kissing Gemini
Twice tould went too for compagny.
On Pegasus thear bye did ride
A Perseus with his sword by's side 20
Like Sagittarius one is born
Another rides for Capricorn.
I had allmost forgott to name
Auriga who in the rear came
And brought after these Deities 25
The rest which we call Pleiades
   Then after this Troop a far
   Ofe came the Great and Less Dogg-starr
   Following their Centaur, who (as dull
   May well be sayd to be half Bull) 30
   Now when all these approached nigh
   The place wher fixd they should lye
   Each 'gan with admiration
   T'extoll the Ciutation
   From whence they might descry the Faire 35
   Cassiopeia in Her chaire.
By whom Thuribulum was sett
Whilst th'Argos-eyd-Traind Bird them mett
And soe conducted in wher they
Found that it had been Pisses day 40
By reason of some Saints which followed
Through blind Superstition hallowed
Thear Lyra was to entertain
The Ears and Feet of this bright train
And what Eridanus affords 45

    Was sett with plenty on the bordes
    Thus shind They all that night; till morn
    Awakt the drowsy Capricorn
    Who with the help of Aries browe
    A Huntsaye to the rest did blowe   50
    Soe shrill that all awoake and spide
    The Vale beneath all Tiffanide
    With Casamour wovn with some few
    Gould threds and sett with silver dew
    For Spangles: whilst the Star of day   55
    Was nor yet come, nor yet away
    His half-face only lett them know
    He was then rising from below
      Then t'make them sport thear harberd were
      Some falling-Starrs, which we call Deer   60
      Which being but exhalation
      Serve but for recreation
      Which once obtain, each one returnes
      And in His proper Zenith burnes
        Now if Corona crown with bayes   65
        This visite she my labour payes

To my very noble Cosen the Earl of Stanford

Broad as thy Gates thy hart is Gray and 'twer
    But just thy purse held true Diameter.

A Dierge For Hasty Ginny

Hor: Ode—28
    Sithence 'tis decreed, the path of Death
Must trodden be by evry thing hath breath
    And that thear is a Middnight drest
Wherin all living Creatures shall take rest
    And sithence again it is most sure   5
That what's most violent will least endure
    Let it less wonder breed to see
The hast of my poor Ginnies Destany
    Who, had the Earth more been her frend
Than was the fier, She'd not soe soon to th'end   10
    Of her race run wher for a prize
The haight of mettle crownes her, as she dies
    How many Jades as slowe and dull
As Bufeloes or Asses, yet are full
    Of years; and though the mark were out   15
Long sithence, at drawing still seem wondrous stout
    O let not such invitement have
To wayt upon my Ginny to her grave
    But if ther be yet leaft a race
Of Coursers, Jennetts, or Barbes to embrace   20
    This service, lett such sacrefize
Some tears heer at their Kindreds Obsequies

Let Peg-a briggs be calld to mourn
And send into the North for Pepper corn
    Lett Bess-a Brackley weep for Her 25
And little Robin with th'red stomacher
    And if ther be of Puppy kind
Yett leaft, let them not leav a tear behind
    Lett Marigould white and Red-Rose power
Forth siths for her: Lett Primrose, Gilliflower 30
    And Tulipe amidst that Dewe
Her herse with their Enameld leavs bestrew
    And for a Favour to this Fate
White Ribband shall that duty personate
    Wherin Her silver haires shall be 35
Wov'n and bequeath'd unto posterity
    That evry one may see and knowe
This was the silken-silver mane did flowe
    From Her thin Crest, and as she went
Shot at the wind out of a bowe still bent 40
    By the controwling raynes did sway
Her Serpent Head, and teach it to obey
    Wherin a pair of eyes were set
Of Lightninges quicknes, though in couler Jett
    Twixt which a forehead broad did lie 45
Stampt with the Signe of Courage very high
    From whence in Label did descend
Her narrow Face and Nose Hawkt towrds the end
    Wher two wide Nostrells did implie
In red wax seales Her Mettles Sovranty 50
    And whilst Her narrow Eares did stur
Her wide mouth lined seemd with minifurr
    And though the breadth which should adorn
Her Buttocks, on Her goodly brest was borne
    Yett take Her alltogeather She 55
Seemd the True Ofspring of a Barbery
    Her strait flatt leggs, high coffind hooves
Did speak noe less, but were suffitient proofs
    Well: now she's gon, who while alive
To top the formost hound soe wont to strive 60
    Now the contentions turnd and They
Ambitious are which shall a fleeter way
    Invent to be revengd. This takes
A lim; th Entrailes t'others feasting makes
    And thus interrd, none can deny 65
But She again shall run, and did not Die.

**Sonnet upon second amorous thoughts
or A challeng to Cupid or my plea.**

1:   Tel me fond Boy
     Why dost thou shoot again

      At me in vain
  Sithence the great comfort and that joy
     Which earst I did obtain
       Is fled and gon
  None of thy poysons I dare entertain
     But chuse to live; soe live alone

2: Be not deceivd
    'Twas not thy shafts command
      Nor fier-brand
    Into my bowells I receivd
     Alone before: the hand
       That governs all
  Of form and goodnes had a chaplet weavd
     To Canonise my Nuptiall

3: If thou want'st game
    To exercise thy art
     Goe strike some hart
  Near yet acquainted with thy flame
    Thus may thy sweeter smart
     A subject find
  Soe much of sugered follies to impart
     As may make others with thee blind

4: But heer I stay
    By vertue bid t'admire
     A second fier
  And to her lawes becom a pray
    Whilst from my late desier
     She strives to serve
  My resolutions to that fancy higher
     May happines to me renew

5: A Saint at least
    If by the powers decree
     I marry thee
  Enrowld I stand: and soe made blest
    A second Jubile
     I may proclaim
  And guive indulgence to my pilgrim brest
     Which soe hath travaild for the same

My tryall and araignment at loves second barr

  Why did not some when first I undertook
  This task of Love again, guive me my book
  The crime is not soe hainous to deprive
  Me of my clergy, though again I wive:
  My years alow it, and those cannot stay
  But each reprive's as bad as cast away
  I did confess at first, soe hoapt to find

A salm of mercy but the Judg unkind
Turnd me to such a leaf and line in Her
That the Caldayck is a caracter
Of more facilety and th'Arab scrall
When pointed (by much) more methodicall
Nay, wher the berth of printing first began
I'le sooner read th'obscurest Chinian.
  First with a little measurer of time
  Clad all in Crystall I did seek to climb
  Up to her favours, that at once she might
  Consider my cleer thoughts and his swift flight
  Next with a ring wherin a ston was sett
  Devoted to her hand or Cabinett
  Wher envy-swoln I wisht oft to have been
  My self a Gyges; soe lurkt ther unseen
    Then did I try (as Feature-caught) how those
    Would work upon her fancy, and soe chose
    A peece or two soe limmd as might express
    How full my hart framd her; drew others less.
These were the bribes I sought with to procure
Eas to my fettred soul: All Courts endure
Like violence and 'tis the face of Kings
Opens all cases: Cabbinetts and ringes
Are of great use too, and a watch to line
Their time to rise up by, to sit to dine
    But this more rigid than all Common pleas
    Yeilds noe appeal, accepts noe prints like these
    Of such devotion as in times past was
    Loves polish't magick through a looking-glass
    But wher the last acts of affection move
    Beginns at first for vertues sake to love
Which though I cannot to my self apply
Yet hence I'm happy that my constancy
Soe firm should be that by reflections view
Your Goodnes seems t'be multeplide on you:
    To love the good is easy but the skill
    Hath ever been to fancy those are ill
    Soe if you mean an Artist to become
    Cast your affections on me for a doom.

To N.B. at Thorp

Ned:
  Can I be at home, and you the same
    Yet neither meet
    The curteous Flame the Flame
    And Streams each other greet
  All though they seem as from each Pole they came
    Or farthest stretcht
    Meridian fetcht

Surely it is but some malignant starr
    That would debarr
      This influence for fear 5
    We should more bright appeer
Soules in conjunction frame the perfect'st Sphear
Soe I to Ned must move, or Ned move heer.

Apthorp.

An Ode to N.B.

The Heathen Poets in the dark could cry
    To this or t'other Deity
    To save from dainger, or bestow
What so'ever They had need of heer below

And shall neglect and sloth soe dimm our sight 5
    As for to turn our Day to Night
    And downwards point our cares, and mindes
Which, Joy in earthly goods alone confines

Noe: Lett our humbled thoughts be taught to sore
    (For by descent ascent's made more) 10
    And by the Fabrick learn t'erect
Praises unto th'Almighty Architect

Then dainger-free, and blest with evry thing
    Boads good, or may contentment bring
    Wee'r sure to be; nor can we want 15
Sooner than He is ready for to grant

Doe This Worlds waves-resembling-Stormes begett
    Fear of a shipwrack being over-sett?
    Hee's both the Neptune of the Seas
And Jupiter who can their rage appeas 20

Or would we send a Vowe, or Prair, to win,
    What our affections most are in
    Let their adress to Him but fly
And 'twill return crowned with Victory

Noe wishes charmd by Enemies Magick shall 25
    Have powre my freedom to enthrall
    Nor wherin others doe excell
Shall fond Ambition hurry me to dwell

I will not sell an inch of that same clew
    Of thred the middle sister drew 30
    For Pelf, but in it pleasure take
Till it be wound up and a Bottom make.

'Tis not the gratefull Soyle that can invite
    My pen in praise of it to write
    But wher both earth and ayre conferr 35
How they may perfect'st health administer

Lett rich Calabria glory in her store
   And both the Indies in their Ore
   Whilst the immoderat Heat doth tell
The Ayres infection in each Paralell   40

What if Sardinia swell with lusty corn
   Or Clusters Calibus adorn
   When as the Sun in Cancer Lies
He sends a general scorching through those skies.

The Merchant full fraight with the hopes of gain   45
   Ventures his bottom on the Main
   And though he send one Pole to bed
To raise the other, yet's unpunnished

This shall not make me venture more
   Than wher my lyrick licks the shore   50
   [*Wittellsy*] shall sett bounds alone
To all my future Navigation

My appetites allurements I'le confine
   T'a sallett and a cup of wine
   Wherto a frend or two shall be   55
Invited to preserve society

And though through Time my youth must wayn
   Into an Age condemnd to pain
   Yet not quite cast Ile sue to have
Some mirth still to attend me to my grave   60

And if the Sisters soe much favour lend
   To Lullworth I my course will tend
   (A Place I fancy most) and thear
The remnant of my borrowed minutes wear

Drawing them longer by that Ayre which fills   65
   The concave 'twixt those brest-like Hills
   Sent out of Thetis lap to show
What Homage to the Castle It doth owe

Round about which the nimble-footed deer
   Trip it as if they Faries were   70
   Whilst Homwards-bound a rowling wood
Far ofe I may descry upon the Flood

Yet not puff't up with Joy, nor Shook with Fear
   Whilst I am noe adventurer
   For Cuntries sake I wish betide   75
Good speed unto the Vessells as they ride

When I the Ankor of my cares would waygh
   To merth bequeathing half a day
   My sailes strait with a land-wind full
Ne'ar slaken till they bring me salf to Wool   80

Wher Tom and I may freely make reports
   What happend in each-others sports
   He with his Doggs, I with my Hooke
What Foxes, Hares or Fishes we had tooke

And thus beguiling Time, Till'ts Blacker winge   85
   Shadows us for a Covering
   At last we part with full intent
The next Dayes Light shall break this bannishment

To David Earle of Exeter after the death of William Ruin-house.

Let Burley Sluggish Deities ore whom
Time and Neglect soe triumpht now become
Awfull again nor longer seem to dwell
'Neath th'dainger of some tottering pinnekell
Awake ye Lares and Confessing stile   5
Your selves the Traytors to th'once Glorious Pile
Changd into Ruines: and sithence gon is He
Who was the Patron build up Soveraignty
In the survivor, for know conquests all
Are not Entaild to names whilst Howses fall   10
But that ther may a David be to sway
The Scepter when a Saul is fall'n away
And to Orecome decayes not by a ston
Out of a sling, but their conjunction
More firmely ciminted that Passers bye   15
May timely wittnes that recovery
   And thus restord at length to what ye were
   Shine and protect the noble Governer—
                  Soe wisheth. W.

A sonnet upon a pretty Gierl her mothers darling .16. compleat by the Easter book

Ripe now for man
   Why dost deny
Thy plump age full satiety
When neither time nor season can
   By a return convaigh   5
Thy Roses to thee being once falln away

Suns sett and rise
   Woods may renew
The pleasures of their summer-hue
But if once thy fair cheeks and eyes   10
   Sink and turn pale the dumb
Though speachless yet will signe that winter's come

Quake not through fear
   Like to the Alpe
Whilst I desier thy limms to grasp   15

>   I am noe Lion nor fierce bear
>   But quit thy mothers wing
>   And by my grouth thou shalt conclude it spring.

A Jorney into Norfolk

Prologue
Disposd to merth and seasond by that time
Invites all sap in plants, all blood to climb
In fleshy vaynes and soe much heat doth ster
That evry thing becomes a travailer
I could not sleep at home but sought to pleas   5
My appetite both on the land and seas
   Soe through the Favour of a brace of frends
   And wind auspitious I obtain my ends

Embarking first at Stand-ground of my own
As fair a gale as ever yet was blown   10
Filld up our sayles and 'thin few houers truce
Brought us to guive a broad-side to the sluce
Wher whilst some seek with dores to curb the wave
I'le undertake their purses windowes have
Whence fair come ofe without too far remove   15
We found good Ankerage in the bay of Love
Wher was one strait creek, if what did appeer
For Beakon may b'allowd discoverer
Yet thence we waighed salf and with morning sun
Clapt spurrs, set sayl again as we begun   20
And past the Line (which through productions grace)
Brought us unto an other Troppick Chase
O what A Rising did it cause to see
In place soe wild, soe much of gravety
For, that the Mayor and Prisons both might fall   25
Under one climat they were wooden all
Yet would he not be hindred this content
To say they sent the first to Parlement
And soe we made it, for heer first began
Th'appropriating of parts to evry man   30
Who should be Speaker, who should draw bills up
Who first saluted be with cap, or cup:
And adding one Frend more unto our score
We became a Committee strait of fower
And with a full agreement that night came   35
To visit the fam'd Lady of Wallsingam.
   Wher we noe sooner did our steeds releas
   Of what they carried, but: (My Lord wilt pleas
   You walk up) was in every Tapsters throat
   Nor could the Chamberlin sing other noat   40
   For sure ther was one lookt for: 't had been cride
   Last Market day their widdow should be Bride
   And Westmorland should have her thus in mists
   Whilst we desire to walk, He stil persists

In prais of her, and usd all art his skill 45
Of drawing out of Vessells and to fill,
To pump out on's one might that stile put on
Discharging th'reckning of's suspition
But all in vain, for whilst of springes he tells
We only sup soe post away for Wells 50
And ther to try the valor of each brest
We goe to sea to make the fish a feast
But not ambitious of a party wher
The Northern blasts, the Southern waves did rear
We were content to steer about and sell 55
Glory for th'hopes again of seing well
And soe along the Coast our Course did stand
Asking for Yarmouth and for Loving-land
Soe soon we did arive wher Stif-ky stood
The postur she requiers the place I would 60
And ther observing hangings all pulld doun
We found such thinges befitted not that toun
For those unproper ornaments were sure
Cast bye t'make way for better furniture
Yet one amongst us curious more than need 65
Would needs enquier a reason for this deed;
And had it thus: as they did understand
She was to marry the Duke of Westmorland
And soe required these movables to come
To London, ther to dress her up a room 70
Thus did report-beguild these Cuntry Spies
Create new Hymens and new digneties
But we out went them, for we came, nor wed,
Nor Dukefide, nor once discovered
Poor Stif-kies nakt, yet whilst that name't may own 75
It need not be ashamd of being shown
Soe up we went perusd each room and stair
The ayr-fild Hall and empty wine sellar
And when we had performd this stil survaigh
We with the stooles and hanginges went our way 80
But usd a severall Compas they to th'town
Soe upward went whilst we were going down.
It was not long, the pleasure of the way
Curtalld the miles, and made a longer day
That we took Rainam in our road to Lin 85
Which by report had soe commended been
We found noe less: For what of art and prise
Nature could claim or judgment exercise
To court that nature, both heer soe agree
As if to make one perfect Cymetry 90
The Hous the Groves support, and make it bear
In a field vert the lively character
Of a ripe witt Bemantled with'select
Fore-casting-knowledg of an Archytect

Instead of Crest the stately Leads supply 95
From whence when each had wearied his eye
On objects fayr, or o'th'remoter lost
Soe hard it was to guess which tierd them most
They were calld home to walkes and Guardens, which
Did all this scuttchion powder and enrich 100
Plaines stood in awe of woods, and those again
Seem t'yeild obedience to the structures raign
Which ore the frutefull mead and clear-quick stream
Did sit like to a costly Diadem
Soe that 'twas hard to judg wher lay the debt 105
Whither in Nature, or the Skill there sett
For both doe seem each other soe to raise
That 'twer a crime for to devide the praise
Nature putts on her best attire, and's swelld
With pride of this Arts-peece-unparalelld 110
Again this Art doth seem to blush as fayr
As Brick can paint, t'others soe singular
Soe least we should be quite bereaft of sence
We stayd not long but took our leavs from thence
    And now our voyage tending to decline 115
    Lodg'd us that night under the torrid Line
    More soe by what our wellcome did express
    In good fresh Butts and a fair Vintneress
    Skearce ripe for trade, allthough her school might teach
    How to pierce high or low, to make a breach 120
    Then stop't again: her tender years noe ill
    Had suckt in, 'less to use the reed or quill
    Be thought soe: nor (on mine) it may be said
    Or sworn she had not lost her maydenhead
Time like a Churle forbids us heer to dwell 125
And sends us to a marchant who did sell
French wines and with them what his power had done
For oft he tells us of a lawe thear spun
How He and others Earles and Lords did sitt
On a Commission for to perfect it 130
Thus edefide both in our eyes and ears
Each on his proper stile and title wears
And soe the Session brake up; nor did rise
Thout much content instead of Subsedies
For every one his part had acted soe 135
As at the graunt thear was not guiven a Noe
    Soe what we would, we freely did discover
    Cloaking the fiery passions of a lover
    Under the name of Smith (my robes layd bye
    Did quite delude the whol touns Minstrelcy 140

Epilogue   All ended 'twas adjudgd my Muse and I
    Should dedicate these as a salery
    To merth and frends, that if again they stray

Into those parts they may not leese theyr way
Nor I their compagny: thus if I err 145
'Tis in becoming a Cosmographer
And Poet too, the first to show my care
That Frendship should not be irregular
The other is to beg by and my sute
You will graunt pardon wher you might confute. 150

An Ode sent into Scotland to a frend

   You that Ar-mine
   How coms't about
Soe many sands run out
Sithence I receivd a line
Unles; because what's worse 5
Again, I am not yours

   Noe Ocean
   Or wall of Pickts
Or China that inflicts
This seperation 10
Say then, doe Posts miscarry
That soe they'd make me tarry

   Noe: sure I am
   Your leisure's strait
And Busnes of more wayght 15
For else we are the same
 And though the clime may sever
 Our bodies, our harts never

   Which made to stere
   But one course both 20
I should be very loth
That either hope or fear
 Might cast an hazy Sky
 Upon our Pilacy

   But as one Pole 25
   Directer is
Unto that Port and this
Wher mutually each soule
A store house hath to lade
Noe wrack befall such trade 30

   'Til in the Urne
   Our Ashes lie
A prize to desteny
After a full return
Heer by Exchange wafts through 35
You Back to Apthorp me to Edenburrough.
                   W.

9.3.18.22.20.17.1.3.

 Cast up in Letters 93
 And 'twill discover who't should be

Upon his Majesties return out of Scottland in November 1641
wrot at Huntington in his passage

 Doth Charles return to make our Climat shine
 And shall not every Spring run Claret wine
 Is not the Kalender reverst, and wher
 Decembers dirt, and th'frost of Janiver   5
 Threatn'd a winter now those sheets display
 Themselves ore frutefull June or Teeming May:
 For thus, as 'thin the Troppicks may we bost
 That two fair seasons have twice blest our cost
 'Ere one whol year ran round: the time He went   10
 Seeming the Springes for-runner or our Lent
 For soe He was but borrowed and we rest
 With his return alone, whose interest
 Suffitient of him self, in which bank lies
 The treasure of His subjects harts and eyes   15
 See how they flock else and with tumbling hast
 Are less content because soe soon He past
  Be satisfide, yea have your Prince again
  Fro'th' North and Charles Triumphant not in wayne.

Epigram Inter Acus et Aculeos pugna

Man like a little world opens a pack
Of government to all such Climes as lack
Wherin those humours that disturb the health
For power doe represent a common wealth
And (Nature uncontrowlable) would trye   5
To Subject all under her monarchy
But in that conflict finds noe small diseas
Whilst all restraind authorities displeas
 Heer may we see as from a Chaos, spun
 Discord at push of pike, and factions t'run   10
 A tilt to break in t'shivers and destroy
 The strict Command of eithers soveraignty
  Yet neither Title need we fear to leese
  Sithence ther's both King and Commonwealth, mongst Bees.

Upon newes of the first beating up the quarters at Leeds and Wakefield

Fax
 All that is Commet like amongst the rout
 That look noe farther: makes these cast about
 For frugal ease and muster Clubbs as farr
 As backt with *Fair* pretext and *Holy* warr
 Cloathing their purpose with such hope as Ledes   5
 T'awake the Feild by their Heroick deeds

Let them not bragg too soon, the day may come
They'L wish they'd kept them stil at wheel and Loome

An Oad sent into Scottland to a Frend by sea
November-3-1643:

Prologue   Frend—   'Cause these Sullen Spheres
Blubber and drench our Southern Sky in Tears
After th'increas of Jelouzies and Fears
Love craves a Cabbin 'mongst the Passengers

My Will—   Affections word's advance   5
Without Elsinges decree Brownes Ordinance
The Armes of Love: soe neither Pike nor Launce
But a pens-point let drop in hast by chance

For had I had more time
To know the Bearer was now changing Clime   10
Than the Alarum of one minutes Chime
Reason had gon along as well as Rime

Alone this Act is sent
To show how Plunder and Imprisonment
Alow not wonted Cloaths for Complement   15
But sequester with Lands the Muses rent

A Bare revenue: yet
Of soe much force and power as to begett
This Confidence that though a Diamond's set
In brass 'tis stil the same, noe Counterfaict   20

So's Love, whose luster lies
Not in the ravishment of outward eyes
By quaint expressions but the Soules surmise
And by that standard it must fall or rise

Impatient left alone   25
In noe case it admitts cessation
But thus by way of recreation
United thinkes of two to become one

Noe protest, Oath, or Vowe
Can such a harmless contract disalowe   30
From whence noe plot doth spring nor project growe
But what an Earl may find to you I owe

Wherfore I Covenant thus
May your Endeavours prove Auspitious
To bring Peace home, yet not the Scot to us.   35

By-Ward to some Cittisens entring the Tower
the 1t of March-1642

Frends, pray forbear: why Croude yea with such hast
To enter: wher some would goe out as fast

Were they permitted, and conclude it too
A benefitt to be as one of you
Free in your own choyce: but fond Nature ties 5
The appetite to fancy novelties
And yea look for them heer? Could not the change
Glut you or th'Lyons ther? 'tis wondrous strange
Yea should affect with soe much care and paines
To see that place which is to others chaines 10
And by free-will turn Prisners for an hower
To say heer after you had seen the Tower
'Tis well yea are noe Docters, if yea were
We'd keep yea for Arminianisme here
But sithence yea are noe degree can own but such 15
As th'Citty guives, I am resolvd soe much
To favour your designes as to consent
Yea should survaigh all thats of wonderment
And that's noe more than what yea see (fond age
When Follies actor all this world the stage. *one of the 20
    Heer are we come past *wher* the *Jaylor dwells*   Taverns
    That's *calld a Gentleman* whose Castle smells
    Soe high of Treason and such other faults
    The Prisners though dischargd lurk stil in vaults
    And soe advanct a pace or two lay ther 25
    A Cannon which the wives soe put in fear
    As they cride out for help, and backward fell
    Saying it will not shoot we hope? pray tell
    Noe, I replide, but when it doth, 'twill shower
    And guards the Traytors guate and bloody Tower. 30
At this One faints, an Other trembling Cries
Pray why soe calld (quoth I) the Histories
Guave then these names, the one as I have read
Entoomd two smotherd Princes (noe blud shed)
The other 'cause it made a way for Her 35
That knew noe Treason t'become Prisoner
To Her Sisers will: then all, as if they'd seen
Her living yett repeat O blessed Queen
And then pull out their Sawm-bookes and again
Proclaim these bad times: Hers the happy raign 40
'Twas well They did Confide else't might be sayd
Idolatrous to say soe much o'th'dead
As They still utterd menacing Grim Death
For taking from them Blest Elizabeth.
Now are we mett by One abates this pride 45
Who seems to swell and offers first to chide
That we might know his place and trust to be
Care of the gates and Porters deputy
And what procurd him this that you may have
'Twas cause He was in truth an arrant K. 50
Some Boyes (were ther) cride when they heard his Name
But I to calm Him took on me the Blame.

Well then we must to the Lieutenant pass
Before we could goe on; and ther, Alas
We meet stern lookes, soe full of rigidnes 55
That when the wind's awake the Byskian seas
Seem as a Bay becalmd the Alpian Land
As if 'twer rowld into an Even sand
Compard to them; nor must it be thought wonder
(Though Winter) when He spake if't seemd to thunder 60
Heer my poor Guests were stricken, though before
They had seen the Bears and heard the Lions roar
This voyce and Countnance had ore them such power
Their harts began to daunce, their eyes to shower
When One of them posessing but a dram 65
Of courage more than Those who with her came
Askt if it were the Office or the place
That Pattent guave for such rough words and face
Wherat I smiling towld her, Customs bring
Oft times our natures to their likening 70
Soe just; that wher a soft and gentler hand
Might serve sometimes, the fierce word of Command
(As learnt by hart) will not guive way at all
To lenety, or to one wrinkles fall.
   Those that had spent their youth in Marses feild 75
   Cannot forget the Musket, Sword, and Shield
   The Buskins were not worn by Comick Actors
   Nor's smooth Phrase usd to Those are Malefactors
   And heer dwelt none but such: besides a rout
   Of Officers took care They got not out 80
One righteous Judge Three Knights condemned are
A Brace of Aldermen, Bishops a paire
Two Earles, Three Kiernes and all to this sad fate
The Times distraction Heer to Celebrat
In much retirdness: neither heard nor tride 85
They linger out a life as if they dide.
   A sad condition: when nor foe, nor frend
   Will help to Triall, that might put an end
   Unto this living Death, or dead reprive
   Wherin they only can but be, not live 90
   Shut up from all society which smothers
   Their best intents towards themselves and others
   And that to Felons Justice not denies
   These are debarrd of th'hopes of an Assise
   Or Jayle-delivery: sithence all mens ears 95
   I'th'Town are filld with Jealouzys and Fears
   What pitty 'twas that any did suppress
   That Court Could make Truths more, but such ears less.
As we advanc't to follow our intent
We measurd out that Crittick Pavement 100
Northumberland layd ther, wherby he found
A way to make a mile thats long turn round

Most proper for these times are soe presize
They walk by standing up, pace Truths by Lies
Soe that when a Survaigher comes to view 105
And search reports, finding the falce judgd true
What may He say but that inventions skill
Is exercisd in framing Fancy will
And what we wish indeed to see or heer
Proves oft the loadston that our faiths doth steer 110
   Next is the house of store or Magazin
   Wher were some Gunns, yet ther ther more had been
   'Fore these late troubles drew them out to play
   And bandy the Militia with th'Aray
   They were the Kings and must be sayd to be 115
   None others yet: noe more than that we see
   Opposes light to shine: Or day appeer
   Benighted under a Vale though near soe cleer
   When they are mounted, leveld at noe mark
   But Him and His, shall we not call light dark 120
   Perswade the hardest marble to be wool
   Bitter thinges sweet, Call empty vessells full
Can we be sure that any thinges our own
When strainger to himself each one is grown
Nor dares think, much less speak, or write, or doe 125
What Nature, and his duty Prompts him to
Though't be to serve his Prince or else the state
It must be as opignion sets the rate
And soe esteemd, if you but Cross the one
Malignancies the Beasts Mark and you'r gon 130
When to oppose the Other in's demands
(Though ne're soe just) will multeply Commands
   The Gossips eyes had now a while been fed
   With th'wardrop and the fower Turrited
   White Tower which guives occation to their tongues 135
   To ask to what use this or that belonges
   I did resolve them thus: I'th'first doe lie
   Beds, Cushions, Chaires, peeces of Tapisry
   Rich Arras work presenting story and
   Embroyderd Cloats of State which or't did stand 140
   Whilst it remaind, now only'are kept to show
   That times to come may work an overthrow
   On these are present, as these have on those
   Are past whose Trophes now yon walls enclose
   For th'other Candid Towring Pile pray know 145
   It carries Gunns aloft powder below
   And soe the linings to this bewteous ston
   Are the Black Cornes bring forth destruction
   Wherby we are confirmd it falls out true
   Oft Darkest mischief's clad in brightest hue. 150
These everlasting Gazers whose delight
Was as insatiat as that appetite

A greedy worme betraies, noe sooner tast
This and the other but seek new: at last
The Curteous Bell informes ther is noe stay 155
For those may out: yet heer again by th' way
I must inform them what the Chappell was
And who stood up ther / faith I cride an—
That was soe great an Enemy to sence
As he had bannisht all Commerce from thence 160
Of Prayers Composd, and by the Church prescribde
By stupid Ignorance and Folly bribd
To vent his own stuff: laying order doun
To gain the approbation of the toun
Then what Could-harbour was? I bade them see 165
Whither the Almenacks did soe agree
To name it, or the scittuation rather
Soe neer the Tems as t'hav't for Godfather
But ther those lodgings were beheld, wher kings
Had kept their Courts now contemptible things 170
And such as for restraint are dedicated
To harbour such as by the lawes were fated
Or doomd for Captives, soe the Change implies
That Time may bring the seat of Joleties
To be the stage of Misery: Ther's none 175
But ere a life spin out must act theron
 Come now unto the out most bounds of all
 Begirt this place and to the limits wall
 I must Coygn something more before we part
 And entertain Them with the Minters art 180
 (They have enough o'th'Printers in the Citty
 Wher they vent Lies for Truths the more's the pitty)
 The Purifiyng furnace we behould
 And see the liquid Silver and the Gould
 Run into Barrs, and as Fair Daphnes doom 185
 (Sought by herself) made flesh and blood become
 A Tree to mock the God soe heer before
 One turnes about that which was liquid ore
 Is turnd to substance and soe firmely knit
 That ther noe small paines goes to hammer it 190
Ther sate the Clippers who like Justice are
Furnisht with Balances to ajust this ware
Saving that these have use of hands and eyes
To Cast them into such Varieties
Of coyn as the wayght guives; in t'peeces gould 195
Or halfs at least that may be soonest tould
Shillings of silver most and crownes that guive
Two stamps to make one whol prerogative
And pass for soe much: single pence for th'poor
Soe now with Beggers we are come to th'dore. 200
 Yet once again diverted by some Plate
 We did espye the Owner to Translate

In t'Cash had thither brought; or's wife converted
By th'last long praier She heard that pride discerted
T'advance the Common Cause which brought about   205
The Publike-Faith repayes all without doubt
   In which Beleef besotted out they pack
   And leav me to my Posture Drinking—

Upon the Suddain rise of my Cuntry Men and their defeat by Collonel Manneringe and Brown the woodmong[e]r July 24. 1643. at Tunbridg.

How Time turnes up-side down and Fortune failes
In favoring the Round-Heads 'gainst Long-tayles
For He that would a skoar of years agoe
'Plac't Heer the Victory, ther the overthrow
Might have grown rich through wagering: how ere   5
The Proverb sets out Kent and Darby-shere
Famous both at one end: the Latter tries
With his round-headed Hills to kiss the skies
Whilst th'Others woods and hedges muster thus
Imbatteld under Generall Orpheus   10
Else had not Conquest now been new: 'ts a thing
Worth noting how their Foes in Mannering
Th'affaires proceed and Countermine their Plott
Which formerly prevaild so strait wayes gott
One verc't in Coal and wood and Him they sent   15
To Overthrow the Sturdy Oake of K.
I doubt They were but Sapling* Undertakers   *35.H.8.17:
Soe ther remain enow to make Wise-Akers
Thus whilst 'twixt head and taile ther are such Bleedings
Ther's left skearce head or tayle in all proceedings.   20

Anglia Hortus

The guarden of the world wherin the Rose
In Chief Comman-ded did this doubt propose
To be resolvd in, whither Sence to prize
For Umpire to create it Paradice
One lead by th'Ear of Philomell tells tales   5
And strait wayes calls't the Land of Nightingales
An other sharper sighted, ravisht cries
O that I could be turnd now all to eyes
A third receivd such raptures from the tast
Of various, dainty, frutes that it surpast   10
A fourth was caught not with perfume Commends
The Indian Clime but what (heer) nature lends
Last if you would Sattins or Velvets touch
For Soft and Smooth leavs can afford you such
   And thus disposd whilst evry Sence admires   15
   Tis Senceless t'plant mongst Roses Thistles, Briers.

Epigram.

The Jealous State with more then Argus eyes
Mustering up it's wakfull misteries
Finds it not safe that either fort or Toune
Ship or the Like be trusted more i'th'Crown
But kept for it by them: because say they   5
Wee'l not confide but i'th'Militia
Yet mark how they'r deceivd upon this skoar
The Crown hath stil one New-Castle's worth more.

The Scottish Pedlers turnd Merchants.

Feb. Sithence all endeavours to advancement move
1646. Why seems it strange Pedlers should Merchants prove
      And triffle out noe more with beads and Rings
      But deal in whol sale now 'twixt states and Kings
      Or that they'r Gamesters grown and come the caster   5
Ent: Eng. At In and In, Fling out, and Loose Their Master
2ce. The Prime of Traitors if we call to mind
      Was but a Petty-chapman in His kind
      Compar'd to these: One Potters Field alone's
      Too small to lay out such a somm upon   10
      And that too great to be returnd. This nation
      Would pleas me to fulfill all imitation
        Had Judas known the Stapeling of These
        Neither the Scribes, nor yet the Pharises
        Should have ore reacht Him: Or did he remain   15
        Alive He'd hang himself for spight again
        He set *soe lowe a Valew* on His Lord   *30d*
        When Heer the Markets *better Rates* afford   *200,000£*
          We hang for wittches people poor and owld
          Forgetting ther's noe sorcery to Gowld.   20

My Far-well to the Court—March-25-1644.
at Merworth

Goe (fond deluder of our sences) find
Some other Objects henceforth, to make blind
With that thy glittering Folly; for noe more
I will be dazled with thy falser ore
Nor shall thy Cyren-songes enchant, to tast   5
Or smell or Touch those sorceries thou hast.
But I will strive first in my self to be
Soe much myn Owne, as not to flatter thee
And then my Cuntries, for whose wellfare still
My native thoughts, prompt to impress my will   10
And that, drawes Action forth wher'by to showe
To whom, and what, and when, and wher I owe
Not as this Nod, or beck, or winke, or glance

Would dictate and imply to follow chance
Fortune, or Favours ever-turning-wheel 15
But to be firme and Constant, backt with steel
And resolution, for to guive the True
God what is his, and Cesar tribute due
And that in Season too, for time and place
As th'one requiers, and th'other affords, grace, 20
Not such as only from vain Titles springes
And turnes to bubble to Court Prince or Kinges
With faignd applauses of what ere they speak
Or doe, bee't near soe frothy, faint, or weak
But what is clad in Truth and dares not lie 25
Though all the world should turne its Enemy
Brand it for want of Breeding and conclude
Because it not disembles therfore 'ts rude
Those dancing dayes are done, nor longer sute
My disposition to the Harp, or Lute 30
Horne-pipe or other Instruments have been
The Commonwealth's diseas, ore swoln Her spleen:
Jocky and Jinny footing may appeer
Most Trim at the next wake in Darbisheer
Gotier sayle from the Clouds to catch our ears 35
And represent the harmony o'th'Sphears
Will Lause excell the Dying Swan: Laneer
Nick it with ravishments from touch of Lyre
Yet uncontrowld by these, I safely may
Survive, sithence not stung by th'Tarantula 40
That tickling Beast—Ambition that makes sport
In our hott Climat Calld the verge of Court.
And soe resolve, dressing my mindes content
Hence-forward to be Calme and represent
Nothing but what my Berth and Calling drawe 45
My Purse out for my God, my King, my Lawe
   And when for These my wearied breath is spent
   Let with my Last-bloods-drop one sigh be sent.

Upon the Babes of Grace or the Saints that seek for their portions in this world.

Why ist we seek from Room to roav soe far
As t' wipe all Saints out of our Kalender
Apostles too, but that as I suppose
For this, we have can wear them in their nose
And make the memory of their lives shine better 5
Than any Rubrick or Dominick letter
For such referrd to Scripture and tould when
Those Glorious martirs first were Fishermen
And that their calling was to seek and trye
How they could catch men with humility 10
But this was time of Owld, and we'r at loss

Unless Gods book admitt another gloss
The cream of Earth all fat things of the land
The milk and hony of our Canaan
Belongs to none but those who by their power 15
Them selves can Canonise and all devower
Inverting quite our Saviours mandate thence
And Compassing this Crown through violence
Which how they Err in 'tis not hard to Trace
When they seek Glory first then after Grace 20

Contemplationes Divinæ:

Cedant Humana Divinis: Et
Longe Majora Canamus

In unitate Trinitas

That Number 'bove the rest
   Be ever blest
   Which God himself doth daine
To branch into, yet reunites again

   For as His providence could tell 5
     When Angells fell
That Man would follow, and ther must be one
   Sent for to make redemption
Soe from that misery did He inferr
   Th'necesity of a Comforter 10

This doth inspire; That did create
The second did regenerate
   Thus though distinct They are
     Yet Singular
   And One wise-ever Powr it is doth tye 15
   This Trebble Knott into a Unety

Cæli enarrant Gloriam Dei—psal: 19

Are we asleep or doe we see
*in the Syrian Noe more than did blind Bartheme
the sonn of Or are our sences charm'd to lie
blindnes Benum'd into a Lethregy
Whilst Sin makes of's a conquest? rise 5
Flesh-buried soule, and from the Skies
Let thy winged thoughts to thee relate
Who 'twas those Structures did create
   Wher in thy Hemisphear at large is pend
   More wonder than Fraile Clay can comprehend 10

Whither a Sun, a Moon, a Star
A Commet, or a Metear
A Various Bowe true signe of peace

Swoln Clowdes that cause the Earths increse
When breaking they distill; the glum 15
And horred beat of thunders drum
We heer or see: why were these sent
But t'shew He is Omnipotent
   That thus in Caracters did write, wherby
   We have a Lecture in Divinity 20

For as Those Great and Lesser Lights
Distinguish Time by Dayes and Nights
Soe was it Day with us; untell
Our disobedient Parents fell
Yet as the Tyncelld Night guives way 25
At th'opening o'th'true Goulden day
Soe did the powres of darknes fly
The Sonn of Righteousnes being by
   And when we Commet-struck in sin had run
   The Father did redeem us by the Son 30

When th'Undertaker first did daine
For to restore His world again
He us'd noe other lock or sluce
I'th'Clowdes but sent a Bow of truce
What did His mercy, less, when we 35
Who are the worlds Epitome
Delug'd in Sin lay breathless drownd
Untill our Saviours pretious wound
   Opend a draine wherwith He layd us drye
   From wickednes into fertillety 40

The Aire imprisond faine would trye
The vertue of more liberty
Yet meeting with a tougher Clowd
'S Constraind to quarrell and speak loud
Soe if we seek our freedom heer 45
We must noe Cloud of fortune fear
But like Bonargeses proclaime
What we profess, and be the Same

Soe shall noe thunder-crack nor dash of wett
Prodigious Commet in us fear begett 50
But the Suns purple, and the silver winges
The moon Putts on bespeaks us Saints and Kinges
Whilst Iris endless peace, the numerous lights
Adorne the night discyfer all delights
Which for to seek to compass and obtaine 55
He that quitts life and all heer makes great gain

The Fallacy of the outward Man.

Are we awake, or doe our eyes
Only wi'th'Glow-worme sympathize

To light the Pismire to his bed
When He through toyle and Labours wearied?

    Doth not the Banke of moss apeer 5
    Crispt up in moon-shin farr more clear
    When Argos-eyd with many a Mite
    It waites upon the Goddes of the night?

    Have not the wanton Fairy Elves
    Their torchbearers light as Themselves 10
    That with our fancies sport and play
    Untill they lead us quite out of the way?

    Cannot a Spangle, Pin, or Bead
    By Candlelight int'error lead
    And representing Treasure claim 15
    A stooping to the Matt, or Bord for th'same

'Tis from noe Other, but from hence
That whilst alone with th'outward sence
We doe behowld and not with minde
We are asleep, or we are blind. 20

    Awake and See: Let Sin noe more
    Lock up the window and the Dore
    To thy fair apprehention (Soule)
    But by His owne alurements Him Controwle

    Let His falce Treasure, Vapour, Sparke 25
    Of Canded dew, shine in the darke
    And the bejeweld worme eschew
    The morn, least that Her Diamonds prove untrue

But lett Thy Luster Foyle-less be
And soe present the Day to thee 30
Lett Sparkes of Grace, and Truths light steer
Thee to Contemplat thy Lord Treasurer

    Who not on bords or Matts did lie
    But did In-Stall Humilety
    Whilst in the chambers of the Inn 35
    One spies a Bead, an other sees a Pin

    He is the Light which doth convaygh
    All wisemen to th'Eternall Day
    Whilst fooles by falce illutians fier
    As in the dark slip into dirt and Mire 40

    'Twas He alone; whose wounded Side
    And Hands and Feet are Glorefide
    Whilst Potentates with Jewells hunge
    But barren Moss bankes are; and filthy dunge

Noe Sweat, noe Travail, nor noe Pain 45
Did His love shun, to win again

Thee that wert Lost. His Mercys shon
Farr above th'glance of truest Diamon

   Wherfore if Thou make use of this
   Wormes love, to raise Thy thoughts to His   50
   If with industrious care Thou bring
   Home to Thyself His suffering
   If, by reflection Thou returne
   Sithinges unfaignd, for Siths, and burne
   In Zeal: noe falsefide delight   55
   Can e're deprive Thee of thy sight
     But with the eye of faith thou maist behowld
     A Crown immortall prizd 'bove purest Gould.

Contemplatio Diurna

When we behowld the Morning Dewe
Dissolve with'rising Sun: what doth it shew?
But that a Sonn to us did rise
Our Fathers hoary Sin to atomize
And when the Flowres displaid appeer   5
To entertain the mounting Charretier
What would they say in that fair dress?
But Mans redemption out of wretchednes
For the shade-shortning Noon can tell
The prowd and such as with ambition swell   10
That whilst upon opignions wing
They seek to soar they work their lessening
And the Prognostique Western sett
May our conditions rightly counterfett
For if we rise, shine, and sett cleer   15
The Day-Starr from above's Our Comforter
If Sinn becloud Us as we fall
   Our next Dayes rise will prove our Funerall
   et quid lachrimabilius?

Ut sit et cogitationibus Verbisque Factisque propitius Omnipotens

Great God in Whom all Justice raignes
    And Truth
   Lett not the raines
    Of youth
   Soe slacken in me still   5
T'enthrall and Captivate my Thoughts to ill

Much less my Deeds, but as thy Sonn
    Begun
   Wher Solomon
    Layd ston   10
  Soe make thy house my hart
And scourge out of it each mecannike part

Neither let wordes that die when spoke
    Provoke
      My Soule to thinke   15
        They'l sinke
    Into Oblivion
Soe soon as they are uttered and gon

Place a sentenell before
      The dore   20
    That by my Chanoin tongue
      Be sunge
    Noe Anthem but thy prayse
Nor let it ever send forth other layes

Thus may my Thaughts and Words which usher on   25
    My Deeds to Action
By thy divine power purg'd fro'th'dross of sinn
Pave me a goulden tract to progress in
    Which if thou crown with grace too, let't appeer
    Dormant, yet watchfull, ceasing never heer.   30

    Annus annulus ex Diminutione Largimur

If the year Serpent-like doth cast its skin
And's stript oth'owld, when as the new comes in
What would't inform, but that w'anew invest
Our selves in Christ, and Adams raggs detest
And if a Janus Bifronted doe stand   5
Looking at once to this and t'other hand
What would he teach our contiences, save this
To see at one view, whence salvation is
And whence our woe was; that for this we may
Our Tribute tears, for that all praises pay   10

Now when the Season blossoms in its Spring
And Time putts on a parti-coulerd winge
Why should not our soules which before did lie
Defil'd through th'smuch of Sin, receiv a die
(Wherat the rose may blush) from that same flood   15
(All streams surpasses) of our Saviours blood
For if that Leprosy we fain would heal
This is our Jordan staind with Cuttcheneal
If from our first Sire we receivd a wound
This is the Spikenard that can make us sound   20

And as th'approaching Sun comes dayly on
For to supplant the Winters garison
Soe should our frozen Harts be thaughd, and melt
When we to mind call, what our Jesus felt
And we deservd; His Zodiak should bring   25
Us to the Troppick of our Sommering
In those warme thoughts, til ripe in faith and hope

Love like a Vale cover our Horescope
For what can we return for His; who rent
The Temples to free us from punnishment 30

O lett the Lustfull Clusters we behowld
Betassel Automn, and those ears of gould-
Resembling Corn, say to us if we thirst
Or hunger: He who is both Last and First
Did tread the winepress for us, and fulfill 35
What was to us due for our Fathers ill
That soe we might be numbred 'mongst those guests
The Lamb invited to his mariage feast
And though we once fell by what one Tree bore
God by an Others frute did us restore 40

Then whilst the Sharpe-breathd-winter seems to lay
Stripes on the patient earth, and blasts th'array
She late was deckt in, spitting on Her face
It's featherd rain (all embling the disgrace
For us he felt who would have known noe shame 45
Had we been innocent and without blame)
Doth't not discyfer how a Lilly pure
Sprang up midst thornes, their scourginges to endure
And how They spatt upon a face that shined
Which prov'd Our eye-salve who before were blinde. 50

Cui in calamitatibus solo sit fidendum

When first the towring Hills the Loftier Pine
Exchangd to ride upon the swelling brine
Neptune prepard and with more active skill
Grew sometimes in the vale, sometimes o'th'Hill
Whilst floating in a compleat tackle drest 5
Juvenal   Shes taught to sayle from Cadis to the East
Satir—x.   Wher Ganges runs, and from those coasts being come
To steer a course back to Ilyrium:
Then was that Coward Fear bannisht the mind
And hart of Man ambitious still to find 10
More worldes and workes of wonder, wherin He
Might trace the Greatnes of the Deity
Hor: ode—3   And as if fortefide with steel and brass
Venturd his Bottom on this field of glass
Soe brickle and unconstant, as't may trye 15
How neer one comes to death, yet doth not die
A small Gale over-fills the Sayles, a Leake
Is sprung in shorter time than I can speak
Then being o'resett above, o'rechargd beneath
What can expected be but present Death? 20
Yes if we seek to him at whose command
Becalmd into Obedience Tempests stand
And rise when he soe pleases, and are gon

	When he planes o're their rugged Motion	
	Whose powres at life exprest, when waight assends	25
Psal: 107—	And all most to the Crystall Skye extends:	
from v-23-to.	And when to follow'ts nature it hath found	
v.30.	Leav, it returnes unto the lowest ground	
	Then are they troubled that on it doe ride	
	Rowling and tottring unto either side	30
	Being drunk through fear and sorrow, nor can tell	
	How many sands shall knowle their passing-bell	
	Thus in a trance dismayd, and quite bereaft	
	Of sence, save of a little spark thats left	
	To kindle hopes, they to their maker cry	35
	Who strait releases them from misery	
	Sending a Calme wherat the liquid plain	
	Becomes to them a looking glass again	
	Soe They in mind restord, have quick access	
	Unto the Haven of their happiness.	40

A Dedication to my Sonn Charles to Him that made him

    Is it not fitt the mould and frame
    Of Man should dedicate the same
To God who first created it: and t'guive
To Him the first frutes of the span we live

    In the worldes infancy could Hanna tell   5
    She ought to offer her Son Samuell
      To him that made him, and refine
      That Sacrefize with flowr and wine?

    Was Abrams longe-expected seed
    From Sara's wombe condemnd to bleed   10
And shall the times now they grow owld conclude
In faithlesnes and in ingratitude

Lett shame awake us, and wher blessinges fall
Lett evry one become a prodigall
    In paying vowes of thankes, and bring   15
    The first and best for offering.

Wher am I then, whom God hath daind to bless
With'hopes of a succeeding Happines
    Unto my house: why is't I Stand
    At th'Altar with an Empty hand?   20

    Have I noe Heards, noe Flocks, noe Oyle
    Nor Incence-bearing-Sheba-Soyle
Is not my Graynry stor'd with flowr thats fine
Are not my strutted Vessells full of wine?

What Temporall thing is lacking, to suffize   25
And furnish out a lively sacrefize.

       Save only this: to make a free-
       Will offring of an Infancy

       Which if I should not doe; that pilde-
       Up wood, wheron lay Saras Childe   30
The Temple would accuse me, wher the Sonn
Of Elkna first had dedication

       Wherfore accept I pray Thee this
       Thou'st guiven and my first Son is
Lett Him be Thyne and from His Cradeling   35
Begin His services first reckoninge

Graunt with His Dayes thy Grace increase, and fill
His Hart, nor leav ther roome to harbour ill
       That in the progress of his years
       He may express whose badge he wears.   40

       A Christmass Karroll
       sung—an—1634

Luke 2:	Awake dull Soule and from thy fowld of Clay	
8-10	Receive what newes the Aingells bring to day	
Luke 13:	Not of a Foxes Cubb whose guile might be	
32	A promise of successive Tyranny	
Luke 2:	Nor o'th'victorious Eagles farr-spred winge	5
1:	The chiefest of the Worlds parts covering	
Jhon 1:	But of a Lambe thats yeand, a Child thats borne	
29:	Noe spectacle of glory, but of scorne	
Luke—2:	For in a house of bread, this Bread of Life	
17:	For Us is come to Joseph and his Wife	10
Luke 2:	And though the Citty Davids were, therin	
11:	His Sonn noe Throne possesses, but an Inn	
Luke 2:	Thear thou mayst find Him, at whose mean, lowe berth	
7	The Mightiest Potentates of all the Earth	
Luke 2:	Nay Oracles are silenced and gon	15
4. 5.	Nor longer serve the Div'ls delusion	
	The Delphian Fin confesses Hees orecome	
	And by an Hebrew-borne-child stricken dumm.	
Dion.	The Letters of th'Owld Law effaced are	
Suidas.	Doun falls the statue of Great Jupiter	20
Nicepharas.	With th'Twinns and their nurcing Beast: which showr	
	Of Prodegies rouse up the Emperour	
	Who thus far in the darke could see t'erect	
	In honeur of th'Almighty Architect	
	An alltar in the Capitall to's Sonn	25
	First born, with the sole dedication	
Paga[nis]m	If Light thus through darknes shon; why is't,	
	That thou who hast the Gospells beams; the mist	
	Of Errors canst not dissipate, but still	
	Becomst Idolater in doing ill.	30

	How doth thy Pride and Envy hatch deceipt	
	And fond Ambition raise thee in conceipt	
	Of Thine owne worth, when all these Honeurs can	
Psal: 44	But make thee to be like a Beast, noe Man	
20.	The Serpents Brood like Twinns doe allwayes paire	35
	Which by thy Beastly Humors Fostred are	
	Thy Tongue noe more thy Harts cross-rowe doth spell	
	Than if thou weart an other Oracle	
	Be silent then, nor longer thus prophane	
1. Chor: 6	That Holy Temple for which Thou art tain	40
19:	But let the Lambes blood wash away the staines	
	And Characters were written in thy vaines	
	By thy first Parents, and which sithence thou hast	
	By thy endeavours into Volumes cast.	
	Throw doun thy self for Him, who meekly came	45
	(Into the world for thee) a Child a Lambe	
	Born to be slain for thee, yet slain before	
	To make the victory or the conquest more	
	Humilety's a Child, a Giant Pride	
	Goliah from the hand of David dide	50
	Soe though like foes, thy ill affections growe	
	Unto immencity, a powerfull throwe	
	Out of the Sling of Faith, of Hope, of Love	
	May all the Monstrous uncooth Brood remove	
	Then shallt thou raign without suspicion, free	55
	As Pharoe did till this Nativety	
	Then shall thy contience Oraclise thy Fate	
	Than was Augustuses more Fortunate	
	Nor in the Capitall but in thy Hart	
	Erect an Altar to Him: Let each part	60
	Express thou art awake, and seing canst tell	
Psal: 14. 11	That now salvations come to Israell.	

El Sembrador.

	All are solicitous who grounds possess	
Mat. 13	To Knowe	
	Both when, and how to sowe	
	That promise may to them the most increas	
	And by the severall seasons; Change, or Waine,	5
	Full, or	
	Increase; to stir them for	
	What might be properest of evry graine	
	Nor doe they search soe deep as for a mine	
	Of Gould	10
	Yet what's the fittest mould	
	For evry seed, can readily define	
	And doth not Great neglect and slouth appeer	
	In these	

    Whom Barly, Wheat, Rie, Pease   15
Afect alone, in being cheap or deer

Whilst that the fallowes of their harts untilld
   Noe more
  Can promise than before
To be with Cockle thoughts and darnell filld   20

For when the Bells doe seem all in to chime
   They'l say
  This is some Holyday
Soe never frame a work unto the time

All that they pray, or heer, or read, or doe   25
   Shall be
  Choak't with the Briery
Cares of this world which they are slaves unto

Before the Reverend Preacher doth devide
   His Text   30
  Some one soon tell'st the next
Yett's robb'd of it; for't falls by th'highwayes side

An Other getts a Point by th'tag, and may
   Goe on
  Till Persecution   35
Declare him Niobe: then He must stay.

As when a Soyle's prepard with art and care
   The Hind
  Such Crops doth allwayes find
As to's endeavours answerable are

Soe let our Harts be throughly wed of Sin   40
   And then
  They'l prove good ground again
And bring us more than thousand proffites in.

ad Corinth: *Trium Gratiarum maxima charitas*
1—13.13
   When all perfections prove
    But like some sound
     Of Brass
  Wherin noe certain noat is found
    Without Harmonious Love   5
What doe we see then more than through a glass

   We may with Eloquence
    Beguild our speach
     And then
  Offer at more than we can reach   10
    And bring in influence
Of workes to raise us: yet we are but Men

  For if provoakt we be
   Wee'l not forguive
    And soe   15
 Forgett the wrong we did receive

  Though it be Loves decree
Untill we can work our revenge in woe

  The Churle through sparing skill
   Denies to feed   20
    The Poor
 And such as stand in greatest need
   Yet thinkes he doth noe ill
Whilst He walkes double on his Ivory flore

  An Other envy-swoln   25
   When once 'twas heard
    By chaunce
 That such a one was new preferd
   Cries, what are Honeurs stoln
Yet in the same tract strives Himself t'advance 30

  This Mushrum may appeer
   When first the Sun
    Doth rise
 But when His Hemisphear is run
   And that the Ev'n drawes neer 35
It shuts up all its treasure and soe dies

  Unless revivd again
   By loves sweet charme
    O're which
 Noe night or va'pour can doe harme 40
   For neither Pride, Witt, Gain
Can make us truly live, or truly rich

  But if affection
   To Truth prevaile
    And say   45
 Noe suffering shall turne the scale
   Nor yet Promotion
This Night will turn into Eternall Day

Love begetts Fear

'Twas of thy goodnes (Lord) I had
Knowledg of what was good, what bad
Yet through the ill of nature blind
I followd Sin and leaft thy fear behind
Soe forfaited a Blessing; till   5
Thou of thy free and gratious will
Sign'dst me a pardon in that stile, repent
And soe eschew all punnishment

Psal: 128

Thus then awakend, I began
Thy Judgments, Blessings, Love, and fear to scan   10
And in a scoal when I them all had waighd
Methought I lov'd (Thee) still, still was afraid.

My Penthouse against the storm of greif

O, how the blasts
Temptation casts
Against my naked ston
Threaten subvertion
   Sithence the decree of late was Thine   5
   To take away my sheltring Vine

   Well: let them blow
      And rain
   Their gusts and showers in vain
      For sure I am   10
   Thou stil uphouldst the frame
      Whilst I behould the olive sprouts to grow.

   With this assurance; to my hart
      I may impart
      A Calm of peace   15
   And that these trialls all shall cease
   If I ride out them: Fear is good
      When it with stands ill, not of ill withstood

My hand-kerchef to dry my eyes

Lord:) sithence the best
   Of thine
   Their portions have
Of Sorrow, Sicknes, and the Grave
   Why should the worst repine   5
Though (Thou) lockst up their chiefest joyes in rest

   Joyes heer but Lent
     And soe
   'Tis of meer mercy we can say
     W'enjoy them for a day   10
Yet whilst we have nothing but what we owe
The land-lord must destrain to have his rent

   This the unthrifty course we take
       Begetts
   Whilst pitty-moovd He tells   15
   Us, Hee'l repair our tottring sells
   And quite strike ofe our former debts
If with contentment, thankfullnes partake

   These against sadnes are
     An Andidote   20

Preventing its could poyson, and
A heat-allaying Jewlipe wher (Thy) hand
Doth (Thy) displeasure in a feaver note:
They stile the Grave whither't be neer, or far
    T'be but a Bed; wherin when all must sleep   25
Let them rest envide; for our sinns wee'l weep.

My Carroll sung upon Christmas Day—1637

When we a Gemm or pretious ston have lost
    Is not the fabrick or the frame
Of fancy busied? and each thing tost
    And turnd within the roome
        Till we the same   5
Can find again, is't not a Martirdom?

Doth vanety affect us soe: yet are
    We slumber-charmd, nor can employ
A thought that backward might reduce soe far
    Lively to represent   10
        Our misery
Who fell, and thus incurr'd a Bannishment?

Shall we leav any corner reason lends
    To guive sence light unsaught, untride?
To find how farr our liberty extends   15
    And how refound we were
        Re-edifide
By th'Shepard and by th'Sonn o'th'Carpenter

May not this skill and love in him requier
    The white and better ston to mark   20
And raise this time above all others higher
    Wherin He came, (though light)
        Into the dark
For to restore unto Man-kind its sight?

Most sure it will: and wher neglect denies   25
    To be observant of this day
It proves not only forfaiture of eyes
    But all parts seem a-sleep
        Or gon a-stray
So's th'house again unbuilt and lost the sheep.   30

Easter Dayes Resurrexit
composd 1640

Set the Cliff higher
    Now
And raise
Each harts key
    To present a Vowe   5

          In praise
    Of Him who lately was our buier
          And of this Day
    Which He makes cleerer far than other dayes

        For look we back and ther   10
            We may with ease
            See what we were
            Transfomd beyond
        All workes did pleas
            The maker   15
                Soe
        That whilst He did commend
        What He had done Man wrought his endles woe
    Nor of those praises longer was partaker.

        Before when known   20
            To be
            By innocencies Livery
        The fairest likenes of creation
            All other thinges
            Were but to him as offerings   25
                Wherby
            He might maintain
        The title of the Worlds true soveraign

        Justice and mercy both
            The King of Heaven   30
            Delights to show
        And in his hands the Scoales doth hould soe even
        That whilst enforc't to punnish, yet He's loth
            To over throw
            And soe a way prescribes wherin   35
        Man may revenged be of sinn

        To this effect
          When He saw time
          His Sonn was sent
        That all disgraces of the crime   40
            On him being spent
        Noe contumely nor neglect
            Might lie behind
        To sink into despair a troubled mind

        Soe sufferd He   45
            To sett
            Man
            Free again
            Whose debt
            Requird noe less   50
            To recompence
            The guiltines
        Of soe great disobedience

Which bond dischargd
      All are enlargd 55
   Who can through Faith arise
      With Him who Clarefies
      Beyond our apprehention
   The splendor this dayes skies
      Put on 60
To Emblem His bright Resurrection.

   My Charroll—1640

   What though't be Could and freez
   Let noe good Christian leese
   Soe much of heat and Zeal
   As not for to remember
   That blest day of December 5
And what to Shepards Aingells did reveal
   Which doth of right claym lay
To all that ever Man can write or say

   A Saviour's born for us
   What newes more pretious? 10
   Wer't but some neighbours sonn
   The bells should straitwayes ring-
   In Cakes for Gossoping
Soe soon the tidings o're the town would run
   And many a light brain tost 15
Amongst the goodwives wher to place their cost

   And shall my frozen hart
   Not thaugh and bear its part
   In jollety for this
   Wherby not I alone 20
   But each beleeving one
May promise to himself eternall bliss
   For such can nere be could
Who have this berth-day in their harts enrould

   But may be sayd to burn 25
   Till some thankes they return
   Which though far short they reach
   The comfort is most suer
   H'hath healing winges to cuer
Not for reward, but to make up the breach 30
   Which soe repaird: 'tis Wee
Must make it good 'gainst Satans battery

   Wherto belonges this care
   In chief and singular
   That stricter guard we keep 35
   Because both night and day
   Th'artillery doth play

Nor doth our adversary ever sleep
And we shall shew therby
Christs favour hath not slipped our memory. 40

Upon St Stephens day—the same year

They w'r of Dewcalions race could b'of noe other
Who ston'd St Stephen Pirrha was their Mother

This is a true saying and by all means worthy to be received that Christ Jesus came unto the world to save sinners of whom I am the chief—Timo. 1—1-15

Be a thing true or falce our Nature lies
   Allwayes soe prone to novelties
That we are caught: and what is done or said
   Tickle, till we have uttered:

*Timoth—1 Yet are asleep *whilst a true saying's come 5
-1-15   (Or else with *Zachery struck dombe
*Luk 1-20 Through incredulety:) allthough't express
   In it the haight of worthines
And this the scoap: that he who noynted King
   Allthough he governd evry thing 10
Contented was of's footstool t'make a throne
   Wher he might work salvation

*Mat 9-13 And soe is a true Jesus; *nor doth thus
Mark 2-17   Become unto the righteous
But to those parties who through sinns decree 15
   Condemned were to misery
Amongst whom the Apostle whilst he'averrs
   Himself as Chief (soe little errs)
What should we judg our selves to be, whose all
   Of Life is but Apocryfall 20
Less than the least of mercies; yet again
   When in our ills we not remain
Goodnes shall cause that scepter to distill
   All-saving grace into the Will
Soe that repaird by this, forgiven by that 25
   We may thus farr be consolat
That Princely clemency and wonted love
   May both the crime and guilt remove

Then though the chiefest of the Chief we be
If we repent this verse will set us free 30

My reveille-Matin—to my wife
an ode composd at Newcastle upon tine:
May 26 1639

Lord
   When the Casements of mine eyes
     To wellcom in

  The morn, first opned are
Graunt that my hart may early sacrefize
   To expiat for sin 5
    Prepare
  And mustring up thy favours and its crimes
Cashire the one, let t'other stand enrowld
To evidence at full that time of times
Wherin Thou ransoms't me who once was sould 10

Let all the drowsy vapours prest
  My fancy down
  Dispell and guive it way
To rise betimes and to be better drest
  Soe dignify and Crown 15
   The day
With Anthems may set forth that Glorious flame
Thy love burst out in when my fault was soe
I h'd line for ere benighted in the same
Hadst Thou not vanquish't and o're come my foe 20

Cause (I bessech thee) that moyst dew
  That falls upon
  My waking temples tress
(By evry yawne thy goodnes taught to shew)
  An Exhalation 25
   Express
  Obaying noe heat save what did proceed
From that most righteous Sonn whose beams alone
Were of full power for t'refine the deed
Our Parents dross't by their corruption. 30

And as my armes unfoulded stand
  To fathom out
  The Latitude as 'twer
'Twixt the beds either side meridian
  Let my thoughts sore about 35
   That Sphere
Unparalelld for Grace: and stretch to be
Embracers of those mercies did extend
Beyond all sounding plummet or degree
And thither all my Kidds and fattlinges send 40

Thus tain by'th'hand by His whose felt
  What mine deservd
  I'm up and strait perceive
The morninges berth bedewd with his whose smelt
  All of perfumes and searvd 45
   T'conceive
Such raptures in me that noe part nor sence
Could be at quiet, till it rose to make
This offring and from a full influence
Inspird of love dull thanklesnes t'forsake 50

Now if my eyes, my hart, my head, my armes
Embrace, contemplat, feeling, seing, charmes
Wher can this exorcisme trulier stay
Than on that Starr which chang'd our night to day.

My Carroll sunge upon Christmas day—1639.

Luke—2—1 ⎫
     2 ⎬ verses
     3 ⎬
     4 ⎭

  Was all the world by Cesar taxt to know
    What wealth each cuntry, Citty, house could show?
  Did that decree extend but just soe far
    As thear Syrenius was governour?
  Yes sure: wher e're the Roman powr bore sway   5
  None could decline the Doom of Syria.
    Soe cam't to pass that He of Davids stem
    Hastned from Nazareth to Bethleem
    With his espoused Mary, and got ther

6}
    "Of whats before time Time's th'accomplisher   10
  Nor would the darknes of those dayes confess
  A Currency unto such pretiousnes
  But hous and Citty, Cuntry all three seem
  To cast upon those Guests the low'st esteem

7}
  And soe the Other straingers well may be   15
  Shuffle these frends into the Ostlery
What doe we less whilst Emprour like each one
Bears o're his lesser world dominion
And freedom hath to tax each sence to bring
Their best of treasures to this offering   20
Yet as asleep or blind through natures light
Wee'r taught to court all objects save the right
And whilst those houses should 'been tricked ore
For this alone they'd lett in Sin before
The Citties of our Harts possest with vice   25
Will not change garrison at any price
Soe what the region of our soules can graunt
Is t'appeer rich in ill, all good to want;
Yet though this Province, Fort, and Sconces all
Taken, betrayd, and under Satans thrall   30
'Tis not presumd, but that by Fayth being led
All these may easly be recovered
Nay all are won allready to that brest
Prepared is to wellcome this new Guest.

A morning Fancy upon the Berth of my Sonn Mildmay the 3d of December-1640. And the hopes of My owne recovery of the smallpox

Mark but the Sluggerds shame, the Change
Wher Pissmires numerously doe range
  And you'l conclude noe sight soe quick to trye
  Distinction in those Creatures industry

See but a showre of motes that seem to beat
Some busy traffick in a Sun-beams heat
   Then tel me what eye's soe distincticall
   As for to single one out of them all

This and much less is man whose numerous frye
Fills the world to preserve posterity
   And yet ther is an Eye both frownd and smild
   A sicknes heer, and ther a lovely Child

Singling out one, to show at once the room
Wher's mercies doe his judgments overcome
   And when the Fatherly chastisement's don
   Crownes him the joyfull Father of a Sonn

What can be heer returnd? the full expence
Of a whol sumers toyle and providence?
   Or such a part of lighter merchandize
   As in the sun delight to exercise?

These, and noe better are what we can raise
To shew our thankes, saving a hart of praise
   Which God himself must guive, and then'ts noe more
   Than t'borrow of one to pay the same a scoar

Yet Lord heer be my Creditor and lend
A Soul that may soe much to thankes pretend
   That whilst I seek thine own but to restore
   Thou, through acceptance maist create it more.

Psal. 124 turnd into meeter

Had not the Lord declard Himself for us
   May Israell now repeat
When men rose up that were malitious
   And Threatned all alive to eat
Such waters had exceeded soe their bound
As that our soules for ever had been drownd

Those Streams (I say) boyling with wrath and pride
   Had overwhelmd them quite
But be his name at all times magnefide
   Who savd us from their Jawes and might
And as the Fouler of the bird doth miss
When the snares broak, Our Soul escaped is

Let then this Help that it may bear true date
Ascribed be to His name did Create
Both Heavn and Earth that soe our thankes put on
Noe falce endorce or superscription.

My Figg Tree

The thankfull Soyle manurd and winter-drest
Returnes the Hind an Automn interest

For all his care and labour: nor denies
To be uncloathd to deck His graneries
Soe doth the youthfull vine those prunings owne 5
When as her blossoms are to Clusters grown
Nor (to shew thankes) doth spare her blood to spill
That soe the planters vessells she may fill
This vegitable lecture may indeed
Cast a blush ore me whose return for seed 10
Soe farr comes short as not for every one
To bring an ear but for a whol seed-time none
Noe not that corn again was left in trust
And harrowed up under my barren dust
But Nature doth in pregnancy soe raigne 15
That with wild oats she Choakes the truer graine
And wher my gratefull hart should die my press
It's all besmeared with unthankfullnes
Nor can a thought, a word, or act proceed
Out of my Clay that turnes not strait to weed 20
And before my frutes ripenes is begun
Abortive like its witherd in the sun
Of self conceipt: Lord prune again this vine
Luke—13-7:   And plough this ground least th'figtrees doom be mine.

My Looking-Glass

Foe to ill faces for thy truth, be free
And shaddowe back my soules deformety
Thou'lt pleas me better far than that which can
Return a Raven white, and black a swan:
For if thou shouldst like to thy self rubd ore 5
Guive all for Moat-less that come thee before
I might suspect (that, justly) whilst thou'rt sett
To me'n Diameter for Counterfett
horrid   Soe ugly black my contience doth present
My guilts complexions night Firmament 10
Not Tincelld with one starr of Grace, or spark
Of goodnes, but sin-clouded-ore and dark
How shall I then presume to claime a right
To any dawne of mercy and of light
Unless my Faith guive credet for the loan 15
And soe God's Sonn lend fro'th'reflection
Of His bright merits soe much power to say
My Pardon's seald and night is turnd to day
And then and not before I may seem drest
When His Great Favour, my Great Sin's confest. 20

My Charroll Sung—1641

Arise Arise
Dull fancy from the bed of Earth

          And that lowe strain
            Besotts thy vayne
        That soe thou maist devise   5
Some record of that famous berth
    Which about this time as our date will have
    One sonn for all the rest the Father guave

          Leav to the Be
    To set a valuation   10
            On this or that
            Fair guarden platt
    Ther t'brouse some flowr or tree
And to some forraign nation
    To crown their Annalls with the Pellican   15
    Or far-fetch Cordiall Mirrabolan

    Heer's Comfort more
A guift that's farr beyond all worth
        The Curious mind
          Could ever find   20
In what a Plant e're bore
Or barren wildernes brought forth
    Sweetnes exceeds the Bee's bagg and such good
    As prov'd our strong restorative by's blood.

The attributes of true love

1. Chor.   We call that patience, when provoakt we can
Cap—13.   Deferr revenge but 'tis True Love in Man
            And when with open hand we would express
            Our bounties Tribut some stil't Lavishnes
            But they Mistake as far as those despise   5
            All steps wherby another man doth rise
            Yet think they have Love too, and boast noe less
            Than that She is their constant Patrones:
        If Her Decrees be not to seek Her own
        Praise, as not seemly, whither are such blown   10
Ver—5:   That soe would tempt her anger when 'tis taught
        She is not to be moovd to an il thought
        But's ever pleasd and doth rejoyce to see
        Truth to triumph over iniquity.
            As She sustains and is contented stil   15
            With what wind blowes soe doe her hopes sailes fill
            When from the windowes of Beleef doth breath
            A steddy Gale t'advance her course beneath
                Til by the Saints transplanted and above
                Sh's moord within that port and call'd True-Love.   20

My Reformation

        If all the span
        Of dayes,

    Lent heer to man,
    To Pilgrim in,
  And in times Kalender enrowld,   5
     God should but skan:
  What might he find, in waight, and measure,
But pounds, and pecks, of this, and t'other evil:
    Noe one, markt to his praise,
     But spent, or sould,   10
   For proffit, or in pleasure,
     By whole-sale
      Unto Sin:
     And by retail,
  Unto the Flesh, the world, the Divel.   15

    If the immence
     Goodnes
    Did not dispence
    It's power, upon
  Our frailties, that like Clay, or glass,   20
    Makes noe defence
Gainst Potters, or the Glasiers skill:
What could we promise, to withstand such loss:
    Or miseries redress,
     Unless, (alas)   25
   His Sonn, he let them kill,
    Soe, himself t'pay
     That, by one
    Which one all lay,
And t'expiat, through greef and Cross.   30

    Heer, am I lost
     Soe small,
    Yet soe much cost:
  Wherin, the debt
  Would well nigh drive into despaire,   35
    Had not the most
Of me been dross, and soe unfitt,
To take the stampe, of any grace, or good,
    Until, He that made all
     Did too, repaire   40
   My crackt estate, and knitt,
     By His paine
     Wherin mett
   To sett againe
That Breach for Balme, His pretious Blood.   45

    Captives yea know
     Are led
    Into much woe,
    And sufferance,
Until, by ransom they get free   50

Again, and soe
Noe more are bound, but to those wayes.
Wher lies my bond, and obligation, then,
To sin was cancelled,
But stil with thee 55
My Saviour, whose Bayes
O're Deaths sting,
Hel, and Chance,
A Conquest Bring,
To sett me at full Liberty again. 60

Not what I will
To speak,
Or doe my fill:
As appetite,
Not reasons fescue, shall direct: 65
But with that skill,
Thy Gratious mercies shall infuse,
To make me truly censible of those:
Whilst I, the fetters break,

And doe detect 70
That, which did me abuse,
My yong years,
Which were light,
Too voyd of fears:
That soe, I might the rest for Thee compose. 75

My Invocation

Great, and Good God of Justice, Love
As that to fear soe graunt this move
My Trembling Hart, til it retain
Some sparkes of heat and life again
   Sithence my Creation Fuell's don 5
   Lighten the Turf by thine own Sonn

What hopes of this? unless I may
In awe to that find a decay
Of such lewd thoughts, words, Acts did bring
My whol man to a wintering 10
   In Lust and Sin, and growth in Grace
   T'assure a spring tide in the place

How's that attaind? By heat not Could
'Tis that the Bounteous Marigould
Displaies its Treasure, and kind showers 15
Not Frosts befrend both frute and flowers
   Thaugh then my Brest til't open Zeal
   And let my eyes those sigths reveal
     In raine, that my Affections may subdue
     Soe from my Owld Congeald Clott raise thoughts new. 20

My Closs Committe

    How busied's man
    To seek and find
An Accusatian
    Against all those
He deems his bodies good, or Goods oppose 5
And winkes at such as hazard soule and mind

    Nothing of late
    Is done or spoak
But either King or State
    Concerned are 10
The while each 'gainst his neighbour wages warr
Soe'r all the bonds of Love and Frendship broak.

    And how comes this?
    But that we doe
Or utter what's amiss 15
    In every thing
Making each Fancy Lord, each Will a King
And all that checks not Reason, Treason too:

    Wer't not more wise
    To lay about 20
Which way for to surprise
    That Traytrous band
Of Sinns that in our bosoms bear Command
And entertaining Grace, cause thos t'march out

    Our Lust, our Pride 25
    Ambition
Or what somere beside
    Seems to guive way
To that unjust Militia and Array
Bring we t'our Closs Committees inquisition 30
    Thus when Our harts These for malignants brand
    Committ them not but bannish Them Thy Land.

In Natalem—1643.

If nothing else; may not This Season move
Or Time become true Chronicle of Love?
And soe alay the Fury stint the Rage
And Madnes doth predominise this Age?
When for to ransome Man (whose least Offence 5
Was Characterd in Disobedience)
He who knew noe sin came, that, to fullfill
The mercy statute of His Fathers Will:
Thus He Forguave, and Guave, to let us know 10
What to our very Enemies we owe
By His Example; and decrees this Fate

       To the posterety unfortunate
       Of too-beleeving-Adam, that They must
       Guive Themselves over to noe Other Trust
       Than what His word assures; nor to make less   15
       That first of sinns Create them numberless
       In Envy, Malice, and Ambition:
       But joygn to Charety Contrition
       For by-past faults and resolutions raise
       To spend the Future in our makers praise: 20
       Obey Him first; Then Those His glorious Powers
       Shall Substitute for Our Superiours
       And with our own Condition whatsome're
       Content, Enjoy a full harmonious Sphere
       Leaving noe Orbe for Discords fond increas   25
       Sithence He that's born for Us was Prince of Peace.

Jhon—16-20: *They that sow in Tears shall reap in joy. Psal 126—5-6*

Math: 13-3: As in the Cuntry Parable it's found
       God to be Husbandman and Man the ground
Mark 4-14: His word the pretious seed that doth excell
Luke 8-11:   All others, and our harts the Arrable
       Soe would't informe we should our soyle prepare   5
       To recompence soe great a Seedsmans care
Math 13-7:   And neither prickt with Pride, stupid like stones
  5:    Layd Common to all wicked motions
  4:    Be unprovided t'save, much less t'afford
       Increase against the harvest of the Lord   10
Gene—3-17: Wherfore as Earth 'thout Culture sithence Mans fall
  18:   Is of Frutes barren, Thistles Prodigall
  19:   Soe doe the dispositions and desiers
       Nature brings forth abound with Thornes and Briers
       Which to correct the Masters strict Command   15
       Is to break up again the Fallowe land
       And by Contritions Coulter and Plough-Shers
Matt—26-75 To dress our mindes, furrow our Cheekes with tears
       Of true repentance—and those thus destroy ⎫
Gala—6-9: root* The weedes* of Sin; shall surely reap in joy. ⎬ Psal-51-8 20
                     ⎭

           In Natalem—1649
Postnata   *A Great mistery Christ manifested in the flesh* Timothy 3-16

       When wonder struck, Amazement ceasd
       At what Our God to frame was pleasd
       Soe that one Age the other tels
       The Glory of his Miracles
       Though those may end yet will not I   5
       Leav noating of one Mistery
       Soe far excelling all the rest
       As worthily to be the best
       And therfore 'tis a Great one stild

   Though swaded in a little Child   10
   The King of Heaven daind to come
   On earth thorough a woemans wombe
   Mans lost condition to refresh
   Was, manifested in the flesh
    Let flesh again soe much afford   15
    Of incence to this Gratious Lord
    As to exchange the world and all
    Its trash for treasure spirituall
    Keep A Berth day for him through fayth
    For ther's noe more that scripture sayth 20
    And wher that finger silent is
    If man attempt he steers amiss
    For nothing fit to be reveald
    Must be presumd is ther conceald

  Ascensus Gratiarum descensus Gratiarum. Mr Call[am]y
                up[pper]
If ther be any Vertue left that can   Tha[me]s
Pull Blessinges down, 'tis Gratitude in Man April-9 1644.
And to be humbly thankfull that alone
Makes Him true subject for Compassion:
All other Graces as Asistants sitt   5
Upon the wool-sacks for to farther it
In representing how the Lawe concludes
On Gods rich bounties Our ingratetudes
Soe ther upon impeachment's drawn to showe
Delinquencies and what He guives, we owe: 10
First then unless dejected care posess
The Hart and Soule for by-past wickednes
And stir up resolutian to become
Hence forth more righteous, ev'n to Martirdome
In vaine it is to hope or yet surmise   15
The Acceptation of such sacrefise
From Him whose all-discerning-eye doth pierce
The very Center of the Universe
And Knowes before we Think; Let our thoughts flye
To overtake His Providentiall Eye   20
And we shall strait be conquerd and confess
His Treasures, but our own unworthines
And like the Eagle first such flight beginn
From the Lowe Contemptible Vale of Sinn
Until Confession and Amendment rayse   25
Our stretcht out Pignions to the Cloudes in praise
  And then when all is done that we are able
  Stil we must knowe we'r but unproffitable.

      Cordis renovatio

Postnata   *Cor novum crea in me Deus. Psal.*
   Cor mihi Carnale est Saxoso durius, adsit
   Gratia, sic Carnem mollificare suam

My hart of flesh is harder far than ston
Let Grace asist to mak't a fleshy one.

    The Hart must needs obdurat be
    When Carnall thoughts doe Petrefy
    But those removd: It to refresh
    God frames again a hart of flesh
    Whose substance like soft wax receives
    The same Impression He guives
       Soe that who ere shall it reveal
       May know the writer by the seal

Whilst on mans owld hart Natures season lies
Noe wonder though it covet novelties
In food, apparrell, pleasure of each sort
To which a world of vaneties resort
Soe lulld asleep by these how can't discern
Those properties a better change concern
Til prompted from above? then taught by Grace
Man seeks a new one in the Owld harts place.

Upon Easter day—1644: at Stifky

    Sin-buried Soule awake and rise
      Let not the Conquered more
    O're Thy affections Tyrannise
    All that this world affords for Ore
    But drossy is, nor the Least might
    Of happines in Fleshly Appetite

    The Divel from the first was stild
      A Lier and hath stil
    Improvd his malice, soe beguild
    Us as our Parents to his will
    Each word we utter, thought conceive
    Or Act, all serve but t'help him to deceive

    Noe marvail then if Thou wert bound
      When 'twas a three-fould cord
    A Trident mischief that doth wound
    Requird a Trebble patience to afford
    Releef: with which we heer were sped
    When th'woemans seed did break the Serpents head

    First 'twas one God in Three compact
      Vouchsaft to work this Cuer
    Though't seemd the Sonns alone this Act
    Both Father and Spirit were ther most suer
    For 'tis with out contention
    All Three in one workt mans Redemption

    They were three wisemen from the East
      Conducted by a Starr

Refusd noe travail for this guest
But came with presents from a farr
To Court Heavens munificence
With Gould, with Myrrh, and Frankinsence 30

Those Three indeed bewitch our sence
  And what could men bring rather
Fayth was in infancy, and thence
It chose to sute the guift I guather
As wherby t'shew what dawning 'tis 35
That entertains the blossoms of our bliss

The frute comes after: and that was
  When He who knew noe sin
Condemned yet Contented as
A Malefactor great had been 40
Not only born, but born to bear
Our Crimes became for men a Sufferer

Suffer He did and was interrd
  And shall fond man refuse
To die for Him or be afeard 45
To bear, nay t'see his cross, and chuse
Rather to pass a moments pleasure
Heer than partake of such a lasting treasure

Shame rouse us, and as He did sleep
  Three dayes within the grave 50
Soe let our sins be buried deep
That they noe more domignion have
Nor hang like plummets on our thyghs
When with our blessed Saviour we should rise

Who for our sakes this Conquest won 55
  O're Hel, the Grave, and Death
Three that sought Mans confusion
Til Man-with-God-unite beneath
So far prevaild as first to Die
Then rose again to Crown the Victory. 60

at Rainam   *An Ode to Mr Waple a great Faulkner upon*
July-18. 1644   *Prince Ruperts defeat neer York*
                and the thankes guiving day for it

True Victory on Fames winges taught
    To flie aloft
  Soe Covers all the Plash
Or stream wherin herr falser tidings wash
    That none of them more rise 5
    Upon our Faiths to Tyrannize
  But put to plunge what shift to trie
Shunning the hawkes-pounce, meet the pole, soe die.

Now as in Aqueducts the Source
      Must guide the Cource   10
  And to the same degree
Haighten the reach of its humidite
    Soe 'tis but just and even
    That Benissons sent down from Heven
    Should Thither rise again in Praise   15
And fill each Calender with Holy-dayes

Not such as 'wont make red-inke deer
      Charging the year
      In memory t'express
This or that man's a Saint, Could die noe less   20
    But by such duties t'showe
    Our thankfullnes and what we owe
  As from that place alone we can
Conclude our spring of Blessings first began

Thus whilst for praise we set apart   25
      Both Day and Hart
      And sweetly doe embrace
Gods mercies meeting in his holy place
    'Thout question He'l goe on
    To perfect the Conclusion   35
  And Crown the Conquest farther, soe
That that nere more be our Frend, He counts Foe.

In Diem Natalem etiam et Jejunalem—1644
quoniam Mercurialem mensis ultimam.

A Holy-Day Thou wast, and art soe still
For Holy-fasting saves, when Riots kill.

In Sanctam Cœnam Domini
Epigram

Kings—5-10./	Wash and be clean, Eat, Drink This, and 'twill save
Jho—9-7	Soe easy is the sute our Lord doth crave
Math—26-26.27./	Yet with the heald Cripple back Hee'l call thee
Mark—14-22.23./	And bid Thee sin noe more Least worse befall thee.
Luke—22-19-20./	
Jhon—5-14./	

Qui te fecit sine te non te salvabit sine te August[ine]:

He that made man without man will not now
Save man without man put His hand to th'plough.

An Ode—upon the times—February-20-1644

    Awake Thou best of sence
      Intelligence

And let noe fancy-vapour steer
Thy Contemplation t'think that peace is neer:
   Whilst warr we doe bemone   5
   Ther's nothing less left in intention

England that was, not is
   Unless in Metamorphosis
Changd from the Bower of bliss and rest
To become now Bellonae's interest   10
   In dainger of a funerall Pile
   Unless some happy swift means reconcile

Which how to bring to pass
   Beyond Mans hopes, alas
Therfore Be pleasd (Thou that didst make   15
   Attonement for His sake)
To silence this un naturall spell
As Thou didst once the Delphian Oracle.

The True Bread of Life—Jhon—6-48:

Levit: 26-26:/ Bread is the Staff of Life, and Life's the Scoap
Of every Mans Desier, Ayme and Hope
Gen: 5-25; Yet He who was the Spoyle of Death (for soe
The Syriack renders Him) yeilded Therto
And after more than any else ere sawe   5
Of Years and Dayes did at the last withdrawe
To shew the fraile condition heer beneath
Of Those who in their Nostrells bear their Breath
Soe that Compar'd unto Eternall bliss
A Shadow, Bubble, Span all Emblem This   10
Why then should Thoughts be tosst to Court such Clay?
But that Our natures Mandate we obey
And may doe soe whilst Appetite puts on
Nor other Garb 'save Moderation
The Bounty that from Ceres Goulden ear   15
Scatters to bless the painful Labourer
Comes from above too, yet when ground and bread
'Tis but our Tabernacle's nourished
And that but for a while: The Soule must be
Behoulding to an other Grainery   20
Not that which Moses Praier Causd to fall
To Satiate the Israelites withall
Nor of such Barley loavs grew on the Earth
2 Kings—4- Wherwith Elisha fed some in a Derth
42-43./ These might have hunger after: but They'r blest   25
With the True Batch of Life may ever rest
Soe satesfide as with the haight of store
For Such shall never need to Hunger more
But an Eternall Life enjoy, wherin
Noe Darth or Famine is, but that of sin: 30
Plenty and Joyes for ever more dispose

Themselves to be the Comforters of Those
And whilst one's Faith makes that a Life indeed
The other to trust is a broaken Reed
   Afflictions sower that Temporall bread with Leven   35
Which This is freed of, for it comes from Heaven.

For Mr Conyers Darcy
At Merworth March—11: 1644

  If I must needs discover
I am in Love: be Christ again my Lover
  And let His Passion bring
My Actions to their Touch and Censuring
  Who in this world was Borne   5
Liv'd in it, and was put to Dearth with skorne
  That I to sinn might Die
Being borne again; soe Live Eternally
  Thus I'le noe Longer make
Addresses to my Glass for This Curle's sake   10
  Or that Quaint Guarbe wherby
I may enchaunted be with Flattery
  Nor on Luxurious vowe
Becircling Rose-budds Crave to Gert my Browe
  But with a Melting Thought   15
Bring Home the Ransome, wherat I was bought
  In Contemplation
Of that same Playted Crown He once had on
  And when my Glove or Shooe
Wants Ribbond, Call for th'nailes that pierct Him too   20
  Else farther to be Drest
Borrow the Tincture of His naked Brest
  Nor wash but in Soule-Pride
Then use noe other Bason than His side
  Soe up, and Redy, Think   25
How He, for Me Lowe in the grave did sinke
  That I again might rise
With Him that was both Priest and Sacrefize
  To make attonement in
The difference 'twixt His Fathers wrath, Mans sinn.   30
  Wherto it must remaine
That I through Faith requite this Love again.

A reveille-Matin Ode to C.E.H.
at Merworth March 15 1644

  As the Black Curtain of the Night
    Is open drawn
  By the Gray-fingred-Dawn
    To let out Light
  And bid good morrow to the Teeming Day: 5
  Soe let all Darkned Thoughts through Sin
    Call in

Their Powers that led them in a blind fowld way
  And Rows'd up from Securety
Bring Better Frutes unto Maturety.   10

  For now the Fragrant East
  The Spicery o'th'World
    Hath Hurld
A Rosy Tincture ore the Phœnix nest
  And from the Last Dayes Urne   15
    An Other springes
      And Brings
With it a Charrettier too in its turn
  Soe that by this new Fier
Be Goodnes hatcht, all Wickednes expire.   20

Then, as This Prince of heat doth rise
  In Power and in Might seem stronger
  Proclaiming that 'tis night noe longer
By vanquishing (the witchcrafts of the Skies
  The Spelly-Vaprous-Mists)   25
    Soe let th'enlightned soule
      Controwle
Our Actions that noe farther They persist
  To follow sence, wherby t'invite
Ruine, the sawce t'unruly Appetite.   30

  Thus Now it's Cleer
Out of all Question
The world's unmaskt and all of Valeing Gon
Phebus Triumphant ore our Hemisphere
  Let us not therfore in Disguise   35
    Seek, or Bravado
    To Shaddow as 'twer under Maskerado
      Soe many Faults and Villanies
        Knowing that He who made the Light
        Cannot be destetute Himself of sight   40

But though His Providence
  Did This begett
That suns that rise should sett
And in appeerance Vanish hence
Yet doth he Clayme for th'interest   45
  Of Day lights bliss
    We slumber not amiss
When as our light is borrowed by the West
But the Choice Cabbinett of Mind adorn
With Contemplations may befit next morn.   50

  In Quadragessimam—1645

When all the Dayes w'have borrowd are mispent
Had we not need to beg more time were Lent

                    And not to suffer This too, to be gon
                    Because Abusd through Superstition:
                       A knife to Cut is Good but if to kill   5
                       It be abusd we say that then 'tis ill
                       All thinges are made for use; Abuses came
                       But as Usurpers to Deprave the same
                       And in some kind or other All we doe
                       Speak, Think, or have those have their moralls too   10
                    Our Pampred Bodies oft such Thoughts put on
                    That They Become like to Proud Gesseron
                    And when our minds from full Cups are exprest
                    'Tis Like to Baltashasser at His feast
                    Our Actions too Loaden with Temporall good   15
                    Cannot permitt t'Aspire at Spirituall food
                    But Over-fed we surfet and becom
                    Like to the Beast in all thinges, 'save being dumb
                    Tung-tide we are not when we would express
                    Our Enmety fro'th'Root of Bitternes   20
                    Nor yet uncharitable: 'less in this
                    To Judg that Those who hunger doe amiss
                    And such as Thirst too: whilst our Cups run ore
                    And Bellies are made Magazins of store
                    It should be otherwayes if we would shun   25
                    The hevy Doom of Sad Temptation
                    And as the Meat and Drink of Faith, prepare
                    A Holy-Fasting-Sanctefying Praier
                    Cookt from our Cornerd Harts and not the streets
                    A Sacrefize Incenst with Love for Sweets   30
                       And Thus performing what is Lent aright
                       We'l fear nor Scismatique, nor Ankorite.

1647.   *Use and Memory Parents to Wisedome*
Usus et memoria: *Epigram.*

                    Use out of Date and to Remember
                    Our Saviours Berth' (wont bless December)
                    Cride downe: what may we Judg by these?
                    But this: that Wisedome's in decrease
                    And certainly must Folly owne   5
                    When as Her parents are not known.

                    Upon a very wett St Stephens day 1647

                    God would his Saints should be bemond
                    Soe the Day weeps for Stephen Stond.

                          To Easter Day—1646: Ode
Math—28-1   Wellcome Blest day wheron
Mar—16-9.   The sonn

Luk—14-6	Not of the Sphers alone	
	Did rise	
	But that of Righteousnes who shon	5
	Our True Light, was our sacrefize	
	For 'thad been night	
	With us	
	Dark, Everlasting, Dismall, Vaperous	
	Entaild from our first Parents Appetite	10
Jho—9-5	Til by the power and might	
Jho—12-46.	Of This Light of the world our shades took flight	
	Death, Hel, the Grave	
	That ever crave	
	And never satesfied appeer	15
	Noe longer their Dominions have	
	Sithence vanquisht by This Conquerer	
	Who doth enlighten every Faythfull Sphere	
	Now that each Orbe consenting prove	
	The while	20
	And trulier might feel those Comforts move	
	From soe great light, such pretious Love	
Mat—25-1.	We must back on our selves recoyle	
	To see what in each lamp one hath of Oyle	
	For without doubt	25
	Their Share is darknes Let their lights goe out	
	And wher again	
Math 5.16:	Ones Light doth shine through vertues before Men	
	'Tis true Divinety	
	Our Heavenly Father's Glorefide therby.	30

Upon The great Mercy of God in the Deliverance from the Gunpowder Trason on the Fifth of November.

Am I in Kent? and can I be noe more
Befrended than to want a Ston to Skoar
That Skape from dainger which had it orecome
At once had Conquerd Kent and Christendome
Die-mans all though not rare now: Rubies are   5
Through our discentions made peculiar
Blazners of Vertues Heraldry: nor can
The Tincture serve of the Cornelian
The Topas, Sapher, and the Emrode may
On Fingers worn, Proclaime it Holyday   10
But I must find a whiter though it came
Not far but whence Fayer Albion took its name
The Cliffs of Dover on whose Canded brest
I shall presume to share an interest
On This occation, that noe Rubricks spell   15
May henceforth in some Bookers Chronicle

Eclips its glory or exempt its prayes
By ranking it amongst the workedayes
Surely the Die that black design put on
Would crave the best of all and whitest ston 20
To mark the Providence that did prevent
The Mischief of that Vaporing Element
   Hatcht Low as Hel should our Conceptions rouse
   In that before it grew pernitious
The shel was crackt, and soe that enterprize 25
Was vanquisht with the abortive Cocketrise
First to the Great deliverer and then
A freedom of acknowledgment 'mongst men
That everyone may as their fortunes are
Spend something on a Solemnising care 30
And as the Powder should have been our chance
Now Let't express loud our Deliverance.

Upon Mans Frailty

What Permanence to Earth or Clay is due
Fond man Consider for that Emblems you

Hodie vidi: This Day brings humane flesh under Deaths yoak
Heri vidi: And yesterday I sawe a Pittcher broak
   Our Forms are diffrent, Substances the same 5
The subtil artist doth both vessells frame
For honor and the Contrary, and thus
Our Great Creator moulds and Fashions us
   If we would then Our makers praise set forth
   We should take Care to becom those of worth. 10

After a weekes sea voyage for pleasure
an Observation—May-3-1645

Though Every thing we see or heer may raise
   The Makers praise
For without Lightning or Thunder
   His workes are all of wonder
Yet amongst Those ther's none 5
   Like to the Oceon

Wher (not a Catalogue to keep
Of Severall Shapes Inhabiting the Deep)
   Let but our Thoughts Conferr
With what once gravelld the Philosopher 10
   And we must strait confess
Amazement more, but apprehention less

The Fier, for heat and light
   Most Exquisite
And the All-tempering Ayer 15
   Beyond Compare

  Earth's Composition and Sollidity
  Bountifull mixed with humidity
   But heer for proffit and Content
  Each must guive place to th'liquid Element   20

   Whose Admirable Course that steers
  With in twelve howers both Mariners
    Owtwards and Homewards bound
   May be suffitient Ground
  To raise Conclusian from thence   25
  At once of Power and Providence

   For as the Cynthian Queen
  Her Bewty less or more vouchsafes 'be seen
   Soe by Her wayne she bringes
  The Tides to neaps and by her full to Springes   30
   Yet not but as He pleas
  Who set Her thear chief Governess of Seas

   Which understood
  Truly by such would seek for Traffique good
   They must their Ancors waigh   35
  Out of that Osy dirt and Clay
   Earths Contemplations yeild
And hoysing sayles theyl straitway have them filld
  With a fresh mackerell gale whose blast
  May Port them in true happines at last   40

   Ther 'thin a Bay of Bliss
  Wher a sweet Calme our wellcome is
   Let us at length the Cables veere
  Afore and Aff that may our moorage cleer
  From warp or winding soe ride fix upon   45
   Our Hopes sheat Ancor of Salvation

May—7. 1645:   *My Poole of Bethesda or*
    the effusian of Christs Merits to heal our miseries

When Childeren would goe, or Cripples stand
Cruttches and stooles are framd for Arme and Hand
To rest upon: least such attemping shall
With out like props occation Them to fall
  What are the Sonns of Adam? if we trie   5
  Condemnd to Lamenes and to Infancy
Through sin and soe disabeled to pace
The Paths of Vertue, tread the steps of Grace
Til God of's Mercy pleased to conferr
A Standing-Stoole as if fro'th'Carpenter   10
Though He Himself was Artist and did frame
The remedy for those were weak and Lame
Soe that without a farther Inquisitian
We all were and are such, Christ's the Phisitian.

The 5. Porches to Bethesda

August—16:   Man is Bethesda and's five sences be
1646   Porches unto that Great Infermery
               Wher Divers Cures are needfull, yet not one
               Attaind, but through an Angells motion
               Grace powred on the hart: Which whoso can   5
               Improve, becommeth strait a perfect Man
               But Those who Opportunety Neglect
               Must not an other Saving help expect
                  For as the Crippple thirty eight years lay
                  And had don more, had not Christ come i'th'way   10
               Soe whilst these powrd out waters we would try
               Others step in Prophane their Sanctety.
               Lusts both our Ears and Eyes and Pallets charme
               Through nostrells and by fingers we doe harme
                  And 'cause all over leprous and defil'd   15
                  We'd faine be cleansd, to health be reconcil'd
               Yet cannot get soe soon into this tide
               Afford us of that Jordan from Thy side.

A Morning Thought—May-10-1645.
Ode

Psal: 104. 23.   Sithence it is guiven
              To Man to follow's Labour til the Even
                  And when that starr doth close
              Up Day: then to seek quiet and repose
                  Let us what's of our own   5
                    Learn to make known
                        To be
              But soe much cash of purchasd Misery
                    All else confess
              (Of Love and Providence) true happines   10

                  For as our soules had been
              A Combating all Day with flesh and sin
                    And then for Captives led
              In slumbers Fetters, Prisond in a bed
              Soe by the Nights exchange again to Day   15
                    They may
                  Set free, take up Their Armes
                  And having overcome those Charmes
              Bowldly Conclude the Victory to keep
              When as They warr for Him kept Them asleep   20

                  Noe other Ransome need
                      To speed
              This Liberty but once awake
                  Into our thoughts to take
                    What such confinement might   25

Administer of Dainger in one night
    And how th'all-wakefull eye
  Provided had for Our delivery
Which on the winges of Contemplation raisd
Again w'are mounted, whilst His name is praisd.   30

Man Levens the Batch

Mr Calla[my
1. Chor-11-28

Let every one
examin himself

God made all thinges for good; 'tis Man
Sowers and worsts Creatian
Who Levend by his Father, thence
Becomes all Disobedience
Noe thought, noe word nor Action He   5
Contrives can owne integrety
To Him that made him, for by deeds
As words and Hart his growth's in weeds
Which whilst neglected doe express
Gods Grace, but Mans unfrutefullnes   10
Now if again He would bear Corne
Man must himself a weeder Turne.

Catena Causarum ad Salutem pertinentium

Man's hart's soe linkt to sin wedded to vice
It needs a chaine to bring it unto Christ

Ode Occationed upon my sonn Veres sicknes

In my recall
from Apthorp
Septem 10 1647

What ever Gods Divine
    Decree
Awardeth unto mine
    Or me
  Though't may seem ill: 5
    With Patience
I am resolvd to undergoe
Nor to His purpose once say noe
But moderate both minde and will
  And Conquering th'Rebellions of sence   10
  Place all Content in True Obedience

  Thus I Create it Good
    When His
  Correction's understood
    Which is   15
  Not to destroy
  But to reclayme
And t'cause me turne a new-leafe ore
Count all an Error-writ-before:
Soe find the sting of flattering Joy   20
  Making the Scoape of all my future ayme

To Reverence and Glorify his Name
Thus when our God will frowne if we waigh it
In Judgments Skoales we make't a Benefit

*Occationd upon the Communion
when it was a snowe—Januar-18-1645*

A Hymn:

Invited now to supp with Thee my God
All that I am is at a Period
    How to be fittly drest
And soe t'become a worthy Guest:
      For 'tis preparde alone, 5
For such as have the Wedding guarment on:
    Which thorough gilt I want
And all my subsance to buy it is too scant.

Make me a Purse then, from His sacred skoar
Whose Institution 'twas; and will doe more 10
    For those beleev His name
That to redeem us sinners came
      Into the world: and shed
His pretious Blood, for to stand all in stead
    By a quick Faith applye 15
The Soveraign Ballsam of His Agony

For like the Man mett Theevs we all were left
Naked and wounded, Spectacles of Theft
    And Rapine too, wherin
We welltring lay a pray to sinn 20
      Till th'True Samaritan
Passing this way Redemption began
    Not sparing Wine, nor Oyle,
Out of His hands, and feet, and side the while

Thus now upon recovery again 25
Bound up in His Grave-Cloaths, brought to our Inn
    And earnest left, to prove
His high Compassion, and Love:
      What Care should be, t'express,
In all our future Actions Thankfullnes 30
    Which, noe waye's better spent
Than in partaking right this Sacrament

Which without Clensed Harts; and mindes that Can
Turn a new leaf, (with the Centurian
    More of a Christian showe), 35
    Made white as is the day with snow,
      And like the Prophetts sute
Purged with Hissop from what doth polute
    We cannot hope to doe
Nor that, 'less prompted by Thy Grace therto. 40

Wherto (I pray Thee) soe much mercy add
That I may have some Balme from Gilead
    To heal my Leprous sore
    Whilst humbled for my sinns before
        My Future dayes may be   45
The inventary of more Piety
        My forehead bear Thy stamp
As Servant, having Oyle stil in my lamp.

De Maria Magdalena Casimiri Lyric:

She wearieth the Starrs with Her sad Theam
And waters Her soft cheeks in a salt stream
And as Impatient Hurried preferrs
The desert Hills and Caves for Partners
Why did these Tears soe prodigally flow?   5
That Magdalen might sayle in Her own woe.

Upon Dives and Lazarus

Ther was a certain mighty Rich man had
Noe other name (in Scripture) allthough Clad
In Purple, who deliciously did fare
Dayly for which ther neither Cost nor Care
Was spard to feed His Gluttony with store   5
Of what the Seas did yeild when galed ore
And what somere both Earth and Ayer afford
Seemd Heaped Tributes to His quainter bord
Soe that noe Element to His desier
Was Niggerd 'save what was reservd the Fier   10
Yet This Man died and on that sleepy skoar
Was buried   and noe more—

Ther was an Other whom spare diet made
More specticle for Charety, being layd
Naked and Could before the Rich mans gate   15
Who full of sores and all disconsolate
Saving from what the licking Doggs apply
Concludes all this worlds Pomp but Flattery
Then He dies too. but as in Life These were
Nothing akin, soe in Diameter   20
Death Their Condition states for now't appeers
What heer was sown in joy, ther's reapt in tears
And He who by hard Fate was heer opprest
In Abrams Bosom finds an Interest.

Upon Moses put yong to sea
or hid in an Ark of Bullrushes

This sonn of Amram soon as born did find
Pharo a Tirant but the Midwives kind

Exod—2	Soe being from that bloudy Doom set free
2	Becomes His Mothers care and Huswivry
3	Who to his safety that She might conferr 5
	More hopes she makes him first a Marriner
	A good presage wherby it was implide
	His people He through the red sea should guide

Ad Quendam tam Potentia quam Intelligentia et Doctrinæ Divitijs æque ac Nobilitate et Honoribus praeditum. Epigram.
Englisht thus

Thou art a witty Man, nor's every one
I'th'world for Power Thy Compagnion
In Berth and Riches all Thou dost out fly
And exc'lent Parts backt with Authorety
On Thy arear this only now may fall 5
Thou render These to th'Lord who guave them all.

The contempt of this world raises the esteem of the other

When all the Vertue we can Heer put on
Is but Refined Imperfection,
Corruption Calcinde: A Minerall Vayne
Wher Clay (to be more prizd) some Ore doth gain:
Why doe we not Employ our best of Care 5
To Learn wherin Truest Contentments are
And how attaind? The Jewellers command
O're art, is how to Foyle the Diamand
As may add Luster to it: Soe who tries
Less to esteem of This Worlds Flatteries 10
Setts Higher Valew on the Other, wher
Perfection is th'Eternall Jeweller.

Upon the Berth of my Sonn Henry the 13th of August at 11 a clock at night—1646

Luk. 18.13	When I (O Lord) Thy mercies skan	
	Stooping unto the Publican	
	Standing afarr ofe, and didst dain	
	To guive, that he might aske again:	
	(For not the owtward-beaten-brest	5
	Nor down-cast-look could make him blest	
	But 'twas Thine owne Power did controwle	
	His former vice, stampt new His sowle)	
	Me thinkes I am soe far set free	
	From all sinns bonds and Tyranny	10
	As that raisd up in hopes, noe more	
Luk 19-4	I need Zaccheus *Sycamore*	*or wild figg tree*
	But though a Dwarf in grace conclude	
	I see Christ 'bove the Multetude	
	Calling me down as if to say	15

He meant to be my Guest to day
And (though a Sinner) crowne my wish
Bringing an Olive branch for's Dish.

Cordium Concordia vera.

It is not meant that three in One should be
But in each hart Triple Capacety
Wherwith to serve ones God, ones King, ones Frend
To which assignd and for noe other end
    In Flaming Zeal upwards to mount again 5
    In Loyalty to owne a Soveraigne
    In mutuall Love society t'maintain.

To Mall

Psal 119.71.   If David found it good He'd been in Trouble
Jerem.   What should I learn that am a sinnfull Bubble
But that Afflictions we meet with heer
Are sent to steer us to our God more neer
Who thus improves his thoughts on thinges goe cross 5
Without a Riddle makes great gaines of Loss

Emblem Two Turtles billing and Death standing over them with a sithe redy to sever them to whom this Divide et Impera

Nature hath ore Affection soe much won
To knit a knot never to be undon
Whilst Life remaines. but Death to shew his power
Cutts and Devides soe becomes Emperour
Yet the Relict for to prevent Fates charmes 5
Doth Volontary fleck into Her armes

Emblem
Amoris Sigillum

Mans hart lockt up within his secret Brest
Cannot by Tongue or Gesture be exprest
For what's of soe great worth we must suppose
It is a work of Power to disclose
Such Harts as make Men faithfull and upright 5
Are those at once both face and mind unite.

A quid retribuam
before a sacrament

Poor-Sin-bound-Naked-Creature-Man nere knowes
What to return for that His God bestowes
But as Propereties encrease goes less
In retribution of Thankfullnes

His eyes not opned but with Clay made dimm 5
Renders that Miracle not wrought on Him
Remaines soe stupid, but wher Faith's declind
To unbeleefe such are for ever blind
   Now that I may like judgment stil prevent
   By entertaining True-Soules Nutriment 10
Not Poyson, let example spurr me on
To take the Cup filld with Salvation
And praise His Holy Name that did prepare
Such Cates For Those heavy and Laden are
Sinns Dromidaries swift by nature led 15
To run to evil heer unburthened
By One that bore both Cross and shame to free
The plyant Branch of Eves Posterety
(Soe have I tender Saplins seen unbroak
When Tempests have o'recome the sturdier Oake) 20
And if in sacrefize we'd pass degrees
The best for Acceptation's from the knees
Outwardly and inwardly exprest wherby
To notefy unfaignd Humilety
For such deny to shew repentance thus 25
Surely forget Christ came from Heavn to us
And Those of that slack memory may know
Their Portions earth, They shall not to Him goe
   Who's Riches, Rayment, Food and all releef
   To Them Contemn This world make Him Their Chief 30

    My Cuntry Audit   April. 25. 1647.

Blest Privacy, Happy retreat, wherin
I may Cast up my Recknings, Audit sin
Count o're my Debts, and how Arears increse
In natures Book towards the God of Peace
What through Perversenes hath been wavd, or don 5
To my first Covenants Contradiction
How many promisd resolutions broak
Of keeping touch (allmost as soon as spoak)
   Thus like that Tenant who behind-hand cast
   Intreats soe ofte forbearance til at last 10
   The summ surmounts his hopes and then noe more
   Expects but mercy to strike ofe the skoar
Soe heer Me thinkes I see the Land Lords Grace
Full of Compassion to my drooping Case
Bidding me be of Comfort and not greevd 15
My Rent His Sonn should pay if I beleevd

Humiliation without Reformation is a foundation without a building
Reformation without humiliation is a building without foundation

    Best Architects whither in brick or ston
    Cast first to lay a suer foundation

Then raise the fabrick; confident therby
T'assign't a tearm of perpetuety
While lesser artists failing of that care 5
And skill erect them Castles in the ayre
An Element unconstant which betrayes
To ruine whatsomever ther they raise
 Such and noe other are those soe profess
 To add by reformation happines 10
 Yet want the basis they should build upon
 To make it last Humiliation
  When Others are cast doune upon the flore
  Yet are reformd noe better than before
Soe heer foundation without building is 15
And ther a building on a precipice
   Wherfore let me be humbled first and then
   Reforme soe as never to sin again
   Blending these two together with intent
   To build an Everlasting Monument. 20

Translation

Psal—1. Buchan[ani] Paraphra[sis]

Happy is He whom from the right wayes Lawe
The wicked Multitude could nere withdrawe
Nor led by error would He lend an Ear
To Scoffers, or Partake of their Curst Chaire
But dilligently searching how to find 5
The means to better Life, revolves in Mind
The Lawes of God which He alone doth prize
And makes them's Nightly and Dayly exercise
 He shall be like a Tree that's planted by
 The Rivers Brink which lets it not stand drie 10
 But Heat-and-Could-free Prodigally bringes
 The Hind reward in frute and Blossomings
 Nor doth it feed the Masters empty pride
 With Flattering Hopes alone whilst 'tis not dride.
  It's otherwayes with those not understand 15
  The Holy Covenant and Divine Command,
  Bring Heav'n into Contempt: Like Dust such are
  A whirlwind strait Careers into the Ayre:
Wherfore when as the Righteous Judg shall come
I'th'Clowds to Sentence every one their doome, 20
Ungodlines retire with sad lookes must
Nor once presume t'appeer amongst the Just
 Whose Fraud-free-Paths our Heavnly Father knowes
 And markes whilst wickednes He overthrowes

Unus quisque sanctus Altare Domini in se habet; quod est Fides.
To man an Epigram

        Hard harted man what canst thou say
        That thou thy self hast turnd to brick thy Clay
        But that thy hopes are built upon
sent   His promises *squeesd* fountaines out of ston
        Wherfore to Sacrefize to Gods desire   5
        Mans Hart must be the Altar sighths the fier.
                A broaken and contrite hart
                  The Lord will not despise.

Psal—114. Buchan[ani] Paraphra[sis]

When Israells lookes all homeward bent did stand
Being quitt of Pharao and His Barberous land
Hatefull alike, to Juda God Alone
Becomes of safety and Protection
Which the sea sees and with a trembling Tide   5
Commands Her waves astonisht to devide
And Jordans current noe more nature-led
Presses the waters back unto their head
Great mountaines now their craggy tops advance
In measure as the Flocks Pride leads the daunce   10
And Lesser Hills their heavy foreheads shake
Like Lambs that in the meadowes Pastimes take
    What sawst thou Thetis that thou thus laydst dry
    Thy channell? and Kind River tel me why
    Thy Purlings back to seek their fountain went?   15
    And mountaines struck as with astonishment
    How com'st about yea seem to play like Ramms
    Whilst Lesser Ridges imitate the Lambs
    But thus: the God of Jacobs presence spoak
    Terror to th'trembling world, whilst Altares smoakt   20
    He that to Liquid use turnd hardest ston
    Changing the flints hot vaynes to Helicon.

Psal—133. Buchan[ani] Paraphra[sis].

Nothing can Paralell that prizd delight
When Mutuall Love doth Brothers harts unite
'Tis not the Ayre-perfuming Balm was spent
On Arons sacred head yeilds like Content
Though in a wellcome showre disperct about   5
It Lav'd his beard and Costly tier through out
Nor yet that Dew whose pregnant Powers distill
Embroydery o'th'Gras of Sion Hill
In Twin-born flowers: Noe nor those vapours fall
T'inebriat faier Hermons top with all   10
Fertillety: for wher Fraternall peace

Inhabiteth, Gods right hand sends increase
Of Riches and of Children; to which He
Adds a succession of eternety.

Psal—134. Buchan[ani] Paraphra[sis].

Yea servants of the Lord that can enstile
Your selves His Houses Life Guard, when the while
He shends you from all harme send praise to's name
And let the silent Night Concent the same
Amidst the which both Hart and Hand appeer 5
Lift up in Blessinges to the Heavnly Sphere
And then the Lord (as in returne) will make
Both Heavn and Earth send Comforts for your sake
He who Alone made'um. and Sion sees
Bestowe His favours on Thy Pedegrees. 10

Psal—137. Buchan[ani] Paraphra[sis]

Whilst far from home with sadnes overprest
By Babilons Euphrates we seek rest
Our troubled thoughts suggest a world of care
That we noe more to Sion should repaire
   We wept; and Greef supprest our stammering words 5
   Whilst to our barren brests each eye affords
   A showre of mollefying tears: Those stringes
   To musique stretcht once, now like silent thinges
   Hang by ther, on the willowes: which express
   In their green branches our forsaken-ness. 10
Then the Fierce Lord Rich Solimis thus spoild
Requires a song of us that are exild
And that we should our Bannishments reherse
(As we were wont when Free) in Syons verse
When as Her Kingdomes prosperously stood 15
The Envy-mark to all her Neighberhood.
   Would this Prophane soyle in derisian raise
   The holy Keyes of our Diviner Layes?
   Jerusalem? Shall any Age suppress
   The Memory of Thy fayer Courts access 20
   And Holy Temples? First I wish, and Pray
   My right hand may forget on harp to play:
   May voice forsake my Tongue, whilst thorough drouth
   That becomes furrd soe sticks unto my mouth:
   Rather than I Thy prayses should not guive 25
   O're all my merth spetiall prerogative.
But Thou O Father bear in mind the cries
Of Edoms race over our Miseries
How They prescribd our Ruines, to Confound
And equallize all Pallaces with ground: 30
   Thou shalt O wicked Babilon receive

Reward like wise of what thyself didst guive,
For happy shall he be to us doth joygn,
And pay Thee mischief in thy propper coyne:
Yea Blest, that tears Thy Sucklings from their brest 35
And with their braynes prepares the stones a feast.

Psal—120. Buchan[ani] Paraphra[sis]

Hence warrs Beleaguer me, whilst Envy stands
Advancing Thence Reproaches Fier-brands
Wherfore to Thee to whom all Creatures owe
Their beings I alone for refuge goe
Which by an humble voyce when I express 5
Thou art not slowe to guive my praiers access
May thy protection be an Antedote
'Gainst th'Poyson of th'deceiptfull Tongue, and Throat
That utters lies. O Tongue what gain will't be
To hope to blast with falce Impiety? 10
Arrowes are Poyson-Piled noe more can
Infect though shot by a fierce Sythian
Nor's any Fier half soe bad and cruell
As such a Tongue when made of serest fuell
My life's opprest with sorrowes For I tread 15
The mountaines til now uninhabited
And soe those Cottages frequent wher none
Deodates But *Muscovite* and *Arab Theeves* are known
notes upon   My mind is vext my Annalls to reherse
the place.   Sithence they have been with those to Peace averse 20
Such enemies to quiet as when I
But mentiond it 't hath whet their Cruelty
And a word utterd but on Concords skoar
Their warrlike Dispositions haightned more.

Poemata Quaedam Postnata

To a Glass of wine set before one
Ego non capiam Te, ne tu Capias me

Why art thou set heer to surprise
At once two sences Tast and Eyes
And with Thy sparkling witchcrafts spell
Setst upon Tempers Sentinell
Seeking t'corrupt the Guards and win 5
The outmost Port and soe get in
  But Thy Deceipts are too well known
  Thy Ayme is to make me thin owne
  Yeilding unto Conquest soe
  In taking Thee myself t'forgoe 10

Be not mistaken Blush for shame.
I'le never for Thee change good-name.

*On the Philosopher who not apprehending with the eye
of Reason Naturall the cause of the flowing and Ebbing
of the sea cast himself into it with these words
Quia Ego non Capio Te, Tu capies me*

Phylosophy may This averr
But 'tis noe Christians character
Who knowes that to Creation went
Nothing but was of wonderment
For soe Diviner wisedom strove 5
To set his drift our reach above
That Awfull Reverence alone
Might bound our Contemplation
And wher His writ word silence keeps
He is Presumptious that peeps 10
For nothing's left out ther that can
Befit His Glory, Proffit man.

Senec[a] Agamem[non] 1. Chor[us]

O the deceipt
Of Fortunes bayt
Which oft times brings
Ruine to Kings
Whose very Crown 5
Alone waighs down
And scepter prest
They take smal rest
One care coms on
As t'others gon 10
New Tempests wind
Tosses their mind
More than ere lay
On Biskian Bay
Or doth Controwle 15
Under the Pole
The freer main
Neath Charleses wayne
 Thus doth Her wheele
 Make monarchs reele 20
 Who feard would be
 Yet Thence fear see
Noe night to those
Affords repose
Nor slumbers charme 25
Once shends from harme
Which else would bear

Sway over care
  What Castles strong
    May not ere Long   30
  By Trechery
  Dismantled Lye?
  Though They hould out
  Til force Them rout
    At Last They yeild   35
    To Conquering sheild
      Loves Holy Tye,
      With modesty,
      And Lawes, Courts fly
But in Their sted   40
Bellona's sayd
With bloody hand
To bear command
Wher Envious Pride
Loves to abide   45
Which one howers space
Brings to disgrace
  Graunt warr should cease
  And subtil Peace
    Noe more prevaile   50
    But both strike sayle
      Greatnes alone
      Is such a one
      Whose very wayght
      Will sink it strait   55
What Fortune rears
She feales and bears:
When hoyst up sayles
Meet prosperous Gales
As Those doe fill   60
They most fear ill
And Turrits high
Seem t'kiss the Skye
To Southwest drops
Submit their Tops   65
Whilst woods of Shade
Fierce Stormes invade
Til Their owld stocks
Are turnd to Blocks
And torn and rent   70
Noe more consent
To Perch the higher
Winged Quier
Bright Lightning drills
The Tops of Hills   75
When the boult flies
From Thundring Skies

Bodies are Thick
Prove oftnest sick
Whilst the lean heard   80
Is not afeard
The Fatter dies
For Sacrefize
And what we see
Thus raysd to be   85
As Fortune heavs
She but deceives
And Haightned Fates
Precipitates.
Thinges that presage   90
A longer age
Are Governd by
Indifferency
And He is blest
Above the rest   95
Who quiet grown
Doth hugg his owne
And Courts that Breeze
Which best agrees
To waft him neer   100
Wher He may steer
Within His bay
And never waygh
To trust to Seas
Are merciles   105
But by the shore
Contentment more
Doth find wherfore
Ther wetts his ower

Senec[a]: Hippolitus—4 Chor[us]

How many Chances meet to dress
And Spin out Humane Busnesses
In Smaller things Fortune goes Less

   It is Obscureties high price
   She Mistreses Secureties   5
   Which in a homely Cottage lies

Whilst the aspiring Tops soe high
Above the Clowds seem t'kiss the Sky
Subject to Stormes and Tempests lie

The moister valey doth not know   10
The mischief of a Thunder blow
But is preservd by being lowe

    When Caucasus that Giant Hill
    Lay trembling to feel the ill
    From the loud Thunderers bowlt and will   15

    Nor could the Phrygian grove be free
    Honerd with Fame of Cybele
    Neernes in Jove bred Jelousy

But the low sell and Cuntry roof
None of the Greater Motians moove   20
Soe such are wind and weather proof

    The active hower with doubtfull wings
    Flies fast away and seldom bringes
    To pass fond Fortunes promisings

    Yet He that lookes the Starrs upon   25
    Behoulding Day when night is gon
    Puts on sad Contemplation

    For nights return; and worse than Hel
    Concludes it to see now the sell
    And house wher once his frends did dwell   30

Pallas th'Athenian Goddess Thou
Canst nothing to thy uncle owe
For Theseus hath made a vowe

He that accounts Himself for thine
The Stygian Lakes for to decline   35
And Heavn look up to wher Gods shine

As for the Tyrant swayes beneath
He hath his number, yet what breath
Comes from above in mournfull ditty
Sure Phedra's mad seeks her owne death   40
Yet willfullnes deserves less pitty.

Janus

    What would the Season now inferr
    By the approach of Janiver
But that the Owld guives place to the New year
    December now is past
    O let man then at last   5
        Consider
How He the Ten Commandements hath broak
    Nor longer lie under sins yoak
    To make the breach the wider

    But casting of a beak and Skin   10
    With th'Eagle and the Snake begin
To live anew to Grace and die to sin

       And This obedience drawe
       From Him fullfilld the Law
          Like-wise
Chasing all ev'l Affections out of dore   15
  Whilst that our harts defild before
      With lust we Circumcise

  This be alone our skoap and Drift
  And let it serve for New years guift
That from our selves we thus desier to shift   20
     Cutting ofe those delights
     Bewitcht our Appetites
        To stray
Til entertaining better in their room
  We are renewed and become   25
    Sonns not of night but day

And He that winnowes thus his secret mind
Bringes forth good wheat and finds his Land lord kind.

A Carroll—in 47.

   Awake mine eyes
    Stand ope
    And view
    The Trew-
    Est scoap   5
   Of misteries
Unswaded heer for you

  Leav not a thought
    Of hart
    Or mind   10
    Behind
    T'impart
  Who 'twas me bought
And prov'd soe wondrous kind

  Let evry sence   15
    Be movd
    And ston
    Each one
    Improvd
  To rayse from hence   20
Fit Contemplation

  This is the time
    Wherin
    As we
    Agree   25
    'Tis sin

    And held a crime
To bannish Jollety

      But few are those
        Can tel   30
        Why 'tis
        That this
        Befell
      And soe expose
    Their Busied braines amiss   35

      Plum-broath and Brawn
        Minct Pies
        These are
        The care
        Heer Lies   40
    What Heathen dawn
For Bacchus did prepare

      But Christians were
        More blest
        And soe   45
        Did know
        The best
    Way to that Sphere
Did Cast true light below

      2 d: pt:

        For how could sky   50
        Beclowded lie
When as the Day Star from on high
      Bestowd on man a visit
        Which not alone
        In Jury shone   55
    That Gentiles might not miss it

      Yet though this light
      Did shine most bright
    Some Darknes did preferr
        And ther are stil   60
        Soe prone to ill
Will by noe means those rights fulfill
Should soe great mercy Kalender

      May ther be such
      My Harp, my Lute   65
    I shal not cease to touch
    And with the Prophet them confute
For if ther can be joy for temporall things
    I will not spare my stringes
But warble out the benefitt This brings   70

          An Infant's born
          To bear our scorn
        And can we e're forget
          Who ransomd us
          When we were thus   75
        Enthrald to sin, in graces debt
        And but for Him, had been forlorn

          Noe; may His name
          Stil be my Theam
          It's wine and Oyle   80
        A Balsam that can heal
        Man's lost Estate and Conquered Commonweal
          This sonn, This Child
        Born for us, and heer guiven to reconcile

          Beg we   85
          That He
          Then would create
          In us new harts
          To bear our parts
          Become again o'th'nurcery   90
        For Innocency, and Regenerat

          With Him begin
          Take up our Inn
        Be truly humbled under sin
          Skorn all thinges smile   95
          For they'l beguile
          And count it Loss
        Not t'bear for Him who bore for us the Cross.

A Carroll in 1648.

Thrice as the antient Roman stories skoar
A lock was set on Janus Temple dore
In Numas Glorious time first it was thus
Next under Consul Titus Manlius
Lastly when Cesar swayed to which increase   5
Of Happines was born the *Prince of Peace*
And doe we stil in violence run on
To out-vie Heathens with Confusion?
When heer such were whose morall vertues rayse
The Olive branch above the Conquering Bayes   10
And in Prophetick mist thus would Implye
What 'tis makes up the tru'st felicety
Peace upon Earth whence Love proceeds and brings
Eternall Glory to the hi'est of Kings
Who to conclude it Acceptable sends   15
Into the world his sonn to seek his frends
Were lost and out o'th'way; which clue hath in't

*Imperante
Augusto natus
est Christus*

    The rediest way out of sins Laberinth
      And therfore worth remembring what it cost
      By any one that would not stil be lost.   20

Mat—11-19   *Wisedom is Justefied of her Children*
          on the Epiphany

Mat—2-1:   To Justefy themselves three wisemen came
       Out of the East to Holy Bethlehem
       The Heavens were their call, a starr their guide
       And soe the Twylight of their fayth was tryde
        Herod did raign yet These their presents bring   5
        Not unto Him, but to an Infant King
        They were prophetick and did surely know
        That from the root of Jess a branch should growe
        To Scepter Juda and by Law compell
        The stubborn hart of stiff-neckt Israell   10
        And that the Jewes might not alone heer sit
        Under this light they come and Gentil it
        Implying that restriction should be none
        In the wide work of mans redemption
        But Jew and Gentile, Bond alike as Free   15
        Are not exempt from this Capacety
         For's mercie's over all, and wher we miss
         Of ransom 'tis our faults, and none of His.

         A good morrow fancy.
           to E. H.

     At the first Glimmering Dawn the morn sends forth
     What can ther be of more Esteem and worth
     On Contemplations skoar than to indite
     With Holy David praise to th'Lord of light
      And though my viall and my Harp stand stil   5
      I shall awake my Hart, my Tongue, my Quil
      To Regester what may be rought or sayd
      From Meditating thoughts begot a bed
      And in the stead of mischief thence contrive
      The amplitude of his Prerogative   10
      Who Governs all whilst with Obedient rest
      I doe conclude what ere befalls me best
       When under that Protection, and my bliss
       Whither I sleep or wake to be found His

          Mundus Vanitas

     Of all the Divels wichcrafts ther is none
     More Huisherer unto Temptation
     Than the beGuilded nothings of delight
     The world howlds forth to cheat mans Appetite

       Which masking under Pleasures subtil name 5
       Or proffits spell, soon Captivates the same
       When as Those Comforts what somere they be
       Should be made soe by a Conformety
       To him that guives them and in usage raise
       The Contemplation to the Doners prayse 10
         First as we grow in Substance to provide
         Our Gratious God may be stil Glorefide
         Else Riches are but Snares: for better 'twas
         Without them to be Blest with Lazarus
         Than over-whelmed in too great plenties store 15
         With the rich Glutton Torturd ever more
           And wher Contentment's Sugerd baytes entice
           We should beware as if we trod on Ice
           Soe Slippry's their foundation heer and all
           Their Favorites They doe but rayse for fall 20
           Whilst if we call to mind what Scripture bears
           That Those shall reap Joy; first have sown in Tears
           We would Ambitious be our Cares to turne
           From Piles of laughter to those sells that mourn
             Wher finding wisedom we may easly see 25
           That all This worlds Pack is but Foppery.

Homo Vanitas
Fons aquarum viventium
Christus

       When This world seems to court me with a smile
         I'm tickld all within the while
       Then in a Cloud of Crosses if it frown
         I'm every whit as soon cast down
       'Tis too too true that in mans nature lies 5
         A million of Infirmeties
       Shaken by th'wind, and soe entitled thence
         To weather-cock-Obedience

         Knowing not what to hope or fear
       Whilst all its motians are Irreguler 10
         Shot betwixt wind and water thus
       We may expect the doome of Icarus

Psal—42-1:   But as the Hart or chased Roe
       Unto the waters for refreshments goe
         Soe if in hott'st of Trialls we 15
Psal—87.7:   Can find our fresh springes out (Jesus) in thee
         Ther's noe pursute of Time or chance
       Shall fright or chase us into variance.

       But in the gates of Sion whilst we dwell
         Ther'l need noe scout nor Centinell 20
       For safety from above the Lord intends
         To Those become His Cittisens

        Players on Instrumments and singers ther
           What ere Delights and Comforts are
        Shall not be wanting to fullfill   25
           Predictions of that Holy-Hill
           Wher His Foundations Layd: t'Ascend which mount
        Each must below goe less in's owne account.

        Upon occa[sion] of Mr Sharpes text in Great St Bartholmes
Isay 55-1:   *20:-2-1649.*

        The Mart is Ope, the Prophet is The Crier
        And every one that Comes heer may be buyer
           The merchandice is water, milk, and wine
           Which must be bought without a price or coyne
        But This Condition He implieth first   5
        Ther must be want before one comes and Thirst
        Faith on the Appetite must set an Edge
        Ere capable of soe Great Priviledg
        As This now offerd: and our needs express
        Before we purchas can this Righteousnes   10
           We must not bring our sorded Baggs along
           Like such as into Fayers and Markets Thronge
           To Truck and chaffer wares: These price-less goods
           Extended heer for nutriments and foods
           From a free hand of bounty are held forth   15
        To all that freely can Esteem their worth
        Others (for Silver bought) we tast, and then
        (Though for a time quencht) drouth returnes again
        But when the Pallet *is* refresht with these
        It's freed from all Distempers can displeas   20
           And thus by Him Who was the heavnly bread
           We gain eternall Strength being nourished
           And cheerfully rejoyce t'have Sin abhorr us
           Whilst we drink Him that trod the wine press for us
                Then quaffing from that well of Life the water   25
           We may be satesfide, nor ere thirst a'ter.

           Upon occation of a Sermon
           on the 2d of Peter—1-10.

        He that would build, soe prove an Architect
        Before He doth his wall and Pile erect
        Digs for a Rock, and having found the ston
        Grounds to Himself a suer foundation
        And guathering all Confidence from thence   5
        Materialls mustred are with dilligence
        To Cut out windowes and to frame the Dores
        Sutable to the stories and the flores
        To guive each Room and stayre proportion due
        For haight, bredth, length, and point each Timber true   10

Unto its mortice, lay the side-wall-Plate
Wheron the Cuppelings to Elevate
To joygn the rafters place the Tiles in riggs
For covering pind to the Laths with priggs
Then wind and weather proof he may conclude   15
He's safe because with providence endude
(This for a Temporall Structure):
                                                Which agrees
   Soe neer with that of Spiritual edefice
   As that there must much paines be usd and care
   Before one can such bewteous building rear   20
The Rock must by a lively fayth be found
Before we can have good foundation ground
And then the Ground-sel and the floores should lie
Squar'd right and Leveld by Humilety
That each ascent might answer to its story   25
Grace must begin the work that ends in Glory
   And now to cover all that man had done
   He that Elects, redeems us by his Sonn
   And thus that Building to his heavnly call
Answers shall stand for ever, never fall.   30

'I must heere tell Sr. Robert Nanton'

I must heere tell Sr. Robert Nanton
That of the Queens servants heere I want one
For as her Exchequer proclaim'd her fame farre
   Sot was it not without a Chancelar

A Farcy.
wrot when K. Charles the first was Prisoner
to his Crewell Rebell Subjects

The Prologue   When Neptune's ploughd and Earths turnd Liquid
Sharp counted round and Round calld Picked
And Contraries posess each thing
We may have Peace without a King

   By the broad a God man coth the Scot I'st nere endure   5
     My near born King s'ad be Captive and pure
       But while my bonnets blew
         Though Tase tu ethers to Him i'st preve trew
     And with my dog, my whinyard or Switch
     Seek tu restear Him t'us right privilidg   10

Cotts Pluttre nayles co Taffy up tat
Up Tis, up toder, up I know not what
As Hur's a Shentilman and must never goe less
Hur will not put up such barberousnes
   But wit Hook and Tacker Hur sweares to maintain   15
   T'at Hur must have hur none King again raign

Else hur shall make hur to know
All will not soe well goe

Diel a my sall cries Blew cap Brother
Come ye in o'th' ea side and ist in o'th'other 20
Sea weest gar the English Lounds
Ken weele The due exceed their bunns
For tu effect through reformation
Sud gang the denoyr of every th'ilk nation

By Cot and by St Patrick Ile sheath my skean 25
In any that shall to Anarky lean
And paune my mantle, my broages and my trous
Nor leav any harbour about me for louce
Before I'le guive way my King and my master
Should liberty loose and in Prison lie faster 30
And though for a Rebel some at me have spurnd
I'le shew them at last the tables are turnd

Cot's Sacramant coth the Dane who brookes noe jest
Why take I Sloap-drink whilst my Cosens opprest
Up Hulst up Elsnore and Coppen-haven 35
Te sound be my frend too tat I may saven
Men, Mony, nor shipping spare I shall
To bring my Good nephew again to white hall

Then out comes Butter Box and pleads a free state
Yet would not have England such at any rate 40
For though but the yonger sister shed be
As her state would be more soe shed be more free
And Envy in Rivalls affection all smothers
The one is stil Jealous of the fortune of t'hothers

Catt so cries Pantalone—if I not sayle 45
Digneties growing now like a Cowe tayle
For Dukes unto Kinges wont upward to looke
And now ther's a King shrunk less than our Duke
Then picking his teeth out comes Cankero
Capita many heads make one but a Toe 50
That may get again power to kick and then These
Aymèe (allthough Hydraes) may meet Hercules

As neighbour to that though not of Opignion
Geneva steps forth the Hugenots Mignion
And doth profess and profess and profess 55
That she wont to Envy Englands happines
Under a Youth a Mayd and a Man
But now their Disorders She cannot wel skan
That seeke to Reforme to Reforme, to Reforme
Til casting ofe Government all's turnd to storme 60
Like one that his Cloak or Cassock throwes bye
When Tempests arise and yet would ride drie

Up rise the Haunce Touns all together
And calling a Diet dispute it whither
They should account London a sister or noe   65
But that question Brake ofe and noe farther could goe
For Waller and Massy and Poynes and the rest
Of the fugetives tould them that Citty was a beast
And had wittlessly yeilded to Parlements Yoak
At Armies Command without striking stroak   70

The Emperour, Pole, and such of Election
Begin to rouse up and think the infection
Of Populer Power may ill consequence bring
That the one noe more sway nor t'other be a king
Soe to Their Brother send pitty not scoff   75
For Ayd they can none they are soe far ofe

But Monsieur in Querpo cries par ma foy
À Cheval à cheval to help the Black boy
Yet stops his career when once he considers
That we have allredy heer too many riders   80
And'ts certain a Cuntry with it self falls out
To'ts neighbour great benefit bringeth about
Soe He comes not on but claps hands cries ça ça
Let disorder confound both the Church and the Lawe
'Twill for his advantage heerafter be plea   85
If he seekes to revenge the attempt upon Rea

Por Todos Los Santos comes Don out in huff
Streatching out's whiskers to measure his ruff
And with a scornfull back looke ore the same
Sees the point of his Rapier half as long as his name   90
Who i'th'muster rowle of's dominions did find
The whol world was too little to fil up his mind
Yet least that his stomach ore charged should be
Naples and Portugall send remedy
Though He want his extents to reach the worlds ends   95
Yet now his Condition will not help his frends.

Benedicito cries His Holines
If things run on thus my three will goe less
For if they clip Crownes as now they begin
I shall be accounted the Man of Sin   100
And all my Indulgences, Bulls, Pardens thus
Will become Skarr Crowes and Ridiculous
My Eldst Sonn allredy in Calabria goes worser
And soe I am like to leese homage and Courser
And as the People prevaile in their tricks   105
I shall be condemned even by hereticks

Last the Grand Signior brings up the rear
And by His Mahomet Lowdly Ginns swear
That with his shash, his Turbant and drumm

He'l shake hands with Perce and view Christendom 110
And seek to extend his Power and Dominions
Ore those soe devided in hart and Opignions
And bring this Iland too into his world
Which out of the Owld the Poets had hurld
And soe to th'South East the North West he'l pull 115
To make a whol Orbe and His half moon a full.

To My Cosen Mistress F. F.

Cuss-   Shall I tel with whom and wher
    I would rub out the silent year
    It should not be in Camp or Hall
    Though to be Judg or Generall
    Clients at Barr, and Rendevous 5
    Ile never for Contentment chuse
    Nor sequester my judgment soe
    As to partake with frend or foe
    When the house smiles and Army frownes
    Until they ease Them of their Crownes 10
    Dismember them or threten knocks
    As if with heat They'hd gott the—
*Quæ supra   *These are above us: nor is't fitt
nos &c: To open whilst committees sit
    With pen or tongue to speak or write 15
    'Gainst Those have teeth for such will bite
    But with a Frend one may call soe
    I shall into the Cuntry Goe
    Ther Chuse myself within my Sphere
    Or house the first knight of that shere 20
    Whilst that my wellcome doth express
    My neighbours too are Burgesses
    Thus when I have Lent-all their Q
    The Speakers place belongs to you
    Females, and to the Chirping Frye 25
    T'express alowd their noe or I
    When as the questions verdit lies
    In Rodds Plum Cake or Apple pies
    Then all my martiall Feats are known
*Fortior est   *By Conquering my self alone 30
qui se &c.   In which Exployt as much I shine
    As if a Walled Town were mine
    Ther place my Guards that vice and sin
    May meet repulce nor enter in
    Yet Entertain what Freedom lends 35
    Of Conversation to Frends
    Which is Drawn out Discoursing wayes
    In Censuring This or in Thats praise
    Wherin the Discepline soe well
    Observd as that noe Bird can tell 40

    Then to draw out my Park preferrs
    Thes Scouts and Those field Officers
    The Trembling Deer of Fallow hue
    Closs in the Fearn doe lie perdue
    Til Gallant with his Party Charm   45
    Th'Eccoing woods guive alarm
    Then Jupiter shootes from his sphere
    Clowder that Thundring Cannoneer
    And Singers heard whilst bullets fly
    Then Conquering Cesar mends the Crye   50
    Dutches and Juno of a speed
    Fleetly run in and doe the deed
    Whilst by a valley th'game is known
    And Peerles ruines them alone
    Tomboy the favorite of the Gierles   55
    Casts quick about and nimbly hurles
    To catch the sent Then Famous sped
    Hits ofe the fault or nayle o'th'head
    And wher the doubling game had gon
    Leavs not t'vent from ston to ston   60
Thus when their quarters are broak up
And we in Garrison a Cup
Of Nut-brown Ale or radiant Sack
Strait fournishes with all we lack
Meat, Drink, and Cloth; the Hall and skreen   65
Are Courts of Guard and Celler Magazeen
Which I'de not change with Cardnall Mazareen.

Ebsom Well to Cuer sicknes—July-24-1645

    Ease and Luxurious Appetite
    Invest diseases, Ebsom how to—
    And that infection might have less power
    Ore Corpulency heer I teach to—
    Clensing the Intrailes that one would think   5
    All savours were suppresst, saving to—
    Wher that noe fiddle string might want its part
    Tenner or Treble—base, each Gut doth—
    In Diapazon and in Long and Largë
    Skoar out the Key and Cliff as in Dung—   10
    With Quavers-semy-Demy whilst the Gutt
    In Brief is troubled til you mountup—
    Now 'Cause Degrees in shooting doe controwle
    All shiting Level's random from the—
    And guives the Charge 'thout other Fife or Drummer   15
    Than what Arse-hole Fizells when you—
    Both white and Brown are Founders and present
    As from their forge a reaking Funda—
    Whilst nature thus assaulted must confess
    She's her own Conquest thorough shit—   20

All Misdemeanour's liable to scourge
Soe doe malignant humors need a—
And what deceiptful Tast doth recommend
Unto excess must out at t'other—
Cures are not wrought but by the Contraries 25
Wher Stomack's over clad ther bare thy—
And if with sicknes Helth be growing skearce
Be not ashamd i'th'Common t'shew thy—
For 'tis noe jesting matter those that Come
To Drink of me must often turn up— 30
Before the Timpany or Dropsy source
Abate and Ebb-out of that Lower—
All those that thirst for health come heer and quench
Whither swoln Matron or wanton w—
That is all Aier, for all diseas of wind 35
By water prest Evaporats be—
One drinkes soe many Ownces, t'other pledges
Until at last they both run through—9—
Could but this smock tel tales and t'other shirt
That which was Haytegoe they'd christen sq— 40
And what before the fluxes wont unsluce
Of Belly-Gripings now it is this—
This pretious Liquor; that can cuer and save
When husbands are too slack what wives would—
For at pretences door heer whilst some knock 45
They Find the surest way's to change the—
And soe one swelling whilst abatement swayes
An other comes t'exalt the horne of—
Ladies are nice and dress them at a Glass
But ther's noe shi-ting place like to the— 50
Whither Profitients, or yet to learn
For their Back-Faces-fan the best is F—
And she that of me many Pottles takes
'Tis odds her Belly Twattles in the Br—
For 'twas approvd with out bought words or fayle 55
That all Obstructions sally best from—
Which Postern gate or Caz'emat alone
Huyshers the road unto port Esk—
When forc't by me, and their condition such
Their Coulers flying all the Common s— 60
And soe display like fetherd rain in flakes
That doe proclaime the Conquerer A—
As if Ulisees quite had left the field
Ajax seemd armd with Agammnons—
And soe unconquerable 'less in this 65
Wher all must yeild their nose to T. and P—
Which once admitted tis without all doubt
I can doe wonders turning inside—
Discover smelling Treason in a word
Discypher Plotts and them defeat in T— 70

More might be spoaken in my Fountains praise
But He that houlds too long himself be—
Therfore let this suffize and when you—
If't mend the stool I'm payd then wipe with it.

Epigram

I flow to make some Ebb and Ebb to fill
Soe run my Tides without Lucinas skill

Upon a Coyne Stamp't at Newarke dureing seige there of the valew of 9d.

          Whilst Newarke lay beseig'd twas nothing strange
          Her nobles she to ninepences should change
English   For being belegred by each nation
Scotch   She durst not stampe a shilling, marke, or Pun
          For feare of trechyrie as I suppose   5
          Knowing that thistles prick soe doth the rose
          And therefore all such mintage to confound
          A coyne created is, thats square not round
          For so it signifies thus cornerd seene
          To manifest the straights that she was in   10
          C: R: a Crowne imperiall, the reverse
          O. B. S. Newarke and the date reharse
          Soe that besides condicon without doubt
          Those letters spell, obedient, bowld, and stout
          Which with the Governour soe well agrees   15
          As that hee's rightly stild Lord Bellassize
          For what can more of beautyfull than this
          When Royaltie to prowesse coupled is
          Valour with love so spun on vertues wheel
          That mildnesse and good nature shine through steele 20
          And to these added all that nature can
          Compass to frame a goodly faire yong man
          Thus though this be but ninepence I'le averr
          It must remaine a noble Character

Ms Urselye—alius Arslys Triumphs

Vide Ben.   Some Frends to make themselves and Others merry
Jhonsons   Upon a time took water in a Wherry
workes   At Puddle Dock; and thence 'thout other wind
pag: Than what the Collick fournisht from behind
            Constant Nose-East to Holborn-bridg they huff   5
            At One Spring-Tide and take the Coast in Snuff
            Honors (Cry They) through perills must invite us
            And wee'l row on allthough they doe—
            The Haight's well known, wherat the Breaking Clowds
            Of this Horizon doe bespatter shrowds   10

	And what Those Powers are, They cannot Sink us	
	Only Their showre may stayn and soe be—	
the Kings	This to sett forth least any pen should lack	
yearly	Ben, undertakes it: not from's *Butt of Sack*	
salery	But from the Barrell, for it best agrees	15
to him	With Turn-ups Ale: to write of dreggs with Lees,	

A Kinderkin's suffitient t'make a Solon
In Poetry when as the subject's Colon
 Braynes washt in Beer, or layd a steep in wort
 Thorough Port-Eskelon make Cannons sqwort 20
 Which hazard all within that Gulf doe trade
 Of Poysoning if not of being be—
  The Radiant fier of Sherries nobler spirit
  Or any of that Race that doe inherit
  One Drop of Helicon must heer guive place 25
  We write of that is Contrary to Face
  For as th'Antipodes to us doe Ranke
  Their Feet to Feet, soe Countnance heer's point Blank
A Turn-gutt Clark with other Petty-foggers
Produce their Client at the Barr of Boggers 30
A Jaxes Common Pleas, wher sentence feeles
Justice when overflown run down by th'heeles
Which Court as Others Crowded is with Craft
Soe Ms. Ursely sells heer mornings-draft
Two Far-s one Fiz-l 3. back—belc–s more 35
Proves currant coyne to satesfy the skoar
And since I name Her I must needs disclose
Her features, They'r two Cheekes without a Nose
 Soe that for Goodman Snott He must forbear
 And only kiss the pocket Handkecher 40
She needs noe Looking-glass soe goodman Jorden
Lest a Stale-Frend Her Vessels to put T—in
If you will have me say what ere I can
 Of Her: she is Natures Philistian
 And beggers all those Empericks indite 45
 Their recipes in Characters to sh—
 Noe Citty Bands soe readely discharge
 Their peeces (when the powder's dank); nor Barge
 Laden with Dunge more Fragrancy doth spare
 When Emptying; for to perphume the Ayre 50
 This the Bear-Guarden-quite putts down for smell
 And Jack that sh—soe far at Epsom Well
  If you for more look let the Stigian Lake
  And Akeron sweat prayses for Her sake

Sola Bella che piace

'Tis but a folly to be nice
Sithence Liking sets on bewty price
And what we doe affect alone

Becomes to Each his Paragon
All Couler, shape and form we know 5
Improves to best to those think soe
And wher Esteem its Anker wetts
Ther grows true Pearle noe Counterfetts
 Were she as crooked as a pin
 And yet could Love it were noe sin 10
 To love again for writers tel
That Love hath in't the Loadstons spell
Were she proportiand Like the Sphere
Noe limm or Joynt Irreguler
Yet to my fancy if she Jarr 15
I shall not sayle by such a Starr
Did she out vie the newborn day
Or th'richest Treasury of May
Soe that what Skies and Flowers put on
Guive place to her Complexion 20
I'le sooner deem a Black wench white
That's suting to my Appetite
 Well in Conclusion hath she fayer
 Or brown or Black or Goulden hayer
 If one be Cupit struck—Venus is ther. 25

In Effigiem Caroli 2di.
Englished

If any one to recken ore's Enclind
Thy vertues Cesar and the Guifts of mind
He'l find Thou far Excellst all Monarchs past
And Trajans Adage fittlier on Thee plac't.

MS WESTMORLAND (A) 6.VI.1
POEMS, 1643–51

De Fœdere Nationale, February 1643

The English, Scottish Irish knit; increase
By a firme League the hopes of lasting peace
And as their Faith, their Lawe their King's but one
Contrive their safeties into union
Graunt Thrice-one-God these Three-fould-People may   5
Weavd into One onely to Thy name pray
Whilst the Scott Prelates let the Irish send
The Popedom packing, England both. Amen
                For I have heard it often spoak
                  A Trebble Cord's not easly broak.   10
                          W

In novi anni—1644. Diem primum

If Eagles shifting but their Bills have made
Their Youths return, soe years seem retrograde
And serpents by devestment of one skinn
Resumd another thus their age t'beginn
Or whilst th'eleven months like food appeer   5
To satiate the hungry Janivere
    Why should not Man this Riddle too unfould
    And be renewd by putting ofe the Owld?
                          W

An Epitaph on Sir Thomas Nicolson Knight a famous Civilian

Like to that Tower whose Light the Seamen guides
To shun the daingers of the Lybian Tides
Such was this Nicolson His Cuntries pride
A goulden Lampe of Heavnly fier beside
Hermes begot Him Pitho gave him pap   35
Whom Themis bore Apollo took in's lap
The First gave Him His wand, the Third a Hart
One Eloquence the Other Musicks Art
Justice and Retorike are silent made
Now the rod's falln and Phebus Lawrells fade   10
These spoyles like monumental Trophes were
Bequeath'd to Earth whilst He enricht the Sphere
Soe that the Gods these humane ashes turn
And by their Power innoble grave and urne.
                          W.

Epithallamy

Startled awake as if bespoak
  Not by the Crowing Cock
    But from the steeple
      And Casements ope
        I see the People 5
          Guather and Flock
Together as some show were nigh
The Sorceress to Commonallety

    And soe't did prove
For the fierce God of warr 10
    Whose day it was
    Yeilding up Armes to Love
Like a poor Captiv'd Prince did pass
Not for a Planet but a Common starr
    Whilst that the Waggish Boy in spight 15
    Had stoln His Beams, to guive His Torch more light

Soe't proves noe longer Training-day
  But as the wanton pleas
    To order and direct
      The whol Militia 20
        According to such Dialect
        And Discipline, that These
He strictly doth command to be Obeyd
By every one that would not die a—

Now 'cause howers spin and wast
  They are drawn out 25
    In ranke and File
  And in that posture to the Temple hast
    To reconcile
  And bring all questioning past doubt 30
That 'tis noe longer Marses spirit
Raignes heer, but Tounshends matcht with Tyrwhit.

Ther They joyne hands
  Nor is't a wonder
  Two Champions should doe soe 35
When Prowess evermore Commands
  Like Curtesy to frend or foe
And harts thus Grasping are not put asunder
  ('Save at the Destenies request
  In Clayming of their interest). 40

  Then as by way of pledg
    To fix the first seal on
    And signe that holy vowe
  The Bride-groom takes the Priviledg
  Before um all to teach them howe 45
The Turtle whispers its Compagnion

        Who with a melting kiss
Exchange and shew what Transmigration is.

   Thus two soules leapt
    Into each others brest 50
   They sound Retreat
For each solemnety must needs be kept
And space alowd to raine a shower of wheat
   To Emblem out Increase upon the rest
     And that the Cake broak ore the Bride 55
   Guive Leisure for a dining time beside.

Which done, the Revells next
     Take place
   And squadron out the Roome
   In figures: yet without pretext 60
    Of any Conjuration to come
But what might add unto each Party Grace
Yet shew that wher ther wants no fuell
One may seem in such kindnesses too Cruell.

For why alass 65
  Poor soules I guess
    They stand on Thornes
    And think the hower glass
     Envies or skornes
By standing stil, their happines 70
And that Bright Barneby is heer
Bequeathing His Long day to Janivere.

Yet ther's this comfort still,
  That hath its night
    And soe shall this, 75
  When now the Art and Skill
Of Groom that was, and of his Misteress
Is for to come from drilling to closs fight
And ther engaged in each others Armes
Vanquish and put to flight all other Charmes. 80

But Envy yeildeth not
   To this designe
  But labours of protraction
Soe stil contrives this and that other plot
   T'adjorne and put off satisfaction 85
With Jonketings and possetts made of wine
Yet when the stocken's thrown we'r sure
These hindrances much longer not endure.

But with the Lamps retire
     Whose modesty't appeers 90
   To wink and stile it late
   That soe the nobler fier
Noe longer may seem separate

                    But in Conjunctive Spheres
                    Entoomb each other and become one flame   95
                    As Rivers when they meet prove but the same.

Upon Sir Anthonies incomparable peece wherin are most faithfully set down Divers Passages of Court and State During the raigne of K. James. 1.

                    That 'tis Well-don who is't that dares deny
                    If ever read in Men or History?
                    (Both liable to Flattery); yet heer
                    Nor derth of Truth in One, or Courage neer
                    To bid defiance to the others ill   5
                    Soe steddy in'ts dementions as to Skoar
                    At Life most passages not long before
                    Without enclining partially to spare
                    Any Transgress how Great somere they are
                    Nor yet in Times-observancy to be   10
                    Guilty of such smooth-fac't Idoletry
                    As Favorites wont Clayme: when as their rise
                    Is but the reddiest way to precipice
                        This shall enduer and may all times be known
                        Wherin such times as these are tould their own. 15
                                    W:

The Genius and houshold Gods salute the little stream brought to run into the moat by Captain Stanlies Art and industrie.

                    Rivlett of Glass whose liquid Crystall can
                    Soe freshly fall into this Ocean
                    And chose the Fish drink nectar understood
                    Before noe Current save a sea of mud
                    Thou that dost such a pretty purling keep   5
                    As pricks the Gammuth-Are unto sleep
                    Not like a Torrents fall (to wake and fright
                    Thy waters serve: allthough Rone swift in flight
                    Speaks lowd: Thou art content Heer for defence
                    To yeild This-Iland-sell munificence   10
                    And as the Sea beguirting world around
                    Soe seemst Thou to this little world a Pound
                    Let that famd Guarden-God bring of the best
                    And Pan out of his flocks present a beast
                    Thou old Silvanus shalt strew Flowrs between   15
                    That Loves may heer be forgd by th'Cyprian Queen
                    Noe God or Goddess must have power to be
                    Unmindfull of Thy Splendid purety
                    But in their mutuall suffrages Combine
                    T'exalt and add Thee to th'eleventh signe   20
                    That soe Thou mayst not scruple or seem nice
                    Of being presented with this Sacrefice.

Upon Sir Thomas Fayer-Fax whose vertues make
Him shine a bright star in our Horizon.

Great Alexander makes the World appeer
Less ('Cause noe more), soe Curbs the Conquerer
Yet Cesar found His Bayes to Amplefy
(People fro'th'World apart) in Brittany
      Who without Cesars Armes and Pignions too   5
      Soe Great a work in soe short Time could doe?
      Nor Any but of Mighty Power Compact
      Could Iterat Bellerophons Great Act
Let the Cleer Moon bost of Her borrowed light
Fair-Faxes Star desert shines far more Bright   10
Phebus the Dark-Ill-Vapours may expell
But this is He Ill-humors doth repell
      Clowdes and Night-chasing-Light whose splendid Ray
      Is the Faier-Blazon of Our hopefull Day.

Translations

Out of Martiall Ep.-21-Li-5 To Martiall

Might I enjoy my time with thee
(Deer Martiall) in securety
And soe dispose of vacant howers
As for to make life truly owrs   5
We should indeed but strangers be
To Towers of magnanimety
And steer our course alike as farr
From Crabbid strife and the sad barr
Nor with Statue Pride Familiar   10
But riding out into the feild
Discourse of that our bookes doe yeild
Or else at home what the house hath
Enjoy In shades in wench in bath
These Places we should still Posess   15
Make This alone our busines
But now (alas) soe times enthrall
None lives unto himself at all
Good Dayes are fled and truly soe
To us that sufferd them to goe   20
      When any one knowes how t'live best
      Ther let him fix and set up's rest.

Ep.-90.Li:2   ***To Quintillian***

      Great master of the Roving Youth of toun
      Quintillian Glory of the Roman gowne

>   Guive leav that I though poor may hast to live
>   Since ther's soe few clayme this prerogative
>   Let them differ Their Joyes who will for me   5
>   To become great in Publike History
>   A Fier 'neath such a Roof as may preferr
>   A good Black smoak to be its shadower
>   With a quick spring and herbes from Nature's store
>   I will but aske one slave to wayt noe more   10
>   Let not my wife be learned but create
>   My night for rest my day without debate.

Ode—To a frend in Imitation of these 1648

            Ned—might I sit
    In a black Chimny Corner closs by Thee
                With comfortable Ale and Tost
                Brown as the Berry Nutt, or Rost
    Presented in a Bowle Resembling it   5
    With what Content, with what Securety
                Would I imbalme my quiet and Conclude
                All Fortunes else to be but Interlude

                Thorp when I name
    The Neen, the Ancient Burrough and the Meer   10
                Clayme Their remembrances as due
                And though remote bring back to you
    That hart and that Affection's still the same
    All of distrust and Jealousy to cleer
                Soe that when hopes our Contemplations rear 15
                To second meeting they may banish fear

                That's Incident
    To those Great places in the State posess
                Whither Imployd to Furle, to Hale
                To Trim to Steer in every Gale   20
    The Great Rich Carack of the Parlement
    Which as it out sayles all soe all goe less
                Yet ther's left happines for him that can
                Neither be Chayre nor yet Committe man

                A good warme herth   25
    With a Plump, Buxom, Blith, and Bonny Lass
                For nature's help, and the fier fed
                With wood had nere been Sequestred
    To yeild a cleerer Flame to truer merth,
    Next the Great Loafe, and Rib of Martemas   30
                To which when Hopps are cheap and malt grown deer
                Wee'l quit our nut brown Ale and drink March beer.

[*A Christmas Carroll to the*
Earle of WestmoreLand

Now Christmas comes
But for the plumbs
T'enrich the pie
No one have I
Wher's now the tree 5
Of Rosemarie
To grace the Brawn
(As cleare as Lawn)
Whose proper wine
Is Muscadine 10
Or capring sacke
All which I Lacke
Wher's now the Beefe
Of Viands cheife
The Porke the veale 15
That glutts the meale
The Goose the Grice
The birds of Price
Nor thes nor those
My table know's 20

But you have Sir the Pheasant
The Riffe the Raile
The cock the Quaile
And other fowles as Pleasant

And to this store 25
You may have more
To glad your geniall Table
Which I poore I
Can never buie
Because I am not able 30

Poor Larr as yett
Do's starving sitt
(Much like a here)
Expecting still
To have his fill 35
Of boild or else of Rost-here

Then doe noe worse
But ope your purse
And bounteous Lord remember
To give us that 40
Will make us fatt
And frolike this December]

His answære to the Caroll

Robin—Like Copper guilded ore
The sheafe of plenty at the dore

             Whenas within
             A meger Larr and thin
             Leaves thee no more t'in-heritt   5
         'Save a quicke ayry fancy spiritt
         I shall conclud it is not meate alone
Or drinke yelds contentation
But wheire the Muses doe bestow
Their doles, thence true contentments flow   10

Cherish—and entertaine this good time then
With wine from Hippocrene
                 And let that Twinny Hill
Thy Pies in stead of Plumms with Disticks fill
Till they create   15
A well dish't feast to satiate
Those pallates that have not their relish lost
But can taste dainties where there is noe Rost
Nor at Pie corner meete
To rifle newgate market, Gratias streete   20

Thes—the Gods knew not: why should wee
Deale in this sorded Higlery
Skim Cheape side Kettles to become
More perfect sonnes of Christenome
A Caroll sung   25
In the wide Hall with Holly and Ivy hung
Flagons of Beere
Now wine is deere
That had not kist the brew fatt since last yeare
With bacon I confesse shall not want here   30

For—whilst the Gracchi and the fulvii strive
At once t'put down and strech prerogative
I will not Judg't a misse
To kisse my Tub like to Diogines
Keepe closse at home   35
For he lives well that doth soe as say some
Yet to the end
My Robin not despaire of one poor freind
He Pumps his Magazin and checker tries
To adde unto his Lyrickes some plumbe Pies   40

Upon the Death of the Lord Hastings sonn to the now Earl of Huntington   1649

Is ther a Bright starr fallen from our Sphere
Yet none sets out some newer Kalender?
Doe the Orbs sleep in Silence? is the Skeam
Struck dumb at th'apprehention of such Theam?
I shall not challenge Booker heer, nor will I   5
Call up the Mathemat-like dreams of Lilly
To search the reasons, sift Prognosticks out

How this soe sad disaster came about
Since that to every one it is well known
The Best and pretiousest will soonst be gon   10
Such Greef by th'cause is haightned to excess
And wher that falls expression goes less
Yet if we'd skan why thus He's Hasting hence
His Name may guive you some Intelligence
   The world with Him this opposition had   15
   He was too Good for it and that too bad.

In Fallacem Leguleium Epigramma

No one might plead til he first swore to th' Crown
Fallax did swear and then put on the Gown
But when the Covnant's up, Allegianc down
Fallax did Covnant and puts on the gown
At length th'Ingagement runs about the town   5
Fallax engaged and put on the gown
Nay should the Divel charge him with his frown
Fallax would doe it to keep on his gown

Upon min Hostes Bland at Tousester

Trust not too much thy flattring Bland but know
Thy Evning frend may prove thy morning Foe.

HOUGHTON LIBRARY, HARVARD:fMS.ENG.645
POEMS, 1637-61

Upon the Strange adventure and memorable voyage of Prince Tomaso ali:
Black Tom from wansford bridg to London the 29th of October-53

I'le bring noe foreign Voyage on this stage
From Mandevil or Purcas Pilgrimage
Nor will I rake Tom Coriats ashes ore
To coast the Lybian or Atlantike shore
My pen a subject home-bred cannot want   5
Whilst a brave squier goes up to Troy-novant
And for to guive both purce and body ease
Makes choice o'th'fower-wheeld-common passages.
    Wherin now mounted stately He exceeds
    The Fiery Pallfries with his eight good steeds   10
    At length drawn out whose every step they tread
    To the next comming wayne is registred
    In well tun'd bells (Squerrells incag'd some times
    I've herd present their Patrons with like chimes:
To consort with the thirsty Axel creaks   15
And faignes as if for Licker more it speaks
Such harmony seems plaintife making mone
As swine when their nose jewells they put on:
    Though these goe slow they'r sure, a pace preferd
    In state espetially when musik's heard   20
    For all the Triumphs Potentates are in
    Ought not to vanish quickly, but be seen
    Soe in a grave solemnity requier
    Noe swifter march than that o'th'Pismier
Thus then enthron'd this worthy wight appeers   25
As Prince to all the other Passengers
Commands and all obey: whom for to help
One straines ambitiously to serve his whelp
As a dry nurce; yet that she may guive milk
Before they part, He shews he is not Bilk   30
Hath some cards worth the owning, Hers turnd up
The game goes on they play their Tricks and sup
You'ld judg as in that Leather shell they sate
T'had been the Lobster Lady and her mate
By sun-burnt-russet-Packs the hue's exprest   35
Of that same crawling monster e're't be drest
Though like the horses time drawes out in length
He sate secure and fortifide with strength
Of double Packs like Gabions on a wall

To damp a shott or any harme might fall 40
Him or his Puppy, and soe stowd for worth
The Curtaines drawn He noe wayes peepeth forth
For fear of a discov'ry (Gould thats fine
Lies deepest in the Caverns of the mine
And soe to set upon him self more price 45
He thus incoacht shunns all discoveries
    Jhon had not bought an ambling nag to ride
    To Paris could He'ha'been thus coachefide
    'T had saved Lepton horse-flesh, paynes, and work
    For once within his week he had seen York 50
But those were silly Travailers of owld
Could not reach this Invention, save their Gould
And in more state and ease contrive to be
Transported with like great solemnity
    Now when one Prince unto an other sends 55
    Embassadours attended by their frends
    Accoast his court wher met with Lords and Gentry
    They'r huisher'd in as They first make their Entry
That this with His she frend as he draws nigh
The suburbs may not want Civility 60
And due respects but met with a like Train
I doe proclaime their Entry Carter-Lane.
                                  Basta

Upon a mischance or fall

    As dark as pitch
    The night in which
Noe moon nor star appears
    A Doctor Bowld
    His steps mistowld 5
Soe tumbled downe the stears

    Twas in October
    And he was sober
For as if thirsty he fell
    And brused his head 10
    That he lay for dead
At the dore of the Fresco sell

    Soe He never spoak
    Though his pipe it was broak
His box of Tobacco and all 15
    His browe and his eyes
    Did suffer likewise
Was not this a terrible fall?

    Yet at the length
    He guatherd some strength 20
And came to himself again

  Complaines his director
  And Lant-horn protector
Had plotted to beat out his braine

  Why should we then skorn   25
  The Light or the horne
When those of such use may be
  To save and defend
  As the daylight doth end
And conduct in securety   30

  I will noe more wonder
  Though't lighten and thunder
We uppermost Fates must endure
  And yeild to all's don
  Heer under the sun   35
Soe Phisitian thyself thou mayst cure

  To H.T. into Nor[folk]

My Noble Holl
 Nor Kate nor Doll
 Nor Gibb, nor Hodges Mary
 Nor Ruth nor Bess
I shall express   5
 Nor Jone looks to the Dairy

But my desire
 Is set on fire
To tell Thee some good story
Yet it shall not   10
 Speak Coriot
Nor Ambeling Jhon Dory

There is a Knight
 Whose spurrs shine bright
And thus I doe Embrace him   15
When thither I goe
 Though't be noe snow
You redely may Trace him

'Tis not Ban Bon
 Nor Watt, but Jhon   20
Though Cunny oft awaks him
He seldom Knocks
 Until the Fox
Catch him and speachles makes him

Then out He's led   25
 Unto some bed
Or couch neer to the same
Where again up start

  He cries sweet hart
   I fayth I am very lame   30

  He came t'afford
   His owld Land Lord
  His Company not Rent ho
  Til as I sayd
   He was well payd
  And a good lodging stent to   35

  Whence the next day
   He slips away
  As silent as the swimmers
  For being so Kind
   He'had utterd's mind   40
  Before, after some Brimmers

  His dry soule up
   Calls for a Cup
  Then mounts his steed noe Trotter
  And Gallops home   45
   Wher fittly come
  He may teach Docter Potter

Hug Gross: Epigram to J. Douse of the Woad of Holland taught English

  That I some miracles may rowse
  To tempt the strangers Faith my Dowse
  Know that allthough noe flocks heer stray
  Minnerva's Spinsters seldom play
  We dwell in Touns are very good   5
  Though in a Cuntry bears no wood
  All's Pasture, Ceres field we lack
  With heaps of Grain yet barnes do crack
  Our Sellers full with Vessells stand
  Yet heer no vines for th'Pruners hand   10
  Heer Flaxen stalks are very rare
  Yet tel me wher more Hollands are?
  Our Dwellings to the waters joygn
  Yet Douse our thirsts we quench with wine
              W

Song or Ode
Upon the speakers of either houses leveing their charges and runing away to the Army

  The Parliment sat soe long without head
  Til never a speaker was left in each house
  Jack Presbiter made his will and was dead
  And all was ordaind, prov'd not worth a louse

Sing round about every one to's trade a gaine
Let shoomakers noe more exceed their Last
Nor Princes obey that Subjects might raigne
Lest thes become all long Letters at Last
How comes it about there was found of Late
A trick to put all authority downe
But that some would change a Monarch to State
And with their mil breath Blast the Flowers of the Crowne
   Sing round about let us forget to speake Duch
   And let our Mother tongue beare Command
   Let Insolence want necessities Crutch
Wherefore God bless the King and his Peeres
And all Loyall Commons what soever they be
That whilst Citty and army are goeing by th'eares
The Subject againe may have's Liberty
   Sing Round about Babilon twill be thy fall
   With Multitudes thou both houses dost awe
   Till now thy great army and Generall
   Doe seek to give thee and the Kingdom the Law
What proffitts it now magna charta to read
What of Foresta or the Petition of Right
Wher time Devoures all things upon them doe tread
And the best understanding is how to fight
   Sing Round about looke to thy owne and be wise
   Leave ofe to solicite thy cause in a forme
   Beleivt there will be neither sessions nor size
   But all will be under confusions storme
Unless by a timely returne from our sinn
Wee be able ore feavere soe much to prevaile
That as Members goe out our King may come in
Cutting of perpetuity in the intayle
   Sing Round about let the Just sphers and the skies
   That overlooke all below heere provide
   For the time thats to come wee become the more wise
   And Let the known Lawes alone be our guide

To Sir A W Clerk of the Kitt[chen] to K J Upon his well cookt Dish—now in print calld the Gut of K. James.

Reader behold what past times did afford
Heer set before ye on this dresser-bord
Where thou mayst find both Coke and Bacon which in
Good Diets Clerkship would commend the Kitchin
Then tell me ever if thou Knewst a Man
Write stronger from the spitt or dryping pann

Grace before meat and after to my L: Ch:

Gratia { gratis data / gratum faciere }

With Thankfull cap in hand you'l bring Grace under
But if Grace make you thankfull 'tis a wonder:

3. Graces

Fayth–Hope–Charety
Fayth I beleeve, and tis noe sin at all
To Hope that pride at length may have a fall
Yet Charitably I'le dispose my wish
That soe much Grace may never coole your Dish

Upon my falling Lame under suspition of the Gout only in December 1650

Excuses all but bootless are
When Payn becomes a Conqquerer
Since then I cannot put on boot
I forced am to goe on foot
And that denide too by the same   5
Reason I halt and soe goe lame
Now what is left to stand in stead
But t'goe on Crutch and ride a bed.

My taking Phisick to cuer my lamenes I make the Doctor speak

Courage my Lord: let not your fancy skan
The mixt complection of your Potian
Though it be nautious in tast and smell
Those first must suffer ill that would be well   5
Let not a female squeamishnes conclud
You weak but putt on manly fortitude
And roundly take it up then doun your belly
Then gutts will rumble and arse squirt I tel yea.

To my Frend Mun: gon to London to play at Tennice

Mun
  I that am thine, and thine all
Wish myself now a Tennice B—
Or else some wanton Lasses P—
For ther thou lovst to keep thy racket   5
But seing distance wo'nt afford
These let me be the Grid or Bord
That whilst thou cutst the Line with grace
Thou Hazard hitst or nickst a Chase
Equivolent to cause dispaire   10
Be th'service guiven nere so fayre
And if all this yet will not doe
Ile covet t'be some Madams troü
Soe slightly guarded that with ease
Thy B—s may find their passages   15

                Thus when thou winst and guivst me set
                I cannot Leese whilst Thee I get.

         In Rem publicam. Epigram that which is publike is Common

                    Res is a harlot Publique's Common
                    Yet They'r overcome by noe man
September-7°   Whilst Fayth is Drawn in to be
1651.   Of the same Sisternety
                    Beleef henceforth I shall averr   5
                    To be an Adulterer
                    Whilst of Truth it doth begett
                    No thing now but what's Counterfett.

                              My Lottery

         Cast crosse or Pile draw cutts that wee may see
         Once more what Lawes and what Religions bee
         Sithence Coupling time that Jealousies and feares
         Doe Valentize all things increase to payers
         As if that every star governd this Skie   5
         Borrowed its influence of Geminie
         Why Plunder I the spheres when our state falls
         Within a Packe for Gleeckes and Mornifalls
         Of Toms and Ases t'other coates Lay beare
         Out of our hands Ruft out and Tidied are   10
         For the Least Trumpe soe Qualifide may give
         A heave to the bests Cards Prerogative
         And warrant it whilst the Groom Porters mess
         Proves Authors Ephe to all passages
         Remarkeable, whither Diarnall ones   15
         Or else nocTurnall Lucubrationes
         Tis for Election Generally they fight
         And sitt in Counsaile to turne Day to night
         To say they floct or Covide might mainetaine
         They would submit to birdes of pray againe   20
         Or hearded (like the Gaddrens swine) were worse
         For that in titles to the Divells cursse
         What if I make them Bevy so akinn
         Unto the Dwarfy Elvish Gobbeline
         I shall not be mistaken whilst one Round   25
         Greene headless Tracts both their Contrivments found
         But be they more or fewer (to Conclude
         Their Powers from the Giddie Multitude
         Confusions Taskemasters like Pharos Press
         For truth and Peace yet Covet nothing Lesse   30
         When 'tis impossible whilst love they smother
         That Righteousnesse and peace should Kiss each other
         Disorders Favorites that faine would find
         A means to Calme the Sea by raiseing wind

Sell snow for fuell make Newcastles Tine 35
Send Coales ('thout Barkleyes leave) to coole their wine
Screw up impossibillities and then
Replant the Olive branch by raiseing Men
Or not by Laying downe armes again of those
So raisd, though enemie thers none t'oppose 40
Bring the King Home-by weeping X and thus
In stall him prisoner soe more Glorious
Than on his Throne where nothing he could awe
But travers by ascent Ordinance to Law
Canonick that would with its owne waight fall 45
And Create Scripture of Apocrifall
Stampe Majestie upon their Idoll Bell
And Dragon too in spight of Daniell
Thes be devouring beasts and must provide
For Preists and wives and Children beside 50
What ever Law and contience assayle
Blinde Tobits fawning Dog will wag his Tayle
In hopes by some new Levit to be read
And Text his first endowments maydenhead
If one be guifted stild by women soe 55
There is noe neede such goe to Jerico
Smoth face suits best unto a buterd tongue
And tis noe matter what soe he be yongue
Thus runs the female verdict, neighbours say
Wast not a rare yong man stood up to Day 60
In sooth methought his Teaching Did eclips
Suzannas story with her Elderships
O for a salique Law that might deny
The Petticoate and smocke supremicie
Judg if there were not Righteous Doings ment 65
When two together met with one intent
T'assault her chastity with Lust to th'Brim
And soe Set Antelers on Joachim
Yet this noe insest here our Mother is
Most shamefully polluted by the miss- 70
Created Independence alone
Whose Fancyes Law and will Religion
And thus free quarter and the Pulpit bring
A kind of Matrimony 'thout a Ring
Despisd cause Concords Emblem and the Gowne 75
By Buttend Preists and swords in belts put downe
A watch or clocke Growne fowle through age and rust
Condemned to a slower Turning must
Guive way to Time but here the Wheeles smoth worne
Precipitate the motion and scorne 80
To Stay for Time yet each alike comes under
The artists hand againe to take't asunder
None other must: O did wee thoroughly see
How many artless soules reformers bee

Of State and Churches wheles wee might mainetaine 85
They'd broken that they neare can set againe
For whilst they make Religion pretence
And order Law those both are driven hence
Wich when wee would restore I think't first good
The one were truly Knowne t'other understood 90

A game at Tables

Whilst wee play Rebells all at Levelcoyle
Who ist that Laughs ins sleeve the while
But Devill Pope and Turke
And is not this mad worke
Wee'd seeme to fight not Liberty to loose 5
Till I thinke Hells broake Loose
And all Conditions sexes and Degrees
Contend for Pedegres
To Blazon out in argent feild
A Dart Gules thats with malice steeld 10
Of the first house from Caine and of noe other
Soe's thought distinction from an Elder Brother
Only that he his Brother, wee our King
Must sacrifice helpe out in offering
And Call God t'wittnesse too: pray Fates 15
Wee find not Cains reward prove runnegates

Honos alit Artes

Arts all will pine now honours must goe downe
Though one once changed A sheepe hook for a Crowne
Had I as many Crownes as ere were borne
I'de pawne them all for one small barley Corne
Three Letters of the Alphabet the Nine 5
Recond forth first the twelve and the fifteen
Which Like a powerfull spell should straight untie
The Scepters mistick Knott of Monarchy
And Leave the Comon Wealth unlac't to ease
Her dropsie and Anarchicall disease 10
Untill each humor did breath out and then
The State being Cur'd I'de be myselfe again

An Independents Coate Blazond

Hee beares partly per pale Atheisme and Turcisme chargd with Liberty of Contience for Croysant or new Light soe is of the yonger House to Lucifer: his Hypocrety in devotion intitles him Enemy to the Crosse in Generall as well Salter as other though otherwise his avaritious dispositian makes him the greatest Idolater in the world Where they backe the Kings Image he 5
withstands all Goverment and soe carries noe Bend or chevern in his escuttchion a Dexter would doe him too much right and though indeed he may

seeme to deserve a sinister for Base yet his Intentions for truth the wrong
way discharge that too his Supporters are Popery and scisme which divide
his senclesse coate and soe would rend the seamless one. His mantle the 10
inspiration of his owne Phranatique fancy Under the cloake of Piety to cover
his—&c, his crest the Tower of Babell his word Confution he sekes to make
order or Discepline A Malignant and soe for delinqency endeavours to
imprison and beare it in a Canton crying downe peace as well as truth that
his upstart honors might mocke the honerable title of Baronett and prove 15
by Pattent hereditary and soe beares a bloody hand as well as heart in the
Centre of his Attchivements.

Upon New-Lights

What truths expectable truth to expound
When Mothers are crid up and Fathers downd
Nor Herolds-worth any credit though set by
With Browne-Brick Attlas of Divinitie
Austin and Jerom Ambros and to summ 5
Up all that Giulden-mouthed Chrysostom
Blasted for Popish obsolete beside
By those who seeke some newer Lights for guid
And Though the Scripture to it selfe preferr
The truest glass and best in-terpreter 10
Yet there are some soe mad inspird that will
Question the dictates of that sacred quill
Brand it Humane tradition and that those
Prophets or Patriarks in verse and Prose
Noe more then what the Egyptians schooles has gott 15
Or Jesses fruitfull Lawrel soe much wrote
Wonder of ages when the Lie is given
To truth it selfe how seeke wee after Heaven
And to shun Hell where all the misteries
Tend to promoate the Father of all Lies 20
But thus methinks like as each motian sent
To seeke its center proves more violent
By how much it approaches so't appears
The Divells Raign is in declineing yeares
And there upon he bends more rageing skill 25
To Bring more proselites in sak's to's Mill
Wher he may Grind all good in Tonle free and
Sever the Apostle Peter's flower from Bran
Syms-sonn Confute and call His Prophets nye
With Coale man to make warme his Forgery 30
Corne well may here begrownd and Brighter made
By Grinding too a Cousning shefeld Blade
Blacke well befits this story and the night
A favorer to every newer Light
Where Wills-sonn with a wispe Jennys Burnt arce 35
Seduce into that Dick or that Salt March

From such unholdsome moory grownds alone
Those Meters have Brought-on confusion
And Lest this Sacrament or tother should
Keepe faith and Charitie from waxing Could   40
These respit either as notorious crimes
That seeke to falsefie thes Later times
Whilst Disputations flow truths watters ebb
And thus our Church hath spun a faire webb
For Questions are raysd many none she thurroughs   45
More Like to Combs of Bees then Cunny Burroughs
Notorious Rogues whither elsewhere or Kent
That Dare deny the Blessed Sacrament
In either Kind whereby wee must put on
The fertile Hopes of our Redemption   50
But ye are all one graine and soe become
One Batch of Leven to sower Christendome
And if your Master that setts you a worke
Had don w'yea heere I'de wish yea with the Turke
Or Caniball to preach'em Tame and Civell   55
For like to lik saith Collier to the Divill:—

16-December 1641

Bishop for up goes soe that game is done
And all must be reformd to Henderson
The church was sick o'th'collect now receives
More comfort from what praire each brest conceives
And then of windy Instruments sett free   5
Admitts noe anthemes in her Lithregy
But Rubrickes Letany and compos'd prayer all
Contem'd and Condem'd Apocrifall
And second service (out upont) it's worse
Then Brawne and mustard servd for second course   10
The mimicke guarb and gestures speake noe Less
When Coppefide then Hocus Pocussis
And the superfluous sarke wore one the gowne
In penance for the whoredome of th'whol towne
With that of Babell need noe more be knowne   15
Sithence that we're purgd of superstition
What needs the hood and capp to shew degree
The mas is mas without such sophestry
Was not that plott a poore and silly one
To call a table made of oake a stone   20
For such were alters and to make a pownd
As if't had trespast in some neighbours grownd
When raileing better doth the Pulpit suit
Where other waye some Teacher would be mute
And choake fo want of Matter to be spun   25
With hawkes and humms untill the glasse be run
This Emblem of humanity ere I passe

I must acquaint theirs scandall too in glass
But tis the britler sex would thee expell
It may be cause in paint they them excell 30
And crave more adoration from the eye
Sithence by that crosse wee live by theirs wee die
Or is it thus such windowes call on night
And then themselves they'd have the Church more Light
Or Thinke they not they can be of renowne 35
Though they be up unlesse the glasse goe downe
Fond undertakers if your feares and Joyes
Were rightly plact yea need not straine at toyes
But your delights unsteady and your feare
Least her being allwayes drest yea come Late there 40

Epigram In Idem

My neighbour though to satisfie desire
Would of the steepel ring the Bells i'th'quire
And being offended much with what was wont
Of owld, ordaines the Belfrey for the font
Thus giveing innovation noe ease 5
Wee'r halfe transformed into Antipodes

Upon Master Alexander Henderson's Death and the Preaching Coachman

Greate Henderson the Scot is gon
Who Knockes downe now Roomes Babilon
If in such Boughs perch Jus divine
How ist the Trunck should thus decline
Unlesse prevention heere had end 5
To save the weight of such a freind
And Nature to deny this Clay
Desert, quits it the Common way
Soe he lies silenced and dead
Who would have Bishops Silenced 10
Where are wee now who strikes the stroake
To resett Government thats broake
A Clock that is in sunder tain
May goe a gaine if Pinns remaine
To sett the wheeles together butt 15
Those lost it cannot move one jot
Forme was before reforming skill
As accon's still succeed the will
But that wee might more Passions Know
Heere wee'd run first then Learne to goe 20
Lay downe all government before
To take up one on a new scoare
Religion Bankerouted I feare
Ther's few can tell th'account to cleere
But in arithmatick goe on 25

Noe further can then Fraction
Or if they Multeply at all
Tis mischeife how t'make others fall
Divisions easy and the high-
Way, unto cheife authoritie   30
Not as our Saviours rules advise
By going Less to seeke to rise
But skiping up at once and there
As greate as John the Presbiter
Why was the buildings corner stone   35
Joynd with a Rock foundation
Of greatest proofe gainst wind and storme
If vertue was not raisd by Forme
Or did that seamlesse garment once
Christ chose to put on for the nonce   40
Emblem division I should bee
Convinc't wee ought not to agree
But as the twisted cords define
The truest seale of discepline
Soe let the Gospell changers all   45
Whose Doves have more then others gall
Expect whilst they exceed their last
Presumpsion chase them out as fast
For I beleeve that many Knocks
May beate a Coach man of His Box   50

To Northampton

A Garison? what else: dost thou not heere
The sufering drum awake the shoomaker
To March beyond his Last, and chang his worke
To fight against the Cawy: worse than Turke
And though there never were more Hides then now   5
Tis not the weell tann'd skinn of Horse or Cow
Hee seeks to purchase naught stands him instead
Save Cavileeres skinns soundly Curried
Of such he covets to gett many a Dicker
For winter waere because theile take their Licker   10
Calves-skins is his owne cushion and the fells
Of the flockes bleaters he at market sells
All but what heads the Drum and those hee keeps
Quiets disturbers enemies to sleeps
With the revelia March and the tatoo   15
Wich by Instinct he learnt from boots or shooe
Why are there scooles for Artists to Commence
When here a bylke hath such intellegence
Nay to Divide the tex of discipline
And measure out the flanker curtaine line   20
With such Dexteritie as one might swere
That Mars had spawn'd these meteors from his sphere

Let all their trade from Etna can derive
Looke to their Venusses Lest those they—
For tis most sure where inspirations been 25
Concupiscence is but a veniall sin
Like good Arithmatitions here they trie
How to Substract that they may multyply
And by Divisions Logerisme show
Those were but siphers now for figures goe 30
Counting from one to hundreds the while
Tis hundreds to one but they beguile
Both state and Church and as the Proverbe say
Chuse in thes sunshine Daies to make their Hay.

The Cosmography of this County

It alwaies in former times stood distinguished by Longetude of east and West and yet held paralell the Hundreds to all services but now it is Lancht wounded and cut through by so many miridian Lines hott fiery Zealots or rather bonte feux firebrands of Cisme and seeds men of all seditions that it accknowledges noe bounding Tropicks but strives to Lay Levell in the 5 Equator both Day and night a Like Pesant and Peer noe difference twixt Thrones and Coblers Bulkes nor is it girt thin other then the Torrid Zone and Soe spitts Flames-fire and Sword gainst Crowns and Scepters, all authority but what such Preach would Deeme their Pulpits Poles soe make Charles Wayne the which without prevention, that timely too will set al soe on fire 10 by the rash attempts of these state Phaetons that wee shall becom moores soe blacke through Guilt of Fond conceipt and all Disloyaltie that noe streams of our Masters grace and mercy (who is an ocean of such) shall wash us white soe make us innocent to God, to Him, ourselves but whilst thus vayne wee may proclaime our Labour and endeavours to bee noe lesse and 15 rest at the unprofitable ridiculus signe.

An invective against Gould the corrupter of all

Why doe wee Lay the blame to that or this
Of any thing is acted heere a miss
And the true cause pass by why all states move
To cherish hatred and to banish Love
The Mortals God is nothing else but Gould 5
Wherewith all happinesse was bought and sould
Can reach noe higher then this world preferrs
Unto its sence beguilled Pasengers
This hath a Place an other would it guet
Brothers of Tindarus one star must set 10
To elevate the others Pole and here
Envy the orbe Contention fills the sphere
And all this from below earth but refin'd
By influence soe workes upon mans mind
That without difficulty Ide mainetaine 15

Affections captivd in a goulden chaine
Lawes and Religions are but traines to draw
Weaker capasaeties under this Awe
When neither truly meant becom once skand
Youl find them only steps to rayse command   20
Increase Possessions highten Pride untill
All Soveranties comprised 'thin the will
Of Him that to such riches can attaine
And Powre as t'mak this world his Soveraigne
But though pretence with a faire Light may shine   25
Whilst not etheriall't shall not be mine
Nor will I from my first foundation err
But Keepe a Rowland for an Oliver.

Epigram on the times

A-Peace A-Peace whilst every one doth seeke
It spells noe peace, if wee but turn't to Greeke
Wherefore A-Warr A-Warr I would mainetaine
Which is noe Warr. then 'twould be peace againe

On King Cromwell

It doth comend the stampe of every coyne
When't beares resemblance with it's Soveraigne
I wish that wee awaken not that old
Base Romish mettalle Tinkers trash for Gold
For if our Charles not fill up but still waine   5
Leaveing not C.R. but K.C. to raigne
His Brazen face and Copper Nose will runn
For Currant better then a Harrington
Those were but Tokens but for these we're sure
They'l turne a Plague that will admitt no cure   10
Then Lord have mercy on us who alone
By speedy Power can worke prevention.

To Hugh Peters

Hugh 'twas a grosse mistake when men did call
The Peter's, for thou more belongst to Paule
And strivs't to make the scripture good from hence
Heavens Kingdome is attained by violence
Tis force not Keyes must the strait gate unbarr   5
And soe thou art becom a sonne of warr
Canon-Bonerges if there doe not want
Faith to beleeve their's few soe Valiant
As thou hast beene, cutting of men 'thout feare
As each had been but Malchus'es right eare   10
This thy owne Sarmants speake and in a word
Thou married hast the Pulpit to the sword
This to maintaine that that hath been thy skill

To Draw out this to murther slay and kill
But if thou wilt Pauls Masters will mainetaine 15
Thou must leave striking and Put up againe.

To Sir Thomas Fairfax

Though thy pretences may for fair stand
Black Tom the rest in Latine's fire brand
And soe I feare thou art who prict with fame
Embroylst thy native country in a flame
In vertues schoole those doe not more excell 5
Who conquer; than who manedg Conquest well
non minor est virtus &c

Upon Jack, Tom, Will, and Dick

Jack would live Batchelour yet neds must wive
Tom goes although hee'l neither Lead nor drive
Will from his charge roavs and Condemned is
Dick stayes at marke and that is judg'd a miss
Will Tom Dick Jack may well examples bee 5
To point out this worlds mutability.

For A Treaty

Shall's treat what else for there in may be found
Means to In-treat the King to be uncrown'd
Soe ordinances to doe may have noe-more
When St: John's Will, and Martin hath his whore
Without controwle each member else (uppright 5
As reformation) may speake or write
What witt or Fancy dictates, and therein
Though it crosse disposition 'tis no sinn
For that the Breach of Law imployes when here
Noe forfeit of a Cabb: or Covenanteer 10
Soe much imports as may the Kingdomes Jarr
Reiteraite and imbroyle in second warr
If the King more or Parliment have lesse
To say, who is't that is the misteris
That Governs all (but freedom) to that still 15
Example Led is fostered by will
For wher the Prince obeyes the People sway
Soe Subjects oft times Soveranties betray
Yet wher noughts sought but what the Lawes require
Hees tyrant and no King doth more desire 20

Upon Madam Severa

I shall not spare when I severa praise
For I then write of Rosemary and Bayes
Nor must the Sun shine but the Heavens all vow

To Sympathise her sullen Lowry brow
Smiles all call'd in noe cheerefullness once dare
In such ore shadowed night-peice to have share
But when thick clowdes open too much of light
Ile borrow for my Inke the darkest night
Where Batts and Skreech owles from their wings shall Lend
Me velom and a Pencell to Commend
Her rare endowments that are inward spent
Upon her selfe in fostering Discontent
Yet Like t'a bird new scapt out of a cage
They'r fledg And breake sometimes int'open rage
Bring her a child to Tyrannise upon
And then the Rods her recreation
Which on the suffering buttocke she employes
Untill they blush to see her cruelties
Then if a Servant man or maid doe err
She proves both Divell and the cungerer
And what her wand or fist cannot effect
Their sure to have it from her Dialect
For that small weapon fæmales armd withall
Which was the cause of Tantaluses fall
She wilds soe nymbly and soe sharply whets
That all mens valours seeme but counterfetts
To her high Prowes; thus she conquest brings
By hooke, by hand, by tongue as snakes by stings.

Upon Madam Severa and her Gierle Friskin

Like medlers lockt up safe when they are gotten
Not to prove only ripe for foode, but rotten
Soe did Severa to her girdle tye
Her Darling friskin for securitie
And hatcht this chickin still under her wing
Till the wingd God found means to cast his sting
Through her feathers and the gierle mans meate
Resents the Operation of his heate
And become Gamester, strait on payes her box
Then Like a Rotten Peare she's ripe with pox

Upon the Petitionall rising in Kent June-1648 and their defeate by Fairfax

Is Kent orecome? their enterprize dispatcht?
Twas cause they'd count their Chickens fore their hatcht
And Build on fruit abundant ere they knew
Whither or noe there should arise mill dew
Might Blast their hopes and nip such budding skill
Of coupling to humillitie free will
First thei'd Petition, or at Least pretend
In humble sort their sutes to recommend
To higher powers then of armes possest

Thei'd turne that to a warrant was request 10
And mustering up the glory of their power
That had withstood the first King-Conquerour
Monopolize that tytle as not meant
Of any County save (unconquered) Kent
But mark the Issues those before did err 15
Being vanquished by Browne the wood monger
Thought noe dishonour now nor sham at all
To take a Route from the Lord Generall
And thus retireing each unto his home
Some to their Long, some to their short are come. 20

To Captaine Minous after his returne the 9th time from the East Indes

Minor thy name alone goes lesse
Thy actions more of worth express
For though th'whole gloabe it self hath been
Travild by thy Countrymen—   {Drake
Yet 18 times to pass the Line   {Candish 5
Could be non others act but thine
Wherefore let those thrice Sisters Three
Record ye to Posteritie
Who nine tymes hast observd the Tyde
Where Ganges waves and Indus slide 10
That whilst thou Heaven and Seas found Kind
Letters Befreind may with faire Wind
To give encouragement whereby
Majors may Minus fortunes trye.

Upon Breaking the Seals because of the Kings Image on them.
or the states Polecy
Ego frangam te ne tu frangas me

Whilst policy doth thus provide
Better Destroy than t'be Destroy'd
More pitty I than wonder Lacke
For Seals and all that goe to wrack
But how will thos hence forward drive 5
On their design'd prerogative
Unless they doe a new one gett
May be their owne, noe Counterfett
Which should I proffer I'de not seek
To other caracter, then Greeke 10
That alphabet hath some one Letter
May for their pardons graunt serve better
Than any now our King is gon
Bears Longer Superscription
Than when they doe for mercy call 15
A Letter Long may conclude all

A Summons to Frank Beumonts Gost upon reviving one of his owld playes

Beaumont arise slumber no more in Clay
It's Lawfull to revive a good owld play
Heere such a one from thy Prophetick Vaine
A King and no King's acted ore againe
Whilst Cap and Knees cheap loyalty doe poynt 5
A Soveraigne whose power out of joynt's
Bereft of strength, yet like a legg or arme
Which are noe less the same for any harme
Through mischance this Majestie still bears
The stampe of his renown'd Anchesters 10
For Trumpets sound then enter King with ease
And Ratefie what ere thy Subjects pleas
By a great suit greatness is understood
Then here wee may conclude noe ebb, but flood
A full high sea which from the Deeps belch forth 15
Soe many Pibbles stones, and shells of worth
As crave his stooping to, whilst they begett
The Private strictness of a Cabbinet
Opend for wonder sake, then shut againe
Not as himselfe pleases but as his Train 20
Where nothing can distinguish him a hayre
From them but as the stage allowes a chayre
And guards afore and after which relate
To Prince and match captivitie to state
Yet in this Dreame he (Patience tryd) snores out 25
In hopes (spectators weary) t'bring about
An other scene wher in the world to show
His Kingdomes loss is his own overthrow
And therefore to maintaine himselfe and them
Resolved is against all streams to stem 30
Advise the contrary and gives consent
To's minds concurrence with his Parlement
Things once thus brought to pass (if I but durst)
I would conclude Exit K. Charles the first

Some playes like Ladies would implore 35
A Prologue usher them before
To speak the greatness of the Plott
Here such prevention needs not
This is of that transcendent skill
It goes for good though acted ill 40
Nor Revel Masters place nor those
Call'd the Townes witts once dare t'oppos
It doth in Bishops posture sitt
And silence every Cittrick witt
The Scoape thereof both sets apart 45
And sequesters the Cream of art
Soe that all expectations tend
To nothing now but t'marke the end
Which if good her'l be noe cause

> For Epilogue to beg applause 50
> (Worth will reward it selfe) but base
> Will alter quite the skoals and case
> Whilst Baldnesse needs a Perrewigg
> Clownes will not laugh without A Jigg.

To invite my Lord to walke in the Tower

> A Crop of honor tis he reaps
> Who walketh in his Fathers steps
> Wherfore my Lord I pray think't fitt
> To act something may merit it
> For none but prisners now walke there 5
> And I would have you his true Heier

Upon Prince Charles riding in the Downes

Rides Charles i'th'Downes and doe wee warpe and wend
As if our Everlasting had noe end
Is all the Ayme wee drive at and the scoap
To lie at Anker and be moord i'th'Hope
Unfurle and let us waygh for shame to meete 5
With Love and Loyaltie this featherd fleet
Whos Lading doth containe of Treasure more
Than Jasons Argo brought from cholchos shore
His was a fleece if wee may credit Tayles
But hers a mine of Gould a Prince of Wales 10
Adorn'd with such rich vertues as comprise
The wayghty mas of Thousand treasuries
Hoyse up your top sailes Gallants and create
A wind may ever more be fortunate
To him and his designes and such a one 15
As may new christen each day Halcion
When as the stormy Gusts of discord cease
And stile our Ile againe the Bay of Peace.

On the Mayor of Evsham

> Hee is him selfe a beast or worsse
> That calls the Mayor of Evsham horse
> For those can only prance and Kick
> But he had lernt an other trick
> To strayne the saddle make it wider 5
> And soe at last to cast his Rider
> For thus the staffe and mace mainetaine
> Vice gerent ship to soveraigne
> And hee to'th'haight of Justice bent
> May chance be come a President 10
> Now Gentle Sir what ere men call ye
> In shop or bulke where ere they install ye
> That word when meant of thee at least

Can signifie nothing but beast
Soe tis a controversy whither 15
The Mayor a greater beast be or the other

Upon the Perfume Pembrooke left when he was sent to bid this world good night The Second of May 1649

Have you observd the poysoning breath   Fama mendax for
Of a Corps sequesterd by Death   he outlives the day
Or beene made happie with the sent   not the Perfume
Of a Draught full of excrement
Smelt you e're savory fumes arise 5
From the gold finding mis'eries
Or Candles snufte after the flame
Was spent, even such is Pembrokes fame
Now he is out who living tride
To pawne his honor e're he died 10
But that had blasted beene before
Soe sweld to nought but chancelour
Of a great schoole who cannot passe
Censure for chusing such an—
Whos parts and learning bound in one 15
Make but a Gotam Alkeron
Now though the fates decreed his set
He could not die in vertues debt
For he soe little had of her
With eas he turnd a Commoner 20
And there in displaid his Jewel's Banner
Whilst his contention was w'th'tanner
Soe as St George the Dragon slew
Hee becam Knight and foyld this few
Then for his hatt band he Kept it 25
To compass in his little Witt
Yet he houlds worth to be employd
In the successfull Conquering side
And would each fellow peere invite
To be a State Hermophrodite 30
Which through liberties pretext
Might chirish most the thriveing sex
And those ye thus yeild way to fall
May gaine at length the Devill and all

    Cause Oxford's silent this I Wright 35
    To prayse its Chancelour Barksheirs Knight

Cambridge and Oxford

How com'st about when Sisters are coheirs
Ours hath but one but theirs hath Chancelers

Or why did fate make different in the power
Send one to'th'feild the others to the Tower
Unless the plot this double sence affords 5
Minervas th'one th'others for th'records
Were sent to search t'Apollo did belong
Soe that sought fame those others but a song
Yet doe I find there was in this some skill
To make th'one sister like th'two headed hill 10
And least the others bridg should pass the broke
Or ford the Parliment an order tooke
To keepe them safe that if the bill should bee
Passing to give the King a subsedy
Neither might suffer but preferrment find 15
One voated first before the last behind
Now whilst both houses to Keepe fast the praise
Belong to'th'one let t'other weare the Baies.

On Pembrokes Languishing Diseas

Hee is not out: but howlds up still one eye
One heart one hand against integrity
To Church and state and like a Candles winking
flame goes in and out soe more doth stinke
Had he kept silence when first voyced dead 5
His speeches had noe more gainst sence beene read
Nor Personages of honor rackt and rent
To heere him chatter downe owld government
In praise of that wherein noe stampe is seene
But Lyberty for Envie, malice, spleene 10
To vent without an oath which hee forbears
Before the Saints else like a Divell swares
As he was wont yet not in body well
Noe more then witty is not ripe for Hell.

Upon Gutt A Greate Glutton

Of all the meate doth fatt increace
Ther's none like owld beans and peas
The Bacon Hogg weene nothing good
For all the graines without such foode
And Leistersheir of all the rest 5
Of Counties can afford the best
Wonder not therefore Gutt dwelt there
Where from the Tith of double beere
And black eyd flatt corne he cast up
A Bellied Round provender tubb 10
Soe as A Mule that Traviels goes
With Laden basket at her nose
Hee (but a Kin to her) Commands
His Struted bin up with his hands

                And broaken winded breaths uneven   15
                As he was Atlas and his Loade the heaven

                If with a Child or such a thing
                God bless him It must be guttling
                For soe the Spawne preserves the Kind
                Of Fish and men as piggs doe swine   20
                The Gaddarens of him might boast
                Who Chas't their King out of their coast
                And he would Know who by this same is meant
                Heede goe noe further but conclude it—
                                                out of Christendom   25

The Prologue to the Dream

Robd of my vessell by that PiRat fate, and left but with 2 long boats and a
Cock, I cast a bout where to be furnished, to set to sea againe, and what by
Freinds, what by my owne endeavours, I lit on, a: crick, where bottomes
Lay yet such as had, great want of yards else were they Ridg'd enough, which
to supply whilest I did not despaire, I guest I mought at easy rate have   5
Boughton At last this vapour fancy vanished:

                Into a Dream which if you can afford
                A single smile I'me Laden and aboard.

My Dream the 8 of September 1637

As I passt by the Downes methought I mett with A fleet consisting of a
Pinass called the Royall Fancy and 3 whelps, at first I put forth false Colours
at which the Pinass or rear-Admire-all (for soe it seemd shee had been in
her younger time and might be still by her Command) bearing a flagg staffe
on her misen and the second whelpe calld the safeguard (soe ill built that   5
shee heeld much and therefore it were noe prise to take her) hald me to
Larbord of them to know whither I was bound which soone Resolvd I passt
them /—but I had skearce made a board or two but the wind tackt soe
about that I was perforce driven under their Lee againe soe that Then I had
noe other way to avoyd their great and less shott (being all this while sus-   10
pected) but to discover myselfe by my scarlet Ensigne to be A Merchant
adventurer their Countryman Friend and not an Enemy Then did they all
unvale unto me and afford all curtesie saveing to suffer me to com aboard
on of them which for some curiosity I affected yet therein finding difficulty
I made the best use I could of bearing up with them .3. Daies soe left them   15
to their course whilst I tooke mine, The yongest whelpe I chrisned the true
Paragona The Admire-all off the whelps as I had it of the pin-ass was calld
the Repulse: a proper vessell shee is yet seems as if her Bowsprit lay too low
and forecastle did stoope soe yet shee carries not an even Keele but yet being
lancht Farther for all that sheele prove snugg and draw more at the poope   20
or stearn then at the head she is high carv'd and Therefore would require
the larger compass in her sides or Ribbs which when I had surveighd
Methought I found the timbers not soe due proportioned as I had seene yet
warantable enough and like to sayle well soe that she have good store of

stones to ballance her which yet she wants she was not guilt at all yet, but
in hopes to be soe in revertian Then how trim'd for the present I shall lean
on you to Judge her cloths be smootty as if weather tride allready surely she
is not leaky although noe Savour ill rise from her pumpe her Decks were
plaine yet comly and her Launtorne open to shew 'twas darke for light shee
bore none the mast was first set in her now was spent and she was Riggd
anew to the pinasses forme and bore noe Crosse at all but o'th' s' top gallant-
flag for pennants streamers, and like galentry. she put not forth cause it was
worke day and soe shee Knew her Taske, her ports were closse shutt downe
that you would sware she might ride out with safty and repulse the highest
Sea within the bay of Biskey yet some scuttle holes under her decks I judge
: were open At her first launching Ankers were put forth to bring her to her
Ana- moorage but they all finding the ground *les-sur came home againe yet she
gram without them hath obtained her end, her cheifest now's the hope she hath
Vessel to be broak up at Last and built againe upon some Prinses bottom noe ship
else of all the royall Navie will Content her and soe twere fit she were for
upon triall made I find her good only before the wind now and nothing
yare at helm at all: with under Decks unseene I guesse but ordinary only
for feare to lessn and soe spoyle her selfe-love Cabbin she would not admit
on any tearms of bearing of .2. My-sons: her sights or wast-cloths died were
by despite into a Tawny and soe suted best to Emblem what the Rage of
time might doe upon her beauty for neglect to it:

She had noe ordinance savd What the Pinass pleasd to afford her who gave
fire to all only for two chase peices she had stowd under her peack-head
Will a Demy Can-non and Resolution but a Mignion she had noe mur-
therers abord that I saw: she went before such a conceipted-wind that Maine
sayle top sail and s'top gallant too with fore sayle spright sayle and the Mison
were filld to the streach untill the sheets did crack soe she did goe a tripp:
Though many tides prov'd contrary shed steere stoutly against them till she
win aport then though she ride in berth but third to the chaine, shes first
fro'th'Church; what gibing by her boards procur'd were her owne sayles were
the best interpreters If she but hould this play a yeare or two shee'le fittest
be to coast the narrow seas soe be proclaim'd a Man of warr at least for by
that time shee'l beare an ancient o'th'stearne and soe may well be say'd to
wayt too long upon the Pin-asses stere-age. I think if any then shall goe in
her they'l find themselves I'th' straights: I thought her to have found the
Happie Enterance and Swallow too but it seems they were designd some
other coast yet in this fleet besides there Rod a Frigott calld the Baga-cara
and two ould gully foysts I never examind their Ladings for I saw never a
Catch amongst them all: twas not the North but an Eastar was guide unto
their Pilotts soe it wanted Pole and I did seek to Joygn on.* My Fleet con-
sisted but of .5. in all first for discovery was the Confidence where in I tooke
the van and went first on the second was the Dread naught, third the Defi-
ance (both very Stout and Dareing vessels) they did serve to make the fight
good and the Convertin did bring me ofe but being slow of sayle I shifted
into the swiftsure: And imbarkt in her soone I lost ken of them and soe
awack't finding my selfe not at the Downes in Kent But with my hounds
on Stamford heath yet thence I saw deale-faire which from the other
Downes by reason of a fogg vapord from prid and foly skerce appeard. They

loost ofe me as I conceivd to make the Coast of Devonshire and soe turne
fishers after Folly (Their owne I mean) yet then methought they mought   75
have sav'd that Labor for they were soe frighted with the same kind of Mer-
chandise allready as If thei'd tane a huge and mighty draft of't).

Epilogue to the Dream or an Epigram upon a thrice faire peece

When first upon my East-star I did looke
I found her fixt yet I was plannet strooke
And wondreing which o'th'seaven she might bee
Methought shee could be non but Hecate
For what of beauteous feature nature Lent   5
Was well enricht by arts Imbellishment
Then for to add to both a treble price
Sh'had learnt for to be fooleish, Coy, and nice,
Soe at this marke, I durst noe Longer stick
Feare t'be transform'd into a Lunatick.   10

Me nive Cadente petijt mea Julia, rebar
Igne carere nivem, nix tamen Ignis erat—Ovid

Snow falling Julia Me did press
At which I 'gan admire
The heat in snow, yet found noe less
That snow itself prov'd fier.

Unto a Lady: that refus'd her amorous Knight his Aproaches for him

Be-vile as is thy Name now I have sworne
To hate as much as I did love before
Thy other name although by blood thou'rt half
A rich proclaimes the but to be a Calfe   Es.
For were faith pinnd to fame thy Damms a Trull   5
Soe was thy Sire for certaine made a Bull
Or sithence the forrest strecht its bounds soe farr
As P[ir]goe he becam of Antler
A goodly stagg, lett him goe change his ground
When the King comes to Hunt least he be found   10
But for thy selfe thou needs't not take that care
I'le nere uncoupell wher thy footsteps are
Nor break myselfe of sleep more for to seeke
A Harts returne from a Deceiptfull cheeke
    fronti rara fides   15

Upon the Scotsh business—1638

Without an interposing Sea or wall
The Picts doth into disobediance fall:
Nor will conform: what is the cause? how is't?
Why thus he is become a Sepratist

Yet all His Covenant-Conventicles are 5
For a defensive not ofensive warr
Soe were my counsailes heard I should perswade
Not with the Drum and Trumpet him t'invade
But with Cope, Ephod Rochet, hood, and all
Tippet and Cap, and Robe Cannonnicall 10
And Miter too soe should he not be free
But straight submit unto our Litregy
Else stand suspended: to performe this may
Our Bishops all be sent, our people stay

Writ at the Campe at Birkes

Two various factions of the present time
Shuffle the Cards, and soe the King's at Prime
And haveing lost by stakes he thinks it best
To vie noe more butt set up the rest
Now that he may encounter truer spotts 5
I'de counsaile him for to discharge all Scotts

The Pedegree of Bay Wastnes as I had it from Sir Hardolph

Yong Puppie sonne to owld	Gascoygn Mare Daughter
Puppy that beate sawcy Jack	of Sir William Gascoygns horse
and came of the Famous	by Robins Sister
Mare Witherington	by Freak

Yong wastnes a Puppy by the Sire and soe a Kin to wanton? And Although he want yet that part of shape being very yong he is by the Dam a Gascoygn: soe is he Likewise by the halfe blood for all his youth a Witherington: and as much a Robin which might promise him to prove a good Buckhunter and to ride well in the woods but that he hath of Freak 5 in him and therefore I feare will prove too Caprichious: although Not black he hath a graine of peppercorne in him and will bite: being a Bay he gives much hopes of calme riding yet whilst Zein all of one colour and without marke he can have none of Rainbow nor Peacock in him, yet for speed (when tried) may equall an arrow and then shew his tayle to traine to what 10 horse soever shall ride against him he is too large to come of a Crickett: and I'me assur'd heth noe part of a Killdeer in him (for soe not I him by trayning but he me by complaining might make fine) espetially sithence the Last proclamation. Lastly in hopes he is a Blossome promising (when matcht) the fruites of a Conquerer and if for Plate to prove a Cup-Carle, if for mony 15 a soop-Stakes.

Upon the Rebells assault upon the Cass of Lough Gear

Sithence that the Rebells now are ther
Let my L. B. looke to's lough Gear
For certainly theil goe about
To win the fort and thrust him out

And then the Issue will be clear 5
He handled, but theil occupy his Gear

  Nor shall it for a wonder be accounted
  When hee had neer a peice of Cannon Mounted

In Eundem supra maneriam suam De want-age

That my Lord B. is yong who can't deny
When want-age is his owne (I rod it by
Yet that this L. noe manly courage lack
I'de wish he bore, his Manner on his back
'Twer point of Gallentry and I'le mainetaine 5
Though's rentalls loss 'twould prove his wives cleer gaine

Commissioners for the Irish affaires

Whilst all those Lords and Commons heads ere round
Intrusted are I'th'Irish affairs
Let such as list for me venter for ground
My head as dealing's square: I'le to my prayers
And thos shall be, that whilst wee conquest muse 5
Wee not forget what Christ prayed for the Jewes.

To Capt Fra[nk] Court[u]p A Huntsman

Let us noe Longer now goe on
To question transmigration
Sithence (Court up) I can find in thee
A Treasure of Antiquity
And though all Poets silenct were, 5
Asleepe each Histriographer
Thy worth sufficient is to call
To mind the Antient wortheys all
Neither from greece did thy soule come
Nor Room alone but Ilium 10
True Trojan (yfaith) and thus
O'th'famyly of Julius
Cæsarian visag'd and a Nose
Puts Naso downe though fit'st for prose
Allmost Heroick, I'le Maintaine 15
In thee ten Cæsars live againe
Titus delight of human race
Nor yet Augustus speaks thy face
The other tyrants thou dos't mock
When as the Subject proves the Smock 20
For like to Agrippina's blood
Att Belly ripping thou art good
And in plain dealing maist compaire
With his Successor to a haire
Othos effemynacy's out gon 25

When as thy Perriwidgens on
Caligula seems too controwld
By Thee who wallowest more in gould
Vespation Claudius and the Other
Thou dost Resemble as a Brother   30
And when thou list play the good fellow
Biberious was not halfe soe mellow
Thus art thou all ore Emperour
Sprung from Queen Didoes Paramour
Now for thy Love to hunting game   35
It calls up owld Sir Tristram
St Hugh Acteon, Robin Hood
Or all that ere in Greene wood stood
To see how thou those toyles gost through
Ore hill and daile to Cunny burrough   40
Others the Sticking place is wont
To make fleet hounds by inches hunt
And that thou lovst nor is it harme
When the sent's could to find it warme
Within the hole who oft time tride   45
Makes thee thus Emperour Deifide

To Sir Abram Williams upon his Barge Call'd the unthrift wherin I found him Fishing

Thrift, how applid I leave to Judge
Not to Philosophers who Grudg
At others happiness, nor prize
But what themselves Monopolize
Let such all Laugh or weepe anew   5
For what the world sends to their view
I shall obey noe other Charge
But that of Wonder at thy Barge
Some in th'Olimpique Games Delight
Some favor Peace some love to fight   10
The Campe, the Trumpet, and the Drum,
The Hawke the Hound bewitching some
Thers nothing suits soe with my wish
As to betray the Silent Fish
Ther with noe other thoughts of harme   15
But to Invite them with a Charme
First baite the Ground and then the hooke
Till they scull in and bite are tooke
Thus what i'th'open river Dwell
Thou Dost Confine within thy well   20
Untill thy Dinners Ordnance past
They'r Sacrifiz'd unto thy fast
Heer whilst Contentment Rides a drift
What Richer gam? what greater thrift?
Nor is this Carak nam'd a miss   25
By an Anteparistisis.

To my Lady Kat[herine] Scot

Sithence faithless man
        Is growne
Soe that noe protestation
Or Covenant alone
        Can tie 5
His wonderings from mutability
I shall for Ever hence forth vowe
To love a Scott, but non but you

That Nations Trot
        To this 10
Must Challenge now noe other oath
But what Negative is
        And soe
I am Contented to pay what I owe
Swere to my power never more to be 15
Behoulding to the *Scottish* Pedlery   *Blewcap.*

But to advance
        The Force
O'th'selfe denying ordinance
I doe without remorse 20
        Conclude
I have noe power but whats from you endude
And in that Posture doe desire to stand
You shall alone approve of and Command

To which I'le Call 25
        for Pledg
Not the Securing Goldsmiths Hall
        Or any Priviledg
        That saith
I may be bowld upon the Publique faith 30
Noe, my assurance by your Goodness signd
Bids mee presume you will not prove unkind

And then whats sayd
        Or done
Heer in shall never mak afraid 35
        But that oblivion
        May Pass
To pardon all the Sinn what e're it was
And by free grace from your Diviner will
Create a Rapture from my rustick quill 40

To Fayre Mrs Doll Peckam

Had I Appelles pencell and Could Draw
The Lively traicts of fresh yong Helena
When glory of the Greeks the Boy

First stole her thence to beautifie his Troy
Or should I chaffer with the fragrant Morn 5
For Heavenly Orient Colours to adorn
The best of natures workmanship and ther
Comprize within the spring the rest o'th'yeare
I might attempt to call thee yong and faire
But that thou art beyond all this Compare 10

Out of Martiall

But fower teeth Elia had which Caughing shee
At twice spat out soe she may now cough free
Out all her Daies and most securly too
Sithence thers noe more left for a Third to doe

To Fran[k] Coortup

Frank
   I Returne thy hounds with thanks
   Take too this Line of all their Pranks
   For intrest, sides a hardle more
   To add unto thy Kennells store

Luther Confuted Belloer-min 5
(For such the staggs in rut time beene)
Nor Could The Horned Pompey stand
When Caesar bore the Cheife Command
Set up at Bay that did employ
Awhile Natuers Artillery 10
Till feirce of Conquest this rusht on
And wounded made it Rubicon
Wher they encountered soe died
The streame from th'honor marke ofs side
If Lucan were againe to write 15
The Art and Strategems of fight
Now with a swifter stile t'enforce
The on-sett by th'Couragious horse
Then sound retreat to winn new breath
That might more tirannize ore death 20
His owld straine should give way and yeild
To blaze this new Pharsalian feild
Soe feirce the pass and venies were
Twix ones teeth t'others anteler
And as once Cesars sayd to high 25
Over the Seas for Anthony
Soe this with speed into th'Pond went
To give his mates encouragement
Tracing the very places ore
That swam on the Alexandrian shore 30
As ther one book that did preserve

So this a Volume doth deserve
Wherfore be Proud whilst Cesar his part playes
At Cobbam Lett noe trees florish but bayes
Thus for a Valliant Prince Whilst I Commend him   35
A Gunner and a Courtyer must attend him
And when Pride doth my Dutches A Queene make
I'le begg a straine for Cleopatra's sake

To Mr T.T.

Two Tees may poynt Tawtology
Soe Tom of winfred I'le prayse thee
Not Tom of Odcombe or odd Tom
That wandering Jew of Christendome
Noe Hee of Crudeties did write   5
But thou dost higher strains indite
Thy storyes only to relate
Would bring one straite unto surate
Noe part o'th'world where Zodiack line
Leads Phebus car is hid to thine   10
But Goa Bantam and Ormus
Alike to thee Propitious
Thou art as well read in the peas
That grow amongst th'Antypodes
And with noe less of Ease dost pullem   15
As if they grew hard by at Fullum
Thou dost noe other fruite Surmise
T'have bene the first of Paradise
But Kentish Pippin and out votes
A Million of Coriots   20
This is the age and thou dost raine
As true and mighty a Soveraigne
As any those who ere they bee
Rais Lies to throw downe Monarchie
The Scoutes not halfe soe diligent   25
To bring news to the Parliment
The Scottish Dove Thou dost out flye
Teaching the Olive branch to lye
The Northerne Post thy tongue out rides
And all Diurnalls else besides   30
Yet as a horse thats good may stumble
Within thy Chops thy Dictates fumble
Soe that thy speech as much doth vary
As if that Minshios Dictionary
Had beene thy foode for with much ease   35
Thou speakst at once nine Languages
And Drunke or Sober none can tell
Distinction in a Syllable
Prag: Brit. Elenct: and all Devise
From thy greate art their mercuries   40

　　　　　Yet like a fowle whose feathers gon
　　　　　Thou flaggst neath sequestration
　　　　　And art not satisfide at all
　　　　　That truth should bring thee to the hall
　　　　　Courage: lett Patience steere and then noe doubt　　　45
　　　　　Thoug thou rush in her hand will bring thee out

To Rob[in] Oliver after his coming ofe from his troubles congratulatory

　　　　　Like streams that blend their currant silver, such
　　　　　Proves mutuall Friendship that endures all touch
　　　　　For as the waters whence somere they run
　　　　　At length into a web of Cristall spun
　　　　　Make one fayre glass: soe may we best descry　　　5
　　　　　The perfect temper of true amety
　　　　　When each for other soe concerned is
　　　　　As to participate in cross or blis
　　　　　　Soe Robin I who fore times trod the way
　　　　　　To troubles now am glad thou'st got the day　　　10

Ad P.C.
To Take Time when one may is always best
Lest that let slippe one Lees ons interest
Post est occatio Calva

Prol[ogue]:　　　Waygh: and lett wind ore Cloth prevaile
　　　　　　　Ther'l need noe skeet to stiffe your sayle
　　　　　　　For Constancyes your owne make her your gaile

　　　　　　　In voyages it ought Deceives
　　　　　　　To be too long in taking leaves　　　5
　　　　　　　Nor doe the ships that Gold bring ore
　　　　　　　Leese time in Lingering neer one shore
　　　　　　　But with their Canvas wings stretcht out
　　　　　　　Clipp o're the maine to fetch't about:
　　　　　　　To be embay'd when stormes arise　　　10
　　　　　　　May suite some weaker Policies
　　　　　　　But when the Gust is past well nigh
　　　　　　　At Anker t'ride would sloth imply
　　　　　　　And Moores that Bark at Ruins Coast
　　　　　　　Letts opportunity be lost　　　15
　　　　　　　Hoys up your maine saile then I say
　　　　　　　Hale taught the sheats when once away
　　　　　　　Each glassy wave Curld by the Tide
　　　　　　　As't heaves you on shall be your guide
　　　　　　　Nor need you Rock or shelfe to feare　　　20
　　　　　　　Whilst Right's your Pilot that doth steere
　　　　　　　The Rudder and the Rudders bond
　　　　　　　Will turne all yare at your Command

Then (not before) all those your Iles possess
May find good ground i'th'haven of Happiness. 25

Upon my reaping Day the 28th of August 1648

    Hayle to that sylver hand
      At whose Command
   The orient Pearle of Dawne
Like lillies sprung up under whitest lawne
Appeares t'inrich our hopes that soe wee may 5
Put on the assurance of a fayer Day
And promise noe more raine to Dash our plenty
Since tis already august th'eight and twenty

    Up then and Ceres bless
      With full encrease 10
   Of goulden eares of well filld Corne
Till every sheafe at once bee borne
Into the barne and their of Comforts raise
Whilst they fill up the empty bayes
And tel us that their shall noe more be want 15
In winter whilst wee Imitate the Ant

    Yet their will more goe to't
      Words will not do't
   But hands employd must bee
And sickles usd with rakes and furmety 20
And binders too be gott
With the black Jack and flagon pott
That whilst with working each doe sweate
Those may allay and temper heate

    And for to add to thes 25
      The bacon peas
   The sith and pitching-forke
Must all in season too be sett a worke
Nor the browne Lusty lass
In her straw hatt must here unmentioned pas 30
But every one in their Compartments Come
And reape and binde and loade my Hock Cart home

    Thus have I seene a streame before
      All Coverd ore
   With swans as now each one 35
His Doublet ofe did seeme the feild upon
And Like to poppy in a lilly bed
White waste Coates mixt with petty Coates of red
Soe that to plentyes store it might appeare
Beauty had been Contributary heere 40

    The Mare and fillyes and the rest
      That must be drest

        As puppet Jack and Gill
        With Serimonies mirth to fill
        And as rewards unto the swaines   45
To mak them sport after their toyle and paines
I must alone (by business Calld away)
Leave to the Gierles and children to defray
Yet that they better may this task goe through
Let them find Gill I'le find them Goldsburrough   50

A Letter to L.L. at Co. after A yeares absence from each other

Shall freindship wayn becaus the world goes less
As age Creeps on't In shining faithfulness
Doe wee not see the Moon decrease and then
Though but with borrowed light fill up againe
For still she hath a body Cannot bee   5
Deprivd of Created Entety
Noe more may Change in states unsteady sway
Unspheare true love; or make affeccions stray
Out of their Course as the good will of tymes
Befrend or not their must be waynes and primes   10
Distance to shew our sublynary state
Is lyable to Variations fate
All orbs though darkned doe the same remaine
Till opportunities cleer them againe
Soe prime of those to whom my aspects owe   15
Tribute of mutuall smiles by Thes pray know
I doe salut you under noe pretence
Save that from kindness takes its influence
And that you may the same you did still know mee
I rest   20
                      Your humble servant
                      Senza Nome

Upon James Martins house at puttny being robd his Brother kiss[ing] all the while

At Jameses putny theirs a hole to start in
Wher Will. his brother Martin
Sculct and lay Close whilst theiving Canalers
    Went up the staires
And what hole should this bee but without wonder   5
    The same hee wont to plunder
Soe whilst those were for booty scratching
    Hee was a Cunny Catching
See what the Easterne parts produce of Treasure
Whilst others are feare struck hees at his pleasure   10
And Travilers may lie some say but hee
A Masters growne in spelling. O.Q.P.
                Vita Proba

Robin for Poesy to a wedding ring hath CUPIO *or I desire*

  Surely the God of love did him inspire
  With a Conceipt that must not be said noe
  Whilst that but symbol was o'th't'other thing
  Wishes as thoughts are free
  Let O be Alpha and Omega P.   5

My Dedicatory at the end of Beaumont
and fletchers playes now sett out 1646

It well becomes the glory of the press
And poetry their surfrages to dress
At these two Lawreats shrine whos works despise
The Thunder boults of blackmouthd Callumnies
For whilst they teach the world upon a stage   5
To tread true measure and each personage
Either to cast smiles here or frowne threats ther
As vice and virtues sit Diamiter
This corner of it (from the rest by some
Divided) is Apolloes I'le become   10
For the nine sisters noe where else doe dwell
But where such Raptures rais an oracle
For my poore vaine which never could produce
Of that Inspireing fountaines Nectar Juce
Nor yet entitle to that power or skill   15
To Crop a spell branch from parnassus hill
Is far to meane, unless some Reader lookes
Upon this as the Carrier of their bookes
After them not in Print but wrot with quill
And soe the last Page may not deem them ill   20

Upon Ben Jonsons Playes calld his workes

Why do we stile Those workes which wer but Playes
But that to Fancy ther goe severall wayes
Some born to Raptures fluently distill
Their sacred Numbers to adorn the quill
Others ther are bring forth with paines and sweat   5
So Head and Braines into an Anvile beat
Of Those, was This, whose deep Conceptions Lurke
Therefore we'l turn His Playes into a worke.

Invited to exceed Limits

  Cupid although a Child's
   Soe stronge
  That neither Craft nor wile
   Prison nor Chaine
  May him detaine   5

  Nor thong
   Can hould him
Whilst of restraint
I made Complaint
And of some Jealousies and scruples tould him   10
Hee bad mee not to feare but Come a long

 For why
 Quoth hee
 It Cannot bee
But those affections moves   15
To trace the sphere of turtle doves
  Should bee most free
From all the Fetters and the tye
  Of any other
Law, but what nature likes, to die   20
 One for and with the other

Loves Negative

Noe tis not beauty must Confine
Loves Votaries to venus shrine
 Nor any specious good
 Of flesh and blood
The fairest then would only know   5
The benefitt of Cupid's bow
  And Natures Courser Clay
  Is Throne away

Noe tis not soules divinly joynd
In sweetest hermony of mind   10
 Nor sympathy of hartes
 That love imparts
Then equall thoughts would ballance soe
The highest Virtues with the Loe
  That who soe doth excell   15
  Must not doe Well

Noe tis not wealth nor birth nor fame
Nor privilidge by fortune's Claime
 The poore and loe borne men
 Would want it then   20
Nor fates nor minds nor bodyes give
Loves Monarch this perogative
  Only by nature linckt
  It is Instinckt:

Loves Affirmative

Yes, wher less Virtue shines
To Venerate fond Venus shrines

Ther is the greater neede
Of beauties Charme to doe the deede
   Else 'twere a geer 5
As if to love a thing that were not ther
   When faire or good
Or both in all affections Understood
And as a supplement defects to smother
The one is rais'd by'th'setting of the other 10

Yes, I agree that soules may place
Their mutuall simpathizing grace
Shot from each hart through eyes
Like Influences darted from the skies
   Yet neither bee 15
   Guilty of partialitie
But all Contentions bind
Within the perfect Circle of the mind

Yes, whilst humanity doth steer
Both wealth and birth, and fame, are neare 20
   To guide the Rudder
   And make a pudder

Yet ther is none borne meane and Loe
But fortune fonde may soone outgoe
   The rich or greatest hee 25
   What soe ere hee bee

Soe that her wheeles advance
   Gives Lowest spoakes preheminence
And true Concurrence finds
The Cheifest nutriments from Conquerd minds 30
And if I would a woeing goe
Ide Chuse a Hellen for my bedfellow
   Unless Ide leape and winke
Then nature should provide me by instinct

F. The L. M.

Horace Carmina   I hate the vulgar dietyes
Lib: 3 Ode 1   With their Ar[se] hole Plebeities
Odi prophanum   Let not my muse fall in their wayes
vulgus et arceo &c: Whose garlands stinke, are not of Bayes
   For all that ever such comend 5
Bewray the vaine foule fingers end
Smell all of tallowe and of Greace
Noe whit of oile the Lamps increase
Tearme Rapture madnes and a floud
Of Christall layes but Channell mud 10
Prophane all by the sisters spun
Or what Apolloes Preists have done

When I those sacred vestments were
That could enthrone me in that sphere
Whence I might dart a ray of verse 15
Nor tyme before did ere reherse
   To ad more fire
   To yongue desire
Touching my sweet soft Lesbian lyre
Then let noe rustick note wage warre 20
Upon my strings to make them jarre
But by the Cliffe the Key the Eights
Each one observer of there leights
In Diapason true expresse
How concords raysd from differences 25
Soe people set in tune againe
May owne there lawfull soveraigne

Ad RemPubl[licam] Bel[lum] Civil[em] reparantem

Hor: ode 14   Shall a new tyde of differences
lib:1   Carry againe my bark to seas
O navis referent   Farre better were it to defray
in mare te novi   That charge and ride safe in a bay
fluctus o quid   There to a calme of Peace conforme 5
agis? &c   After a tempest and a storme
How doth the foaming angry maine
All substance wast and treasures drayne
And in despight of Canvas wings
Cordage with other tacklings 10
Though riggd she be when Nereus frownes
My vessell sinks and quickly drownes
Be at the length experience taught
'Tis not too late though dearly bought
And let her misteryes teach this 15
Shees good though but hard mistres
Better it were in tyme belay
Wett ankers and the frett obey
Then to persist and therein finde
The furious madness of each winde 20
Summoning up in liquid rage
The witchcrafts of there Parentage
These thy first deityes are gone
Nor serve more for protection
And though thy Planks and keele may boast 25
They grew on Calidonian coast
Thence raysd thee fame yet these may erre
'Lesse fortitude be Passenger
For though highe Carvd with decks thou be
Beguilded in each gallery 30
On the maine top a flag, to Call

Thee at the least highe admirall
With antient Pennants streaming farre
From every yard like man of warre
And on thy boult sprit head a Jack   35
Yet canst thou not be free from wrack
Unlesse through Pilacy to these
Thou ad, to shun the Cyclades
Those more then fivety Islands lye
As if conspiring Jeopardy   40
To any bottome that doth steere
And yet forgets to cry noe neere
But grant thou lanch into the deepe
And wilt not in a harbour sleep
Though faire envited take advise   45
Doe not too farre Præcipitise
Mark well your Fires how they are plac't
Most advantageously when chas't
Or in pursuit as you come after
To give a shot twixt winde and water   50
Then when a broad sides given next
Dismount that Cannon call'd Pretext
And winning winde proclaime th'event
None's like Monarchike government.

Upon Lamb[er]ts repo[rted] to be Gen[eral] &c: s.x. before

'Twas not in vaine the Antients all
Usd Ramms to batter down a wall
Since now our modern warrs doe teach
The use of hornes to make a breach
And Cuckolds prove the only Thinges   5
To rayse Rebellion, put down Kinges.

A Riddle upon Tobacco

Not drunk yet Drunk by People tain yet not
I was not food yet from west India got
When drunk I increas more thirst: I'm vulgers prey
Rowld up, thence cutt and dride I'm burnt away
Men sat together and each hand did bring   5
As from Heavns bounty to my suffering
One part but from the Rowle, an other shred
And dried by th'fier at last is Mastered
Those who shun Idlenes to us resort
And with great care small busnes doe in sport   10
I'm lost by what I'm taken and that dore
Of mouth receivs me whiffs me ever more
Which thou who dost the Clenlier Chimnys dress
Accept in Spittle from my sufferances.

Sonnet February: 1659

Though Munks assume what Powers They will
  And Monestaries Keep such free
And Parlements their houses fill
  Yet ther's Sovraign Posterety
    Will not be wiped ofe Their right   5
    Though Monks and Traytors still should fight

Courage St George for England yet
  And let the Dragons Twisted *Tayle*   *or Rump*
No Mastry, ore Thy Spear beget
  Nor 'gainst thy Loyalty prevaile   10
    But shew Thou canst aswell bear Arms
    For lawfull Right as t'shend from harms

Freedom is chiefly Mans desire
  And if he fayle of this He's lost
No more of Thee George I requier   15
  But that this Serpent Rump be Crost
    Who Pride-inspird assume uponum
    To Level All, turn All to Common

From Netherlands Thou didst extract
  Thy Discepline and feats of warr   20
Let due Obedience Thee contract
  Into a Subject Regular
    And then I'le say no Covant can
    Produce a better Christian.

Epigram on the Rump

A Tumer's raysd in Counsailes Rumps
Much like Prides Timpany or Mumps
Which to asswage again, lay flatt
Nothing save *Monks-hood's* good for that
                     a garden simple

To welcome home Veronia or to the Spring on May day 1650

Welcome faier Season that dost bless
Again the fields with newer dress
For wher of late lay flakes of snowe
Ther fresh grass springs and flowers growe
  The fortune-tellers heer appeer   5
  Getting the mayden head o'th'year
  And by some even leafs discover
  What shall betide to evry lover
Next of the same complexions die
T'enrich more natures tapistry   10
The guilded cowslip shewes its head
And soe the Mead's embroydered

  Corn grounds with Poppy-rubye's set
  Inameld green like Carkanet
  Bejewel Earth whilst on each hill   15
  White fethers grow of Daffadil
And every plain deserves its prayses
For pregnancy in silver Dazies
  The bottom of a hedg begetts
  Esteem from Saphir Violetts   20
  Whose purple-mantelings maintain
  They of all else are soveraign
  Ther being none for sight or smell
  That howld with them true paralell
    Allthough the guarden would out vie   25
    In painted Tulips sophestry
    Or dappld Gilleflowers produce
    Faint coulerd Pink, or flower deluce
    Great Crimson Pionyes or all
    The wives delight growes still by wall   30
    Graunt it in healing balm be fertil
    Or houlsom sage or greener Myrtle
    Blew Lavender and herb of grace
    Mint, savin that with some takes place
    Or that which ore all thinges will come   35
    Time, savry, or sweet marjerom
    The charmes most mortall cares controwle
    (Soucy in french) our Marygould
    Whose radiant leavs their welths' display
    At th'opening of the Orient day   40
    Then shut again as sable night
    Her curtain drawes to bannish light
Kitt run-by-street or litle pancy
Party per pale to sute each fancy
  Crispt Camamil whose worths exprest   45
  In thriving best when most it's prest
  And like a worthy of renown
  Growes better for being trodden down
    Yet none of these shall ere reposum
    Wher Violet may in Her soft bosom   50
The woodbine to bewitch the sence
Of smelling bears preheminence
Yet 'cause its figure under is
It cannot claym soe great a bliss
    Though Nature wills Ther be contest   55
    Mongst these which look and sent the best
    Unto which suffrage she Discloses
    Those which in both excell the Roses
    Damask, and White, and red: yet nowe
    Veronia's lip, her cheek, her browe   60
    Drawn to my mind soe farr surpass
    All those again, as those doe grass.

Epigram
Senes bis pueri

  When Infants first into the world doe come
  Crying and sucking is their proper doome
  And what doe men when unto age grown ripe
  But crye 'tis time to suck 'tis time to pipe
Whiffing   *Dancing* away their last howers in bravado   5
  Whither Virginia please or Trinidado
  The diffrence is not much I must confess
  Children are fooles and aged are noe less.

Cogit amare Jecur Lyvor wort procureth love

  As opposite as are the Poles
  This Livor is that man controwles
  For it in Latin doth imply
  Malice and Envies infamy
  When as the English gently moves   5
  The breath of sights the noats of loves
   Thus each to others tongues betroth
   Englisht and Latin'd Livor's both.

Upon a course in the padock between Swan Sir Hor[ace] Toun[send's] red pide dog and a Blew Academ[ic] or Camb[ridge] dog of Will[iam] Spen[cer]

  As Pricket ore the Course did trip
  Two Gray-hounds tride their footmanship
  But neither could the pray ore-take
  That bargain they forgot to make
  Yet Swan not swam but seemd to fly   5
  And allmost pincht he came soe nigh
  The other seen in Morals more
  Deemd fit the best should goe before
  Soe read in Logick strait defind
  In forrests Arts should come behind   10
  This as a scholler dog he Knew
  It was his place to come ofe blew
  And Heraldry this truth begetts
  Poets guive place to Barronets
  Yet if their had not Ladies been   15
  Spencer had raysd his Fayry Queen.

Upon the Generall the Lord Fairfaxes resigning up his Commissions to Oliver Crumwell

  Upon account it's understood
  When Theevs fall out one comes by good
  And what doe all men but be sh-t'um
  When Generalls conclude with Itom

For soe their reckening but small is 5
If cast up without summa totalis
Pounds, Crownes, and shillings to a farthing
In Auditings are worth reguarding
And though misplac't ther may be reason
To judg it is but for a season 10
To try their skil whose fayths amount
Unto an Exchecker account
Wher figures their owne places fill
And Cifers remain Cifers stil
Which in Arithmaticks schoole fall 15
Or rise but as additionall
Set them alone I dare averr
'Ts like Rowland changd to Oliver
Signefies that ther doth remain
Nothing saving the same again 20
When we ought drive a greater skoap
On Pounds and Crownes to fix our hoap
Whilst swords make plowgh shears, let Hemp R—

Ad Geo: Fane: in commemorationem natalitij Reg. Car:
2^{di} in cellula vulgo vocata Le Grotto scriptum vigilium
scilicet maij 28 1650 Englisht thus

Under what Planet in what clime
Should he thats master of his time
Improve it better to posess
A dowry of true happines
Than wher my houshould Gods dispell 5
All cares within the Grotto sell
Wher the free ayre and pure as it
May by two running fountains sit
Which are enough to rouse up witt
   Noe place on earth for merth and jest 10
   Can trulier challenge interest
   Than underground heer wher ther runns
   Fathers full blessings to his sonns
   Til gratitude inspiers the mind
   To a requiting thankfull kind 15
   And this awakes the future morn
   Wheron our noble Charles was born
   Wherin Joves favour doth appeer
   T'have blest this land this twentith year
Hence from the bottles and the hart 20
Soe many joyous motions start
Whilst as in shades securety
Each one is blest we that enjoy
Soe much of light as may return
Comfort but neither scorch nor burn 25
From the suns goodnes, and such wind

As may but coole, n'ere prove unkind
By which refresht the active Spel
Rousd up awake from couch or sel
Ascends his brittle throne and thence 30
With Couler and tast controwles our sence
    Heer is noe need of bush of prayse
    Nor snow nor Ice that heat alayes
    Noe Mirtle, rose, nor oyntment
    But 'tis King Ralphs wine yeilds content 35
    And what had been long bottled up
    To fill such a rejoycing cup
    Better by far then that imparts
    Through mixture all the vintners arts
        Count twice the time of Troyes distress 40
        And then you'l find his years noe less
        Who now writes man and wears that goun
        What though his father were put doun
        He as successor to the Crown
        May with undoubted right increase 45
        His peoples good by bringing peace
Then I'le noe more seek to command
That bottle had layn long in sand
Nor think I doe great matters rayse
Courting my pallet severall wayes 50
Whilst I neglect not Terrene seas
To bring me wine my tast to pleas
As the Albano of account
And that of Fiascone mount
Verdea and what not to be 55
My partners at this Jubile
    For soe great state 'tis properer
    Apollo be my vintner
    And the Castalian well my wine
    For whilst Solemnety's divine 60
        With a light hart and without odds
        I would drink nectar with the Gods.

marginal note: When bottles leak and fountaines run the while/ One writes, it needs must prove a fluent stile.

A Ballet 3: September 1658.

Owld Olivers Gon Owld Olivers gon
    O Hone O Hone
And has left His sonn Richard
That Pretty yong Prick-Eard
    To Govern These Nations alone alone: 5
The Counsail and State
He Commanded of late
    O Hone O Hone
But the Tables turnd quite
Those Govern This wight 10
    And turns our rejoycing to mone to mone

Thus with Their Consent
Thers calld Parlement
      O Hone O Hone
Soe 'twixt Swede and Spruce 15
Ther'l be made a Truce
      And Wrangle be Generall'y Known
The Cuntrys are quiet
Fates bless their good Diet
      O Hone O Hone 20
'Tis a pittifull thing
Three Kingdoms noe King
      And Estates to be rackt skin and bone
Yet we live in hope
To conquer the Pope 25
      O Hone O Hone
When souldiers and Clowns
Fall at Odds about Crowns
      Then True men may come by their Owne

Of Man to W[illiam] Ar[mine]

Noe wonder 'tis that man loves fights
Since He's composd of Opposites
  His fleshy parts at once comprise
  Fowr Elemental contraries
  On which Affections excess 5
  Beget an Issue numberless
  Which nurced up by Humors brest
  In Fancies school clayme interest
  Wher for a leson They let in
  The Common-place or Head of sin 10
  Whilst Appetite noe Rhet'rick spares
  To scatter 'mongst the wheat some tares
  Soe choak the Harvest, and with rain
  Let loose, sowes Cockle for true Grain
Now over these to rule and sway 15
He that created Night and Day
Endowes the Mind over the sence
With Knowledg for Preheminence
Exalting Reason 'bove the rest
As He did Man ore every Beest 20
  And thus installd why is't the mind
  Strives from its Limits unconfind
  But that in search of a new berth
  Man would create his Heavn on Earth
  Fix on the Creatures all content 25
  When God who is Omnipotent
Is evermore at hand to be
Protector 'gainst all injury   }Philip: -4-5-6.
  Be Patient then, nor care at all

For what in Temprall Things befall 30
Make him acqainted with thy state
And fear not to be fortunate
  Whither by Prayer thou sendst request
  Or guivst Him thankes for all the rest
  Thou dost enjoy; stil let it be 35
  Soe seasond with sincerety
    That that which all thinges goes beyond
    His Peace in Christ may be thy frend.

To a frend from Apthorp in a great Snow

                         January-6: 1650

How we fare if you would know
That are now Condemnd to Snow
Frozen up in Winters Geaile
Without or mainprize or Baile
  On the Peak high summer 'tis 5
  All the year in shew of this
  And Compard to it alone
  Scithia's in the Torrid Zone
Noe couler seen nor other die
But Caucasus white Livery 10
The Grampion or the Lomans Coat
Or night cap of owld Cheveot
Wherwith invested we advance
The Pole starrs Badg and Cognisance
  And Like his Minstrels doe retire 15
  To the good Ale and Tost and fire
  Whence bannishing all Discontent
  Each one tunes up his Instrument
  And playes soe well that we forget
  The seasons Could amidst such heat. 20

The North Wind

The newes from north blowes very rife
They are transporting men to Fife
But Charons bottom not yet ther
The General must plye that Fare
And to that end a fleet prepares 5
To waft ore thousand passengers
 Poor silly soules that hud winkt come
 To find out ther Elizium
 Wher Scottish mists and vapours fell
 Deny the Least content to dwell 10
  Let this Presumpteous Pylot hast
  Least Charon ore take him at last
  And for his pride and other Tricks
  Ore-set and leav him sunk in Styx.

Upon the rumor of his departure though faigned Epitaph.

Heer lies he was dide in Grain
Chief murtherer of his soveraign
Bane to his Cuntries peace and good
The horse-liech covetor of blood
One whose high spirit naught could pleas 5
But fishing in the troubledst seas
Of a Tempesteous mind was tost
Ambitiously to rule the rost
Til the all-conquering-Fates by doom
Causd Atropos cut ofe his Loom 10
  And whilst his busnes hee's about
  I'th'northern Clime his fier goes out.

The Rump

Tom C: hath been in Italy and swears   January: 1659
He's for the Rumpe, Contemns All other wares:
And deems it best of Pleasure that is stole
So Day appeers thorough a little Hole
For Trading in the Citty's grown so Common 5
Since Adam was a Man and Eve a Woeman
That He despises the Owld way to Sinn
And must a new pass find to bring it in
'T may be for that His fancies All Conspire
To let us know a Burnt Child dreads the fire 10
And evry box of ware hath in't some Trick
To Cheat and Cousen Oftentimes Jack P—
When He is Crest faln out of hart and Poore
Drivn from the fore-gate to seek the back Dore
Or Broaken-Snouted needs a Dildo prop 15
To Reinvest Him Foreman of that Shop
Yet guiv'n to Gaming stil Tom turns up Trump
And Shunns the Belly for to Court the Rump.

(C. for Challoner)

To the Countess of Exeter upon her brach Lemons whelping An Ode or Song

Lemon has whelpt O Joyfull newes
  Enough for to create a Muse
    Out of the dullest block
That can to hunting sport pretend
  Wherfore pray Jove some Nectar lend 5
    Apollo Helicon unlock

Ther is noe hound for nose and speed
  Allthough of Creet or Sparta breed

   Could ever hunt soe well
Or drive a Chase wher Pan doth Keep   10
  (The Huntsmans curse) his flock of sheep
   Soe she's 'thout paralell

That fancy is but poor and silly
  To court a whelp that comes of Lilly
   Her strain's not half soe rare   15
For though she some times well may run
  She cannot match this Paragon
   She wants a M[istres]s care

And heer I'm ravisht with a Spell
  The Greater happines to tell   20
   This Creature soe befrended
As t'be intiteled and Crownd
  Not my Lord's Brach but Ladies Hound
   Wherwith her Fame's ascended

Some doe goe farr and pas the seas   25
  For Lemons, and for Oranges
   And ventrous Jorneys take
I wish from hence they'l stay at home
  And only to this Kennell come
   More proffit sure they'l make   30

Others doe deem't a trick of bliss
  If they can Compass but a Kiss
   Of what is more precise
Which makes the Vicker of the toune
  Doft Girdle, Casssock, Hose, and Goune   35
   For to Monopolize

Such suer doe howld the Proverb true
  That better horse-flesh is their due
   Soe clayme it for a fashion
And judg the crime but Light not hevy   *Ang.* 40
  Thus to part *Tiths*: with Tribe of Levy *Thies*:
   To help on Reformation

For 'tis not fit that He alone
  From Pulpit-Elevation
   Such Canaan should discover   45
When Bewty bountifull transferrs
  Her flames into th'Parishioners
   Inspiring each a lover

But heer's enough; nor This nor That
  Must Coupled be at any rate   50
   Unto my Lemon heer
Diana and her Nimphs nere knew
  Soe Saint-Like hound for sent and View
   Nor like Containes the Spher.

A Ballet To x.x.x. upon his pond on wittring heath and the Iland bower and fish house ther

    Some to the Lucrine Lake bequeath
        All prayses for the fishing
    Guive me the pond upon the heath
        Might I but have my wishing

    For ther doe scull in sholes along
        Dum Creatures armd with skales
    Whose squadrons of Finns soe strong
        Over the wave prevailes

    As Geering Carp and Gyant Pike
        A stand for hawkes and Bream
    I think noe poole can shew the like
        Or guive an apter Theme

    Yet thers an Ile some wonder claymes
        As in the midst it lies
    Which sometimes doth abound with flames
        From bewties misteries

    When the fayer Mistres of that Bower
        Graces it with Consent
    Frank-Ly to spend a summers hower
        Amidst that Elament

    O how 'tis hard then to discover
        Which is of dainger higher
    Leander-Like to dround a Lover
        Or to consume with fier

    Who would not his Abid-os quit
        To court soe fayer a queen
    Allthough he wrackt in ventring it
        By a Hellespont between

    But for to quench that heat again
        Ther is a house stands by
    Wher the Lord will you entertain
        With all Civilety

    Ther to his mess some Trouts apeer
        His neighbour Lord and frend
    The Barronet he loves soe deer
        Phil: wood for the bords end

    These doe retrive a chirping cup
        Such as the Gods nere knew
    And whilst they doe carouce all up
        With snakes their years renew

    First to the Nimph protects the place
        Then to some other bewty

Til chapeau-bas with cheerfull grace
   Each one hath done his duty

Bridgwater and his noble Spouse   45
   Must not heer be forgot
As long as Bacchus frends the house
   With bottle, glass or pott

Will any more Peggs lodg frequent
   Or skulk in Saraes hole   50
Which only huffcap Ale doe vent
   The senses to Controwle

Neckar and Coblins on the Rine
   Squeese out their Lustfull Clusters
And Deal to us their Juice divine   55
   To fournish out our Musters

Then Captain Glass full to the brimm
   Presents a Lusty charge
Whilst Bottles from their Sanadrim
   Awakt apeer and march   60

Nor is France wanting though denide
   Our Appetites all meet
To judg that best is done aside
   And stollen pleaseure sweet

In fine what need we travail soe   65
   To feed our Observations
When heer is more than what we goe
   To seek in other Nations

Constance and that of Gardo too
   With Lake Leman must yeild   70
For though their Citties finely show
   This hath a braver field

It were a wittless thing indeed
   For to commend the meer*
When all that in those waters breed   75
   Are in more plenty heer

And that wherwith I wil conclude
   Excelling all the rest
The owner with such love indude
   As cannot be exprest   80

His freedom opes the sluce and way
   Of Liberty to some
Who otherwayes confined lay
   Within 5 miles of home

Wherfore in Tribute to present   85
   Thanks worthy any had I

> Without or food or Complement
> God bless the Lord and Lady
>   *wittles ile meer

To Cleveland before the first interview at maneby

> Though Childing women may oft long for this
> Or that nor yeild a reason why it is
> Yet my desiers rank-wingd have hither flown
> That I to Cleiveland, He to me were known
> Whose raptures are soe elevate by art   5
> As that each science in them hath its part
> And yet in Him not got with *anvile* pain
> But flowing Like a Torrent after rayne
> Which every one wher fancy credit getts
> Strives to procuer inbankt int'Rivelets   10
> T'imbellish his discource, and make it thus
> To relish and come ofe facetious.
> Ther's an owld Tale I did beleev but talk
> That Soules int'bodies Transmigrated walk
> On Earth again after they had been dead   15
> And from their proper carcass sequestred
> But since that Eminency of strain I find
> In Thee I'm grown quite of an other mind
> For tis not one but all that ere wore bayes
> Thou dost with thy Syraffick numbers rayse   20
> Thou buildst owld Roome again, and dost rehears
> Her Antient Bards so famous were for verse
> Nay; thou out bidst them with thy genuine skill
> And bringst this Ile nearer Parnassus Hill
> Than Those ere dwelt, whilst that Thy quil may own   25
> To be a Pipe drawn from true Helicon
> I will not rack or torture with delay
> The forward hopes I have put on to day
> To have my wish but bootes and all put on
> I'le mount away to Stephen Anderson   30
> Whose Hospitable parts, noe other end
> Clayme but to be belov'd, and love his frend
> Which doth soe well with Poesy agree
> That's house may seem Apolloes nurcery
> Wher Learning's cherisht and the Arts revive   35
> Under his bounteous roofes prerogative
> For verses evermore delight to dwell
> With a free hart; yet in retired sell
>   *Carmina cecessum.*

Jhonson- (marginal note at line 7)

To Him again in return for a letter he wrot upon the former

> Not like the bird whose bewteous train
> Being praisd is more displayd again

Nor of the Academick witt
Is raysd by Humms to cherish it
When (as it thrives) it must at best 5
Have Scrattching store to mak't a Jest
Would I appeer: but Favours say
They clayme acknowledgment for pay
Which I heer offer to the skan
Of all great Arts Leviathan 10
For now I shall noe longer looke
Whence Hobbs intiteled his booke
Though surreptitious and by stealth
Since thou'rt above all commonwealth
Thy Straines Monarkike, nor can bear 15
Th'affront of a Competitor
Wher Science Liberall is who guives
Not unto All prerogatives
Over the Tongue and Pen but brings
Those best deserve to be her Kings 20
Yet what are such if left alone
Nor Honord by Subjection
Whilst 'tis the great'st alay to power
When ther is noe inferiour
And nothing soe much Luster Spoyles 25
In Diamonds as to want their foyles.

An invitation to my Askanius a true Trojan ifayth

   My George were not the tie
   Of Consanguinety
   Of greater force than Reason
Or else the Lawe of Nature would impose
I should conclude you guilty of more Treason 5
    Than e're Sir walter Earles nose
       Could disclose
   For envying us thus long the sight
   Of your fayre Starr that shines soe bright

   Surely 'tis not the West 10
   You live in but the East
   For soe such Rayes imply
You raysd to Guild that Climat and to bless
That side the world whilst we in darknes lie
    And under Midnight of distress 15
       Posess
   Noe more of Day to guive us ease
   Than's guiv'n to your owne Antipodes

   But since the world 'round is
   On hopes 'tis not amiss 20
   To feed the fancies appetite
That certain revolutions heer and ther

> May bring about a Day to chase the night
> And soe illuminate our Sphere
>   From fear 25
> Of any mist that may portend
> Dainger through th'absence of a frend
>
> Of this I'd have you sure
> Each Plaister's not a cure
> To evry wound, for Paris 30
> Transports to Troy what He makes Gretians want
> But you unmercifully take what rare is
>   Not only from our *Troy-novant*   London
>   But skant
> Afford your owne territories 35
> Matter to fill up their stories
>
> Up then away and come
> From western Ilium
> Bring Hellen safe whose Eyes
> Hath warmd suffitiently that watry coast 40
> And let them favour now these Northern skies
>   For want of bewty that allmost
>   Are lost
> For 'twer a Sin too long to stay
> And soe deprive us of more Day 45
>
>   Let Thy julus come along
>   And burthen with a cry this song

A Ballet of Dedication of the new Academy or Musike room by the Back Gates—to Phil: Wood.

> What various stories men invent
>   T''amuse the weaker braynes
> When Musike ne're had Instrument
>   Like that good wine containes
>
> Some Vialls that de Gambo are 5
>   Commend, Others the Lute
> The Viall Glass shall be my care
>   Or else the steeple Flute
>
> Who can beleev that Sacred Layes
>   Or Ditties that have fier 10
> Apolloes art alone could rayse
>   And Bacchus not inspire
>
> They write how Pan with oaten quill
>   First did all musike frame
> And how the Tritons Trumpets stil 15
>   The wild waves into tame
>
> How Dolphins and the other tresur
>   Of the great Deep advance

After Arions Harp in measure
    As Each had Learnt to dance   20

Alike of Orpheus we read
    Vulcan and's Cyclopes
In wine ther's truth to stand insted
    Of all such lies as these

Juball and Tuball Brothers were   25
    As well in Art as blood
Imposing Gammuths on the Spher
    Fore Grapes were understood

The Juicy Grape of purple die
    Chief Glory of the press   30
First parent was to Melody
    Conceipt and Jovialnes

How far from consort doe those rove
    The Toun wayghts would bring in
Or think a bagpipe far above   35
    A curious Violin

Ther are High boyes in merth doe well
    Joyned with Sack-butts shugg
And for the Base double Curtell
    Guive me a double Jugg   40

The trebble cornets note soe shrill
    Cannot with this Compare
When Ganimed Joves cup doth fill
    That proves the choisest ayre

Ther is noe magick art or spell   45
    Can work in power like this
It doth all other charmes excell
    Turning all Crass to bliss

His Fame but flaggs who over beast
    Stones, Trees, is sayd had power   50
When one wine glass well fild at least
    Installs one Emperour

Cesar and Alexander too
    Had long since been forgot
But that they both knew how to doe   55
    In Counsail, Armes and Pott

What were the Labours men ascribe
    Unto Alcides might
But that His Glasses twelve did tribe
    To doe his Mistres right   60

Could Sampson ere have been soe strong
    To pull down Gates and Tours

But that with Foxes brought along
   The fields too he devowres

O brave deluders of our sense   65
   Controwling every vayne
With what Supernall Influence
   Do'st act the Soveraign

Soe that of all the Arts that be
   None rules the Rost and sitts   70
With greater state and Majesty
   In the Conclave of witts

Of whom a Jury if you call
   When verdict they guive up
Their billa vera it will fall   75
   Upon a Chirping Cup

And for a Sessions house to plead
   This Legis Latine power
To th'Musick-Room let this you lead
   Next to the back gates Tower.   80

Upon Dabbling or Fishing

As many men, soe many minds
  To which the Proverb's Mother
Fancy's best pleased with sevrall kinds
   This that sport likes, this t'other
         One thinks the Hare   5
         Beyond compare
         An other deems it trouble
         Because poor watt
         Before a sqatt
         Non plusses Dogs with double   10

Others ther be of High degree
  The Harts chase doe espouse
And say thers noe such Melody
  As when Hounds Eccho rouse
         Yet thers again   15
         That doe maintain
         Noe pas time to the Cony
         And love the hole
         That doth controwle
         Both Ferret and ther mony   20

Some love t'pursue the Boar thats Wild
  Others the Wolf soe fell
I would in noe waise Hunting stild
  A Dainger but a Spell
         Which by a Charme   25
         That bodes noe harme
         Might over time prevaile

> To Cosen't soe
> Noe care or woe
> Should triumph but strike sayle 30
>
> More Innocent and harmless more
>   What can be namd than this
> Which can our health and strength restore
>   When warping both amiss
>   Wherfore or Brocks 35
>   Or wily Fox
>   Whatsoever we pursue
>   Ther's none embrace
>   Soe well the chase
>   As Phil: wood *Layd** Perdue   **sett*. 40*
>
> The Trojan Horse cride up by fame
>   If wood might call him Cosen
> For ther Lurkt hidden in the same
>   Brave Gretians by the Dozen
>   And who would seek 45
>   A merry Greek
>   Let him accost this shore
>   Hee'l Pipe and sup
>   A Chirping Cup
>   Like any Emperour 50
>
> His then the glory of my wish
>   Of late times did befall-us
> He may all hunting change to fish
>   Which Exercise may mall-us
>   When ther's noe stint 55
>   But what Tom Flint
>   That Magazeen doth carry
>   Wherwith posest
>   Noe Place for rest
>   Like Portall Dormitary 60
>
> This was a Bird whose age might well
>   Avoyd the snare or gin
> Had He but thought of Sentinell
>   To keep his Temper in
>   But 'sted of chaff 65
>   Whilst He did quaff
>   His Brindases soe fast
>   He's caught, and tain
>   Forfets his brain
>   And soe's captivd at last. 70

An Invitation to R. H: to change the Citty Life for this in the Cuntry April 8. 1651

> Robin if thou but kiss or sip
> In a Good-fellowes fello-ship

Me thinks it might such spirits rayse
Not to be layd the common wayes
  Truth is when Conjuring comes in fashion 5
  Figures are usd and Circulation
  T'amuse and confidence supplant
  Posessing of the Ignorant
  But what the Times and Age puts on
  Ripens to more perfection 10
  Than any Cube or witchcrafts spell
  Can alter in a sillable
Citties and fencing walls were good
When freedom less was understood
And soe agayn those raysd the cause 15
Whence first we did derive our Lawes
  I shall not sound deeper to reach
  At what Antiquety doth teach
  Only prescribing by the way
  That Aintient Customs ought t'bear sway 20
There was not known a sute for Rents
In Jabals time who dwelt in Tents
Nor ever durst Presumptions lie
Open 'neath Heavens Canopy
But when our Guilts increasing calls 25
For vengeance that claymes sheltring walls
  Thus fortefide without all strife
  Ile guive the Ball to th'Cuntry-life
  And swear all entertainments less
  Though the City hath more Venusses 30
For may not that deceive withall?
Cuckoos come in with Nightingall
And 'tis a Lesson to discover
Wher on may meet Joy in a lover
Some to the Scholler-ship advance 35
But then that Grammer's Ruld by chance
Wherwith when governed we be
Our helth proves but Infirmety
    I should be sorry (living ther
    At rack and manger as it were) 40
    You should through Pampering despize
    The Cuntries full satieties
I yield you may some Guarden call
Your bliss to court the Spring withall
But sure I am Her bounties yeild 45
Thousand times more to evry field
Nor may you cloyster up that treasure
Is Blossomd out heer without measure
For though with Graces overspred
Those seem wher Bewtie's mustered 50
Yet doe the wholsom Milkmayds Arms
Stript up assault with noe less charmes

Or is not Rapture then begott
Under her tuckt up Petticote
When she her strait white ancles shewes 55
Daggled and washt in morning dewes?
   You may perchance take course in Park
   Hide stollen pleasure in the dark
   Game not at Ruff but Picadill
   And ther Bowle out and Rook your fill 60
   I dare avow that none of these
   Out-vie the yards, the Chase, the Leas
   Containd within this lower sphere
   Wher noe Star seems Irreguler
   But mutuall Influences joygn 65
   To make the day of frendship shine
      You'r but Irradiated half
      Whilst trading at the Sun with Ralph
      Nor (wer't at full) could your half moon
      Prevaile to make of midnight noon 70
      The puer Elixar Juyce divine
      Needs not the Comment of a signe
      But wher its vertue's understood
      Without a bush Ile call it good
What though you have a River ther 75
To waft your thirst ore to the Bear
And a Trade wind whose privilidg
Constant from Westminster to th'Bridg
May fill your Sayles trimd and prepard
To take in fresh watr at Stillyard 80
You must have care in passing by
Of Sirens in this Pilacy
For ther's a Tribe Enchantment pumps
As you accost wher Dwelt Duke numps
Then what befell Ulisses cast 85
Who tide himself unto the Mast
   When heer the Musike of the Groves
   Tund to the Keyes of birds make Loves
   To which our whelps seem t'add a grace
   As they are following their Chase 90
   The Ecchoing wood in ho-mul ho-
   All other Gammuths quite out goe
   And when we are from hunting come
   Heer's a resounding Musick Room
   To solace in; wher for content 95
   Hangs this and t'other Instrument
As the Theorbo, Viall, Lute
With Harpsicon to these a Flute
Whose rich Concavety containes
The Pretious Treasure for the Vaynes 100
Wher with Sublimd our thoughts aspire
And carry us 'bove Ela higher

Then heer's a Pond too and a Boat
A shed therby to wash your throat
From any Fish-bones harm or worse 105
Catt-killing-Care, or any curse
The hardnes of the Fates or Times
Create to Cancell merth and rimes
   Ther in a Counsail whilst we sit
   To propagate noe state but witt 110
   Like Court of Justice we dispence
   High verdict censures 'thout offence
   And all Malignant humors drive
   Out of Contents prerogative
   That noe disasterous breth impayre 115
   By dialect that wholsom ayre
   Wherin we breath and are as free
   In mutuall society
Thus with one Frend and two; noe more
Than makes up just the Count and Skoar 120
To freedom and to merth belongs
You may rest happy out of Throngs.

To Phi: Wood upon my Lady x x x going To London and Leaving these parts

Shall we Leese Exiter and with Her all
We can true Joy or Conversation call
And doth the Fancy sleep? is the pen dry
That should record in Dierge or Elegy
This soe hard hap? wherby our Comforts flight 5
Leavs all this Lesser Clime heer Ankorite
Secluded from the world and set apart
Alone to feel the rigor and the smart
Of the Times hevier tred? did Fates devise
This knack to make us all Philosophise? 10
Turn Stoicks? walk Cross-buckleing our armes
As if we were a meditating Charmes?
Not one word from the Tongue, but from the Eye
Or Brow wrinkled into Severety.
All objects transmutated seem t'posess 15
The direfull figures of some hideousnes
To fright us from our selves, and more to try us
Each Shaddow's like an Evil Aingell by us
Now that our Better's going: so't begetts
A Time of darknes when our day light setts 20
   Such will beshade all heer by Her remove
   (Princes of Frendship, Quintessence of Love)
   Wher left as 'twer in Vassellage (noe less)
   To Forrest Beasts and to their wildernes
   With Hob and his Compagnons Puck the Mare 25
   Such Goblins as our Sence deluders are

And play their Reaks with mortalls whilst the sky
Becoms Closs mourner in nights Livery
  Yet as the glimmering light of dawn appeers
  To ransom all out of those bonds of fears   30
And huisher in the morn; soe may't prove now
My intercession to the Powres, and Vowe
For Her return to shorten this our payne
Quickly to bring us home our day again.

Ode: My Valedice to x x x^r going to London may.5.

      But must Frends part awhile?
        Can noe reprive
      Guive longer hopes to live
        Than one poor day?
          Say may   5
  We not this difference reconcile
    And Jubelise the same
  Unto affections sacred name
    Count Fivety years but one
And that a month, a week, a Day and none   10
Til you return to leav's noe more alone

  For brooks that swell we see
    Severd by Iles
  For very many miles
    Yet met again   15
    Maintain
The usuall Current Liberty
  And Circling embrace
The frutefull medow with more grace
    The t'other Element   20
How ever seperated in its ascent
Unites and becomes one i'th'Firmament

    Soe let what will betide us in our course
    Love's sayd to guather strength by short divorce
    And all I wish our parting prove noe worse   25

In Obitum and transportationem per Wainsford Corporis Amicissimi mei Gul: Armin Baronetti &c: Ad viatorem May-8-1651

What ist thou wonderst at soe much? to see
A Triumph clad all in one Livery?
And whilst Dame Flora natures Law obeys
In painting out her bounty sevrall wayes
To add unto the Meads and Guardens prayse   5
              How com'st about
Ther thus should march soe Black a mourning rout?
  Tis a true Funerall prepar'd alone
  For Greef to set out Sorrowes action

Wher in the last farewell and service due 10
From Frend to Frend to testefy the true
And former Loves noe Ceremonies have
More waight than those attend them to the Grave
    Now who in Frendship ever did out vie
    Our Armin heer? whose great Civilety 15
    To all he knew, (matcht with a studious care
    To be his Cuntry's too Advantager
    For which He's born; til Envious Fates by stelth
    Would neither spare Him us nor th'Commonwelth
    Soe dide He: Leaving this behind: that as 20
    Th'example of his frendship did surpass
    Soe Greefs occation seldom greater was.

To Phil: Wood at London.
Ode:

Time hath its Seasons. Soe hath Love
For evry absence or remove
    Frends from ech other make
        I take
To be the winter Tropick wherin Dayes 5
In Frend-ships Zodiack shortned severall wayes
    These future Comforts raise
    That by return they'l bring
The happy tidings of a joyfull Spring

The wool-pack Clouds of Fleesy snow 10
That threaten us a Storm below
    And Blanketings to cover
        All over
The Damask of the meads And fields soe green
Til neither grass, nor flowr, nor blade be seen 15
    What doe they other mean?
    Than that when once blown ore
The fragrancies by much will seem the more

I cannot tel (my Phill) when we
Broak ofe our Late society 20
    And Burley emptied was
        A-las
But that the months all backward seemd to stray
The weather Lowrd and night prevaild ore day
    Contentment to betray 25
    Yet let a word or Letter
Signe a returne we shall be pleased better

Then what remaines of us as yet
Condemnd to winters stormy swet
    Under deprivements skoar 30
        Noe more

Of June or Julies summer feel I swear
Than Those within the Artike Circle, wher
   They'r 'frended with the Bear
    Unless some quick reprive   35
Huisher us hopes of Heat to make us live

To the same after return upon receipt of a second token of Toba[cco]

Whilst I desier your frendships understood
  Phil: I protest I'm in a wood
Not in Dodonas grove
  How all somere
  That might present in Trees a Spher   5
  With interwoven leavs
  Though thence may be
  Extracted sylvane sympathy
Nor in those shades our Forrests yet retain
  To keep their guests from Being slain   10
For I am soe and more since thy kind hart
  Doth stil fresh curtesies impart
  Well then as from the root of love those spring
  Lend me one branch or bough for covering.

Rosseus Vaticinus
Englisht

October 1659

Fear wayts on those who doe Loves stings approve
Time swallows All things, let's then yeild to Love
Shall my Ears tingle stil and n'ere reply
Oft did the Chaugh proclayme my Destenie
From th'hollow willow that at Home I had
A father kind but wife was very bad   5
I married am and doe bemone my Fates
Yet Comfort 'tis t'have some Assotiates.

The Ivy—twine

Vivamus mea
Lesbia &c:

Come my Cordelia let's not Leese
The frutes of youthfull passages
Time is a Theef and steals away
The Blessings that befrend each day
And Like a rank-wingd hawke in flight   5
Trusses the pastimes of the night
Soe that what's past is past recall
And what's to come conjecturall
It is the present tence alone
Guives life to true fruition   10
  Graunt we may spend the lighter howers
  And make the Day Platonick ours

Wee'l find the Night in darkned skies
T'sute better with Loves misteries
When in a soft embrace we meet 15
And crown all stollen pleasure sweet
    Then we may sport and toy and play
    Free from what scandelous censorings say
For Curtains drawn, the Valence will
Be silent, nor detect for ill 20
What is well meant: Let's banish fears
Since sheets and Blanckets have noe ears
Nor can the frame or Bed-cords speak
Unless by whispering a creak
Which can noe other signefy 25
But that those live who theron lie
And active bring all parts to joygne
In consort with this Ivy-twine
Far sweeter than the Eglantine.

Upon the Castle in the Ayer and Bower of Bliss to Phi: Wood:

    Whilst some delight
    In warrs to fight
        And make the Camp their cheefest care
    Others ther are
    Shun Discords Jarr 5
        Soe build their Castles in the ayre

    Ther be Likewise
    Who to devise
        More freedom on Contentments skoar
    A Bowre of Bliss 10
    Create which is
        Severd by waters from the shore

    Heer harmless merth
    Skearce known on Earth
        Is dealt from evry whiter sowle 15
    And mutuall Love
    Doth gently move
        Without a whirlwind of controwle

    Ther freedome true
    Like to the view 20
        Or prospect that fayre fields discovers
    Yeilds noe consent
    To Ambushment
        Or circumvention of Lovers

    Who that had these 25
    Would cross the seas
        And seek content in forraign parts
    Or range and rome

From house and home
   To practise Marses bloody arts 30

(*Flint)   *Fill me a glass
Then let it pass
   Til evry Lip hath done the same
In silent stelth
Of frends and helth 35
   Performd alike and without name

This done we'l part
Though not in hart
   Stil placing hopes above despaier
And will be well 40
And we may dwell
   In Bowres and Castles in the Ayre

Sonnet

Some for their sport
   To woods resort
Wher kenneld lies the wily fox
   Others delight
   I'th'moonshine night 5
To boult the Cunny, sack the brocks

   Some say the fields
      More pass-time yeilds
In following Watt that dies for fear
   And ther's again 10
      A Stoick train
Place all content in a Carear

   But all such err
      I dare averr
And doe their minds with froth confound 15
   For ther's noe chase
      But must guive place
Unto the Race on Stanford doun

   Wher Cripple lies
      And Jack-straw flies 20
And Marigould amongst the rest
   With Cooper matcht
      Is soon dispatcht
For that horse wins that runs the best

   Ther Logger-head 25
      Must not be sayd
To measure out in vayne the course
   Since he's to start
      With one of Art
A Cambridg Academick horse 30

    'Sides a bald steed
       Ther is indeed
Cost half a hundred and more
   Suted to dance
      As well as prance   35
Wearing white pumps on his feet 4.

    But he is yet
       For training sett
And soe but looks upon the game
   As I suppose   40
      Least he should lose
Soe rob Pick-pocket of his name

    These met together
       Wind and weather
Lords and Ladies all agreing   45
   Noe recreation
      To Conversation
Which crowns that Life else were but being

    Poor Sorrel's beat
      Soe we retreat   50
Yet thus our future hopes display
   Since Holl's of age
      It doth presage
That Westmorland will win his day

The second part to the same tune.

    This may suffize
     But when the prise
Or cup is to be run for then
   I'd have none heer
      Soe voyd of fear   5
As not to yeild to Lincoln men

    We are but Majors at the sport
But when those blades to it resort
   Each is a Collonell
And hath the speed as I suppose   10
And heeles in swallow of all those
   That cannot drink soe well

    Some doe soe little lap endure
They yeild and pay a forfeture
   Rather than leese their main   15
Nor can that horse however quick
Run out his course when he is sick
   Allthough of Fennick strain

    Ther is a Brother of the Nett
Were He put in I judg would get   20

> The plate from any other
> For He noe sooner starts and's up
> But he must have his chirping-cup
>   His cares to drownd and smother
>
> Then rise up Peg and waygh thy Ale
> Was brewd last night soe is not stale
>   The word Saint George is guiven
> They come apowder and amain
> Now St Jhon has't now Bob again
>   To make thy Lodg their hevn
>
> Ther Bully Watt swears he will meet
> And judg which of the two's more fleet
>   For He's a Jocky right
> Til they have all the Ale-stoops past
> And now retird to th'Chimny at last
>   Sit nodding ore a pipe

Upon Buck[ingham']s and his Duch[ess']s Visiting Apthorpe and stay ther from November the 17th til the 28th

> These seven dayes I last did pass
>   Appeer a week of wonders
> Wherein was left nor Cup nor glass
>   Of ale or wine for Plunders
>
> Skearce any meat to fill the Mawe
>   But All was clean devowred
> As if by new prescriptions lawe
>   My spits were to be scowred
>
> A Noble Duke and's Duches bright
>   En passant came a pransing
> Until they turnd the Day to Night
>   And Night to day in Dancing
>
> God bless me from such Guests again
>   Whose Modestie's a pleasure
> That house and home I may maintaine
>   In Comfort more and Leisure
>
> That wine and Ale again may fill
>   My sellers and my Diet
> Servd up in proper howers stil
>   To ratefy my quiet
>
> My wood yard too not disposest
>   Of what should keep me warme
> 'Fore with new loggs I reinvest
>   To shend from winters storme
>
> Thus if my Frends befrend I'le say
>   Thei'r All most walcome come

Else Charety goes out o'th'way
  Which ought begin at home

Frendships Salamander to x. x. x.

Whilst all the world is on a flame
  And each bethinkes him wher to wander
True Frendship should remain the same
  Turn Nature into Salamander
    And from those fiers of spleen and hate   5
    Grow fatt and more incorporate

Thus my good Lord wher Frends once are
  Knit in affections bond together
Noe hot alarum from the warr
  Should be of power to startle either   10
    But by how much such discords rise
    The more t'make Neighbours Sympothise

Arrowes soon break when they unquiver
  For strength unite is of more force
When smaller streams meet in a river   15
  Then add they glory to their source
    And not before whilst bankes of moss
    Their liquid Intervenings cross

Such Jealosies and fears appeer
  Stil whispering some disastrous fate   20
To make a man his shadow t'fear
  And deem misfortune at the gate
    When nothing can that soule offend
    Is constant to himself and frend

'Twas when the blustring storms awoke   25
  Not blest beneath a sunshine skye
The Travler lapt him in his cloak
  For t'other had causd him t'throw it bye
    Soe 'tis Afflictions prize alone
    To siment faster Union   30

Then though the thundring Canons roar
  The Trumpetts sound and Coulers fly
I am stil wher I was before
  Much more in love with amity
  Whose Trophy I would raise as soon   35
  As others horse doe and Dragoon

Ad Protectorem—January-30-1653.

Brave Captain though thine honor gaind increase
By war let all concluded be in peace
'Tis commendable after Pallas spear
Had brandisht been Her Olive branch to wear

For being Protector and anoynted thence 5
All suppling lenatives He should dispence
Unto the People; make the sword to bend
Into a sickle, th'Helmet to defend
Hive like the laboring Bee; if this He'l doe
I'le say He shall be my Protector too. 10

Upon the death of my Good nag: Fox

The Fox is dead, if subtilty with him
Interrd 'twer happy: and a Sanadrim
Of well composd conceptions to apply
The Happy fate of this sad desteny
Then would ther be noe more Plotts to controwle 5
Our Enterprises whither in bush or hole
Launds or their Circumvalls, but all agree
The fox is dead, henceforth wee'l sober be

An Epigram upon His Highnes entertainment in the Citty translated

Let all rude Triumphs seace of Cesars Roome
A new Star shines, a better Cesar's come
And Greater too, whilst thus He shuns the same
Leavs Others t'snatch at Crowns; He'l only Fame
T's enough t'have power: and if presage speaks right 5
This other Cesar may Rooms Gods afright
Heer fall my Lot Thy Capitalls t'Ascend
And bring Thy neck to Brittish yoak to bend
That soe't may tame the Triple Tirants rod
And strike a fear into the three-crownd God 10
Thou Brittish Queen let thy advance increase
  Now Cromwell favours and guives lawes to th'Seas
  Call out the Blew Gods, Let the Naydes agree
  All heer to bring their Consort Thams to Thee
  And Thou New Troy minting thy Forme a new 15
  Weave Garlands for soe Great a Princes due
He who soe many Crowns despisd, seeks you
The harts of men, nothing of stage or shew
He brings his own bayes, broaken scepters yeild
That Liberty He guave might take the feild 20
  Now are yea first made Cittizens, time past
  Were servants unto Kings; learn this at last
  To yeild to th'reigne of those whose power who skans
  Shall find them but your fellow Cittizens
The Conquring souldier's deaf but yet He knows 25
How to change armes int'Lawes and making showes
And thence puts on the Gowne, soe what of late
A Chaos lay a new world will Create
  Forthwith all things as at the first you'l see
  And Plato shall my Great Apollo be 30

Let his year bring about the goulden age
Of Saturne's reigne whilst Sol treads heavens stage.

De Regulo—Martial L: 1 Epigram 82.

This Tarrace turnd to Rubbedge doth express
The Trophies of some great unhappines
Yet mark with what safe misteries and Charme
It fell that Regulus might take noe harme
Who lately had been walking ther, whose worth   5
Orecome by: soon, its weaknes it brings forth
And after that its Master was gon in
To tumble doun it thinks it then noe sin
(Regule) after such a scape who dare
Deny but that Thou art to th'Gods a care   10
For whose sake soe Great Ruines harmless wear.

William Martin
Anagram
A Mart in mi Wil.

Pullin and Tompson spare your paines
And goe no more to Frankford Mart for books
  For heer at home He'l find more gains
  Who on my Persian Travailer but looks
    The Vatican and Bodlies leavs   5
Fade and strike sayle when His Volumenous lungs
  But utter what His hart conceives
Out of his study in the Eastern Tongues
  If Any be more Curious stil
Tel them they'l find a Mart heer in mi Wil.   10

Veritas Odium parit—Horace.
to Nol: February: 1654

Since Truth breeds Hate Thou must not tak't amiss
I love Thee Nol: in whom soe little is
For should I say I hate Thee, that revers't
Might get more Truth than's fit to be reherst
But whither I Thee love or Hate, 'tis true   5
Thy Cake is Dowe and soe thou mayst goe Brew
For having pleasd all states alike They cry
Thou art a Villain; that's noe flattery
But, what they think, Fayth cousen them and fling
Away thy weapons huisher in the King.   10

A Dialogue between a Hunting Swayn and
a Shepardes weeping the Loss of Pan

Hunt: Fair Shepardes why dost thou weep
      Since ther's an end of winters could

	The Season now invites thy sheep	
	To blanch the Mountaines, quit their Fould	
Shep:	O tis too sad for to be tould.	5
Hunt:	Make me acquainted with the cause	
	Of this distemper, and I'le Vowe	
	To tear out of the fell wolfs jawes	
	What s'ever Lamb h'hath tain from you	
Shep:	This might proov Jest, wer't not too true.	10
Hunt:	Yet cause thy greef speaks thus in tears	
	Torture me not with long delay	
	But tel, soe rid me of those Fears	
	O're all affections now bear sway	
Shep:	Why then in short, thus I obey	15
	Ther was a time when our Great Pan	
	And Flocks Protector kept these plains	
	Making them like th'Arcadian	
	Wher all Securety stil reignes	
Hunt:	Let me partake of what remaines.	20
Shep:	You shall: ther stept out of a wood	
	(As they were Mad) of Giants race	
	Who envying our Kidds that good	
	Chas't all protection from this place	
Hunt:	That was a sad and dismall case.	25
Shep:	Thus ever since we open lie	
	To what blast the intemperat wind	
	Can threaten towards our misery	
	Afflicting us in Corps and mind	
Hunt:	How could the Fates prove soe unkind?	30
Shep:	Only for this, as I suppose	
	Our offrings did displeas the Gods	
	Who in their anger did impose	
	For our Correction these rods	
Hunt:	'Twas soe 'twas soe without all ods	35
	Then for to dry thy Tear-drownd-eyes	
	I shall advise for time to come	
	We offer better Sacrefize	
	To bring our Pan back to us home	
Shep:	That should pleas all, but will not some	40
	Wherefore I'le crave thy hunting art	
	To tuft the thicks and find those out	
	Who thus have causd my Lambs to smart	
	That they may safer feed about	
Hunt:	These are but foxes without doubt	45
	But were they wolv's though clad like sheep	
	Lions in Lamb-skins to beguile	
	I'le not dispair, nor think of sleep	

               Til I this difference reconcile
               Provide the Hevns subscribe the while   50

Shep: Thanks noble Swain my greefs Alay
            That buried hast in hopes my sorrow
       All happines attend thy way
            And cause us t'meet again tomorrow
       The rest let expectation borrow.   55

A Sonnet Pastorall between Coridon and Phillis

Corid: Phillis fayr, and why soe Coy?
            Doth the wingd and spightfull Boy
             Soe contrive His cunning Art
            To make Thy Comelines my smart?
            Or is it thus? must Thou become   5
            Chief Glory of my martirdome?

Phill: Noe (fond youth) be not unkind
            To thy self, since Cupid's blind
            And endeavours main and might
            For to bereav us of our sight   10
            Until we groap as in the darke
            Th'out other light 'save from His spark

Both in   If it be soe, then let's be wise
Chorus   Nor farther prise
                  Those misteries   15
           Presented only to the eyes
               When 'tis the hart
               That must impart
               Those sacred fires
               Of chast desires   20
              And thus agreed in one
           Phillis again may like her Coridon.

Two Seafaring men invoak the Springs return

1:   How doe the winds
        Torment our minds
           And storms stil rise
           And Tempests rage
    The foggy vapours mist the skies   5
    Tel me what is't can this asswage?

2:   Arise and bring
      To us our Spring
          Great Phosphorus
          And assure us   10
    That those Damps are soe propostrous
    Shall guive way to Yong Arturus

Both: Then we again
Shall on the main
Ride happily   15
As erst before
When as our Polestar we espye
To guide our Barkes unto the shore

Til when through dout
We'l not put out   20
Least evry Tack
Should threaten knocks
And soe at last we prove a wrack
And split upon presumptions Rocks

To my Lord of Portland for a nights Lodging at his house in Wittlesey as I past for Norfolk the 20th of August 1661—in whose absence I was freely entertained by his servant Cole.

In Time of Owld when smiling Fate
Crownd this or That Day more Fortunate
The Custom was to skoar it on
With better marke from whiter ston
Instead of which least I pass bye   5
My happy Luck's Conveniency
None other than a Cole I'le Use
To help my Pen and Prompt my Muse
In rendring Thanks and Prayses due
Unto your Servant House and You—   10
                                W

A Pepper-corn or small rent sent to my Lord Campden for the Loan of his house at Kensington 9: February: 1651

Ingratetude's the worst of ill
Wherefore I shall not dip my quill
In its black Inke, but timely owne
Your favring Obligation
That with such Freedom now have Lent   5
Me this your Princely Tenement:
    Wherin I may survaigh at ease
    What Travailers by Land and Seas
    With toyle and trouble seek to gain
    Allthough at home I stil remain   10
Campden that wrot his Cuntries praise
Most worthily deserves the Bayes
But Frendship must Intitle you
To the true Laurell as your due
Who have not only plac't me heer   15
But makes me Emulate the sphere

Become Compagnion with the Sun
Soe round about the Gloab to run
In sevrall Pictures that declare
How it is framed Circular 20
   Nothing within its Compass falls
   But either on the Stayrs or walls
   Hang Trophe-like to represent
   The figure of each Continent
   That one may freely say or swear 25
   Drake, Forbisher, All had been ther
   Who to discovries bent their minds
   And Courted had, both Seas, and winds
   Heer larger pleasure on me wayts
   Than Magelans, found out the Strayts 30
   Making all vaine and falce the while
   I'm reading Sir Jhon Mandevile
   For These with story more engage
   Than Purcas in his Pilgrimage
   Or what was either sayd or wrot 35
   By Sands or by Tom Corriott.
Heer the fowr Seasons Mustred are
And what's to Each peculiar
With evry Nations sevral dress
Suting them to their Provinces 40
   Ther Other Landskips are display
   Thout Clock the parts of Night and day
This Room's defence, are men in Arms
That Other's blest with Sybells Charms
And the Fam'd Poets did devise 45
Stories of owld now held for lies
Adorn the Entry doth invite
To th'Place can conquer Apetite
And as their Raptures held divine
Soe doe they seem to guard the wine 50
That was Ralphs once but now is Mine.
   Thus evry Corner soe compleat
   As if each were a Flora's seat
   Tablets of Potts and Flowers rare
   Present a Guarden on the Stair 55
   Wher sits Tom Piper whose stil Layes
   Not to the ear but fancy playes
   And such a hand and Lute Him by
   As might the Lesbian out vie
   Whilst the heads posture speaks as much 60
   As keeping time with evry touch
   Ther for to Netefy the Roome
   The pretty Mayd Stands with her broome
   And Sempsteres somewhat above
   Both shew what postures They approve 65
   An Owld nakt Father 'thout a Coole

Heer puts Devotion to Schoole
Whilst on a Crucefix ther lies
Only a Painted Sacrefize
A Maudlen too that fain would crye 70
But that the Coulers now are drie
Ther farther fetcht soe more admir'd
See how a Turkish Bride's attir'd
And if it be not held a crime
To cherish order in this time 75
Cast but your eye a little farther
And you may see that of the Guarter
From the first Infancy and since
How it hath come from Prince to Prince
As sovrains of It and those Peers 80
Admitted been their Partners
Now ere I have with staircase don
A Frier ther doth shrift a Nunn
Or in probation at Least
Casts a Sheeps eye and stroaks her brest: 85
Whilst in a ston-bow One doth shoot
The wench houlds up that he may do't
Now that the Flesh may not begett
A surfet heer's a Fish-market:
An Emblem Picture tels you how 90
Owld Age with Iö's made a Cow
You'ld judg that Equity's not far
Wher's one and t'other Chanceler
Yet in a Proverb I was tould
Each thing that Glisters provs not gould: 95
A Bedchamber 'tis leads from hence
T'a Room of State and Audience
Wher Roe soe much o'th'world did see
Admittance hath and place to be
Yet Modestly his Spech forbears 100
(A Vertue Rare in Travailers)
So's Embassy's not heard but seen
As He presents it 'fore the Queen
Yet when my Lord would silence break
Heer is an Organ that can speak 105
Not quite demolisht though some notes
Have felt some stops from the red-Coats
Whose Drums all Musike else defye
Making it silenc't Ministry
And such at first began this dance 110
Of Discord and of Variance
A Coppy ore This doth express
The Labours of Great Hercules
Whilst in an Other Coign a Peace
Soe Rarely done to life that Greece 115
Nay all the World wher Pallas swayes

With Art did ne're more Nature rayse
Wher two faire Nimphs 'neth sheltering Bowres
Seem to delight in picking Flowres
And with a smiling Look imply 120
They'd guatherd them for those pass by
    He would not melt at this fair sight
    Might worthely turn Ankorite
    Bury Himself alive, see none
    But Earth beneath, about Him Ston 125
    Which brings me to such Tables as
    For Curious Marbles all surpass
    Wherin Art doth the Coulers dress
    Into Mosaik and Pedri-commess
    Appropriating to evry ston 130
    His wayght of Admiration
A Table in the Hall besides
That shewes how from one silver glides
Ther round about Those Gossips meet
Frequent Cheap side and Gratio's street 135
With Cock and Hen, Partridg and Phesant
Or other Cates to diet Plesant
And though we are not fed therby
These cure the hunger of the eye
    Whilst All within dores I commend 140
    I'de not forgett as you ascend
    Unto this structure to display
    That Claudian like or Appian way
    Soe due Proportioned noe Feet
    That ever Trac't out Wattling-street 145
    Of Antient Romans Cost and Pride
    Fram'd any one more qualefide.
To shew the Sovranty at Gate
A Lion and a Lions Mate
In silence stand, nor Roar to fear 150
Th'approach of any Passenger
Orchards on either side of these
Not yeilding to th'Hesperides
Gardens and walks that seem to me
Bestrewd with Curiosety 155
Whilst Nature's not of Arts help nice
But Both conclude it Paradice
Which that I might soe more beleev
Heer's Pictur'd too Adam and eve
Beasts Birds and Fishes making-one 160
Sampler of the Creation
A Wilderness too but in name
Less fit for wild things than for tame
And for to add to all this Tresure
A little Park walld in for pleasure 165
    These and a thousand more delights

Ravish my sence and Pen that writes
And would (as 'twer) bewitch and bring
Me 'thin a Circle and a Ring
Not to depart but heer to dwell 170
Enchanted through such Magick Spell
Such stately Mausolean flore
Tarassed and Ballkoned ore
With Pergola's claims wonder
Whilst to Each Guarden ther lies under 175
Grottos and Pavements that discover
Happy Retirements for the Lover
His fires in Secret to express
Unto his backward Misteress
All thats ascribd to Fortunes wheel 180
In reference to our weak keele
Disciferd is with curious art
And the Nine sisters sevrall part
Yet ere I can conclude this story
A virgin hand adds soe much Glory 185
To all the rest in Limning touch
Apelles skearce could doe soe much
In my opignion't doth out goe
Rubin and Michel-Angelo
These Traits and Lineaments are truer 190
Than Van-Dike drew or Albert Dure
And Gelthrop (alas) is Poorer
Fitter to hang than draw before her
Only my fears increase in this
Least Pallas should take it amiss 195
To see Her self too overcome
Soe dam Her to Arachnes doom
Now as a Merchant Factor that
Trades to Bantam, Ormus, Surat
Such Ports as of Greatst Riches are 200
Makes some return to shew his care
Soe heer my Lord think it noe skorn
I send you this poor Pepper-corn
Leases are held soe and doe bind
Cheefly when service rests behind 205
And that you may of this be suer
None shall obey and serve you truer
Than
W:

Wrot the 5ᵗ of November-1657.
Sonnet

This fiv't of November
As some may remember
Our Church and our State

                    Was neer a sad Fate
                        And should have been blown up with Powder   5
                But God did prevent
                That wicked intent
                    Discoverd the Plot
                    Sent the Traytors to th'Pot
                        Yet since we feel that speaketh Lowder   10
                Now by Civil Jarrs
                Our Peace turnd to wars
                    The Lawes in a word
                    Struck dumb with the sword
                        What Misery then is ensuing?   15
                The King and his Throne
                With Kingdome are gon
                    And Common-welth come
                    To rule in their roome
                        And is not this a good brewing?   20
                Noll with his frend Pride
                And others beside
                    The matters soe spun
                    That All are undon
                        But of their Own Occupation   25
                For now we have heer
                Nor Prelate nor Peer
                    Yet Parlement summon
                    To see what will come on
                        I'le tel you: to Blow up the Nation.   30

Upon our Lady's Day or The Anuntiation—1652

With what Laborious Care and studied Paines
Doe we torment ourselvs and beat our braines
In Combs and Glasses, Gould and silk aray
To trick and bewtefy our Lump of Clay
When in the Potters hand our doome is red   5
This to be honerd, that dishonored
And the like mettel sev'rall wayes imployd
Yet Both doe Crown the Workman Glorifide
  As I have seen from the same fountain flow
  Rivers that various Parts o'th'Compass goe   10
  Yet each adds to the Sea in t'which they fall
  And from whence first they suckt Originall.
Heer a Selected Vessel by decree
Restoreth Adams lost Posterety
When as the Herald Aingell did express   15
Out o'th'same Sex to rayse a Blessednes
Causd first our ruine, and that Rib to bear
Our Cure by whose advice we wounded were
Soe for to Close the broaken flesh again

Heer was disclosd a medson soverain 20
An Oyle that from a Virgin Taper might
Add remedy to th'Scorpions deadly bite
Save all but such as wantonly despise
The hidden vertue of Fayths Misteries
Guided by outward sence, and such with shame 25
For vessells of dishonor I proclaime
Incurable; Then that we shun their Fate
Let us not scruple to Commemorate
Though not Adore the Blessed Mary's womb
Opend to shut our everlasting Toomb. 30

Upon an Eclips of the Sun the 29th of march-1652
Voyced by Prognosticators to turn Day into night allmost
the moon soe obscuring his beams yet found nothing soe.

Mark how each Apprehentions on the rack
Looking to see a Sun-Shine Day turn black
Without any other inquisitian
Than that o'th'moones interpositian
Soe Natural as that it justly falls 5
To Christen such behoulders Naturalls
Who 'Cause Lucina's in the story read
Would fancy something to be brought a-bed
And soe heer 'twas for all run out o'th'house
To see a Mountain propogate a mouse 10
A wonder in Expectance, shrunk soe small
As that it prov'd noe wonderment at all
And yet the Timerous Sex noe peace admits
Until it on this subject forfait witts
Start out of bed as if mare-rid and then 15
Though fast asleep rise, walk and talk agen
   Doe not Astrologers mistake and err
   Or is't stil March, not rather Midsummer?
   Soe many Moon-led fancies roav' and stray
   After Eclips and to find Night by Day 20
Thus have I observd a new start Hare to skip
Out of her forme devoyd of foot man ship
(Through fear at first benumd) but softly goe
Yeilding approaches to her yelping foe
With one ear up the other closs doun layd 25
Telling the furlong how she was afrayd
As heer and ther woemen amazed run
To view the Late irradiated sun
Soe they supposd 'twould be but look how farr
These were deceived by the Kallender 30
Expecting Midnight, when it prov'd noe other
Than Cinthias fayer dessigne to kiss her Brother.

Upon a blessed shower from heaven after a drowth

    When the eternall hand of love
      Opens it self above
    In any showre of temprall good
      What should be understood
        But scripture thence   5
    Of true Obedience.
      And that vild Clay
      Should Powres Obey
    And in a thankfullnes for what is guiven
    Exalt the Doners prayse, look up to heaven   10

Corporis Anima Tutela—1652:

As two great fleets of potent neighbours strive
Whither shall win the Seas prerogative
Affections move in man and would controwle
The active pow'rs of Body and Soule
  Heer the fond worlds allurements doe invite   5
  To waygh, hoyse sale, and follow appetite
  Ther with the glass of promise we descry
  The various perills of its flattery
    And fearing shipwrack wher such dainger's layd
    Conclude the body safe when Soule's imbayd   10

Mereworth   **Upon my Sonn Charles return from his first 2. years**
April 20: 1654.   **travailes in Holland Fland[ers] and Brabant.**

Doe the fresh streams pay tribute to the Seas
  And glad the green Meads in their passages
Doth heavns dew cause the grass and flowrs appeer
  In thankfullnes to th'season of the year
And evry Plant its livery blossoms bring   5
  To wayt upon their Shrief this forward Spring
And doth the clumsy winter stil remain
  Over my Inke and fancy Soverain
Locking up both; when as my sonns return
  Should all unfreeze my hart and make it burne   10
In gratitude for incense to that Throne
  Afforded had soe great protection
Thither I'le fly then humbly and confess
  The mercy that vouchsafes this happines
And though I have nor Kid nor Lamb to kill   15
  Make him my Isack off'r him to God still.

1652   **Upon Good Friday**   at Aston.

    Meet we heer with cares and crosses
      Tribulations beside

Know we not our Saviour dide
And that Sea the Merchant tosses
To his Proffits port's the guide
    Nothing of gain
    But's mixt with pain
    Whilst heer below
We all are placed not to reap, but sowe

Doe not Captives when released
  Cherish Liberty the more
  For th'condition went before
  Ought not our Joyes t'be increased
  On our blessed Masters skoar
    Who sufferd thus
    To ransome us
    And set us free
Who were enchained to sins slavery

  Mark but a Prisner at the barr
    When cast and condemnd to death
    He spares noe cost, noe frends noe breath
    But doth importune neer and farr
    Til a reprive he gotten hath
      Heer 'twas his will
      All to fullfill
      And to procure
Our Pardon did himself the paynes endure

  Let us noe more besotted then
  Cark and beat our braines in vayn
  Crouching under evry payne
  With the meer worldly sort of men
  As if Glory all were slain
    When over Hell
    The conquest fell
    Sin and the grave
He vanquished, was lost awhile to save.

In Pascam 1652

Triumphant Passover Divine
Wheron the Lord of light did shine
And being raysd dispelld the charms
Of Darknes vanquishing deaths armes
  How foolish was the peevish Jew
  To think he could in Toomb subdue
  Him to whom toombs obeyd and guave
  Those up again had lien in grave
Yet thus allthough he were unknown
And made a stranger by his own
He did vouchsafe his glorious ray

To light the Gentiles into Day
And soe (night past) let evry one
Cast ofe black deeds, put brighter on.

At Dover the   of June-1652
Staying 3 dayes for a Passage for my sonn and nephew

Dij maris   God both of Seas and Land
et coeli   If't be thy will
                Command
              The winds be stil
           Nor quarrel any Longer   5
Whither the wave or they should seem the stronger

       For Heer we lie embay'd
          And full of doubt
              Afrayd
          To venture out   10
Whilst the fresh Gales maintain
A Tempest to disturb the Liquid plain
      Lay Thy great power upon
         What's in thy fist
            That none   15
       Of These resist
     Thy mandate but appeer
Benign to Us and Evry Travailer

     Which though we cannot sue
        Nor yet plead for   20
          As due
       Thy Grace is more
    When it's Layd out to bless
With favour Those are in the most distress

To the Suns accosting our Troppick and huishering
in the Spring–April: 19-1654

Wellcome wellcome Glorious light
That not only conquerst night
But putst winter now to flight
  'Tis thy presence with thy rayes
  That again ad'st howers to dayes   5
  Blessing our Climat sevrall wayes
For its Thy auspitious hand
Stroaks pregnancy all ore the land
That Teeming is at thy command
  Soe the silver Dazy's seen   10
  To enrich that bank of green
  With guilded Cowslips between
Such as nere on Tagus shore
Glistering 'wittches, nor such ore

From Inds mines digged; but far more 15
  Up-start at your approach Primroses
      The chief ingredient to Poses
      And captivate both eyes and noses
Then to redeem this Fate again
The purple Violet I'le maintain 20
Sits ore the rest as Soverain
  Who shall now Protector be
      Ore such Treasures Soveranty
      But O-liver? O that is He.

Upon William Sharp a Colliers' ploughing the Moulhill or sandy bank neer Apthorp bridge.

Sharp witted Will to occupy some land
Enterd a Tenant to the sand-
      y moulhill at the bridg
One would have guest it like the shore
But He did make it bring forth more 5
      by's Colliers priviledg
Wherfore since he proves undertaker
Though't measurd be by foot not Aker
      soe much his labour's blest
As that a Crop it brings him forth 10
And of pains taking shews the worth
      which payes with interest
He is himself both Plough and Share
Smal husbandry's Great manager
      'thout yoak and Cattles Jossel 15
What from an handfull on the ground
Was first bestowd again he found
      increast unto a Bushel
Nor had he need of Barn with bayes
When all the Corn he gets he layes 20
      in some smal payle at best
And then to thresh it doth noe more
Than of his shovel make a flore
      his famely to feast
Which doth consist of These 'thout strife 25
One Dog one Cat Himself and wife
      barrend through time and age
Noe full bords to invite a Mouse
Nor any riches in the house
      a Theef for to engage 30
But whilst he doth enjoy the ease
Of a safe life which best doth pleas
      his houshould Deities
Free as the ayre he breaths all care
Of Sequestration and warr 35
      he utterly defies
Soe when the Evning shuts up day

He doth his wearied limms display
   upon the bed of sleep
Judging all Cedar of the hill   40
In vaine when as light-strawe-thatch will
   him dry and warmer keep
He careth not for flower of wheat
Cockle and wild oats are his meat
   which boyled in a pan   45
Or Pipkin rather, not in folio
Least soe his pottage mock an Olio
   Well smackt with Onion
For the next meal't maybe he'l guather
Sharp nettles or smooth mallowes rather   50
   fro'th' common mead therby
To's neighbour River make adress
For water when he's in distress
   through thirst and very dry.
(Though poor he doth noe Cattle lack   55
For some are crawling on his back
   yet such as noe plough tugg
Which with their six feet nimbly pass
Til at the last they'r turnd to grass
   with an Italian Shugg)   60
He hath noe heards of 's own but free
Can others as they straggle see
   all ore the fields to wander
And wondring all men not consent
(Whilst Nature is with les content)   65
   to be their own commander
But prostetuting Theirs alone
Not only to each motion
   of news that treads the streets
Each covets and therin seems wise   70
Entitled to all avarice
   which he in noe sort meets
In the meantime he'l not resist
Knowing wherin his good consists
   but happines declare   75
To be alone dowry to such
As content having not much
   rejoyce with shorter fare.

To the tune of   *Upon the horse race at Newmarket*
Cock Lawrell   *between the Earle of Suffolk and*
        Sir Horatio Tounshend Barronet
        the 4th of November 1652.

   As through Newmarket I passed of late
   A muster of Jockyes I ther espide

That came to run mony and not for the plate
And all the Cracks went on Suffolk side

The Town is devided soe ther's a dispute
  Thick arguments layd doun in yellow and white
But those lodg'd in Suffolk did Cambridg confute
  And guave them a non plus 'ere it was night

The Pegasus Steed that bore the great fame
  Soe pittifull poorly and hobling rides
His sides were well guilded for all's thundring name
  And Northumberland ran short of Silver sides

Ther was such confidence that he would win
  As to the stoop they were leading him out
That all the house of the Howards and kin
  In betting their pockets disperced about

The other as He approached the post
  As meaner far and of mortall race
Had but some five or six frends at the most
  To back him and counsail him t'run apace

In a plain sheet and blanket as bad
  He was accoutred as if doom'd to lose
When Tother a stall soe victorious had
  As silver could make bespangled with Oes

Besides the fayer hands his ribbons tide on
  Was enough to discourage the other side all
For Bewties charmes we say yeild to none
  But win the day wher ere they doe fall

I thought well that Wallsingxam would not have been
  'Gainst Norfolk, yet soe it appeered he was
And though in such riding he's very well seen
  They borrowd an other to take the disgrace

A fellow cut out for the nonce you would say
  As if all his gutts into one were spun
Soe lank, had a pudding but lien in the way
  Some verely think that that He'd ha won

I will not say to whom he belonges
  His Lord is my frend and soe I forbear
Yet all are acquainted with rimes and with songes
  Know well they may clinch, not prick though come neer

One Neighbour I had too that was soe bould
  Because he had cast a figure or Spell
To tel him what's done, he lookt for my gould
  But't fel out I should prise his silver aswell

Ther were of Lords some poor and some Rich
  Some that drank wine and some that drank Ale

Yet ere they ran none propheside which
  Should win before him that came from Skars-dale

That name raysd a dampe; soe when they all mett
  And making the stakes that bets might abound   50
He bravely steps out and guives the onsett
  Soe eased his pockets of many a pound

What Care I quoth Jack that Corpulent Squier
  I never sawe any match but one lost
And this may perchance draw the Barronet higher   55
  Creating him Jocky to his noe small Cost

Soe strikes in a new an other to make
  Which is accepted and our side agrees
To run with the Barb and to double the stake
  And venture two hundred to win or to seese   60

Sir Cotten and Soams and the rest that were ther
  Our opposites had soe great a defeat
For wheras they hoped to carry it cleer
  They found those hopes blasted when as they were beat

The Russels came in their Tunshend to back   65
  And ventured far his side to maintain
Besides some of his own name were not slack
  To throw at the Caster and venture their main

Ther was a (Collonell) man of armes
  As He himself reported that came   70
Against us, whose Dice had they had noe more charms
  Than heer he had luck, his welth had been tame

Sir Ned too that Elder I must not forget
  He wanted some Crowns his pockets to fill
And soe he came posting from London to bet   75
  And yet his pockets were empty stil

Now that record of this course might be taken
  Honest Sir Sim: and his Poet were by
But as soon as they found they all were mistaken
  They quencht their own thirsts but left their quite dry   80

Wherfore least any mistakes by report
  Should issue in prejudice of what was done
I guave my Pen this freedom to sport
  And thus you have all who lost and who won

additional or 2^d part to the same tune

Now that I may guive each Jocky his stile
  As they marcht up and doun the toun
Some Reeling out of their ranks into file
  When Barly-corn-broth had seised the Crown

Owld Willson, Owld Soresby, and Owld David Heard 5
  Three principall members of that cheating raff
Who had rod matches since Adam wore beard
  Yet now like yong birdlings were caught with chaff

Whilst Bignall and Desborow aymd at the prise
  And started ofe the skoar on a sudden 10
The first gaind the Ditch in all mens eyes
  And soe the last came as if post for a Pudding

In Effigiem Urbani Octavi Papæ præterit

If Piety to witt be put to schoole
Thou wast the Eight wise man and that speaks—

In Effigiem Innocentij Decimi nunc Papæ—1652.

Father why Innocent? when most men know
Thy rules at best are th'Churches overthrow
For whilst St Peters Keyes the Heavns unlock
Thine shut the passages unto Christs flock
Of owld the Tenths were held the Clergies due 5
Soe th'Divel a Clarke may take his Tithe of you.

In Rempublicam—1652

All's common now since Commonwealths bere sway
And warr in Earnest's become Rebells play.

In Cardinalem Wolsæum

Whilst Laicks glory in descent of Blood
Why shouldst not Thou in Titles shine as good
Great Clergy Prince? whose Fathers house might die
In Crimson grain all His posterety
Hence came't about Purple adornd thy head 5
And more to blush Thy Vestments all were red
Thus from the Shambles wher much blood doth fall
Thou didst become a Tyrant Cardinall.

In partem Capitis vicessimi primi
S[anc]ti Mathæi   April:3°-1653.

When towrds Jerusalem our Saviour went
He chose noe state nor Pompous ornament
But rather on an Asses coult did ride
To cast a more contempt on this worlds pride
Yet multitudes their garments spredding lay 5
And cut doun Palms to strew them in his way
How seasonably was this done when He

Dessigned was a speedy Victory
The bloody Day approaching which should tell
His Conquest over Death the Grave and Hell.   10

Upon suspition of the Gout to Doctor Bowles

What pride of humor doth my feet command
That those but now stood, can noe longer stand.
Soe have I markt some members faile in drink
But I am free from Bacchus (as I think)
How ere this Comfort stil supports my shrine   5
Though all else shrink one member'l not decline.

September 3-1657   ### Upon a Gent: calld F.F. and his Kittling

Mark heer what Sympothy is hatcht
She loves to Scratch He to be Scratcht
And 'cause his Fancy to enrich
He would be scratcht wher't dos not itch
He hath made choyce of this poor best   5
To signe Reward for evry Jest
Pregnant abroad and in the house
This Kittling (Peace) can catch a Mouse
Soe that Conditions Paralell
Towsing and Mousing both like well   10
And for to pay a Mistres due
He'l leap and Catch whilst she cries mewe
If a Gib-cat this Kittling prove
I'le Envy, not upbrayd His love.

Upon the Lady Margaret Marchioness of Newcastle her Rare Poems new come forth—1652.

Noe wonder 'twer though Schooles went doun
Now Learning shifts from Goune to Goune
Whilst Petticoat and Kertle may
The Banners of the Nine display
And Atomize what ere the Quill   5
Recorded from the Twin-like Hill
Make Wit and Fancy soe combine
In Numbers true and feet to joygne
As if all Dance and Musikes art
Were heer brought in to bear a part   10
(For the contrivement I'd averr
'Twould pussel a Philosopher)
The Stile, the Method and the Phrase
Doe haighten soe the Authress prayse
That I should too Injurious be   15
To cast into such Treasury
For all the Graces heer are mett
To make a Pearle of Margaret.

'Upon a Time it did befall'

Upon a Time it did befall
Peter was stript to Cloath St Paule
And then not many years by gon
He's robd again to pay St Jhon
The question heer is in a word   5
Whither Opes best the Keys or Sword
That whilst it keeps all things in Awe
Perforce must guive the Keyes the Lawe
Those then as picklocks to our purses
Open indulgencies 'gainst Curses   10
If so th'Conclusions pregnant thence
Heavn Gates are Opt through Violence.

'Both Creame O'th'Poets and of Clergy He'

Both Creame O'th'Poets and of Clergy He
To Whom Cremona was a Bishops See

Upon the History of Great Brittan by Willson

When a great Kings Court doth recorded stand
Under a Clark O'th'Kittchens hand
What can the Hungry-Curious think or wish
But for a tast of such a dish
Which when they have obtain and ore it ran   5
They'l find it tast ill, though Welldon

But Heer Like to a Second-Courses charme
That guives to Female Appetites Alarme
And Quainter Pallats I'le suppose a mess
Of Godwitt, Phesant, Quaile, or Partriges   10
And though I have not read my Willson ore
The Subject can afford noe less, but more.

Upon the Death of Mr Jhon Selden the great Antiquary—1654.

We sayd when Symon Dews subscribd to Fate
Death did some Owld Record Obliterate
But what shall we say now that Learned Jhon
The Patron of Antiqueties is gon
We will conclude (noe Age like this) ere sent,   5
A Subject fitter for a President ~ ~ ~
                        in what sence you will:

[Set up under the Gen[eral's] Picture at the Chang as was reported—

Ascend 3 Thrones Great Captain and Divine
By the will of God, O Sion for they'r thine
Come priest of God, bring Oyle, bring Robes, bring Gould
Bring Crownes and Scepters, it's high time, unfowld

> *Your Cloystred Baggs you State-Cheats least the rod* 5
> *Of Steele and Iron of this King of God*
> *Pay ye'all in's wrath with intrest kneel and pray*
> *To Oliver that Torch of Sion Starr of day*
> *Shout then you Marchants, Citts and Gentry sing*
> *And all bare headed Cry God bless the King.]* 10

An Answer to it

Skales fower times 3 ascend Arch Traitor Thou
By th'will of Satan becom Hell hound now
Come Gregory bring Ropes int'Snittles tide
To fitt this Hammon would be dignifide
Let not the Gibbet be to seek, wheron 5
This Princely Peece may hang, not sit on Throne
But if a Pardon may in favour be
The Axe and Block prove His Catastrophe
'Twill be retaliation beside
That the same Fate should haunt a Regicide 10
 Then Merchants Citts: and Gentry all may say
 With their Capps on that Justice crownes the Day

veni ⎫
vidi ⎬   **Shrove Tuesday-1654. when Fra[ncis] Palmes**
vici ⎭   **came to visit me at Apthorp was**
     wellcome won mony &c:

Squier Palms to Apthorp Threshowlds welcome came
Might Cesars Palms deserve to crown his name
For first He Came; Then sawe, Then won, all Three
Innobling Th'Garland of True Victory
 He out of frendship came, Sawe the Gierle too 5
 And won my mony (fortune being my foe.

To the Impudency of Monsieur de Militiere who dedicating his book to our Royall Master thought therby To Triumph indeed in bringing him to the Romish Church but was deceived

Why should thy Triumphs flourish which are vayn
Nor conquest bear over our Soveraign
Though sheets of fond allurements might entice
Thy warfare's mean, His is of greater price
For being instructed in the true Church wayes 5
He cannot daunce unto your Romish Layes
But is for Christ whilst with Mass magick spell
You fight against Christ soe Milier farewell

October 1: 1653   **At Newmarket horse race wher all the Rookes**
     of the Toun were guatherd together

It's allwayes held a signe of chang in weather
When as soe many Rooks doe Flock together

O that this would howld Influence too ore Fate
Soe that we might at last have change in state.

To Will Martin after a Mischance by a fall

Will—though Mischance hath made thee lame
In frendship stil thou shinst the same
For say uneven ground or stayrs
By a Misstep thy strength impairs
Those cannot hurt the feet Divine　　　　　　　　　　5
Are consecrated to the Nine
A Martin is a Bird we knowe
Will thither fly wher't cannot goe.
　　　　　　　　　　quoniam brevipes.

To Mr Levite of Ashwell of that Tribe too

Levite Thou art aswell by Name
As by Profession too the same
Soe Thou for Ancestor
Hadst Aron when H'asisted Hur
To prop up Moses at the fight　　　　　　　　　　5
'Twixt Israell and th'Amalekite
　Thus if that Tithes at all be due
　They doublely belong to you.

Anagram
PROTECTOR
OPORTET C.R.

Catelinus　　　It is decreed, nor shall thy Fate O-Crom=
redevivus　　Resist my Vowe. C.R. again shall come
　　　　　　　Though Hills were set on Hills and Seas meet Seas
　　　　　　　To guard Thee, He will through all Passages
　　　　　　　And plough up Rocks, and lave the Brittish Flood　　5
　　　　　　　To expiat and revenge his Fathers blood
　　　　　　　He'l reach Thy head, thy head Prowd Conquering Fin
　　　　　　　And by attempting that shew Thee thy sin
　　　　　　　He feels a spirit within Him that commands
　　　　　　　And chides His neighbour Princes sluggish hands　　10
　　　　　　　And sayes Those have deservd to mak't their owne
　　　　　　　And in a short time too t'be overthrown
　　　　　　　For He's a man born Great as Heneries name
　　　　　　　With Jameses Prudence could present to Fame
　　　　　　　Equall to All Her worthies and of right　　　　　　15
　　　　　　　May clayme the Lowdest of Her Trumpets might:
　　　　　　　Was He of all the Princely brood markt out
　　　　　　　For such repulse and skornings of the Rout
　　　　　　　And Rabble? Thus Condemnd to Exile too
　　　　　　　By Thy decrees, who dar'st noe other doe　　　　　20

For Thyn owne safety, Horrid Regicide,
Since thou hast lost thy Loyalty through Pride
Know He can loose Compassion towards those
That doe his Crown and Dignety oppose
And mak't appeer at last such Marses frye   25
Are All but monstrous and a Prodegy.

Sent to W. Cope when Monke came into England with
a Scottish Army upon account of the Owld cause

Cope loves a Monke, Monke loves a Cope again
Soe Bishops once more England may maintain
When it obtaines its Lawfull Sovereign
  Then Tippetts Rochets when such shall put on
  Be stild no more the Raggs of Babilon   5
  Nor of that Whore or Superstition
But deemd a Comely dress to worship in
Confound Scismaticalls slovenly sinn
In serving Him in Whom all Orders been.

FULBECK HALL MS 3
POEMS, 1649–65

Solus Deus protector Meus
               W:

Nulla Dies sine Linea.//

A Jove principium:

A Reveille Matin wrot at Copt Hall.

    In the first place when Day
             Appeers
I'le rayse my thoughts above the Sphers
         My Vowes to pay
To Thee my Gratious God, whose might   5
Hath watched over me this night
And brought me to an other Light

    Then I'le consider th'wayes
             Wherin
I have benighted been through Sin   10
        Thee for to prayse
Who after Dawning thus dost trye
To Shine in Mercies Majesty
And rayse poor worme above the Skie

    In Caverns though alive   15
            I h'd line
Without this Great Prerogative
        Of being Thine
Which when Thou wilt but owne, and say
For what I sue for now and pray   20
Is granted; Night is turnd to Day.

      Sursum corda

    High as the Sphere
  My Muse Thy fancies rear
     A ditty frame
  May Harmonise the same
    And Sympothise   5
   With Heavnly Misteries
That whilst the Angells Halaluias sing
Above, below heer we may touch that String

    Eucaristia.— h noe letter
        Anagr.
      Te via Caris

Christ is the way and Heavn the Place of Bliss
Such as are Thankfull He will owne for His.

Eucharistia
Anagr.
Situ Ei chara

Fear not my Soule. He that ordaind this food
If thou be'st deer to Him will make thee good.

A Christmas Carroll—1655

Must Jewes come in
And is it not a sin?
To goe about
To cast Christ out?
I will not say   5
That This the Day
With selebration we adorn
That He for us was born
Because the Scriptures therein silent be
As dictated by God's Decree   10
But sure I am such Love such Mercy and Grace
In Hart in Thought, in Pen doe claim their Place.

Psal: 108—Awake Lute and Harp I my self &c:

Sleep no more, sleep no more
My Harp and Lute
But Confute
Evermore
Those that are mute   5
For Thy prayse
O God all wayes
I would express
And by my Early Layes
Make my adress   10
That Thou my God again
Since help of man is vain
Wouldst of thy favour daign
Not to despise
This my poor Offering   15
Which in a Song I bring
To Thee my Lord and King
As my Harts Sacrefize
For it is Thou alone, for it is Thou alone
Treadst down mine Enemies.   20

January 1:   *The Scepter Shall not depart from Juda*
             nor a Law guiver til Shilo come

The Scepters gon the Law's fullfilld
When as the Jewes our Saviour Killd

Shilo is come indeed yet They
Blind and Hard-harded Stil doe stray
Expecting a Messias when 5
God had inspir'd each Prophets Pen
To set it down and to fore tell
This High Misterious Miracle
   Angells the Heralds of such newes
   Might serve for to confute the Jewes 10
   But that as yet it doth not fall
   Within the Time of Their recall
   Such undeserved Mercy's sett
   Alone in His closs Cabinet
   Who All things at the first did frame 15
   To prayse and glorefy His Name
   And that His Mercies might out Shine
   All other Attributes Divine
   Sent us His Sonn of Juda's Race
   To cancel th'owld Lawe, bring in Grace 20
   For Circumcision He endur'd
   Wherby beleeving Sinner's Cur'd
And bearing Conquest over Death, Hell, Grave,
Was Lost Him Self awhile Our Soules to Save.

Psal: 50–10:/   *Cor Mundum crea Mihi Deus:*   Jer:

When our white Linnen's staind with bloud
   Or any soyle Defilement lends
We strayt way send it to some Floud
   Or Cristall Stream that Filth to Clens
But our poor Soules with Sin and Vice 5
   Besmeared ore we let to lie
Forgetting that 'twas bloud the prise
   Should Clens Them from their Leprozy
Water and bloud Excelling far
   All Jordans, Abanahs or Farfar. 10

The Yong man and Christ

A Yong Man that sought Heaven to Christ came
And askt what He should doe t'obtain the same
Christ wills He should's Commandements approve
And as Himself His Neighbour that He love
That from my Youth I thought I'd done replide 5
The Yong man strait; what is't remaines beside?
Our Lord then Counsailes Him to sel his store
And freely to distribute to the poore
Soe mayst thou be with Heavnly Tresure blest
Wherat He's sad and cannot that disgest 10
For He was Rich: and Such whilst They Look high
Can seld or never trace the way to th'Skye

It is easier for a Camell to
goe through the eye of a needle &c:

Optimus Thesaurus Cœlestis

The Covetous seek Riches, To that Man
Struggles with peril on the Ocean
Desier of Gould is sacred, and doth bring
Both Sayles and Tackle to th'winds whisteling
Soe goes the world: but why? when Heavn hath store   5
Of Riches ought to be desird much more;
Ther's Heavnly Faith and Hope and Love which three
Resemblance make unto the Deity,
These though with noe small Labour got and care
Tullus and Ancus but poor fellows are   10
For Those are gon: whilst heavnly clouds deny
That Treasure Layd up ther should ever die.

On Collonel Ed[ward] Pellam[s] death.

He's gon he's gon
What shall we say
The Fates have trac't the way
To us that follow, and we must Jogg on
First I and then an Other anon   5
Nothing can over Desteny bear sway
seu cito   But Soon or Later All must to their rest
seu sero   As God decrees either accurst or blest.

Carroll—1656.

Psal: 110:   Like as the pregnant Morn distills its dew
v.3:   And adds refreshment to the tender grass
Soe did Thy blessed comming Us renew
    And that Great Work of Wonders bring to pass
        Taking Our natures on Thee and to die   5
        To Ransome Us out of Captivety:

Our Fathers Disobedience had Entayld
    Soe Great a Curse on all Man kind, that 'twas
Noe little Paynes nor Labour heer prevaild
    To cut it ofe, soe He who noe sin has   10
        Contented was 'mongst Sinners to appeer
        To Cancell bonds and our Accounts make cleer:

Happy that Contemplation can afford
    Reflection on so Great a Benefitt
And pay due Vowes and Offrings to the Lord   15
    That High Triumphant over all doth sit
        Curbing Those Powres whose wily crafts had been
        Our Parents first, and now our Bayts to sin:

    All under Christian Light are full of this
      And must acknowledg Mercy above all   20
    Noe place on earth, noe time be thought amiss
      To celebrate our Great Redeemers fall
        To rayse us up again were lost and gon
        Without the Power of such Redemption:

Wherfore if Parcht through Unbeleef we lie   25
  And in Contempt seem to neglect and scorn
The Memory of This Nativety
  Noe Dew Distilled from the fragrant Morn
    Will add refreshment to that Grass and Hay
    Tramples upon soe Great an Holy day: 30

The best Meditation is that of Death
Wishing for Heaven   Despising Earth

As Frend to Death all byepast Merth and Jests
I doe renounce with all their Interests
Casting them into th'Crittick sensuring seas
To be tost up and down as the winds pleas
Whilst thy Could Coast is feard of evry sowle   5
Pale Death that doe inhabit 'neath the Pole
Why should my Last hower then soe me afright
Who am secure entirely and in good plight
O Thou who dost greatly rejoyce to see
Those carefull minds full of Integrety   10
Pluck me some Heavnly Joy and Comfort down
And for my Panting Soule get me a Crown
Sweet Rest. For nothing servs my Fayth 'thout Thee
That sign'st Reward unto Fidelity
Hence a New Life I may and shall attain   15
Exchanging this for an Eternal gain.

O Lord thou art my Portion   Mr Yates
&c.   November 1-1657

Whilst Thou'rt my Portion, what's all this worlds pleasure
He's truly rich makes Godlines his Treasure.

Solatur se etsi Naturaliter Miserum, Faelicem tamen Gratia,
ex Passionibus Christi fore

Rom. 7:24   How miserable Men are
                Caught in Sin and Natures Snare
                By what means then may I
                Free my self of this Fates Captivety

                    The body of Death in me doth reign   5
                    Unlawfull Lusts my mind doe strayn
                    But I the wily Fox will joyne
                    To th'gentle Lamb ere t'encline

More to Adulteries Dessign

So't pleas my God: who's pleasd and kind 10
To the Confessing Penitent Mind
From Whose meer Grace its Pardon's signd

When Satan Me with Baytes did trye
I strayt considerd Liberty
And Who it was for me did die 15
Then for His Suffrings My Self Crucefy.

*A cursing the Civel warr waged in the flesh by the Divel
and a cheef means of casting out the Tempter.*

Whither amend you wicked Lust
 To whet the Divel a sword?
Was not our Fathers fall but just
 To make thee t'be abhord?
That with incontinency stil 5
 Thou dost inflame our harts
And by intemperance of will
 Seekest to drownd our parts?
Help (good Redeemer) now I pray
 With thy right hand repayre 10
Th'own Image chase that Divel away
 By fasting and by Prayre
The powre of bewty hurries blind
 Ther's wichcraft in the tast
Let thy abstemiousnes prove Kind 15
 Th'Example make me chaste
And kill that swelling wicked pride
 That in me stil doth Reigne
That soe Converted I abide
 Free from Deaths Soveraign. 20

What Profiteth it a Man to Gain   Mr Allen
 the whol world   of Sibson
 and to Loose his Soule   June 5. 1659

The Merchant flyes ore Neptunes Plain
To Lard His ware hous and for Gain
The subtil Statist breaks his Rest
To add more feathers to His Nest
The Bowld-fac't Souldier for his Pay 5
Ventures to Cast his Life away
Yet few of These consider what
Is of a far more pretious rate
The Soule I mean of such esteem
As the whol world cannot redeem 10
For that to loose concerns one more
Than All rich Pearle or Indian Ore
Pleasure and Honers, Proffits are
The Sensualists Peculier

    But wher the Soule in Ballence lies 15
    Which is Immortall never Dies
    Who doth not All things else despize
    Comparatively is not wise.

On Good Friday-1659

    How are we tost in minde
        To finde
    To whither Passion
    Sorrow or Joy we ought to be Enclind
    For Him who died our Propitiation 5

    Our Sin for which He came
        Casts blame
    Upon Our Soules Betrayd
    And Craves Contritions Tear t'expunge the same
    Yet by His Passions Greef ought t'be allayd 10

    For what to me or you
        was due
    By Mans Transgresion
    He underwent, yet Death and Hell orethrew
    And now for Us makes Intercession 15

    Let's for our Selves alone
        Make mone
    That stil for want of Power
    In Grace are left soe to Temptation
    That we afresh Afflict our Saviour 20

    This Day then bring to pass
        A Glass
    Wherin we may descrye
    Cause of Rejoycing whence Salvation was
    And for Our Frailties to Lament and Crye 25

    Reason of Sorrow and Joye both heer
        Appeer
    Whilst we consider howe
    We have offended Him to us drew neer
    And Thus to's Foot stoole Earth the Heavns did bowe 30

    Then let a Canceld Debt
        Beget
    Such Husbandry and Care
    That All our future Industry be set
    A work in This Redemption to have Share 35

    That the Owld Man of Sin
        Wherin
    Thus Lost and Damnefide
    We had from Our Originall being been
    Be with the New Mans Suffrings Crucefide 40

That Powrs of Darknes may
    Guive way
And Lewd Affections cease
Since This became the Reconciling Day
That with the Father the Sonn made our Peace   45
  Let's now take heed noe more Those debts increase.

Text:/ Labour not for the meat   Mr Cooper of
    that Perisheth &c: Tudly and Capell:
        Morning Exercise
Those Labour more for Plentious bords
And what this fraile short life affords
Than to attain at Spiritual foode
Which Everlasting Life makes good
But wash the moore which when they've don   5
Are stil but wher They first begun—at the signe of Labour in vaine.

Text:/ A new Commandment I guive unto you   Afternoon
    that yea love one an Other as I loved you   Jhon. 13.34:
Were We some Owld Precept Enjoygnd
Nature to Novelties enclind
Mought make Obedience slack and drawe
Our sensuall Thoughts to Court Her Lawe
But heer Our Saviour wisely knew   5
Since His Commandement was Newe
'Twould take us more; and from above
Descends Himself to teach us Love.

Wrot at Raynam June-23-1659.

  Lord in whose hand it is
To make a Metamorphosis
  And whose sole will creats
A change in Kingdoms, Powers, and States
  Smile on This sinfull Land   5
Nor let Oppression bear Command
  But Now in these Our Times
Cancell the Guilt of all our Crimes
  Let not the Conquering Sword
Prevaile, but Sunshine of Thy word   10
  Still light us in our wayes
To bless and magnefy Thy prayse
  That All Tunes may agree
Under the Vine, Fig, Olive Tree
  Concentrating in This   15
That to Serve Thee Chief Freedom is

      And Peace and Truth as One
      Accomplishing the Diapazon
        Each may Enjoy his Due
      From Thee whose sole Edict is True.   20

Wrot at Mereworth June-9-1661.

    Most Mercifull and Gratious Lord
        Who dost Afford
        A Time wherin
    If Man repents him throughly of his Sin
        He may a Pardon find   5
        Graunt me such Grace
        As to Efface
        Those Blots and Staines
        My youthfull vaynes
        Contracted had   10
        Which were so bad
    And rectify my crooked mind.

        Cause me t'look back
      To what of it I then did lack
      And for the future Grant   15
        I do not want
        That forecast may implore
        I sin no more
    But in the Evning of my Setting Dayes
    Throughly Repent, Amend, and guive Thee Praise.   20

Preces et Lachrimæ Sanctorum Oblationes

September 4:   On Broaken harted Altars Saints express
        In Powerfull Prayrs and sorrow melting Tears
    That Syon mourns, Jerusalem's in Distress
        Tost 'twixt two Rocks of Jealouzy and Fears
        T'implore a mercy and deplore the Cause   5
        That hath bereft both Church and State of Lawes

    Once This a Glorious Kingdom when a King
        Endude with Vertues All Times mought admire
    Governd the Scepter and such Peace did bring
        To Church and State as None could more desire   10
        But too Good for such people Heavns decreed
        As just reward for Their sinns He should bleed

    What Greater Cause of Sorrow then remaines
        To blubber Those with Tears would Saints appeer
    Wherby to wash away that guilt, those Stains   15
        Self Interest and Ambition Count soe deer
        And to beg Pardon with incessant Cries
        At Heavns bright Throne for such Impieties

'Tis quickly sayd but done asks much more time
   The Subtil Statesman must Consult His Treasure,   20
His new-born Greatnes, both which seem to Chime
   In Power and Proffit by which Skoales He'l Mesure
      What sutes Him best, then Skoar Himself a way

   For what He lists either to weep or pray
Thus doth Hypocresys deluding Paint   25
   And Varnish ore This Lump of Clay new-raysd
Who fain would be esteemed a Holy Saint
   Claym Adoration and to be praysd
      Of All, yet in conclusian Guilty of Evill
      This Saint is Metamorphosd into Divell   30

Peace is the Object of this holy Prayer
   The Churches downfall Subject of our woe
Which warr and Thousand scisms now impaire
   And Greevous suffrings cause Her t'undergoe
      Wherfore God showrs Prosperety on Them   35
      Through pitty shew They love Jerusalem.

Math—6-33:   *But seek ye first the Kingdome*   Doctor Sutton
                 of God: &:

The Invitiation's kind
Search first, then we shall find
What ever need requiers
To satiate Desiers
And if we would improve   5
Such a Transcendent Love
We must not wishes shrink
To what we'd Eat or Drink
Or so our Thoughts Employ
How t'use our Drapery   10
But how our Soules mought be
Fixt to Eternety
Gods Kingdome being of Prize
And Righteousness suffise
   For thus All things may Cherish true Content   15
   Will added be to an Accomplishment.

   Upon Candlemas day or the Purification—1664:

For a Child born the Custom was to bring
By th'Richer sort a Lambe for Offering
Two Turtle Doves the Poorer 'wont present
To ratefy the Voat of their Intent
Virgin why bringst thou with thee birds from nest   (Luke 2:)   5
Is't not enough that Lambe lodgd in thy brest.

A Voyage to Heavnly Canaan:

Man like a Ship by wind and weather tost
Would fain double this Cape, attain that Coast
Wher Happines abids, til Running neer
Two Rocks of Equall Danger both appeer
Presumption, and Dispair, the One pleads This 5
I have done well, nor ever steerd amiss
The other deviating too far, implies
Ther's no help left to salve its Miseries
And through This Bosphorus our sayles make way
Til Anker of Hope let downe we cry belay: 10
  In steps the Pylot then to Consolate
  Our sad Condition, proves our Advocate   1 Jhon 2
To's Father for Remission of our Crimes
Pleads the Corruption of our Natures, Times
And All things else betray us to this Evil 15
The worlds Deceipts, the Fleshes, and the Divel
And by His praier and Sacrefize alone
Offers Himself Propitiation
For All our sinns: Let not Despaire prevaile
To make us take in This or t'other sayle 20
In Christian Duties, Nor presume so much
That what we doe can merit, or bear touch
With what we should doe: but with Fear Confess
How much His Suffrings shrink performance less
On our side: And Salvation worke out 25
With Trembling Care until we bring't about
To Comfort those that Assurances may guive
That in and through His merits we shall live
Mauger All storms and at the last posess
Through Faith in Him the Haven of Happines. 30

Sturbridg Fayer

—What is a man profited if he shall gaine the whol
world and loose his owne soule—Mathew-16-26:/

  The Faire's Proclaimd, and evry Bulks Devise
  Or Signe is to set out it's merchandise
  The Docters all in Scarlet doe proclaime
  And Learnedly Authorising the same
  Guive high Encouragement to those who are 5
  Buiers and Sellers at this Mart and Fayer
    Some sell Some buy as needs requier; Each one
    Seeks to guive Others satisfaction
    When All the Gaine Those make seems but to be
    A Guilded nothing to Eternety 10
One Swears and Damms himself his ware's o'th'best
An Other willing to quit's Interest
In what it Cost him, so he may obtain
Your Custom is Content to pass by Gaine

Thus this world dandles mortalls, whose lowe pitch 15
Ayming at nothing more than to be rich
Mistake their Marke, when All this world presents
Are but Enchanting Farded Complements
Set by th'Immortal Soule, whose prise is more
For loss of that Speaks all the world else poore 20
   Ex quolibet ligno non fit Mercurius
   sed ex Re qualibet Contemplatio Divina.

Coritanum Regio Vel Comitatus et Agris Darbiensis Descriptio.

These Hills are Pregnant, and when brought a bed
What proves their Issue but Sowes Piggs of Lead
Not Mice Ridiculous Those elswher must
Their Kindred seek, not in such Pondrous Dust
For mountain vertues through Ambition swell 5
Whilst under ground the Richer Treasures dwell
Whenc may be learnd the Inmost parts to trye
Nor to be caught with Joyes that Pearch soe high
When Riches All incentred Lowe doe Lie.

Upon Sir Jhon Prettimans Change in Fortunes

  A Goodlike man some did presage
  When I was borne and Came to Age
    Yet under Cloudy Fortune cast
    I am but Pretty man at last
  It howlds in due Proportions Paralell 5
  That those who buy All, All at last should sell

To Sir F.F: neer Darby Shire upon Prince Rupert the Duke of Cumberlands Voyage to Ginny set out in Octobr. 64:—and Captain Homeses success against the Hollanders upon that Coast A Ballet.

Strike up the Horn-pipes play some Giggs
For we shall now have Ginny-Piggs
Instead of Darby Sowes of Lead
Since Project now is brought a bed
And Cumberland dispatched hence 5
To curb the Hogens Insolence
Teach Butter-box to know his Bred
Through Our Protection's better spred
Into Obedience Mogens t'Bring
To Fear a Monarch Prise a King 10
And in a short space shew to view
How they may Bake as They did Brew
And Pay those Cruelties before
They'd acted on Amboynas shore
Usurping All of India's Bounds 15
Wher those set footing on the Grounds
  Away yea Water-Ratts away

  Teach Porposes 'Gainst storms to Play
  Pack to your Element and Homes
  For now that warlike Captain Comes   20
  To bid your Petty Friggot, Pinke
  Strike Sayle (or in two words) goe sink
  And that yea wander no more Erring
  Vittle with Poor Jhon Pickle Herring
  And fortefy with Brande-wine   25
  As yea are Tost upon the Brine
   Upon the wave our Castles swimm
   With their spred Canvas in a Trimm
   Not built i'th'Ayre but carrying Fire
   With Which presenting from Each Tier 30
   Such Prowesses on purpose sent
   T'Amaze and guive Astonishment
   To the Behowlders; quell the Pride
   Of such a Traytrous Brood beside
  Beef, Porke and Peas Our Fleet preferrs 35
  For Hart and Strength to mariners
  And souldiers too: which mustred heer
  With Canns of Wholsom Double-Beer
  Will Animate and thus prevaile
  Causing All Fish Eaters strike sayle   40
   Back to your Harbours I advise
   Come not Abroad if ye be wise
   Into our Channell least we make
   Yea food for those so fain y'ould Take
   For 'tis our Kinge's sole Lord of These 45
   As rightfull Patron ore's owne Seas.

    Post Script to the Voyage

  Let Hollands Fleet no more be Feard
  When Ours is got beyond Cape Vert
  And Noble Rupert in a Trim
  With his Triumphant Vessells Swim
  The Pride of Hogens to Abate   5
  Coasting by th'Hands fortunate
   Up Dam come down De Ruttier Steer
   Your Course Aloofe and come not neer
   Least yea Encounter Shelvs and Rocks
   And Butter-like be payd in Box   10
   Whilst Homes and Lawson guive yea Knocks.

   Concordia Res Parvae Crescunt October 1664:
   Discordiâ Maxima Dilabuntur:

  The Martiall Turk, Grim Tartar both agree
  To Rowse the Emperour, pass Danube

Threaten Vienna and at length come
A Scourge and Terror unto Christendome
Whilst Princes All Those Miscreants should withstand 5
Together linked are like Roaps of sand
So that as Fame relates and story tels
Ther's small power left to Curb Those Infidels
Cleer up those Parts again since Count Sereine
Missing Encouragement lays down Dessigne 10
But Treaties meditated to Asswage
By way of Truce that Fury and that Rage
  Surely the Rumors of this war portend
  The world Decrepid is and neer its End
  When through Ambition, Envy, Malice, Hate 15
  All Christian Princes prove Degenerate
  And not Unite in Concord to Resist
  So Vanquish quite those Enemies to Christ
    But Privat-Intrest-Biast cease to worke
    And guive Check mate to Tartar and to Turke. 20

Upon the Death of the Most Heroick and thrice Noble Princes the Owld Countess of Darby of the House of Tre-Moulle in France

  Thrice wet in Greef, how coms't about
  The Taper of thy years goes out
  But Fate-turnd-downwards it appeers
  Snufft and so drowns it self in Tears
  First for thy Loyalty depriv'd 5
  Of Hand, means, and last unwiv'd
  When Boulton that rebellious Toun
  Upon thy Verteous Mate did frown
  And not a Man with in thy Ile
  Administred one help the while 10
  But with the Plague of All this Nation
  Thou w'rt lyable to Sequestration
  Leaving an Offspring to partake
  Of thy just Sorrows, and to make
  In Gushing Streams such flowds to flow 15
  As Current Speak mishap and woe
    Yet Crownd with Constancy again
    In Love to Husband, Soveraign
    And Frends Thy Name can never dye
    But Treasurd up in Memory 20
    Cause Treble Fountains from each Eye.
      First the Court mourns for loss of such
      As for its sake had done so much
      Then Children, Frends, and all that knew her
      With their salt showrs come and bedew her 25
      Nor sorrow with in Banks contain
      For that which was their loss, her Gaine.

To Prince Maurice.

Maurice coulst thou but Joygn
To the Rich Elme thy sheltring vine
Thou wer't a Prince thy Grapes should muster
Not Branches only but in Cluster
   But now (Alas) Thy Could Adress   5
   Blasts all Those hopes of Happines
She's fled she's gon to Others kind
Thus woemen mock th'unconstant wind
And you may catch the One in hand
As well as t'other to Command   10
   Take but a Slippery Eele by th'Tayle
   You may ore it as soon prevaile
   Then what remains thy thoughts to feed
   But that th'whol Sex is falce indeed.
Hadst thou not had More-Ice than Fier   15
Thou hadst not fayld of thy Desier
But sung an Anthom in the wido's Quier
   Tres sum though three thou'rt calld thou art but One
   So Stil must rest content to lie alone.

To Morice Upon Sir Francis Comptons marrying the widdow and raising up her Belly

Since Thou'rt come ofe an Other is Comd on
And Frankly swore she should not lie alone
Making good musike with her trebble string
Scrud up and Tund unto his warbeling
   Which a Dull Elme could never reach so high   5
   She did out pitch his weak Capacety
This martiall knight hath done the feat and so
She's better pleasd than all thy Ramms could doe.

In Tricessimum Januarij Diem in quo serenissimus Ille   wrot
Rex Noster Carolus illius Nominis Primus Nulli pietate   1663
secundus a subditis suis inhumaniter obtruncatus erat.

Let the Castalian well be overflown
And sad Melpomene express her mone
Whilst comes to mind the Cruell murthering
Of an All verteous and magnanimous King:
O wickedness before thes times ne're known   5
Of a kind Prince by's People overthrown
Who knew no Gratetude: His memory rears
This day, a solemn feastivall for Tears
And fasting fit: that such a King being set
We mought no more that Tragedy forget: 10
Nor of those Regicides malicious Rage,
But Reger't up, as Horrid Age, to Age.

To the Society of *Phanaticks* or more truly *Jesuits*

Phanaticks what are yea that thus swarme
And bring to King and Kingdome so much harme
Imprudence 'tis, Mischiefs and Malice sway
To cause yea thus All lawes to Disobey
And to your Cuntrymen such daingers bring   5
As to foment fresh war against your King
And Cuntry too: if Faith hath any share
Or Godlines in you, 'tis to impare
Both Godlines and Faith that you alone
Mought raise that Idoll superstition   10
Whilst King and loving People yea delude
By Conventickling in a multetude
And Jesuite-like those principles put on
May swallow All up in Confusion
   It is enough: Goe packing hence t'infect   15
   Some Forraign Cuntry with Thy cursed sect
   Or else forget thy lewd Opinions vile
   And Peaceably demean thy self the while
   Bring no more Dainger on thy self and frends
   Nor more resist the Lawe; But make amends   20
   For what is past, Conforme in evry thing
   Fear God and yeild due honer to thy King
   So from that fond Phanatick mood Thou'lt be
   In t'mutuall Love and Sobernes set free.

Fortunæ

   O how unconstand are thy wayes
   Fond Fortune that to th'haight dost rayse
          Those wickednes posess
   When to the faithfull honest brest
   Thou saist goe set thy hart at rest   5
          And him dost more oppress
   Not yeilding succor to that spirit
   Glory and Prayse for worth doth merit
          But pardoning the Guilty
   Guiving stil more to Greedy Swaynes   10
   On Pride and Mammon set their maines
          Til all things turn to filthy
   So what to Cesar Glory got
   Are layd aside these dayes God wot
          as Counsailes now Combine   15
   And if one hide a Candle so
   Under a Bushell who can know
          That ever it did shine
   He that is Poor shall be so stil
   Whilst Guifts the Rich mans Coffers fill   20
          Wherfore let suffrers use

        Great Patience to overcome
        And those deserve with sadnes come
              On such hard haps to muse
        But whilst the world round as a Bowle   25
        The various Fates do it controwle
              Nor's this lifes State ere Stable
Subject to Change, what need we doubt
But that kind hopes may bring about
              Future Dayes Comfortable   30
        That Those this Daye in Triumph sit
        Exalted for their mass of witt
              High Subtilties and Pride
        The next may see cast down and Lowe
        Not knowing well whither to goe   35
              Their Falcities to Hide.

Upon the Death of his Excellency Thomas Earle of Cardigan an Epitaph Who Died the 15th of September 1663

        Woulst thou enquir heer passing bye
        Who tis interred thus doth lie
          Cast but thin Eye
        Upon this Marble Ston
            And Thou'lt find One   5
        Was All of truest Frendships Paragon

        Thomas Earle Cardigan heer lies
           After His Obsequies
        Intoombd: and Doubts arise
            Now Natures payd her skoar,   10
        Whither his Titles did adorn Him more
        Or haight of Merits he enjoyed before

           For 'sides the rest
           His frendly Brest
        Entitled Him of Frends the Best   15
        And in All Literature well seen
        Partner to many years had been
          Living to Seavnty and five teen

        Now Dead and from this Lifes sad ends
        Restord to Rest, bewayld of Frends   20
         Most worthely his memory guave
        Me subject to bedew with Tears his Grave
                        W:

Counsail and advice to a Frend how to make Could weather appeer warme and to dissolve Frost and Snow with Fier, Wine, and good Cheer.

        What thou shouldst doe whilst Phebus hides his Rayes
        In a Thick Snow-filld Cloud these whiter Dayes
        And Evry Mead is coverd ore and lies

Under white Blanketings for Tapissries?
  Let Bacchus Crown thy Glass, Dry wood incline 5
  To warm thy Chimny, make thy harth to shine
  And let choice Foule unto thy bord impart
  What ere pertains unto the Foulers Art:
    So, though the Heavens Lowre, to Thee they'l smile
    Thou'lt pass time ore and stamp it mild the while. 10

'Astroites Lapides Belvi-Oris Inveniantur'

These Astroite Stones, on Belvoyr Coasts appeer,
And in five Coynes, starrs representing Cleer
Will move to Joyne (as some men doe averr)
If you but cast them into Vinegar,
And never rest, untill they meet, and thus, 5
They seem becharmd and led by Orpheus:
(If't be beleev'd) who carries these in warr,
Oft overcomes, so becomes Conquerer,
And wins the field of honer, as some note,
Who ever doth enjoy this Astriote: 10
  So it appeers, the Lord of Belvoir, bent
  To manners, makes known help, to th'Indigent.

To my frend Sir William Davenant upon his Opera called the Seege of Roads

Could Chaucer Die and Spencer be forgott
Whilst Will's alive? delineates a Plot
Of fresher witt, and of a newer straine
Than ever flowd from Shakespears lofty brayn
Beaumonts and Fletchers, or my owld frend Ben 5
Sweating produc't; to dignefy his pen,
Adorn the Stage, and make the Busken tread
In a Majestike Posture o're the Dead
And wher the Comick scene did love advance
Ther with the sock to propagate a Dance 10
  Thy new invention therfore clayms more prayse
  For it out vies th'Out Landish Operas
  Shunning the Common Roads or beaten way
  Of longe Disputes which Academicks sway
  It brings on Roads it self and thence preferrs 15
  Th'attchivements of the brave Knights Templers
  In honer of the Cross, and to maintain
  That Ile, and t'shrink the half moon into wayne
  And the least Light of all: whilst Sultan swells
  Concluding Jealouzy a payne of Hels 20
  So reconcil'd to Roxolana, He
  Sets by Hyanthe, and Alfonso's free
Thus heer whilst New found Art thou dost express
All Theaters and stages else goe less.

Upon the Chimny Act

What ever Cole or wood afford
    The houshould Gods to warme
The thankfull People to their Lord
    And King do now Conforme
For out of evry Harth a part   5
    Of Loyalty doth shine
And this the Altar of Each hart
    Brings in a Silver Mine
Each Chimny sends not only forth
    Vayn Smoak soon turnd to Ayre   10
But Silver Treasure of more worth
    In Shillings made to payre
Thus hath our Pious Parlement
    Decreed to serve their King
And to that Generall Consent   15
    Alltars and Chimnies bring.

To a P.K: that sent to me for 2 Peeces R.W:

Robin two Peeces did request of Me
I sent him eight so to his sute prov'd free
But when those eight in silver he had tould
They shrunk to One whilst He expected Gould
Thus Thrifty-prodigall in what I guave   5
Under eight half Crownes t'other Peece I save.

Upon a chip of the Royall Oak sent me by a frend F F: for a stopper

The Glory of a Forrest and Joves Tree
What fitter Plant to Shelter Sov'ranty?
From Briars and from Pop'lar Shrubs of late
Sought to supplement our Sedars growth in State?
Let the word Dris make All hence understand   5
The Hamadrydes are All at his Command
And Evry Branch that Famous Tree did sprout
Peace and eternall Happines point out
That when what's writ and sayd or can be spoak
Comprisd in This Enstall it Royal Oake.   10

May 1662   *Upon the Heroike Lady the Markiones of Newcastle her Incomparable Playes newly set out.*

Of All the weapons I have read
    To Female Sex belong
Are These, the Needle and the Thred
    Besides the Use of Tongue

But heer the Mirroir of our Times   5

Adds Pen and Inke to rayse
In Crittacisms and in Rimes
   This Conqueresses Prayse

Who All the Bards of Ages past
   For Fancy, Witt, and Stile   10
Surpasses far so now at last
   Those strike sayle and Recoyle

Yeilding up Bucklers to her Layes
   Composd with so much Grace
That as Her due th'Immortall Bayes   15
   From them to Her Shifts place

The Thing so misapplide to skowld
   She manages so well
That Rhetoritians of Owld
   To Her strains yeild the Bell   20

In stead of Needle Sharp Conceipt
   Draws admiration to it
Toucht with a Loadston to that haight
   Makes evry one to woo it

And when she writes she cutts a Thread   25
   And Spinns a web so fine
Pallas herself mought heer be sayd
   To Emulate Her Line

Bens Playes mought well be works indeed
   On Anvile Hammerd soe   30
When from her works such Playes proceed
   As doe not drop but flowe

Her morning Tresses and her Hayer
   Decheveld's not more free
Than are her Raptures may Compare   35
   With wit of hiest Degree

But 'bove Her Sexes Worthys All
   So brightly She doth shine
That though Her we a woman call
   Her Pen Skoars masculine   40

To the Highly approved Statesman and best of Servants to his Masters two Incomperable Kings of Great Brittany this Age hath produced the Lord High Chancelor Sir Edward Hide now Earle of Clarington.

Ned Hide, how can I hide thy Offerings
In Faith and Loyalty to two Such Kings
As Charles the first and Charles the second are
With whom the Christian world houlds no Compare
Only I'le count those Patriots most wise   5
Can Emulate such Gratefull Sacrefize.

Upon Sir Jhon Lawsons Eminent Services in the Levant to the Glory of our Nation—1662

Laws-Sonn? I am mistaken: ther appeers
He's Neptunes sonn and heier: wittnes Algiers
Wher He Those Pyrat Robbers did reduce
To such an Amicable Frendly Truce
As that our English Merchants mought not want   5
Securety in Traffike i'th'Levant
His Valour, Prudence, Wisedom wrought this work
That Christians now guive Laws unto the Turk.

To the Markiones of Newcastle upon her book of Orations

Madam: if All the Rhetorick were gon
    That Tully wrot or Famous Xenophon
Demostenes, or Chrisostom of Owld
Dropt from his silver Pen in words of Gould
'Twer All at life restor'd in the rich vaine   5
Presents it to the world in flowds again
Of so great Eloquence that All must say
Though you come last, you taught Those first the way
                                                      W:

To Docter Brown a Phisitian maried to Mistress South widdow at Cliff the 9:th of May-1665.

Brown bread a white neck would inferr
But wher such is allredy in Her
What Loaf can rayse it to more bliss
Than wher before it placed is
    East West North South as soon may meet   5
    To Conquer this or t'other Fleet
    As you be parted now 'tis known
    You doe to Either Others Owne
She as Infirme directs her mind
To see if Gallen would prove kind   10
He not a Trewant in his Art
Seeks to advance and Rayse his Part
So that all Gouty'Infirmety
May end in two leggd Timpany
    Which that it may my wishes are   15
    To end the Conflicts of this warr
Cuer first her Foot then make her Belly swell
And then I'le Swear (brave Doctor) th'hast done well:

To my Cosen T.F.

Thou feedst on Bakon I admire
Thou art no fatter then

Nor like unto thy Dam nor Sire
　　But Skelliton of Men

Yet since thy Features well agree　　　　　　　　5
　　With His that wears a Crowne
It were Presumption in me
　　To Coat thee 'thout Renowne

Thy Parts I must confess excell
　　All Theirs of Thy Alies　　　　　　　　　　10
Such wit and Learning in Thee dwell
　　Thou bearst away the Prise

Though in thy meagre Cheeks appeer
　　Deep furrows Lines of Grace
By learned students held most deere　　　　　　15
　　As honoring the face

Philosophy in Thred bare weeds
　　Sets forth Her Clients so
That Praises should from inward deeds
　　Not out ward Glittrings flowe　　　　　　　20

Fare well deer Cosen this suffize
　　To make the world Confess
Thou art not only Kittchen wise
　　But fed with Sciences—　　　　　Basta:

In Jesuiticum Ordinem

Nola the Bow Fair France the Arrow guave
Who'l guive the Roape that Those deserve to have?

In Prayse of a Cuntry Life

Who so Enjoyes the Cuntry Ayer
With Hounds in Couples, Frends a Payer
Or more, and seriously can looke
Sometimes into a Harmles Booke
Need not contemplat what the Barr　　　　　　5
Molests, or stratagems of warr
Produce, nor on Ambitions winge
Seek to sore up to Court and Kinge
But with a Comp'tency Content
Pass All his Dayes in Merriment　　　　　　　10
Yet with such Care, Those let not in
Temptation or the least of Sin
But both to Body and the minde
Like Solaces appeer most kinde
Infeofing either with such Health　　　　　　　15
Is prisable above all wealth.
　　　　　Non est vivere sed valere vita

Queen Katherine Landed at Portmouth in Hampshire the 14 day of May 1662:

Landed a shore: what follows now 'save Praiers
To multeply unto this Princes Heiers
That ther may neither wanting be to rise
Some one to Guard our Houshold Deities
Of the Imperiall Line: Nor More we may 5
B'exposed t'Immoderate Common Peoples sway
But the true Father of his Cuntry Reigne
And openly acknowledgd Soveraign
Let Heiers then boast they till their fathers Lands
Succession brings to Charles Scepter Commands. 10

Ode: ### To the Royall Fleet sent out of the Downes into Portugall to fetch home our Royall Queen Katherin.   December 20: 1661:

Hayle to that Floating wood
Rides swelling ore the Floud
Prowd to be so Emploide
To bring Great Charles his Bride
Who once heer set on Shore 5
I'le Brag-and-say no more:
   But let all streets with Bonfiers shine
   For Joy of our Queen Katherine:
And evry Clapper Ring
A thankfull Offering
To rayse our hopes upon 10
Future Succession
May cuer again and heale
This late hurt Commonweal
   And so produce like Gileads Balm
   After a Rugged Storm, a kind Smooth Calme. 15

Upon His Majesties resolution to Dissolve the Parlement and the Lower house desiring to sit longer til Plots are discoverd

You see your Senate on their Insteps stand
Who hath your Subjects purses at Command
   Which skearce can bear that Load
Til wicked harts Reveng and Plotts devise
Sharpnes of malice for to Exercise 5
   And t'Hazard your Aboad
Dissolve that Congregation and Pack
With Royall Majesty as Supream Act
   Then draw fower hundred out
Grown Owld with sitting (Monarch Just) 10
And leav the rest to th'Citties trust
   Your Enemies did rout

So that your Crown not shaken may appeer
Nor troubled more the Faithfull Cavaleer
  But whats to come Embrace   15
And Treasure up in store, then make't your gaine
As incident to your Auspitious Reigne
  Whilst you good fortune Trace
Despise not Prince the Cyprian Queens delights
Nor Dauncings, whilst you yet enjoy the rights   20
  Of youth nor Hayres change Couler
But be inflam'd and pass your time in Love
And pretty nightly whisperings approve
  To make soft kisses fuller
Nor let the Father-killing-Traytor more   25
Trust to his Corners, but now pay his skoar
  Of All his Mischief ment
And for Catastrophe to his sad Fate
Become a Convert though it may seem late
  When to the Gallows sent.   30

  Sapiens Dominabitur Astris.   Wrot September
What shall I say? when Each String Jarrs   11. 1650
Hes only wise can govern Starrs,
Count ore the Gammouth that extends
Unto the Spheres, at fingers ends
Compose an Ayer may Controwle   5
Both Artike and Ant artike Pole
As if Each Noat its Cliff and Key
Had borrowd from the Milky Way
To trace a smooth white path wherby
His Life mought All prove Harmony   10
Fixt Constant on a Fimament
Of so much quiet and Content
Whilst Planets Rove, that nothing thence
Shall cause to Him ill Influnce
When He himself to mirth Resignes   15
He's Conversant with All the Signes
And if abroad He would be sped
The Dog-Stars are uncoupeled
To start and run the Timerous Hare
Court Cassiopea in her Chaire   20
Mount Pegasus and wings Display
In refuge of Andromeda
Dance to Orions Harp and Skip
After Bootes and his whip
Make the fower wheels in Charlses wayne   25
Fier their Axel tree again
As once they did when Phaetons pride
Phlegon and th'*other three would guide: *Piroeis
Take the Bull by the Eye and wrest   Eous Æthon

    The Lions Hart out of its brest: 30
    Contemplating admire the Swan
    With its new Constellation
    Butt with the Captain of the Flock
    And at the Virgins dore-sels knock
    Rectefy Cancers Crawle and Trye   35
    To disunite kind Gemini
    Poyse Libras ballance and bring on
    Alay to Fiery Scorpion
    And Chirons double shape betray
    When Saturn horsed Philera   40
    Bringing the Lustful Goat to mind
    When winter Solstice proves unkind
    And for to drayn Aquarius send
    For undertakers of the Fen
    That Fishes may enjoy their ease   45
    In larger scoap in boundles seas
    And Cetus satiated thus
    Swallow and spout Eridanus
    Play with the Dragons twisted tayle
    And Gibe fayr Argo's Unfurld sayle   50
    Mount with the Eagle, ther Comprise
    The Voted Locks of Berenice
    Observe the Dolphin when stormes neer
    How He becomes Irreguler
    Adding Corona unto These   55
    Call down sweet showres from Pleiades
    Causing the Earth with Hevns dew blest
    Participate with All the rest
    Whilst He who shuns debate and warrs
    Is truliest sayd to Govern Starrs.   60

To my Tutors Ghost Doctor Travers:

When Skillfull Gunners ayme a Mark to hit
They mount their Ordnance first then Travers it
To find true Levell, and all Art express
The quadrant yeilds with Caloping Compasses
Then they guive fier, and not before, to trye   5
The Conquering force of their Artillery
    So did Thy Riper Judgement Lectures use
    To frame Delighfulnes unto each Muse
    My youthfull Stubbernes could skearce disgest
    And didst beguile m'into Apolloes feast   10
    At unawares, so running ore the fare
    Wher evry Dish appeerd most Singuler
    My Tender years, weak Judgment had posest
    To chuse the lighter Cates, refuse the best
Which was my fault alone, and not thy will   15
Would have directed to more power and Skill.

August-16: 1660: *Upon the little parler Garden at Mereworth*

    My Parler window doth descry
    The malice of Presbitery
    For wher of Owld Houshoulders sate
    To watch the entry of the Gate
    The stinking Elders rayse their head   5
    So all my Optike's sequestred
    Or so debarr'd my Gates to find
    That (like thier Tenents) I am blind:
    Joynd to these wall-plants little higher
    Growes Eglantine and the sweet brier   10
    Making't a Guarden, yet all These
    Stamp it not the Hesperides
    Those were of greater bounds, but This
    Only by Inches Measurd is
    Like Martialls Farme which did extend   15
    From Lupus to reward his frend:
   So that a Marigould or Rose
   Before their Tresures they disclose
   May haply live in Bud to be
   Remoovd to other nurcery   20
   To court the Sun which never heer
   Can bless them from his fulgent Sphere
   Wher it is winter all the year:
   Six Daisies that 'mongst Flowers goe less
   If to more number they increase   25
   Must sue to be transplanted by
   Some Habeas-Corpus subtilty:
  The ground's so small a Mouse got in
  And judging it some Pantlers Binn
  Solac't her self on Eggs of Ants   30
  Til at the last driven to wants
  Rather than Hunger starv'd t'be found
  Leapt into th'moat and ther was drown'd:
  Judge if one mouse such wants sustaine
  How many wants This would maintaine   35
  Or Skipping Grasshoppers supply
  With force for their Agilety
Erewiggs I doe confess that shade
Mought harbour and a whol Brigade
Of lesser vermine to devowre   40
On freedoms Quarter frute or flowre
If ther were any; but that fear
Is needles since none found are ther:
  The Bees attchievments heer must flagg
  for want of that should fill her Bagg   45
  And Spiders in some Corners spin
  To snare some fly within her gin:
The Room's so narrow it would pussell

Two Butterflies to meet, not Jossell
If Caterpillars five a brest 50
Should march, skearce space left for the rest
Ordaind to follow; that the while
Their Rankes spake five three deep in file
They mought a Compleat body weave
To wage a warr 'gainst frute and leaf 55
 The Lady-gould with studded winge
 May heer sometimes seek harbouring
 (Her house on fier) yet find but small
 Hopes of Encouragement with all
A shole of Bussing Gnats that fly 60
Over this lesser Husbandry
Present unto the Crawling Crewe
So many wild geese by their view
And if a Dorr but issue out
To Humm and Drumm the Ayre about 65
It seems the King of winge and Joves
Over this Paradice that Roves
Scorning to make a stooping at
A worme, a Spider or a Gnat
At which though some doe strain yet swallow 70
Whol Camel-Caravans that follow
I cannot guess it less to be
Than Gross and Fond Hipocresy
 And thus from Presbiter I skip
 With His unhallowed Eldership 75
 For though he hides me from my Gates
 My hopes still build on better Fates

Upon Jack Prick at North[ampton]

Jack Prick marcht in Northamton Toun
In feeble Posture up and doun
Yet was not Drunk but could not stand
And when the matter I had skand
I found 'twas thus the stones of might 5
Were pulld doun should raise him upright.

Upon Doctor Crafts his Sermon at Court the 24th of June-1660. out of the 4th verse of the 45t: Psalme wherat some Exceptions was taken by the King.

He was not his Crafts Master that would bring
Ought of Exception 'fore a Gratious King
In whom exception none is, but a True
Pattern of what the Text presents to you
Majestique Greatnes Prosperously brought on 5
To sit at last upon his Fathers Throne
Wher Truth and Meeknes, Righteousnes did reign

And are by him Instaled new againe
    Thus much unto the Preacher I'le say then
    The Greatest Clerks are not the Wisest Men.   10

To a Frend upon my Pallace and habitation in one of the New houses in Portugall Rowe in Lincolns Inn fields London

Wher I abide, or whither Fled
If you would know, let These be read:
    At first to Durram Yard I range
    Yet finding that Place neer the Change
    I soon remoovd wher more Ayre yeilds   5
    Content and Pleasure into th'Fields
    And tooke a house which though't not shine
    To me's a Pallas because mine   Casa mia Casa mia
    Thence I behowld and view at ease   p. piccola che tu
    What Travailers on Land or Seas   sia tu mi para   10
    Can boast they'v seen, as water store una Battia
    And mountains too before my dore
        The Terrene Sea nor Ebbs nor Flowes
        Is not Comparable to Those
        Black Standing Liquids heer remain   15
        An Ornament unto the Plain
        Compast about with Alps preferr
        The Great Toyle of the Scavenger
        Wher 'sted of wolves of Boars and Bears
        The Croaking Frog and Toad appeers   20
        Raising their heads above their Sire
        Of putrid Dirt and Dung and Mire
        Yet at th'approach of Rat or Mouse
        This and That leavs his Mud-wald house
        And Skips or Crawles into the wave   25
        That stands hard by Himself to save
        So People It for fish since none
        Of the Skal'd Tribe was ere ther known
        Who would not Judg Himself neer Nile
        And each of These some Crocadile   30
        Or in the King of Egipts chamber
        Wher such quick Cattle once did clamber
            That was a Curse; now marke and see
            Through Times strange Mutabilety
            How Changes prove; we count of These   35
            As Blessings Eyes and Ears to pleas
            Whilst Colon comes, presents, guives fier
            To Top these mountains, make them higher
            And whence some Urine-Torrents make
            The waters rise with in the Lake   40
            Like Genver Zee whose waters Growe
            As Great St Bernard sweats his snowe
Judg if the vapours hence arise

　　　　Must not needs Densefy the Skies
　　　　And make the Ayre with health abound   45
　　　　Wher such a Prospect may be found
　　　　　　Howere to These we must be debter
　　　　　　Cause Cuntry seats will seem the better

Upon a fine Shower that fel on the 16th of Aprill-1660.

　　　　　　Drop down Thy Power
　　　　Thou kind and Grass-refreshing Aprill Shower
　　　　　　That Every Flower
　　　　Participating Thy Auspitious Dewe
　　　　　　May truly Shewe   5
　　　　Forth May in Triumph, when perfum'd again
　　　　With Rose and Lillie Guardens Soveraign

　　　　　　But Sinke and Drownd
　　　　That Sterill, Poisnous, and Malicious Ground
　　　　　　Wher naught is found   10
　　　　Save Nettles, Hemlock, Henbane, or such weeds
　　　　　　As Mischief breeds
　　　　That such no more rise up to Choak and Spoile
　　　　The fertile Hopes of our Brittannike Soyle

　　　　　　Whilst in Their Roome   15
　　　　Let Trees-frute-promising with Coulers Come
　　　　　　Displayd and Bloome:
　　　　And meads in Natures Jewells deckt appeer
　　　　　　To Grace This year
　　　　With Daisy, Couslip, Primrose, Vilet, more   20
　　　　Than Any Season had ere Teem'd before
　　　　　　For Joy of His Return unto our shore.

Post Tenebras Lux:
Apres La Plüie Le Beau Temps:

　　　　After a Dark and Dismall Night
　　　　The Sun arising in his Might
　　　　So dissipates Those Clouds of Tears
　　　　　　For His Decease
　　　　As Clarefies again our Spheres   5
　　　　　　With hopes of Peace
　　　　After a sad Intestine warr
　　　　Restoring His Succeeding Star

　　　　It was no slight Dew or small Raine
　　　　Showrd for the Loss of Soveraign   10
　　　　But a whol Cataract to destroy
　　　　　　At once our Joy
　　　　And sinke our Barkes, til now at last

                    The Tempest past
            We may enjoy again faier weather   15
            When *Clouds pack all away together   *Knaves

            Scenes have their Changes, Moon Her wayne
            Those vary, she fills up again
            So after suffring Darknes, light
                    Appeers more bright   20
            And now our Charles from's wayne doth rise
                    He far out-vies
            All other Orbs changing this Land
            From Egipt to a Canaan

            His Presence, and His Peoples Love   25
            Those Black Nights and These Storms remove
            We Hud-winkt had so long lien under
                    That Calm and Cleer
            A work wrought by the God of wonder
                    All might appeer   30
            At His returne whose faier Aspect may guive
            To Each His due t'Himself Prerogative.

                Upon George Munks routing the Rump &c:

                    Our Husbandry must needs goe on
See the new   Whilst we have George (that's Husband man)
world of   (Once Tribune 'neath our Soveraign
English words   Charles This Iles Dioclesian)
                Who thorough Prowess store and Might   5
                Against that Serpent Rump did fight
                So rescude Those our Virgin Lawes
                Out of That Poysnous Breath and Clawes
                Restoring back the True Intents
                Of Lawfull and Free Parlements   10
                Wherin Each free born Subjects care
                Ought to Participate a share
                Nor Longer shuffled out stand by
                Mute and Enslav'd by Tyranny
                And hard Oppression but gain force   15
                To set the Saddle o'th'right Horse
                Invite His Presence to bring on
                The Sacred Tie of Union
                To us His Subjects so long Time
                Secluded quite this Northern Clime   20
                    Then shall that Poysnous Berry worke
                    No more calld Cauphe by the Turke
                    But Like true Christians our Gaines
                    Will better Harringtons light Braines
                    For Oceâna that fond Prize,   25
                    An Ocean of Felicities.

Aug: 3: 1659   *Upon a Rumor of a Generall rising*

         At Rising Chase not far from Lin
         Wher Vessels are bound out and in
         I ther espide a Lad whose Fate
         Through wandering Unfortunate
         Had driv'n Him Thither to implore   5
         Asistance from His Native Shore
         His Comely Features did presage
         That Offspring from Royal Parentage
         He should again restored be
         To's Antient State and Dignety   10
         Mauger All Opposition, when
         True Faith posest His Cuntry men
         Which that it may my wishes are
         And happy Peace succeed unnatural War.

To my Neph[ew] Gerr[ard] after his return from
Constantinople and Room to Paris

Cœlum non Animum mutat &c:

I hope y'are Constant and not Gibe by Change
Of mind whilst often ore the seas you range
Though through the Dardanelles you did pass
Bizantium view in Venice Looking glass
After behowld prowd Roome in Pomp and State   5
I guess These cause you not Degenerate
But that at your returne we may confess
You stil an honest English Hart posess
If ther be any such yet left? if none
Then you'l appeer this Iles sole Paragon   10
When to your God and Sovraign you prove true
And pay to Frendship what to it is due.

To the People of England—June-5-1659.
An Abhorring the bloudy Civill warr begun by Popular fury under S.X.
T.FX. and O.P. and Continnued Under Fleet[woo]d Lamb[er]t
Va[ne] Heisel[rigge] Coss: &c:

     Whither O wicked Brood do'yea run   Hor: Epod.
     Is't not enough what was begun   7:
     In a mad Fury but do'yea still
     Invent new Fewds and how to kill
     Must Sword be drawn again t'appeas   5
     As if on Land and on the Seas
     Of English bloud ther had not been
     Enough yet spent or Malice seen
     Must warr prevaile ore Peace and Truth
     Whilst evry London Prentice youth   10
     Is taught to skorne and Trample downe

The Clergies Rights and Lawmans Goune
And that which to our Enemies we
Mought wish, as that They not agree
By home discention we preferr 15
To be our owne Executioner
   Thus doe not wolves nor Lions rage
   'Less 'gainst some Other Parentage
Are we more fell than Beasts? doth Power
And Force incite us to devower 20
Each Other? is not Fury blind
To Cause us t'rush on our owne kind?
Or is our Sin soe great; noe Fate
'Save This may serve to Expiate
Bereft at Once of speach and sence 25
What may be read or guathered thence
But that for Remus bloud once split
Posterety should feel the Guilt

   Martialis Prophetizans
    Lib: 7. Epig: 10   May-1659
  To Olus and the Owld Cause

Harry was Sick and Martin Lame
'Twas the Owld Cause procurd the same
   But what is This to Thee or me
   'Less the New Cause smell Sovranty
Richard Adresses Thousands had 5
Yet at the Length He's poor and sad
Lambertus in the Day doth feast
Whilst Night Sport sutes his Consort best
The state to Cittisens much owes
Guive not nor lend a Mite to those 10
But what to thee doth most belong
And which not rightly stated's wrong
Thou Owst a loyall debt Owld Cause
To vindicate our Broaken Lawes
And to restore again to Health 15
Neath Soveraigns sway this Commonwelth
   Else All betroth'd Pretences are
   But Prostetutes to men of warr
   And the the Issue of such power
   Will be the Cause must pay the Dowre 20
I many times mought recken ore
Owld Cause what rests upon Thy Skoar
But that (Exempt from power) I leave
Both what Thou guivst and dost receive.

    Acrosti[ch]

  O-ver This World He Conqueror is
  R-eckons not of It's Change amiss

  M-inding more Heavnly Joyes and ther
  O-re topping evry Orbe and sphere
  N-or need He doubt to appeer wise   5
  D-are match in Loyalty with Skies—
    Sapiens dominabitur Astris

  To The countess of Ruttland upon Her New   Belvoyr
  reedefying of Belvoir after it had been ruined   May-10.
    by the Late Civil warr   1659

  Iam Seges est ubi Troia fuit—Belvorius ante
   Destructus Bello iam Renovatus erit.

Wher Troy once stood (some say) now Corne doth growe
Fertillety thus springs from Overthrowe
 Had Belvoyr not been crusht by our late quarrell
 It had not shined now in such Aparrell
 As Its Reedefying hath put on   5
 To Shape the Frame into an Union
Thus have I read the Phenix bird to die
To rayse an Other to Posterety
And out of perfumd Ashes to restore
That wonder to the world admird before   10
As Heer you see out of a Rubbish-heap
(Made soe by warr) a Stately Pallace leap
Again to entertain Peace may't be had
To make the Patrons, and Their best Frends glad:
 Wher All to Architect prescribe may see   15
 Their Observations and their Cymentry
 So well Skoard out that It might give content
 To Curious Wootten and His Element:
 The Quaint Contriver forming All a-Newe
 To Challenge Admiration from the View   20
 Of the Behowlders Rayseth such a Pile
  That Smooth-hewn-Ston seems pleasd, and windows smile
  The Bounteous Vale Adoring It the while:
Heer on the Frontespice One may descrye
The Sevrall Scuttchions of Heraldry   25
This Elevated Mount and Sharp-rais'd Hill
At first belongd to, and belongs to still
And that I need not Heer the Owners name
Manners and Ancient Honer speak the same
 Which that They may enjoy long and commend   30
 From Age to Age shall be my wishes End.

   Le Monde Renversè
   Jordanus Retrorsum

The Humors of This Ile turnd Topsy-Turvy
Who could but guess that All would prove but Scurvy

And As the Sea our Bullwark did defend us
We must implore the same again to mend us
Nature must not be wanting now to Showe
To Whom our Natures and our Duties owe
Though Princes Startle at this Showr of Fate
The Loyall Subject's ne're Disconsolate
But that in Peace the Empire will accrue
To Him, to Whom All Titles makes it Due
And what of Late in Civil broyls was spent
For time to come his Conduct may prevent:
Noe Paralell, Meridian, Tropick Line
But will Approve of This soe Just Dessign
And from Two-fowld Emprisonments acquitt
That of an Ile and of Restraint in Itt
The Ocean's wide, Let not us straiten Hope
Ther flowes a mercy from the Horescope
May bring home Those who yet Abroad Distrest
Will make the Conquest Glorious and us blest
And from this Ile to th'Continent restore
What wrongfully had been Usurpt before
Why name we Hercules the Fablers might
Let what will come Right will ingender Right
Let us Obey not worship least Therby
We run the sensure of Idolatry
   Our Romulus is lost: our Roome noe more
   The Giddy Storme Us root and branch up tore
   Fortune's as Wind's inconstant and may blowe
   That uppermost again that now lies lowe
     Wherfore let none despair: This Loss may bring
     Our Hopes to Ank'rage; and that send a King.

For a Gentleman whose Mistresses name was Ara-bella.

Fair-Altar from whose Fabrick doth arise
Enough to fournish out a sacrefize
Whither that Aleblaster we Admire
Thy Flesh Enshrin'd in, or that Sparkling Fier
Thy two bright Starrs shoot from their Orbs to light
Thy Other Features into Exquisite:
Or Turtles-like Those Twinny Brests appeer
To Expiat at full Loves Character:
When from the fowlds increas ther needs a Lambe
Thy mild Sweet Countenance presents the same
Away with Sulferous wichcrafts Salt and Hayre
None such must to This Altar dare repayre:
Nor from the Heard I'l fetch a Goat or Kid
Wher Chastety's Enthron'd in Those Parts hid
But from Those Dores which Cherries Ripe out vie
And Cast more blush upon Vermillions die
From whence such Spices India never knew

Like fragrant Incense is perfum'd from you
Ther's only Your acceptance Crav'd to bring
This my poor Offer to an Offering   20
And t'make me happier than the Persean King.
   Persarum ut verè sim Rege Beatior

Sapit qui sibi sa-pit

At Kinton fight I sawe a pit
Wher a Great Lord was hid in it
I askt the Reason: He replies
He's wisest that t'Himself is wise.

The Cutt-Purses Faier—November-1658
Ballett

Whilst many a True man felt the Fate
  When Oliver did Reign
To be depriv'd of's Estate
  And ne're to see't again
His Royall Herse (he being Dead)   5
  The Cutt-Purse Crewe may bless
For that did stand Them much in stead
  In Causing many a Press
Wher wattches store and Other things
  Those made their Gaine and Prize   10
Mony Key Chaines Bracelets and Rings
  From such as showes made wise
Soe whilst Alive He provd a Bane
  To Honest Cavaleers
Inherst He raysd That Noble Trayn   15
  And made Them prick up Ears
Alive and Dead, Dead and Alive,
  A meeting Place shall be
But wher and How and which will thrive
  Then, Ther's the Mistery   20
Yet Scripture tels; and All men know
  Ther must a Judg appeer
And All shall Reap as they heer sowe
  Cutt-Purse and Cavaleer.

Nec Sicca morte Tyranni

In Peace, at home, in bed to die
Cannot sound Guilt of Tyranny
'Cause not imbude in Blood but drye
 Yet mark what follows (Truth being started)
 This man of Garth Golia Farted   5
 Beshit his bed and soe departed
    Leaving a Savour behind him &c:

Fullbeck
—Sic magnis componere parva—

Since Lesser things with Greater may compare
And in Proportionable Praises share
Let Fullbeck (though beneath the Cliff) not hide
Its Patron's Glory thus re-edifide
Wher All such Architecture doe express 5
They marry Bewty with Convenientnes
Whither to Parler, Hall or other Roomes
We would apply our just Encomiums
And so confine them to the Seelings, Dores
The Windowes, Stair-case, Chimnies and the Flores 10
Or let them walk abroad and take the Aire
Wher the Par-terra'd Guardens Dainties are
(And that you deem not Flora heer alone is
Ther's Statued Venus Paramour Adonis)
Or on the Twinny Orchard spend their might 15
Wher All of Frute and Shade afford delight
Which like a Life-guard to the Pallace stand
To guide the Passenger on either hand
Whilst a fayr even Walk conducts him strait
Upon the Frontespeece and out-most Gate 20
   All These and more when duely skanned strike saile
   Unto the Nobler Prospect o're the Vale
   Wher soe rich Soyle at one View may be seen
   Gould-ears Enameled with Medows green
   And sevrall Parishes and Touns amidst 25
   Known and distinguisht by their Pyramids
   That Graves heer might not Judg his time lost quite
   To write of These who'f Egipts once did write
   What Alexandria doth committ to Fame
   Grand-Cayr or Memphis heer to Nottingam 30
   Newark and Southwell now Transplanted lie
   And Claym a revrent wonder from each eye
   And fertile Nile ore come heer by assent
   Confess its water's barren to our Trent:
Thus Least I leese myself on Joyes beneath 35
I must wing Fancy, sore up to the Heath
Wher if on Earth we may what Poets faigne
Enjoy: then sure Ther's the Elizian Playn
Wher All that Mortalls for content may find
Presented is to Satiate the mind 40
And guive the body to preserve its health
Of Exercise a Scope and Common wealth
   Whither Poor Watt his Clotty Forme forsakes
   And to his nimbler leggs his fear betakes
   When swiftly followd by the flattring crewe 45
   Of well nos'd senters that their Pray pursue
   Soe hot and closs they break sent into View

Or else a Cony from some Grotten Spring
To trye the Mastery and power of wing
With some high-towring-Hawke whilst nimbly ther 50
She stoops and Trusses 'thout a Canceleer
   These and a thousand more delights concurr
   To prove the vertue both of whip and spurr
   When the Beasts need them, whilst nor Gate nor Hedge
   Stands ther t'restrain Their Running Priviledg 55
   But whither Hawke or Hound in swiftnes win
   The Rider may resolve by Riding in:
I'le say noe more but Judg All these Comprize
And Christen Fullbeck Earthly Paradice

Upon 29th of may Di[es] nat[ivitatis] Carol[i] wrot-1659

   Born on the Twenty Ninth of may
   May I but Live to see the Day
   Of Thy Restorement to thyn owne
   And May to me shall stil be Blown
   Nor will I owne any other Die 5
   Than Green and White for Livery

Upon the Death of Oliver Crumwell Lord Protector of the 3 nations who departed the 3d. of September-1658.

   The Rose and Thistle overcome
   The Olive Plant took up the roome
   Which Joynd with Lillies grew soe strong
   The Harpe could play no other song
   Til Pale-fac't Death steps in the way 5
   Then Musike Stops and Plants decay.

Unto his Sonn the Lord Richard Crumwell chosen Protector in Succession to his Father

   Thou Rich-art t'whom Succession brings
   Power to sit in Skoals with Kings
   Gaind by Thy Fathers Conquerings
   Who born aloft on Fames Rank-wings
   Yet could not Scape Deaths Sith nor Strings 5
   But Left Thee to Protect All things.

Upon immoderat Rayne falling a little before the Funerall day of O: being the 9th of October. 58.

   Least ther should want a Hallowed Tear
   T'accompany our Great Lord Oliver
   Unto His last home: mark how Heavns and All
   Conspire to sanctify His Funerall
   And from their Full Swoln Clowds bestow 5

A Cataract upon us heer below
To sink us into sorrow: might it hap
This Ile were Danae into Whose Lap
Not only Jupiter (as once) would Raine
But bring our Treasure C: to us again   10
   Then should we wipe our eyes and noe more mourne
   When we find that long wisht for doth returne

Upon the Death of our late famous English Orator   May
and Poet Jhon Cleveland.   1658

Is Cleveland dead? Could noe Rich Fancies Spell
Work a Reprive, and stop the Passing-Bell:
The Fates Decree noe Mortall can withstand,
Nor may our Threed skape Atroposes hand:
Riches and Honors, Parentage, and Berth,— (*nec Tullus*   5
Can naught avayle, Earth must again to Earth: *Dives et*
But the Sublimer Raptures Crownd This One, *Ancus*: Hor:
How could They fall asleep? b'Entoombd in Ston?
When All that knew Him, bowldly may averr,
None e'er wrot Like, soe He was Singuler: 10
And Jhonson, Spencer, Jeffery, and All
Poets, to Him, seemd but Apocriphall,
His the True Text Invention desird,
To make Apollo, and the Nine Admir'd:
He Tund Their Numbers, to a Newer strain   15
Than e're was heard on the Arcadian plain,
Prickt Noats of wonder, that Fames Trumpet Shrill,
Might carry Them, above Parnassus Hill:
(Beyond, or This, or T'other Grove belowe,
Wher Venus Myrtles, Phebus Lawrells growe)   20
Up to the Spheres, as Ditties, only may
Sute, with the Ayres, Orion Ther doth play:
Or soe Seraphick, that the Spheres, and Those,
One Ditty, Ayre, and Harmony compose:
Soe did He-leav-Land, Water, Ayre, and Fier   25
(Wherof Compos'd), t'Enrich a Nobler Quier:
Whilst we, one letter, from his name obtain   C:
To Skoar our Loss an Hundred through His Gain.

The yong Protector unprotectd. *May 1659*

Well mayst thou be Crum; but Crum-Well
How can that howld True Paralell
When Thy Cake now is turnd to Dogh
Without a Forraign Frend or Foe
Rich-art Thou stil and soe remain   5
Since that Contentment's greatest gain
Wherby Thou mayst out-soar the Pitch
Of Flattering Fortune soe be Rich.

Upon the Immoderat Use of Pastime.
or rather abuse

How shall we pass the Time away
Cryes evry Mouth and hart of Clay
When Time is wing'd and ther with all
Flies swift away without recall
    The Morn's awake and Cocks doe Crowe 5
    The Hunt is up and Hornes they blowe
    The Balling Currs forsake their rest
    To Coast the woods and Rowse the Beast
The Allys Mow'de and Rowld soe's fitt
To Trundle Time away on it 10
The Match is made and Those who win
Forget that Loss of Time steals in
    One sings away with't let's be merry
    Drownd sorrow and sink Cares in Sherry
    When as the Reckoning for These 15
    Proves Remedy worse than Diseas
For God made man for Other End
To Fear His Name and love his Frend
And to improve those Howres are lent
Will ne're return when gon and spent 20
    What Rocks afford in Pretious Gemms
    And Seas yeild Pearle deck Diadems
    Who is not Greedy to obtain
    And t'spare noe Peril for such Gain
Only what is more Pretious sure 25
Time that Delays cannot Endure
We Triffle out Consume in Wast
Imping more Plume unto its Hast
    Til having Been, not livd, we dye,
    Debters stil to Eternety. 30

To Mr Anthony Hungerford

Some Hunger after Riches, Honers some
Some follow Venus and some Marses Drum
But when the Rivers Deepest, in a word
Guive me the man that Hungers for a Ford
Mark-Anthony heer in Biumvirat 5
When Mars and Venus are conjoignd in State
And you will find none fitter to resort
To this Gods Temple and the Others Court
An Amorous Youth, yet Noble Cavaleer
That knowes to draw his Weapon, brandish spear 10
Make a fierce Onset: And be sorry for't
That Sport that is soe sweet should be soe short.

Upon taking up of Severall Persons of Honer and quallety by the Maior and souldiery and securing them at Northampton the 14th of Aprill-1658.

Not like the Gentler Spring whose purle-like dew
It's Tyssue in the Rivolets doth shew
Or those Heat-Drops an Aprill showre distills
From Clowds of Tiffany upon the Hills
My sorrowes are, but Torrent-like they flowe 5
From my two windows as doth Alpian Snowe
I'th'Dog dayes when the Sun with Trebled flame
Shoots Rayes that melt and soe dissolve the same
Or like some Cataract or fall of Nile
That threaten Deluge and a wrack the while 10
They Roar and Break, My sadness is noe less
To see soe many Frends now in distress
And noe cause showne, nor help, nor succor neer:
(Enough to force from Marble ston a Tear)
Or t'Petrify the Stupid sence to see 15
Such needless Fear and Causeless Jelousy
As now posses the Mighty of the Land
Who howld the Raynes of Sovranty at Command
(The Sword I mean) whose Conquering Blade and Edge
Hath gaind this powre and claymes this priviledg 20
That who so doth withstand its force is sure
To be excused of dying by Calenture
Surfet or Ague whilst the Twisted Hemp
And Axes chop from all disease exempt
Traytor's a name soe common grown of late 25
Since Kingdom is Transformd into a State
That 'tis less wonder Hydra like surmise
Deems whence heads ofe thence other heads should rise
Soe to make all Cock suer and without strife
Guive me the privat sell and Cuntry life 30
Wher in a Minors Fortune I'le posess
More than All Maiors envied happines.

Upon Owld Char[les] Cotton who died in December 58.

How Cottens it now Charles is dead?
All merry witt is Vanished
Nor can our Ile be sayd to be
Longer the Muses Nurcery
   Room stole from Athens, we from them 5
   The Lawrell Wreath and Diadem
    'Wont Crown the Learned: Heer was One
In All the Arts Perfection
Not only merited the Bayes
But what All Science guave for Prayse 10
Him the Acuter Genius lent

A Hone to whett Accomplishment
To such a Sharpnes might infuse
A quicker strayn in Evry Muse
Rayse the two-hedded-Hill more high 15
Drayn the Castalion Fountain drye
Soe Rare and Eloquent His stile
Predominized in This Ile
  But he is gon: we that remain
  Noe other Comforts can retain 20
  Than Those shall bring us to our rest
  Wher He and All Good Soules are blest.

Upon the Extream winters Cowld and hopes of a future Spring.

The winter fierce with Could doth rage and blowe
Whilst evry herbe lies Candide now in snowe
The milk white fields a Thousand sparks have on'um
When Phebus casts a radiant smile upon'um
And tam'de through Cowld floods run not now but stand 5
All waters yeild to Ice that bears command
The Leavy wood hath its proud head soe dight
With fleesy locks which render it all white
That neither Aged Oake nor prickly Brears
Can challenge now precedency in years 10
The wood alike all Owld in hoary layers
  But when the Spring its Uthfull Season brings
  And with't restores both heat and life to things
  The purple Vilet, Couslip and the rest
  Peep forth and clayme each one its interest 15
  In this new change; The Marygould likewise
  And Melilot offer their sacrefise
  Then will the pleasant Grove repaired be
  That lookt soe wan in new green livery
Soe aptly doth the year by months provide 20
That evry Season should be dignefide.

In Niuem profundam et Gelu Frigidum.

The Feilds, and Meads, and fleesy woods all three
Servants to th'Season wear one Livery
And whilst Could reignes and Earth's intoombd in snowe
Our strength seems aged, and doth feeble growe
By what means then might I dissolve this frost 5
And bring warmth back again that now seems lost
But thus: with th'help of Bacchus mighty charme
And Ceres, spells alone keep Venus warme:
To build of owld wood such a fier may shine
And thaugh again those stupid nerves of mine 10
Then to prepare good Cheer and wine the best
And a white Lass to grace both man and Feast

Soe then noe Could nor Snowy Showre in Flakes
Can hurt, when 'tis my Nest her white brest makes.

Dum Spiro Spero.

Some may Aspire to sit in State, and ther
The wayghty rod of Sovranty to bear
But therfore 'tis my Lowly Cell presents
Me with more solaces in True Contents
Heer I live quiet whilst Cares make Cares sport 5
In troubling those exalted are in Court
'Tis safer on this Obscure stage to Act
Nor shall my Soule by foolish Pomp be rackt
But whilst the Fates drawe out Lifes woaff to me
I'le ne're despaire but better times to see. 10

In Domum Parlementi Alteram sive Novam a Protectore Editam—20° January 1657.

I am not now soe much engag'd
To Lamenes since the Could's asswag'd
Yet 'Cause the Ould howse is my due
To sit in, cannot fadg to th'new.

Philomelæ ac Citharædi Concertatio

Famian: Strad: pag: 308:

Claudiani:
Stylus:

The Sun declin'd and taking leav of Day
Sent a more moderate fier now from his Ray,
When One in musike skilld to Tiber gets
Wher drowning Cares and Shelterd from all heats
By th'shady cov'ring of a well grown Tree 5
Presents the Ayre with Ayres and Harmony:
Which heard by One in the neer Grove did sit
(Who was the Siren and the Muse to it)
She neerer skips, though hid in Leavs, to find
What sound it was: Then troubeled in Mind, 10
At Last what His hand did disclose in Noat
She did again returne Him from Her Throat
   The musike master finding ther was One
   Answerd his Tunes with Imitation
   Was pleasd to guive the Nightingale content 15
   And soe more bowldly strikes up's Instrument
   As to a fresh encounter: and runs ore
   The Strings with more Dexterity than before
Nor is she slow to answer, but replies
In Thousand Noats prickt to varieties: 20
   The Lutanist in Skorne to be out done,
   Over the Quavring Strings doth nimbly run
   With his right hand, ordring his fingers soe

  As some times to strike high, and some times Lowe
   Then stops: 25
Which she observing sutes her part,
To answer Key for Key, and Art for Art,
Now in a wilde Noat she drawes out her strain
Then calls it in with a Jugg Jugg again
And varieth soe her Gammuth as she sings   30
You'ld Judg All musike harbourd 'neath those wings
  The Man admires, that soe much Art and Skill
  Of sound, should issue from so small a Bill
  And soe with Might and Main prepares to try
  A new attempt, in more variety   35
  Of Flatts, and Sharpes, and Mooding Time aright,
  Smooth Touches hath for Peace, and harsh for fight
This like wise Philomela sings, and proves
By sweet sweet-singing the sweet flame of Loves
And yet not willing to be overcome   40
Varies again her Noats to Fife and Drumm:
  The Minstrell blusht, and warme with anger, cries
  Thou Lutanist to th'Sylvane Deities,
  If This one tune I goe to play, Thou doe,
  I'le break my Lute and yeild up Bucklers too: 45
  Soe 'thout more words, he guave his Lute a Touch,
  Surpast All Imitation t'doe soe much:
  For flying ore the strings with Active hand
  He had both These, and Those, so at Command
  That evry Diapason did present   50
  More Pride of sound, and higher wonderment
  To All the Quier, and having got this prayse
  He stands expecting which should wear the Bayes:
But She (poor Bird) whose voice had thus been stretcht,
Impatient to be soe far overreacht,   55
Musters up All her Force, and when she sees
'Twixt His Strings, and Her Native Faculties
Such Disproportian, and that 'twas 'gainst Fate
That Lesser Ayrs should Greater imitate,
Checks Bowldnes, and Impartiall, for greef dies,   60
And falls unto His Lute a Sacrefize,
As Overcome, Then shews entoombd thus,
How Emulating Vertue deals with Us.

Upon the Lord Gray of Grooby yellow haired being Cutt and Guelt of one Ston for a Rupture he died Bleeding

  A Sorrell Gray which you might guess a Bull
  With Cruelty and Lechry Pamperd full
  Would needs be cut of's Rupture got of late
  Breaking into an *Other Mans* Estate   Lo: Cravens
  The Surgion Bowld His Testicle out drew   5
  And sayd ther'l need noe more of breed by You

At which such streams of Blood ensude: that He
Pay'd the reward of Blood and Cruelty—
     Satiatus est Sanguine quem sitijt

'To which his wiser Lady sayd'

To which his wiser Lady sayd
My Lord is cut, my Lord is dead
 But since 'tis thus
 I must cheer up again with Guss:
For He's the Man must stand in stead   5
  Of Him thats gon
  Had lost a Ston
 His Comfort to me will be more
And pleas my Sex with Prick and Praise good store.

Thorp Pallace a Miracle

Who so desiers, that, earnestly to see
The statued marbles of Antiquety
And wher with Times past Impt the wings of Fame
Ambitious is to Celebrate the same
Let Him to Longthorpe goe ther He may find   5
Subject enough to satiate His mind
Ther stand such Trophies wher in He'l descry
The Lively Figures of Owld History
 Whither H'observes Huntsman Adonis ther
 And by him Venus Mirtle growing neer   10
Or else the Thunder God with threatning hand
Not far from Whom the Sturdy Oake doth stand
Cratippus represented Heer as one
Was Athens Glory Moveless now as Ston
And therfore noe Paripatetikon   15
Ther a Roomes Fencer whose stern Lookes strike fear
Allthough He hath noe sword to hurt with there
And in the midst of These soe wondrous Great
And Bewtifull Faire Livia takes her seat:
Not wearied with walking (as we talk)   20
But Labours Hercules o'th'right hand walke
As Gardian stands (the Dragon killd) ore these
And solely now protects Hesperides
And that these Earthly Trophys reach the Sky
Behould o'th'Stayrs ther's winged Mercury.   25
On the left hand some water nimphs ther are
Who Grace a spring Cleerer than Cristall far
Upon whose Brinke both heer and ther in Lines
The Fir trees growe being set with Guarden Pines
On evry side such Unety befell it   30
That I Judg ther is nothing can Excell it

And yet these All must yeild and Servants be
Unto the Pallace, Uniformety
Sitting in Triumph ore them, and the Roomes
Enricht within with such Encomiomes 35
Asthat whilst we this one peece would Compare
To th'Roman Circus, Ampitheater
Niles Piramids parts of the wonders seaven
We must add this to make that number even.

Octavo Huic Miro Septem Miracula Cedent

Seav'n wonders to this eight guive way
   To let the Owld world see
Antiqueties the new arraye
   In its Owne Livery
Which Edefice for art and skill 5
   The Master may compare
With All that stand on vale or Hill
   He'l finde ther's none soe rare
Heer are with Judgment Trophies spun
   To mark out to this Age 10
What the wise men of Owld had done
   Soe brings Them on our stage
     Methinks it seems just to add this waight
     Unto His Wisedom and Count him the Eight.

Upon the State of England at Present—July-12-1659

About a Government ther is much strife
Yet few ther are can Govern well a Wife

   Wher Aristocrasy bears sway
   The Nobler Rule the rest obey
   Wher Oligarchy rules the Rost 5
   Tribute is payd unto the Most
   But wher Democracy Clayms power
   Number select proves Governour
     Now shuffle these and tel me then
     If woemen Gain not all of men 10

   First They're select Endowments rayse
   All can be sayd of them in Prayse
   Next what somere be't ne're soe Common
   Man yeilds unto because a woeman
   Then to conclude whilst She bears Rule 15
   A man's the Ass and she the Mule.

Epitaph of Sir Foulk Hunkes who died at Cliff the 6. of November-1657

Bred in the Schoole of Mars he did appeer
As born too 'neath noe other Star or Spher

Wilding his sword with that prudentiall care
As stil to Clayme in Acts of Honer Share
Yet with reflection on the Truth and word   5
As for that Cause alone to draw that sword
Though many wounds receivd He rests content
Knowing for Him more pretious blood was spent

To Robin Brudnell Keeper of the Red Deer Park in love with Mall Exon.

Ripe now for Man Mall yeilds to Loves fair charmes
And (Cautious though) conceives more Joyes than Harmes
Thou with thine Arrow Case makst noe Delay
To bend thy Bowe and follow Her for prey
Enough then since the Blind God both posest   5
And wounded hath with's gould-pild-shaft each brest
Let Mall cast through Loves Flame a favring smile
On Robin, He returne the like the while
Love's wingd strike up the match 'thout more a doe
Let Him his standing find; she'l prove the Doe.   10

September 27   ### To Mistress Mary Fairfax sayd to be
1657:   ### married to the Duke of Buckingam

'Tis happily resolvd (Faier Star) to cast
An Aspect on Him honers You, at last
And by your Influence to a new Create
One happy had been soe Unfortunate
As T'leese all that he had, yet to obtaine   5
In You (far more than e're he had) againe
Howses, and Parks, and Riches though some pleas
His Lucks increase is; that depriv'd of These
He may enjoy You, and in You posess
What may make All of Fortunes brood goe less   10
As when the Sun Shines Lesser Orbs are fled
And Phebus up Those All seem gon to bed
Soe He illuminated by your Ray
Bids All his Midnight Chance recede to Day
And's Crosses to guive way to this Content   15
Of Freedom to Serve You for Bannishment
  The Graces Three enthron'd in you, His came
  Made up a Fourth, to Crowne You Buckingam.

To the Noble paier of kinsmen the two Edward Mountaques the One Admirall redy to put to sea, the Other lately returnd from Travaile and taken with the Bewty of the Excellent Lady Diana Rich as was conjectured.

Whilst Thou dost fright the Sea God with thy Armes
And with Thy navy guardst the Land from harmes

The Paphian Queen a suddain Flame doth rayse
And strikes thy new come kinsman with its blaze
Thou follow'st Mars, He's now turnd Venus guest 5
(That other warfare doth become Him best)
   Whilst thou dost seek our fierce Foes to restraine
   And Thundrest with thy Ordinance o're the Mayne
   He is Loves Captive, caught in Cynthias nett
   And to Diana Owes a Servants debt: 10
   Thus both your Fates in doubtfull Starr doe meet
   He must be raysd by Her, thou by the Fleet.
Thou Sea-borne-Venus now in woods ador'd
Let both be to their wished aymes restor'd
May One have bewty, Victory the Other 15
Compleating Fortune, Mars and Art together.
Art stears the Ship, and Art too guideth Love,
And without this Mars cannot valiant prove:
Both from one stock are sprung, let Heavns then be
Propitious to them both in each degree: 20
Let mony boast her wealth, beyond all measure
Diana's bewty is the richer Treasure
   Riches by Sea may faile, He that gets Her
   Shall ne'er be poor; whilst Luck and Name concurr.
                     W: M:

A Sonnet upon the same Subject

The woods and seas at odds
   To Goddises and Gods
        Appeale
For a precedency in Commonweal

   Venus the Offspring of the Flood 5
   Commands the Whistling winds to play
      And t'Curle their Liquid way
        Whilst woods
         And Groves
   Blest with Dianaes Skill 10
On the sharp mountain Top or Hill
Prove the Retirements for Sacred Loves

   Neptune with's Trident Anger showes
And then Each Triton his Shell Trumpet blowes
           'Til all the Mayne become 15
           A Froath and Foame
     Yet through the Loadstones Ayde
     Sylvanus will not be afrayd
        Whilst Love* is such   *magnes amoris Amor*
But wher Dianaes Quiver guives a touch 20
In skorn of all tempestuous waves and seas
Will Bowldly venture on all Passages.

To a frend in the Citty
Sent out of the Cuntry.

The word of Kindnes: how I doe
This or that Other Frend would know
Nor body I nor Mind impaire
'Thin the infectious Citties ayre
I hatch no Plots at any rate   5
Of prejudice unto the State
But what the Cuntry doth afford
Contentments Tresure up I hord
Heer with a harmless book or frend
My howers I pass my time I spend   10
And with my own Estate content
Ambitious thoughts and cares prevent
   I view my herds my flocks my corne
   Which the green Meads and fields adorn
   My towles of trees and pleasant Groves   15
   Wher all the winged Quier make loves
   Pomonaes Laden boughs I see
   With Floraes bewteous Tapessry
   Without a Dragon for to guard
   My Guarden, Orchard, or my Yard   20
   But as my Appetite doth rise
   These all pay Tribute and Excise
   When heat or Could seem to invade
   The woods afford both fire and shade:
When Recreation would be found   25
The docile horse well senting hound
High soaring hawke are my delight
Wher with I send all Cares to flight
Yet Use These not with that Excess
As t'make them my sole busines   30
But to prepare both body and mind
For better things to be enclind
And though exempt from publike Care
Wherin my past-times busied wear
I have a Wife and Children store   35
All which my best thoughts doe implore
And He Those cherishes not well
Is worser than an Infidell.

De Quator magnam importantibus pacem

An Others will before thine owne commend
And less than more to have let be thy end
Seek the Low'st roome, and Others to advance
Wish and pray all wayes, Gods will be thy chance
Such a man shall inherit rest and Peace   5
Whilst troubles vex All such as seek inrease

This saying's Breef, yet much in it containes
In Speech Short, full in sence, frutefull in gaines

To Julius Martiall

Things that would frame a Life to pleas
Most wellcome Martiall are these
A free left means not gained through paines
A field that yeilds increase of graines
A chimny warme throughout, and mind 5
Averse to sutes, to rest enclind
Wit in abundance health noe less
To cherish innocencies dress
Frends of the same ranke, home bred fare
A Table not by art made rare 10
Noe night in wine drownd but soe free
As that noe cares with it agree
Noe bed of sorrow yet wheron
Chastety spreads pavillion
And ther such slumber may import 15
The Shadowing season to be short
    Be what thou wouldst be nor contend
    To hast through fears or hopes thin end.

Of an Owld Hagg that desired Verses.

What doth she seek? a verse of prayse?
To crop a Spell-branch from the Bayes?
    Fresh Aprill flowres you may remember
    Pul in their heads at Sharp December
Could cannot be comprised in 5
Those numbers wher the Muses been
For like to Janus all Her Graces
Consist through baldnes in two faces
Time with his plough bewrinkling thorough
Her Tawny skin hath run his furrough 10
    Between Her Squint Eyes that seemd fled
    For Age soe sunk into her head
    Erected was a Nose that's flatt
    Yet wheron Promontary satt
    With which a Downy Chin half met 15
    Include Her speaking dore of Jet
    Soe that heer represented are
    Some Narrow Strayt and Nuttcracker
Now being Tooth-less Gumms Sh'intreats
To doe their Office, chew her meats 20
Which when sent to her rotten Panch
Again in Belch and Fart doe lanch
Whence riseth such a Damp and Breath
To Those approach as threatens Death

In evry Yawne such sulphers dwell 25
As Etna hath not more nor Hell
  The Rume which through a Could distills
  Hangs at Her nose like Icecles
Frame Her all winters Could, yet in
Her Chops through leannes hollowed Thin 30
The fiery Carbuncle in Red
Pimples like moulhills shews his head
That you would think't the Goddess fell
Drank of that Macedonian well
But if with Her lookes you compare 35
Phebus the Great Worlds Travailer
You'l find Him fixt Even and Morn
To th'Tropike Line of Capricorn
Nay rather soe Dark doth Sh'appeer
As 'thin the Artike Dayless Sphere 40
That who so doth behowld and see
This spawn of Baselisk may be
Ever of stil Mortallety
And if her Stammering tongue but hiss
The Screech Owle or night crow it is 45
  To Her Crook Neck Her Shoulders sute
  To joyne the Belly of her lute
Soe that She seems O-wrions harpe
Her body all soe much doth warp
That you may judg Her Age to be 50
From Cleanlines and True Joy free.

To Leucone inviting to cherish pleasure and omitt care for the future

Hor: L-1.
Ode-11
        Wouldst thou informed be,
        (My Leucone) what end the Gods decree
        In life assigned hath, to Thee or me?

          Break not thy braynes, to trye
        The Babilonian Astrology, 5
        The better to submit to Desteny:

          Whither more winters shall
        Pass ore thy head, or this, prove last of all,
        Thou wouldst desier to know, before it fall:

          Take to thee wine that's prest, 10
        Straynd wine, which evermore is counted best,
        And leav ofe care th'disquieter of rest:

          Then, with thy Lifes short thred
        Cut ofe those future hopes wher with 'twas fed,
        For, whilst we speak, our Envious age is fled: 15

          Soe, the Time present Use
        And let not whats to come Thee more abuse,
        For All must die at Last, and cannot chuse.

Upon a Very fayer Lass

  Fayrer She is by much
Than snow caps Caucasus noe hands ere smutch
  The Rosy Morn doth Glowe
To see upon Her Lips ripe cherries growe
  In Dimond Chaines she ties   5
To Her observance all Behoulders eyes
  Fanning Continnuall Love unto Her Spies

  And from Her Nobler Browe
Like to the Milky Way i'th'Sky or Bowe
  Such high Bewitching Snares   10
She shoots, as Captivate All unawares
  Whence Her Heads covrings fayer
More gracefull far than Bereneeces hayer
Which ore her milk white neck discheveld are

  That haighten might desier   15
To Compass sight of that we but admire
  Her Skin: which softer is
Than the Swans downe or the Segovian Fleece
  The Lilly Laune soe thin
Her Body Cloaths softer than the worms spin   20
And Sphere like True all Her Dementions been

  Now if she sing or speak
The Nightingale outsunge her hart doth break
  And Orators struck dumm
With heering of their Eloquence orecome   25
  In Equall rewes Teeth met
'Thin Her sweet mouth are in such order set
As th'Orients Pearle seems to them cunterfet

  And from Her Breaths Perfume
The Ayre its Gumms and Spices doth assume: 30
  Such fiery Beams doe move in
Her eyes that You'ld think for to carry Love in
Sh'had Borrowd Phebus carr;
That Bewty that Enflamd the Trojan warr
And Ilia—were but meteors to this Star.   35

October 24 1656

Upon a hunting match defeated by wett weather wher I was to have met my Lord Ros, Servant to Ms. Mary Fair-Fax to whom I dedicate this advice

  Alij Lepores sequantur, Ego Lepôres.

  Before we hunt, what weather is't
  Some Silver drops or Scottish mist?
  Poor Wat in form may couch her ears
    This Season bannishes her fears
      Yet if the Poets ere say true   5

Thou mayst be blest with Goulden *Dew**   *Ros
Fair mayd o'th'North; and in thy lap
Partake thy fill of Danaes hap:
Meet with thy Jhon, and Him Embrace
'Twil far out strip all other chase: 10
Noe sullen weather can deny
The youthfull God's dexterety
But as He meets with Crosses store
His fier brand will flame *much more*   *Amantium Iræ &c:*
As sometimes Contraries appeer   15
To trebble Force when *placed neer*   *Contraria*
Venuses Mate the Lame God's heat   *inxtase &c:*
Would soon goe out wer't not for wet
And Love let loose abroad takes could
When kept within dores Brisk and Bowld   20
He Skips from eye to lip and nose
Then takes a tast stil as he goes
Of evry Feature evry part
Til by his subtil Magick art
Enchanted Nature yeilds and's won   25
To strike up into Union
    Then be the weather what it will
    Tempesteous Rayne, or what's as ill
    Could rigid Frost to Hunters Game
    With fertile Dew you'l be the same   30
    For wher Affections Mutuall are
    Ther'l reigne noe Could, nor weeping Star.
        quod fac sit &c:

To my Sonn Charles in prayse of Horsemanship.

Hor: L.1:   On Hunting some, on Fowling Others muse
Ode: 7:   Or else else commend the Craft that Fishers use
    Suting Each Season with a Pass time fit
    Wherin Variety mought sweeten it
    It sores above my Patience to wayt   5
    Upon the Fowlers Net or Fishers Bayt
    Or to be caught with Hunting and the Hound
    But with that horse which Justly beats the Ground
    Thence I th'Elixir of Delight and Pleasure
    Drawe out, and of all Others deem't a Treasure   10
    And t'be Esteemd of Exercise the Prime
    Deserving best a Verse and well tund Rime
    O for a Muse now wear propitious
    To dip my Pen i'th'Spring of Pegasus
    Wherby I mought preferr before the Rest   15
    This noble Art of Horsemanship as Best:
    Fair Junoes Throne Rash Icarus did prove
    And Phaeton His Fathers Chariot drove
    To Their Destruction both, with winged steed

Andromeda by Perseus was freed 20
Both Witt and Skill to Alexander came
When He Bucephalus first strove to tame
Diversities to Divers best agree
But 'bove all Science This best sutes to Me
To Ride well, and soe moderate my hand 25
And Leg, that Horses may be at Command:
He that by Venus Power enfeebled is
Or Bacchus Charmes cannot accord with this
But He whom Temprance doth commend for wise
Alone's the Master of This Exercise 30
Noe weather hinders This, noe Rayn, nor Snowe
Nor whither the winds Mists or Frosts doe blowe
But as the weather's Coulder it invites
More Aptitude unto These high Delights
Which if One would with Other Arts compare 35
Then waigh them in a Ballance regular
He should this art of Horsemanship then finde
For Health to Body and for Good to minde
Soe far out strip All Others without trouble
As Cedars Shrubs, or Lofty Pines doe Stubble. 40

'This life when at the best'

This life when at the best
Is but on Natures Interest
And if we not improve the same
    We are to Blame

All Exercise is Good 5
When it impaires not Livelihood
And draws not Inconveniencies
    To Prejudice

That Health which solely makes   *non est vivere*
A Happy Life without Mistakes   *sed valer vita* 10
Is wher the Mind and Body agree
    In Harmony

Tis not a Tennice-ball
Can so Bewitch my Thoughts with all
As that I Toss away the Time 15
    Whilst in its Prime

But graunt me Temper such
That Exercising not too much
I may and that at Once health find   *ut sit mens sana*
    In Body and Mind   *in Corpore sano* 20

Lessianum

He a spare diet keeps and doth despise
The wichcraft of His pallats Luxuries

Nor in all sumpteous feastings takes delight
But layes Restraint on His Wild Appetite
And shuns the Tables costly are and rare 5
Replenished with Jonketings for fare
May praise the simple foode that's easly had
And ther with make both minde and body glad
Whilst Heliogablus in excess did err
Cornarus He and Lessius may preferr. 10

To my sonn Bill upon his Entertainment at Cane-wood at the Christning of his Daughter Diana June the 14th 1661.

The Various Canes from Severall parts are brought
Some for Eye, some for support are bought
But those of Cane-wood appertain to Bill
Were sugar-Canes whence Each mought suck his fill
Of such high Entertainment as did rayse 5
Content in All, and to the Doner prayse.

'Sir: That to You I never fayle'

Sir:
That to You I never fayle
In what all Frendship may Entayle
Know that My wishes sayle as far
As t'prosper stil Your Man of War
That when you shall your Ankers waygh 5
May noe Thwart Hazer stop your way
But all things fitted in a Trimm
Let your Triumphant Forrest swim
Then Lanch into the Deeps and find
Your Unfurled Canvas Court the wind 10
Looming before it, til it make
Your Halliers stretch and shetes to crack
Soe Ride a Trip, and in that Guise
Speak Terror to Our Enemies
And stiffly Stemm the Tide what ere 15
Without a Back-Stay or Lanere
Mean while Each Watery Pow'r admires
The Order of your Trebble Tires
Blew Tritons Their Shell Trumpets bring
To pay you Musike Offering 20
As you Glide 'long their confines, and
Orions Harp b'at Your Command
All of Disastrous Brood (fore tell
A Storme) to bannish and expell
   Noe Sea-Swine Skale-less Porpos rowle 25
   Thes Charmes of Safety to Controwle
   Nor any Foule of Witch craft Feather
   As Augur Hern or Crane, together
   With Cormorants Chime in Fould weather

Bear Flag on Main-Top wher withall 30
Y'appeer the Fleets High-Admirall
And from Each Yards end Streamers fly
To Notefy your Gallentry
Your Coulers too You must not Lack
Antient O'th'Stern, On Bowlt Sprit Jack 35
 Make Neptune startle at the wonder
 To heer such Arteficiall Thunder
 As from your Broad-sides You present
 To All the worlds Astonnishment
Your Decks too wast cloaths having got 40
Powre Thence a Peal of Smaller Shot
Ther Let noe Deadmans eyes appeer
But what's fram'd to the Fore-mast neer
Nor any Shot prove soe unkind
As t'Cause a Leak 'twixt wat'r and wind 45
Run on your Course nor Tack-about
Til you have found the Roavers out
Would Rob us of those Honers due
Unto Our Nation Ships and You
Steer then Aloofe to quell Their Rage 50
In gayning of the weather-Gage:
Wherin whilst Sayles Gibe known it is
How Yare at Helme Your Vessel is
Which very much Her Prayses rears
When She's Crank-Keeld and nimbly stears 55
 Last Cabins, Hammackoes All down
 Set naught before you 'save Renown
 Til having Them in Chase ore'tayn
 You pay Them Tributs to the Mayn:
Those sunke and All things brought to pass 60
You had Dessigned on Liquid Glass
A Mild and Favring Gale maintain
Your waftage back to us again
Spooning before it, til it bring
You safe a shore on Conquests wing 65
 Then Cables bent to evry Beam
 Belongs to Anker, Cadg, Shete, Strem,
 Those hang a Cock-bell water neer
 Redy to wett when Cables vere
Ther may you leav your Ships to Ride 70
Brought to Their Moorage Ebb and Tide
And all the shore with wonder pleas
To see a standing wood o'th'seas

 Unto These Voats Ile add but This one Peece
 Like Jason too You bring the Goulden Fleese. 75

Post Scrip:

Pen.   Frend I salute you with my Pen

Venables.	Not t'Govern you but you your Men	
Buller.	And that your Trophies may prove fuller	
Blague.	I'le send nor Venables nor Buller	
Askwe.	A Blague's enough his Judgment keep in store	80
	It will siffize and I'le Ask-you noe more.	

'For Hispagniola it is gon'

For Hispagniola it is gon
But rich Jamaica's our own
And those with Gould themselvs would choak
Coat Rawly and the Oranoak
That Enterprize doth best maintain   5
It's priviledg when Crownd with gaine
    Finis coronat opus

'Whither for th'Strayts or else Un-furld'

Whither for th'Strayts or else Un-furld
To seek some Gould in t'other world
I'le not conclude all though the case
Be that they seem Synonimaes
Hazard in either: Vertues tel   5
That's hardliest got that doth excell
And Conquest allwayes haightned is
From difficulties Precipice—
    Qua pulchra difficillima

A Sonnet to my Mistress

A Groat a day some one May-erne
 And some a Pound by th'week
This lesson only would I learn
 I May-erne Her I seek

Noe Orient Pearle nor western Gould   5
 I would attempt to Gaine
Soe that I might in Armes enfowld
 This pretious Prize my Main

I'de envy not fond Midas wish
 Nor Croseus glittring store   10
My pallat's framd to other dish
 Wherin I look for more

Vertue and witt Comprized in one
 Bound up together wher
Shines such a Constellation   15
 Might darken t'other sphere

Thus though some years her Labans will

    I servd have and obeyd
    Yet wages now direct my quill
      To crave what for I stayd   20

    Smile on the Sute I thus commend
      And let me call you wife
    Not only twice seavn I'le attend
      But serve you all my Life
                    as Becomes
        The humblest of your Servants:
              Cha[rles]: Le-de-Spe[nser]

To my Mistres. La Debonaire

    Shall I commend a Rose
Or write the Tinctures that the morn disclose
  In Currall and in checkerd Amber
When Phebus rises from his watry Chamber
    And how we are with bounties blest   5
    Of Fragrant Spiceries fro'th'East

    Shall I those Pearles preferr
Wher Natures self sits chifest Jeweller
    Hang on the tender grass to shew
    The pregnant Indies of her morning dew   10
  Or Lilly, Primrose Vilet bring
  To deck Her 'gainst some Reveling

    Noe I'le conclude all these goe less
When I behould my Misteress
Whose evry dimple, evry smile   15
Whilst I contemplat the while
Me thinks as Master peece I see
Opend a Bank and Treasury
  For Sweet and fayre
  Beyond Compare   20
  And though the Sun
At haight of noon doe shine
He must must confess that she hath wonn
  Whose Rayes are more divine

'Candida perspicuo numerantur Lilia vitro'

  Glasses Transparent Lillies white disclose
  Soe Cristall cannot hide the Blushing Rose
  A woemans body 'neth a silk smocks seen
  As Pibbles in a clear Stream numbred been.

To Her again. La Cruelle

  Am I with any thoughts opprest
  What shall I seek for cure and rest?

  In haight of Greef noe tears appeer
  I shall then borrow from the Deer
  The slain Stag that did newly fall   5
  Some say that such are Medsinall.
  I'le take the bone too from his hart
  To see if Thine that guives mine smart
  Will softer prove and pitty showe
  Before my totall overthrowe   10
  If not to Powder it I'le grind
  Then take one dos to Thee unkind
   And wher I want sobbs to bemone
   The mandrake shall lend me a groan
    A sigth the Nitingall   15
    Contribut shall
    And evry thinge
    Of Plant and winge
     Bear part
  To signe my woe; and how Cruell Thou art.   20

On Judg Ask.

Maydston Mar:-17: 1655

  Who ist that Rides our Circuit? Ask
  And you may quickly read his name
  For 'tis in noe Disguise nor Mask
  But As with K: spell heer the same
   And to's Profession This relates   5
   Whilst t'other His Nature denotates.

Taken with Love of Adriana His misfortune thus He bewailes

  O cruell Nimph fayre Adriana, how
  Dos't stil Thy Ears stop to my praiers and vowe?
  Thou art soe many wayes by Venus grac't
  Soe many Cupids Mustring in Thee plac't
  As that noe Lillies can more white disclose   5
  Nor fresher Tincture bears the blushing Rose
  Than thy cheekes wear: it may be Thou art Coye
  For this, Least too much bewty should destroy
  Soe wear'st a Vale; the Sun too takes delight
  To mask in Clowds some times, t'appeer more bright   10
  When those blow over: Lay distrust aside
  Let noe such Twylight thy fayr Graces hide
  From me thy Servant, nor suspitions guive
  Thee cause to doubt: (that soe again I live)
  For by this kind unkindnes thou dost more   15
  Inflame my hart and Venus wounds prove sore:
  Whilst Hopes are Languishing as Times wear out
  And yet delayes Thou findst to bring't about
  In Labour and in Travaile what dost less
  Than make me to act over Hercules   20

Or Ixion-like dost make me Torture feele
In being turned on a restless wheele
Or being condemnd to Syciphusses Ston
That Rolled is without sessation
Or Tantalusses fate, (whose thirsts though great   25
In waters languish) and Hee's starvd 'midst meat
Thus Rackt's my soule Graunt mercy now for lawe
That I noe more in sinn my water drawe
Let Him by Travailes made the world his owne
Be soe far blest as t'lodg with in Thy Zone   30
And moor his vessel ere it be too late
At Those Thy Ilands calld the Fortunate
   Let Hymen cause his sweeter Torch to shine
   And quench that deadly flame (Cupid) of Thine.

MS WESTMORLAND (A)
6.VI.3/26

Charles Darbyes Coppy taught English

Long whilst we pray and doubtfully would [brin]g
Our wishes and our hopes from Languishing
Our Eyes run ore the Main and Curled Seas
Whilst fayrest of all Objects that Mought pleas
Like blushing Morn and Neptunes Spouse was seen   5
To rise out of the Ocean Brittans Queen
Rejoycing to make hast to come and t'be
Partaker of New beds Felicety:
Now All to Triumph's raysd, the Creeky strand
Proclayms its Joyfull Ioes ore the Land   10
Which the Cragd Rock send Ecchoing out of Holes
And from its Concaves whirles up to the Poles:
The Frequent Concurse too Trooping along
Beget in Evry quarterd Street a Throng
And wher somere we turn us, we conclude   15
The foot paths beaten sore by th'Multetude
Th'Horse Guards in file draw out that Evr[yone]
Mought Bewties Miracle fix eyes upon
And pay from prying Looks Devotion:
No less than when some fiery Commet burns   20
With Glittring Beam All to Amazement tu[rns]
Or when some New Starr shines and doth a[rise]
Amidst the rest i'th'Orbs of Twinkling Skies
The flock of Common People ope their [eyes]
Ravisht to look and see such Miracles   25
The stedfast Gazings Gale the seas, yet find
They want not View though fill not up the Mind:
    But She herself at first in Pretious Stons
    As Saphirs Rubies Sparkling Diamons
    And Gold Shines so, She sends the Day to flight   30
    As Unacquainted with such new born light
    At which the Sky astonnisht wonders t'see
    That Earth produces such a Galexy
    Mought Emulate its Starrs and make Compare
    With Phebus Rayes, when Those the brightest are   35
Then Her suite follows what for Riches worth
And Flowr of youth brave Portugall brings forth
And what somever formerly had been
Hid in the entrails of the Sea now's seen
Or happy Bowells of Each Indies Store   40
Or what seems rosted from the Affrike Shore

Under the Torrid Zone or Lybian Sands
Gatherd together heer Shine at Commands.
The Queen accompanide with such a Train
Set foorward ore the Cristall Liquid Plain   45
Rallies her forces as Diana led
Her Virgin Nimphs in Dances where shafts sped
So tript the Cretan Gierle ore fields and Grovs
Of fair Idea ther to cherish Loves
Untill at last Apollo meets her Brother   50
And then They joyn their Choruses together:
The wood Nimphs are inflam'd, those of the Hills
Assemble so that All rejoycing fills
Made up with People of Arcadia plain
And Dryopes their feastings doe maintain   55
And hand in hand thus Court thir Soveraign:
    The English Youth and Portugese so joygn
    In Choruses that feet and harts combine
    From heavn a shout resounded throogh the Ayre
    The Forrest woods new musike now prepare   60
    Whilst neath Triumphant Arch the way with ease
    Is trod leads to the Princely Pallaces
    Followd with Vowes which did these words express
    For ever flourish Katern our Princes:
But now Great King what Augurs need we t'bring   65
Their Prairs and wishes to this Offering
To Crown this wedding shall I the Dove noat
Flying the Spanish Puttock to thy Coat
In Innocencies dress and free from Gall
Exchanging swarty Lysbon for White Hall   70
Nor is't in vain I call to mind the Fate
Ulisses underwent: Thou from thy State
Like Him was banished yet now we see
Like Him thou meetst thy Chast Penelope
May bring thee Offspring and those chast Loves cherish   75
May faun Thee mutuall Comforts nere to perish
What shall we hope of Dowre? Such lucky Dooms
Makes England truly rich when Tagus comes
To wed with Tamasis and to the Bandes
Of Matriminy brings its goulden sands: 80
    Henceforth let All Prognosticators led
    By This or t'other Star be silenced
    This Year of wonder certains more betide
    When Charles is coupled to his fairest Bride
    Foretould Above whence Powrs Divine had guiven   85
    This certain rule that Mariage comes from Heaven
        Hither then (best of Kings) we hurried fly
        With our Ambitious prayrs that Progeny
        From your most happy bed may spring to sway
        The British Scepter in Successive way   90
        So long as Titan Cleer and Cynthia bright
        Guive light unto the Day and to the Night.

YALE CENTER FOR BRITISH ART:
SAXON'S ATLAS

'I am but Saxton and soe toule the Bell'

I am but Saxton and soe toule the Bell
For Cambden that described These soe well
   And though an Age before him I did write
   Time ripened His to be more Exquisite
   Wherin All Trauailers may vnderstand   5
   How to direct their Voyages by Land
   If any more you would desier to know
   Turn o're Mercators Atlas, let that Show
                                             W

The Soft and Just Support of Brittans Crown
Behold in Portreture lively set downe

Whilst 'neath sad warr All Nations wearied Lie
And Errors blindfould ore the world do flye
With longer Peace thou dost thy Brittons bless
And Truest Piety (Brave Sovereign Bess)
Howlding the Reins of Government so well   5
And wisely too that Justice bears the Bell
   Beloved at Home, Reverenc't abroad Posess
   This Kingdom longe, t'other of more happiness
                                               at Last

APPENDIX I

A doubtful poem and summary list of English poems by other authors

A doubtful poem: Davenant and Hudson

The full text of these two poems is given because it is possible that the second one, Jeffrey Hudson's reply, is in fact by Fane: the style is consonant with his, no other copies have been traced, and Hudson is not known to have written any poetry. The first poem is also unknown elsewhere, but there is no reason to reject Fane's attribution of it to Davenant, for whose other poems on Hudson see n. The two poems are transcribed by Fane in *F3* on pp. 62–3, following *In Tricessimum Januarij Diem* (see p. 312).

An Epitaph wrot by Sir William Davenant Long Since upon
Jeffery Hudson the Queens Dwarf:

Let no rude hand remove this Ston
All though it be a Little one
And hath been in a Thumb-ring worne
For under it doth lie forlorn
The Prince of Dwarfs brave Jeffry hight 5
Who hand to wing in single fight
Did Dunkerk Turky undertake:
And slew him for his Cuntry's sake
 Wherfore to this Ston be kind
 Though under it no bones you find 10
 For when they layd him in his Grave
 A Giant Worme an hungry slave
 Let Creep at him and at one bit
 Consumed winding sheet and It
 Finding the Matter full as Small 15
 As Jonas was unto the Whale.

Jeffreides or Jeffery the Dwarfs answer to Sir William Davenant
in revenge for the Epitaph he wrot long since on Him.

I'm Stil alive as I suppose
And have both use of Eyes and Nose
Though my Dementions are small
Mine hath a Bridg that will not fall
But frame an Arch may be thought fitt 5
To grapple with thy Giant witt
I was forgd small in evry part
Saving the Structure of my hart
Too big to be in Thumb-ring set

It calls to mind Plantagenet 10
Famous in Stories and Renound
For Prowes: so whilst I lie Bound-
Up in small volume thus, Ile sell
For Homers Iliads in Nut shell
Whilst sheets of large extent goe less 15
Tiring both Readers and the Press
  If ther were more of the wingd Crew
  To fight with I'd resign to you
  Who could not chose but something kill
  You have so sharp a witt and Quill 20
  And such Knight Errantry to spare
  Justly you may with Worthyes share
    Now though you made me pay Death Skoar
    Long since the worme lies at your Dore
    Judging it hazardus to Venter 25
    On your sweet self before he'l enter
    Least that such Bowldnes cause mishap
    Guiving Him with your Flesh a Clap
    As for your Bones I must confess
    Thei'r shrunk so much through Rottennes 30
    Ther'l need no winding sheet nor Lead
    But what your vertues merited
    Saving that sheet which Covers shame
    Suting Thee for Repentence Game
      Then let that Ston thy Toombe shall be 35
      Snevel out, Heer lies Lechery.

Summary list of English poems by other authors

Titles (where appropriate) and first and last lines are given. All poems, and the names or initials with which they are subscribed, are in Fane's hand unless otherwise stated.

F2

p. 218. *A letter to C. B. from Epsam Wells*

    1. Sir though our flight deserves noe care
  112. Cald long taile from the man of Kent.

First printed anonymously in Sir John Mennes and James Smith's compilation *Musarum Deliciæ* (1655), p. 3, as *To a friend upon a journey to Epsam Well*. Attributed to Mennes by Raylor, p. 221, an attribution apparently confirmed by Fane's reference to 'Jack that sh— soe far at Epsom Well' in *Ms Urselye—alius Arslys Triumphs*, p. 192, l. 52. The version in *F2* is in a secretary hand that is probably Fane's, but which only occurs once more in *F2*, transcribing *Upon a Coyne Stamp't at Newarke* (see p. 192, *Title* n.). The same hand is found in *N*, transcribing Herrick's *A Christmas Carroll to the Earle of WestmoreLand*: see p. 202, *Title* n., and Cain, *Christmas Carol*, p. 133.

N

51. *Upon the K. murthered*

    1. Heer wants that King who ruld as he thought fitt
  20. Frighted with horror at the Parricide.

Signed 'Cap. Jackson'.

11r.1. *Epitaph on Buckingham by the Lord Faukland*

   1. Reader stand stil and look loe heer I am
   6. That you beleeve two Kings before a slave.

See Crum, *Index* R63. Found in many manuscripts, but not attributed to Falkland elsewhere: that Falkland was a neighbour of Fane in St Bartholomew's gives the attribution more weight.

11r.2. *On Baken*

   1. If you will know
   12. And made his Breath soe stinking.

11v.

   1. Marie my Love, my Life, my Deerest Bliss
   20. Be I in Thee, and Thou in me—I rest.

Signed 'R.T.'

16r. *Upon the worthy Authors discourse and observations concerning the reign of King James.*

   1. Reader heer view A Picture of our times
   10. Prerogative's whole life, the Kingdomes death

Signed 'R.B. grati animi ergo apposuit'. Follows Fane's *Upon Sir Anthonies incomparable peece* (see p. 199), and like that refers to Weldon's *Court and Character of King James I*.

23v. *A Christmas Carroll to the Earle of WestmoreLand.*
By Robert Herrick: for full text see p. 202, and Cain, *Christmas Carol*.

27v–28r. *To my Lady Morton on new years daye 1650.*

   1. Madam new yeares may well expect to finde
   40. Her princely burthen to the gallick shore.

Signed 'Ed: Waller'. First published as a broadside (1661). See Waller, *Poems*, p. 134 (which has eight more lines); Crum *Index*, M29.

28v–29r. *The Scale of love or the sences festivall*

   1. I saw a vision yesternight
   78. Who would not dye upon the Spot?

Signed 'Cleveland'. See Cleveland, *Poems*, ed. Brian Morris and Eleanor Withington (Oxford, 1967), p. 47: *To the State of Love, or, The Senses Festival*. First printed in *Poems* 1651, p. 1. Crum, *Index*, I179.

29v.1. *In Fallacem Leguleium Epigramma.*

   1. None could unles first sworn plead publik cause
   8. Fallax would do't and his gown new transpose

Vilvain, *Enchiridion* pp. 128r–v translating Latin epigram by 'Anonymus'. See Fane's version, p. 204. Crum, *Index*, N305.

29v.2. *Michelbourni Heptades ad Crispum.*

   1. Frend Crisp I send you verses only seven
   7. Which that you'l pay, seven verses I bestow.

Vilvain, *Enchiridion* (p. 142v), translating Edward Michelbourne's Latin epigram.

H

p. 179. *In Answer*

      1. Whilst our Kings Court doth now usurped stand
      6. From both their Princes name, Crum-well.

Signed 'S.D.' Not Sir Symonds D'Ewes, whose name occurs in *Upon the Death of Mr Jhon Selden* (p. 293), the poem immediately following this. D'Ewes died in 1650, too early to refer to Cromwell usurping the court.

p. 180. *Set up under the Gen[eral's] Picture at the Chang as was reported*
See p. 293 for full text. Another copy in MS Harl. 3991.

F3

p. 62. *An Epitaph wrot by Sir William Davenant long since upon Jeffrey Hudson the Queens Dwarf.*

p. 63. *Jeffreides or Jeffery the Dwarfs answer to Sir William Davenant in revenge for the Epitaph he wrot long since on Him.* See above.

p. 114. *A Flye that flew into his Mistresses Eye by Tom Cary—page—63*

      1. When this Flye liv'd, she usd to play
     20. Funerall Flame, Tombe, Obsequie.

See Thomas Carew, *Poems*, ed. Rhodes Dunlap (Oxford, 1949) p. 37. First printed *Poems*, 1640. Transcribed facing Fane's Latin translation.

APPENDIX 2

Calendar of Latin, French and Italian poems and prose

Unless otherwise indicated, items listed are in Latin verse and are attributed to Fane. Page or folio number is given first, followed by *Title* (in italic) or 'First line' (Roman, within inverted commas), Fane's marginal notes to titles or first lines [*italic, in square brackets*], and number of lines. In the many cases where a Latin poem also provides the title for the following English version (not always a close translation), the latter usually just headed '*Englished*', the Latin title is retained in the text, together with relevant marginalia; such poems are marked here with an asterisk, as are those which, though having a separate title in the English version, are still translations or variant English versions of a Latin poem. Poems by authors other than Fane (though copied in his hand) are placed in square brackets. Many Latin items in *F2* are impossible to summarise adequately: they are akin to Apollinaire's *Calligrammes*, 'concrete poems' in which drawing, acrostic and layout of words are combined; some were printed in *Otia Sacra*.

F1

f 2r–3r (2v blank) *Le favore*. [*at Paris—1623*]. Sixty lines.
11r. *In Dom: Roger: Sobrium sed et asinum*. [*at Mereworth—1625*]. Four lines.
13r. *Ad Theseum suum mare tantum divisum*. [*at Orleans—1622*]. Four lines.
15r. *In socium suum tam pinguedine quam moribus abundantem et chastissi?* (text cropped) [*at Orleans—1622*]. Four lines.
15r. *Ex quibus elementis nutriatur*. Two lines.
15r. *Navis in tempestate*. [*upon the sea—1621*]. Two lines.
16r. *In quendam nomine Stonhouse*. [*at Paris*]. Two lines.
17r. *In mortem sui Thesei cum in nuptias sororem suam ducere appropinquasset*. [*At Geneva—1623*]. Ten lines.
17r. *In Noctem futuris nuptijs dicatam*. Two lines.
18r. *Lutetia apud insignem cassis hoc 21° die Novembris—1624*. Ten lines.
19r. *In filiam piscatoris Genevensis eximia forma præditam*. [*At Geneva—1623*]. Twelve lines.
20r. *In Pot & Top*. [*at Orleans—1623*]. Two lines.
20r. *Nox Diem sequitur post tenebras lux*. [*at Geneva—1623*]. Two lines.
20r. *In quendem millitem panem in dorsum portantem*. [*at Paris—1623*]. Two lines.
20r. *In Civitatem Genevens*[*is*] [*1623*]. Two lines.
21r. *In reditum Principis ex Hespe*[*ria*]. [*at Paris—1624*]. Twelve lines.
22r. *In filiam Hospitis a Geneva*. [*at Geneva—1623*]. Four lines.
22r. *In Dom: Field*: [*at Paris—1624*]. Two lines Latin, followed by four-line French version.
23r. *In parvo magna* [*at Paris—1624*]. Four lines, with Latin prose annotation.
23r. *Ad prisci temporis Poetam* [*1624*]. Four lines, with Latin prose annotation.
24r. 'Gaudia quis possit sero suæ condere vultu' [*1624*]. Sixteen lines, with Latin prose annotation.
24v. *Ex Martialo*. Two lines, with Latin prose annotation.
25r. *In pluvias Decembrales—1624*. Two lines, with Latin prose annotation.
25r. 'Queris aquas sitiens? nescis quod flumina cuncta' [*1624 at Paris*]. Two lines, with Latin prose annotation.
26r. *In Dom: D'Holl*: [*at Paris 1624*]. Ten lines.
27r. *In noui Anni 1625 diem primam* [*at Paris*]. Two lines.
27r. *In Regem quendam Regis alterius Subiectum* [*at Paris*]. Two lines.

27r. *In G-G.* [*at Paris 1625*]. Two lines.
27r. *In quendam tam nomine quam re arenosum* [*at Paris 1625*]. Two lines.
27r. *In mutationem sui ipsius nominis* [*at Paris 1625*]. Two lines.
28r. *Ad Hen: Martin* [*at Paris—1625*]. Four lines.
29v. *dal Pastor fido*. Six lines, Italian text.
30r. *ex pastore fidele*. Four lines, Latin version of the former.
30v. *Ex Virgilio.* Two lines.
32r. *In H. M.* [*at Paris—1625*]. Two lines.
32r. *De seipso ad Dom: Martin* [*1625*]. Four lines.
32r. *De seipso* [*1625*]. Two lines.
33r. *De amico* [*at Paris—1625*]. Four lines.
33r. *In Dom: de Knock: cui Guber: Matth: vinosus & admodum rixosus* [*1625*]. Six lines.
34r. *In obitum Regis Jacobi* [*at Bollin—1625*]. Eight lines.
35r. *In M. H—ancillam* [*at Apthorp—1626*]. Four lines.
35r. *In chartulam peregrinationis meæ in Gallia* [*1626*]. Two lines.
36r. *De Comitessa Oxonien: nuperrime viduata* [*at Apthorp—1626*]. Four lines.
39r. *De igne suo Fama tantum conflato cum Comitessa Oxoniense Cui nomen Diana.* Six lines.
39r. *In seipsum.* Two lines.
39v. **Orimur & Morimur.* Thirteen lines.
58r. *Hæc cum carne feri*[*n*]*a missa ad Ro: Ward unum ex procuratoribus in nundinas vulgo Sturbridg nominatus. An.D. 1626* [*at Apthorp*]. Six lines.
58v. *In W.K.* [*at Apthorp 1630*]. Six lines.
59v. *In mortem Anno—1629—Ætat: suæ-49.* Eight lines.
60v. *'*Dum dubitat natura marem faceretæ puellam*' [*1627*]. Two lines.
62v. **TheoD Bezæ Epigramma In Pontem Gardi* [*Paris—1625*]. Ten lines. See *Vita Authoris*, p.
64r. '*Quem Domus Austriaca ab Patrijs secluseret oris*' [*Apthorp 1632*]. Twenty lines, with Latin prose annotation.
65r. *In obitum nobilissim. Principis Mauritij Hassiæ Landgravij—1633* [*Apthorp*]. Ten lines.
68r. *Ad N.B.c* [*1632*]. Prose, twenty-four lines.
73v. *ad Robertum suum.* Prose, nineteen lines.
79v. '*Numina non Nummos me dum cernis*'. Two lines.
80r. *Insula Britannica In Classem Naualem 1635 Mense Maij Littora solventem.* Twelve lines.
80v. *Unto Sr. Thomas Roe chancellor of the guarter upon his word Tramite vere.* Two lines.
81r–v. *de la vie de Henry 3me de Valois le 62me Roy de France.* French prose, twenty-two lines.

F2

pp. 1–7. *Vita Authoris*. Prose, with some verse (see pp. 36–45).
9–10. *Oratio in diem Inaugurationis Regis Jacobi, Anno Salut: 1619*. Prose, ninety-three lines (Fane's MA oration).
11–13. *Epigrammata*. A sequence of twenty-four numbered epigrams.
14.1. *In Piscatoris Genevensis eximia forma præditam.* Twelve lines, fair copy of *F1* f. 19r.
14.2. *Insula Britannica In Classem Naualem 1635 Mense Maij Littora solventem.* Twelve lines, fair copy of *F1* f. 80r.
15. '*Inclyta forma illi, celeri cui vincere cursu*'. Eight lines, preceded by drawing of ?galloping horse.
16. *Muiopotmus.* Twenty-two lines, preceded by drawing of summer landscape.
17.1. *Navis in Tempestate.* Two lines, fair copy of *F1* f. 15r, preceded by drawing of ship in storm.
17.2. *Lugduni Ciuitas.* Two lines, preceded by map showing confluence of the Rhone and Saone.
18.1. *In Pueros Bethlehemitanos quos Herodes morte Ch*[*rist*]*i causa multavit. Mat. 2—16.* Two lines, preceded by drawing of hand from clouds holding out a wreath.
18.2. *In Mot: Amicissimi Thæ: Rho. Ordinis Gart: Cancel:* Two lines, preceded by drawing of a Roe deer. Fair copy of *F1* f. 80v.
18.3. p.e.l.i.c.a.n.u.s. Acrostic (nine words) arranged beneath drawing of a bird feeding on its own breast.
18.4. *Ad Galli Cantum.* Two lines, preceded by rudimentary drawing of a cock.

19.1. *In Davidem Lapideum or Upon the Chimny peece in the Gallery at Apthorp*. Four lines, preceded by faint pencil drawing of the fireplace and statue.
19.2. *In Horologium nimis celere sonans*. Ten lines, preceded by drawing of clock.
19.3. *Placet in vulnus maxima Cervix*. Eight lines, preceded by rudimentary drawing of man shooting at a tree.
21.1. *In parvo magna*. Four lines, fair copy of *F1* f. 23r.
21.2. *In pluvias Decembrales*. Two lines, fair copy of *F1* f. 25r.
21.3. *Ad Comiten de Clare Fratrem suum*. Four lines.
22.1. *Naumachia*. Twelve lines.
22.2. **De Imperatorum Julianorum lineæ ultimo Et Sulpitij sive Electorum primo*. Ten lines.
23.1. 'Quem Domus Austriaca ab Patrijs secluserat oris'. Twenty lines, with Latin prose annotation. Fair copy of *F1* f. 64r.
23.2 *Ad Amicum super 4or Anni Tempora & 4or Ætates hominum comparative*. Ten lines.
24. **Tragicomædia vitæ humanæ*. Fourteen lines.
27. *Pastor Fido: /* 'Si peccare grave est placidum simul; integra non est'. Four lines, fair copy of *F1* f. 29v. (Italian text, inc. 'Se'l peccar è si dolce' facing.)
28.1. *'Omne Bonum presens minus est, sperata videntur'. Two lines.
28.2. *'Fallere fallentem non est Operosa Puellam' [*Ovid*]. Two lines.
28.3. *In Nasutum*. Two lines.
28.4. *In eundem Euro sufflante*. Two lines.
28.5. *Ben Jhonson Drunk*. Two lines.
29.1. *In adventum meum ad antiquos Lares Abthorpienses May-20 1646*. Six lines.
29.2. *Ad Scoto Brittannum cui Carolus noster novum operaturus Opus se subtraxit—May-5: 1646*. Four lines.
36.1. *In mortem suius Thesei J.D. An: 1623. Cum cum* [sic] *sorore sua appropinquassent Nuptiæ eius*. Ten lines, fair copy of *F1* f. 17r.1.
36.2. *In Noctem futuris nuptijs dicatam*. Two lines, *fair copy of F1* f. 17r.2.
37.1. *In obitum F: C: W. pa: me: Anno: 1629—Æta: 49*. Eight lines.
37.2. *In Obitum nobilisimi Principis Mauritij Hassiæ Landgravij. An: 1633*. Ten lines, fair copy of *F1* f. 65r.
38. **Over the Chimny in the great Chamber at Merworth. Oxford*. Eight lines.
57.1. *Ad F: s. F.F. ~ De P. s. F. P. W.* Four lines.
57.2. *Ad Eund De Eod: Frs. Vo:* six lines.
57.3. *Ad Eund*. Two lines.
74. *Ad N.B.* Prose, sixteen lines.
89. *Dialog: inter Judic: et Ratio: Decemb.—1642*. Prose dialogue, sixty-one lines.
90. *Quædam Videntur et non sunt Quædam sunt et non videntur*. Prose, twenty-one lines.
91. *Temporis Mutatio*. Prose, thirty-one lines.
92. *P.R.O.L:* 'Me qualem capiat iudice formulam'. Sixty-four lines.
95. *Sorte Tua sis Contentus*. Thirty lines.
96. 'Est mihi iam fulvo Cognatus cognitus Auro'. Twenty-eight lines.
97. 'Si campo indulges, hostem canibusquem sequeris'. Thirty-two lines.
99.1. *Upon the Earle of Straford Lieutenant of Ireland his Triall in Westminster Hall before the Peers & the Committee of Commons who had impecht him of High treason—wher the King was pleasd to be present incognito*. Ten lines.
99.2. *Elogium Strafordianum*. Sixteen lines (see p. 52).
101.1. 'Numina, non nummos Me dum cernis meditantem'. Two lines.
101.2. *Verbum Dei manet in æternum et transitoria spernit*. Two lines.
111. *Quid maxime semper in Votis habeat*. Eighteen lines.
113. E U C H A R I S T I A G R A T I A R U M A C T I O. Acrostic, set out diagonally from bottom left to top right, one word for each initial letter.
116.1. *In Diem Natalem Dom[in]i* [*1633*]. Ten lines.
116.2. *In Eandem* [*1635*]. Six lines.
116.3. 'Dabit Deus his quoque finem queis hic frumas seu plectimur miserijs'. Three lines, acrostic of GOD.

117. *Natus Damnatus Necatus Glorificatus*. Prose, twenty-five lines.
119. *Soliloqia ad Salvatorem*. Twenty-eight lines.
122. *Decem precepta*. Twenty-one lines, acrostic of *Jehova Deus*.
123. *In Passionem et Resurrectionem Domini*. Fourteen lines.
123.2. *Non in Ligno Sed in Signo*. Pattern poem, set in drawing of a cross.
124. I N R I. Full page drawing of Calvary, containing acrostics (Plate 4).
125. J E S U S. Full-page drawing containing acrostics (one word for each letter) of *Jesus*, above a swag with *Pij Regis Compassio* emerging from a cloud; below it a hand emerging from the same cloud holding a swag containing *Jerusalem* above a drawing of a walled city (? garden), with to the left a cross lying on its side, containing acrostics on *Christus* and *Simon*.
127. *Soliloquia cum meliore partem suam amisisset*. Thirty-one lines.
129. 'Corpore si (Tu) agrotas'. Eighteen lines.
130. *Æliter cum Domino: A cum Principibus huius mundi Negotiandum*. Twelve lines, the title set in a swag down the left side of the verses.
131. CARO SPIRITUS. Acrostic, two words to each initial letter, each of the two initial words set in a swag held by a hand emerging from the margins on opposite sides of the page.
132. 'Alipes Astra petens (sic Fabula) Gramina rumpit' [*1636*]. Ten lines, with Latin notes.
133. *Asssensus, Sensuum, Ascensus*. Acrostic of *Jesus Augot*, set out as sides of one large and two small pyramids, with two lines of verse below.
134.1. *In Sa[nc]tu[m] Stephanum Protomartyrem patientem et duritiem Cordium Judæorum Lapidantium*. Two lines.
134.2. *In Novi-Anni Diem primam Dialogismus*. Four lines.
134.3. *Aliud in eandem. ad Adamum sive totam humani generis stirpem*. Six lines.
135.1. *In Epiphaniam sive Manifestationem Domini*. Ten lines.
135.2. *In Natalem Domini* [*1638*]. Twelve lines.
137. C.R.U.C.I.F.I.G.I.T.U.R. Acrostic, twenty-four lines, the initial letters at the beginning of the hexameters.
138. *Necesse est ut*. Diagrammatic meditation.
141. *In Epiphaniam anno 1640 extemp*. Two lines.
146. *Bona*. Analytic table.
147. O P E R A. Analytic table of opposing attributes and results of good and bad works, set on opposite sides of two shields.
151.1. Untitled diagrammatic list beginning *Quare—quæritis Non—est*.
151.2. Diagrammatic lists of opposites headed *A Deo A Diabolo*.
154. 'Charitas'. Columnar list of virtues (Latin) each joined by English prose commentary showing how one leads upward to the next.
155.1. *Quid vita vera Quænam Mors certissima*. Diagrammatic list.
155.2. *Temporibus hisse maxime discendum*. Seven lines, prose.
155.3. *Verus Christianus sit*. List of arms of the true Christian, with accompanying drawings. Nine lines.
156. *Causa sine qua non*. Analytic table.
159. *Regula nullo modo Spernenda*. Analytic table.
164. **In Diem Natalem etiam et Jeiunalem—1644. quoniam Mercurialem mensis ultimam*. Two lines.
165. 'Aperi Domine, ut Ingrediar'. Acrostic on twenty letters of alphabet (missing *j, k, w, y, z*). Prose, twenty-two lines.
178. *Ineffabilis Amor atque Admirabilis Christi Admiralis*. Fourteen lines, headed by drawing of an anchor.
179.1. *Non est Bonum Ludere cum Sanctis*. Twelve lines.
179.2. *Amasse Licuit, quem peccasse penituit*. Twelve lines.
181. *Ad Angliam in quinti Novembris Feriam Annualem*. Thirty-seven lines.
184.1. *Quid perficiet Homini si totum mundum lucretur et perdat Animam suam*. [*Upon occation of a sermon of Mr Obedia Sedgwicks in Covent guarden Church the first of February 1645.*] Six lines.
184.2. [*Such as stand upon falce bottoms in saving of their soules.*] Twelve lines.
184.3. **De Maria Magdalena Casimiri Lyric:* Six lines.
185. *In Divitem et Lazarum*. Twenty lines.

185.2. *In Mosem ad huc Infantem Amne Abditum.* Two lines.
186. **Ad Quendam tam Potentia quam Intelligentia & Doctrina Divitijs æque ac Nobilitate & honoribus praeditum.* Six lines.
188. 'Creatio—prima—Gen:—1-26'. Analytic table p. III.
189. Κοσμοζ. Analytic table.
190. **Emblem Amoris Sigillum.* Six lines, acrostic of *condia*.
194. *Decem Hac Altaria Fument.* Ten short passages from Church Fathers.
203. *Postnata.* Thirty-five lines.
204. *Vaticinium de ruina Troiæ novanti.* Thirty-three lines.
207. 'Heu quam Lubrica'. Fifty-five lines.
232. **In Effigiem Caroli 2di.* Four lines.

N

f1v. In/Et} tuetur} *Omnia.* Four lines.
2r. *Quindecem Lapsus Petri.* Prose list with biblical references and English prose annotation.
5v. 'In Malis minimum eligendum'. Two lines.
8r. 'O Anima, assiduis vitæ iactata procellis'. Seventeen lines.
8v. *Quam diu Domine.* Forty-one lines.
[9r. *M.S.* (epitaph 'Extat in Templo de Puttny Marmor hoc. 1643. Ben Jon. Comp'.). Nine lines.]
[10v.1. **De Foedere Nationale, February: 1643.* Six lines signed 'E.H:' (?Edward Harley).]
10.v.2. *In Pictura Elizabethæ Reginæ extant hæc.* Four lines.
[11r. *Roma Anagramma.* Twelve lines, signed 'Ge. Herb:'". See Herbert, *Works*, p. 417.]
[12r. *Sic transtulit J.T.C.* Eight lines, referring to preceding English poem *In novi anni—1644.*]
[12v. *In Obitum clarissimi viri Eduardi Rosseteri Equitis Aurati*... Thirty-three lines, signed R[owland] Woodward.]
[13r. *Dom Thomæ Nicolsoni Equitis* [?*Squiris*] *Aurati*. Fourteen lines signed 'G.F.' See *An Epitaph on Sir Thomas Nicolson Knight*, p. 196.]
[15r.1. *Extat in Templo de Brocklesby Inscriptiones Hæ.* Ten lines, prose epitaph on Sir William Pelham 'Miles' (d. 1587) and his wife.]
[15r.2–15v. *In Eodem*, twenty-two lines, prose.]
16v. *Ad Comitem de Clare de Vita Rustica.* Prose, nineteen lines (subscribed 'De Castello Merwordiano mense Maij 1645').
17r. *In Literas Frequentiones C. ?N. ad P.S. miss: in Va:* Six lines.
18r. **Genij Huius Laris & Penatum Salutatio Ad Rivulum Stanlaicum nuper in stagnum hoc Merwordanum Ductum.* August—*1645.* Twenty-four lines.
[18v. D.O.M.S. Twenty-two lines. Epitaph on James Martin, dated 2 December 1652, by his brother William. Cf. 30r below.]
19r. *In adventum Charoli ad Parlamentum suum.—10ᵇr 1645.* Prose, forty-three lines.
19v. *Oratio.* Prose, forty-five lines, on how Charles's return will bring peace.
20r. *Panegyrica.* Thirty-four lines, on same theme.
[20v. *Epiced. John. West. Arm.* Signed 'F. Fane'.]
21r. *Januarij Prima—1645.* Forty-four lines.
22r. **In Thomam ob Pulchram Virtutum Facem Splendidissimum Equitem etiam et Auratum.* Fourteen lines.
27r. 'Quicunque Regno fidit et magnam potens'. Thirty-eight lines.
[29v. **In Fallacem Leguleium Epigramma.* Eight lines. See Appendix 1.]
[29v. *Michelbourni Heptades ad Crispum.* Seven lines, by Edward Michelborne. See Appendix 1.]
29v. **Upon min Hostes Bland at Tousester.* Two lines.
[30r. D.O.M.S. Second copy of epitaph on James Martin, this one dated 2 December 1651, otherwise identical.]

H

pp. 2–3. *Dialog: inter Judic: et Rationem December 1642.* Prose, sixty-six lines.
4. **De Mirandis Bataviæ ad J: Dousam.* Fourteen lines.

5. *Temporis Mutatio.* Prose, twenty-five lines.
7. *Fabula* [*January 22 1641*]. Prose, twenty-three lines.
8. *Caracter acrostichis.* Prose, seventeen lines. (Acrostic spells *Horativs Tovnshend.*)
9. *Saegri: Gazetasticon inter Mil: and Robert: Suum.* Prose, eighteen lines.
10. *Causa sine qua non: September—1: 1643.* Tabular list of policies and results. Prose, thirteen lines.
11. *Quædam videntur et non sunt / Quædam sunt et non videntur.* Prose, twenty-three lines.
63. *Hor: lib: 1. ode 15ª: Nerei Vaticinium de Ruina Troiæ.* [*Meum Novantis.*] Twenty-nine lines.
64. *Rogatus quare Ludicra ab antea non preparasset.* [*Hor: L. 1. ode 37.*] Thirty-five lines.
65–6. *Quo magis sævit Populus eo magis Deo et Pietati indulgendum Carolo. dicato 2do.* [*Hor: lib 1 Ode 9 / 1 January 1649.*] Forty-five lines. (With marginal annotations in English.)
66. *Ænigma in Petum.* Fourteen lines (trans. as *A Riddle upon Tobacco*).
67. *Paraphras: Psal:1 vel Flaccus Evangelisans.* [*Epod-2.*] Twenty-four lines.
68–9. *Ad Horatium filium.* [*Hor: ode 11 lib: 2.*] Forty-four lines.
70. *Ob Cuius ex Exilio reditum gaudio exultat.* [*Hor. Car. L:1: ode 36.*] Forty-two lines.
71. *Ad Car: filium cuius instinctu concitatus quædam carmina Lyrica de Augus: et Patria est dicturus.* [*Hor L:-3: ode:-25.*] Thirty-eight lines.
72. *Alij alias Laudant conditiones.* [*Hor: L: 1 ode—7.*] Thirty-one lines.
73. *Ad Urbem infantam de indole.* [*Hor L—4 ode—4.*] Twenty-eight lines.
74. *Ad Amicum de mutandi damno.* [*Hor: L—1: ode—20.*] Thirty-two lines.
75. *Non prodest moderatio.* [*Hor. L. 1 ode—24.*] Thirty-one lines.
76. *Amænitate pacis restaurandi.* [*Hor. L 1 ode 4.*] Twenty-six lines.
77. *Ad Car: Spes futuri.* [*Hor: L. 4: ode—7 / Apres La Pluie Le Beau Temps Post tenebras Lux.*] Thirty lines.
78–9. *Ad Augustissimum Car: 2:* [*Hor: L 4:ode—14.*] Sixty-two lines.
80. *Ad Fontem meum.* [*Hor—L—3 ode—13.*] Twenty-seven lines.
81. *Ad P Pettum.* [*Hor: Epod 11. Ode.*] Thirty-two lines.
82. *Ad Restituandam Regis authoritate.* [*Hor. Car. L.4 ode—12.*] Thirty-six lines.
83. *Ad reditum Caroli. M: Hor. Ode—2.* Forty lines.
84. *Hymnus Omnipotenti Deoque Optimo maximo.* [*August 1651.*] Twenty lines.
84. *Character quiusdam.* Prose, twenty-six lines.
85. *Ad Cognatum meum T Fane Armiger.* [*October—25: 1656 / Hor. L.1. Ode 37.*] Thirty-two lines.
90. **Ad Geo: Fane: in commemorationem natalitij Reg. Car: 2ᵈⁱ in cellula vulgo vocata Le Grotto scriptum vigilium scilicet maij 28 1650.* Fifty-seven lines.
92–3. *Magnæ Britanniæ transfiguratio.* [*1650: August:.*] Forty-one lines.
93–4. *Ad Illud quod Parlementum Perpetuum alequi appellare voluerunt Nuperrime 20ᵒ: Aprilis An 1653 a Milite dissolutum.* Fifty-six lines.
95. 'Scotia dum Carolus dum basis and Ipse columnæ'. Headed by emblematic drawing dated 1650. Thirty lines. At foot of page is: *Introitus Acta Probavit Maÿ 29ᵒ 1660.*
96. C C. Twenty-seven lines.
97. *RELIGIO Acrostich.* Tabular, three columns.
97. *PATIENTIA Acrostich.* Tabular, four columns.
119. **In Obitum and transportationem per Wainsford Corporis Amicissimi mei Gul: Armin Baronetti &c: Ad viatorem.* [*May-8-1651.*] Twenty-six lines.
121. **Rosseus Vaticinus* [*8r: 1659*]. Seven lines, acrostic of *Rosseus.*
122. *Ad Hor: Toun: and Tho: Cre: in Conven: Parl: asiste: recusantes etsi a Patria Elect:* [*1656.*] Prose, twenty-two lines.
122. Untitled acrostic on '*Protector*'.
123. *Prævaricatio quædam.* Forty-two lines.
129. *In funestum Septembris diem tertium Ubi Scotorum Rex cum suis were put to the worster* [*1651 / Hor L.3 ode 28*]. Thirty-two lines.
130–1. *Ode Ad Amiciss. Ed: Harl: 7r. 7ᵇ 1651* [7r. 7. 1651]. Fifty-six lines.
131. *In Effigiem Oliverij Cromwell Ducis Plebei Exercitus Generalis nuper excusam &c.* Six lines.
132. **Ad Protectorem* [*January-30-1653*]. Eight lines.
134. *Ad Phoebum.*
136. **De Regulo Martial L:1 Epig: 82.* Eleven lines.

APPENDIX 2　373

137. *In Natalem Domini ad Carnem superbiente Ann° 1651.* Acrostic of CARO. Four lines.
137. *In Actum Oblivionis Sine Gratiæ.* Eight lines.
150. *Unus ex Nobilibus Iunioribus a Nobilibus Minoribus Gradu sine dignitate Nuperrime viz: 25 mar; 1652 privatus sic cecinit.* [A: *Persei Prologus.*] Sixteen lines, with English annotations.
153. **In Pascam 1652.* Eight lines.
155.1. *Ad T.T. post longu Literarum internallum.*
155.2. *In Temporis Istive Discordiam.* [*Hor L 1: Ode 31:*]
157. *Ne plus æquo dolendum Amici exitum quoniam omnes una manet Nox.* Thirty-seven lines.
158. **In Guilielmum Sharp Carbonarium grumulum arenaceum arantem iuxta Apthorpianum Pontem.* Fifty-five lines.
163. *Tempora mutantur et nos mutamur in illis.* Twenty-seven lines.
164.1. **In Effigeiem Urbani Octavi Papæ præterit.* Two lines.
[164.2. 'Dum mea me Pietas, mea me sapientia notum'. [*Turnd to his prayse by a frend.*] Two lines, initials S.D. Variation on 164.1.]
164.3. **In Effigiem Innocentij Decimi nunc Papæ 1652.* Six lines.
164.4. **In Rempublicam—1652.* Two lines.
165.1. **In Cardinalem Wolsæum.* Eight lines.
[165. *Turnd to his prayse by a frend.* Eight lines, initials S.D. Variation on 165.1.
[165. *In the Popes praise.* Six lines, initials S.D.]
166. *Regnaldas Polus Cardinalis.* Sixteen lines.
167. *In Tho: Cromwellum.* Sixteen lines.
168. *In Libellum nuperrime editum Hagæ-comitum cuius titulum Regij sanguinis Clamor ad Coelum adversus Paricidas Anglicanos.* [*1652:*] Twenty-seven lines.
169.1. **In partem Capitis vicessimi primi 8ʲⁱ: Mathæi.* [*April:3°—1653.*]. Ten lines.
[169.2. *Alluded to the Kings sufferings by a frend.* Ten lines, initials S.D. Variation on 169.1.]
170.1. *In Poemata Maphæi Cardin: Barbarini Postea P.P. sub nomine Urbani Octavi.* Twelve lines.
[170.2. *Alluded to C[romwel]ls Actc[ion]s.* Twelve lines, initials S.D., variation on 170.1.]
171. *In Diem Passionis Christi: 1654.* Twenty-two lines.
172. **Upon suspition of the Gout to Doc[to]r Bowles.* Eight lines.
174.1 *Qui in Rure venatur Tempora et omnia jure lucratur.* Twenty lines.
[174.2 *Qui in exercitu versatur, Jure vel injuria cuncta lucratur.* Twenty lines, initials S.D. Variant on 174.1.]
[175.1. *By a frend in answer to those wrot upon Tho: Cromwell pag 167 in allusion to O Crom.* Sixteen lines, initials S.D.]
175.2. *In Civitam: Lond: ab Illa quæ fuerat maxime mutatam.* Ten lines.
176. *Die Passionis Christi 1655 April: 14.* Twelve lines, acrostic of *Passio Cristi.*
176. *Die Resurrectionis 1655. April: 16.* Ten lines, acrostic of *Resurrexit.*
177. *Psal:—91:* [*Palm sund: April: 8 1655*]. Sixteen lines.
178.1. *Vida Anagram Diva.* Six lines.
178.2. *Vida Anag: Diva.* Four lines.
[179. *Responsio.* Six lines, initials S.D., responding to 178.2.]
180. **Shrove Teusday 1654. when Fra: Palmes came to visit me at Apthorp was wellcome won mony &c:* [*veni, vidi, vici*]. Six lines.
181. **In Libellum Domi: de Militier.* Eight lines.
182. *Ad Aurelium Prudentium Clementem Poetam Antiquum æquæ ac eximium.* Ten lines.
182. *To W.W. with a token I had promised but not performd.* Six lines.
187. *Psal.—137* [*10r-1656. Lon.*]. Prose, twenty-two lines.

F3

p. 1. 'In manus tuas Me meosque remitto (Domine)'. Four lines.
3. 'Quo usque tandem abuti Patientia tua Me finis Domine'. [*Psalm 1.*] Prose prayer, partially imitating versification of Psalms. Fourteen lines.
11. 'Ut petit a Domino quanam ratione salutem'. [*Mat: 19 / Mr: Calamy.*] Twelve lines.
11. *Optimus Thesaurus Cælistis.* [*Ver Harc:.*] Twelve lines.

12. *Psal: Davidis secundum Textum in Hexam: et Pentam: Versus.* [*July 5 1657.*] Twelve lines.
12. *Nam si secundum Carnem Vixeritis futurum est ut moriamini: sed si Spiritu actiones Corporis Mortificetis vivetis.* [*Rom 8–13 / Mr Wallis August 30 1657.*] Eight lines.
13. *In Funus Eduardi Pellham Armiger et Generis mei prædilecti Cantus Lugubris.* Thirty-three lines.
15. *Ad Deum Immortalem* [*In Imit. Hor Ode 1*]. Forty-three lines.
16. *Mortis Meditatio Optima.* [*Hor: L: 1. Ode-26.*] Twelve lines.
17. *Paraphras: in Psal 1: Vel Flaccus Evangelisans.* [*Hor: Ep Epod: 2.*] Twenty-four lines.
17. **O Lord thou art my Portion &c.* Two lines.
18. **Solatur se etsi Naturaliter Miserium, Falicem tamen Gratia, ex Passionibus Christi fore.* Sixteen lines.
19–20. *Prædilecto et Unigenito Dei Filio Laudibus Omnibus Dignissmo* [*Hor: L: 1. Ode-12: / Decr: 25 1656*]. Sixty-four lines.
21. *Me met ipsum e nequitia reditum sic consolor.* [*Hor: L:2: Ode 7:.*] Twenty-eight lines.
22–3. *Divino præsidio e periculis Erebi ereptum se dicit eodemque tutum semper fore sperat.* [*Hor: L:3. Ode: 4.*] Eighty lines.
24. *4. Psalmus Davidis secundum Textu in Hex: et Pen: Versus.* [*apud Wrest July 1657.*] Eighteen lines.
25–6. *Virum Religione præditum nihil extimescere.* [*Hor: L: 3. Ode 3:.*] Seventy-two lines.
27. **Execratio belli Civilis in Corpore humano a Satane gesti: et fuga Damonum Oratione et Jeiuncis maxime impetrata.* [*Hor: Epod: Ode: 7:*] Twenty lines.
29. *Carroll—1657 Dies Natalis Acrost:* Sixteen lines.
53. **Coritanum Regio Vel Comitatus et Agris Darbiensis Descriptio.* Eight lines.
59. **In Vicessimum Nonum* [added *Tricessimum*] *Januarij Diem in quo serenissimus Ille Rex Noster Carolus illius Nominis Primus Nulli pietate secundus a subditis suis inhumaniter obtruncatus erat.* Eleven lines.
64. **Ad Societatem Fanaticam vel verè Jesuiti.* Nineteen lines.
66. **For—*[emblem: wheel]*—tunæ.* Twenty-nine lines.
68. **In Obitum præclarissimi Thomæ Comitis Cardiganensis Epitaphium Qui Decessit Decimo quinto die Septembris Ano: 1663.* Twenty lines.
70. **Ad Amicum Xr.* Eight lines.
71. **Astroites Lapides Belui—Oris Inveniantur.* Twelve lines.
74. **In Actum Focarium.* Twelve lines.
75. *Northantoniæ Villulæ præsens Status sive Northantonia Imminita.* MDCLXII. Two lines.
79. **In Jesuiticum Ordinem.* Two lines, by 'Ferrier' (see note to English text).
81. *Votum In Adventum Regina* [*Aprill 2: 1662*]. Six lines.
81. *Salutatio Votifera post accessam 140: die Maij.* Eight lines.
82. **'Vides ut Alta mente composita'.* Twenty-four lines.
108. **In Frigus Hyemale prasigne et Spem Veris futuri.* [*February 15 1657.*] Twenty lines.
110. **In Niuem profundam et Gelu Frigidum.* Eight lines.
111. **Dum Spiro Spero. January: 24. 1657.*
111. **In Domum Parlementi Alteram sive Novam a Protectore Editam—20° January: 1657.* [*Aeta: 56.*]
115. *Ad Celiam et Muscam in Oculum eius Volantem:* [*January. 9 1657*]. Sixteen lines: Fane's Latin version of Carew's *A Fly that flew into my Mistress's Eye*, transcribed on the previous page. See Appendix 1.
116. **Miraculum hoc Anglicanum Mundi Octavum.* Thirty-five lines.
118. **Octavo Huic Miro Septem Miracula Cedent.* Six lines.
120. **Ad Bellonam.* Twelve lines.
121. **Ad Robertum Bru: Amore Mariæ x⁻: Captum.* Ten lines.
121. *Upon a very great snowe Epiphany—1657.* Six lines.
124. **Ad Eduardum de Monte Acuto Archithalassu Littora soluente et Cognatum suum eiusdem etiam Nominis Amore Proclarissimæ ac Nobilissimæ Dom*[in]*æ: Dianæ Rich Captum.* [*Juli-18 1657.*] Twenty-four lines.
126. *Ad Olivarium Nostrum Ang: Sco: et Hiber: protectorem Eximium Regis Titulum etsi a Parlamente* [sic] *suo ut sibi iam sumeret multoties deoratum Recusantem.* [*May 1: 1657.*] Six lines.
126. *Pacis Trophæum.* Six lines.
126. *Ænigma.* [*1657: March: 11:.*] Four lines.

126. *Miles Anag: Limes.* Two lines.
127. *Ad Olivarium Nostrum nuperrime ab Assatinatione premeditata Liberum.* [*February: 20 1656*]. Thirty-two lines.
128. *Miratur Insulam Quandam in Pace et Concordia antea Stabilitam ad Militiam transisse.* Sixteen lines.
130. **Martial—L:—10. Epig:-47./ Ad Julium Martialem.* Thirteen lines.
130. **De Quator magnam importantibus pacem.* Seven lines.
132. **De Ano Deforme Carmina Petente.* Forty-four lines.
134. **In Filiam Eximiam Formam Praditam.*
138. *Gratulatur Montifacuti Amicimæ et Postremæ Expeditionis maritima ex Generalibus Unius faustum in Patriam reditum—8br 1 1656.*
139. *In Collegium Emanuelis Epigram.* [*April-13 1657.*] Twelve lines.
139. *In Annales Veris vere Dignas.* Fourteen lines.
140–1. **Ad Carolum Filium in Arte Equestre pritissimum.* [*Hor: L: 1. Ode: 7. / 10r 1665.*] Forty-five lines.
145. **Lessianum.* Ten lines.
150. **'Candida perspicuo numerantur Lilia vitro'.* [*Martial*]. Four lines. A version of Martial VIII. 68, 5–8.
152. **Captus Amore Adrianæ sic Infortunium plangit.* Twenty-seven lines.

Saxton's Atlas

Coritanum Regio Vel Comitatus et Ager Darbiensis. Eight lines. Text identical with *F3*, p. 53 above.

NOTES TO THE POEMS

An asterisk indicates that the note contains information which supplements that in the *OED*.

F1: Fulbeck Hall MS. Poems, 1621–35

To his Mistress   8. part stakes] share.
Me nive cadente petijt mea Julia   Title] 'My Julia sought me as the snow was falling. I used to think that snow lacked fire; and yet snow was fire.' The same two lines are used as title on p. 230, where they are attributed to Ovid. Alexander Brome, *Songs and other Poems* (1661), p. 179, translates the same passage, and Thomas Philpott, in a collection dedicated to Fane, has a similar poem (*Poems*, 1646, p. 3), but the source (probably not Ovid) has not been located. Cf. also *An owld man married a yong lass* (p. 62, ll. 5–6) and *La resverie or Loves Winter Seege* (p. 65, l. 15).   4–6] Cf. *Upon a hunting match defeated by wett weather*, p. 348, ll. 16–7 n.   10. exasperate] Aggravate, magnify the effect of.
An Invitation to R.H.   Title. R.H.] Robert Herrick; for an account of the context of this and *To R.H. with some Venison* (p. 61), see Cain, 'Robert Herrick'.
An ode To N.B. an angler   Title. N.B.] Ned (Edward) Beecher, b. *c*. 1575, apparently still living 1648 (see *Ode—To a frend in Imitation of these*, p. 201). Of Howbury Hall, Renhold, Bedfordshire, and Peterborough; matriculated at ?Peterhouse *c*. 1592 (Venn). See also *A tinder-box for Ned: Beech[er]* (p. 62); *A Letter sent to E.B. from Apthorpe to Howb[ury]* (p. 89); *To N.B. at Thorp* (p. 112); and *An Ode to N.B.* (p. 113). References to his age (ll. 15–20) confirm it is him, and not his great-nephew of the same name, who matriculated at Peterhouse the year of this poem.   28. Clubbing] Social meeting, not necessarily in a club.   29. purle] Decorate, as in ornamental edging.   30. my Lord's] Fane was styled Lord Burgersh when his father became Earl of Westmorland, 1624: a Latin epigram in *F1 In mutationem sui ipsius nominis*, dated 'At paris 1625' notes the change: 'Fanus dum fueram nondum cognatus: at ipso / Tempore quo Burgersh sum fiat affinitas.' From 1626 to 1629, he was Lord le Despenser (*Peerage* XII, pt 2, p. 568).   38. Tom. Blotts] Thomas Blotts, of Barmwell All Saints, Northamptonshire, 'Husbandman', d. 1633 (NRO, *Index to Wills Proved in the Consistory Court of Peterborough* I, f. 7r).   40.1. Ex Scotia missa] 'Sent from Scotland'.
The Savoy—Excetter house   Title. The Savoy] On the south side of the Strand, near Charing Cross, approximately on the site of the Adelphi. The old palace was much let and sub-let. Fane's father and uncle had bought ten messuages and three gardens in the area in 1605 (*Survey* XVIII, pt 2, p. 4). This or a nearby part of the liberty of the Savoy in 'Durham Yard' was the family's London home in the early 1620s, probably while Sir Henry Hobart rented the house in St Bartholomew's Close: see E. A. Webb, *The Records of St Bartholomew's Priory and of the Church and Parish of St Bartholomew the Great West Smithfield* (Oxford, 1921), p. 266, and 'A Howshold Booke' from Mereworth (W(A) Misc. 15, f. 15v): 'sent to the Savoy to my Lord a pidgeon pye, a capon pye and 6 rabbetts' (July 1625). Cf. *To a Frend upon my Pallace and habitation*, p. 325, l. 3, and *My Fidelia with whom I had been cross the Street at Devotion*, p. 93.   Excetter house] On the north side of the Strand, backing on to the old 'Convent Garden'. Frances, the dowager Duchess of Richmond and Lennox, aunt of Fane's future wife, Grace Thornhurst (see *A Valentine for my Lord Savage*, p. 70, ll. 10–11) was one of a number of tenants following the death of the first Earl of Exeter, 1622. Grace must have stayed with her while in London (ll. 1–2).   2. turretts] Begun during the reign of Edward VI by William Cecil, Lord Burleigh, Exeter House was a heavily tur-

reted mid-Tudor building.   5. strait] narrow.   14. terreine] earthly.   21. *actiom] axiom (not in *OED* in this form).

Mine eyes Ember weekes fast   *Title. Ember weekes*] One of the four periods of fasting and prayer following (1) the first Sunday in Lent, (2) Whitsunday, (3) Holy Cross Day (14 September), (4) St Lucia's Day (13 December) Though 'Papist' (l. 1) they retained favour with Presbyterians as well as Anglicans, being observed punctiliously by the Harley family at Brampton Bryan.   *fast*] See above, *The Savoy—Excetter house*, l. 19.   *Margin.* Mereworth] Mereworth Castle, Kent, one of the two main country houses of the Fanes. It was rebuilt during the eighteenth century and now, unlike Apethorpe, bears no resemblance to the house Fane knew. See also *To my Cosen T.F.*, p. 318, *Title* n., and *Upon the little parler Garden at Mereworth*, p. 323.   9. delia] The moon.   13–16] Proverbial, cf. Tilley, C442.

To R.H. with some Venison   *Title. R.H*] Robert Herrick (see *An Invitation to R.H.*, p. 58, *Title* n.).   2. Obberon] Herrick wrote three fairy poems involving King Oberon: see Cain, 'Robert Herrick', p. 315.   10. blow] Blossom, placing the poem in spring 1626 or 1627.

'If one but anoint the sword'   *Title*] Referring to the 'weapon-salve', the principal ingredient of which was moss from a skull. Applied to the weapon which had made the wound, it would cure it by sympathetic magic. *OED* s.v. *weapon-salve* quotes Dryden, *Tempest* 5.1: 'Anoint the Sword which pierc'd him with this Weapon-Salve, and wrap it close from air till I have time to visit him again.'

An owld man married a yong lass   Cf. Henry King, *Paradox. That it is best for a Young Maid to marry an Old Man* (*Poems*, p. 180); R. Fletcher, *An old Man Courting a young Girle*, in *Martiall his epigrams Translated. With Sundry Poems and Fancies* (1656), p. 177.   *Margin.* apthorp] Apethorpe Hall, Northamptonshire, Fane's main estate. Though his father did not inherit Apethorpe until the death of Sir Anthony Mildmay in 1617, Fane implies in his *Vita* that he moved there in his 'third year', 1604–05.   1. December . . . married] Proverbial, Tilley, M768.

'He who such strong lines wont compose'   2. Atropos] 'She who is not to be averted', one of the three Moiræ (Fates), the 'blind Fury with th'abhorred shears' of Milton's *Lycidas*, l. 75. Cf. *Upon the rumor of his departure*, p. 252, l. 10, and *Upon the Death of our late famous English Orator and Poet*, p. 335, l. 4.   4. Sir Simion] Sir Simeon Steward, of Stuntrey, Cambridgeshire (d. 1629), of an East Anglian family, kt 1603, m. Grace St Barbe. He wrote *The King of Fayries Clothes*, and was an associate of Herrick, who probably knew him as a resident of Trinity Hall, where he kept a room for many years after his graduation: see Herrick, 126.3, *A New-yeares gift sent to Sir Simeon Steward*.

A tinder-box for Ned: Beech[*er*]***chafing***   *Title. Ned Beecher*] See *An Ode to N.B. an Angler*, p. 59, *Title* n.   *chafing*] Becoming angry.   4. leese] lose.

Upon an Escheater   *Title. Escheater*] 'An officer appointed yearly by the Lord Treasurer to take notice of the escheats in the county to which he is appointed, and to certify them into the Exchequer' (*OED*).   1. cousnedg] cozenage, cheating.   2. Es] Ease.

TheoD Bezæ—Epigramma   *Title*] 'Epigram by TheoD Beza on the Pont du Gard'.   *TheoD Bezæ*] Théodore De Bèze (1519–1605), French poet and theologian, succeeded Calvin at Geneva. Named by Donne as 'the best linguist' in *Satire IV*, l. 55, but also known, like other Presbyterians of his period, as a proponent of contractual monarchy. Fane owned both *Psalmi duplici poetica metaphrasi* by De Bèze and George Buchanan (1581) and De Bèze's *Summe of the Christian Faith*, trans. R. Fylls (n.d.), both now at Fulbeck. This poem is not in them, nor in his *Poemata*.   pontem Gardi] Fane visited the Pont du Gard in 1625: see *Vita*, p. 38.

'Goe to the signe o' th Hen and Cock'   4–6. Rushen . . . Worth] Though 'not worth a rush' was a common phrase, Fane seems to be punning on the name 'Rushworth'. John Rushworth (1607–90), later Fairfax's secretary, was 'neere of kin to Sir Thomas Fairfax' (Aubrey, II, 207–8), and was thus to become distantly related to Fane from 1638. Later still (1664), Rushworth's daughter Hannah m. Fane's nephew, Sir Francis Jr, but there is no evidence of Fane's knowing him in the 1630s.   10. *Nabir] ?'Neighbour'; if so, an eccentric spelling even by Fane's standards (but cf. *OED* 'nebber' and 'neiber'). It may not be coincidental that it is 'riban' (l. 12) spelt backwards.   13–14. rest . . . crest] Not an anagram of 'horn' as might be expected.

in eandem   *Title*] 'On the same'.

A lecture to be mild in love 17] Echoing or anticipating Herrick, 'The Coming of Good Luck' (100.2), ll. 3–4.   29. kie] kye, plural of 'cow'.   30. tapisry] Variant of 'tappissery', early form of tapestry.

La resverie or Loves Winter Seege   Title. **resverie*] Reverie, here in its developing seventeenth-century sense of a fanciful notion (*OED*, 3).   1–2] Gustavus Adolphus of Sweden, having consolidated his control of Finland and the Baltic States, invaded northern Germany in 1630 to counter the threat posed by Wallenstein's Catholic army to Protestantism and Swedish hegemony over the Baltic. He over-wintered on the Rhine in 1631–32.   22. Hannibal . . . Vinegar] Livy describes Hannibal blasting an Alpine cliff out of the way by heating it and 'pouring vinegar over the glowing rocks, so that they crumbled' (XXI. 37).

Public record Office: S.P. 16: 437.60

Upon the Scotch Sermon that compared the Kirke to a horsse   Title] Addressed 'for his Majesties speciall affaires To Mr. Secretarie Windebanke', i.e. Sir Francis Windebank (1582–1646), se cretary of state since 1632. From a Lincolnshire family, Windebank may have been related to the Fanes: the Dowager Countess addresses him during the 1630s as 'cousin'. He was one of those on the Privy Council 'earnest to put the King upon a war' with the Scots (Earl of Northumberland to Strafford, 23 July 1638, quoted in Masson, II, p. 24). The sermon has not been traced, but the poem must date from 1637–38. It differs markedly from *Upon the Scotsh business* (p. 230, dated 1638) and was presumably written to please both Windebank and the King.   2. sea] so: imitating Scottish pronunciation.   4. Cope carle] A 'cup carl' was a fast, perhaps a difficult, racehorse (not in *OED*, but Fane uses it thus in *The Pedegree of Bay Wastnes*, p. 231, l. 15). Here a pun on Presbyterian opposition to the clergyman's cope as prescribed for Scotland in the Laudian *Book of Canons* (1635) and *Service Book* (1637), a 'cope carle' being a person churlish, violent or niggardly over copes.   8. dolefull] Clothed as if for mourning: here in the plain black gown of the Presbyterian minister.   *Jockies] This use meaning 'riders' antedates the first *OED* quotation of 1643. There is probably not a pun on 'Jock', 'Scotsman', which is not recorded before the nineteenth century (*OED* and Partridge).   9. paces] The gait of a trained, controlled horse.   tint] Lost: Scottish dialect.   gane] gone.   10. The feind] ?Misspelling 'fiend', as a Scottish curse equivalent to 'the Devil a . . .'.   Strack] Pace, speed (*OED* s.v. *strake n*1, 5b).   gang] go: Scottish dialect.   12. my bird] Evidently used as typically Scottish term of endearment, but cf. *Tp.* 4. 1. 184.   14. mare] more, with a pun on 'mare', female horse.   15. pace] Walk, amble.   16. Canterbury] The 'Canterbury gallop' (hence 'canter') supposedly used by mounted pilgrims: here also both Laud (who became archbishop 1633), and Anglican Church discipline in general.

F2: Fulbeck Hall MS. Poems, 1623–50

Brook House Bay trees   Fane's note in *H* ('Comp[osed during] interm[en]t &c Lon./ December. 13. 1643') indicates it was written when the conditions of his house arrest had been relaxed: in August 1643 the House of Lords 'ORDERED, That the Earl of *Westmerland*, giving his Word upon his Honour to remain in safe Custody, shall have Leave to ride out, and take the Air, within Five Miles Distance from *London*, for his Health Sake' (*Lords' Journals* VI p. 185).   Title. *Brook House*] Probably the one in Hackney, which had a larger garden than Brooke House, Holborn; both were within five miles of Bartholomew Close. Evelyn found the garden 'one of the neatest, & most celebrated in England: The House also well furnish'd, but a despicable building' (*Diary*, 8 May 1654, III, p. 96). Cf. Fowler, pp. 233–4. There is a pen-and-ink drawing of a semi-circle of trees beneath the title in *F2*.   1. Joves Plant] The laurel was sacred to Apollo, but was supposedly immune to Jove's thunder, and thus a common symbol of survival in adversity.

In Davidem Lapideum Title] 'On the statue of David'. Chimny peece ... Gallery] An elaborate fireplace, still in the Long Gallery at Apethorpe: photographs and description in *Country Life*, 27 March 1909, pp. 452–3, and *Country Houses*, p. 65, fig. 74C. *F2* has a very poor and faint pencil drawing of the fireplace beneath the title. 6. daunce] II Samuel 6. 16: 'Michal, Saul's daughter, looked through a window, and saw King David leaping and dancing before the Lord.'
Upon the Clock going too fast Title preceded in *F2* by pen-and-ink drawing of a clock.
A Valentine for my Lord Savage Dated 'London—1627' in *F1*. In *F2* title is followed by a tiny (20 mm^2) pen-and-ink drawing of a rose and lily surmounted by a coronet.   Title. *Lord Savage*] Thomas Savage (*c.* 1586–1635), second bart 1615, created first Viscount Savage 1626, married 1602 Elizabeth, daughter and co-heir of Thomas, Lord Darcy of Chiche. His daughter Anne married (1640) Robert Brudenell, probably one of Fane's gentleman attendants, later second Earl of Cardigan: see *To a P.K: that sent to me for 2 Peeces*, p. 316, Title n.   3. Rose and Lilly] Cf. Herrick, *Upon one Lillie, who marryed with a maid call'd Rose* (44.1).   10–11. Lennox ... Richmond] Frances, then dowager Duchess of Richmond and Lennox (married 1621, widowed 1624), daughter of Thomas, Lord Howard of Bindon, and aunt of Fane's first wife. There was a portrait of her at Apethorpe (George Bridges, *History and Antiquities of Northamptonshire*, 1822–41, II, p. 424), and she lived in Exeter House in the Strand, near the Fane family, from 1625, dying there 1639 (see *The Savoy—Excetter house*, p. 60, Title n.).
A Hart Enamelld white to Nel. G. Dated 'London—1627' in *F1*, where it is entitled *Fama Mendax*, ('Rumour is false'). In both manuscripts, the title is followed by a tiny pen-and-ink drawing of a heart. The poem imitates Jonson's 'Have you seen but a bright lily grow', *Underwoods* II, 4, 21–30 (*Poems*, p. 129); cf. *Sonnet Comparing Fid[elia] to the 4: Seasons*, p. 94.   Title. *Nel. G.*] Unidentified.
Upon a small occation of 10,000£s disburcement   Title. *raptim*] Suddenly snatched away.   1. Portians] Marriage portions: £5,000 was the sum Fane was contracted to give as dowry with his sisters and each of his six daughters in 1650 (W(A) Misc. 15, f. 77v; cf. Stone, *Crisis*, p. 213). In 1648 he still owed £4,000 for his sister Rachel's dowry, though a proposal by her husband, the Earl of Bath (July 1648) to sequester his estates until it was paid seems to have been abandoned (*CCAM*, p. 636). Another sister, Katherine, died in 1649, shortly after her marriage to Conyers Darcy, with £4,000 of her portion unpaid (see *For Mr Conyers Darcy*, p. 159, Title n.), while between 1645 and 1650 Nicholas Crisp of Rutland and his son John were demanding £2,000 owed to them on behalf of 'several daughters of Crisp' (*CCAM*, pp. 544–5).   2] Fane had been fined £19,000 by the Crown under the revived Forest Laws in 1637, later reduced to £2,500 (W(A) 7 xvii 41). He was assessed for a fine of £3,000 for delinquency in 1643 (*CCAM*, p. 665). The Committee for Tendering the Covenant resolved (23 March 1644) that since he had 'expressed his good affection by staying in town upon his honour, by taking the Covenant, by paying 2,000*l.* since he was brought up upon his 20th part, and by voluntarily paying all other assessments; and that as he has dealt freely, they should deal freely and nobly with him. As he has suffered much by soldiers, has many children, and was one of the first Lords that took the Covenant, they recommend that he should enjoy three-quarters of his estates, and pay the remainder to Parliament's use during pleasure of both Houses.' The Goldsmiths' Hall Committee confirmed this, noting that 'he had been in actual war against Parliament'. They called him before them four days later, demanding the balance: 'fine set at 1,000*l.*' (*CCC*, p. 832, 26 and 30 July 1644). His accounts record the payment of the £1,000 only, but later references confirm he paid £3,000 in all (see e.g. *CCAM*, pp. 66, 119).   3. Howses ... Confiscat] His estates were confiscated 1642–44. He was able to use Mereworth from August 1644 (W(A) Misc. 7, f. 12r), but did not return to Apethorpe until May 1646, two years after his release: see *In adventum meum ad antiquos Lares Abthorpienses*, p. 78.   hould out] continue, survive.   4. Bankerout] Bankrupt.   5. shuffling's delt] 'Shuffling' implies cheating at cards; cf. *Ham.* 3. 3. 61–2: 'There is no shuffling, there the action lies / In his true nature.'
De Imperatorum Julianorum lineæ ultimo Title] 'On the last of the line of the Julian Emperors, and the first of the Sulpicii'. Latin version has marginal note 'Tacitus histor: lib.', i.e. Tacitus, *Histories*, Book I.   1–7] C. Julius Vindex led a rebellion against Nero in AD 68, joined by Sulpicius Galba, governor of Hispania Tarraconensis, whose claim to be emperor Vindex sup-

ported. Vindex was killed, but Galba was supported by the Praetorians, and Nero committed suicide. A few months later Otho persuaded the Praetorians to kill Galba.   2. not in bed] Cf. Juvenal X, 112–13: 'Few kings descend to Ceres' son-in-law except by sword and slaughter, and few tyrants die a bloodless death.'   5. him . . . Roome] Nero.   8–9] Galba was hated for his meanness, and his part in the massacre of a group of marines.   9–10] 'Caesar' was thought to derive from *caesaries*, hair (Isidore, *Etymologiarum* IX. 3. 12).

The Tragecomedy of Mans Life   Dated 'Apthorpe: 1633' in *F1*, and therefore possibly relating to Fane's sister, Grace, Countess of Home, whose death at Apethorpe in April–May 1633 would have coincided with the pregnancy of his wife with their daughter Isabella (b. November 1633).   9. Left-hand file] 'Then shall he say also unto them on the left hand, Depart from me, ye cursed, into everlasting fire, prepared for the devill and his angels' (Matthew 25. 41).   11. right winge] 'Then shall the King say unto them on his right hand, Come ye blessed of my Father, inherit the kingdome prepared for you from the foundation of the world' (Matthew 25. 34).   12. Bridegroomes] Christ's: Matthew 25. 1–13.   13. Catastrophe] Conclusion of a play.

Vita Humana quid?   Title] 'What is human life?'   1. span] A short space of time, especially of human life; cf. *Tim.* 5. 3. 3: 'Timon is dead, who hath out-stretcht his span.'   4. Enameled May] Cf. Herrick, *A Nuptiall Song*, 112.3, l. 2: 'Injewel'd May'.   10. Lachesis] 'The Allotter', that one of the Fates who allotted man's span, and predestined future events.   19–21] Cf. Donne, *The Canonization*, l. 21: 'We are Tapers too, and at our owne cost die' (p. 95).   25–7] Cf. Herrick, *Divination by a Daffadill*, 38.1, ll. 5–6: 'Secondly, I shall be dead; / Lastly, safely buryed.'

Horace: Ode: 10 : Lib 2   5. The golden mediocrity] *Aurea mediocritas*, the 'golden mean' between the extremes of wealth and poverty.   19. ne] nor.

Horace: Ode: 38: Lib: 1   6–7] Horace does not make this claim for the myrtle (the bilberry), nor do the English herbalists; in Horace it is 'simplex', presumably because of its ubiquity and its low growth. It was sacred to Venus.

Horace: Ode:13 : Lib:3   8. *butted] Equipped with horns.

Horace: Ode:7: Lib:4   15. wrags up] ?'Rolls up, compacts'; this meaning is not in *OED* or Baker, but 'Rags up' in the sense of tearing up (*OED*, s.v. *rag* VI), does not fit with the 'frozen ball' (l. 16).   18. Phœbe] Diana as goddess of the moon.   23. Tellus . . . Ancus] Tullus Hostilius and Ancus Martius, third and fourth kings of Rome.   31. Minoes] Minos, judge in the underworld.   38. Hyppolitus] Killed by his grandfather Poseidon at the behest of his father Theseus, who wrongly believed him responsible for the death of his stepmother, Phaedra, whose advances he had resisted. Diana told Theseus the truth too late.   39. Theseus loose Perithoes] Theseus and Perithous tried to carry off Persephone from the underworld. Theseus was rescued by Heracles, but Perithous was left behind.

Horace: Ode: 9: Lib: 1   Addressed *To My Lord Gerrard my Brother* in *F1*; Dutton, third Baron Gerard of Gerard's Bromley (1613–40), m. Fane's sister Mary (1606–34) in 1632 (see *Epithal[amium] in Nup[ti]as: Sororum*, p. 99, n). Fane became guardian to their son, Charles (see *To my Neph[ew] Gerr[ard*, p. 328).   6. faire Avons] *flumina* (streams) in Horace.   10. blinking] ?sleepy   Ned] Perhaps generic for a drawer, perhaps addressed to Gerard.   Leonard] ?Name of a landlord or brewer, or the beer itself.   12. Diota] Fane thinks this was a Roman wine (a reasonable inference from the Latin): in fact it was a 'two eared' wine jar that held the Sabine wine.

Martial: Lib: 10: Epigram: 47   Cf. Fanshawe, *A Happy Life Out of Martiall* in *Shorter Poems and Translations*, ed. Bawcutt (1964), p. 67.   3. Molde] soil.

Pastor fido   Heading] '*The Faithful Shepherd*'. Tragi-comedy and proto-opera by Guarini, first performed July 1598. Fane made these translations in Paris, 1625 (*F1*).

'*They are true kisses*'   *Pastor Fido* 2. 3. The Italian text is copied opposite the translations: 'Son veri bacci ove mutuo vuglis / Tanto dona altrui puarto si taglie' (for 'son veri baci, ove con giuste voglie / tanto si dona altrui, quanto si toglie').

'*Fayre Mistress, lett's rejoyce and sing*'   *Pastor Fido* 3. 5: 'Godiam sorella mia / Godiam, che'l tempo vola, e posson gli anni / Ben ristorar i danni / Dela passata lor fredda reckhiezza / Ma s'in noi giovinezza / Una volta si perde / Mai piu non si rinverde / Ed a canulo, e livido sembiante / Puo ben tornar amor, ma non amante.' Fane's text does not differ significantly.

Martiall. Lib. Epig. Title] Aparently imitating rather than translating Martial.
Martiall Lib—7. Epigram—38   VII, 39 in modern editions; Fane owned the Plantinus edition of Martial (Antwerp, 1568; sold Sotheby's, 1887, lot 394).   12. fast] Stuck, unable to escape.
Fallere fallentem non est operosa Puellam   Title] Modifying Ovid, *Heroides* II, 63: 'Fallere credentem non est operosa puellam,' 'To cheat a trustful girl is not a work of great difficulty.' *fallentem*] cheating.
In nasutum   Title] 'On Nose'. Latin version has n. 'Martial Lib', but probably to suggest *imitatio*, not a translation.
In eundem Euro sufflante   Title] 'To the same, an East wind blowing'.
Ben Jhonson Drunk   The implication is that the Latin epigram Fane is translating is by Jonson himself: 'Sta pes, sta mi Pes, ne Labere mi pes / Sta pes aut Lapides hic tibi lectus erint.'
Horace Epod. 2   5. *dept] debt.   12. poppler] poplar.   20. kie] Plural form of 'cow'. The translation is unfinished, apparently abandoned and lightly crossed out.
In adventum meum ad antiquos Lares Abthorpienses   Title] 'On my return to the old household deities of Apethorpe'.   *May—20: 1646*] W(A) Misc. 7, records for 18 May 1646: 'Taken with me to Apthorp for my jorney thither [£]30 wherof brought home again 5li' and for June 'My expenses in a 3 weekes jorney to Apthorp & back set down in the former month when begun' (ff. 34r, 35r). On 15 August 1643 a petition 'That he may have leave granted him . . . to go to his House in Noth'tonshire' was refused (*Lords' Journals* VI, p. 181). Fane's estates were freed from sequestration on 13 September 1644, but he remained based in London and at Mereworth until 1646. It may be that troops were garrisoned at Apethorpe, as they were to be at his London house in 1650–51 (W(A) Misc. 15, f. 76v).
Ad Scoto Brittannum   Title] 'To the Scoto-British, to whom our Charles has withdrawn himself, being about to work on a new Enterprise'. The King had given himself up to the Scots at Southwell, near Newark, 5 May 1646, after leaving Oxford disguised as a servant ten days earlier.   2. borrowed] Charles had been born in Scotland.
To Sir Jhon Wentworth upon his Curioseties   Title. Wentworth] Sir John (1574–1651), m. Anne Soame, Herrick's first cousin (1599). He 'inclined to the Parliamentary side' but 'during the Lowestoft rising of 1643 he behaved suspiciously and was arrested' (Fowler, p. 230). See Rosemary Laing, 'The Literary Relations of Mildmay Fane's Sir John Wentworth', *Notes and Queries*, 230 (1985), 167–8, for the suggestion that this poem provided a model for Marvell's *Upon Appleton House*. Fane had visited Wentworth before: see *A Jorney into Norfolk*, p. 116, l. 57.   *Summerly in Lovingland*] Somerlyton Hall, near Lowestoft, on Lothing Land (Lovingland), 'an island formed by Oulton Broad and the river Waveney' (Fowler, p. 230). Fairfax visited in 1648: 'On Tuesday last [12 September] he came to Sir John Wentworth's House in Lovingland, where he had great Entertainment, and the greatest varieties that are to be seen, for Ponds, Water-works, Groves, Conveniences of Coy-Ducks, that are to be seen in the Kingdom of England' (Rushworth, IV. 2, p. 1263).   1–3. *Margin*] Fane's house arrest in London had apparently been lifted, perhaps following the favourable report of the Committee for Tendering the Covenant (23 March 1644); he was also at Wimbledon in April (W(A) Misc. 7, f. 7r), and at Putney in May (f. 8r). See also notes to *Upon a small occation of 10,000£s disbursement*, p. 71, and *In adventum meum ad antiquos Lares Abthorpienses*, p. 78.   4. timbering] 'nesting' (*OED* s.v. *timber* vi.b); cf. *Her Lading*, p. 93.   6. Spiceries] The Phoenix built its nest of aromatic material, which was ignited by the sun.   8. Barbery] North Africa.   15. contracted vertue] The essence 'contracted' from a substance was believed in medieval and Paracelsian theory to have powerful 'virtue'.   26. Candy] Crete, from Lat. *Candia*; cf. Fane's play, *Candy Restored* (1641).   27. Daphne's groves] Daphne was turned into a laurel to save her from Apollo (Ovid, *Met*. I, 490–567).   28. Tempe] A valley in Thessaly, home of Daphne's father, the river Peneus; hence any place of great (pastoral) beauty.   34. Faires] Fairies.   43. Satyrs] Woodland spirits of Greek mythology, here in the mischievous or malignant sense used by Reginald Scot, *Discoverie of Witchcraft* (1584) VII. xv: 'witches, urchens, elves, hags, fairies, satyrs, pans, faunes, sylens' (Arundel, 1964 ed., p. 139).   45. past] paste.   47. *Firr-deal] The fir tree, from which deal (normally meaning a wide plank) is made. Cf. Fuller: 'Somerley Hall . . . well answering the name thereof; for here summer is to be seen in the depth of winter, in the pleasant walks, beset on both sides with fir trees, green all the year long, besides other curiosities' (quoted in Fowler, p. 231).   49–50. Like . . . distance] Cf. Marvell, *Upon Apple-

ton House: 'While, like a *Guard* on either side, / The Trees before their *Lord* divide' (ll. 619–20). 51. Glob's] Globe's; Wentworth had 'a pair, celestial and terrestrial, summing up the disposition of the elements [l. 52]' (Fowler, p. 231). Cf. *A Pepper-corn or small rent*, p. 277, ll. 18–20 and n. 58. Meander-like] The river in Phrygia from which the word derives; such walks were a new feature in English gardens. 63. Natures helper Art] 'a central georgic theme' (Fowler, p. 231). 63–8] There was evidently a sophisticated system of water gardens and 'works', whose control would have been especially important in Summerly's wetland situation. 69–70. bracelet... Carkanet] A bracelet could describe an ornament worn other than on the wrist, here hung from a necklace: see *OED* s.v. *bracelet*, 2. 80. made a Coast] Finished the voyage. 94. Castle] Probably a neo-gothic fantasy castle (Fowler, p. 232). 96. Cod] 'The narrow closed part or bag at the lower end of a trawl-net or other fishing net.' *OED*. 96. Euterpes nett] Euterpe was the muse of the flute, her net presumably the entrapment of music. Fowler notes that 'in mannerist gardens, such tricks as automatic or hidden music were common' (p. 232). 97. Lesbian Lute] Music of Orpheus: his dismembered head was washed ashore on Lesbos, still singing. 99. table] In 'table-music' the parts were set at right angles on the same page, enabling performers to read them seated around a table. 103. Gammuth] Gamut, 'the "Great Scale"... analogous to the series of spatial intervals of the planetary spheres' (Fowler, p. 232). 104. Tickebrack] Tycho Brahé, Danish astronomer (1546–1601). 111. Humanety] Obligingness, courtesy.

De sene Veronense Title] *'Of an old Veronese'*. Margin. Claud—pag—231] A fairly close imitation of Claudian, Alexandrian-born Latin poet, d. *c.* AD 404. His epigram of this title is *Carminum Minorum*, 20 (cf. Fane's *Philomelæ ac Citharædi Concertatio*, p. 339). It was also translated by Cowley (*Works* I, p. 477), Randolph (*Poems*, ed. G. Thorn-Drury, 1929, p. 49) and Vaughan (*Works*, ed. L. C. Martin, Oxford, 1957, p. 655). 12. soldad] Anglicised form of *soldado*, a soldier. 12. Baytes] Contentions. 18. Pole] Sky, heavens. 19. Casts... Consults] The Roman year was denominated by the two consuls elected. 27. Ile] 'proxima... Verona' in Claudian. 30. Standground... meer] Fane owned land in Stanground, Farcet, and Whittlesea Mere, south of Peterborough; 'Benacus' in Claudian.

Epigram: Upon one Beal a minister Title. *Beal*] The most likely candidate is Theodore, Vicar of Ash Bocking, Suffolk, ejected by the Earl of Manchester (perhaps Fane's source) in July 1644. Matthews gives a long account of his selective ministering of the Covenant and unorthodox marriage guidance to parishioners, one of whom he (allegedly) told 'to put away his wife for objecting to come up to rail to be churched, he should keep a maid and give her 5£' (*Walker*, p. 327). 1. Covenant] The Solemn League and Covenant established Presbyterianism in England; it was negotiated with the Scots in 1643 by commissioners led by Fane's friend, Sir William Armine, and his distant cousin, Henry Vane Jr. On 1 February 1644 Parliament offered delinquents a pardon if they took the Covenant and compounded. Fane was one of the first Royalist peers to subscribe, on 14 February: 'And the House appointed the Earls of *Rutland* and *Stamford* to tender the Covenant to him presently; and accordingly they went forth; and the Earl of *Westm'land* took and subscribed the Covenant' (*Lords' Journals* VI, pp. 425, 427). His meditation justifying Covenants, dated 14 February 1644, is in *N*, ff. 32v–31v (manuscript reversed; folios not numbered). Ludlow believed Fane's defection was inspired by the Kent MP Sir Edward Dering's on 2 February and counted it an important moment in the war (*Memoirs of Edmund Ludlow*, ed. C. H. Firth (Oxford, 1894), I, p. 84). For Dering's decision, see Everitt, pp. 205–8.

The Times Steerage Title. *Steerage*] Guidance or government of the State. July 1643] Fane was released from the Tower in March 1643 but was still under strict house arrest in St Bartholomew's Close, the conditions being lightened in August: see *Brook House Bay trees*, p. 70, n. 2–3. Cavallier... Bowle-Noddled-Crue] William Lilly recorded the first use of 'Cavalier' and 'Roundhead' at Christmas, 1641: 'The Courtiers againe, wearing long Haire and locks, and always Sworded, at last were called by these men Cavaliers; and so after this broken language had been used a while, all that adhered unto the Parliament were termed Round-heads; all that tooke part or appeared for his Majestie, Cavaliers, (*Monarchy and No Monarchy*, 1651, p. 107, *OED*). Rushworth is even more precise, saying 'the first miniting (*sic*) of 'Roundhead' was on 27 December 1641 by 'a reformado' named David Hide (III. 1, p. 463). 14. Patist] Intellectual (here ironically), from 'pate', meaning 'brain' (*OED* s.v. *pate*, 1). 15. Statist] Politician, especially a Machiavellian one. 19–22] Cf. Fane's 'Query' in *N*, f. 39v: 'For a King as Gods substitute... [should not] encline to the seducement of His own privat will & affections, which may as he is a man entitle Him to failings, nor yet to Those Dalila respects may deminish together with His own the strength & happiness of His Dominions.' 23–7. Discerting . . . State] Deserting his councils, the two Houses of Parliament and thus making them suspect his intentions. 26. woffe] thread or fabric. 28–31] The traditional Norman French of the 'Bodies' of the lawyers and courts, including Parliament, has been replaced by the Latin of the Roman Catholic Church and the modern French of Henrietta Maria's coterie. Fane describes the King in one of the prose 'Riddles' in *N* as 'reduced to soe uncertain Tearms as not to Judg skearce when & wher to keep the Tearms [of Law and Parliament]: in the Owld Courts or New Colledg Camps to turn the Martiall Law the only extant now into true Lattin & French to geer the other' (f. 37v). 32. Leav them] Charles had left London in January 1642. 32–50] Riddle no. 13 in *N* accuses Charles of giving 'such encouragement to his subjects whom he calld together for his ayd in Counsail towards government, til He refusing their advyce as being raysd to a strayn of too much command by His own gratiousness at the first, They refuse at last all government save that of their own decrees & Counsailes without His ascent' (f. 37v). 34. Petitiond humbly] Perhaps referring ironically to the Grand Remonstrance of November 1641, which demanded major concessions of the royal Prerogative. 37–9. Cesars . . . perpetuall] Caesar was appointed dictator for life in 44 BC. 40–5] Parliament took control of the militia and the right to appoint Lords-lieutenant from the King in March 1642, by the issue of the Militia Ordinance, claiming that the power of the King remained vested in Parliament, whether or not he was himself present. 48. Le Roy Le veu[l]t] The words in which the royal assent is given to an Act of Parliament. 50. Soy't faict comme ils desirent] 'Let it be as they wish,' replacing 'Le Roy Le veult.' 51–4] The publication of speeches and bulletins of the week's debates increased greatly after the abolition of the Star Chamber in 1640. 55–6. Bannish . . . Crosses] Crosses in London and Westminster were demolished by order of a Commons committee, headed by Fane's friend Sir Robert Harley. 58. Henry Elsing] Henry Elsynge Snr, Clerk of the House of Lords, wrote *Modum tenendi Parliamentum apud Anglos*, published under parliamentary authority 1641. His son, Henry Jr, was Clerk of the Commons 1640–48; cf. Cleveland, *To P. Rupert*, ll. 11–12 (*Poems*, p. 33). 60. Brown] John Browne, Clerk of the House of Lords March 1640 until its abolition in 1649. 62. *Kakt] Reformed into a cake (here implying 'baked', not in *OED* thus). 65. Free-States] Of the recently independent Netherlands. 66. Arminious] Jacobus Arminius (Harmensen), Dutch theologian (1560–1609), rejected the Calvinist doctrine of absolute predestination. 71. pan] skull. 2. tinkling] tinkering (*OED* s.v. *tinkle v2*.) 73. under-sett] prop up. 74. *Lay-Prop] ?Give unqualified support in both Church and State. 75. bear up] carry. 78. Tutelar] Tutelary, protective. 83–5] Between June and August 1641 the Long Parliament abolished Ship Money, the prerogative Court of High Commission and the ecclesiastical Court of Arches; Fane welcomed these moves 'to lay asleep all Arbitrary Courts . . . & all such exorbitant prerogatives' (*N*, f. 37r, Riddle 20). He also singles out Ship Money, 'which is above law' in Riddle 16. 88 Paraters] Paritors, summoning officers of ecclesiastical courts. 90. 'thout bones] Without scruples or hesitation (*OED* s.v. *bone n*8). 95–6. article . . . rule] The Thirty-nine Articles of the Church of England, threatened in 1641 by the Root and Branch Petition, which condemned the Book of Common Prayer as 'Romish'. 102. Take . . . fall] Many believed that biblical prophecies of the 'last times' and the fall of the Antichrist were being fulfilled: some sectarians (such as the Adamites) were accused of combining such millenarianism with sexual freedom. 118. Supersedious] *Supersedeas*, a writ commanding the stay of legal proceedings. 119. Table] On which motions, petitions etc. are laid in the House of Commons: the Mace is placed on it when the Speaker is in the chair, removed when the House is in committee (l. 125). 121. Patents] Monopolies or other privileges conferred by royal letters patent, largely abolished by the Long Parliament in 1640–41. 124. Closs] Close committee, one that meets in secret; the accusation is that the affairs of the kingdom are in the hands of Pym and a few others (cf. ll. 155–68), and that the courts of law have been superseded. 132. a T. . . . —] 'A turd that's stirred will stink.' Proverbial; Tilley, T603. 137. Those] The ships, forts and towns of ll. 135–6. 138. Chevalier du guet] 'The Captaine of the watch' (Cotgrave). Hence a severely limited contractual monarch. 146. to—] 'rope'. 152–4. quintessence . . . Authorety] A basic principle of alchemy. 171–8] During the summer of 1642 Parliament raised money to pay its troops by loans and gifts from the City.

190. his Excellencies] The Parliamentary Lord General, at this date the Earl of Essex.   195. Dun i'th'mire] Proverbial for being stuck, 'Dun' being a horse: Tilley, D643. Cf. Chaucer, *Canterbury Tales*, Manciple's Prologue, 4–5, and *Rom*. I. 4. 41.   196. Brick-Hill's] Little Brickhill, on the Watling Street. Clarendon says that in May 1643 Essex left his army 'quartered about St Alban's' (VII. 85), while in July 'his whole army [was quartered] within ten miles of Oxford' (VII. 120). In either case, his main army was forty to fifty miles from Little Brickhill.

Upon the King and Queens happy meeting again   *Title*] Henrietta Maria returned to England in February 1643, having left a year earlier to raise money, arms and troops in Holland. Fane, as a messenger of the House of Lords, had witnessed her departure (see *Vita*, p. 43).

Cloris Complaint—July-25.-1644   *Title. Cloris*] Since 'Chloris' was a pastoral pseudonym for Henrietta Maria, it has been suggested (Loxley, *Royalism and Poetry*, p. 239) that, especially as she had left England again eleven days earlier, she is the speaker. While this may have been a starting point for the poem, the desire for reconciliation in the closing lines is not characteristic of her, and the 'wave' of l. 21 is more likely to be the metaphorical one of Fane's own acceptance of the new *de facto* order: the poem was written the day before the Goldsmiths' Hall Committee recommended Fane's estates be freed from sequestration on payment of the last part of his fine (see *Upon a small occation of 10,000£s disburcement*, p. 71, *Title* n.).   26–30] Cf. Fane's petition of February 1644 to the House of Lords, where he resolves 'for the future to sacrefize Life and Fortunes to the reall service of King and Parlement for which he was borne' (*N*, f. 31r; *CCC*, p. 832).

Over the Chimny in the great Chamber at Merworth   *Title. Merworth*] Mereworth, the Fanes' main house in Kent. *Oxford*] Either written at Oxford or referring to one of the de Vere Earls of Oxford, probably the nineteenth earl (d. 1632), who claimed the title in a celebrated dispute in 1625, and to whom the sentiments of the poem might thus well be applied. The Oxford de Vere connection would also give more point to the Latin title in *OS*, *Virtus vera Nobilitas*. Fane was related to the de Veres through his second wife, Mary Vere.

An Epitaph for Wimarke   *Title. Wimarke*] Edward, of Luffenham, Rutland, a village close to Apethorpe. MP for Chippenham 1597, 1601 (a seat in the gift of Fane's grandfather, Anthony Mildmay). Wymarke 'kept some sort of register of concealed lands, reimbursing himself from the amount recovered by the government' (P. W. Hasler, *The House of Commons, 1558–1603*, 1981, III, pp. 666–7). He was a friend and informant of the letter writer John Chamberlain (see *Letters*, *passim*). He d. 1634, a date which fits the placing of this poem in *F1*. The John Wymarke who matriculated at Emmanuel in 1618, the same year as Fane, and who died 1620, may have been his son.

In Histrionem quendam   *Title*] 'On a Player' (*OS*).   Dated '1626 London' in *F1*, making it almost certain the poem refers to Edward Alleyn, who died 25 November 1626. See *Playhouse Wills 1558–1642*, ed. E. A. J. Honigmann and Susan Brock (Manchester, 1993), pp. 150–4.

In Obitum Ben: Jhons[on]   *Title*] 'Upon Ben. Jhons[on's]s death 1633' (*F1*). Jonson did not die until August 1637, but the newswriter John Pory thought Jonson 'had been dead' in September 1632. This poem is inscribed in Fane's hand on p. 1015 of his copy of the Ben Jonson 1616 Folio (Sotheby's, 1887, lot 658) now in the Beinecke Library, Yale: see *Upon Ben Jonsons Playes*, p. 240, n., and Joseph T. Roy Jr and Robert Evans, 'Fane on Jonson and Shakespeare', *Notes and Queries*, 239 (1994), 156–8.

He is not dead yet: but Dull   *Title. Dull*] Though Jonson had a stroke in the winter of 1628–29 which left him partially paralysed and bedridden, the sense here is of mental deterioration (cf. ll. 6–8).   10. *farcey] farce; this spelling not in *OED*, but cf. *A Farcy*, p. 186.

A Letter sent to E.B. from Apthorpe to Howb[ury]   Dated 'Ap[ethorpe]. 1632' in *F1*. *Title. E.B.*] Edward Beecher of Howbury, Bedfordshire. See *An ode To N.B. an angler*, p. 59, *Title* n. Cf. *A tinder-box for Ned: Beech[er]* (p. 62); *To N.B. at Thorp* (p. 112); and *An Ode to N.B.* (p. 113).   1. Chast Grecian Dame] Penelope.   21. Simoes] Simoeis, a river near Troy: *Iliad* V. 774–7.   23. sweet Thorp] Apethorpe.   25. Gentle Stream] The river Nene (l. 38) rather than its smaller tributary, the Willow Brook, which runs through the village and nearer to the Hall.   26. Phlebotomy] Blood letting.   32] Punning on the old standard measures of perch = $5\frac{1}{2}$ yards, ell = 45 inches. 'Yard' was an alternative name for the pintle fish; 'Pickrell' was a young pike; 'ell' perhaps also puns on 'eel'.   33. Formia's] Fashionable (in classical times) coastal resort south of Rome.

35. prospective] Of the view, prospect.   36. middle Region] One of three into which the air and thus the 'prospective' was divided: cf. Bacon, *Sylva* (1626), p. 81.   37. Scene] Seine.   49–50. Trowling] Trolling, fishing, usually for pike (ll. 57–8)   Kemp] A small eel used as bait.   55. Sewlhey Poole] At Sulehay, on the Nene, due east of Apethorpe Hall. Old Sulehay Forest survives.   71. Perioding] Concluding.

A woollen night cap sent to the same   Dated 'Ap[ethorpe] 1632.' and signed 'Your true frend / W.' in *F1*.   Title. *Les estrennes*] Étrennes, Christmas or New Year present.   2. hand-kacher] Handkerchief, perhaps reflecting Northamptonshire pronunciation: *OED* quotes *Northamptonshire Notes and Queries* I. 77, 'hand-carchaes' from 1583.   3. *wax-book] ?A collection of wax tablets.   4. *Gossopings] Originally a Christening feast, but here the gift of a Saturnalian (i.e. Christmas) present.   7. Quier] Of paper (l. 3).   15. die] dye, colour.   17. Could] Cold.

Upon the Death of My Fidelia a farewell to wine   1. Margin. St Peter] Added in a different ink. The feast of St Peter is 29 June, confirming that this and the following poem refer to the death of Fane's first wife, Grace, who died 29 June 1636 (see *Vita*, p. 40). The subtitle *'a farewell to wine'* is also added in (another) different ink.   3. Margin] The Sun is in Aquarius from 20 January to 18 February.   7. fish ... swimms] Pisces (19 February to 20 March).   14. Doggs] The 'dog days', associated with the constellations Canis Major and Minor, last from 3 July to 11 August.   2. Grace's three] Grace Thornhurst's name evokes similar associations in the *Vita*, p. 40.   25. Thornes ... nails] Of Christ's passion.

In praise of my Fidelia   In *F1* the untitled versions of this and the following poem are surrounded by poems dated 1626, the year of Fane's marriage to Grace Thornhurst. The following ten poems, with the exception of *Upon Fidelia only to be admired not drawn*, which is dated 1632, constitute a series of courtship poems, presumably sent to Grace before the wedding on 6 July. To those that follow here should be added *The Savoy—Excetter house 1626* (p. 60), *She is sick* (p. 60), *Mine eyes Ember weekes fast* (p. 61), *'If one but anoint the sword'* (p. 61), all from *F1*, and *Upon the Lady of my second adventure Verania*, p. 97.   8. Hesperian] Western, here a fleet sailing from the West Indies or America.

Her Lading   2. Alcinous] King of the Phæacians, whose orchard Odysseus admired (*Odyssey* VII, 112–35).   3. timbering] See *To Sir Jhon Wentworth*, p. 79, l. 4 n.

My Fidelia with whom I had been cross the Street at Devotion   Dated 'at London—1626' in *F1*. For the proximity of the two houses, see *The Savoy—Excetter house*, p. 60, *Title* n.   1. B:] For Lord Burgersh ('Burwash'), Fane's courtesy title between 1624 and 1626.   12. Leese] Lose.   19–21] Jove raped Danae in the form of a shower of gold (Ovid, *Met.* IV, 611; VI, 113).

Amor non patitur Moras   Dated 'at London 1626' in *F1*.   Title] 'Love does not suffer delays'. Fane uses the same phrase about this marriage in his *Vita*; see p. 40.

Sonnet Comparing Fid[elia] to the 4: Seasons   Cf. Jonson's 'Have you seen but a bright lily grow', *Underwoods* II, 4, 21–30 (*Poems*, p. 129).   3. Phylomele] The nightingale; see *Upon a fall which Ms. F: C: had*, p. 98, l. 4 n.

Sonnet: She is Fair and Verteous   1. sleaved Silk] Silk thread teased out into smaller, floss-like filaments for embroidery, fishing flies etc. Cf. Donne, *The Bait*, ll. 23–4: 'curious traitors, sleavesilk flies / Bewitch poor fishes' wandring eyes' (p. 117).   10. tiffany] Transparent silk or muslin.   11. Delia] The moon.

Having suffered an absence from my Fidelia   Dated 'London—1626' in *F1*, where it is called *An example by the 4 Elements upon a short absence from ones love*.   7. Joves ... Kingdom] The sky (and the element of Air): Juno was worshipped as the queen of heaven.   9–11] Prometheus stole fire from the sun, hence its desire to be reunited.

Upon Fidelia only to be admired not drawn   Dated 'Apth[orpe]—1632' in *F1*.   2. Apelles] Greek painter, famous for the precision of his drawing.   strait] ?'Precise' (*OED* s.v. strait *a*1.3) rather than 'straight': 'not crooked'.   3. Limmd] Drawn, painted.   5. Fethred Pencill] Quill pen.   6. Thespian spring] Source of tragedy, here the highest kind of literary art.   11. piece of Rubines] Picture by Rubens.   14. As ... 'tis] Labelling the painting to indicate what it represents.

Sonnet   In *F1* dated 1626.   2. Phebe's] The moon's.   3. Brothers Carr] The sun, chariot of Phoebe's brother, Apollo.   7. Bowld Triumpher] The sun.

Fidelias Title to the Empire of the World   Dated 'at Paris 1625' in *F1*.   1. Phebus] The sun.

To the County of Kent   Title. *June-1-1644*] Fane was at 'Quinborow' (Queenborough in Sheppey,

Kent), probably fishing, in June 1644 (W(A) Misc. 7, f. 9r), and was apparently able to use Mereworth from spring 1644: see *To Sir Jhon Wentworth upon his Curioseties*, p. 79, ll. 1–3 *Margin*, n. The poem's emphasis on Kent's freedom from the immediate impact of war reflects the growing disaffection of moderate Parliamentary and Royalist Kentish gentry to the war as then being conducted in the rest of the country: see Everitt, pp. 204–12.   2. Freequarter] The obligation of having to provide free board and lodging for troops.   6. Welldon] Punning on Sir Anthony Weldon, who rented land from Fane (see W(A) Misc. 7, f. 48). A leading Parliamentarian in Kent, where his home at Swanscombe was not far from Mereworth, he had been Clerk of the Kitchen to James I, and published a malicious history, *The Court and Character of King James I* (1650). Cf. *Upon Sir Anthonies incomparable peece*, p. 199.   14. bye] The 'Bye plot' against James in 1603, so called to distinguish it from Raleigh's alleged 'Main' plot.   21. T'unbridg] A Royalist uprising had been suppressed at Tonbridge, 24 July 1643: see *Upon the Suddain rise of my Cuntry Men*, p. 126; Everitt, pp. 190–200.

Upon the Lady of my second adventure Verania   Dated 'at Mereworth—1626' in *F1*, where it is entitled 'An allay in love upon sticking at portian'.   *Title. Verania*] From Vere, the maiden name of Fane's second wife, Mary. The title in *F2* is written in a different ink from the body of the poem, which *F1* shows to have been written twelve years before his marriage to Mary Townshend. The early date and the original title's reference to delay over agreement on the bride's marriage portion indicate the poem was first addressed to Grace Thornhurst and recycled for the second countess.

Upon the fairest Webb that Nature ever Spun   *Title. Webb*] In *F1* she is '*Ms: Webb. jnr*'; the poem is there signed 'W', indicating a date after March 1629. There was a Kentish family of Webbe, seated at Frittenden, and at Fordwich, near Canterbury.   13. Goddes new] ?Britannia, who first appeared on a coin of Antoninus Pius, *c*. AD 160.

Upon a fall which Ms. F: C: had from her horse hunting in my park   Dated '1632 at Apthorp.' in *F1*.   *Title. F.C.*] Not identified.   1. balletts] ballads.   3. Daphne] See *To Sir Jhon Wentworth*, p. 79, l. 27 n.   Acteon] Actaeon was turned into a stag and killed by his own hounds because he had accidentally seen Artemis/Diana naked (Ovid, *Met.* III, 138–252).   4. Prognes] Procne, metamorphosed into a swallow after taking revenge on her husband Tereus (who became a hawk or a hoopoe) for raping her sister Philomela (nightingale) by feeding his son to him both roasted and stewed (Ovid, *Met.* VI, 426–674).   6. cum privilegio] *cum privilegio imprimendi solum*, the formula used to give the sole right of printing certain books.   7. Cynthias Revells] Title of a play by Jonson; here, the hunting revels of the moon goddess (Artemis/Diana/Cynthia).   14–16] Cf. Marvell, *Upon Appleton House*: 'Or turn me but, and you shall see / I was but an inverted Tree' (ll. 567–8); but the topos was a commonplace: see A. B. Chambers, *Studies in the Renaissance* 8 (1961), 291–9.   22. *Enlawnd] Covered by a fine, transparent material, here water: cf. Herrick, 'Halfe with a Lawne of water hid', *Upon Julia's washing her self in the river*, 294.4.   24. Brothers of the horne] Either huntsmen or the deer they hunt; both would be ruined by plunging into the 'Cristall Spring'.   29. sleaved Silk] See *Sonnet: She is Fair and Verteous*, p. 94 l. 1 n.   33. Daughter of Pandion] Philomela, the nightingale.   36. Terean] Of Tereus, punning on 'tree'.

Epithal [amium] in Nup[ti]as: Sororum   *Title*] 'Epithalamium on the marriages of sisters celebrated at one and the same time at Westminster'. For the double wedding of Fane's sisters Mary (1606–34), who married Dutton, third Lord Gerard, and Elizabeth (1608–69), who married Sir John Cope of Hanwell. The date 'London 1631' in *F1* is for 14 February 1632.   1–2. time . . . guive] St Valentine's Day, as l. 16 and the title in *F1* (*Epithal: Valen:*) make clear.   8. Lares] Roman household gods.   11] Echoing Herrick's "Tis she! 'tis she!' (l. 11) and 'See where she comes' (l. 21) from *A Nuptiall Song, or Epithalamie, on Sir Clipseby Crew and his Lady* (112.3). Crew's marriage took place in 1625: for contact between Herrick and Fane in the 1620s, see Cain, 'Robert Herrick'.

The like in Medly for F.F.   *Title. The like*] Another epithalamium.   *F.F.*] Francis Fane (1611–80), brother of Mildmay, MP for Peterborough 1624, KB (with Mildmay) 1626, inherited Fulbeck Hall in 1632, Commissioner of Array, Lincolnshire, 1642, commanded the King's forces at Doncaster and Lincoln (1644). Taken prisoner at fall of Lincoln, compounded 1645. He rebuilt Fulbeck *c*. 1659. After the Restoration he refused to persecute Nonconformists; became FRS 1663, died 1680.   1] 'Sparing not at all, the Fates'.   2. owld Lord Darce] John, Lord Darcy of Aston, d. 1635.   3] 'Cupid, the son of Venus.'   4] Francis ('Frank') married Elizabeth, widow of Lord Darcy, 1636; she brought him estates at Aston, near Sheffield, where they are both buried.   7] 'Both the old man Laertes and the boy Telemachus'; Laertes was father of Ulysses, Telemachus the latter's son.

A Posy upon a weeks absence from her   Title. her] Elizabeth West.   1. dampe] Depression.

Χαλεπα τα καλα εστιυ   Title] *'What is good is difficult'*, quoted by Socrates as 'an ancient saying' in Plato's *Cratylus*, 384. Cf. Herbert, *Providence*, l. 97: 'Hard things are glorious; easie things good cheap' (*Works*, p. 119).   F.F.] Francis Fane.

The North-West Passage   Title] Punning on the name West.   3. Diameter] On the diametrically opposite side of the world   6. Davis] John Davys (?1550–1605), navigator, made three voyages to Greenland and Canada in search of the North West Passage.   11. Buttons Bay] Baffin's Bay.

Upon the names of her various sutors   Title. her] Elizabeth West.   1–9] The other suitors appear to have been called Howard (l. 1), Temple (2), Knowell/Noel (4), Waller (6), and perhaps Fairfax (7) and Leek/Lake (9).   8. hausar] hawser.   12. Vain] Vane was an alternative spelling of Fane.

A Caracter of Newmark[e]t   Dated 1633 in *F1*. It had been established as a fashionable racing venue by James I. Cf. *Upon the horse race at Newmarket* (p. 288).   3. flurting] darting.   6. stoope] Post, possibly here 'finishing post', but in *Upon the horse race at Newmarke*, l. 14, clearly 'starting post'.   7. crack] Usually 'talk', with suggestion of exaggeration, but as in *Upon the horse race at Newmarket*, l. 4, it seems to mean 'tips' or 'money laid'.   9. Dutton] This and following names are probably those of horses rather than jockeys or owners.

Upon Ms. B West Widdow to the Lord Darceay   2. Take West-moreland] Punning on her family name (West) as well as his title.   7. Dare-say . . . F] Punning on Darcy, with B for Beth (Elizabeth) and F for Francis, and U standing for W[est].

A Fishing Sea-Voyage from Lin to Boston   *F1* adds: *To myBro[the]rs the Lords Gerrard and Cope* dating it '1633 at Sea'. For his boat and later voyages, see *After a weekes sea voyage for pleasure*, p. 163; for Gerard and Cope, see *Epithal[amium] in Nup[ti]as: Sororum*, p. 99, Title n.   Title. Lin] King's Lynn. Fane owned land in Norfolk a few miles east of Lynn, at Langham, Stiffkey and Stibbard. This 'sea voyage' took him a few miles across the Wash to Boston, Lincolnshire.   5. Nereus] Sea god.   Phebes] Phœbe's, the moon's.   13. Tritons Cabinett] Triton, son of Poseidon and Amphitrite, lived with them in a golden submarine palace.   16. Mayd] 'A name given to the Skate and Thornback (*Raia batis* and *R. clavata*) when young' (*OED*).   17. *threvy] ?Tending to come in shoals: a threave is a large number, a multitude (*OED* s.v. *thrave, threave* n2).   18. *Butt-fish] ?'Butter fish', the gunnell.   19. Mouse] The sea mouse.   Damsells] 'damsel-fish, a small brightly-coloured fish of the family *Pomacentridæ*' (*OED*).   20. Hedghogg] Hedgehog fish, the sea porcupine.   salf] safe.   36. Shroudes] Rigging.   39. Halcedonian] Calm, tranquil.   41. Beak-head] Prow.   43. glass] Sand-glass, on ships often measuring half or quarter hours.

My adventure, or a new discovery under the Bear   Title. Bear] The constellations of the Great Bear and Little Bear. Here also the Bear at the Bridgefoot, an inn on the south (Bankside, l. 13) end of London Bridge, kept in 1650 by Cornelius Cooke. On 10 October 1648 Fane recorded 'The Book at the Bear crost   £2–13–8' (W(A) Misc. 7, f. 64r), a large bill, more than the annual wages of some of his servants.   Pole Artick] The Arctic was so named from the Bear stars (Greek *artikos*, 'pertaining to the bear'). The Pole Star is part of the Little Bear, almost marking the North Pole. Here, a phallic *double entendre*.   1. Astrolabe] Instrument used to take astronomical measurements.   2. Tickhobrack] Tycho Brahé, Danish astronomer.   5. Cygnas] Cygnus, changed by Apollo into a swan and placed among the stars: Ovid, *Met.* II, 367–80.   11. Argo] Jason's ship in the quest for the Golden Fleece.   13. bank-side] Bankside, the Southwark bank of the Thames, opposite the City, well known for brothels as well as playhouses.   15. Aspects] The relative positions of stars from Earth at any given time.   23. near] ne'er.   Tyndarian race] Stars: Tyndareus was the father of Castor (Zeus was father of his twin, Pollux).

The Peake. ode   Called *My return out of the Peak forrest with incitement thither again* in *F1*.   4. wimbles] Type of auger used in mining.   10. Sharper Hill] ?Sharplow Point ('low': 'law', hill) but possibly not a place name at all.   13. Mun] The Mun family of Bearsted, Kent, were neighbours of the Fanes at Mereworth (Hasted, V, pp. 509, 527); see *To my Frend Mun: gon to London to play at Tennice* (p. 211). 18. Had-on] Haddon Hall, in the Peak District, belonged to Fane's relatives, the Manners family.

My Fox-huntinge Dated 'Apthorp 1632' in *F1*. 1. Cynthias] Artemis/Diana, goddess of hunting. 2. Brothers Laurells] Apollo, whose plant was the bay. 3. Delphos] Delphi, site of Apollo's chief shrine. 4. Candy] Crete. 18. Volpone] A fox. 20. potts] Of ale. 21. cunnies] conies, rabbits. 27. Laxon] Laxton, four or five miles west of Apethorpe. 29. Finsett] Fineshade, forest four miles north-west of Apethorpe. 30. canvassed] attacked. 31. Hogen-Mogen] Strong drink (*OED*, s.v. *Hogen-Mogen* B.3). 39. double] step (in dancing).

Upon his Majesties late jorny into Scottland   *Title*] Charles had gone to Edinburgh for his belated coronation as King of Scotland on 18 June 1633. 23. Elevation] In astronomy 'The altitude or angular height of the pole, or of any heavenly body, above the horizon' (*OED*).

The Basse   *Title*] The Bass Rock, in the Firth of Forth. 1–9] The annual battle between pygmies and cranes is mentioned by Homer (*Iliad* III. 1–6) and elaborated by later writers along the lines Fane describes, but the 'Far North' was never the location. 17. Lowden] Lothian 18. Tantallon] Castle on the Firth of Forth, home of the Earls of Angus. 24] The rock is a nesting site of sea birds. 28. two Cubits] About 3 ft. 32. Sollen-Geese] Solan geese, commonly used of gannets. 40. formerly'] A Jonsonian 'metrical apostrophe', indicating that the three syllables of the second foot are elided into two beats.

A Buck-hunting Jorny to Belvoyr   *Title. Belvoyr*] Belvoir Castle, Lincolnshire, home of the Earl of Rutland, to whom Fane was related. See also *To The countess of Ruttland upon Her New reedefying of Belvoir*, p. 330. 12. Junoes Bird] The peacock. 13–14. Great ... head] The star Aldebaran. 14–15. wheat ... hand] At the centre of the constellation Virgo. 15–37] All references to constellations or individual stars. 38. Argos-eyd-Traind Bird] Hera/Juno put Argos's hundred eyes on the tail of the peacock when he was killed by Mercury. 40. Pisses] Pisces. 44–9] Referring to stars and constellations. 49. Aries browe] The horn of Aries, the Ram. 50. *Huntsaye] Variant of 'hunt's-up', a song played or sung to waken huntsmen. 53. *Casamour] Gossamer. 59. harberd] Harboured, in stag hunting tracing a deer to its covert to start the hunt. 61. exhalation] Both a falling star and an ephemeral vapour.   Corona] The Southern and Northern Crowns, *Corona australis* and *Corona borealis*.

To my very noble Cosen the Earl of Stanford   *Title*] Henry Grey, first Earl of Stamford (1599–1673), Fane's puritan neighbour and 'cousin' through Grey's mother, Elizabeth, daughter of Edward Neville, Lord Abergavenny. He was a notoriously unsuccessful Parliamentary general, defeated by Hopton at the battle of Stratton (1643) despite holding a near-impregnable position and outnumbering Hopton's Royalists by more than two to one. He was said to have led the flight, and was mocked by Cowley in *A Poem on the late Civil War*, ll. 431–2: 'How oft has vanquished Stamford backward fled, / Swift as the parted Souls of those he led!' (*Works* I, p. 478). Cf. Denham, *A Western Wonder* (*Works*, p. 131). He declared for the King in 1659. He was father of the enthusiastic regicide Thomas, Lord Grey of Groby: see *Upon the Lord Gray of Grooby yellow haired*, p. 340.

A Dierge For Hasty Ginny   *Title. Hasty Ginny*] A grey (l. 35) barbary horse (l. 56). 1–2 and *Margin*] Horace, *Odes* I. 28, ll. 15–16: 'sed omnes una manet nox, et calcanda semel via leti.' 2. drest] prepared. 6. violent] intense, hot-spirited. 20. Coursers ... Barbes] All types of fast horses. 23–5] Names of horses. 29–31. Marigould ... Tulip]. Though echoing Milton, *Lycidas*, ll. 142–51, these are probably all horses: 'Marigold' races on Stamford Down in *Sonnet* (p. 269, l. 21), and a horse called 'Primrose' is mentioned in Fane's accounts (W(A) Misc. 4, p. 23; July 1652). 33. Favour] Token for the funeral. 52. minifurr] Miniver, soft white fur. 63–6] The horse is fed to the hounds.

Sonnet upon second amorous thoughts   This and the following poem refer to Fane's second marriage in June 1638 to Mary Vere (1608–69), daughter of Sir Horace Vere, Lord Vere of Tilbury, and widow of Sir Roger Townshend of Raynham, Norfolk (d. January 1637). 36–8] In the Catholic Church a jubilee year (in Fane's time every fifty years) allowed pilgrims to visit Rome to obtain an indulgence.

My tryall and araignment at loves second barr   2–4. book ... clergy] Benefit of clergy: convicted men able to read Latin from a book, usually from Psalm 51 (cf. l. 8), could escape punishment; it saved Jonson's life in 1598. 10. Caldayck] Chaldaic. 11. *scrall] scrawl. 14. Chinian]

Chinese.   15–16. little . . . Crystall] A watch (cf. ll. 31–2).   20. Cabinett] Jewel case.   22. Gyges] King of Lydia, owned a ring that made him invisible.   25. peece . . . limmd] Miniature portraits.   46. doom] Judgement.

To N.B. at Thorp   Title. *N.B.*] Ned Beecher: see n. to *An ode To N. B. an angler*, p. 59.   Thorp] Apethorpe, about fifty miles north of Howberry, Beecher's home.

An Ode to N.B.   29. clew] Ball of thread.   30. middle sister] Lachesis, second of the Fates: see *Vita Humana quid?*, p. 72, l. 10 n.   Bottom] Nucleus on which the ball of thread is wound (*OED*, 15.a).   37. store] abundance.   42. Clusters] Of grapes.   Calibus] Cales, modern Calvi, on borders of Campania in wine-growing area.   51. [*Wittellsy*]] Whittlesey Mere, south of Peterborough, part of Fane's estates. The word is scratched out in *F2*, but nothing is substituted.   54. sallett] salad.   63. Lullworth] Lulworth Castle, Dorset, overlooking Lulworth Cove, belonged to the family of Fane's first wife, coming to him as part of the marriage settlement. It was sold in 1641 (this poem was probably written in the 1630s), but Fane's brother-in-law Thomas Thornhurst owned land in the area, and the two men remained friends after Fane's remarriage: see *To Mr T.T.*, p. 236.   67. Thetis lap] The sea.   80. Wool] Village north of Lulworth.   81. Tom] Thomas Thornhurst.

To David Earle of Exeter   Title] David Cecil, third earl (?1604–43), m. Elizabeth Egerton. When he succeeded his father William 'Ruin-house' in 1640 the estates were 'much impoverished by the portions of the three co-heirs and the dowers of two widowed countesses' (Barron, p. 33). His son John, fourth earl (1628–78) married Fane's daughter Mary in 1670. Cf. *To the Countess of Exeter*, p. 252, and subsequent poems to the family.   1. Burley] Punning on 'burly'; Burghley House, Stamford, home of the Earls of Exeter.

A sonnet upon a pretty Gierl her mothers darling   Title. Easter book] An account book kept by the parson for recording the dues payable to him at Easter.   14. Alpe] bullfinch.

A Jorney into Norfolk   Title] See *A Fishing Sea-Voyage*, p. 103, Title n. for Fane's land in Norfolk.   9. Stand-ground] On the river Nene. See *De sene Veronense*, p. 81, l. 30 n.   12. sluce] Where the Nene flows into the Wash, west of King's Lynn.   21. the Line] King's Lynn.   23. Rising] Castle Rising, east of King's Lynn; cf. *Upon a Rumor of a Generall rising*, p. 328, l. 1.   36. Lady of Wallsingam] The shrine of the Virgin Mary at Walsingham Abbey.   38–9] Using brackets to indicate speech.   42. their widdow] Mary, widow of Sir Roger Townshend of Raynham: see *Sonnet upon second amorous thoughts*, p. 110, Title n.   50. Wells] Wells-next-the Sea, on the Norfolk coast.   58. Loving-land] See *To Sir Jhon Wentworth upon his Curioseties* p. 79, Title n.   59. Stif-ky] Stiffkey, near Wells; the Townshends owned a house there. A phallic pun follows in ll. 60, 76 (natives, sensitive to such nuances, call the village 'Stewkey').   69–70] The marriage took place in Hackney, north-east of London.   85. Rainam] Raynham Hall, south of Stiffkey, main seat of the Townshend family.   86–94] Sir Roger Townshend had a new house built c. 1620, possibly by Inigo Jones.   92. field vert] In heraldry, 'field' is the surface of a shield, here vert (green), on which the 'charge' is displayed.   93. Bemantled] 'Mantling' is the ornament around the achievement.   114. torrid Line] In the tropics, i.e. south of King's Lynn.   139–40] An earl would normally have travelled in style: see Gladys Scot Thomson, *Life in a Noble Household 1641–1700* (1937), pp. 216–17, for the Earl of Bedford's use of 'music morning and dinner' to accompany him when travelling in state. The last entry Fane ever made in his accounts was: 'To wittny for mending the Trumpet   00.3.00' (W(A) Misc 8, f. 70r, 21 January 1666).

An Ode sent into Scotland to a frend   1. Ar-mine] Sir William Armine (1593–1651), of Osgodby, Lincolnshire, MP 1621–51, was in Scotland as a commissioner from the Commons in 1641 and 1643 (see *Epigram: Upon one Beal a minister*, Title n.). A prominent oppositionist throughout (he had been a friend and ally of Sir John Eliot), he refused the forced loan in 1627 and was imprisoned for a year. In 1647 he fled to the army with other political Independents. He declined a summons to the High Court in December 1648, but played a prominent part in the Rump and Council of State from 1649 till his death. The mention of Apethorpe in the last line confirms this poem was written on Armine's first (1641) visit to Scotland, when he was one of a group sent by Parliament to shadow the King.   24. *Pilacy] pilotage.

9.3.18.22.20.17.1.3   1] The numbers add up to 93: a simple seventeenth-century alphabetical code produces 'icsxurac', meaning 'I see Essex you are a C', the C probably meaning 'Cuckold': see *Upon Lamb[er]ts repo[rted] to be Gen[eral] &c: s.x. before*, p. 244, l. 10 n., which also uses this abbreviation. Written just below this, separated by a line, is a still more cryptic riddle, whose abbreviations are as unclear as its meaning: 'Noe T[urd?]. with out a P[iss?]. thats the stile / Mark how't occurrs without a match—/ Noe sent—good nor [?]p^cr that can [?]Car^e / Imp. Powr but αλ and αρ.'

Upon his Majesties return out of Scottland in November 1641 Title] Charles was in Scotland trying to consolidate support there in August to November 1641. Leaving Edinburgh on 18 November, he would have been at Huntingdon on or about 23 November, the day the Commons passed the Grand Remonstrance. 14–16] Charles received a warm welcome on his return to London, and probably also on his journey south. 18. Triumphant ... wayne] By November 1641 the King had recovered some of the popularity lost in earlier months, and moderates like Fane looked forward to a reconciliation with Parliament.

Epigram   Inter Acus et Aculeos pugna Title] 'A fight between pins and stings'.

Upon newes of the first beating up the quarters at Leeds and Wakefield The whole poem is deleted in F2, perhaps because of Fane's changing attitude to his brother-in-law (see p. 23), who took Leeds and Wakefield in January 1643.   *Title. beating ... quarters*] 'to arouse, disturb; colloq. to visit unceremoniously' (*OED*). 2 *Margin. Fax*] Latin, a comet. 3. Clubbs] Fairfax's army was reinforced by local volunteers called 'clubmen' because of the weapons they used. 4. *Holy* warr] The strong religious motivation of the local volunteers was well exploited by Fairfax. 5. Cloathing] Both towns produced woollen cloth.

An Oad sent into Scottland to a Frend by sea Title. *Frend*] Sir William Armine; see *An Ode sent into Scotland to a frend*, p. 119, l. 1 n.; cf. 'My Will' (l. 5) 'Covenant' (l. 33) and peace mission (l. 35). 6. Elsinges ... Ordinance] See note to *The Times Steerage* p. 82, ll. 58, 60. 7. Love] Either Christopher Love, a leading Presbyterian, later (1651) executed for conspiracy, or Nicholas, also a puritan minister, an MP in the Long Parliament and a regicide. 14–16] Fane was imprisoned in the Tower from October 1642 to March 1643, and was then under parole in London until his sequestered estates were restored in 1644: see *Upon a small occation of 10,000£s disburcement*, p. 71. 33–5] The Covenant had been agreed in August (see note to *Upon one Beal a minister*, p. 82), but Armine was evidently one of those who stayed on to negotiate for a Scottish army to advance into the north of England, which did not take place until January 1644.

By-Ward to some Cittisens entring the Tower Title. *By-Ward*] A gate tower on the outer wall, one of the main entrances. For Fane's imprisonment, see *Vita*, p. 43, and *An Ode sent into Scotland to a frend*, p. 119, ll. 14–16 n. 7. change] Either Gresham's Royal Exchange in Threadneedle Street (1571) or Cecil's 'New Exchange' (1608–09) in the Strand. See *To a Frend upon my Pallace and habitation*, p. 325, l. 4 n. 8. Lyons] Henry Parrott's *Sine Flamma combustus* similarly combines 'The *Tower*, the *Lyons*, and the new *Exchange*' among London's leading attractions in his *The Mastive, or Young-Whelpe of the Olde-Dogge* (1615), n.p. There is no record of a menagerie at the New Exchange, but lions were certainly kept across the road at the later (1676) Exeter Change, where the menagerie remained until 1830. 13–14] The Bishop of Ely was one of Fane's fellow prisoners. 35–8] Elizabeth, sent to the Tower by Mary. 39. *Sawm-bookes] Psalm books. 62. Bears] Also part of the Tower menagerie. 81–3] These included the Bishop of Ely, Lord Montague of Boughton and the Earl of Bath, the latter Fane's brother-in-law, still waiting for his wife's dowry to be paid following his marriage in 1638 (see *Upon a small occation of 10,000£s disburcement*, p. 71, *Title* n.). 83. *Kiernes] ?'Kerns', Irish soldiers. 100–2] Henry Percy, ninth Earl of Northumberland, was imprisoned from 1605 to 1621 on suspicion of complicity in the Gunpowder Plot. 100. Crittick] Combining the senses 'precise' and 'skilful, learned'. 114] The London Militia, for Parliament, and the Royalist troops raised by the Commissions of Array of 1642. 130. Malignancies] Active Royalists were described as 'malignants' by Parliament. 145. Candid] White. 179–80] The Royal Mint was in the Tower. 185. Fair Daphnes doom] See *To Sir Jhon Wentworth*, p. 79, l. 27. 191. Clippers] Of coins (legally) at the Mint. 200] Fane has noted the line number here, the only occasion he does so in any of his extant manuscripts. 208. —] Sack.

Upon the Suddain rise of my Cuntry Men Title. Manneringe ... woodmong[e]r] Randall Mainwaring, 1588–1652, mercer and colonel in the London Militia, and Sir Richard Browne, d. 1669, Parliamentary general and 'woodmonger' of London; they led troops which put down a Royalist rising at Tonbridge, where Fane owned land (Everitt, pp. 190–200). Later Browne became a

Royalist and was one of the City deputation sent to invite Charles II to return.   3. Long-tayles] Kentish men, said to have tails; cf. Oldham, *Satyrs upon the Jesuits IV*, ll. 175–8: 'Becket's Bones, and Hair, For murd'ring whom, some Tails are said to wear; As learned Capgrave does record their fate, And faithful British Histories relate.'   6. The Proverb] No proverb connecting (or opposing) Kent and Derbyshire 'Famous both at one end' survives.   sets out] proclaims.   10. Orpheus] Because he could command 'woods and hedges' to move with his music.   12. Mannering] A seventeenth-century form of 'manuring', as well as a training in manners.   13. Plott] The rising was connected with 'Waller's Plot' of May 1643.   15. Browne was derisively known to Royalists as the 'Faggot-monger' (whoremonger; the word did not have its modern American meaning) as well as the 'Woodmonger', the latter being his own description of his peacetime occupation.   17. *Margin.* 35.H.8.17] 'An Acte for the preservacion of Woodes', concerned with restricting the felling of young growth: *Statutes of the Realm* (1817), III, pp. 977–80.

Anglia Hortus   Title. *'The Garden of England'.*   1–5] Leishman, pp. 283–4, notes these lines are echoed by Marvell, *Appleton House*: 'Oh Thou, that dear and happy Isle / The Garden of the World ere while, / Thou *Paradise* of four Seas, / Which *Heaven* planted us to please' (ll. 321–4).   5. Philomell] The nightingale. See *Upon a fall which Ms. F: C: had*, p. 98, l. 5 n.

Epigram   Probably dating from May 1642, when by the Militia Ordinance Parliament took control of the armed forces of the kingdom (see ll. 3–6; cf. *The Times Steerage*, l. 40 n.).   8. New-Castle's] The Earl of Newcastle, who became Royalist Commander-in-Chief in the North in 1642.

The Scottish Pedlers turnd Merchants   In December 1646 Parliament agreed to pay off the Scottish army in Newcastle, to whom the King had surrendered in May. In a move seen by all Royalists as obviously related to the receipt of the money, the Scots then handed Charles over to the parliamentary commissioners at the end of January 1647.   6. *Margin.* Ent: Eng. 2ce] The Scots entered England in 1640, and again in 1644.   in-and-In... Master] Games: in-and-in was played with dice; others not identified.   17. *Margin. 30d*] Judas's thirty pieces of silver (Matthew 26. 15).   18. *Margin. 200,000£*] The sum paid by the English Parliament towards Scottish soldiers' back pay.

My Far-well to the Court   Title. March... 1644] Lady Day, the old New Year's Day, and just over a month after Fane had subscribed to the Covenant. The language is similar to that of his petition to be allowed to take the Covenant, and to that in his *Vita* (p. 44). See Cain, 'A sad Intestine warr', pp. 39–40.   Merworth] The order of August 1643 limiting Fane to exercise within five miles of his London house had been relaxed by spring 1644: see *To Sir Jhon Wentworth upon his Curioseties*, p. 79, ll. 1–3 n.   10. native] Innate; Fane uses the Latin *nativa* to make the distinction between public duty and intuitive promptings of conscience in discussing the same issue in his *Vita*, p. 44.   24. near] ne'er.   29. Those... done] Fane was not a particularly assiduous courtier in the years before the war.   33. Jocky] Usually applied to country people: cf. 'The country Jocks and Jennies at the fair' (*OED* s.v. *Jock*, 'Mod.').   35–7] Court musicians: Gotier (Jacques Gualtier, d. before 1660) was a French lutenist (cf. Herrick, 39.3, *A Lyrick to Mirth*, and 276.4, *To M. Henry Lawes*); William Lawes, composer brother of Henry, was killed at the siege of Chester, September 1645 (cf. Herrick, 288.3, *Upon M. William Lawes, the rare Musitian*); Nicholas Lanier (1588–1666) was Master of the King's Music 1625, and introduced the new *stylo recitativo* to England; he was also a painter, acting for the King in buying much of his collection.   37. Dying Swan] Proverbial, Tilley, S1028; cf. Cicero, *Tusc. Disp.* I. 30. 73, and Browne, *Pseudodoxia Epidemica* III, 27: 'they sing most sweetly before their death' (*Works* II, p. 254).   40. Tarantula] Cf. John Rowland, *Moufet's Theater of Insects* (1658), p. 1061: 'All those that are stung with the Tarantula, dance so well, as if they were taught to dance, and sing as well as if they were musically bred' (*OED*).   42. verge of Court] The area around the court: in particular, the precincts of Whitehall.

Upon the Babes of Grace   Title. Babes... Saints] 'Born again' puritans, newly convinced that they are among the elect, or 'Saints' as the Independents in particular called themselves (cf. I Peter 2. 2 'Like newborn babes, long for the pure spiritual milk' and Acts 9. 32, 'he came down also to the saints that lived at Lydda'). Cf. Jonson, *An Epigram on the Court Pucell*, l. 44 (*Poems*, p. 195).   1. Room] Rome.   4. wear... nose] Jokes about Cromwell's nose were common: Henry Tubbe wrote a whole poem of 220 lines on it: see *On the Dominical Nose of O.C.* in *Oxford His-*

torical and Literary Studies V, ed. G. C. Moore Smith (Oxford, 1915), p. 89. Needham's newspaper *Mercurius Pragmaticus* was similarly inventive on the 'Almighty Nose'.   6. Rubrick ... letter] Both marked Saints' ('red letter') days in the Christian calendar.   18. Compassing this Crown] Cromwell had discussed kingship with Whitlocke in 1652, and was in a quasi-regal position after the expulsion of the Rump Parliament in April 1653, but Royalists had accused him of seeking the crown from 1649. This poem must belong to a later date than most in *F2*, a dating supported by the fact that it is copied in different ink in a space at the foot of the page, and by the presence of a copy in *H*, most of which was transcribed 1651–55.

Cedant ... Canamus   Title] *'Mortal affairs give way to the divine, and we sing far greater things'.*
In unitate Trinitas   Title] *'On the unity of the Trinity'.*
Cæli enarrant Gloriam Dei   Title] *'The heavens declare the Glory of God'* (Psalms 19. 1).   2. *Margin*. the Syrian] Reflecting the current belief that the Syriac versions of the Gospels were in the form of Aramaic in which Jesus spoke.   Bartheme] Bartimeus (Mark 10. 46–52).   49–50. dash ... Commet] ?A comet bringing rain: cf. 'þe wete sterre arture' (*OED* s.v. *wet a*2.c).   47. Bonargeses] 'Sons of thunder', the name given by Jesus to James and John (Mark 3. 17).   53. Iris] The rainbow.

The Fallacy of the outward Man   3. Pismire] Ant.   9–12] Friedman, p. 146, notes Marvell's possible indebtedness in *The Mower to the Glow-worms*: 'Ye glow-worms, whose officious flame / To wandering mowers shows the way, / That in the night have lost their aim, / And after foolish fires do stray (ll. 9–12).   39. illutians] illusion's.   54. Sithinges ... Siths] Variant forms of 'sighing' and 'sigh', the latter recorded by Baker as Northamptonshire dialect.

Contemplatio Diurna   Title] *'A Daily Contemplation'*.   19. *et quid lachrimabilius?*] 'and what more worthy of tears?', perhaps recalling Salvianus, *De Gubernatione Dei* 6: 'quid lacrimabilius hac stultitia'.

Ut sit et cogitationibus Verbisque   Title] *'That the Almighty may be gracious to thoughts, words and deeds.'*   7–10. Sonn ... ston] According to Luke 2. 41–9, Jesus began his teaching aged twelve in Solomon's Temple.   12. mecannike] base, vulgar.   21. Chanoin] The spelling (from French *chanoine*) suggests Fane is thinking of the canons of a cathedral chapter, who sang anthems (l. 23).   28. tract] Path, but also in heraldry a line (*OED* s.v. *tract n*3.III).   30. Dormant] In heraldry, represented lying or sleeping.   watchfull] Translating the heraldic *regardant*, looking backward.

Annus annulus ex Diminutione Largimur   Title] *'The Year a Serpent We invest from its decrease.'* (Cf. ll. 3–4).   18. Cuttcheneal] Cochineal, scarlet dye.   20. Spikenard] Aromatic ointment used by Mary Magdalen to anoint Jesus's feet (John 12. 3). It was not used for curing wounds.   35–6] Isaiah 63. 6: 'I have trodden the wine-press alone,' prefiguring the Crucifixion.   44. *embling] Embleming, representing in emblematic form.

Cui in calamitatibus solo sit fidendum   Title] *'Who in extremities may alone be relied on'.*   5. tackle] rigging.   6] Translating Juvenal X, 1–2, 'a Gadibus usque / Auroram et Gangem'.   13. *Margin*] Horace, *Odes* I. 3, ll. 9–12.   14. Bottom] Hull.   15. brickle] brittle.   19. o'resett] overcome.   26–7. *Margin*] ll. 21–40 are largely a paraphrase of this psalm.

A Dedication to my Sonn Charles to Him that made him   Title. Charles] Fane's eldest son, b. 6 January 1635, became third Earl 1666, d. 1691. Charles I was his godfather: see p. 14.   5–8] See I Samuel 1. 24 for Hannah's dedication of Samuel.   9–10] Referring to the proposed sacrifice of Isaac (Genesis 22. 1–14).   18. succeeding Happines] Reflecting the importance of a male heir to succeed to land and title.   22. Incence-bearing-Sheba-Soyle] 'To what purpose cometh there to me incense from Sheba?' (Jeremiah 6. 20).   24. strutted] distended. (*OS* version of this poem provides the sole example in *OED*.)   30–1. Childe / The] An 'and' is elided between the lines: the wood on which Isaac ('Saras Childe') was to be sacrificed *and* the Temple where Samuel ('Sonn Of Elkna') was dedicated would both accuse him.

A Christmass Karroll sung—an—1634   3. Foxes Cubb] Jesus calls Herod 'that fox' in Luke 13. 32.   5. victorious Eagles] Of the Roman empire: Luke 2. 1 refers to the decree of Augustus 'that all the world should be enrolled'.   7. yeand] born.   9. Bread of Life] John 6. 35, not given in Fane's marginal references.   15–17] The pagan oracles were said to have fallen silent for ever at Christ's birth: cf. Prudentius, *Apotheosis*, 435–3; Milton, *On the Morning of Christ's Nativity*, ll. 173–80, *Paradise Regained* I, 455–9; Micah 5. 12.   17 Fin] Fiend (Apollo).   20–1] The statues of

Jupiter Capitolinus and of Romulus and Remus were said to have collapsed at the moment of Christ's birth. The myth may derive from wishful misreading of Prudentius, *Apotheosis*, 444–6: 'The very Capitol at Rome laments that Christ is the God who sheds light for her emperors and her temples have fallen in ruins at her leaders' command.' In fact the first temple of Jupiter was burnt down in 83 BC, a second one in AD 69.   21 *Margin*. Dion.] Dionysius of Halicarnassus, Greek rhetor and historian; the reference is to his *Roman Antiquities* IV. 62, which mentions the 83 BC burning of the temple.   Suidas] Tenth-century Byzantine ecclesiastic, compiled a Greek *Lexicon* which contained earlier literary and biographical material from classical times on.   Nicepharas] Callistus Nicephorus, c. 1256–c. 1335, whose Greek Church history from the birth of Christ was translated into Latin by Jean Lange (Basle, 1553).   22–6] Suetonius describes Augustus's building of a new temple (in fact he restored the old one) and prophetic dreams concerning him and the temple (*Divus Augustus*, 29, 94). This combined with the prophetic lines in Virgil, *Eclogue* IV, read as messianic by Augustine and Constantine, to enable later compilers to Christianise Augustus's restoration programme. Jacobus de Voragine popularised the story of Augustus asking 'the gods to make known to him who would reign after him; and he heard a voice saying: "A heavenly Child, the Son of the living God, born of a spotless Virgin!"' Whereupon he erected an altar beneath which he placed the inscription: 'This is the altar of the Son of the living God' (*Golden Legend*, trans. Granger Ryan and Helmut Ripperger, New York, 1969, p. 49).   34–5. *Margin*] Referring to pagan beliefs in general: 'If we have forgotten the name of our God, or stretched out our hands to a strange god; Shall not God search this out?' (Psalms 44. 20).   37. cross-rowe] alphabet.   40. Holy Temple] 'Know ye not that ye are the temple of God, and that the Spirit of God dwelleth in you?' I Corinthians 3. 16.   62. *Margin*] In fact Psalms 14. 7, 'Oh that the salvation of Israel were come out of Zion!'

El Sembrador Title] OS provides Fane's translation: '*or, the Sower*'.   1. *Margin*] Matthew 13 contains the parable[s] of the sower, on which the whole poem is based.   20. Cockle . . . darnell] Both weeds found in corn: the 'tares' of Matthew 13. 25–6.   31. tell'st] recites by heart.   33. Point by th'tag] Punning on 'points and tags', short cords with metal ends used instead of buttons to fasten, e.g. doublet to hose.   36. Niobe] She was turned to stone by Zeus.

Trium Gratiarum maxima charitas Title] '*Of the three graces, the greatest is charity*', paraphrasing I Corinthians 13. 13: 'And now abideth faith, hope, charity, these three; but the greatest of these is charity.'   2–3. sound . . . Brass] Cf. I Corinthians 13. 1, 'Though I speak with the tongues of men and of angels, and have not charity, I am become as sounding brass.'   6. through a glass] I Corinthians 13. 12: 'For now we see through a glass, darkly; but then face to face.'   Churle] Miser.   24. double] bent over.

Love begetts Fear 5. *Margin*]. Psalms 128. 1: 'Blessed is every one that feareth the Lord; that walketh in his ways'.   11. scoal] scale.

My Penthouse against the storm of greif OS adds: '*occasioned upon the Death of a dear Friend*', almost certainly Fane's first wife, Grace Thornhurst, d. 29 June 1636 (see *Vita* p. 40). Penthouse] shelter.

My hand-kerchef to dry my eyes OS adds '*after the loss of a most dear Friend*', again referring to his wife.   16. sells] Cells, the small dwellings rented from the 'land-lord' of l. 12.   22. Jewlipe] Julep, cooling sweet drink, sometimes (as here) medicinal against fevers.   24–5. Grave . . . bed] Derived from Isaiah 57. 2, 'He shall enter into peace: they shall rest in their beds, each one walking in his uprightness'; used similarly for his wife by Henry King, *Exequy* (c. 1624), 'Sleep on, my love, in thy cold bed, / Never to be disquieted' (*Poems*, p. 70, ll. 81–2).

My Carroll sung upon Christmas Day-1637 16. refound] By the 'Shepard' of l. 18.   20. white . . . ston] See p. 162, *Upon The great Mercy of God in the Deliverance from the Gunpowder Trason*, l. 20 n.

Easter Dayes Resurrexit 1. Cliff] clef.   32. Scoales] Scales.

My Charroll—1640 Gossoping] Christening celebration.   15. tost] agitated.

Upon St Stephens day—the same year Title. St Stephens day] 26 December, not known as 'Boxing Day' until the 1830s. Stephen, the first martyr, was stoned to death in AD 33 (Acts 7. 59). St Stephen's Day was retained in the Anglican calendar after the Reformation.   1–2] Deucalion and his wife Pyrrha were the only mortals saved by Zeus in the Greek version of the Flood myth.

When their ark landed, they were told to repeople the earth by covering their heads and throwing stones behind them (Ovid, *Met.* I, 318–415). Fane is suggesting that those who stoned the first martyr were unwittingly causing a new race of Christians to arise.

This is a true sayng and by all means worthy to be received 11. footstool ... throne] Isaiah 66. 1, 'Thus saith the Lord, The heaven is my throne, and the earth is my footstool'. Cf. Donne, *Good Friday 1613, Riding Westward*, l. 20, 'It made his footstool crack, and the sun wink' (p. 241). 13–14. *Margin*] 'for I am not come to call the righteous, but sinners to repentance' (both Gospels substantially the same). 17. Apostle] Paul, the author of the epistle. 21. Lest ... mercies] Genesis 32. 10, 'I am not worthy of the least of all the mercies ... which thou hast shewed unto thy servant'. George Herbert's motto, according to Nicholas Ferrar. 26. consolat] consoled.

My reveille-Matin—to my wife Fane joined the King at Newcastle for the first 'Bishops' War'; this poem, presumably sent to his wife, implies that she did not accompany him, as she did to York when war was again imminent in 1640 and 1642. See p. 23. *Title. reveille-Matin*] Alarm clock: cf. 'the Alarum of one minutes Chime', *An Oad sent into Scottland to a Frend by sea*, l. 11. 40. Kidds and fatlinges] Cf. Psalms 66. 15: 'I will offer unto thee burnt sacrifices of fatlings, with the incense of rams; I will offer bullocks with goats.'

My Carroll sunge upon Christmas day—1639 46. Syrenius ... Syria] Luke 2. 4: 'And this taxing was first made when Cyrenius was governor of Syria.' 10. *Margin*] Luke 2. 6: 'And so it was, that, while they were there, the days were accomplished that she should be delivered.' "Of] Gnomic marking: not used thus elsewhere in Fane's manuscripts, nor in *OS*. 15–16. well ... shuffle] The sense here is either '[it] well may be' the other visitors 'shuffle' them out into the stable, or that they 'well may shuffle' them out; *OED* gives no example of 'maybe' in this latter sense. 23. tricked] marked. 29. Sconces] Small forts.

A morning Fancy upon the Berth of my Sonn Mildmay Title. Mildmay] Fane's second son, d. 1655: see *Vita*, p. 41. *smallpox*] Fane missed the opening of the Long Parliament, 3 November 1640: see *Vita*, p. 53, n. 43. A relatively mild attack of smallpox kept Evelyn in his room for five weeks: *Diary* II, pp. 521–2. Pissmires] Ants. 7. distincticall] capable of distinguishing (*OED*, s.v. *distinctiall*, the only example being from the version of this poem in *OS*).

Psal. 124 turnd into meeter 16. *endorce] endorsement. superscription] address, heading.

My Figg Tree Title] See note to l. 23, *Margin*. Called '*Sham'd by the Creature*' in *OS*. 15. pregnancy] fecundity. 17. press] In sense of wine press, cider press etc. 24. *Margin*] 'Then said he unto the dresser of his vineyard, Behold, these three years I come seeking fruit on this fig tree, and find none: cut it down; why cumbereth it the ground?'

My Looking-Glass 8. Diameter] Opposition. 9. ugly*] 'horrid' was the reading preferred in *OS*. 18. Pardon's seald] Perhaps recalling Donne, *Holy Sonnet* 4 (VII, 1635), l. 14: 'As if thou hadst sealed my pardon, with thy blood' (p. 175).

My Charroll Sung—1641 9. Be] Bee, a common early spelling. 15. Pellican] Fabled to feed their young with their own blood (cf. *Ham.* 4. 5. 146–7). 16. Cordiall Mirrabolan] Emblic myrobalan, *Emblica officinalis*, an expensive 'cordial', whose flowers were used as a laxative, the leaves and bark against dysentery.

The attributes of true love 11. *Margin*] I. Corinthians 13. 5: '[Charity] Doth not behave itself unseemly, seeketh not her own, is not easily provoked, thinketh no evil.' 13–4. Cf. I Corinthians 13. 6: 'Rejoiceth not in iniquity, but rejoiceth in the truth.'

My Reformation 65. fescue] 'A small stick, pin, etc., used for pointing out the letters to children learning to read' (*OED*).

My Invocation 1. Great, and Good God] Cf. Jonson, *To Heaven*, l. 1: 'Good, and great God', *Poems*, p. 119. 6. Turf] Here as a fuel, but with the secondary suggestion of the turf on the grave. 14. Marigould] The flower opens when the sun shines on it; cf. Herrick, 164.2, *To Daisies, not to shut so soon*, ll. 5–6: 'No Marigolds yet closed are; / No shadowes great appeare.' 20. Clott] Clod (of turf).

My Closs Committee Title] Committee of Parliament meeting in private, often in the City of London. Used in the Long Parliament; cf. Alexander Brome, *A new Diurnal ... 1 June 1643*: 'This business was handled by the Close-Committee, / That privately met at a place in the City', in *Songs and other poems* (1661), p. 129; Denham, *A Speech Against Peace at the Close Committee*:

'So many nights spent in the City / In that invisible Committee; / The Wheel that governs all' in *Works*, p. 124. See *The Times Steerage*, p. 82, l. 124.   30. malignants] Used in such committees to describe Royalists.

In Natalem—1643   Title] 'On the Nativity'.   *1643*] At this date Fane was under house arrest in London, and about to take the Covenant: see *Epigram: Upon one Beal a minister*, p. 82, l. 1 n.   4. predominise] Predominate, in the transitive sense 'dominate over'. The only quotation in *OED* is from the version of this poem in *OS*, but cf. *Upon Owld Char[les] Cotton*, p. 337, l. 18.   21–2. Those . . . Superiours] In this context, the King.

They that sow in Tears shall reap in joy   Title. Margin] The verse from John echoes the Psalm: 'Verily, verily, I say unto you, That ye shall weep and lament, but the world shall rejoice: and ye shall be sorrowful, but your sorrow shall be turned into joy.'   17. Coulter] The straight cutting blade of the plough.   Shers] Shares, the curved blades which turn over the soil cut by the coulter.

In Natalem—1649   Title. Timothy] 1 Timothy 3. 16: 'Great is the mystery of godliness: God was manifest in the flesh.'   *Margin. Postnata*] 'Born after', i.e. written later than the poem above it on the page (*They that sow in Tears*).   10. *swaded] Apparently meaning 'wrapped' or similar, and therefore a form of 'swadled' (swaddled); see *A Carroll—in 47*, p. 180, l. 7.   19–24] Parliament had decreed, in 1645 and 1647 respectively, that religious and secular celebrations of Christmas should be abolished.

Ascensus Gratiarum descensus Gratiarum   Title] 'The ascent of grace, the descent of grace'.   Margin] Mr Call[am]y] Edmund Calamy the elder (1600–66), moderate Presbyterian divine and Cambridge contemporary of Fane's. A leading member of the Westminster Assembly, his 'lectures' at St Mary Aldermanbury (very near Fane's London house), where he was 'perpetual curate', drew large audiences throughout the 1640s. Fane's copy of his *Elegant and Learned Discourse of the Light of Nature* (1652) 'ex dono Guliel: Dillingham' of Emmanuel College is at Fulbeck Hall. up[pper . . . 1644] On this occasion Calamy was apparently preaching at one of the four churches in Upper Thames Street, although Fane records that on 9 April he gave 'At Al.[derman] Ber.[y] to a Collec   1.2.0.' (W(A) Misc. 7, f. 7r).   5–7] Judges sat on the woolsack in the House of Lords to give advice, but did not vote.   26. Pignions] Pinions, wings.

Cordis renovatio   Title] 'The renewal of the heart'.   *Cor . . . Deus*] Psalms 51. 10: 'Create in me a clean heart, O God; and renew a right spirit within me.'   *Margin. Postnata*] See *In Natalem—1649*.   1–2] Translated in ll. 3–4.

Upon Easter day—1644: at Stifky   Title. Easter . . . 1644] Accounts for April mention 'my journey', presumably from London to Norfolk (W(A) Misc. 7, f. 8r).   Stifky] See *A Jorney into Norfolk*, p. 116, l. 58 n.   5. might] Probably meaning 'virtue, strength', but possibly 'mite', though *OED* does not give this as a variant spelling.   7–8. stild A Lier] Because derived from Greek διάβολος, slanderer, and because he is introduced in Genesis 3. 1 as 'subtle'.   9–10. beguild . . . Parents] 'And the woman said, The serpent beguiled me, and I did eat' (Genesis 3. 13).   14. three-fould cord] Of thought, word and deed (ll. 11–12), and 'Hel, the Grave, and Death'.   18] 'And I will put enmity between thee and the woman, and between thy seed and her seed; it shall bruise thy head, and thou shalt bruise his heel' (Genesis 3. 15).   34. guather] conclude.

An Ode to Mr Waple a great Faulkner   Title. Waple] ?John Walpole (pronounced 'Wapple') of Spalding, Lincolnshire, who was assessed at £200 in May 1649, and compounded in July that year (*CCAM*, p. 1073), or (more likely, given the location 'at Rainam') one of the Walpole family of Houghton, Norfolk.   Prince Rupert] Of the Rhine (1619–82), created Earl of Holderness and Duke of Cumberland by his uncle, Charles I, January 1644. Cavalry commander, and commander-in-chief of Royalist forces from November 1644 to October 1645. He relieved York on 30 June 1644 but was subsequently defeated at Marston Moor 'neer York', the battle referred to here, on 2 July.   thankes guiving day] On 8 July the Commons resolved 'That Thursday come Sevennight shall be set apart and appointed for a Day of publick Thanksgiving to be rendered unto God for his great Blessing in giving the great and full Victory over Prince Rupert's Army in Yorkshire' (*Commons' Journals* III, p. 554).   *Margin*. Rainam] See *A Jorney into Norfolk*, p. 116, l. 84 n.   July-18] Fane left for London the following day (W(A) Misc. 7, f. 10r).   3. Plash] A marshy pool.   8. pounce] talons.   pole] ?polecat.

In Diem Natalem etiam et Jejunalem   Title] 'On Christmas Day being also a Fast Day'.

In Sanctam Cœnam Domini   Title] 'On the Holy Supper of the Lord'.   Margin] References are to

II Kings 5. 10, 'Go and wash in Jordan seven times . . . and thou shalt be clean'; John 9. 7, 'Wash in the pool of Siloam'; Matthew 26. 26–8, 'Take, eat; this is my body. And he took the cup, and gave thanks, and gave it to them, saying, Drink ye all of it. For this is my blood of the new testament, which is shed for many for the remission of sins.' (Mark 14. 22–3, Luke 22. 19–20 both describe the same episode.) John 5. 14, 'Afterwards Jesus findeth him [the 'heald Cripple'] in the temple, and said unto him, Behold, thou art made whole: sin no more lest a worse thing come unto thee.'

Qui te fecit sine te non te salvabit sine te Title] *'He who made you without you will not save you without you'*, a slight misquotation (?from memory or mediated by Presbyterian authors) of Augustine, *Sermones de Scripturis* CLXIX, chapter 11: 'Qui ergo fecit te sine te, non te justificat sine te' (Migne, *Patrologia Latina* XXXVIII, col. 923).

An Ode—upon the times Title. *Februar . . . 1644*] On 20 February 1645 (1644 O.S.) the Uxbridge peace negotiations between Royalist and Parliamentarian commissioners, begun in January, were deadlocked. 3–6] It was widely thought that each side was determined to continue the war.

The True Bread of Life Title. *Jhon—6-48*] 'I am that bread of life.' 1. *Margin*. Levit: 26-26] 'And when I have broken the staff of your bread, ten women shall break your bread in one oven . . . and ye shall eat, and not be satisfied.' (Cf. Psalms 105. 16, Ezekiel 4. 16). 3. *Margin*. Gen: -5 -25] (in fact 5. 25–7) describes Methuselah's life and death. 4. Syriac] Translation of the Bible into Syriac began in the second century AD, but there was a common belief that the language reflected the Aramaic which Jesus (and the writers of the Old Testament) spoke. 21–2] The manna in the wilderness, Genesis 16. 4–18. 24. Like the manna, the bread provided by Elisha miraculously fed as many as needed it.

For Mr Conyers Darcy Title] Conyers Darcy, later second Earl of Holdernesse, married Katherine, Fane's youngest sister, at Mereworth, 14 May 1645, two months after this poem was written. She died 1649, at which point £4,000 of her £5,000 portion was still unpaid (W(A) Misc. 15, f. 77v). It was presumably of this portion that Darcy's father wrote to Symonds D'Ewes: 'I am sory my Lord of W. needs spurringe to that which becomes a man of honour and conscience to doe freely, especially when that on our parts is so freely performed. My daughter[-in-law]'s journey to this end was designde more then a yeare since, and diverted (as rather obstructive) by her brother Sir. F[rancis] who stayd her at his house in the way, since which time my Lord spoke with my daughter, and hath receaved very moovinge letters from her; so that I doe not see what can be done more, if his own noblenes and worthe cary him nott on: and beleeve it, Sir, the very delay (as our condition is at present) will be as much loss as the sum comes to.' (D'Ewes, II, pp. 315–16, 17 April 1649.) Fane at this period faced the prospect of paying eight marriage portions of £5,000 each; he estimated his total debts in 1649–50 at £23,361 and annual income at just over £7,000 (W(A) Misc. 15, f. 76v), though the parliamentary commissioners had assessed it at £6,000. W(A) 2.IX.1B. is the quit claim of Darcy 'of Swillington co. Yorke esqr.' for the balance of his portion of £2,250. For the Earl of Bath's similar problems 'in right of his wife' and those of the 'several daughters of Crisp' see *Upon a small occation of 10,000£s disburcement*, p. 71, l. 1 n.

A reveille-Matin Ode Title. *C.E.H.*] ?Colonel Edward Harley (1624–1700), who became a colonel of foot in the Parliamentary army aged eighteen or nineteen, and a general of horse 1646. A strong Presbyterian, he was hostile to Fairfax and Cromwell and, like his father, Sir Robert, was secluded from the Commons in Pride's Purge (1648). He joined his father and brothers in declaring for the King, December 1648, was imprisoned, and continued to be excluded through the 1650s, but became a member of the Council of State in 1659. He met Charles II at Dover and was made governor of Dunkirk in 1660. 18. Charrettier] Charioteer, from the French *charrettier*. Here Helios, the sun god, who drove across the sky each day. 25. Spelly] Full of spells: the version of this poem in *OS* provides the only example in *OED*. 33. Valeing] Veiling, obscuring. 36. *Bravado*] To show bravado; not recorded as a verb before 1800. 43. suns . . . sett] Quoting Catullus V, l. 4, 'soles occidere et redire possunt'.

In Quadragessimam—1645 Title] 'On Lent'. 3–4] Lent, especially Ash Wednesday, was seen as superstitious by Presbyterians and like other fasts and festivals was abolished by ordinance in 1645. 12. *Gesseron*] Jeshurun (for 'Israel'), which 'waxed fat, and kicked: thou art waxen fat, thou art grown thick, thou art covered with fatness: then he forsook God which made him, and lightly esteemed the Rock of his salvation' (Deuteronomy 32. 15).   14. Baltashasser] Belshazzar: see Daniel 5. 1–9.   29. Cornerd] In the sense of secret, hidden.

Use and Memory Parents to Wisedome   2. wont] accustomed to.   3. Cride downe] See *A Carroll—in 47*, p. 180, ll. 22–8 n.   5. *owne] Acknowledge as superior (*OED* s.v. *own v*6c: first example 1695).

Upon a very wett St Stephens day   *Title*] See *Upon St Stephens day*, p. 144.

To Easter Day—1646   1–3. *Margin*] All refer to descriptions of the empty tomb and the resurrection of Jesus: the reference to Luke should be to 24.   6.   2. The sonn . . . Sphers] The sun. 11–12. *Margin*] 'As long as I am in the world, I am the light of the world' (John 9. 5); 'I am come a light into the world, that whosoever believeth on me should not abide in darkness' (John 12. 46).   23. *Margin*] Matthew 25. 1–13, the parable of the wise and foolish virgins.   28. *Margin*] 'Let your light so shine before men, that they may see your good works, and glorify your father which is in heaven.'

Upon The great Mercy of God   1–2] The title in *OS* explains that Kent is '*a stony Countrey*'.   2. Skoar] Mark.   4] Kent was 'unconquered' by the Normans, William having agreed 'To ratifie the lawes of Kent such as they were, and be' (Warner, *Albion's England*, 1602, 5. 23, l. 91). 'Kent and Christendom' were often conjoined, e.g. by James Howell, *Poems On several Choice and Various Subjects* (1633), p. 22, partly because of Kent's early conversion, partly because of alliteration.   5. Die-mans] Diamonds, the first of the stones with which he might 'score' the escape from the Gunpowder Plot, but also punning (awkwardly, since this is not a seventeenth-century spelling of 'diamond') on the fact that dead men are now common.   5–7. Rubies . . . Heraldry] Because blood-red, and because associated with Mars (cf. Randle Holme, *The Academy of Armory*, 1688, III, p. 1).   12. Albion . . . name] From Latin *albus*, 'white', for the cliffs.   13. Canded] From Latin *candidus*, also meaning 'white'.   15. Rubricks] Derived from Latin *ruber*, 'red', and used to mark holy ('red letter') days in the Church calendar: here the red must not be allowed to obscure the white marking 5 November   16. Bookers] A writer of books: the latest quotation in *OED* is dated 1205, making it all the more likely that a reference to the astrologer John Booker is involved (see *Upon the Death of the Lord Hastings*, p. 203, l. 5 n.).   18] 5 November became a holiday by Act of Parliament in January 1606. A service for the day was in the Anglican liturgy, abolished (along with the holiday) in 1645 by the Presbyterian *Westminster Directory*.   20. whitest ston] Romans used a white stone to mark propitious days in the calendar; cf. Herrick, *His age*, 132.3, ll. 39–40: 'mark each one / Day with the white and Luckie stone'.   22. *Vaporing] Usually meaning 'boastful' (*OED* s.v. *vapouring*), but here combining the old medical sense of vapour as a harmful exhalation (*OED* s.v. *vapour* 3a) and the smoke associated with the (here) hellish element of fire.   23. Conceptions] Apprehensions.   26. abortive Cocketrise] The cockatrice, identified with the basilisk, was supposedly hatched from cocks' eggs by a venemous reptile: see *OED* s.v. *cockatrice*.   31–2] The day was celebrated as now with bonfires and fireworks (notably in Lincoln's Inn Fields), as Pepys noted in 1660 (I, p. 283).

Upon Mans Frailty   3–4. *Margin*] 'Today I saw'; 'Yesterday I saw'.

After a weekes sea voyage for pleasure   *Title*] Fane's accounts contain two entries in May and July 1645 for fishing voyages 'to Margate' (W(A) Misc. 7, ff. 22r, 24r). He owned his own boat: 'By sea in my vessel to London & back fishing &c' (March 1649, f. 69r).   10. gravelld] perplexed. Philosopher] Aristotle, who was supposed to have thrown himself into the sea because he could not understand the working of the tides (cf. *On the Philosopher*, p. 176, *Title* n).   27. Cynthian Queen] The moon.   39. mackerell gale] 'a strong breeze such as mackerel are best caught in' (*OED*).   43. veere] pay out.   45. warp or winding] Both forms of cable.

My Poole of Bethesda   *Title*] John 5. 2–4 describes in Jerusalem 'a pool, which is called in the Hebrew tongue Bethesda, having five porches', in which 'at a certain season' the blind, halt and withered could be healed.

The 5. Porches to Bethesda   4. Angells motion] The pool was curative only when 'an angel went down at a certain season into the pool, and troubled the water' (John 5. 4).   6. Improve] Avail oneself of.   9–10] The cripple had waited by the pool for thirty-eight years, unable to take his chance of getting in the pool when the angel came: Jesus told him to 'Rise, take up thy bed, and walk. And immediately the man was made whole' (John 5. 8–9).

A Morning Thought 1. *Margin*] 'Man goeth forth unto his work, and to his labour, until the evening.'

Man Levens the Batch   *Title. Margin*. Mr Calla[my]] See *Ascensus Gratiarum descensus Gratiarum*, p. 154.   1. Chor-11–28] 'But let a man examine himself'.

Catena Causarum   *Title*] *'The chain of opportunites leading to salvation'*. The text is surrounded by a drawing of a chain, with short Latin reminders of six 'opportunities' leading to salvation ('Passio Christi', 'Fides' etc.) inside each of the links.

Ode Occationed upon my sonn Veres sicknes   *Title. Vere*] b. 13 February 1645, d. 1693, became fourth Earl on the death of his half-brother, Charles, 1691.   1–3. *Margin*] Vere stayed at Apethorpe: 'To Docr. Colledon [a fashionable London physician of French origin] came down from London to Vere   5.0.0' (W(A) Misc. 7, f. 51r, August 1647).   24. Skoales] Scales (cf. 'Scoales', *Easter Dayes Resurrexit*, p. 141, l. 32).

Occationd upon the Communion when it was a snowe   9. skoar] In the sense of 'credit given', 'debt owed'.   17. Man mett Theevs] In the parable of the good Samaritan, Luke 10. 30–7.   34. Centurian] See Matthew 8. 5–13.   26. Bound . . . Grave-Cloaths] Lazarus was resurrected 'bound hand and foot with graveclothes' (John, 11. 26).   37. Prophetts sute] David's prayer that God would 'Purge me with hyssop, and I shall be clean; wash me and I shall be whiter than snow' (Psalms 51. 7).   42. Balme from Gilead] Genesis 37. 25, Jeremiah 8. 22.

De Maria Magdalena   *Title*] *'A Poem of Casimir on Mary Magdalen'*.   *Casimiri*] Matthias-Casimir Sarbievus (Sarbiewski), 1595–1640, Polish Jesuit, published *Lyricum Libri Tres* (1625) and *Lyricorum Libri IV* (1632). A selection with parallel translations (not including this poem) was published by George Hils, *The Odes of Casimire* (1646). For his influence in England, see Røstvig, *passim*; on Fane, pp. 220–3.

Upon Dives and Lazarus   *Title*] The poem is based on Luke 16. 19–31.   10. Niggerd] Niggard, 'given grudgingly'.   11. skoar] reckoning, debt owed.   15. Could] Cold.   20. in Diameter] in direct opposition.

Upon Moses put yong to sea   2–4. *Margin*] In fact based on Exodus 1. 15–2. 3.   8. Exodus 14. 21–2.

Ad Quendam tam Potentia quam Intelligentia   *Title*] *'To one endowed with as much power as wit, and with riches of doctrine equally with his nobility and honours'*. Latin text has marginal notes: 'Cor: Wil^{sr}, [?Cornet Wilsford] 'ap: Mayd[stone]: Apr:-23-1646. / Parts / Power / Riches / Honor / The espetiall guifts of God & to be employed by such as enjoy all or either of them to the honor & praise of His great name alone.' The Wilsfords of Ileden, Kent, were a wealthy family, involved in the Kent risings of 1648 and 1655: see Everitt, pp. 64–6, 303–4.

Upon the Berth of my Sonn Henry   *Title*] See *Vita*, p. 44.   1. *Margin*] The parable of the Pharisee and the publican, Luke 18. 10–14.   12–16] Zaccheus the publican 'climbed up into a sycamore tree' to see Christ, who said he would go as a guest to his house (Luke 19. 1–10).   13. Dwarf in grace] Zaccheus was 'little of stature' (Luke 19. 3).

Cordium Concordia vera   *Title*] *'The true harmony of hearts'*. Poem is untitled in *F2*: title from *OS*. In *F2* headed by pen-and-ink drawing of three hearts overlapping with flames rising from their centre (cf. *OS*, p. 145).

To Mall   *Title*] Fane's familiar name for the second Countess: see e.g. W(A) Misc. 7, ff. 8v–9r (June 1644); his daughter Mary (b. 1639) and neice and ward Mary Gerard are, however, also 'Mall' occasionally (*ibid.*, November 1645, f. 28r, W(A) Misc. 8, ff. 11v–12v, December 1660).

Emblem Two Turtles billing   *Title. Emblem*] It was never drawn.   *Divide et Impera*] *'Divide and Rule'*.   6. Volontary] Voluntarily.   fleck] fly.

Amoris Sigillum   *Title*] *'The sign of love'*; the Latin version is headed by an emblem in the shape of a shield with a heart surrounded by the letters 'CON DIA' (cf. *OS*, p. 148).

A quid retribuam   *Title*] *'Ah! How shall I repay?'*

My Cuntry Audit   *Title. April. 25. 1647*] Written in Wiltshire, where Fane had land at Laycock: on 22 April he noted, 'Taken with me into Wiltshire   50.0.0' (W(A) Misc. 7, f. 46r). See p. 4.   5. wavd] omitted.

Psal—1. Buchan[ani] Paraphra[sis]   *Title*] *Paraphrasis Psalmorum*, Latin verse paraphrases of the Psalms by the Scottish humanist George Buchanan. Fane seems to have used his *Paraphrasis*

Psalmorum, Jephtes et Baptistes (Amsterdam, 1618; Sotheby's, 1887, lot 61), previously owned by Rowland Woodward, and now at Fulbeck Hall. The copy is not annotated, but the page containing Psalm 137 (see below) has the corner folded down. Fane also owned *Psalmi duplici poetica metaphrasi T. Bezœ et G. Buchanani. Accedit Buchanani Jephthes Morgiis*, 1581 (*ibid.*, lot 732), and Buchanan's *Opera Poetica* (Heidelberg, 1609; *ibid.*, lot 56). While his translations are of Buchanan's versions, rather than the biblical ones, he makes no attempt to imitate Buchanan's variety of meter.   18. *Careers] 'carries rapidly'; not in *OED* in this transitive sense.

Unus quisque sanctus Altare Domini   Title] 'Each single saint by the altar of the Lord; which is Faith'. 4] Exodus 17. 6. 'Behold, I will stand before thee there upon the rock in Horeb; and thou shalt smite the rock, and there shall come water out of it, that the people may drink. And Moses did so in the sight of the elders of Israel.' Cf. also Psalms 114. 7–8.   6.1–2] Psalms 51. 17: 'a broken and a contrite heart, O God, thou wilt not despise'.

Psal 114   13. Thetis] A marine divinity, hence 'thou sea' of Psalms 114. 5. Not used by Buchanan.

Psal—134   3. shends] shields.

Psal 137   11. Solimis] Cf. Buchanan, 'Ecce ferox domine Solymæ'. The name is not biblical.   28. Edoms] Edomites, descended from Esau: Genesis 25. 30.

Psal—120   18–9. *Margin*. Deodates] Giovanni Diodati (1576–1649), Calvinist theologian, uncle of Milton's friend Charles, published (1607) *Annotationes in Biblia*. In March 1645 Fane paid £1 4s. 'For a Bible in Italian by Deodati with noats' (W(A) Misc. 7, f. 5v). This was the 1643 English edition of *Pious Annotations Upon the Holy Bible* (Sotheby's, 1887, lot 234), not 'a Bible' but notes on it. The relevant passage reads: '*Mesech* is *Moscovie*, and *Kedar* is *Arabia*; not that *David* ever was in those countryes; but he called those nations so amongst which he was, by reason of their fierce barbarousnesse' (p. 153). Fane probably came across Diodati in Geneva in 1623; his stepson Sir Roger Townshend died at Diodati's house there in 1648 (see *To H.T. into Norfolk*, p. 208, Title n.).

Poemata Quædam Postnata   Heading] 'Certain Poems written later'.

To a Glass of wine   Title. *Ego . . . me*] 'I won't capture you, unless you capture me.'

On the Philosopher   Title. *Philosopher*] Aristotle: for this common apocryphal version of his death, see Lancelot Manning's commendatory poem to Thomas Heyrick's *Submarine Voyage* in Heyrick's *Miscellany Poems* (1691), pp. xix–xx: 'Take Me (He cry'd) and with an Eager Leap / Plunges into the Swelling Deep.'   *Quia Ego non Capio Te, Tu capies me*] 'Since I cannot capture you, you may capture me.'

Senec[a] Agamem[non]   Title] A translation of the first chorus, ll. 57–107. Fane owned the 1624 edition by Thomas Farnaby (Sotheby's, 1887, lot 779).   26. shends] shields.

Senec[a]: Hippolitus   Title] ll. 1123–55.   5. *Mistreses] Gives, bestows, translating *præbet*.   16–17. Phrygian . . . Cybele] Pessinus, in Phrygia, was the chief sanctuary of Cybele, the mother goddess.

Janus   Title] The Roman god who presided over the beginning of the year. Beneath the title in F2 is a pen-and-ink drawing of Janus Bifrons.   2. Janiver] January.   7. Ten Commandements] Appropriate because December is derived from *decem*, ten.   10–11] Eagles were thought to renew their youth by breaking off and regrowing their bills, as the snake its skin; cf. the Sternhold and Hopkins version of Psalm 103. 5: 'Like as the Eagle castes her bill, Wherby her age renueth'. Cf. *In novi anni—1644*, p. 196, ll. 1–4.

A Carroll—in 47   Title. 47] Probably written at about the same time as Fane received Herrick's *A Christmas Carroll to the Earle of WestmoreLand* and wrote *His answære to the Caroll* (p. 202 and Cain, *Christmas Carol*). Metre and verse form are strongly reminiscent of Herrick.   7. Unswaded] Unswaddled (cf. *In Natalem—1649*, p. 153, l. 10 n.).   17. ston] 'stoun', be stupefied, astonished.   22–8] Agreement over the celebration of Christmas was signally absent in 1647, when a parliamentary ordinance of June had outlawed secular celebrations, the *Westminster Directory* having abolished the religious festival in 1645.   36–7. Plum-broth . . . Pies] Perhaps prompted by Herrick's list in *A Christmas Carroll*.   41–2] Christmas festivities were recognised (especially by puritans, who disapproved) as derived from the Roman Saturnalia. See e.g. Joshua Stopford, *Pagano-Papismus* (1675), pp. 233–7.   55. Jury] Jewry.   60–3] Turning the accusation of preferring 'Heathen' darkness against those Presbyterians who were hostile to the celebration of Christmas.   67. Prophet] David: cf. Psalms 33. 2–3: 'Praise the Lord with harp: sing unto him with the psaltery and an instrument of ten strings. Sing unto him a new song; play skilfully with a loud noise.'   95. things smile] 'things that smile', i.e. look favourable.   98. bear] Carry a burden, but with secondary sense of 'bear witness'.

A Carroll in 1648   1. skoar] record.   2–5] The gates of the Janus Geminus were locked when Rome was at peace, and open when at war, forming what Livy, from whom Fane derives these lines, calls an 'indicem pacis bellique' (I, 19. 2). They were thus locked throughout Numa's reign, after the first Punic War (when Titus Manlius was consul), and after the battle of Actium, when Augustus was emperor (Livy, *ibid.*, 3–4; Varro, *Lingua Latina* V, 165).   6–7. *Margin*] 'Christ was born in the reign of Augustus': cf. Luke 2. 1–7.   *Prince of Peace*] Isaiah 9. 6: 'For unto us a child is born, unto us a son is given: and the government shall be upon his shoulder: and his name shall be called Wonderful, Counseller, The mighty God, The everlasting Father, The Prince of Peace.'

Wisedom is Justefied of her Children   Title. *Margin*] 'The Son of man came eating and drinking, and they say, Behold a man gluttonous, and a winebibber, a friend of publicans and sinners. But wisdom is justified of her children.'   *Epiphany*] 12 January, the feast commemorating the star which guided the Magi (cf. ll. 1–3).   4. Twylight ... fayth] Because not lit by revelation (as available to the Jews).   9. Scepter Juda] Cf. Genesis 49. 10: 'The sceptre shall not depart from Judah, nor a lawgiver from between his feet, until Shiloh come.' See also *The Scepter Shall not depart from Juda*, p. 299.   10. stiff-neckt] Acts 7. 51: 'Ye stiffnecked and uncircumcised in heart and ears.'   12. Gentil] Punning on 'gentle', of which this is an old form.

A good morrow fancy   Title. E.H] ?Edward Harley: see *A reveille-Matin Ode*, p. 159, *Title* n. He was visiting the Fanes in September 1651 (see *Upon the horse race at Newmarket*, p. 288, l. 73 n.). Fane records contacts with him at various other times in the 1650s, e.g. 'To Ned Harley's foot boy 5-0-0' (August 1653, W(A) Misc. 4, f. 48r).   5] Cf. Psalms 33. 2: 'Praise the Lord with harp: sing unto him with the psaltery and an instrument of ten strings.'

Mundus Vanitas   Title] '*The World is Vanity*'.   2. Huisherer] Usherer.   14–16] See *Upon Dives and Lazarus*, p. 168 *Title* n.   22] See *They that sow in Tears shall reap in joy*, p. 153 *Title* n.   24. Piles ... sells] Large and cheerful houses, small and mournful ones.

Homo Vanitas   Title] '*Man is Vanity: Christ, the fountain of living waters*'. Cf. Jeremiah 17. 13: 'they have forsaken the Lord, the fountain of living waters'.   13. *Margin*] Psalms 42. 1: 'As the hart panteth after the water brooks, so panteth my soul after thee, O God.'   16. *Margin*] Psalms 87. 7: 'all my springs are in thee'.

Upon occa[sion] of Mr Sharpes text in Great St Bartholmes   Title. Mr. Sharpes] Probably Geoffrey Sharpe, lecturer at St Andrew Undershaft and St Martin-in-the-Fields until ejected 1643; then at Barking, Essex (ejected 1647). Rector of Colmworth, Bedfordshire, 1651, d. 1675 (Matthews, *Walker*, p. 57). The Rector of St Bartholomew the Great 1644–*c*. 1655 was John Garrett.   *Margin*] Isaiah 55. 1: 'Ho, every one that thirsteth, come ye to the waters, and he that hath no money; come ye, buy and eat; yea, come, buy wine and milk without money, and without price.'   1. Crier] Auctioneer.   13. Truck] Barter, exchange.   chaffer] Cotgrave, 'Barguigner, to chaffer; to bargaine.'   24. trod ... press] From a neighbouring chapter of Isaiah (63. 3); cf. *Annus annulus ex Diminutione Largimur*, p. 133, ll. 35–6.

Upon occation of a Sermon   Title. 2d of Peter ... 10] 'Wherefore the rather, brethren, give diligence to make your calling and election sure: for if ye do these things, ye shall never fall.'   11. side-wall-Plate] Timber placed on top of wall to support roof timbers.   Cuppelings] Timbers connecting rafters.   13. riggs] Ridges or rows.   14. priggs] Nails for tiles.   23. Ground-sel] Foundation, especially of timber-frame building.

I must heere tell Sr. Robert Nanton   This doggerel verse is added, apparently as an afterthought, at the head of a short prose account of Sir Walter Mildmay, unsigned but probably also by Fane ('much more might be said of him by me were I not too neere him').   1. Nanton] Sir Robert Naunton (1563–1635) became secretary of state through Buckingham's patronage: he wrote *Fragmenta Regalia* (*c*. 1630), an account of the Elizabethan court and of the Queen's favourites, which omitted Sir Walter Mildmay.

A Farcy   Title. *Farcy*] Cf. *He is nor dead yet: but Dull*, p. 88, l. 10. From 'farce', but this spelling not in *OED*, which does not record use for literary forms other than drama, or figurative use (still referring to drama) before 1696.   wrot ... Subjects] Charles was a prisoner of the Scots in Newcastle, May 1646 to February 1647, then of Parliament and the army, effectively until his execution in January 1649. 2. Picked] Pointed. 5. broad a God] ?Beard of God. coth] quoth. 6. near born King] Charles was born in Dunfermline. pure] poor. 7. bonnets blew] Scots soldiers wore blue caps; cf. l. 19 and *1H4* 2. 4. 357. 8. Tase] ?False or 'teize', headstrong, aggressive. 9. whinyard] Short sword favoured by the Scots. 9. Switch] Whip. 11. Cotts Pluttre nayles] ?God's blood or nails. 15. Hook and Tacker] Hook and Tackle. 16. none] known. 19. Diel a my sall] Devil have my soul. 21. Lounds] Lands. 22. bunns] bounds. 24. denoyr] denier. 25. skean] Irish dagger. 28. louce] louse. 34. Sloap-drink] ?Slop drink. The Danes had a reputation for drunkenness: cf. *Ham*. 1. 4. 8–22. Cosens] Christian IV (d. 1648) was Charles's uncle (cf. l. 38). 'Cousin' was often used for such relationships. 35. Hulst] ?For Holstein, then part of Denmark, rather than Hulst, a small Flemish town west of Antwerp. 39. Butter Box] Dutchman. free state] Applied commonly to the Dutch Republic. 45. Catt so] Italian *cazzo*, penis, current slang in seventeenth-century England; cf. *Upon suspition of the Gout*, p. 292, l. 6 n. Pantalone] A Venetian. 49–50. Cankero Capita] Minsheu gives 'Cancaro' as Italian for 'Canker' (cancer); here ?the Duke of Savoy and Piedmont, a Catholic neighbour of Geneva (ll. 53–4). 52. Aymèe] Ay me! 57. a Youth...Man] Edward VI, Elizabeth and James I, the three Protestant rulers of England. 63. Haunce Touns] Towns of the Hanseatic League. 67. Waller...Poynes] Presbyterian Parliamentarian commanders of the London Militia in its opposition to the largely Independent army in 1646. 68–70] Fairfax's army entered London without resistance on 6 August; Waller, Massey and Poyntz fled abroad. 71. Election] The seven Germanic princes entitled to elect the Holy Roman Emperor. 76. Monsieur] The King of France (l. 86). in Querpo] Undressed: *OED* quotes Fletcher *Love's Cure*, 2. 1: 'Boy: my Cloake and Rapier; it fits not a Gentleman of my ranck to walk the streets in Querpo.' 78. Black boy] Charles I. 86. Rea] Ile de Ré, attacked unsuccessfully by an English expeditionary force under Buckingham in 1627. 87. Por...Santos] 'By all the saints!' 92] Spain still claimed hegemony over the Americas, as well as controlling large areas of mainland Europe. 94. Naples and Portugall] Both had rebelled against Spanish dominion in the 1640s. 98. my three] The triple crown of the papacy. 103] Eldst Sonn] Philip IV of Spain. Calabria] South-West Italy, from where Spain had been dislodged by Masaniello's rebellion of 1647. 104. Courser] ?'Coursey', courtesy, obeisance. 107. Grand Signior] Sultan of Turkey. 109. shash] sash. 110. Perce] Persia.

To My Cosen Mistress F.F. *Title. F.F*] Not identified, probably a 'Frances Fane'. 13. *Margin. Quæ...&c*] Latin proverb, 'Quæ supra nos, nihil ad nos', 'What is above us is nothing to us'; quoted by Fane in a letter to the Earl of Cardigan: 'let it fall wher it will all Circumstances must be left to those governe in the spheres for Quae supra nos nihil ad nos' (8 April [1661], Brudenell I. x. 17). 19–20. Chuse...shere] Elect myself knight of the shire in my own private House of Commons. 22. Burgesses] MPs representing towns. 23. Lent-all...Q] William Lenthall was Speaker of the Commons in the Long Parliament. Hence, when he had mustered all his friends. 26. noe or I] The form in which dissent or assent ('Aye') in a vote is expressed in the Commons. 28. Rodds] Presumably here for fishing, not punishment. 30. *Margin.* Fortior ...se] A version of the Latin proverb 'Bis vincit qui se vincit in victoria' (Publilius Syrus, *Mimi Sententiæ*, 64). 44. perdue] As sentinel in a dangerous position; cf. *Upon Dabbling or Fishing*, p. 260, l. 40. 45–57. Gallant...Famous] Names of hounds. 58. Hits...fault] Rediscovers the scent. nayle o'th'head] 'Hits the nail on the head' in the sense of picking up the scent. 60. vent] Search for the scent. 63. radiant Sack] Cf. Herrick, *His fare-well to Sack*, 45, l. 13: 'More radiant then the Summers Sun-beams'. 67. Mazareen] Cardinal Mazarin (1602–61), effective ruler of France through most of the 1640s and 1650s.

Ebsom Well to Cuer sicknes *Title. July...1645*] Between 17 and 24 July, Fane records: 'To Ebbsom—at Puttney & Tunbridge 4.10.0' (W(A). Misc. 7, f. 24r). 2. Invest] Install. 4. to—] scour. 9. Diapazon] Harmony. 10. Dung—] ?Dung barge (cf. *Ms Urselye—alius Arslys Triumphs*, p. 192, l. 48). mountup—] mountup scut, tail. 16. you—] you scummer. 36. be—] behind. 38. 9—] 9 ?pages. 40. *Haytegoe] 'Hey-to-go' a hunting call to hounds to encourage them to move faster; cf. *OED*, 'Hey go-bet', s.v. *hey* n3a. 54. Twattles] Farts; *OED* quotes Fane's acquaintance Cotton, *Scarronides* (1650) I. 15: 'The Winds burst out with such a rattle, As he had broke the strings that twattle.' 56. from—] from tail. 57. Caz'emat] Casemate, an embrasure built in the ramparts of a castle, esp. for cannon. 58. *port Esk—] port Eskelon:

the anus, presumably from 'ex' or 'exit' and 'colon' (cf. *Ms Urselye—alius Arslys Triumphs*, p. 192, l. 20), but not in *OED* or Partridge. 60. Common s—] Common slutch: mire, dirt. 62. A—] Ajax (a jakes: a lavatory). 66. T. and P—] Turd and Piss. 72. be—] ?bemaze.
Epigram 2. Lucinas] Diana, the moon.
Upon a Coyne Stamp't at Newarke This poem is one of two in *F2* written in a secretary hand that is probably, but not certainly, Fane's own: since the other poem, *A letter to C. B. from Epsam Wells* (see Appendix 1) is not by him, it is possible that this poem is not his either, but it is included here because all other circumstances point to his authorship: it is apparently unique to *F2*, it is stylistically consonant, and Fane is consistent in indicating others' authorship in all his manuscripts. *Title*] Because of its strategic importance controlling both the Great North Road and the river Trent, Newark-on-Trent, under Royalist control, was besieged without success in 1643, 1644 and 1645: it was surrendered to the Scots by the King's order when he gave himself up to them in May 1646. 2. nobles] A gold coin worth one-third of a pound (6s 8d). 3. *Margin*] The third seige, of 1645, was a joint one by Scottish and Parliamentarian armies under Leven and Poyntz. 4. marke] Silver coin, worth two-thirds of a pound (13s 4d). Pun] Pound. 6. thistles . . . rose] Symbols found on some Scottish and English coins respectively. 11. C: R:] For Charles Rex. 12. O. B. S.] 'OBSIDIUM': a small drawing under the title shows the coin marked 'O.B.S. IX New.' 16. Bellassize] John, Lord Belasyse of Worlaby, Lincolnshire (1614–89), Catholic Royalist general, commanded Newark from October 1645 till its surrender in 1646; his appointment by the King prompted a near-mutiny by Rupert and other officers.
Ms Urselye—alius Arslys Triumphs Title. *Urselye*] Cf. Herrick, 232.4, *Upon Madam Ursly, Epig.* 1–4. *Margin*] The reference is to Jonson's *Epigram CXXXIII On the Famous Voyage* (*Poems*, p. 86). 3. Puddle Dock] At the foot of St Andrew's Hill, just below where the Fleet sewer discharged at Bridewell Dock, the starting point of Jonson's voyage. 5. Holborn-bridg] Crossing the Fleet river slightly east of the modern Holborn Circus. 8. doe—] doe beshite us. 12. be—] bestink us. 13–14. *Margin*] Jonson's Crown pension was increased from 100 marks to £100 plus a barrel of Canary wine ('sack') in 1630. 14. Butt] A barrel holding approx 126 gallons. (Jonson in fact only got a 'tierce', forty-two gallons.). 16. Turn-ups Ale] A 'turn-up' was a whore: cf. as verb, Dryden, *Absolom and Acitophel* II, l. 383: 'As 'tis a Leading-Card to make a Whore / To prove her Mother had turn'd up before.' 17. Kinderkin's] Kilderkin, a small barrel of sixteen to eighteen gallons. 19. wort] Unfermented beer. 22. be—] ?besprayed. 28. point Blank] In sense of short range, up close to. 30. *Boggers] Users of bogs (lavatories, *OED* s.v. *bog n*3). 35. Fiz-l] 'The action of breaking wind quietly' (*OED*). *back—belc-s] backside belches: farts (not in *OED* or Partridge). 41. Jorden] Chamber-pot. 44. Philistian] Philistine, ?here 'bailiff' (*OED* s.v. *philistine* 2). 47. City Bands] Trained Bands, the militias raised on a local basis. 52. Jack . . . Well] Sir John Mennes (1599–1671), author of *A letter to C. B. from Epsam Wells*; see Appendix 1.
Sola Bella che piace Title] 'That only is beautiful which pleases'. 12. Loadstons spell] Magnetism. 13. Sphere] Presumably meaning perfect, not spherical. 11–12] *OS* has marginal n. '*Magnes amoris amor*' ('Love [*is*] love's magnet'). Cf. *A Sonnet upon the same Subject*, p. 344, l. 19.
In Effigiem Caroli 2di Title] 'On a painting of Charles II'. 4. Trajans Adage] Each new emperor was greeted with the wish, which became proverbial, that his reign might be 'Felicior Augusto, melior Trajano', 'happier than Augustus, better than Trajan'. Cf. Tacitus, *Historia* I, 1.

N: MS Westmorland (A) 6.vi.1. Poems, 1643–51

De Fœdere Nationale Translation by Fane of a Latin epigram signed 'E. H' (?Edward Harley). Title] '*On the National Treaty*' either the military alliance with the Scots of November 1643 or the setting up of the Committee of Both Kingdoms in January and February 1644. 10. Trebble Cord] Proverbial with various applications, such as the triple cord of the world, flesh and devil, which ties mankind to sin, or of Faith, Hope and Charity, which does not. Cf. Thomas Jackson *Commentaries upon the Apostle's Creed* (1635) VIII. x. 1: 'The Sonne of God began to untwist that triple cord, wherewith our first parents... were bound by Satan.' 10.1. W] This and the signature to the following poem are not clear in *N*, but the presence of *In novi anni* in *OS* confirms that it is either Fane's 'W' or just possibly a monogram of 'M' and 'W'.

In novi anni—1644 1–4] See *Janus*, p. 179, l. 11 n.

An Epitaph on Sir Thomas Nicolson Knight Translation by Fane of a Latin epitaph signed 'G.F.' (? George Fane). *Title. Nicolson*] Thomas Nicholson (*c.* 1575–1649), Rector of Stapleford Tawney, Essex, was imprisoned by Parliament in 1642 along with his sons over the sequestration of the living, and 'for words spoken against the Parliament' (*Commons' Journals* II, pp. 782, 878, 913; Matthews, *Walker*, p. 160). He does ot appear to have been a knight, or a civil lawyer, but his son John (*c.* 1606–77) was a well known DCL. *Civilian*] A Civil Lawyer. 1–2. Tower ... Tides] The lighthouse of Pharos, off Alexandria, built by Ptolemy II. 5. Hermes] God of prudence and cunning (hence also of perjury). Pitho] Goddess of persuasion and eloquence. 6. Themis] Wife of Zeus, and the personification of law, custom and equity. Apollo] Here, as god of music and the arts. 7. wand] The *caduceus* which Apollo gave to Hermes; the judges' staff of office.

Epithallamy Written for the marriage (*c.* 1650) of Anne Townshend to Cecil Tyrwhitt (d. 1694) of Cameringham, Lincolnshire (see l. 32). The Tyrwhitts were a strongly Royalist, and in many cases Catholic, family, here entering an alliance with the Presbyterian Townshends. 8. Commonallety] Shared function or purpose which unites a group. 10–11. God... day] Tuesday, from Latin *dies Martis*, or simply a militia training day (see l. 17). 12–16] The conquest of Mars (violence, war) by Venus (love, *humanitas*) is a commonplace of Renaissance neoplatonism. 17. Training-day] Day set for the training of militia. 24. a—] a maid. 53–4. wheat... Increase] Cf. Herrick, 112.3, *A Nuptiall Song, or Epithalamie, on Sir Clipseby Crew and his Lady*, ll. 45–6: 'While some repeat / Your praise, and bless you, sprinkling you with Wheat'. Brand (II, pp. 63–4) quotes Thomas Moffet's (Moufet's) *Health's Improvement* (1605): 'the English, when the Bride comes from Church, are wont to cast wheat upon her head', and interprets it as a survival of the Roman *confarreationem*, in which an offering of bread (the bride-cake of seventeenth-century English weddings) marked the marriage. 55. Cake... Bride] Brand notes a custom 'still retained in Yorkshire' where the bride-cake 'is cut into little square pieces, thrown over the Bridegroom's and Bride's Head, and then put through the Ring. The Cake is sometimes broken over the Bride's Head, and then thrown away among the Crowd to be scrambled for' (II, p. 64). 59. squadron] Form up in squares, for dancing. 60. figures] Movements or divisions in a dance. 64. Cruell] Because delaying the consummation. 71. Bright Barneby] St Barnabas's Day (11 June) was in the Old Style reckoned the longest day. 78. closs fight] close combat, esp. engagement between ships; strictly, the area between mainmast and foremast. Cf. Marston, *Antonio and Mellida* 1. 1. 33: 'Stand firm on deck when beauty's close fight's up.' 87. stocken's thrown] Brand quotes Misson, *Travels through England*: 'the young men took the bride's stocking, and the girls those of the bridegroom; each of whom, sitting at the end of the bed, threw the stocking over their heads', trying to hit the bride or groom as a way of predicting their own marital prospects (II, p. 107).

Upon Sir Anthonies incomparable peece *Title*] For Sir Anthony Weldon, see *To the County of Kent upon its condition at present*, p. 97, and *To Sir A W Clerk of the Kitt*[*chen*] *to K J*, p. 210. 6. Skoar] Draw (cf. *To The countess of Ruttland upon Her New reedefying of Belvoir*, p. 330, l. 17 n.).

The Genius and houshold Gods salute the little stream The Latin version, dated August 1645, locates the poem at Mereworth. *Title. Stanlies*] Thomas Stanley (d. 1668) of Hamptons, West Peckham, about two miles from Mereworth (Hasted, V, pp. 60–1). See Everitt, pp. 195–7, for his notable part in the Kentish rising of 1643. For his role as hydraulic engineer, cf. W(A) Misc. 7, f. 25r, 2 August 1645: 'To Cap. Stanly Towards payment of workmen 5-0-0'. The ponds were stocked with 100 carp (*ibid.*, ff. 24r–25r). Cf. 12 September 1651: 'To C Stan: groom brought Mall a guelding 2.10.0' (f. 100r). 6. pricks... sleep] 'Plays the particular scale and air which lead to sleep' (translating 'Somnos musicis susurris'). 12. Pound] An encircling barrier, but 'pound' was also a seventeenth-century form of 'pond'. 13. Guarden-God] Priapus (Greek) or Vertumnus (Roman). 20. eleventh signe] Aquarius, the water-bearer.

Upon Sir Thomas Fayer-Fax The Latin version is dated 16 March 1645 (i.e. 1646). Fairfax (1612–71) had then been 'Lord General' (initially 'Captain General') of the New Model Army for just over a year. He had won the major battle of Naseby (June 1645), had almost been killed storming Torrington in February 1646 and had received Hopton's surrender of the Royalist forces in the West Country three days before this poem was written, just time for news to reach Fane. This is by far the most admiring poem he addresses to Fairfax, who had married Anne Vere in June 1637, exactly a year before Fane married her sister Mary. Fane's own position when taking the Covenant in 1644 was not far removed from that of Fairfax, but references in 1647–48 (*Song or Ode Upon the speakers of either houses*, p. 209, l. 23, and *To Sir Thomas Fairfax*, p. 221) are more equivocal, while *Upon the Generall the Lord Fairfaxes resigning* (1650, p. 247) is clearly hostile, as is *Upon the Strange adventure and memorable voyage* (1653, p. 206). Title. *Fayer-Fax . . . star*] The Latin version translates the pun on 'Fair' (*Pulchram*) and preserves the familiar one on 'Fax' ('star'). 1–2. Alexander . . . Less] Because he had no more to conquer. 5. Pignions] Pinions, wings, perhaps punning on 'pignon', battlement. 8. Bellerophons] Bellerephon was given a series of impossibly 'great acts' to do with the intention of causing his death; the first one, the killing of the monster Chimaera, is probably meant.

Out of Martiall Ep.-21-Li-5 Title] Epigram 20 in modern editions. Cf. The version of X, 47, *To Julius Martiall*, p. 346. 6. Towers of magnanimety] Buildings of pomp and affectation, loosely translating 'nec nos atria nec domos potentum'. Cf. Browne, *Urne-Buriall*: 'the . . . wilde enormities of ancient magnanimity'(*Works* I, p. 170). 9. Statue Pride Familiar] Translating 'imagines superbas', in the form of ancestral busts. 13. wench] Deleted in *N*, but no alternative given. Fane is translating 'umbra, Virgo, thermæ', where 'Virgo' stands for cold baths derived from the Aqua Virgo aqueduct as opposed to hot baths ('thermæ').

To Quintillian Title] A translation of Martial II, 90. 5. differ] defer (translating *differat*). 12. debate] strife (translating *lite*, strife, especially legal).

Ode—To a frend in Imitation of these Title. *these*] The translations of Martial, which are on the facing page in *N*. 1. Ned] Either Ned Beecher, most associated with this theme, though he would have been over seventy (see *An ode To N.B. an angler*, p. 59, Title n.), or, if ll. 16–24 mean he is a holder of political office, Edward Harley, who was an MP until expelled that December (see *A reveille-Matin Ode*, p. 159, Title n.). Other 'Neds' mentioned in Fane's accounts are Bellamy and Pelham. 3. Ale and Tost] In the seventeenth century the toast was usually in the ale. 9–10. Thorp . . . Meer] Apethorpe, the river Nene, Peterborough, and Whittlesey Mere (see *An Ode to N.B.*, p. 113, l. 50 n). 30. Rib of Martemas] Salted beef, 'Martinmas meat': Martinmas (11 November) was the occasion when animals were killed and salted for winter food.

A Christmas Carroll to the Earle of WestmoreLand By Robert Herrick. This is the only known copy of the poem, which was probably written in November or December 1647 following Herrick's ejection from his living at Dean Prior in 1646. For the wider context of this appeal and of Fane's reply, see Cain, *Christmas Carol*. 33] Three syllables (probably 'hungry', 'meagre' etc. 'ghost') have been omitted, presumably because the copyist could not read Herrick's usually clear hand.

His answære to the Caroll 1. Copper guilded] Copper covered with a thin plating of gold or gold leaf, as *Troil.* 4. 4. 105: 'some with cunning gild their copper crowns'. 2. sheafe of plenty] Probably thinking both of a Christmas evergreen wreath of some kind, and of a cornucopia, which, though in the form of a horn, not a sheaf, was commonly represented with corn spilling out of it (see *OED* s.v. *cornucopia*). Appropriate here because 'The sheaf' was also the term for the tithe which Herrick had just lost on his ejection. 8. contentation] Satisfaction, with emphasis on acceptance of one's lot. 12–13. Hippocrene . . . Twinny Hill] See *To my Sonn Charles in prayse of Horsemanship*, p. 349, l. 14 n. 19. Pie corner] Corner of St Sepulchre's Alley, near Newgate; cf. Jonson, *Alchemist* I. 1. 25. 20. newgate . . . Gratias streete] Stowe says 'The Poulters of late remooved out of the Poultrie . . . into Grass ["Gratias" or Gracechurch] streete, and St. *Nicholas* Shambles [adjoining "newgate market"]' (*Survey of London*, 1603, ed. C. L. Kingsford, Oxford, 1908, I, p. 81). 22. Higlery] Trade and wares of a petty dealer in poultry. Cheape side] Site of a major London market: Stow, I, 258. Kettles] Probably here containing milk for cream, the skim being a waste product, sold cheap or given away. 25–6. Caroll . . . hung] Christmas was abolished as a religious feast in 1645 and as a secular one in 1647; for defeated Royalists, great halls like those at Apethorpe or Mereworth where Christmas could still be celebrated in the old style were a refuge from ascendant puritanism. 28. deere] For inflation in Fane's wine bill, see

Cain, *Christmas Carol*, p. 136. 29. brew fatt] Brew vat. 31. Gracchi ... fulvii] The Gracchi, aided rather than opposed by Marcus Fulvius Flaccus, attempted social and economic reforms opposed, finally with force, by an aristocratic party 133–21 BC. The parallels with the English Civil War were obvious. 34. kisse ... Diogines] The Cynic, popularly supposed to have lived in a tub, not requiring anything from the world except for it to leave him alone. 36] Proverbial; cf. Ovid, *Tristia* III. iv, 25: 'Bene qui letuit bene vixit'. 39. Pumps ... Magazin] 'Drains his storehouse'. checker] exchequer. 40] Fane sent Herrick £5 on 5 November 1647 (?suggesting Herrick's poem was written in October), and made a series of payments to him between 1647 and the restoration of his living in 1660 (W(A) Misc. 7, f. 53r).

Upon the Death of the Lord Hastings Title. Hastings] Henry, Lord Hastings (1630–49), whose early death from smallpox was commemorated in *Lachrymæ Musarum: The Tears of the Muses* (1649), in which place of honour was given to Fane's poem. Other contributors included Herrick (his last published poem in his lifetime), Dryden (his first) and Marvell. Cf. *A Sonnet to my Mistress*, p. 353, l. 24.3 n. Huntington] Ferdinando, sixth Earl of Huntingdon. Hastings's death, following those of two younger sons, left him without a male heir. 2. Kalender] Of astronomical data and accompanying predictions. 3. Skeam] Scheme, astrologer's chart. 5–6. Booker ... Lilly] John Booker (1603–67) and William Lilly (1602–81), the leading English astrologers of their age. Fairfax interviewed them both at Windsor in 1647, suspecting rightly that they were advising the King on when to escape. 10] Proverbial, cf. Plautus, *Bacch.* 4. 7. 18: 'Quem di diligunt, adolescens moritur.'

In Fallacem Leguleium Epigramma Title] 'Epigram on Fallax a Timeserving Lawyer'. The Latin version with this title in *N* was published by Robert Vilvain (1575?–1663), in his *Enchiridion Epigrammatum Latino-Anglicum* (1654), pp. 128r–v, as by 'Anonymus', followed by Vilvain's own English version (see Appendix 1). Fane copied out both the Latin and Vilvain's translation, and then wrote his own version under the heading *An other*. It is printed here under the Latin title which Fane took from Vilvain. 3. Covnant] See *Epigram: Upon one Beal a minister*, p. 82, l. 1 n. 5. Ingagement] The Act of Engagement of 1649.

Upon min Hostes Bland at Tousester Title] For male members of the Bland family of Towcester (near Northampton), see *Quarter Sessions Records of the County of Northampton*, ed. Joan Wake (Hereford, 1924), p. 168.

H: Houghton Library, Harvard: fMS Eng. 645. Poems, 1637–61

Short titles of poems in the *Index Libelli* at the end of *H* (pp. 183–6 of the manuscript) have been noted only where they differ significantly from those given in the text.

Upon the Strange adventure and memorable voyage Title. Black Tom] Fairfax (see *Upon Sir Thomas Fayer-Fax*, p. 200, n.) had resigned as Lord General in 1650. By October 1653 there were already signs that he might favour reconciliation with Charles II, and in July 1654 Clarendon advised Charles to offer a pardon (*Calendar of the Clarendon State Papers*, ed. W. Dunn Macray and F. J. Oxford, 1869–1970, II, p. 383). wansford bridg] Near Apethorpe, on the Great North Road. Fairfax may have stayed at Apethorpe on his way from York, travelling on to London (with his dog, ll. 28, 41, not his daughter, as Turner, p. 71, states) in a public coach. Accounts show Fane was at Apethorpe in October. 2. Mandevil] Jehan de Mandeville (pseudonym of ?Jean de Bourgogne, c. 1300–72), author of an early book of travels. Purcas] Samuel Purchase (1577–1626), travel writer and collector of travellers' narratives, published *Purchas his Pilgrimage* (1613). 3. Coriats] Thomas Coryate (c. 1577–1617), wrote a part-facetious account of his travels in Europe, *Coryat's Crudities* (1611). 6. Troy-novant] London, derived mistakenly from the Trinobantes tribe; see Fane's note to *An invitation to my Askanius a true Trojan ifayth*, p. 257, l. 33. Cf. Thomas Heywood, *Troia Brittanica* (1609), dedication, l. 41: 'Rankt next to Troy, our Troy-novant should be.' 8] Public coaches for long-distance travel had begun to appear in the late 1630s. 10. Fiery Pallfries] Horses which drew the chariot of the sun for Helios: see *The Cosmography of this County*, p. 219, l. 9. 12. wayne] agricultural waggon. 13. bells] The lead horse carried bells to warn of the coach's approach. 19. slow] The average distance covered in a day would be about twenty-five miles, though in good conditions the 300 mile journey from Newcastle to London took only six days. 24. Pismier] ant. 30. Bilk] Balked; a bilk is a card which stops an opponent scoring in cribbage. 33. Leather shell] Coaches in the 1650s had leather flaps for doors, and no windows. 34. Lobster Lady] Notorious episode summarised by title of poem by Matthew Stevenson: *Upon a Hosier that carry'd His Wife to give Her a Lobster, and lockt Her up in an Apothecarie's House, pretending her mad, where She was kept Fourteen Days with Bread and Water*. Another poem alleges that the husband 'When Oliver took Horseback, was / His Stirrupholder.' See Stevenson, *Poems* (1673), pp. 109, 113. 35. Packs] Of cards. 39. Gabions] Baskets filled with earth, used to strengthen fortifications. 47. Jhon] John Dory, a traveller celebrated in ballads: cf. 'ambeling Jhon Dory', *To H.T. into Nor[folk]*, p. 208, and ?Denham, *To Sir W. Davenant*: 'And all this stir to make a story, / Not much superior to John Dory' (*Works*, p. 318). 49. Lepton] John Lepton, Groom of the Privy Chamber to James I, who 'undertook for a wager to ride six days together betwixt York and London . . . and performed it accordingly, to the greater praise of his strength in acting, then his discretion in undertaking it' (Fuller, *Worthies* II, p. 543). He was later (1621) involved in a conspiracy backed by Buckingham to bring false charges against Sir Edward Coke, and 'escaped as is thought towards Scotland' (Chamberlain, *Letters* II, p. 412), thus proving wrong Fuller's moralising on the 'discretion' of his earlier journey. 62. Carter-Lane] A triple pun: Carter Lane, south of St Paul's, is a likely destination for a coach entering London from the north; but a 'carter' is also a card player and 'a type of low birth or breeding' (*OED* s.v. *carter* 1 2b, *carter* 2). 62.1. *Basta*] Italian, 'enough'.

Upon a mischance or fall 12. Fresco] Fresh air, thus 'the open-air room'; cf. Jonson, *New Inn* 4. 2. 1, 'Come, let's take in fresco here one quart.' 23. Lant-horn protector] One carrying a lantern ahead of him: London streets were supposed to be lit by the inhabitants, but appear not always to have been. This doctor had both a guide ('director') and a lamp carrier.

To H.T. into Norfolk Title. H.T.] Horatio Townshend (1630–87), younger (the elder being Sir Roger) of Fane's stepsons with his second wife: see *Sonnet upon second amorous thoughts*, p. 110, n. In February 1647 Fane took them to France to begin their tour: 'Layd out in a jorney wth Sr Rog & Horace to Calis & back post £68-3-4' (W(A) Misc. 7, f. 44r). They had leave to travel abroad for three years (*Commons' Journals* V, 14), but Roger died in Geneva, where they were staying with John Diodati (C. H. Townshend, *The Townshend Family of Lynn*, 1884 ed., p. 128; cf. *Psal—120*, p. 175, ll. 18–19 *Margin* n.). Horatio inherited Raynham (see *A Jorney into Norfolk*, p. 116, l. 84 n.) and the baronetcy. He was MP for Norfolk 1656–60, member of Richard Cromwell's Council of State, with the secret concurrence of Charles II, and one of the main organisers of the August Rising (see *Upon a Rumor of a Generall rising*, p. 328, *Title* n.). One of twelve commissioners, led by Fairfax, sent to Breda to invite the return of Charles II, 1660. Became Baron 1661, Viscount 1682. An important link between Fane and Fairfax, delivering to the latter in 1660 a message from Charles II urging him to assemble his old soldiers and march on York. 1. Holl] Diminutive of Horatio. 3. Hodges Mary] Mary Hodges was a servant in Fane's household; Joan (l. 6) Nichols and Bes[s] (l. 4) Seamer are in the same list of September 1650 (W(A) Misc. 15, f. 80r). 11–12] Coriot . . . Jhon Dory] See *Upon the Strange adventure and memorable voyage*, p. 206, ll. 3, 47, nn. 19–21] Ban Bon] Not traced. Watt] A hare. Cunny] Cony, a rabbit, but slang for 'cunt'. 23–4. Until . . . Catch him] Until he gets drunk: *OED* s.v. *fox* I.1.d. 22. Knocks] Copulates: *OED* s.v. *knock v.* 2.d, and Partridge. 36. stent] extended. 39. swimmers] Usually in the seventeenth century swimming birds. 42. Brimmers] Full glasses or cups. 48. Potter] A heavy drinker, 'one addicted to poting' (*OED*).

Hug Gross: Epigram to J. Douse Title. Hug Gross] Hugo Grotius (van Groot, 1583–1645), Dutch jurist and poet, wrote *De Jure Belli et Pacis* (1625), a pioneering work on international law, and poems in Dutch and Latin; Fane owned the *Poemata* (Leyden, 1617; Sotheby's, 1887, lot 361). This poem is based on Grotius's longer *Ad Dousam pro suâ Republica Batava Atheniensi atque Romanæ comparatâ*, pp. 173–5 of that edition. Douse] Jean van der Does (1545–1604), governor of Leyden during the seige of 1575, humanist poet, editor of Plautus and historian of Holland, published his *Annales* of Holland in verse (1599) and in prose (1601). Woad] Wold, a plain: cf. Dutch *woud*. taught English] translated. 3–4. flocks . . . play] The spinners are kept in work despite the absence of sheep. (Minerva and her Greek counterpart Athena were patrons of women's crafts.)   12. Hollands] A hard-wearing linen cloth, usually brown, made from flax (l. 11).

Song or Ode   Title. Upon . . . Army] In July 1647 dangerous rivalry between the Presbyterian-dominated Parliament and City and the New Model Army caused Manchester, Speaker of the Lords, and William Lenthall, Speaker of the Commons (though both Presbyterians), to lead the flight of the army's supporters from London, frightened by a mob which invaded both Houses on 26 July. The division represented Charles's best chance of regaining his throne, Cromwell and Ireton having tried hard to persuade him to accept the fairly generous terms offered under the 'Heads of Proposals' of 17 July. In August the army entered London and restored the two Speakers, but not the King. Cf. *A Farcy*, p. 186, ll. 63–70.   3. Jack Presbiter] Royalist nickname for a Presbyterian: cf. Matthew Stevenson, *Bellum Presbyteriale* (1661), 'You that Malignant call'd the Cavallier: / Who is Malignant now? JACK PRESBYTER' (p. 18). It was presumably suggested by the legend of Prester John; cf. *Upon Master Alexander Henderson's Death*, p. 217, l. 34 n.   4. ordaind . . . louse] Ordinances passed during the period of mob pressure in July were declared null.   6] Proverbial, from Pliny 25. 10. 85, 'Ne supra crepidam sutor judicaret' (Tilley, C480). Used in *Vita*, p. 42.   8. long Letters] The long letter ('verbosa et grandis epistula', Juvenal X, 71) sent by Tiberius to destroy Sejanus, the 'subject' who sought to reign.   12. mil breath] Breath from a flour mill, blasting the 'flowers' (flour) of the Crown, but 'mill' was also slang for a housebreaker.   13. Duch] Dutch, characterised as both republican and broadly puritan.   22. Generall] Fairfax.   25. Foresta] *Charta de Foresta*, granted 1217, founded on Magna Carta (1215). Petition of Right] 1628 attempt by Parliament to curb the royal prerogative. Fane, still an MP at that date, would have seen the difficult passage of the petition through the Commons.   26. time . . . things] Proverbial; cf. Tilley, T326; Ovid, *Met.* XV, 234, 'Tempus edax rerum.'   30. sessions or size] Courts of quarter sessions or assizes.   35. perpetuity] The Long Parliament had voted itself a perpetual parliament.   39. the known Lawes] In his memorandum to the King in 1643 Fane wrote of 'the knowne Lawes of the land (no Arbittrary ones)' (W(A) 6.vi.1, f. 411); see Cain, 'A sad Intestine warr', pp. 34–9.

To Sir A W Clerk of the Kitt[*chen*] *to K J*   Title. Sir A W] Sir Anthony Weldon. See *To the County of Kent upon its condition at present*, p. 97, l. 6 n., and *Upon Sir Anthonies incomparable peece*, p. 199. He became Clerk of the [Royal] Kitchen 1604. Weldon's activities as a Parliamentarian county commissioner in Kent had much to do with the Royalist Kentish rising of 1648.   3. Coke and Bacon] Sir Edward Coke (1552–1634), greatest of common lawyers, became Chief Justice of the Common Pleas (1606–13) and Chief Justice of the King's Bench (1613–16); Sir Francis Bacon, Viscount St Albans (1561–1626), was Solicitor General (1607), Attorney General (1613), Lord Keeper (1617) and Lord Chancellor (1618) under James, until Coke led the Commons in 1621 in impeaching Bacon for taking bribes.   6. dryping pann] The dripping-pan caught drips from the roasted meat on the spit, and was then used for frying.

Grace before meat   Title. L: Ch:] ?Lord Charles Gerrard, Fane's ward. No contemporary Lord Chancellor or Lord Chamberlain had a wife called Grace.   1–2. Gratia . . . faciere] 'Grace given freely to make it pleasing'.

My taking Phisick   1. skan] Pass judgement on.

To my Frend Mun   Title. Mun] ?John Mun (1615–70) of Bearsted, Kent. The family were friends and neighbours of the Fane's, and owned land in Mereworth. A 'Mun' is also mentioned in Fane's accounts in the 1650s, receiving relatively small sums.   3. P—] Packet, perhaps for 'pocket', but with a strong sexual innuendo: neither 'packet' nor 'pocket' meaning female sexual organs is in *OED* or Partridge.   4. keep thy racket] Make a noise, disturbance (*OED* s.v. *racket* n3), usually then with 'keep' as now always with 'make'.   6–8. Grid . . . Chase] All terms from real tennis, though 'board' is not normally used for the court.   12. troü] French 'hole', but Cotgrave also gives 'fundament, nock-androe' and (cf. the tennis motif) 'Trou d'une rets' as 'The mesh of a net'. Fane owned the 1650 edition of Cotgrave.

In Rem publicam   Title] 'On the Republic'.   3–4. Margin] Written four days after the battle of Worcester, and the day after Parliament voted that Cromwell should have Hampton Court as a country residence.   4. Sisternety] Sisterhood.

My Lottery   1. Cast crosse or Pile] Toss heads or tails.   draw cutts] Draw lots; cf. *Com. Err.* 5. 1. 423, 'We'll draw cuts for the senior.'   4. payers] pairs.   8. Packe] Of cards, but suggesting both 'conspiracy' (*OED* s.v. *pack n*2) and a gang (*n*1. 3a). Gleeckes and Mornifalls] Sets of three and four cards in the game of gleek: *OED* quotes Cotton, *Gamester* (1670), vi. 68: 'A Mournival is either all the Aces, the four Kings, Queens, or Knaves, and a Gleek is three of any of the aforesaid.' 9. Toms] Jack of trumps in Gleek. Ases] Aces. coates] 'court' cards. 10. Ruft out] Trumped. *Tidied] Put away; all quotations in *OED* are nineteenth-century. 13. Groom Porters] Officer of the royal household responsible for cards and other games. 14. Ephe] Greek 'he says', formula supposedly used by uncritical Pythagoreans of the doctrine of their master. Cf. *Vita*, p. 37. Here, they authorise (or merely comment on?) newspapers (Diarnalls, l. 15) and tracts. 16. Lucubrationes] Studies, usually nocturnal ones; the many tracts and pamphlets appearing in the 1640s. 19. *Covide] Gathered together, as in the noun 'covey', not in *OED* as verb in this sense. 21. Gaddrens swine] Gadarene swine (Mark 5. 1–15.) 23. Bevy] A company of any kind, not especially of goblins (l. 24). 24. Gobbeline] Goblin. 26. Greene headless] Naive and anonymous. 29. Pharos Press] Punctuation: 'like Pharoes, press for'. The reference is to Pharaoh's inconsistent behaviour in Exodus 8–12. 36. Barkleyes] ?Lord Chief Justice Berkeley, who had pronounced that *rex* was *lex* in Hampden's Ship Money trial. 41. Home-by] Punning on Holdenby (pronounced 'Homeby') House, Northamptonshire, where Charles was held in spring 1647. weeping X] To 'return home by weeping cross' was proverbial for grievous failure. There was a 'weeping cross' at Banbury, south-west of Holdenby. 44. travers by ascent] Pass by assent, but 'traverse' also meant 'contradict' in law, and (beginning the artillery metaphors) moving a gun to aim it. Ordinance] 1 Laws passed by the Long Parliament without the royal assent; 2 artillery. 45. Canonick] Punning on 'canon' and 'cannon'. 46–50] In the apocryphal Book of Bel the 'Babylons' worship both a dragon and the idol Bel, who supports seventy priests, with their wives and children (l. 50). Both are destroyed by Daniel. 52–3] The story of Tobias and the dog is in the Book of Tobit, which being apocryphal will be read only by Levites (the forerunners of contemporary sectarians). 54. Text] To use as a text on which to preach. endowments] Endowed post as a preacher or 'lecturer'. 56. goe to Jerico] Proverbial, meaning 'Go away', 'Go to hell' (cf. Tilley, J39), but here also reflecting its origin in II Samuel 10. 5: 'Tarry at Jericho until your beards be grown,' hence the 'smooth face' of l. 57. 62. Suzannas] The story of Susanna and the Elders is told in the apocryphal Book of Susanna, 1. 63. salique Law] The *Lex Salica*, used to exclude women from succession to the French throne. 68. Antelers on Joachim] Make a cuckold of St Joachim, father of the Virgin Mary, here as the type of an old man, and continuing the theme of apocryphal lore, since he is not mentioned in the Bible and the cult of his wife Anne was a favourite target of the Protestant reformers. 69. Mother] The Church. 71. Independence] Independents, sectarians particularly strong in the army. They believed in the autonomy of each local church, with Christ as the only head of the Church, and all its members equal as priests, attitudes which brought them into conflict with both the Anglican establishment and many Presbyterians. 72] 'Whose Fancy is law, and whose will is religion'. 73. free quarter] Compulsory billeting of troops without payment. 73–4] Army chaplains are now preachers in public churches, marrying military and religious duties. 76. Buttend Priests] Priests in plain buttoned clothes, not the gown of the Anglican Church, frowned on by the Independents, cf. Milton, *Eikonoklastes* xvi, 'How constantly the Priest puts on his Gown and Surplice, so constantly doth his praier put on a servile yoak of Liturgie.' 86. set] mend.

A game at Tables   Title. *Tables*] Backgammon.   1. Levelcoyle] Advanced musical chairs. *OED* quotes Blount's *Glossographia* (1656): 'Level-Coile is when three play at Tables, or other Game, where onely two can play at a time, and the loser removes his Buttocks, and sits out, and therefore called also Hitch-Buttock.'   9–10] Heraldic terminology for 'a blood-red spear tipped with malice on a gold background'.   16. runnegates] fugitives.

Honos alit Artes   Title] 'Honour fosters the Arts'.   2] King David.   3–4. Crownes . . . Corne] Modifying the Aesopian proverb 'A barley-corn is better than a diamond to a cock' (Tilley, B88). 6] In the alphabet of the mid-seventeenth century these letters were 'i', 'm' and 'p', the usual abbreviation of 'Imperator', used on coins and the royal seal.   7. untie] Here make clear, so as to empower.

An Independents Coate Blazond   Title. *Independents*] See *My Lottery* p. 212, l. 72 n.   *Coate Blazond*] Coat of arms described according to rules of heraldry.   1. partly per pale] 'Party per pale', divided by a vertical line. Turcisme] Islam: the Independents were accused, e.g. by Edmund Calamy, of tolerating 'Turcism'.   chargd with] bearing.   2. Croysant] Crescent, the emblem adopted by the Turkish sultans.   new Light] Novel religious belief, with the implication that they are revealed new truths.   yonger House] Arms of a younger son or branch of family.   3. *Hypocrety] Hypocrisy; this form not in *OED*.   4. Salter] Saltire, the St Andrew's cross: the Scots were identified with Presbyterianism.   5. greatest . . . Image] He worships the image of the cross on a coin.   6. Bend] 'An ordinary formed by two parallel lines drawn from the dexter chief to the sinister base of the shield, containing the fifth part of the field in breadth, or the third if charged' (*OED*).   chevern] Chevron, a bar bent at an angle. (Neither is carried because he will not bend to authority.)   7. Dexter] Usually 'right', but in heraldry the left side of the shield (to the spectator).   8. sinister] right.   Base] Lower part of a shield.   9. Supporters] Figures on each side of the shield.   10. seamless one] Symbol of the unified Church, from John 19. 23-4: 'the coat was without seam . . . They said therefore among themselves, Let us not rend it, but cast lots for it'. Cf. *Upon Master Alexander Henderson's Death*, p. 217, ll. 39–44.   mantle] Drapery or scroll-work around the achievement.   11. Phranatique] Frenetic, full of religious enthusiasm, the spelling suggesting 'fanatic' as well.   12. crest] Device placed above the shield and helmet.   word] The motto beneath the shield.   14. beare . . . Canton] A canton was a small square section of the shield, but there is a pun on the Swiss (Calvinist) cantons and the Swiss bear.

Upon New-Lights   *Title*] See *An Independents Coate Blazond*, p. 214, l. 2 n.   3. Herolds-worth] Punning on 'Heralds' and Richard Holdsworth, Master of Emmanuel and Vice-chancellor of Cambridge, moderate puritan and Royalist, ejected and imprisoned in 1643.   4. Browne-Brick] Ralph Brownrigg, Master of Catherine Hall, similarly ejected in 1645.   5–6. Austin . . . Chrysostom] Church Fathers rejected by the new sectarians.   16. Jesses] Jesse, father of David, and thus founder of the royal lineage of Judah down to Jesus; Henry Jessey (1601–63), a contemporary of Fane's at Cambridge, became minister to an Independent congregation in Southwark in 1637, and was a leading exponent of Independency throughout the Interregnum.   27–38] Playing on the names of prominent Independents: Swithune Grindal (l. 27), a Baptist, spent some years in exile in Holland, as did Sidrach Simpson (l. 29; 'Sym' is from Sim Subtle, a crafty man). At Emmanuel from 1616; he was lecturer at St Margaret's, New Fish Street, and at St Anne Blackfriars, and a member of the Westminster Assembly. He was an opponent of Presbyterianism, as were Philip (1596–1672, l. 29) and Henry Nye (d. 1643), both members of the Assembly, Philip lecturing at Westminster Abbey 1646–60 ('a man of uncommon Depth' according to Calamy, p. 201). Nicholas Prophet (l. 29), also at Emmanuel (1617–22), was Rector of Marlborough St Peter and St Paul 1630–68. Thomas Coleman (1598–1647, l. 30), Assembly member, was Rector of St Peter's, Cornhill, and preached an anti-Presbyterian sermon to the Commons in 1645. Francis Cornwell (*c*. 1600–46, l. 31), an exact contemporary of Fane at Emmanuel, became minister of Marden, Kent, where Fane owned land: he was a General Baptist, perhaps protected by Fane's cousin, Sir Henry Vane Jr, to whom he dedicated a book. John Bright (1619–88, l. 31), Parliamentarian commander, served under Fairfax, and was governor of Sheffield (l. 32) in 1644. John Blackwell (d. 1658, l. 33), a grocer from Mortlake, was a patron ('favorer') of Independents. Thomas Wilson (d. 1651, l. 35) Rector of Otham, Kent, suspended for puritanism when minister of Maidstone, is more likely to be referred to than Rowland Wilson (1613–50), an Independent, colonel in the Parliamentary army and a member of the Council of State. 'Jenny' (l. 35) may be Jenny Geddes, who supposedly began the Edinburgh riot of 23 July 1637 against the Anglican prayer book imposed by Laud and the Privy Council, but a pun on a name related to 'Burnt arce' is more likely. John Saltmarsh (*c*. 1612–47, l. 36) religious poet, army chaplain, strong champion of the New Model Army and of religious toleration, was Rector of Brasted, Kent. 'Dick' Marsh (l. 36) may be the Dr Marsh who was minister of St Dunstan's-in-the-East. Hugh Broughton (1549–1612, l. 38) was a famous puritan preacher and Hebrew scholar of an earlier generation, patronised by Sir Walter Mildmay, and target of Jonson's satire in *Volpone* and *The Alchemist*. Andrew Broughton was a regicide, and member of the Council of State in 1653.   27. Tonle] Tonnel, a cask, barrel; not traced as a pun on a contemporary name.   38. Meters] Punning on the meeting of the Westminster Assembly, or on puritan 'meetings' in general.   44.

faire] fairy.   45. thurroughs] penetrates, resolves.   46. Cunny] Rabbit.   Burroughs] Jeremiah Burroughs (c. 1600–46), radical Independent minister, admitted to Emmanuel 1617 (the year before Fane), lecturer at Stepney and St Giles Cripplegate, one of the five leading Independents in the Westminster Assembly.   56. Like . . . Divill] Proverbial (though not in Tilley); in addition, Thomas Collier (fl. 1634–91) was a Particular Baptist, a well known New Model Army chaplain who preached in Putney church shortly before the debates.

16—December 1641   *Title*] In August 1641 the treaty between England and Scotland was signed. Charles I visited Scotland, where the General Assembly was in session, with Henderson (l. 2) as Moderator. Back in London, on 2 December Charles was presented with the Grand Remonstrance, and on 11 December a petition supporting the exclusion of bishops from Parliament was delivered to the Commons. Charles, urging Parliament to pass a Bill to press soldiers to put down the rebellion in Ireland, offended both Lords and Commons in a speech on 14 December. On 27 December the Lords complained of 'a concourse' of people in Whitehall shouting 'No Bishops!' (l. 1).   1. for up goes] ?Breaks cover running up-wind (in hunting: *OED* s.v. *up* prep. 4).   3. collect] From the Book of Common Prayer, imposed on the Scots in 1639; punning on 'colic'.   5. windy Instruments] Continuing the colic theme: accompanied music was proscribed in the Scottish Presbyterian rite.   6. Lithregy] Liturgy.   9. second service] The Communion service, following Morning Prayer.   12. *Coppefide] ?For 'copied'.   Hocus Pocussis] Jugglers and conjurers.   13. sarke] surplice.   one] on (over).   17. hood and capp] Worn by Catholic and Laudian clergy.   19–24] The Laudian Canons of 1640 stipulated that the 'Communion Table . . . may be called an Altar' and that all altars 'should be decently severed with rails' to prevent 'irreverent behaviour', such as putting hats on them. In September 1641 the Commons ordered that the Communion table should return to its pre-Laudian position (not railed off in the chancel), that crucifixes, scandalous pictures, tapers, candlesticks etc. (but not hats) should be removed from it; bowing at the name of Jesus and sports on Sundays were both to be stopped, but preaching was to be encouraged.   20. stone] Perhaps from the dedication rite which read 'Let this stone be sanctified, and consecrated . . .'.   26. glasse] An hourglass, since the sermon was supposed to last an hour.   28. glass] Stained glass windows.   32. theirs] ?Sexual; *Partridge* gives 'to cross' as 'to have intercourse with' from c. 1790, but it may have been current slang in 1640.   33. call on night] Make the church darker.

Epigram In Idem   *Title*] 'Epigram on the same'.

Upon Master Alexander Henderson's Death   *Title*] Henderson died in August 1646.   *Preaching Coachman*] See Robert Heath, *On Whip the Preaching Coachman* (*Clarastella*, 1650, pp. 7–8): 'he contemns / All books except the Bible, and condemns / Each human Authour to the flames'. 3. Jus] juice.   5. end] intention.   10. Bishops Silenced] Scottish Presbyterians, led by Henderson, rejected the Scottish bishops in 1639; see *Upon the Scotsh business—1638*, p. 230.   18. accons] actions.   20. goe] walk.   22. new scoare] New motive (*OED* 12), but also with sense of 'with a clean sheet'.   34. John the Presbiter] Prester John, legendary Christian king supposed to have ruled over an Asian kingdom in the twelfth century.   35. corner stone] Christ: see Peter 2. 4–8.   39. seamlesse garment] The Church: see *An Independents Coate Blazond*, p. 214, l. 9 n. 47. exceed their last] See *Song or Ode*, p. 209, l. 6 n.   49. Knocks] Punning on John Knox, Henderson's predecessor as leader of the Scottish Presbyterians.

To Northampton   1. Garison] The Parliamentary army under Essex was garrisoned at Northampton in August 1642.   2. shoomaker] As a centre of shoemaking and horse dealing Northampton always throve in time of war.   3. March . . . Last] For the proverb, see *Song or Ode*, p. 209, l. 6 n.   4. Cawy] Cavy, for 'cavalier'.   8. Curried] Dressed, treated (of leather).   9. Dicker] a bundle of ten hides.   11. Calves-skins . . . cushion] Bibles, bound in calfskin, used as the 'cushion' (book support) in a pulpit, from which the shoemaker now preaches. There may also be a suggestion of cowardice, as in *King John* 3. 1. 129–33.   fells] hides.   15. revelia] Reveille, beaten on a drum in the seventeenth century.   17. scooles . . . Commence] 'Universities for learned men to take degrees'.   18. *bylk] ?Cheat (not recorded before 1790): context suggests 'upstart' or 'ignoramus', but neither is in *OED* or Partridge.   19. tex] text.   discipline] Any specialised education, here military.   20. curtaine line] The wall of a fortified place.   23] Blacksmiths, Etna being the base of Vulcan (Latin *Volcanus*), smith to the gods, and the god of craftsmen in general.   24. they—] swive, have intercourse: Vulcan's wife Venus cuckolded him with Mars.   29. Logerisme] Logarithm; Napier's *Mirifici Logarithmorum Canonis descriptio* had been published in 1614.

The Cosmography of this County   2. paralell] Parallel of latitude.   2. services] Feudal duties, social obligations.   Lancht] lanced.   4. bonte feux] Literally 'generous fire', its meaning here not clear.   Cisme] Schism.   5. Levell] Referring particularly to the Levellers, who were at their most active between 1646/47 and 1649.   7. Bulkes] Stalls.   Torrid Zone] Region between the tropics.   9–10. Charles Wayne] Ursa Major, the Plough: punning on the wane of the King.   11. Phætons] Phaeton, son of Helios, drove his father's chariot of the sun too near Earth, endangering it before Zeus killed him.

An invective against Gould   10. Tindarus] Tyndareos, father of Castor, Helen and Clytemnestra by Leda, was expelled from Sparta by his brother Hippocoön, but returned to the throne after Hercules had killed Hippocoön and his twelve sons.   28. Rowland . . . Oliver] The proverb 'Give a Rowland for an Oliver' (to give tit-for-tat, Tilley, R195) converted to a jibe at Cromwell.

Epigram on the times   2–4] In Greek the addition of alpha (here 'A') before the word makes a negative, a construction surviving in English in 'amorphous' etc.

On King Cromwell   Title] See *Upon the Babes of Grace*, p. 128, l. 18 n.   7] Cromwell's ruddy complexion, and especially his red nose, were a frequent target of satirists; see *Upon the Babes of Grace*, l. 4 n.   8. Harrington] A brass farthing; cf. Jonson, *Devil is an Ass* 2. 1. 83.   11. Lord . . . us] Traditional prayer in time of plague.

To Hugh Peters   Title] Hugh Peter or Peters (1598–1660), militant Independent minister and a leading army chaplain, Cambridge contemporary of Fane. At Naseby he rode among the soldiers with a Bible in one hand and a pistol in the other. He blessed the 'glorious' trial of Charles I, and, though not a member of the court, was executed in 1660.   3–4] Cf. Acts 14. 22: 'we must through much tribulation enter into the kingdom of God'.   7. Bonerges] Boanerges, 'sons of thunder' (Mark 3. 17), hence a loud preacher, here combining the thunder of canon (Church) law with the cannon of the army.   10. Malchus'es] See John 18. 10.   11. Sarmants] Sermons (an eighteenth-century 'vulgar' spelling, *OED*). A conjectural reading: Wake, the copyist, has written what looks like 'Armatts' (with no cross on the 'A'), possibly misreading both a long initial 's' and a tilde for the 'n'.   15–16] See John 18. 11: 'Then said Jesus unto Peter, Put up thy sword.'

To Sir Thomas Fairfax   Title. *Fairfax*] See *Upon Sir Thomas Fayer-Fax* p. 200, Title n.   1. pretences] Heraldic term for a claim made on an escutcheon.   2. rest . . . brand] Lat. *fax*, a torch, firebrand.   6.1. *non . . . virtus*] Cf. Plato, *Laws* 1, 626, and 'Bis vincit qui se vincit in victoria' (Publilius Syrus, *Mimi Sententiae*, 21).

Upon Jack, Tom, Will, and Dick   Perhaps a variant of 'Tom, Dick and Harry', but the context and tenor both suggest now irrecoverable allusions to specific individuals.   4. marke] Boundary, hence 'at home', but punning on 'target'.

For A Treaty   Title] Called *A motive for a Treaty* in *Index Libelli*. Apparently referring to the Newport Treaty (1648).   3] If the King is there to give his assent, parliamentary ordinances will become obsolete.   4. St: John's Will] Oliver St John, a neighbour at Thorpe, Peterborough (see *Thorp Pallace a Miracle*, p. 341), and a contemporary at Cambridge. Defended Hampden in the Ship Money case, and as MP was Pym's lieutenant and leader of the 'middle party' in the Commons after Pym's death. He wanted to continue treating with Charles after the negotiations at Newport had broken down. Later, became Chief Justice of the Common Pleas (1648–60), but took no part in the King's trial.   Martin . . . whore] Henry Marten (1602–80), called a 'whoremaster' by both Charles and Cromwell, regicide, radical republican and probably atheist MP; he was an opponent of any negotiated peace, leading opposition in the Commons to the Newport terms. He may well be the 'Henry Martin' of Latin poems in *F1* (Appendix 2; ff. 28r, 32r) who was with Fane in Paris, having been abroad in the 1620s at approximately the same time.   10. Cabb:] abbreviating *Caballero*, for 'Cavalier'.

Upon Madam Severa   Title. *Severa*] Latin 'harsh', 'severe'.   2. Rosemary and Bayes] Both associated with funerals.   5. call'd in] cancelled, withdrawn.   6. night-piece] A painting of a night scene, usually melancholy or stormy.   10. velom] Vellum was used for miniature painting in particular.   Pencell] Brush.   22. Dialect] Speech.   23–4] One of Tantalus's many crimes was to reveal the secrets of Zeus.

Upon Madam Severa and her Gierle Friskin Title. *Friskin*] A frisky person, esp. in a woman, suggesting sexual freedom. 9. *payes her box] The dice box of the 'Gamester', hence 'plays the game'; not recorded as sexual (or other) slang in *OED* or Partridge.

Upon the Petitionall rising in Kent Title] '*Suppress by Fairfax*' added in *Index Libelli*. Petitioning for the disbandment of the army and restoration of the King, about 10,000 men of Kent were defeated in June by seven regiments under Fairfax and Ireton. This was the largest of a number of Royalist risings in June and July.   10. a warrant] Writ or order (*OED* 10a), as opposed to the petition with which they had begun.   12] See *Upon The great Mercy of God*, p. 162, l. 4 n.   16] See *Upon the Suddain rise of my Cuntry Men*, p. 126, Title n.   20] Long and short tails: see *Upon The great Mercy of God*, l. 3 n.

To Captaine Minous after his returne the 9th time from the East Indes Title. *Minous*] Captain William Minors, recorded voyages in East India Company records as master of the *Eagle* and the *Scout* (1623–24), master of the *Eagle* and the *Refuge* (1626–27), master of the *Speedwell* (1630–31), captain of the *Discovery* (1637–38), captain of the *Mary* (1642–43) and captain of the *William* (1649–50). Captain Richard Minors (?his son) held three commissions 1661–72.   5. *Margin*. Candish] Cavendish, a common spelling, reflecting pronunciation.   7. thrice ... Three] The Muses.

Upon Breaking the Seals Title] This happened in January 1649. Ego ... me] '*I will break you that you do not break me*'.   11. one Letter] ?alpha as a negative prefix; cf. *Epigram on the times*, p. 220, ll. 2–4 n.   16. Letter Long] Tiberius's letter: see *Song or Ode. Upon the speakers of either houses leveing their charges*, p. 209, l. 8 n.

A Summons to Frank Beumonts Gost Title] Fane can hardly have known Francis Beaumont, who died 1616, but he was in the Jonson/Herrick circle in the 1620s, and owned a copy of the Beaumont and Fletcher folio of 1647, for which he wrote commendatory poems 'on the back and on the fly leaf' (Sotheby's, 1887, lot 270, and *My Dedicatory at the end of Beaumont and fletchers playes*, p. 240). His lack of direct acquaintance may show here: *King and no King* (1611) was a tragi-comedy of which Herrick went out of his way to ascribe 'the rare Plott' to Fletcher (415, *Upon Master Fletchers Incomparable Playes*.)   10. Anchesters] Ancestors.   18. Cabbinet] Already meaning a small council of government, as well as a private room and a collector's display room.   43. Bishops posture] ?Like a censor.   44. *Cittrick] Sharp, tart; not in *OED* in this sense.   52. skoals] scales.   54. Jigg] Here, a farcical interlude within a play.

To invite my Lord to walke in the Tower Title. *my Lord*] Perhaps Algernon Percy, tenth Earl of Northumberland, a powerful supporter of Parliament, whose father Henry had been imprisoned for several years (cf. l. 2); see *By-Ward to some Cittisens entring the Tower*, p. 121, ll. 100–2.

Upon Prince Charles Title. *Downes*] Rendezvous for ships off the coast of Kent. Part of the fleet had defected to the Prince of Wales during the 1648 Kentish rising; in August 1648 they blockaded the Thames, but achieved relatively little in support of the Royalists during the second Civil War. Fane had sailed to the Downs a year earlier: 'Aug 1647 To the Downes & back the 7th in Cap. Petts Delight' (W(A) Misc. 7, f. 50r; for the Pett family, shipbuilders, see Pepys, *Diary*, *passim*).   1. warpe] Pull a boat along by a rope. wend] Float off by turning the ship's head. Both verbs imply slow, indecisive movement.   2. Everlasting] For eternity: cf. Psalms 90. 2: 'from everlasting to everlasting, thou art God'.   8. cholchos] Colchis, where the Golden Fleece was guarded by a dragon.   10–11] Alluding to the Welsh gold mines.   16. Halcion] peaceful.

On the Mayor of Evsham Title] In June 1644 Waller's Parliamentary army was welcomed by the 'evil inhabitants' of Evesham, who, as soon as the King had withdrawn 'repaired their bridge over the Avon to facilitate his [Waller's] coming to them' (Clarendon VIII. 54).   11. President] Punning on 'precedent'.   13. bulke] stall.

Upon the Perfume Pembrooke left Title] '*Owld Pembrokes perfume or his dying fame*' in *Index Libelli*. Pembrooke] Philip Herbert, fourth Earl of Pembroke (1584–1650), who as Earl of Montgomery had in 1625 supported Fane's candidacy as a Knight of the Shire for Kent against Buckingham's nominee, Sir Edwyn Sandys: see *Vita*, p. 50, n. 6.   *Margin*. Fama mendax] 'The rumour is false' or 'Rumour is a Liar'; Pembroke died in January 1650, but was seriously ill in May 1649.   6. mis'eries] mysteries (of alchemy).   9–10] Pembroke had supported Parliament from at least 1640, but many Royalists believed, with Clarendon, that his loyalties were opportunistic.   12–13. chancelour ... schoole] Pembroke had become Chancellor of Oxford in 1641;

in 1647–48 he enforced loyalty to Parliament, ejecting Royalist heads of houses, and provoking much opposition.   15–16] Pembroke was foul-mouthed, bad-tempered and not especially learned.   16. Gotam] Gotham, village proverbial for the stupidity of its inhabitants.   Alkeron] Alcoran, the Koran.   20. Commoner] Pembroke was elected MP for Berkshire in 1649, arousing the hostility and ridicule of many fellow peers.   21. Jewel's] The 'George' of the Order of the Garter.   25. hatt band] Of the Order of the Bath.   30. *Hermophrodite] Hermaphrodite. This spelling not in *OED*, nor is this figurative use recorded before 1659.   35. Oxford's silent] Oxford was silent in praising Pembroke, but a number of satires attacking him appeared in 1648–49.   36. Barksheirs Knight] Knight of the Shire, as MP: see l. 20 n.

Cambridge and Oxford   2. Ours] Cambridge, whose Chancellor was Henry Rich, Earl of Holland, executed in March 1649.   Chancelers] Pembroke had been appointed in 1641, but was superseded by the Marquis of Hertford when Oxford became the King's headquarters (1642); he was reinstated by Parliament in 1647.   4. field] Hertford, who was Charles's 'general-in-chief' in the West.   Tower] Holland was in the Tower before his execution.   6–7] Minerva was patron of men at war, Apollo of the arts.   6. records] Kept in the Tower.   10. two headed hill] Parnassus, sacred to the Muses and Apollo.

On Pembrokes Languishing Diseas   Title] See *Upon the Perfume Pembrooke left*, p. 226, Title n.   6] Contemporary satires on Pembroke alleged his speeches were written by his secretary, he being capable only of swearing.   10. Saints] Here Parliamentary puritans, Pembroke's new colleagues, in general.

Upon Gutt A Greate Glutton   3. weene] think.   8. Tith] Tax of a tenth part.   9. black... corne] Either rolled black oats, or some kind of pulse, as in black-eyed pea, bean.   14. Struted] Strutted: full, distended: cf. *A Dedication to my Sonn Charles*, p. 135, l. 24 n.   18. guttling] A glutton (*OED*).   21–2] Cf. Luke 8. 37: 'Then the whole multitude of the country of the Gadarenes round about besought him [Christ] to depart from them.'   24. it—] ?sent.

The Prologue to the Dream   Some problems of interpretation in this and the following may be due to Wake, the copyist, not understanding the allusions.   1. Robd... fate] Referring to the death of Fane's first wife, Grace, in 1636.   1–2. long... Cock] He was left at his wife's death with two surviving daughters, Diana (b. 1627) and Frances (b. 1632), and a son, Charles (b. 1635). Cock] Small boat, but already meaning 'penis'.   3. *bottomes] Ships, or hulls: *OED* does not record the modern meaning ('The sitting part of a man') until 1794–96, but the apparent sexual pun on bottoms and yards suggests it may have been already current.   4. yards] Spars tranverse to the main mast, punning on 'yard', penis.   Ridg'd] ?Wealthy ('ridge' meaning 'gold', *OED* n2), punning (loosely) on 'rigged'.   5. Boughton] ?Referring to the family of Edward, Lord Montagu of Boughton (1562–1644), later to be Fane's fellow Commissioner of Array in Northamptonshire, and briefly his fellow prisoner in the Tower.

My Dream the 8 of September 1637   1. Downes] See *Upon Prince Charles*, Title n.   2. Pinass] Pinnace, a small ship, presumably punning on 'pin-arse' (pointed), not 'penis' (cf. 'pin-buttock', *All's Well* 2. 2. 18).   3 whelps] There was a series of at least ten royal ships called the (*Lion's*) *First Whelp* etc. (see e.g. *CSPD*, 1636–37, p. 55). This and later references confirm the *Dream* does not refer to Fane's second wife, Mary Vere/Townshend, who had two sons when he married her, 1638. 13. unvale] Unveil, reveal, but with secondary sense of 'vail', lower a ship's ensign as mark of respect.   29. Launtorne] 'Some part of a ship' (*OED*).   31. s' top] ?small top; or Wake may have read *f*' (for 'fore') as *s longa*; cf. l. 45.   42. yare] Sensitive to the helm, light.   44. Mysons] Mizen sails.   48. chase pieces] Cannon set to fire ahead or astern.   peack-head] Forepeak, foremost part of hold, in the angle of the bows.   49. Demy Can-non] Large cannon, about 6½ inches in bore; the hyphen suggests a Franglais pun.   Mignion] Small cannon.   murtherers] Small cannon or mortars.   51. Mison] Mizen.   54. third to the chaine] ?Third in rank. 54–5. first... Church] First-married.   58. ancient] ensign.   61. Happie Enterance and Swallow] The *Swallow* was a royal ship: see *CSPD*, 1636–37, p. 146.   62. Baga-cara] 'Dear Jewel'. 63. gully foysts] Galley foist, a light galley.   64. Eastar] East Star. See *Epilogue to the Dream*, l. 1. ?Punning on a name.   65. Joygn on.*] Fane's asterisk indicates an amendment that was never made.   66–70. Confidence... swiftsure] *Dreadnought*, *Defiance* and *Swiftsure* were actual as well as metaphorical ships: so perhaps was the *Confidence* (*CSPD*, 1636–37, p. 103).   72. Stamford heath] North of Apethorpe. Cf. *Sonnet* p. 269, l. 18 n.   deale-faire] 'Fair dealing', ?but also a fair at Deal, Kent, from where the maritime Downs are visible. 74. loost ofe me] Weighed anchor and left me. 76. *frighted] freighted; this spelling not in *OED*.

Epilogue to the Dream 1. East-star] Cf. *My Dream* above, l. 64. 3. seaven] Of the seven then known planets (including the Sun and Moon, excluding Earth). 4. Hecate] Triple goddess of the underworld, combining attributes of Persephone, Selene and Artemis (through the latter identified with the Moon: cf. l. 10).

Me nive Cadente petijt mea Julia Title] See Fane's use of same lines in *Me nive cadente petijt mea Julia*, p. 58, Title n. *Ovid*] Not found in Ovid.

Unto a Lady Title] '*On a scornfull La:*' in *Index Libelli*. 1. Be-vile] Punning on 'Bevill': Essex Bevill (d. 1658), daughter of Essex Rich and Sir Robert Cheke, married 1 Sir Robert Bevill of Chesterton, Huntingdonshire, and 2 (1642) Edward Montagu, second Earl of Manchester. 4. rich] Her grandmother Penelope Devereux (Sidney's 'Stella', sister of the second Earl of Essex) married Robert, Lord Rich, 1581, and had seven children (possibly by Rich), one of them Essex's mother, and five more with her lover, Lord Mountjoy, with whom she lived openly from 1601, and whom she married 1605 after a questionable divorce from Rich. Calfe and *Margin.* Es.] An 'Essex calf', used contemptuously of natives of Essex (cf. 'Essex girl'). 5. Trull] 'drab, strumpet, trollop' (*OED*), referring to her mother, not Penelope, as might be expected ('dam' is always thus, and ll. 6–8 confirm). 6. Bull] A cuckold, because horned. 9. P[ir]goe] Essex Bevill's father, Sir Thomas Cheke, lived at Pirgo, Essex. 13. uncoupell] Let hounds loose to hunt. 15. Harts return] Stag's (and therefore cuckold's) horns. 15.1. *fronti rara fides*] Misquoting Juvenal II, 8: '*Fronti nulla fides,*' 'Trust nobody's countenance.'

Upon the Scotsh business—1638 Title] Referring to the first 'Bishops' War'; for Fane's (and his mother's) critical view, and for Fane's participation, see *Vita*, p. 41). 4. Sepratist] One wishing to separate from the established Church, and usually (as with the Independents) from all centralised Church discipline. The Scots were Presbyterians, with a clearly defined form of Church government; their separation was from the Laudian version of the established Church. 5. Covenant] The Scots subscribed to a National Covenant to defend Presbyterianism against the imposition of episcopal government and the Anglican Prayer Book in 1638. See *Epigram: Upon one Beal a minister*, p. 82, Title n. Conventicles] Church meetings. 9–11. Cope . . . Miter] Trappings of bishops in particular, and of Anglican and Catholic ritual in general.

Writ at the Campe at Birkes Title. Birkes] The English camp '3 miles from Barwicke [Berwick]': see 'jornall' of Fane's relative, the Earl of Rutland, 23 May 1639 (HMC *Twelfth Report*, Appendix, pt IV (24), I, p. 512). 2. Prime] Holding one card of each suit in the game primero, similar to poker. 4. vie] 'In card-playing: To make a 'vie'; to hazard a certain sum on the strength of one's hand.' (*OED*). set up the rest] Normally to stake one's last money (in primero); here, probably to forfeit the reserve stake agreed at the outset of the game.

The Pedegree of Bay Wastnes Title. Wastnes] *wastnedges* in *Index Libelli*. *Sir Hardolph*] Not identified. 8. Zein] ?sene: evidently. 10. train] 'Course or manner of running (of a horse)' (*OED*). 11. Crickett] A horse: see *A Caracter of Newmarket*, p. 102, l. 9. 15. *Cup-Carle] One who is greedy about winning cups. 16. soop-Stakes] Sweepstakes; cf. *Ham.* 4. 5. 143: 'soop-stake you will draw both friend and foe' (spelling from *Q2* and *Folio*).

Upon the Rebells assault Title. Rebells assault] Essex and Waller combined in May 1644 to take Reading, and their horse were then 'quartered about Wantage and Farringdon' (Clarendon, VIII. 37). *Cass*] ?Castle, or house (*casa*) apparently at Wantage (see next poem), a manor belonging to the Bourchier Earls of Bath. Henry Bourchier, fifth earl (c. 1587–1654), had married (1638) Fane's sister Rachel (1613–80). Although he and Fane were in the Tower together and allowed to 'go abroad in their Sedans instead of their Coaches', Bourchier was still owed £4,000 of his marriage portion in 1648, and seeking to have Fane's estates sequestered till it was paid: see *For Mr Conyers Darcy*, Title n. Lough Gear] 'Low gear': sexual organs, here esp. female: there is clearly sexual innuendo in ll. 6 and 8. 2. L. B.] ?Lord Bath. lough] low.

In Eundem supra manieriam suam De want-age Title] '*On the same as above: his Manor at Want-age*'. Lord B.] Bath (see previous poem and n.).

Commissioners for the Irish affaires 1–2] Referring to the transfer of responsibility for Ireland to the Lords and Commons, 1647, and subsequent proposals that Waller should command an army there, accompanied by parliamentary commissioners. 3] 'As far as I am concerned, those who want to can venture to gain lands.'   5. conquest muse] The proposal was that part of the New Model army, to be disbanded, should be sent to Ireland under Waller: the army objected, with Fairfax and Cromwell taking the army's part.   6] Luke 23. 34: 'Then said Jesus, Father, forgive them; for they know not what they do.' Fane's plea is for forgiveness of the massacres of Protestants carried out in the Irish insurgency of 1641–42. These had been greatly exaggerated in England, making his prayer all the more unusual in its humanity.

To Capt Fra[nk] Court[u]p A Huntsman   Title] 'To the Cunny burrough Elder or Fra: Court: a hunt:' in *Index Libelli.   Court[u]p*] Cf. *To Fran: Coortup*, p. 235. Courthope lived at Cobham, Kent (he rented land at Meopham) though the family lived at Brenchley, near Mereworth (Hasted, III, p. 360, V, p. 293).   14. Naso] Ovid.   20. Smock] Woman.   21. Agrippina's blood] Nero.   24–6] See *De Imperatorum Julianorum*, p. 71, ll. 7–10 and n.   29. Other] ?Domitian.   32. Biberious] Tiberius.   34. Didoes Paramour] Aeneas.   36–7] All post-classical figures who had associations with hunting.   41. *Sticking place] Hunting, where hounds are brought to a check, losing the scent.   44–5. warme . . . hole] Hunting, to find the quarry in its sett, but perhaps with sexual *double-entendre*.

To Sir Abram Williams upon his Barge   Title. Williams] Diplomat: after working in the office of Secretary Winwood, he became agent of the Elector and Queen of Bohemia. Knighted 1625, he was assessed at £50 in July 1643, and no proceedings were taken against him (*CCAM*, p. 194). His house in Westminster had been used by the Bohemian ambassador (Chamberlain, *Letters* II, p. 280) and continued to be used through the 1640s and 1650s, first for committee meetings, then for the entertainment of ambassadors by the Republican Council of State (University of Nottingham, Portland MS Pw2 Hy 37, September 1646; Masson, V, pp. 177–8, 247).   9. Olimpique Games] Recently revived in the Cotswolds by Robert Dover.   17. baite the Ground] Lay ground bait to lure the fish to the area.   18. *scull] Propel; not quoted in *OED* before 1850.   20. well] 'A cistern or tank in a fishing-boat, in which the catch of fish is preserved alive.' (*OED*).   26. Anteparistisis] Antiperistasis, the energy generated by opposition.

To my Lady Kat[herine] Scot   Title] Youngest daughter of the Earl of Norwich; she married William Scott, of Scotts Hall, Kent. He petitioned for divorce in 1656 on grounds of desertion and misconduct. Evelyn met her travelling to and from France ('that pleasant Lady, Scott', *Diary*, 16 July 1649, II, p. 560; 27 June 1650, III, p. 13).   16. *Margin. Blewcap*] A Scot: intended as a possible substitute, not a note; cf. *A Farcy*, p. 186, l. 7 n.   19. selfe denying ordinance] Passed December 1644, preventing members of either House holding simultaneously any other 'office or command, military or civil': it paved the way for the New Model Army by excluding Essex and Manchester from their commands.   27. Goldsmiths Hall] Where the Committee for Compounding with Delinquents met.   36–7. oblivion . . . pass] An Act of Oblivion was proposed in 1647.

To Fayre Mrs Doll Peckam   Title] Probably of Yaldham, Kent, neighbours of the Fanes at Mereworth. Hasted (V, p. 17) mentions a Dorothy Peckham, who married Thomas Chiffinch, but gives no date. This cannot be the future Keeper of the Closet and Keeper of the Jewels to Charles II, who married a Dorothy Thanet (*DNB*).   3. Boy] Paris, usually represented as a youth.   5. chaffer] bargain, haggle.

Out of Martiall   Title] Imitating rather than translating Martial.

To Fran[k] Coortup   Title] See *To Capt Fra[nk] Court[u]p*, Title n (above).   1] See W(A) Misc. 7, f. 41r, 22 December 1646: 'To Cap Coortops man brought me Cesar a hound & Bewty a beagle 0-5-0'. The name of the hound suggested the imagery of the poem; Fane stayed 'At Cobbam one night—in the house' at the same date the hounds were brought to him (W(A) Misc. 7, f. 41r).   3. *hardle] Normally 'hurdle', but here a group of hounds, ? a couple; cf. 'To Fra: Comptons man brought a hardle of dogs 00-5-0' (W(A) Misc. 4, p. 141).   5. Belloer-min] Cardinal Bellarmine, Jesuit theologian (1542–1621), here a stag in rut through a pun on 'bellower'.   15–16] Lucan (AD 39–65) wrote *Bellum Civile*, an epic on the war between Caesar and Pompey. As Smith points out, 'these lines [15–22] imitate those of Walter Ralegh, which prefaced Sir Arthur Gorges's translation of Lucan (1614)' (*Literature and Revolution*, p. 388). For Lucan's importance in the 1640s as a republican writer on civil war, see Smith, pp. 204–7; Norbrook, pp. 23–62.   22. Pharsalian field] Battle of 48 BC; Lucan's epic was often called *Pharsalia*.   23. venies] Thrusts or wounds in fencing.   27. this] The hound named Caesar.   27–31] The 'one book' was Lucan's

Pharsalia, of which Book 10 records (in Thomas May's 1627 translation, but not in Lucan's unfinished original) Caesar's escape from Pharos by leaping into the sea. 36–7. Gunner . . . Dutches] Apparently names of hounds.

To Mr T.T.   Title] Thomas Thornhurst (d. 1678), brother of Grace, Fane's first wife, and a co-trustee with John Holles, Earl of Clare, of his will. Thornhurst's eldest son was christened Mildmay.   2. Winfred] Winfrith Newburgh, Dorset: 'here was formerly an estate of about £100 per annum, belonging to the Thornhursts' (Hutchins, *Dorset* I, p. 437).   3–4. Tom . . . Christendome] Thomas Coryate, of Odcombe, Somerset: see *Upon the Strange adventure and memorable voyage*, l. 3 n.   7. storyes] Anecdotes: Thornhurst did not publish on his travels, but BL Add. 34,216 (one of the Westmorland manuscripts) contains his 'true relation of the land business at Lancerota, one of the Islelands of the Canaries, 1617' (f. 48).   8. surate] Surat, Bombay, where the English traded for calico.   9–10. Zodiack . . . car] Beneath the orbit of the sun.   11. Bantam] Town in Java, important trading centre.   Ormus] Near the entrance to the Gulf, a Portuguese trading centre.   16. Fullum] Fulham, a market-garden area in the seventeenth century.   27. Scottish Dove . . . Northerne Post] Newspapers: the *Scotch Dove* began 1643; there were several 'Posts', but John Nichols does not give a 'Northern' one in *Literary Anecdotes of the Eighteenth Century*, 1812, IV, pp. 33–53.   30. Diurnalls] Daily newspapers.   32. Chops] jaws.   34. Minshios Dictionary] John Minsheu's *Ductor in Linguas* (1617) gave the meanings of words in eleven languages. The copy in Sotheby's 1887 sale was the 1625 edition which had belonged to Charles I (lot 683). It is not clear how it reached Apethorpe, where it appears in the *Catalogue*.   39–40] Names of newspapers: *Mercurius Pragmaticus* (Royalist, began 1647), *Mercurius Britannicus* (Parliamentarian, began 1643) and *Mercurius Elencticus* (began 1648, later anti-Cromwellian).   42–4. sequestration] Referring to the threat, not the fact: in 1651 the Committee for Advance of Money assessed Thornhurst at £150 p.a., and charged him with engaging men of Dorset against Parliament in 1645. His estate was never sequestered, and he was discharged under the Act of Pardon in 1652 (*CCAM*, pp. 986–8).   44. hall] Goldsmiths' Hall, where the Committee for Compounding met.

To Rob[in] Oliver   Title] Neighbour (?and tenant) in Kent, twice mentioned in Fane's accounts: April 1647 'Receivd of Robin Oliver for yong Clark mare 7-0-0' (W(A) Misc. 7, f. 45v), and August 1649 'Received of Mr Robt Oliver £48-16-0 for my wood of 3 akres on Birling Hill' (*ibid.*, f. 73v).   2. touch] test (for 'silver' of l. 1).

Ad P.C.   Title. P.C.] Prince Charles.   *Post est occatio Calva*] 'Opportunity is bald behind' and therefore must be seized before she passes. Proverbial: cf. Tilley, T311, and Bacon, *Essays, Of Delay*: 'Occasion (as it is in the common verse) *turneth a bald noddle'*.   2. skeet] Shovel used to wet sails.   10. embay'd] Laid within a bay (suggesting this was not written when the Royalist fleet was waiting at the Downs: see *Upon Prince Charles*, p. 225).   23. yare] Sensitive to steer.

Upon my reaping Day the 28th of August 1648   Title] Called *My Hock-Cart or Reaping day* in Fane's *Index Libelli*, recalling Herrick's *The Hock-Cart, or Harvest Home To the Right Honourable, Mildmay, Earle of Westmorland* (101).   3] Cf. Herrick, 68, *Corinna's going a Maying*, 'the childhood of the Day has kept, / Against you come, some Orient Pearls unwept' (ll. 21–2).   4. Cf. Herrick, 25, *The Lilly in a Christal*, ll. 3–4.   16. Imitate the Ant] Be industrious and prudent: see Proverbs 6. 6–8, 30, 25.   20. furmety] Frumenty, a dish made of wheat boiled in milk and seasoned; cf. Herrick, *Hock-cart*, l. 34.   22. black Jack] Large leather beer jug.   26. *bacon peas] ?A dish of bacon and peas, similar to pease pudding.   31. Compartments] Divisions of troops, rather than the division of the fields suggested by Fowler (p. 226) following Brand, II, pp. 12–13.   32. Hock Cart] The last harvest waggon home.   41] Cf. Herrick, *Hock-cart*, l. 11.   43. Jack and Gill] Generic names for boy and girl: here the horses drawing the cart are dressed, as in Herrick, *Hock-cart*, ll. 11–12: 'The Horses, Mares, and frisking Fillies, / (Clad, all, in Linnen, white as Lillies).' Brand quotes a custom in Bedfordshire of choosing 'a Jack and a Gill' at the end of harvest (II, p. 16).   44. Serimonies mirth] The Harvest Home ceremonies involved a feast at which there was a levelling of social ranks.   50. Gill] Punning on *gill* as a half-pint measure (where a *jack* was a quarter of a pint).   Goldsburrough] 'my gent usher Gouldborow' (W(A) Misc. 15, f. 80r). Perhaps of the family of Anthony, of Stukeley Magna, Huntingdonshire.

A Letter to L.L. at Co.   Title] *A Letter to L.L. at Cob*: in the *Index Libelli*, suggesting 'Cobham'.

L.L.] Not identified: the poem is too early for it to be 'Lord Lichfield', Charles Stuart, first Earl of Lichfield (1639–72), who inherited the manor of Cobham in 1645.

Upon James Martins house at puttny being robd *Title*] *'To Will Martin'* in *Index Libelli*. *James Martin*] He died 1651 or 1652, aged fifty-four: see Latin epitaphs in *N*, ff. 18v, 30r, and his monument formerly in Putney Church (Daniel Lysons, *The Environs of London*, 1796, I, p. 412). He is perhaps the 'James Martyn of London Lynen Draper' who has a half-brother William in *Visitation of London* (1633–35), Harleian Society XIX (1884), II, p. 84. There are several visits to Putney noted in Fane's accounts, many connected with the Martin family: e.g. September 1648, 'To Puttny & back 0-6-0', followed immediately by 'To Mr Martins man ther 0-2-6'. The connection may have been via the Beecher family, since Sir William was also buried at Putney (Lysons, *ibid.*). If the *H.M.* of Latin poems in *F1* written in Paris is the radical republican Henry Marten (see *For A Treaty*, p. 221, l. 4 n.), then he may have been the link.   *his Brother*] William, a traveller in Persia (see *William Martin*, p. 274, l. 4) and the East (l. 9). A William, elder half-bother of James, is described as 'of Lincolns Inn' and married to Martha, daughter of John Collyns of High Laver, Essex, in *Visitation of London* (see above). In July 1656 Fane sent 'a Buck to W. Mart' (W(A) Misc. 4, p. 111).   1. start] In hunting, to start an animal from its lair.   3. *Canalers] ?'Canaillers', a rabble (*canaille* was spelt 'cannale').   12. O.Q.P.] 'Occupé'.   12.1. Vita Proba] 'The Virtuous Life'.

Robin for Poesy to a wedding ring   3. that] The ring, symbol here of the female sexual organs, as is the 'O' of l. 5, where 'P' therefore stands for Penis or Prick.

My Dedicatory at the end of Beaumont and fletchers playes   Not printed in the 1647 folio edition of Beaumont and Fletcher, but inscribed in Fane's own copy (see l. 19 and *A Summons to Frank Beumonts Gost*, p. 224, *Title* n.)   2. surfrages] Suffrages, both prayers and tokens of approval.

Upon Ben Jonsons Playes   Fane's copy of the 1616 Jonson *Workes* is now in the Beinecke Library, Yale University. This poem is written in Fane's hand inside the front cover (see also *In Obitum Ben: Jhons[on]*, p. 88, *Title* n.). Fane also owned Jonson's copy of Samuel Daniel's 1602 *Works* (Sotheby's, 1887, lot 334; *Catalogue*, 74, f. 24v); it was sold again (Christie's, 5 December 1906, lot 225), its whereabouts now unknown: see David McPherson, 'Ben Jonson's Library and Marginalia', *SP Texts and Studies* (1974), p. 39.

Loves Affirmative   5. geer] jeer, taunt.   22. pudder] Dialect form of 'pother', turmoil, commotion.

F. The L.M.   *Title*] *'Odi prophanum &c.'* in *Index Libelli*.   *L.M.*] There are numerous possible Lord or Lady Ms in Fane's circle, including his second wife Mary, Lady Margaret Cavendish, various Lords Montagu and members of the Manners family.   1. dietyes] deities.   1–4. *Margin*] 'I hate the profane crowd and keep them far away.'   19. Lesbian] Pliant, accommodating (not used to indicate female homosexuality before the nineteenth century).   22. Cliffe] Clef.   Eights] Eighths, octaves.

Ad Rem Publ[licam] Bel[lum] Civil[em] reparantem   *Title*] *'For the republic, again preparing for Civil War.'* This is the title given to Horace's Ode I. 14 in John Bond's 1620 Horace, which Fane owned (Sotheby's, July 1887, lot 394). This poem is a loose and much expanded imitation.   1–5. *Margin*] 'O ship, new waves will carry you out to sea again. O, what to do?' (ll. 1–2). For Fane's choice of withdrawal from the second Civil War, see Cain, 'A sad Intestine warr', pp. 27–32.   10. Cordage] rigging.   11. Nereus] Sea god.   35. boult sprit] bowsprit.   37. *Pilacy] Pilotage. Cyclades] Aegean islands, around Delos.   42. noe neere] 'No near!': 'a command to the helmsman to come no closer to the wind' (*OED*).

Upon Lamb[er]ts repo[rted] to be Gen[eral]   *Title*] *'The use of Ramms in our modern warrs'*, *Index Libelli*.   *Lamb[er]ts*] John Lambert (1619–84), officer under Fairfax, a courteous and efficient minor Yorkshire gentleman with 'a subtle and working brain', he took temporary command of the Northern Army in 1645 when Fairfax became Lord General.   *s.x. before*] Essex resigned his overall command following the Self-denying Ordinance (for this abbreviation, cf. *9.3.18.22.20.17.1.3*, p. 120).   3–4] A 'hornwork' was a type of fortification.   5] Essex had been humiliatingly cuckolded by Frances Howard in 1606; Lambert's wife, Frances Lister (a relative of Fairfax), was less reliably said to have had an affair with Cromwell.

Sonnet Feb: 1659   1. Munks] General Monck entered London, with his Scottish army, the only effective military force left intact, on 3 February 1660 (1659 O.S.). His intentions remained unclear, but Henry Marten's remark that the advance of Monck's army was like a man coming with a pickaxe and a spade to make a suit of clothes neatly summed up the suspicions of radicals.   3] Monck ordered the readmission of the 'secluded members' on 21 February.   7. St George] Monck's Christian name was George.   12. shend] shield.   17. Pride-inspird] Pride's Purge in 1648 expelled around 140 MPs unsympathetic to the army, leaving a 'Rump' of more reliable members; it was these secluded MPs whom Monck ordered to be readmitted, paving the way for the Restoration of Charles II.   23. *Covant] Variant of 'covenant'.

To welcome home Veronia   Title] 'To the Spring on a may day' in the *Index Libelli*.   Veronia] Fane's second wife, Mary Vere: cf. *Upon the Lady of my second adventure Verania*, p. 97 and n.   30. wives delight] ?Not a plant name but a collective epithet for the flowers previously listed.   34. savin] Poisonous evergreen shrub.   43. Kitt run-by-street] Somerset and Kentish name for the *viola tricolor*, the 'litle pancy' (Geoffrey Grigson, *The Englishman's Flora*, 1955, p. 71).   44. Party per pale] See *An Independents Coate Blazond*, p. 214, l. 1 n.   52. 'cause . . . under] 'Because its appearance is less striking.'

Senes bis pueri   Title] 'Old men boys for a second time'.

Cogit amare Jecur   Title] 'The Liver drives to love'.   Lyvor wort . . . love] Liverwort, a name applied to various plants with liver-shaped leaves or parts, was used (because of these shapes) to treat diseases of the liver. In early medicine the liver, not the heart, was the seat of love. Hence it could be used as a love potion.   3–4] Latin *livor*, envy.

Upon a course in the padock   Title. Toun[send]] Fane's stepson: see *To H.T. into Norfolk*, p. 208, Title n.   Will[iam] Spen[cer]] William (1630–88), third son of William, second Baron Spencer, married Fane's ward Elizabeth, daughter of Dutton, third Baron Gerard. His father had founded races at Northampton, 1632 (Hore, II, pp. 127–8)   1. Pricket] Buck.   6. pincht] Bit, seized with teeth (cf. *OED* s.v. *pinch v*3).   7. seen in] Versed in; cf. *Tam. Shrew* 1. 2. 134, 'Well seen in music'.   12. *come ofe] 'come off', apparently to follow, come second to, but not in *OED* in this sense.

Upon the Generall the Lord Fairfaxes resigning   Title] On 25 June 1650 Fairfax resigned as Lord General rather than invade Scotland.   4. Itom] Item, here part of an inventory.   18. Rowland . . . Oliver] See *An invective against Gould*, p. 219, l. 28 n.   23. R—] Rope.

Ad Geo: Fane: in commemorationem natalitii Reg. Car: 2^{di} Title] 'To George Fane in commemoration of the birthday of Charles II, written in the little cell colloquially called Le Grotto, the evening of 28 May 1650'.   Geo: Fane] George (1616–63), Fane's brother, of Callington, Cornwall, and St Andrews, Holborn, a colonel of horse in the Royalist army. In 1640 one of those 100 MPs who offered to 'stand engaged' to the City for a loan to finance the army in the north, preventing the King from dissolving Parliament. In the 1650s he was, like Mildmay, borrowing from Lord Brudenell: see Brudenell I. x. 11 and 12.   Le Grotto] Probably the undercroft below the 'Despenser Room' on the south-eastern corner of Apethorpe. It has 'a high barrel vault with plain ribs and jewelled bosses' and had independent access from the garden (*Country Houses*, p. 65).   16–19] Charles was born 29 May 1630. On that date in 1650 he was at sea, sailing for Scotland after agreeing to take the Oath of the Covenant, and by so doing effectively betraying Montrose to execution.   32. bush] Bushel, under which praise would be concealed (cf. Matthew 5. 15).   35. King Ralphs wine] Ralph King was the vintner who kept the New Exchange tavern in the Strand in 1659; 'Ralph' is also apparently the name of the (?same) host at the Sun tavern in 1652 in *An Invitation to R. H: to change the Citty Life*, p. 261, l. 68.   40] The Trojan War was said to have lasted ten years.   42. now . . . man] A year later the Scots Parliament declared his twenty-first birthday the day of 'the King's Majestic Majority'.   53–5. Albano . . . Verdea] Italian white wines.   58–61. Margin] Added between the Latin and English versions, which are on facing pages.

A Ballet 3: September 1658   Title. Ballet] Ballad.   *3: September 1658*] The date of Cromwell's death.   2. O Hone] Ohone, Scottish and Irish cry of lamentation: 'Alas'. (*OED*).   3] Richard succeeded his father immediately as Lord Protector.   4. Prick-Eard] Roundhead, Puritan.   10] The new council was made up of a number of powerful figures such as Fleetwood, Thurloe and Desborough, not all of whom supported Richard.   13. Parlement] A new Parliament was called in January 1659.   15. Spruce] Prussia, which with other European powers was at war with Sweden at the time of Oliver's death, threatening his Protestant League. Richard was under pressure to assist the Swedes. 17. *Wrangle] Dispute: first recorded thus 1797 (*OED* 3). 23] Probably referring to special taxes to raise £252,000 for support of the armies in Scotland and Ireland. These still left a large shortfall after the forced dissolution of Richard's first Parliament, leading to the recall of the Rump in May 1659. 25] Referring both to the Protestant League and to the continuing war with Spain in alliance with France. 27. souldiers and Clowns] The 'army party' led the opposition to the 'clown', Richard.

Of Man to W[illiam] Ar[mine] Title. Ar[mine]] See *An Ode sent into Scotland to a frend*, p. 119, Title n. 10. Common-place] Topic or text cited in an argument or academic exercise.

To a frend from Apthorp Title. Margin. Jan—6: 1650] Twelfth Night. 4. mainprize] Legal surety. 5. Peak] In Derbyshire, near to where, at Aston, Fane's brother Francis lived. 8. Scithia] Scythia, Russia. 9. couler] colour. 10–12. Grampion . . . Cheveot] Mountains: the Grampian range and Ben Lomond in Scotland, and the Cheviot in Northumberland. 14. Pole starrs badge] Snow: the Pole Star is within 1° of north. 15–20] Referring to the Twelfth Night festivities.

The North Wind 1. rife] Full of disease or bad smells. 2] Lambert crossed the Firth of Forth into the Royalist stronghold of Fife and defeated the Scots at Inverkeithing in 1651. 4. General] Probably Cromwell, who remained seriously ill in Edinburgh.

Upon the rumor of his departure Title] Rumours that Cromwell had died in Scotland reached England in March 1651: cf. *The Diary of Ralph Josselin*, Camden Society, third series, 15, p. 81. 10. Atropos] The Fate who cuts the thread ('Loom') of life: see '*He who such strong lines wont compose*', p. 62, l. 2 n.

The Rump Title] Supplied from *Index Libelli*. 1. Tom C:] Thomas Challoner (1595–1661), republican and regicide, 'as far from a puritan as the East from the West. He was of the naturall religion . . . and one who loved to enjoy the pleasures of this life' (Aubrey, I, 159). He travelled, before the war, in France, Italy and Germany, was MP for Richmond (1645) and Scarborough (1659), when he became member of the new Council of State; exempted from the Act of Indemnity and Oblivion, he died in exile. Margin. Jan: 1659] In January 1660 Challoner was again elected to the Council of State, but the position of the republicans was growing weaker. 5. Trading . . . Citty's] Clearly a euphemism for (vaginal) sexual intercourse, but neither the whole phrase or 'City' for vagina is in *OED* or Partridge.

To the Countess of Exeter Title] Frances Manners (1630–69), daughter of John, eighth Earl of Rutland, married John Cecil, fourth earl, 1646 (only five weeks after her death he was to marry Fane's daughter, Mary, January 1670). brach] bitch-hound. 41. Margin. Thies] Thighs: the anagram is loose even by Fane's elastic standards.

A Ballet To x.x.x. Title. x.x.x] Fane's abbreviation for 'Exeter', here John Cecil, fourth earl: see *To Phi: Wood upon my Lady x x x*, p. 264, n. wittring heath] South of Cecil's Burleigh House, on the route to Apethorpe. 1. Lucrine Lake] Saltwater lake on the coast of Campania, near the Bay of Naples, famous for oysters in classical times. 9. Geering] ?Gyring: revolving, rather than 'jeering'. 10. *A stand] A-stand, hesitating at (*OED* s.v. *v stand* 68.c.). hawkes] fish traps. 19. Frank-Ly] Punning on Frances (see *To the Countess of Exeter*, above, Title n.) 36. Phil: wood] ?Of the Woods of Overston, Northamptonshire, descended from Sir John Wood, and related to the Mildmay family. 37. chirping cup] A drink producing cheer, chirpiness. 40] Proverbial; Tilley, S584. Eating snakes kept one young: *OED* quotes Fletcher, *Elder Brother* 4. 4: 'That you have eat a Snake, and are grown young, game-some, and rampant'. 43. chapeau-bas] Hats off (command in presence of King etc.). 45. Bridgwater] John Egerton (1622–86), succeeded as second Earl of Bridgewater 1649. He was the Elder Brother in *Comus* (1634). A Royalist, he was arrested for a short time in April 1651. His sister Elizabeth Egerton was at this time the dowager Countess of Exeter. noble spouse] Elizabeth Cavendish, daughter of the then Earl, later Duke of Newcastle. 51. huffcap] See *Harrison's Description of England* (1577), ed. Furnivall (1877), I, p. 295: 'There is such headie ale and beere in most of them, as for the mightinesse thereof, among such as seeke it out, is commonlie called huffcap, the mad dog, father whoresonne, angels food, dragons milke.' 53. Neckar] The river Neckar, tributary of the Rhine. Coblins] Koblenz. 59. Sanadrim] Sanhedrim, court of justice in Jerusalem, of seventy-one members. Cromwell's House of Lords, theoretically of seventy members, was sometimes so called. 69. Gardo] Lake Garda. 74. meer] Whittlesey Mere, as Fane's footnote indicates. See *An Ode to N.B.*, p. 113, l. 51.   81–4] Apparently referring to the limits placed on Fane while under house arrest: see *Brook House Bay trees*, p. 70, n. The Cecils are not recorded as having any influence over this relaxation of conditions: the fourth earl was only fifteen when he succeeded in 1643.

To Cleveland before the first interview at maneby   Title] John Cleveland (1613–58), strongly Royalist poet, became Judge Advocate for Newark *c*. 1645, and on the evidence of this poem stayed after the surrender of Newark with Stephen Anderson (see l. 30), of Manby, Broughton, Lincolnshire, the second son of Sir Francis.   3. rank-wingd] strong-winged.   7. *anvile*] Cf. *Upon Ben Jonsons Playes*, p. 240, ll. 25–8. 38.1.   *Carmina cecessum*] 'cecessum' makes no sense: Fane may have mistranscribed his own 'cesserunt' ('The verses have finished'). Cleveland's reply implies that a number of poems were sent (see following note) and were not signed: 'Could you think (my Lord) that your suppressing your Name was able to conceal you, when it is easy to wind you by your phrase?' *Clievelandi Vindiciæ; or, Clieveland's Poems, Orations, Epistles; &c.*, 1677 ed., p. 152; cf. Thorn-Drury, *A Little Ark*, pp. 16–18, in which these two poems were first printed.

To Him again in return for a letter   Title. *letter*] Cleveland's fulsome reply was published in *Clievelandi Vindiciæ* (see note to previous poem). He was 'stupid with Ecstasie. . . . lost in Amazement . . . Such is the Strength and Spirit of your Phancy, that methought your Poems (like the Richest Wine) sent forth a Steam at the opening. What flowed from your Brain fum'd into mine. It was almost impossible to read your Lines and be sober' (pp. 150–1).   1. bird] The peacock, traditionally vainglorious; Fane will avoid such a response despite being told he was 'the Favourite of the Muses. Your Strain is so happy and hath the Reputation for so Matchless, as if you had a double Key to the Temple of Honour' (p. 151).   4. Humms] Hums, used at Oxford and Cambridge to express approbation.   10. Leviathan] Hobbes's 'mortal god' in whom 'consisteth the essence of the Commonwealth', here the commonwealth of the arts (*Leviathan*, chapter XVII).   11–12] *Leviathan* was published in England in mid-1651; for Fane and Hobbes, see Cain, 'A sad Intestine warr'. Fane's copy of Davenant's *Gondibert* (1651) was described as having 'MS. Verses on Hobbes, Waller and Cowley, by Earl of Westmorland' (Sotheby's, 1887, lot 229).

An invitation to my Askanius   Title] '*An invitation to Geo:*' in *Index Libelli*.   Askanius] Ascanius, son of Aeneas.   true Trojan] A good drinking companion, but also by this time a good man in general.   1. George] Fane's brother; see *Ad Geo: Fane*, p. 248, *Title* n.   6. Sir walter Earles] MP for Weymouth, an ally of Pym, and captain of horse in the Parliamentary army. In 1641 he correctly accused George Goring, governor of Portsmouth, of treason to Parliament. Goring, a convincing liar, was thanked by the Commons for his loyalty.   10. the West] George Fane lived in Callington, Cornwall.   33. *Troy-novant*] See *Upon the Strange adventure and memorable voyage*, p. 206, l. 6 n. George's London house was in St Andrew's, Holborn, the parish where Cleveland was buried.   39. Bring Hellen] George's wife was Dorothy Horsey.   julus] Alternative name for Ascanius, whose son was in fact called Silvius: but the *gens* Julia claimed its descent from Ascanus/Julus. George's only son was Henry.

A Ballet of Dedication of the new Academy   Title. new . . . Gates] Fane built on and around the Tudor gate tower at Apethorpe, apparently including a new music room; much of this work was destroyed in eighteenth-century remodelling. Cf. 'the resounding Musick Room' of *An Invitation to R. H: to change the Citty Life*, p. 261, l. 84.   Phil: Wood] See *A Ballet To x.x.x.*, p. 254, l. 36 n.   5. Vialls] At this date the normal spelling of 'viol' as well as a glass vessel.   8. steeple Flute] Tall wine glass.   13–14] Ovid tells how Pan made pipes out of the marsh reeds ('calamos palustres' rather than 'oaten quill') into which the nymph Syrinx was metamorphosed just as he caught her (*Met.* I, 698–712).   15. Tritons Trumpets] See Ovid, *Met.* I, 330–47.   17–20] Arion, a Greek lyric poet, was thrown overboard by sailors, but was saved by dolphins charmed (unlike the sailors) by his music.   21. Orpheus] For the power of Orpheus's music, see Ovid, *Met.* X, 40–8.   22] The giant Cyclopes were, in some accounts, Vulcan's assistants, making the armour of the gods: the music is that of their rhythmic hammering, following Virgil, *Georgics* IV, 174–5 ('tollunt in numerum').   25. Juball] 'Jubal . . . was the father of all such as handle the harp and organ . . . Tubal-cain, an instructer of every artificer in brass and iron' (Genesis 4. 21–2).   27. Gammuths] Scales, the whole range of notes recognised in music; cf. *To Sir Jhon Wentworth*, p. 79, l. 103 n.   34. Toun wayghts] Town Waits, municipal wind band.   37. *High boyes]

Hautboy, the modern oboe.   38. Sack-butts] Forerunner of the slide trombone.   *shugg] ?shog, to jog along, thus here to keep a steady rhythm as bass continuo.   39. Base . . . Curtell] Curtal, a short, bassoon-like instrument.   49–50] over . . . power] According to Aeschylus and Euripides, Orpheus could move stones, trees and animals by his singing.   59. *tribe] Associate, gather together in a tribe: not in *OED* as an intransitive. verb, and only from 1696 as transitive.   63. Foxes] *OED* quotes Nashe, *Pierce Pennilesse* (*Works*, ed. Grosart, II, 82): 'The eighth [kind of drunkenness] is Fox drunke, when he is craftie drunke.' Cf. *To H. T. into Norfolk*, p. 208, ll. 23–4 n.   75. billa vera] Medieval and Legal Latin; a 'true bill' is an indictment found by a grand jury (see l. 73) to be supported by sufficient evidence to justify the hearing of a case.   80. back gates Tower] See above, *Title* n.

Upon Dabbling or Fishing   *Title. Dabbling*] In the sense of recreation, indulging.   8. watt] Hare.   9–10] Evasive tactics by the hare: *OED* quotes Markham, *Country Contentments* I. 1: 'The Huntsman cunning to undoe intricate doubles, Skips, Squats and windings.'   23. noe waise Hunting] An ellipsis, 'in no wise *have* hunting' or 'hunting *was*'.   34. warping] Bending, causing to deviate.   40. *Layd * Perdue*] To lie or set perdue: to wait in ambush.   49. Chirping Cup] See *A Ballet To x.x.x*, p. 254, l. 37 n.   54. mall-us] ?maul us, injure us.   56. Tom Flint] Flint glass, a particularly fine glass made from ground flint. First *OED* quotation is 1675.   60. Portall Dormitary] ?A sleeping place within a gatehouse or partitioned off in a doorway; hence a place of disturbed rest.   61–5. Bird . . . chaff] Proverbial; Tilley, B396: 'Old birds are not caught with chaff.'   67. Brindases] Brendices, cups for drinking toasts.

An Invitation to R. H: to change the Citty Life   *Title. R. H*] Fane's *Index Libelli* identifies him as Robert Harley: 'To invite R. Harl: to a Cuntry life'. This must be the younger Robert (1626–73), formerly major in the Parliamentary army. Like his father and brother, he became a Royalist in the 1650s. He was MP for New Radnor 1647 and 1660, FRS 1661 and Chancellor of the Caribee Islands 1662–64. The elder Sir Robert (1579–1656) is precluded by his age, health and stern Presbyterian values, none of which make it likely that (unless complicit in raising Presbyterian hypocrisy to new heights) Fane would suggest he was taking stolen pleasures in the park (ll. 57–8). The lack of a title also points to his second son, not knighted until 1660.   *April 8. 1651*] W(A) Misc. 4 shows that Fane was then at Apethorpe.   6. *Circulation] The making of the magic circle, within which the conjuror was safe from the spirits he raised. Cf. *OED* 4. Here, the walls of London.   11. Cube] Used, like circles and other figures, in conjuring.   21. Jabals . . . tents] 'Jabal: he was the father of such as dwell in tents, and of such as have cattle,' (Genesis 4. 20).   23. Presumptions] Legal term for seizure of an office or powers without right.   28. guive the Ball] As sign of victory, derived from the golden apple Paris gave to Aphrodite.   32. come in with] Share a nest with.   40. rack and manger] Amidst plenty and profligacy.   45–6] Cf. Marvell, *Mower against Gardens*, ll. 31–2: ''Tis all enforced, the fountain and the grot; / While the sweet fields do lie forgot.'   59. Ruff . . . Picadill] Both forms of elaborate collar, but 'ruff' was also a card game and 'picadill' a pecadillo. Piccadilly itself was unpaved and scarcely developed in 1651.   60. Rook] Cheat.   68. Sun] The Sun tavern, of which there were at least three in London. Fowler (p. 254) quotes Peacham on the prostitutes who were the 'overhot and crafty daughters of the Sun'.   Ralph] Apparently the landlord at the Sun, and a vintner. Probably Ralph King, for whom as 'King Ralph' see *Ad Geo: Fane*, p. 248, l. 35, and *A Pepper-corn or small rent sent to my Lord Campden*, p. 277, l. 51 n.   72–4. signe . . . good] The proverb 'A good wine needs no bush' (Tilley, W462) was derived from the vintner's sign of a bunch of ivy.   76. Bear] The Bear at the Bridgefoot: see *My adventure, or a new discovery under the Bear*, p. 104, *Title* n.   80. Stillyard] The four-acre headquarters of the Hanseatic League, on the London bank, just upriver from London Bridge, and now the site of Cannon Street Station. There must have been some kind of tavern there, since Fane spent the large sum of £4 17s 6d (the annual salary of a middling servant in his household) 'At Stilyard' in June 1652 (W(A) Misc. 4, p. 21).   83–4] The journey by river from Westminster to London Bridge passed the theatres of the Bankside and Blackfriars (then closed) and brothels.   84. accost . . . Duke numps] 'As you come level with St Paul's'. From Duke Humphrey's [Nump's] Walk in Old St Paul's. It may be the prostitutes, or the booksellers there, who are the 'Tribe'.   85. cast] ponder.   91. ho-mul-ho] The 'music' of hounds, rather than the huntsman.   98. Harpsicon] Harpsichord; Fane paid £3 10s 'For mending the harpsicon & stringing it' in January 1651, and another 8s 'for mending a Harpsicon' in April 1655 (W(A) Misc. 7, f. 92r, and 4, p. 87). 98–100. Flute . . . Vaynes] The same play on a flute glass of wine as in *A Ballet of Dedication of the new Academy*, p. 258, l. 8. 102. Ela] Highest note in the gamut. 120. Count] The Speaker was obliged to 'count out' the House of Commons if fewer than forty members were present.

To Phi: Wood upon my Lady x x x going To London Title. *Phi: Wood*] See *A Ballet To x.x.x.*, p. 254, l. 36 n. *Lady x x x*] Lady Exeter: see *To the Countess of Exeter*, p. 252, *Title* n. 10. knack] Trick, device. 11. Cross-buckleing . . . armes] With arms folded. 12. meditating Charmes] Both thinking up spells to bring her back, and meditating on her personal charms. 22. Princes] Princess. 23. Wher] For 'We're'. 25. Hob] Robin Goodfellow, usually synonymous with Puck, but here a separate mischievous hobgoblin. Puck the Mare] A goblin which induces nightmares. 27. Reaks] Tricks, pranks. 33–4] Echoing the closing lines of Herrick's *The Hock-Cart* (101): 'Not sent ye for to drown your paine / But for to make it spring againe.'

Ode: My Valedice to x x xr going to London Title. *Valedice*] Farewell. 7. Jubelise] Celebrate a jubilee, here in sense of a time of reprieve or amnesty. 9. Fivety years] Fifty years was the interval between the original Hebrew and contemporary Catholic years of jubilee.

In Obitum and transportationem per Wainsford Corporis Title] '*On the death and transporting through Wainsford of the body of my dearest friend William Armine, Baronet*'. *Armine*] See *An Ode sent into Scotland to a frend*, p. 119, l. 1 n. Armine's death was marked with ceremony at Westminster by the Council of State, of which he was a member. They ordered that his body should then be transported for burial to his home in Osgodby, Lincolnshire, 'according to the civilities due to a person of his condition' (*DNB*). *Wainsford*] Wansford Bridge, near Apethorpe: see *Upon the Strange adventure and memorable voyage*, p. 206, *Title* n. It was probably a stopping place for the procession (hence *per*, 'through', not 'to').

To Phil: Wood at London Title. *Phil: Wood*] See *A Ballet To x.x.x.*, p. 254, l. 36 n. 5. winter Tropick] The point where the sun is farthest from the equator in the northern winter. 21. Burley] Burghley House, home of the Earls of Exeter.

To the same after return 3. Dodonas grove] Site of an oracle, whose answers were given by the rustling of the trees, and the brass vessels hanging from them.

Rosseus Vaticinus Title] '*Ross the Prophetical*'. Translating Fane's acrostic Latin text, the initial letters of which spell ROSSEUS. John Manners (1638–1711), later Earl of Rutland, styled Lord Ros or Roos between 1640 and 1649, was involved in a famous divorce between 1666 and 1670. Cf. *Upon a hunting match defeated by wett weather wher I was to have met my Lord Ros*, p. 348), dated 1656, where he is called 'John' (l. 9). 4. Chaugh] Chough, at this date any of the members of the crow family, especially the jackdaw: crows were traditionally associated with augury. 6] Roos's wife was Anne Pierpoint (1631–c. 1696), daughter of the Marquis of Dorchester: an Act of Parliament of February 1667 made her children illegitimate.

The Ivy—twine Title] Sacred to Dionysus, and therefore twined around the thyrsus: here, a symbol of entwined bodies (see ll. 27–9). 1–2. Margin] 'Let us live, my Lesbia'; opening words of Catullus V, of which this is an imitation. 5. rank-wingd] strong-winged, fast. 6. Trusses] Seizes in its talons. 12. Platonick] In sense of spiritual, contemplative love; there had been a cult of platonic love associated with Charles I and Henietta Maria in the 1630s, and Stanley published his translation of Pico's *Platonick Discourse upon Love* in 1651, around the same time as this poem was written. 29. Eglantine] Here as symbol of a less purely carnal love: Herrick uses it to remind that 'He who plucks the sweets shall prove / Many thorns to be in Love' (*The bleeding hand: or, The sprig of Eglantine given to a maid*, 88.1).

Upon the Castle in the Ayer and Bower of Bliss Title. *Castle in the Ayer*] Common for fantasising, day-dreaming, since *c.* 1575. *Bower of Bliss*] Derived from Spenser, *Faerie Queene* 2. 12. 42–87, but here a place not of intemperance but of 'harmless merth' (l. 13) that has more in common with Herrick's visionary *The White Island: or place of the Blest* (376.5), but which takes on implied political dimensions in ll. 34–42. 12] Spenser's Bower is approached by water, but a closer analogy is Herrick, 'In that *Whiter Island*, where / Things are evermore sincere' (*The White Island*, ll. 9–10). 25–30] A question: 'Who . . . arts?' 23–4] The lovers in Spenser's Bower are ambushed and circumvented by Guyon and the Palmer: *Faerie Queene* 2. 12. 81–2. 31. *Margin*. Flint] A flint glass; see *Upon Dabbling or Fishing*, p. 260, l. 56 n.

Sonnet 6. boult . . . Cunny] To drive a rabbit from its burrow; apparently a saying, cf. J. Guillim,

Heraldry III. xiv (1660), p. 166: 'You shall say Bowlt the Cony' (*OED*).   sack the brocks] Catch (and put in a bag?) the badgers.   9. Watt] Hare.   11. Stoick] Because standing still while the hawk flies, punning on Latin *sto*, 'I stand'.   12. Carear] The flight of a hawk.   18. Stanford doun] Stamford Down, north of Apethorpe; Fane was at 'Stanford horse match' in March 1652 (W(A) Misc. 4, p. 39). Cf. his hounds on 'Stamford heath', *My Dream the 8 of September 1637*, p. 228, ll. 71–2.   19–49. Cripple . . . Sorrel] The names of various horses.   52. Holl's of age] Sir Horatio Townshend, Fane's stepson: see *To H. T. into Norfolk*, p. 208, *Title* n. He came of age in 1651.

The second part to the same tune   13. lap] drink.   18. Fennick] Fenwick, a horse which Fane sold to 'my Lord Campden' for £30 'in Gould' in March 1652 (W(A) Misc. 4, p. 14).   19. Brother . . . Nett] ?Fellow fisherman.   23. chirping-cup] See *A Ballet To x.x.x*, p. 254, l. 37 n.   25. Peg] A local tavern keeper or ale-wife: cf. 'Peggs lodg' dispensing 'huffcap Ale', *A Ballet To x.x.x*, ll. 44–6.   27. Saint George] The English war-cry, but here slang for a half-crown (*OED*, 4).   28. apowder and amain] Impetuously, at full speed (racing for Peg's Lodge).   29. St Jhon] Either Oliver St John (see *For A Treaty*, p. 221, l. 4 n) or, since this seems extravagant behaviour for a Presbyterian Lord Chief Justice, one of his three sons.   Bob] Among neighbouring gentry, possibly Robert Brudenell, later second Earl of Cardigan. There are many Roberts in Fane's circle.   34. Ale-stoops] Vessels containing ale.

Upon Buck[ingham']s and his Duch[ess']s Visiting Apthorpe   Title] Duk. & Duch: kind visit in *Index Libelli*. Fairfax's daughter Mary (Marvell's pupil) had married the Duke of Buckingham in September 1657 (cf. *To Mistress Mary Fairfax sayd to be married to the Duke of Buckingam*, p. 343). Cromwell opposed the match, since it involved a dangerous Presbyterian–Royalist alliance, and was forwarded as such by the Harleys and Lady Vere, Fane's aged mother-in-law. Warrants for the couple's arrest were issued in October, but do not seem to have been enforced, probably because of Fairfax's intercession with Cromwell. Buckingham later lived under restriction in London, but was arrested in 1658 (Fairfax having an angry meeting with Cromwell as a result) and he and Mary were not together again until 1659. The visit to Apethorpe may thus have been in November 1657, or in or after 1659. The poem is added in the bottom half of the page (*H*, p. 127) and was certainly copied in later than those before and after it. The *Index Libelli* entry also appears to have been added late. Mary was fairly soon discarded in favour of Buckingham's mistress, Anna Maria, Countess of Shrewsbury, daughter of Fane's friend Robert Brudenell, second Earl of Cardigan (see *To a P.K: that sent to me for 2 Peeces*, p. 316, *Title* n.). Pepys said in 1668, describing Buckingham's duel with the Earl of Shrewsbury, that she had then been 'for a great while' Buckingham's 'whore' (*Diary* IX, p. 27).   4. *Plunders] *OED* does not record this plural use.   10. En passant . . . pransing] The heraldic 'passant' could be described as 'prancing', which here also means 'dancing'.   20. ratefy] confirm, guarantee.   25. Frends] Used of close relatives (such as a neice and nephew).

Frendships Salamander to x. x. x.   Title. Salamander] Able to withstand fire (cf. ll. 1–5), the mythical lizard became an emblem of constancy.   x. x. x] John Cecil, fourth Earl of Exeter; see *A Ballet To x.x.x*, *Title* n. He was twenty when the second Civil War began, but he and his mother had led the defence of Burghley against Cromwell in 1643 when he was only fifteen.   6. incorporate] united (*OED* v6a).

Ad Protectorem   Title] 'To the Protector'. January–30–1653] i.e. 1654; Cromwell became Lord Protector on 16 December 1653; many Presbyterians and moderate Royalists saw his installation as a practical necessity. He in turn sought to conciliate his opponents; on 19 January 1654 the Council of State repealed the Act of 1650 requiring subscription to the Engagement of Allegiance. It may well have been this that prompted Fane's conciliatory poem. See also Cain, 'A sad Intestine warr', pp. 48–50.   5–6. Olive . . . anoynted] The Latin version puns on *Oliva* and *Olearis*.   6. lenatives] Soothing medicines or ointments.   8–9. Helmet . . . Bee] Cf. Sir Henry Lee, *'His golden locks time hath to silver turned'*, l. 7: 'His helmet now shall make a hive for bees' (*New Oxford Book of Sixteenth-Century Verse*, ed. Emrys Jones, Oxford, 1992, p. 432).

Upon the death of my Good nag: Fox   2. Sanadrim] Sanhedrim: see *A Ballet To x.x.x*, p. 254, l. 54 n.   7. Launds] Glades, pastures.   *Circumvalls] Things which circumvallate them, i.e. form a barrier around them.

An Epigram upon His Highnes entertainment   Title. entertainment . . . Citty] The banquet in the

Grocers' Hall, 8 February 1654. See Bulstrode Whitlocke, *Memorials of the English Affairs*, 1682, p. 564. This (though a translation) is by far the most conciliatory of all Fane's treatments of Cromwell; his brief flirtation with republicanism was over by February 1655 (see *Veritas Odium parit*, p. 274). 6. Rooms Gods afright] 'Presage' of general policy intentions: in October 1654 Blake's success in the Mediterranean caused fear of an English invasion of Rome; the Pope paid £14,000 in reparation for English shipping seized by Prince Rupert. 9. Triple Tirants] ?King of Spain. 10. three-crownd God] The Pope; cf. *A Farcy*, p. 186, l. 98 n. 11. Brittish Queen] Britannia, a personification of Britain since Roman times, though not appearing on English coins until 1672. 13. Blew Gods] Of the sea. Naydes] Naiads, here sea nymphs, daughters of Nereus and Oceanus. 14. Thams] Thames. 15. New Troy] London: see *Upon the Strange adventure and memorable voyage*, p. 206, l. 6 n. 25. Conquring ... deaf] From the classical proverb 'Victi non audent hiscere', 'The conquered dare not speak'. 26. change ... Lawes] Cf. Cicero, 'Cedant armæ togæ,' 'Let arms give place to laws,' *De Officiis* I. 22. 82. 27. Gowne] Of the law-giver (Cicero's *toga*, previous n.). 29–31] The Platonic year was that complete cycle in which all heavenly bodies would go through all possible movements and thus return to their original positions: hence, a return to the beginning of time, a new start, and a new Golden Age. 30. Great Apollo] As god of the sun. 32. Saturne's] The reign of Saturn coincided with the golden age of Italy. 32. Sol] The sun, ?punning awkwardly on Ol[iver].

De Regulo Title] 'On Regulus'. 1. *Rubbedge] Rubbish (this spelling not in *OED*). 9. (Regule)] Fane has left the Latin vocative, indicating its extraneous status by brackets.

William Martin Title] Of Putney: see *Upon James Martins house at puttny being robd*, p. 239, Title n. 1. Pullin and Tompson] Booksellers: Octavian Pulleyn, active 1620–67, was a warden of the Stationers' Company; in partnership with George Thomason at The Rose, St Paul's Churchyard, 1636–66. Fane bought £10 worth of books from him in December 1656 (W(A) Misc. 4, p. 121). Samuel Thomson (d. 1668), was at the White Horse, St Paul's Churchyard, then the Bishop's Head, Duck Lane. 2. Frankford Mart] Frankfurt had long been a centre of book-buying. 5. Persian Travailer] For Martin's travels, see *Upon James Martins house at puttny*, ll. 9–10.

Veritas Odium parit Title] 'Truth gives birth to hatred'. Horace] Found in Terence, *Andria* I. 1. 41, not in Horace, but, as Cicero implies, it was proverbial (*De Am*. 24. 89). Cf. Tilley, T562, 569. Februrary: 1654] By February 1655 anti-Cromwellian Levellers and republicans as well as Royalists (sometimes in collaboration) were planning armed resistance: Overton, Harrison and other republican leaders were arrested in December and January, and abortive Royalist risings, of which Fane may have known something in February, were to take place in March, in Yorkshire and the south-west. 2. soe little] Truth. 6. Brew] The idea that Cromwell had once been a brewer was part of Royalist mythology.

A Dialogue between a Hunting Swayn and a Shepardes 4. blanch] Make white. 16. Great Pan] Here, Charles I. 32] For the war, and the death of the King, as a punishment for the people's sins, see *Preces et Lachrimæ Sanctorum Oblationes*, p. 306, ll. 7–12. Cf. Cain, 'A sad Intestine warr', pp. 45–7. 42. tuft the thicks] In stag hunting, to search the thickets to start a deer.

Two Seafaring men invoak the Springs return 9. Phosphorus] Morning Star. 11. propostrous] Unnatural, out of place. 12. Arturus] Arcturus, the Great Bear, also called Charles's Wain, hence 'yong Arturus' is Charles II.

To my Lord of Portland Title. Portland] Jerome Weston, second Earl of Portland (1605–63), committed Royalist, compounded on surrender of Wallingford 1646, and thereafter lived at Ashley House, Walton-on-Thames, until the Restoration. By August 1661 he had been restored to his pre-war estates and offices. Cole] Not identified. 1–4] See *Upon The great Mercy of God*, p. 162, l. 20 n.

A Pepper-corn or small rent sent to my Lord Campden Title. Campden] Baptist Noel (1611–82), third Viscount Campden (1643), of Campden, Gloucestershire, and North Luffenham Manor, near Apethorpe, which he defended against Parliamentary troops of Thomas Lord Grey (see *Upon the Lord Gray of Grooby yellow haired*, p. 340, n). Kensington] Campden House, Kensington, built c. 1612, was burnt down in 1862. It was in the area now bounded by Kensington Church Street, Gloucester Walk and Sheffield Terrace, the original estate being around 100 acres. Shown in a drawing by John Thorpe (c. 1590–1600) and, somewhat altered, with the garden approach described in ll. 143–7, in a painting of c. 1660 (both in *Survey* XXXVII, pl. 39). During the Protectorate used briefly by the Committee of Sequestrations for Middlesex. *Februar: 1651*] Fane notes 'My Jorney to London and back', his only entry under 'Disburcements' for February 1652 (£22 9*s* 6*d*, W(A) Misc. 4, p. 13). By 25 February he was at Mereworth (*ibid.*, p. 12).   11] William Camden, teacher, herald and antiquary, author of *Britannia* (1586), had no connection with the Noel family.   16. sphere] Of the heavens, moving around the globe.   18–20] Thomas Faulkner, *History and Antiquities of Kensington* (1820), mentions 'the globe room' in the east wing (p. 417), possibly so called because it contained a globe, or map projections of the continents (l. 24). Faulkner describes the history and interior and exterior of the house, but not its paintings (pp. 414–30).   26. Forbisher] Sir Martin Frobisher (d. 1594).   32–6. Mandevile . . . Corriott] Travel writers; cf. *Upon the Strange adventure and memorable voyage*, p. 206, l. 2, 3 nn.   36. Sands] George Sandys, whose *A Relation of a Journey* (1615) dealt mainly with the Ottoman empire.   37–40. fowr Seasons . . . Provinces] Paintings of the seasons, often with studies of seasonal national dress, were common. Hollar produced both costume and topographical series of Seasons: see *The Strasbourg Views* and his two series of portraits of women, full and three-quarter length (*Hollar*, pp. 40, 78–81).   37. Mustred] Both 'displayed' and 'brought together'.   41–2] Paintings illustrating times of day, especially night scenes, internal and external, were popular in Dutch and Flemish painting. Much of Campden's collection sounds as if it was of Netherlandish origin.   43. men in Arms] Cf. the series of men-at-arms painted on the panels of the wainscot in the Pages' Room, Clifton Hall, Nottinghamshire, *c*. 1632–33 (Croft-Murray, pp. 114, 211).   44. Sybells Charms] There were varying numbers of Sibyls, prophetic figures of whom the most famous was that of the oracle of Apollo at Cumae. Their 'Charms' were their ecstatic prophecies (cf. Virgil, *Aeneid* VI, 77–102), written out in Greek hexameters, but here also perhaps the charms of the female figure. Series of Sibyls were often assimilated with Old Testament prophets, most famously by Michelangelo in the Sistine Chapel, more modestly among the fifty-two figures in Bradninch Church, Devon (Croft-Murray, p. 169).   45–7. Fam'd Poets . . . Entry] Either portraits of the classical poets or '[hi]story paintings' of their subjects, hanging in the ante-room to the hall or dining room. In 1574 Queen Elizabeth's barge was painted with 'five stories of poetry' (*ibid.*, p. 181).   51] Echoing Jonson, *Inviting a Friend to Supper*, l. 30: 'Which is the Mermaid's, now, but shall be mine'. For Ralph as vintner and landlord at the Sun tavern, see *Ad Geo: Fane*, p. 248, l. 35, and *An Invitation to R. H: to change the Citty Life*, p. 261, l. 68.   53. Flora's seat] Dwelling place or temple of the Roman goddess of flowers.   54. Tablets] Paintings on wood panel, here of flowers.   56. Tom Piper] Bagpipers were a popular subject in Netherlandish art; Van Dyck's *Francois Langlois* was a recent (*c*. 1635) variation on the theme. 'Tom' is used generically for a man of the people.   58–61] Perhaps a lutenist in the same picture, or a separate painting.   59. Lesbian] Orpheus, whose disembodied head was washed up on Lesbos, still singing. Cf. *A Ballet of Dedication of the new Academy*, p. 258, l. 21 n.   62–5] Paintings of a maid and a sempstress, both found in Dutch art: see e.g. Schama, *Embarrassment of Riches*, pls 173, 187, 198, 200.   62. Netefy] Make clean, from 'net', to clean.   65. postures] Postures of domestic virtue instead of the sexual ones (*Figuræ*) of Pietro Aretino.   66] A St Jerome the penitent, usually portrayed nearly naked and kneeling before a crucifix (l. 68).   Coole] Cowl.   70. Maudlen] Mary Magdalene. As a penitent, eyes filled with tears, she was a popular subject for baroque art even in Protestant England: Donne owned a version.   73. Turkish Bride] Unidentified: there was a fashion for paintings of sitters in exotic costume, such as Van Dyck's *Teresia, Lady Shirley* (Petworth).   77–81. Guarter . . . Partners] There are numerous such representations: Fowler draws attention to their significance for defeated Royalists, and to Peter Heylyn's *The History of . . . St George* (1633) and Elias Ashmole's *Order of the Garter*, illustrated by Hollar (1672). Fane and his brother Francis were Knights of the Bath, but not of the Garter.   83–5] Probably, as Fowler (p. 243) suggests, a Dutch Protestant piece like Cornelis Cornelisz. van Haarlem's 'A Monk squeezing the Breast of a Nun', in the Hals Museum, Haarlem; an illustration of Aretino's *Ragionamenti* (1534) is also a possibility.   84. probation] 1 The nun's probation as novice; 2 the Monk's try at seduction; 3 his palpation of the breast as in a medical examination.   86. ston-bow] A crossbow that fires stones; it seems also to have had a phallic meaning now lost, probably as the shaft which fires the seed from the 'stones'.   89. Fish-market] There are numerous Dutch paintings from the sixteenth and seventeenth centuries, best known of which is van Ostade's later *Fish Seller* (1672), Rijksmuseum, Amsterdam.   90–1] In Ovid's version (*Met*. I, 588–750) Io is raped by Jove, who turns her into a heifer to hide the deed from Juno. Aeschylus, *Prometheus Unbound*, 561–887, stresses the long wanderings that ensued. The myth was interpreted in terms of a journey to maturity.   92–3] A series of portraits of Lords Chancellor. The last had been Sir Richard Lane (d. 1650); from 1646 to 1660 the office was in the hands of a committee.   98. Roe] Sir Thomas Roe (1581–1644), friend of Donne and Jonson, one of the first Englishmen to explore the Amazon (1610–11). He was ambassador to the Great Mogul in India (1614–18), and to the Ottoman empire (1621–28). He was on close terms with the exiled Queen of Bohemia, who is apparently included in the painting (l. 103).   105–11] Referring both to the general prohibition of music in services and to the destruction of concord in the country at large.   107. red-Coats] Parliamentary soldiers: red had been adopted throughout the New Model Army from its inception.   114. Coign] Corner.   116. Pallas] Pallas Athene, protector of intellectual and moral life, and of agriculture: hence her sway is over the civilised world.   129. Pedri-commess] '*Commesso di pietre dure* or Florentine mosaic' (Fowler, p. 244).   135. Gratio's street] Gracechurch Street, centre of the poultry trade (l. 136); cf. 'Gratias streete', *His answære to the Caroll*, p. 202, l. 20.   136–7. Phesant ... Plesant] Herrick uses the same rhyme in *A Christmas Carroll to the Earle of WestmoreLand*, p. 202, ll. 21–4.   143–7] The paved way which led to the house.   143. Claudian ... Appian way] The via Appia was built by Appius Claudius Cæcus; Livy describes its paving (X. 23. 12, XXXVIII. 28. 3).   149. Lion] The lions on the gateposts, from the Noel arms, were either replaced by or mistaken for dogs when Faulkner described them in 1820.   159–60. Pictur'd ... Fishes] Garden statuary (Fowler, p. 244).   172. Mausolean] Mausoleum-like, hence large and costly.   176. Grottos] Fowler notes the fashion for these (p. 244); Fane had one at Apethorpe: see *Ad Geo: Fane*, p. 248.   180–3. Fortunes wheel ... sisters] Inlaid in the pavements or the walls of the grottoes, or painted on the latter.   185 virgin hand] ?One of Noel's four daughters (Fowler, p. 244).   186. Limning] Painting in water-colour.   189. Rubin] Rubens.   191. Dure] Durer.   192–3. Gelthrop ... her] George Geldorp (*c*. 1590–1665), minor portrait painter, trained in Antwerp, worked in England from the mid-1620s. A friend of Van Dyck, of whose work he made 'numerous copies' (*DNB*), he employed Lely on the latter's arrival in England.   193. hang ... draw] Punning on the gruesome elements in the death penalty; Geldorp was derided by some contemporaries (Sandrart, cited in *DNB*, says he had to trace portraits from others' drawings), and is an anticlimax after the previously named painters.   195–7] Pallas Athene, jealous of Arachne's skill at tapestry, turned her into a spider (Ovid, *Met.* VI, 1–145).   199] See *To Mr T.T*, p. 236, ll. 7–11, n.

Wrot the 5^t of November-1657   9. to th'Pot] To be destroyed, as meat is cut up for the pot.   20. brewing] For Cromwell's alleged brewing, cf. *Veritas Odium parit*, p. 274, l. 6 n.   21. Pride] See *Sonnet Feb: 1659*, p. 245, l. 17 n. Cromwell had knighted Pride in January 1656.   27–8] Cromwell's second Parliament had been summoned in September 1656, with no second chamber. Sixty-three writs for a new 'House of Lords', with members nominated by Cromwell, were sent out around the date of this poem. Eleven hereditary peers were invited, Fane not among them (for a list, see Masson, V, 323–4). Cf. *In Domum Parlementi Alteram*, p. 339.

Upon our Lady's Day   Title] Lady Day, 25 March, was until 1752 (1599 in Scotland) New Year's Day.   5. red] Read, i.e. known by God, the potter.   13. Selected Vessel] The Virgin Mary.   20. medson] medicine.   28–9. Commemorate ... Adore] Steering an Anglican course between puritan rejection of the Feast of the Annunciation and Catholic 'adoration' (worship) of the Virgin.

Upon an Eclips of the Sun the 29th of March-1652   Title. 29th of March-1652] An eclipse ('Mirk Monday') was recorded in Scotland on 8 April 1652.   6. Naturalls] Lunatics (from *luna*, the moon).   7–8. Lucina ... a-bed] The moon, goddess of childbirth.   10. Mountain ... mouse] Proverbial for much effort with little result; Cf. Horace, *Ars Poetica*, l. 139; Tilley, M1215.   15. mare-rid] In the grip of a nightmare.   18. Middsummer] Time of madness, through association with the moon.   19–20. stray After] Search for.   22. foot man ship] Skill and speed in running.   26. furlong] Part of an unenclosed field.   32. Cinthias] The moon's.

Corporis Anima Tutela   Title] '*The soul, the guardian of the body*'.   10. imbayd] Laid up, sheltered, in a bay. Cf. *Ad P.C.*, p. 237, l. 10.

Upon my Sonn Charles return   Title. Charles] Fane's eldest son: see *A Dedication to my Sonn Charles to Him that made him*, p. 135, Title n.   2. years travailes] For Charles's departure see *At Dover the of June-1652*, p. 286.   *Brabant*] The Duchy of Brabant, of which Brussels was the chief city. 5–6. livery . . . Shrief] The figure of the seasons being dressed in appropriate livery is common: cf. *MND*, 2. 1. 111–3, *Paradise Lost* 4, 599. Here, the livery is that of the officers of the High Sheriff of a county.   16. Isack] See Genesis 22. 1–13. Fane had made a similar dedication at Charles's birth: see *A Dedication to my Sonn Charles*, ll. 33–6.

Upon Good Friday   Title. Margin. at Aston] Yorkshire, home of Sir Francis Fane. See *The like in Medly for F.F.*, p. 99.   6–7] Cf. Aeschylus, *Agamemnon*, 176: '[Zeus] fixes fast the law that pain is gain.'   9] Cf. Matthew 25. 24–6.   20. cast] Found guilty.   29. Cark] Burden, vex.

In Pascam 1652   Title. Pascam] *Pascha*, from the Paschal Lamb eaten at the Jewish Passover; hence Christ, the Lamb of God slain at Easter.   5. peevish] malignant.

At Dover the of June-1652   *Title*] The date is left blank in *H*, but Fane's accounts show he was at Dover for three days in June 1652 (W(A). Misc. 4, p. 21).   *sonn and nephew*] Charles (see *Upon my Sonn Charles return*, p. 284) and Charles Gerard (*To my Neph[ew] Gerr[ard]*, p. 328).   1. Margin. Dij maris et coeli] 'Gods of the seas and skies'.

To the Suns accosting our Troppick   Title. April: 19-1654] Cf. *Ad Protectorem* (p. 272, January 1654) and *An Epigram upon His Highnes entertainment* (p. 273, 8 February 1654), which both take a generous tone towards Cromwell.   13. Tagus] The river Tagus, in Portugal, was supposed to bear gold: cf. Jonson, *Poetaster* 1. 1. 75, translating Ovid, *Amores* 1. 15.   15. Inds] India's.   20. purple Violet] Cf. Herrick, 262.1, *Upon Prew his Maid*: 'From whose happy spark here let / Spring the purple Violet' (l. 4).   24. O-liver] ?Emphasising the liver as the seat of passion: the praise seems ironic, but cf. note to the title.

Upon William Sharp   Title. Collier] In Northamptonshire not a miner but a carrier of coal or a charcoal burner.   *Moulhill*] Emphasising the smallness of the hill.   15. Jossel] Jostle, struggle. 46. Pipkin] Small earthenware pot.   in folio] large.   47. Olio] Spanish stew of many ingredients.   48. smackt] flavoured.   60. Italian Shugg] ?A jerky gait (*OED* s.v. *shog v3*). Cf. *A Ballet of Dedication of the new Academy*, p. 258, l. 38.

Upon the horse race at Newmarket   Title. 1652] Races were to be forbidden in 1654 because they were rightly felt to cover Royalist meetings, but continued without royal patronage until then. Fane did well at this meeting: 'won at Newmarket horsematch 20-0-0 /Received of Sir Horace Townshend ther 100-0-0 /Recieved at Stifkey of Felton and Drury 100-0-0 /Received of my Lo: Campden for Horaces bet as due to me for rent from him 50-00-00' (W(A) Misc. 4, p. 30). *Earle of Suffolk*] James Howard, third earl (1618–88), succeeded 1640; one of the peers who remained sympathetic to Parliament, he became High Steward of Ipswich, 1653. For his Newmarket career after 1660, see Hore, II, pp. 260–7.   *Horatio Tounshend*] See *To H.T. into Norfolk*, Title n.   Margin. *Cock Lawrell*] Cock Lorell, ballad about the supposed King of the Gypsies; Jonson uses the same metre for the Cock Lorell song in *Gipsies Metamorphosed* (ll. 1061–137), a performance of which at Burley-on-the-Hill or Belvoir Fane may well have attended in 1621.   4. *Cracks] The context suggests it may mean 'predictions' (tips), or even 'bets'; cf. *A Caracter of Newmarket*, p. 102, l. 7.   8. non plus] State of being unable to answer: ?slang for defeat in academic dispute at Cambridge.   12. Northumberland] Presumably Algernon, tenth earl (1602–68), a contemporary of Fane's at Cambridge, and as MP in the 1620s. He was arguably the most influential peer on the Parliamentary side in the 1640s, but remained largely aloof from public affairs throughout the Commonwealth period.   12. Silver sides] A cut of beef; here apparently of Pegasus's flanks.   14. stoop] Starting post; cf. *A Caracter of Newmarket*, l. 6   24. Oes] Small round spangles.   29. Wallsingam] Apparently a rider or trainer for Suffolk. He should not be against Norfolk because the village of Walsingham is in Norfolk.   30. Norfolk] Probably for Townshend, for whose estates at Raynham and Stiffkey see *A Jorney into Norfolk*, p. 116, ll. 58, 84.   40. clinch . . . prick] Quibble or pun, rather than wound.   41. Neighbour] ?Campden, from whom Fane won £100 (Title n.).   48. Skars-dale] ?Francis Leek, first Earl of Scarsdale (before 1581–1655). His grandson was a keen rider at Newmarket (Hore, III, pp. 28, 369).   49. dampe] Depression: Dugdale (quoted in *Peerage* XI, p. 517) says Scarsdale was so mortified by the King's execution that he had his own grave dug, and lay in it every Friday. Clarendon says he had 'a very unusual and unpleasant face' and presents him as a squalid, reclusive miser (*History* VI, 60).   Jack] Not identifiable.   55. the Barronet] Townshend.   59. Barb] Barbary horse.   60. *seese] Pay up: from 'Seize', put in possession of (legal term, *OED* s.v. *seize*

VI). 61. Sir Cotton] Sir Thomas (1594–1662), or Sir Robert, Evelyn's friend. In 1663 Charles wrote to Sir John Cotton, eldest son of Sir Thomas, about the ground at Newmarket (Hore, II, p. 246). Soams] One of the Soame family of Great Thurlow, Suffolk, relatives and probably patrons of Herrick, who addresses poems to Sir William (131.1), his brother Sir Thomas (176.1) and Stephen (199.1). 65. Russels] For the Russells of Chippenham, Cambridge and their Newmarket connections, see Hore, II, pp. 36–40. 68. throw... Caster] The caster throws the dice: thus, here, either to bet against the bookmaker or simply to 'throw the dice', meaning to bet. 73. Sir Ned] Sir Edward Harley; see *A reveille-Matin Ode*, p. 159, *Title* n. Elder] Because of his zealous Presbyterianism. from London] Harley had been ordered not to return to his home in Herefordshire for ten years from 1650 (*DNB*). A letter of September 1651 shows he had been staying with Fane, and had been 'lately in Norfolk' (*CSPD*, 1651, p. 449). 78. Sir Sim]. The reference to a 'record' (l. 77) would suggest Sir Symonds D'Ewes, antiquarian and parliamentary historian, if he had not died 1650. ?Sir George Simeon, of Brightwell, whose daughter married a keen horseman, Lord Mountgarret (Hore, II, p. 255); 'his Poet' is similarly elusive.

additional or 2ᵈ part   4. *Barly-corn-broth] Strong ale (*OED* and Partridge give *barley-broth*). 5] Names of jockeys. 8] For the proverb, see *Upon Dabbling or Fishing*, p. 260, ll. 61–5. 9. Bignall and Desborow] Also jockeys (rather than John Desborough, Cromwell's brother-in-law). 12. post... Pudding] A post rider in haste for a pudding.

In Effigeiem Urbani Octavi Papæ præterit Title] 'On an effigy of Pope Urban the Eighth'. *Urbani Octavi*] Maffeo Barberini (1568–1644), became Pope 1623. A reformer and politician, he probably most disturbed Protestant Englishmen by his assiduous cultivation of Henrietta Maria, through whom he hoped to re-establish Roman Catholicism in England. The effigy may have been an engraving after the bust by Bernini, of whom Urban was the major patron. 2. Eight ... man] *The Seven Sages* was a collection of Oriental tales which became immensely popular in medieval and early modern Europe. An eighth sage (because of Urban's numerical designation) was a fool.

In Effigiem Innocentij Decimi nunc Papæ 'On an effigy of Innocent the Tenth now Pope'. *Innocentij Decimi*] Giambattista Pamfili (1574–1655), Pope from 1644, implacable enemy of his predecessor's family. The effigy may again be from Bernini's bust, but the most famous image is that by Velazquez in the Galleria Doria (and hence those by Francis Bacon). 6] Varying the proverb 'If the devil be a vicar, thou wilt be his clerk' (Tilley, D285).

In Rempublicam Title] 'On the Republic'. 1. Commonwealths... sway] Following the battle of Worcester (September 1651), England was ruled by the Rump Parliament and a Council of State elected by the Rump. 2] By 1652 Ireland and Scotland were both under Parliament's control, the Royalists had been defeated at Worcester, and the naval war with the Dutch had begun.

In Cardinalem Wolsæum Title] 'On Cardinal Wolsey'. 1. Laicks] Members of the laity. 3–4. Fathers... grain] Wolsey's father was said to have been a butcher. 7. Shambles] Slaughterhouse.

In partem Capitis vicessimi primi S[anc]ti Mathæi Title] 'On part of St Matthew Chapter 21'. *vicessimi primi*] Matthew 21. 1–11 describes the entry into Jerusalem commemorated on Palm Sunday. *Margin*. Palm Sunday fell on this date in 1653.

Upon suspition of the Gout to Doc[to]r Bowles Title. Bowles] Mentioned several times in Fane's accounts attending the family, and in a letter to Brudenell in which Fane excuses himself from attending Charles II's 'winter coronation': 'ther is likely to be a greater separation between me and my wife by her desperat sicknes to which Bowles dares not warrant a Recovery but being for London himself hath advised her to hazard going that he mought have the assistance of other Phisitians' (Brudenell I. x. 20, 17 December 1660). There was a family of this name at Scampton, Lincolnshire, of whom Robert Bowles was admitted as fellow commoner, Sidney Sussex, 1634, succeeded as Baronet 1648 (Venn). 6. one member] The Latin version is annotated 'Cattzo' (penis).

Upon a Gent: calld F.F. and his Kittling Title. F.F] ?Francis Fane, Mildmay's brother (see *The like in Medly for F.F, Title* n.), or the former's son, also Francis, b. 1637. 3. 'cause] Apparently 'to cause' rather than 'because'. 5. best] ?beast. 7. Pregnant abroad] Circulating abroad. 10. Towsing] Tousing, handling roughly, 'To pull (a woman) about rudely, indelicately, or in horseplay' (*OED* s.v. *touse*, *v*). 13. Gib-cat] A cat, here a woman who acts like an adult, and possibly bad-tempered, possibly promiscuous, cat.

Upon the Lady Margaret Marchioness of Newcastle Title. *Margaret . . . Newcastle*] Margaret Lucas (1624?–74), m. 1645 in Paris the Marquess of Newcastle. She visited England in the late 1640s, and may have met Fane then.   *Poems . . . 1652*] Fane must have received his presentation copy early: 1653 is the date of publication for *Poems and Fancies*, and it is the 1653 edition that is listed in the Apethorpe *Catalogue*, and in Sotheby's, 1887, lot 701 'with MS. Sonnet by the Earl of Westmoreland on fly-leaf'.   4. Nine] The Muses.   6. Twin-like Hill] Parnassus.

Upon a Time it did befall   4–5] The cloisters of St Peter's Cathedral, Peterborough, and part of the Bishop's Palace, were demolished and sold 1643–51, and bought by Oliver St John to build Longthorpe Hall (see *Thorp Pallace a Miracle*, p. 341).   8. Lawe] St John was Lord Chief Justice of the Common Pleas.

Both Creame O'th'Poets   This epigram refers to the preceding Latin poem (of which it is not a translation), *Vida Anagram Diva*, on Marco Girolamo Vida (1480–1566), Bishop of Alba, born at Cremona, Latin poet and author of orations and dialogues, *De Arte Poetica* (1527) and *Christias* (1535).

Upon the History of Great Brittan by Willson   Title] Arthur Wilson (1595–1652), follower of the Earl of Essex and subsequently of Warwick, wrote *The History of Great Britain, being the Life and Reign of King James I* (1653).   2. Clark O'th'Kittchens] Weldon, for whose *Court and Character of King James I* see *To the County of Kent*, p. 97.   9. Quainter] More refined.   mess] Prepared dish.

Upon the Death of Mr Jhon Selden   Title. *Selden*] 1584–1654, jurist, friend of Jonson, Donne, Camden, Cotton and Hobbes. Fane may have known him through Amabella, widow of his brother Anthony, who married Henry, ninth Earl of Kent, 1644. The widow of the seventh earl (he died 1639) was Selden's mistress, said by Aubrey to have married Selden secretly. Fane's copy of Selden's *Titles of Honor* (1614), previously Rowland Woodward's, is at Fulbeck Hall.   1. Symon Dews] Symonds D'Ewes (1602–50), a Cambridge contemporary of Fane, antiquarian and diarist of the House of Commons.   4. Patron of Antiqueties] Selden built up a huge library, most of which is now in the Bodleian, and was, like Cotton, important to the Parliamentarian side in his theorising over precedent (cf. l. 6).   6. President . . . will] Playing on 'president' and 'precedent'; not used in sense of head of state of a republic until 1787, but the title of the chairman of the Council of State, and associated in various senses with the idea of a 'governor' from early date. It was not considered as a title for Cromwell, 'King' or 'Lord Governor' being the mooted alternatives to 'Lord Protector' (see next poem, l. 10).

[Set up under the Gen[eral's] Picture at the Chang]   Not by Fane; the poem is also found in British Library MS Harl. 3991, without Fane's *Answer*.

An Answer to it   3. Gregory] The hangman, after Gregory Brandon, hangman under James I, who was succeeded by his son, Richard.   Snittles] Nooses.   4. Hammon] Haman, hanged in the apocryphal Book of Esther, 7. 9–10.   8. Axe and Block] Reserved for the nobility.   11. Citts] Citizens.   12. Capps on] The black cap of the sentencing judge, and the flat cap which was the sign of the citizen.

Shrove Teusday 1654. when Fra[ncis] Palmes came   Title. *Fran[cis] Palmes*] 1607–54, fourth son of Sir Guy, of Ashwell, Rutland, and Lindley, Yorkshire. Matriculated from Wadham 1623, aged sixteen; barrister, Middle Temple, 1634, married Mary, Fane's sixth daughter. He died the year of this poem; she later (1670) married John, fourth Earl of Exeter.   Margin] *'I came, I saw, I conquered'*, Julius Cæsar, quoted in Suetonius, *Divus Julius* 37. 2.

To the Impudency of Monsieur de Militiere   Title. *Militiere*] Théophile Brachet de la Milletière (1588–1665), originally a Calvinist theologian and delegate to the Assemblée Politique at La Rochelle in 1620. He rejected Presbyterianism in 1645 with a *Déclaration* defending his conversion. *The Victory of Truth for the Peace of the Church, to the King of Great Britain; to invite him to embrace the Roman-Catholic Faith* (The Hague, 1653) must have been available before its published date, since it was answered by John Bramhall in 1652: *An Answer to Monsieur de la Militiere his impertinent Dedication of his Imaginary Triumph*.   8. Milier] Perhaps for scansion; Latin version ends 'Militiere vale'.

At Newmarket horse race   Title. *Rookes*] Swindlers, cheats.

To Will Martin   Title. *Will Martin*] See *Upon James Martins house at puttny being robd*, p. 239. 8.1. *quoniam brevipes*] 'Since then short-footed'.
To Mr Levite of Ashwell   Title. *Ashwell*] Ashwell, Rutland, home of Fane's son-in-law, Francis Palmes (see *Shrove Teusday 1654. when Fra[ncis] Palmes came*, p. 294, *Title* n.).   *Tribe*] The descendants of Levi (Genesis 29. 34) became a priestly caste: hence a priest or deacon.   1. aswell] Punning on 'Ashwell'.   by name] Probably Levet or Levit. None of that name are found as Vicar of Ashwell, but among several priests one (Francis) became Rector of Little Carlton, Lincolnshire, 1661; another (Ralph) was Rector of Grainsby, Lincolnshire, 1635 (Venn).   2. Profession] Used in particular of a domestic chaplain (from Micah's Levite, Judges 17. 7–13): this Levite is therefore likely to have been Palmes's chaplain.   4. Aron] 'Aaron the Levite' (Exodus 4. 14), Moses's half-brother, was the Chief Priest of the Israelites.   4–6] As long as Moses held up his hands, the Israelites were able to prevail in their battle with the Amalekites: when he got tired, Aaron and Hur held his hands up for him (Exodus 17. 12).
Anagram   Title. *OPORTET C.R.*] 'C.R. is necessary'.   1–2. *Margin*] 'Catiline lives again.'   2. C.R.] Carolus Rex, for Charles II.   5. lave] ?Empty, pour out (*OED* s.v. *lave* VI, 3–4).   7. Fin] Fiend.   13. Heneries] Henry VIII.   14. Jameses] James I.   25. Marses frye] The children of war.
Sent to W. Cope   Title. *W. Cope*] Colonel William Cope (1612/13–91), of Icomb, Gloucestershire, married 1643 Fane's sister Elizabeth.   *Monke . . . Army*] See *Sonnet Feb: 1659*, p. 245.   *the Owld cause*] Normally used by republicans and Cromwellians, but here the cause of King and bishop.   4. Tippetts] Silk bands worn around the neck to hang down from the shoulders, over a surplice. Rochets] Bishops' surplices.

F3: Fulbeck Hall MS. Poems, 1649–65

Solus Deus protector Meus] 'God alone is my protector'. This motto is on many of Fane's books, sometimes on the spine in the form 'SDPM'.
Nulla Dies sine Linea] 'No day without a line', proverbial, derived from Appelles' reputed diligence in practising drawing every day. Cf. Tilley, D93.
A Jove principium] 'The beginning [is] from Jupiter', who was invoked by the Romans at the beginning of any enterprise.
These mottoes are followed by a table of contents (not transcribed) covering poems on MS pp. 1–33. See p. 30.
A Reveille Matin wrot at Copt Hall   Title. *Reveille Matin*] Cf. *My reveille-Matin*, p. 144, *Title* n.   *Copt Hall*] Near Epping, Essex, seat of the Earls of Middlesex. Fane's sister Rachel (1613–80) married Lionel Cranfield, third earl, in 1655, having formerly been married to the Earl of Bath. Cranfield mistreated her, threatening 'to chain her up like a monkey'. They separated in 1657, Rachel being left by her estranged husband in the empty house in Lincoln's Inn Fields from which she had been married (cf. *To a Frend upon my Pallace*, p. 325). Thereafter she styled herself (dowager) Countess of Bath. This poem must belong to the period around her marriage in 1655. 16. line] lain.
Sursum corda   Title] 'Lift up your hearts'.
Eucaristia   Title. *Te via Caris*] 'You, the Way for your loved ones'.
Eucharistia   Title. *Situ Ei chara*] 'Dear to him in the place'.
A Christmas Carroll—1655   1] Cromwell advocated the return of Jews to England in a powerful speech to the Council on 4 December 1655. Although no formal action was taken by the conference Cromwell called, they were henceforth able to return under his protection. Evelyn recorded on 14 December after visiting Hobbes: 'Now were the *Jewes* admitted' (III, p. 163).
Psal:108—Awake Lute and Harp   Title] Psalm 108. 2: 'Awake, psaltery and harp: I myself will awake early.'   19–20] Cf. Psalm 108. 13: 'Through God we shall do valiantly: for he it is that shall tread down our enemies'.
The Scepter Shall not depart from Juda   Title] See *Wisedom is Justefied of her Children*, p. 183, l. 9 n.   *Margin*] 1 January is the Feast of the Circumcision (see l. 21).   5–8] In this case, esp. Jacob's prophecy in Genesis 49. 10.   11–12] The conversion of the Jews was expected to come at the end

of time, just before the Day of Judgement.   14. closs Cabinet] Secret storehouse, receptacle; *OED* quotes Robert Sanderson, *XII Sermons* (1635), II p. 312: 'That counsel of His, which is lockt up in the cabinet of His secret will'.

Cor Mundum crea Mihi Deus   *Title*] '*Lord, make in me a contrite heart*'. *Margin*. Psal: 50–10] In fact, Psalm 51. 10: 'Create in me a clean heart, O God; and renew a right spirit within me.' It is 50. 12 in the Vulgate.   10. Abanahs . . . Farfar] The rivers Abana (Nahr Barada) and Pharphar (Nahr Awaj) in the Lebanon.

The Yong man and Christ   *Title*] Supplied from Fane's table of contents, f. 1r. Latin version, also untitled, has marginal notes: 'Mat: 19' and 'Mr: Calamy' (see *Ascensus Gratiarum descensus Gratiarum*, p. 154).   1–14) See Matthew 19. 17–25.   13–14] Matthew 19. 25: 'It is easier for a camel to go through the eye of a needle, than for a rich man to enter into the kingdom of God'.

Optimus Thesaurus Cælestis   *Title*] '*The best Treasure is in Heaven*'. Cf. Matthew 6. 20:'But lay up for yourselves treasures in heaven, where neither moth nor rust doth corrupt, and where thieves do not break through nor steal.'   10. Tullus and Ancus] Legendary early kings of Rome, 'rich Tullus and Ancus' in Horace, *Odes* IV. 7, l. 15.

On Collonel Ed[*ward*] **Pellam**[*'s*] **death**   *Title*] Edward Pelham (1619 or 1620–57) of Brocklesby, Lincolnshire, colonel in Royalist army, married (August 1645) Diana, Fane's eldest daughter by Grace Thornhurst (he aged 'about 24', she sixteen). On 2 April 1647 his uncle Henry Pelham, MP for Grantham, who became briefly Speaker of the Commons later that year in 'Pelham's Parliament', writes to Edward that his pardon is sealed and he can now come to London. He advises him to bring a 'handsome horse to ride in Hyde Park as other young gallants do' (W(A) XVII. 11). Fane paid Henry legal fees, probably connected with his petitions for the lifting of sequestration, in January 1644: 'To Mr Henry Pellam Counsail fees 3-0-0'. (Two other lawyers were paid, plus the doorkeepers at Parliament.) Several later payments were made to Pelham in 1644 (W(A) Misc. 7, ff. 4r, 6r) and on 24 June '*Mr Pelham* reports the Business concerning the Earl of *Westmerland* his Composition' (*Commons' Journals* III, p. 540). Several 'tokens' and other payments are made to Diana Pelham and her husband: see e.g. February 1655, 'To my sonn Pellham 30.00.00' (W(A) Misc. 4, p. 83).   7–8. *Margin. seu cito seu sero*] 'Sooner or later'.

Carroll—1656   1–2. *Margin*. Psal: 110: v.3:] 'Thy people shall be willing in the day of thy power, in the beauties of holiness from the womb of the morning: thou hast the dew of thy youth.'   30] Referring to the suppression of Christmas celebrations during the 1640s and 1650s. See *In Natalem—1649*, p. 153, ll. 19–24 n.

The best Meditation is that of Death   3. Crittick] Severely judgemental.   5. Could Coast . . . Death] Combining Virgil, *Aeneid* IV, 385, 'frigida mors', and Horace, *Odes* I. 4, l. 13, 'pallida Mors'.

O Lord thou art my Portion   *Title*] The text was Psalm 119. 57: 'Thou art my portion, O LORD'. *Margin*. Mr Yates] Probably the Independent John Yates (c. 1590–1660), graduate of Emmanuel (adm. 1604, became BD during Fane's time there, 1618); Rector (1622–58) of Stiffkey, Norfolk, in the gift of Sir Nathaniel Bacon, but where Fane also owned land. Yates had attacked the Arminian Richard Montagu in *Ibis ad Cæsarem* (1626).

Solatur se etsi Naturaliter Miserum   *Title*] '*He is consoled that, although he is naturally wretched, yet by grace he is blessed, because of Christ's Passion*'.   1. *Margin*. Rom. 7:24] 'O wretched man that I am! who shall deliver me from the body of this death?'

A cursing the Civel warr waged in the flesh   8. drownd] Fane uses as present infinitive the variant 'drownd . . . widely prevalent in dialectal and vulgar use' (*OED*, s.v. *drown*).

What Profiteth it a Man to Gain the whole world   *Title*] Matthew 16. 26: 'For what is a man profited, if he shall gain the whole world, and lose his own soul?'   *Margin*] Giles Aleyn, Rector of Sibson-cum-Stibbinton, Huntingdonshire, six miles from Apethorpe. June 5. 1659] On the same day Fane wrote *To the People of England* (p. 328).

On Good Friday-1659   30. Foot stoole] Cf. *This is a true sayng and by all means worthy to be received*, p. 144, l. 11 n.

Text:/ Labour not for the meat that Perisheth &c.   *Title*] John 6. 27: 'Labour not for the meat which perisheth, but for that meat which endureth unto everlasting life, which the Son of man shall give unto you: for him hath God the Father sealed.'   *Margin*. Mr Cooper] No Cooper appears to have held the living between 1630 and 1699. The incumbent was Edward Wallis (cf.

Fane's Latin poem of 1657 on his sermon, Appendix 2, p. 374). He was ejected and his estate sequestered for participation in the rising of 1643 (Matthews, *Walker*, p. 227). In 1641 the parishioners had petitioned the House of Commons against him, 'for neglect and Popish practices.' (*Proceedings . . . in the County of Kent . . . 1640*, Camden Society 82, 1861, p. 148). Calamy names two Coopers, of whom William, sometime chaplain to the Queen of Bohemia, and ejected from St Olave's, Southwark, at the Restoration, is the most likely candidate (Calamy, p. 195). Tudly and Capell] Badsell, Fane's birthplace, is in the manor of Tudeley, near Tonbridge. Richard Fane (d. 1541) built a chapel and church at Tudeley (Barron, p. 93). Fane inherited both the land and the gift of the living of Tudeley with Capel (Hasted, V, pp. 256–60). He therefore presented Wallis in 1639.

Wrot at Raynam   Title. *Raynam*] See *A Jorney into Norfolk*, p. 116, ll. 84–93, nn.   *June . . . 1659*] Horatio Townshend, Fane's stepson and the owner of Raynham, was by this date a member of the Rump Parliament's Council of State, following the abdication of Richard Cromwell in May 1659. Charles II and Hyde were making conciliatory offers to former Cromwellians, a strategy reflected in the irenic tone of this poem.

Preces et Lachrimæ Sanctorum Oblationes   *Title*] 'Prayers and tears, the offerings of the Saints'.   1. *Margin*. September 4] Probably in 1659, when Booth's Royalist rising had just been put down (19 August) by Lambert, and Townshend had been arrested in Norfolk, rightly suspected of planning a rising there.   22. Skoales] Scales.

But seek ye first the Kingdome of God   Title. *Margin*] 'But seek ye first the kingdom of God, and his righteousness; and all these things shall be added unto you.'   Doctor Sutton] ?Thomas, fellow of Corpus Christi, Oxford (Matthews, *Walker*, p. 26).

Upon Candlemas day or the Purification—1664   *Title*] Feast of the Purification of the Virgin Mary, celebrated on 2 February.   3–5] Luke 2. 22–5: 'And when the days of her purification according to the law of Moses were accomplished, they brought him to Jerusalem, to present him to the Lord . . . And to offer a sacrifice according to that which is said in the law of the Lord, A pair of turtle doves, or two young pigeons.'

Sturbridg Fayer   *Title*] Sturbridge, Cambridgeshire, the site of a great fair (according to Defoe the biggest in Europe) since medieval times. It lasted from 7 to 28 September (see Brand, II, pp. 268, 270). Here it is a forerunner of Bunyan's Vanity Fair.   1. Bulks] Stall's.   21–2] '[The bust of] Mercury cannot be carved from just any wood, but Divine Contemplation comes from anything at all.' The first part is a Latin proverb: cf. *Vita*, p. 46.

Coritanum Regio Vel Comitatus et Agris Darbiensis Descriptio   *Title*] 'The region of the Coritani, or a description of the county and land of Derby'.   2. Sowes Piggs] Cast pieces of lead, known both as sows and as pigs, probably depending on size.   4. Pondrous] Weighty.

Upon Sir Jhon Prettimans Change in Fortunes   *Title*] Sir John Prettiman (1612–75/76) of Lodington Hall and Horninghold Manor, Leicestershire. Entered Queens, Cambridge, 1631, son and heir of Sir John, of Driffield, Gloucestershire. Lincoln's Inn 1629, succeeded 1638. Active Royalist, present at taking of Cirencester 1642. Incurred great losses and compelled to sell the Driffield estate (cf. Evelyn, *Diary*, 29 July 1654, III, p. 117), the probable occasion of this poem. High Sheriff of Leicester 1653, Bart 1660. MP Leicestershire 1661–75. He d. 1675–76 'in involved circumstances' (*Peerage* III, p. 327).

To Sir F.F: neer Darby Shire   Title. *F.F.*] Francis Fane; see *The like in Medly for F.F*, p. 99.   *neer Darby Shire*] Aston, Francis's Yorkshire estate, was about four miles from the Derbyshire border.   Rupert] See *An Ode to Mr Waple a great Faulkner*, p. 156, Title n.   Voyage to Ginny] Rupert planned to take a fleet to defend the interests of the Africa Company against the Dutch along the west coast of Africa ('Guinea'); it never 'set out' though Fane clearly heard in October that it had.   Homeses] Sir Robert Holmes (1622–92), frequently criticised in Pepys's *Diary*, patrolled the Guinea Coast 1663–64, taking a number of Dutch settlements. In August 1664 he crossed the Atlantic to take New Amsterdam, which he renamed after his patron, the Duke of York. He was notably successful in the Dutch War of 1665, especially in 'Holmes's Bonfire' of Dutch ships sheltering at Vlieland in August 1666.   2. Ginny-Piggs] This coincides with the date of the first mention of guinea pigs in the *OED*.   6. Hogens] The Dutch, from Hoogmogendheiden, 'High Mightinesses', the title of the Dutch States General. Cf. Mogen, l. 9.   7. Butter-box] A Dutchman; see Schama, pp. 130–88, for Dutch appetites (for plentiful butter, p. 170).   13–14.

Cruelties . . . Amboynas] In 1623 the Dutch had executed English factors in Amboina, chief of the Molucca Islands, for an alleged conspiracy. Cromwell (thanks to Blake's fleet), not Charles II, had forced the Dutch to compensate descendants (l. 13).   18–19. Play Pack] ?Act as packbearers.   21. Pinke] A small ship (Dutch for 'blink', hence small: *OED* s.v. *pink* a2 and n7).   24–5] Dutch ships were particularly well 'vittled': see Schama, pp. 175–6.   35] Cf. Schama p. 176 for the 'virile' associations of roast beef as opposed to the less heroic fish (and mixed stews) of the Dutch (l. 40).

Post Script to the Voyage   2. Cape Vert] Cape Verde Islands, in the Atlantic, off West Africa.   6. Hands] Las Palmas.   6. Dam] One of the major Dutch ports of Amsterdam or Rotterdam. De Ruttier] Michael De Ruyter (1607–75), Dutch admiral.   10. Box] A blow, punning on 'Butter-Box': see previous poem, l. 7 n.).   11. Homes] Sir Robert Holmes: see previous poem, *Title* n.   Lawson] Sir John Lawson (d. 1665), republican naval commander in the 1650s until dismissed because of Fifth Monarchist leanings. Returned to command the Channel Fleet 1659, supported Restoration and was vice-admiral of the fleet which brought Charles to England. Led expeditions against the Barbary corsairs 1661–62, 1663–64 (see *Upon Sir Jhon Lawsons Eminent Services in the Levant*, p. 318, *Title* n.). Died 1665 from wounds received fighting the Dutch off Lowestoft.

Concordia Res ParvæCrescunt—Discordiâ Maxima Dilabuntur   *Title*] 'Small endeavours grow stronger through unity, the greatest are broken down by dissension' (Sallust, *Bellum Jugurthinum* 10. 6).   1–4] From 1656 on Turkey, with the support of Louis XIV (see ll. 16–20), had been intermittently attacking territories of the Holy Roman Emperor Leopold. The Turks beseiged Vienna in 1663 and 1664.   2. Danube] Pronounced 'Danubee'.   9. Count Sereine] Anglicised version of Count Zriny, who joined in command with the imperial general, Montecuccoli, and whose disputes with the latter (l. 10) hindered the campaign.   12. Truce] The truce of Vasvár (August 1664) was felt to have wasted the benefits of Montecuccoli's victory over the Turks.

Upon the Death of the Most Heroick and thrice Noble Princes   *Title*] Charlotte Stanley, Countess of Derby (1599–1664), of the French Protestant Trémoille family, granddaughter of William the Silent, cousin of Frederick of Bohemia. She became famous for her successful defence of Lathom House, Lancashire, against Fairfax in 1644.   1. Thrice wet] Punning on Trémoille; cf. l. 21, 'Treble Fountains'.   6–8. unwiv'd . . . frown] The Earl of Derby was executed at Bolton 1651.   9. Man . . . Ile] She withdrew to the Isle of Man (of which her husband was hereditary king) after Marston Moor, but the island was surrendered against her wishes in 1651.   13. Offspring] Nine children.

To Prince Maurice   *Title*] Younger (1620–52) brother of Prince Rupert, and like him a Royalist commander 1642–46, when he was deported. He was lost at night in 1652 in a hurricane off the Virgin Islands whilst privateering with Rupert, but there were persistent rumours that he had survived as a slave in Algiers or a prisoner in Puerto Rico. Clarendon says 'he had never sacrificed to the Graces . . . He was not qualified with parts of nature, and less with any acquired' (*History*, Appendix 3L). Since Maurice left England for good in July 1646, this poem must refer to a marriage proposed before that date. There was an attempt in 1643, supported by the King, to marry him to the French heiress Mlle de Rohan, but this does not fit with any of the circumstances of this and the following poem.   2. Rich Elme] A widow, probably from the family of Elmes of Green Norton, Northamptonshire, must have attracted Maurice's condescending attention: see following note.   5. Could Adress] Maurice 'maintained at least the full state of his birth' towards men (and perhaps women) 'of the best condition, with whom he might very well have justified a familiarity' (Clarendon, *ibid.*).   18. Tres sum] 'I am three' ?because Maurice was the third son and was born on 6 January, the Feast of the Three Kings.

To Morice Upon Sir Francis Comptons marrying the widdow   *Title. Francis Compton*] Fifth son of Spencer, second Earl of Northampton. Of Hamerton, Huntingdonshire, and Kew Green, Surrey, kt December 1661. Granted administration of George Fane's will, as creditor, 1673. Fane gave 5s. 'To Fra: Comptons man brought a hardle of dogs' October 1657 (W(A) Misc. 4, p. 141).   1. Comd on] Punning on Compton: Fane sometimes uses a 'd' where the modern reader would expect a 't'; cf. 'unconstand', *Fortunæ*, p. 313, l. 1.   5. Dull Elme] Cf. 'Rich Elme', previous poem, l. 2, still punning on the name of the widow.

In Tricessimum Januarij Diem   *Title*] 'On the 30th day of January, on which Charles, that most serene

King of ours, first of that name and second to none for Righteousness, was inhumanely beheaded by his subjects'. *Tricessimum*] Written above *Vicessimum nonum*, but neither word deleted. The King was executed on 30 January 1649.   2. Melpomene] Muse of Tragedy.   *Reger't] Register it.

To the Society of Phanaticks or more truly Jesuits   1. swarme] Catholic priests returned to England at the Restoration, tolerated by Charles II, who proposed a Declaration of Indulgence which would allow him to override the less tolerant 'Clarendon Code'. The House of Lords rejected his proposal, largely because of its favourable attitude to Catholics, but the court was perceived by many as being filled with Catholics and crypto-Catholics, Charles himself among the latter. 12. Conventickling] The Conventicles Act of May 1664 outlawed meetings 'of more than five' for religious purposes other than Anglican services. Fane attended the House of Lords that May (*Lords' Journals* XI, p. 593) for almost the last time.

Fortunæ   Title] There is a small drawing of a wheel between *For* and *tunæ*. A letter of 8 April ?1661 from Fane to Lord Brudenell expresses similar disillusionment to that expressed here: 'The Glory now preparing is not in Excelsis Which my Age & infirmities make me more look after The distibution of Ho[nou]rs hath brought on Contempt I were [wear] Spanish Breeches so need noe Garters & for the Bath I have been in Friers weeds & a Knight alredy yet I send a Spawne to supply my place [?at the Coronation]' (Brudenell I. x. 17). For the exceptionally large Garter ceremony of April 1661, immediately before the coronation, see Antonia Fraser, *King Charles II* (1979), p. 197.   11. set . . . maines] Place their bets.

Upon the Death of his Excellency Thomas Earle of Cardigan   Title] Thomas Brudenell (*c*. 1578–1663) of Deene, Northamptonshire, and Doddington, Huntingdonshire. Convicted of recusancy in 1626, but the King leased two-thirds of his forfeited lands to Francis Fane the elder, Mildmay Fane, and Francis Earl of Rutland, at a nominal rent of 2*s*. They reassigned the income to Brudenell, who became Baron Brudenell 1627. A zealous Royalist, imprisoned in the Civil War (cf. *Upon taking up of Severall Persons of Honer*, p. 337, *Title* n.), he became first Earl of Cardigan 1661, the title promised to him by Charles I in 1648 at the reasonable rate of £1,000 (*Peerage* III, p. 13). Fane borrowed from him in the 1650s. A letter of 7 June 1658 asks Brudenell for £500 (see *Upon taking up of Severall Persons of Honer, Title* n.). In 1656–57 he had borrowed at least £200, repaid in two instalments of £100 each (W(A) Misc. 4, p. 138).   15. Frends the Best] Cf. letter of July 1658: 'My Best of frends & noblest lord' (Brudenell I. x. 6).

Counsail and advice to a Frend   Title. Frend] The Latin version is headed *Ad Amicum Xr* (Christopher) and dated 'Decem: 10 1662'.   4. Tapissries] Tapestries.

Astroites Lapides Belvi—Oris Inveniantur   Title] *'Astroite stones appear at Belvoyr.'   Astroites*] 'Star stones', a gem or fossil shaped thus. The Latin version has note: 'Cambden—Fol: 403:'. Cf. Holland's translation of Camden's *Britannia* (1610): 'Stones called Astroites, which resemble little starres joyned with one another.'(I, p. 536)   2. Coynes] Angles, points.   7. (If . . . beleev'd)] Latin version has note 'Georg: Agricola:', probably referring to the *De re metallica* (Basle, 1530) by Georgius Agricola (1494–1555).   10. *Astriote] *OED* gives *astrion*, 'little star'.   11–12] bent . . . manners] Manners was the family name of the Earls of Rutland, who lived at Belvoir.

To my frend Sir William Davenant upon his Opera   Title. Davenant] Apart from his inclusion of *An Epitaph wrot by Sir William Davenant Long Since upon Jeffery Hudson the Queens Dwarf* and 'Hudson's' reply elsewhere in *F3* (see Appendix 1), this is the only evidence of any contact between Fane and Davenant, who resumed in 1661 the laureateship he had been awarded in 1637 on Jonson's death. He had been in Hobbes's company in exile, but had been captured in 1650 on his way to Virginia, spending the next two years under arrest. Benlowes, for whose *Theophila* Davenant wrote a commendatory poem in 1652, was a common acquaintance. Fane also owned a copy of *Gondibert* (1653, *Catalogue* no. 76).   *Seege of Roads*] The *Siege of Rhodes*, 'the first English opera', first performed in September 1656 at Rutland House (which Davenant had rented) with libretto by Davenant and music (now lost) by Henry Lawes, Matthew Lock and others.   5. owld frend Ben] Jonson, whose friendship Fane clearly valued: he is mentioned more than any other English poet in his work, though almost always with emphasis on his labour: see e.g. *Upon the Heroike Lady the Markiones of Newcastle*, p. 316, l. 29.   12. Out Landish] Foreign, especially foreign language.   15–22] A plot outline.   18. half moon] Of the Turks.

Upon the Chimny Act   Title] The 'Hearth Tax': on 3 March 1662 Pepys noted that 'this day the

Parliament hath voted 2s. [cf. 'payre', l. 12] per annum for every chimney in England as a constant Revenue for ever to the Crowne' (III, p. 41). Fane did not vote for the tax: he seems not to have attended the House of Lords at all in 1662. In the Hearth Tax Returns for 1674 Apethorpe was assessed for the huge number of forty-eight hearths. The tax was abolished in 1689.

To a P.K: that sent to me for 2 Peeces   Title. *P.K.*] Park keeper: Robert Brudenell, gentleman of the ch[amber] (?or ch[ase]) in Fane's household (W(A) Misc. 15, f. 80r, November 1650), is called 'keeper of the Red Deer Park' (p. 343), but 'R.W.' suggests this Robin (l. 1) is Robert Ward, to whom Fane sent game with a Latin poem (see p. 368).   *Peeces*] Variable according to the metal: here, half a crown (2s. 6d) in silver, hence eight in a (gold) pound (ll. 3–4).

Upon a chip of the Royall Oak   Title. *Royall Oak*] The oak in which Charles II hid after the battle of Worcester. See *Vita*, p. 45.   *F.F.*] Probably Francis Fane, brother or nephew.   5. Dris] Drus: from Greek Δρῦς, 'he of the oak tree'.   Hamadrydes] Tree nymphs.

Upon the Heroike Lady the Markiones of Newcastle   Title. *Newcastle*] See *Upon the Lady Margaret Marchioness of Newcastle* p. 292, Title n.   Playes ... out] Plays written by ... *The lady Marchioness of Newcastle* were first published 1662. No copy is recorded in any of the Westmorland sales, or in the Apethorpe *Catalogue*.   23. Toucht ... Loadston] Magnetised, made to attract.

To the Highly approved Statesman and best of Servants   Title. *Brittany*] Britain.   *Sir Edward Hide ... Clarington*] Edward Hyde (1609–74), first Earl of Clarendon, moderate Parliamentarian 1640–42, supported Charles at outbreak of Civil War and became an increasingly important political and intellectual figure in Royalist party. In exile with Charles II, became Lord Chancellor 1658, and his chief Minister 1660–67, when his enemies forced him from power. In exile in France he completed his great *History of the Rebellion*, which had a disproportionate influence on the predominantly Royalist interpretations of many subsequent historians.

Upon Sir Jhon Lawsons Eminent Services in the Levant   Title. *Lawsons*] See *Post Script to the Voyag*, p. 310, l. 11 n.   *Levant*] In 1661–62, following the acquisition of Tangier by the marriage treaty with Portugal, Lawson's squadron, sent to the Mediterranean to combat serious piracy from the North African 'Levant' coast, captured a number of corsair ships from Algiers (l. 2), Tunis and Tripoli, regencies of the Sultan which had become quasi-autonomous pirate States.

To the Markiones of Newcastle   Title. *Orations*] *Orations of divers sorts, accommodated to divers places* (1662). A presentation copy given to Fane, with 'commendatory verses' (?this poem) on the flyleaf, was sold for 1s. to Ridler (Sotheby's, 1887, lot 702).

To Docter Brown a Phisitian maried to Mistress South   Title. *Brown ... South*] Fane paid fees to 'Doctor Brown' (not Sir Thomas) in April, May and June 1663 (W(A) Misc. 8, ff. 37–9), and occasionally later. The Souths were a relatively wealthy local family.   Cliff] King's Cliff, near Apethorpe.   9 ... 1665] This is the last dated poem by Fane, who died nine months later.   1. white neck] The last sheaf of corn cut at harvest.   15. two leggd Timpany] Pregnancy: *OED* quotes Tarlton, *News from Purgatory*: 'The maid fell sicke, and her disease was thought to be a timpany with two heeles' (1844 ed., p. 78).

To my Cosen T.F   Title] Thomas Fane, 1626–92 (his birth date sometimes given wrongly as 1602), Mildmay's cousin, son of Sir George Fane of Burston, Kent. Halsted says wrongly that the Mereworth and Burston estates were inherited by Thomas through Sir George, the first Earl's younger brother (V, pp. 78–9): Mildmay treats them as his own (see e.g. 'My Parler window', *Upon the little parler Garden at Mereworth*, p. 323, l. 1, and *The Genius and houshold Gods salute the little stream*, p. 199). Hasted also says (V, p. 258) that the first Earl 'did entirely' reside at Mereworth. Thomas was a colonel in the (?Royalist) army and MP for Maidstone 1679, 1681 (Barron, p. 96; Hasted, V, pp. 152–3). He died unmarried, and was an executor of Fane's will.   1. Bakon] As a philosopher (l. 17) he admires Francis Bacon (punctuation: 'Bakon: I admire Thou art ... .').   admire] wonder.   6. His ... Crowne] Charles II at the date this poem was transcribed.   8. Coat] Place in a coat of arms.   *Renown] Display (cf. *OED* s.v. *renown* n1c, but not as apparently here a heraldic term).   10. Alies] Often at this date relatives rather than e.g. his fellow philosophers.   24. Basta] Enough.

In Jesuiticum Ordinem   Title] 'On the Order of Jesuits'. Based closely on a passage from Joseph Hall, *Quo Vadis? A Just Censure of Travel* (1617), pp. 73–4: 'The Jesuites, amongst much change of houses, have two famous for the accordance of their names; one called *The Bow* at *Nola*; the other *The Arrow*, (*La Flesche*) in *France* .... Their Apostate Ferrier ... plaid upon them in this distich: *Arcum Nola dedit, dedit illis alma Sagittam / Gallia; quis funem, quem mervere, dabit? Nola the Bow, and France the shaft did bring: / But who shall helpe them to an hempen string?'* Fane transcribes Ferrier's Latin but then gives his own translation. Jérémie Ferrier (*c.* 1560–1626) was a French theologian, originally Protestant, who changed religion in step with Henri IV.   1. Nola] Town south of Rome, with a seminary founded in 1549, presumably with a name derived from *arcus*, bow.   Arrow] La Flèche, Pays de la Loire, home of earliest Jesuit college in France, the Prytanée.

In Prayse of a Cuntry Life   15. Infeofing] Putting in possession of.   16.1] *Non ... vita*] '*Life is not just living, but living in health*', Martial, VI, 70, l. 15.

Queen Katherine Landed at Portmouth in Hampshire   Title] Catharine of Braganza (1638–1705), daughter of John IV of Portugal, married Charles II at Portsmouth on her arrival, 13 May 1662.

To the Royall Fleet sent out of the Downes into Portugall   Title] The fleet was commanded by the Earl of Sandwich (see *To the Noble paier of kinsmen*, p. 343, *Title* n.), Catharine travelling in his flagship, the *Royal Charles*.   6. Brag-and-say] Pun on 'Braganza', perhaps reflecting English pronunciation.

Upon His Majesties resolution to Dissolve the Parlement   Title. Dissolve the Parlement] The 'Convention Parliament', the only one dissolved by Charles during Fane's lifetime, ended on 29 December 1660. Some members expressed surprise at the notice given them on 22 November that it would end in 'about a month'.   1. on ... stand] From the phrase 'high in the instep', meaning haughty, proud.   2] Parliament was debating ways of raising annual revenue of £1,200,000 promised to the King.   9. fower ... Owld] The approximate number of MPs in the Convention Commons. There was some feeling that, as the Convention Parliament had not been called by the King's authority, its legislation could be questioned.   11. rest] ?Of his revenue. 19. Cyprian Queens] Venus's. Charles was still unmarried at this date (though this was to make little difference).   25–30] One of the last Acts of this Parliament was the attainder of the regicides, with the gruesome addition to the Bill of a successful motion to disinter and hang the corpses of Cromwell, Ireton, Bradshaw and Pride.

Sapiens Dominabitur Astris   Title] '*The wise man will govern the stars*'.   3. Gammouth] Gamut, scale: see *To Sir Jhon Wentworth*, p. 79, l. 103 n.   7. Cliff] Clef.   18–56] Referring to most of the named constellations (not all annotated).   18. Dog-Stars] Sirius (Canicula), in the constellation of the Greater Dog, the brightest fixed star, and Procyon, in the constellation of the Lesser Dog.   19. Hare] The constellation *Lepus* is said to be running from Orion's dog.   20. Cassiopea ... Chaire] The constellation takes the form of a seated woman.   23. Orions harp] Apparently confusing Orion the hunter with Arion the singer (see *A Ballet of Dedication of the new Academy*, p. 258, ll. 17–20 n.).   24–6. Bootes ... wayne] Boötes, the Waggoner (or Herdsman) appears to drive Charles's Wain, the Great Bear.   28. Phlegon ... three] The four 'winged horses of the sun' in Ovid, *Met.* II, 153–4.   29. Bull ... Eye] Aldebaran, largest star in Taurus, forms the 'eye' of the bull.   30. Lions Hart] Regulus, star forming the 'heart' of the constellation Leo. 32. new Constellation] Cygnus, son of Apollo and friend of Phæton: he so grieved at the latter's death that Apollo turned him into a swan and placed him among the stars.   33] Aries, the Ram. 39. Chirons ... Philera] The Centaur, offspring of Saturn and Philyra, placed among the stars by Zeus as Sagittarius.   44. undertakers ... Fen] Those who financed, or speculated in, drainage of the fens, which was especially active in the seventeenth century: see Stone, *Crisis*, pp. 355–7, 377–8. Jonson satirises such undertakers in Meercraft in *The Devil is an Ass*.   47. Cetus] The Whale.   48. Eridanus] Constellation named from the river god (in Ovid the river Po: *Met.* II, 324).   52. Voted] Promised. Queen Berenice's hair was stolen from the temple in which she had 'voted' it to Venus for her husband Ptolemy III's safe return, and made a constellation, in Fane's time the southern star Canopus.   55. Corona] There are now two constellations, the Southern Crown and the Northern Crown.

To my Tutors Ghost Doctor Travers   Title] Elias Travers, scholar of Emmanuel 1603, fellow 1609–21. Rector of Thurcaston, Leicestershire, 1621–41, d. 1641. The date at which he resigned his fellowship suggests he may have been the tutor who accompanied Fane on his European tour 1621–25, though during that period he contributed Latin poems to the Cambridge volumes on the marriage of Charles and Henrietta Maria (*Epithalamuim Caroli et HenricæMariæ*, 1624) and on the death of James I (*Decessio Jacobi Successio Caroli*, 1625), signing himself as of Christ's College. His correspondence with Lady Knyvett, the grandmother of another student, Sir Thomas Knyvett, is in BL Egerton MS 2715, ff. 137–83. Extracts are in *The Knyvett Letters* ed. B. Schofield, Norfolk Record Society 20 (1949), pp. 19–22. This poem is a warm tribute to his ineffective teaching. 4. Caloping Compasses] Calliper compasses, used to measure calibre of shot.

Upon the little parler Garden at Mereworth 2. Presbitery] Since the Vere family, the Harley family and many of Fane's own forebears were prominent Presbyterians, this characterisation is significant at a date when many Royalists, especially the returning exiles, were suspicious of the Presbyterians who had initially opposed Charles I, then from 1648–49 supported the monarchy. 5. Elders] Punning on the shrub / tree, and the officers of the Presbyterian Church, who were teaching elders (ministers) or—the more usual meaning—lay elders. 6. Optike] Visual power: cf. Sir Thomas Browne, *Religio Medici*: 'Nor is it in the Opticks of these eyes to behold felicity' (*Works* I, p. 55). 8. Tenents] Beliefs, tenets: cf. Browne, *Pseudodoxia Epidemica*, 'received tenents' (title). 12. Hesperides] Garden in the west containing the golden apples given by Ge to Hera at her marriage to Zeus, and the title of Herrick's 1648 collection. 15. Martialls Farme] At Nomentanus: a '*rus minimum*' in *Epigrams* IX, 18. l. 2; see also VI, 43; VII, 31. 16. Lupus] The donor of Martial's farm, if any, is not known: Lupus figures in Martial only as a moneylender (XI, 108) and debtor (VII, 11). 22. fulgent] shining. 29. Pantlers Binn] Bread Bin. 35. wants] moles. 56. *Lady-gould] Ladybird. 58. house on fier] From the children's song 'Ladybird, ladybird, fly away home / Your house is on fire, your children all flown'. 60. Bussing] Buzzing. 64. Dorr] Loud buzzing insect, e.g. a hornet.

Upon Jack Prick 5. stones of might] testicles.

Upon Doctor Crafts his Sermon at Court Title. Crafts] Herbert Croft (1603–91), DD and royal chaplain 1640, at Restoration nominated to see of Hereford; he was an outspoken anti-papist, having been a Catholic convert early in his life, and a champion of tolerance of non-Anglican Protestant groups. 4th verse . . . King] The text gave scope for offence: 'And in thy majesty ride prosperously because of truth and meekness and righteousness; and thy right hand shall teach thee terrible things' (cf. ll. 5 and 7).

To a Frend upon my Pallace and habitation Title. Portugall Rowe . . . fields] The fields to the west of Lincoln's Inn were built on from 1638, a large area being partially enclosed by the beginnings of a projected square of houses, never completed in the seventeenth century. Portugal Row was on the south-west side: see bird's eye plan in *Hollar*, p. 137. Fane's sister Rachel was married from a house there, probably the one referred to here, in 1655 (see *A Reveille Matin wrot at Copt Hall*, p. 298, *Title* n.). It was a fashionable development: Lord Brudenell (see *Upon taking up of Severall Persons of Honer*, p. 337, *Title* n.) and the Earl of Sandwich lived there. 3. Durram Yard] See *The Savoy—Excetter house*, p. 60, *Title* n. 4. Change] The Earl of Salisbury's New Exchange on the south side of the Strand, built on the site of the stables of Durham House: see *Survey* XVIII, pt 2, pp. 94–6. It was celebrated by Jonson in *The Entertainment at Britain's Burse*. 8–11. Margin 'Casa . . . Battia'] Tuscan proverb, 'My home, however tiny you may be, You seem a paradise to me'; cf. Tilley, H780. 11–18] The open Lincoln's Inn Fields were crossed by sewers and ditches in the late sixteenth century. They had been laid out with walks by Inigo Jones in the early seventeenth century, but apparently retained the sewers at this date. 18. Scavenger] The 'Rakers and Scavangers' collected rubbish put out in the streets, apparently dumping some of it in Lincoln's Inn Fields. 31–3. King . . . Curse] See Exodus 8. 1–8. 37–40. Colon . . . Lake] The dumping of the contents of cesspits by householders and night-soil men. Genver Zee] Lake Geneva. 44. *Densefy] Make dense; first *OED* quotation 1820.

Upon a fine Shower that fel on the 16th of Aprill—1660 Title. 16th . . . 1660] Written when as Evelyn recorded 'every body were in hopes & expectation of the Gen: & Parliaments recalling' Charles II, who returned in May (III, p. 243).

Post Tenebras Lux Title] '*After the Darkness, Light: After Rain, Fine Weather*'. Cf. Tilley, R8, S908. 5. Clarefies] Lights up. 27. Hud-winkt] Blindfolded, and thus deceived.

Upon George Munks routing the Rump Title] See *Sonnet Feb: 1659*, p. 245. 2–4. Margin. See . . . words] The Apethorpe *Catalogue* includes 'Florio's Queen Anna's new world of Words, 1650'. There was no 1650 edition, but the first with that title (1611) gives '*Georgia*, Culture or tillage of the earth'. 4. Dioclesian] Diocletian (d. AD 316), became emperor 284, associating Maximian with him (as 'Caesar', but perhaps what is meant by 'Tribune' here); his career had some parallels with Monk's, but his restoration of order to the empire after years of chaos makes Fane associate him with Charles.   21–2. Poysnous ... Cauphe] Coffee, regarded as intoxicating, and drunk by Harrison's Rota group (ll. 24–5); for this spelling, cf. Sir Henry Blount, *A Voyage Into the Levant* (1637), p. 42: 'One brought a Porcelane dish of Cauphe' (*OED*).   24–5. Harringtons ... Oceâna] James Harrington (1611–77), whose *Oceana* (1656) proposed a republic, 'anno 1659 ... had every night a meeting ... at one Miles's, where was made purposely a large ovall-table, with a passage in the middle for Miles to deliver his Coffee' (Aubrey, I, p. 289). A copy of the 1656 *Oceana* was in Sotheby's 1887 sale, lot 628.

Upon a Rumor of a Generall rising   Title] A 'Generall rising' was planned for 1 August by Charles and his supporters in exile, and by the Sealed Knot in England. Thurloe uncovered the plan in July, and only Booth's rising in Cheshire, suppressed by Lambert, actually took place.   Rising Chase] Castle Rising, near King's Lynn, overlooking the Wash and the Ouse estuary. Clarendon says the taking of King's Lynn was 'most like to succeed' of the whole conspiracy, partly because of Horatio Townshend's influence: he 'was of very worthy principles, and of a noble fortune, which he engaged very frankly to borrow money, which he laid out to provide arms and ammunition; and all the King's friends in those parts were ready to obey those persons in whatsoever they undertook' (*History* XVI. 24).   3. Lad] Charles, who waited in Calais: there is no suggestion (other than this poem) that he sailed to King's Lynn, though that may have been the plan.

To my Neph[ew] Gerr[ard]   Title] Charles, fourth Baron Gerard (1634/35–67), succeeded 1640, matriculated at Emmanuel 1649; in France from 1652 (see *At Dover the of June-1652*, p. 286). Fane became his guardian in 1640 (*Peerage* V, pp. 635–6; *CCC* I, p. 90). A letter from Gerard to Fane, in elementary French, is dated from 'Angers: Feu:rij 21: 1655' (i.e. 1656: BL Add. 34,217, f. 11). *Peerage* V, p. 636, probably confuses him with Lord Gerard of Brandon in making him a gentleman of the bedchamber in February 1649.   *Cœlum non Animum mutat &c*] '*Cœlum non Animum mutat, qui trans mare currant*', 'He changes his clime, but not his mental state, who travels across the sea'. Horace, *Epistles* I. 11, l. 27. Quoted by Fane in his *Vita*: see p. 37.   1. Gibe] Gybe, alter course.

To the People of England—June-5-1659   Title. June ... 1659] Republicans led by Vane and Haselrigg and army officers led by Lambert and Fleetwood had engineered the recall of the Rump Parliament on 7 May, forcing Richard Cromwell to abdicate on 25 May. The rumours of renewed war in early June grew from fears that France would support the Cromwellians against the Rumpers in an attempt to restore Richard.   S.X. T.FX. and O.P.] Essex, Thomas Fairfax, Oliver Protector.   *Fleet[woo]d*] Charles Fleetwood (1618–92), Parliamentary general, married Cromwell's daughter Bridget; commander-in-chief Ireland 1652–55, and of army in England 1659, but retired in disgrace at Restoration.   *Lamb[er]t*] See *Upon Lamb[er]ts repo[rted] to be Gen[eral*, p. 244, Title n.   *Va[ne]*] Sir Henry Vane Jr (1613–62), a cousin of Fane's, committed and radical (though undemocratic) republican and champion of religious toleration: he refused to take part in Charles's execution, but was nevertheless executed at the Restoration.   *Heisel[rigge]* Sir Arthur Haselrigg (1601–61), MP (Leicestershire) throughout 1640–59, an Independent and leader of the war party in the Long Parliament with Vane and Cromwell. Governor of Newcastle (1647), he opposed the execution of the King, and led parliamentary opposition to Cromwell through the 1650s. Retired from politics at the Restoration.   *Coss:*] A puzzle: nobody whose name begins thus was prominent in this period, nor does a comment (such as 'Cossenors' for 'cozeners') seem plausible.   1. *Margin*] The poem is an imitation of Horace's *Epode* VII, part of Fane's strategy of confronting and understanding the Civil War in terms of classical precedent, in this case the Roman civil wars: cf. *Ad Rem Publ[licam] Bel[lum] Civil[em] reparantem*, p. 243.   21. Fury blind] 'furorne cæcus' in Horace, 'the blind Fury' in Milton, *Lycidas*, l. 75; the Furiæ were represented with bleeding eyes.   27–8] The curse on Rome for the fratricidal crime with which it began, Romulus's killing of Remus, is linked with the parricidal killing of Charles I. For Cromwell as Romulus, see *Le Monde Renversè*, p. 330, ll. 23–7 n.

Martialis Prophetizans   Title. *Martialis Prophetizans*] '*The Prophetising of Martial*', whose *Epigram* VII, 10 this poem imitates loosely.   *Margin*. May-1659] For the political context, see previous poem, Title n.   *Olus*] The addressee of Martial's epigram.   *Owld Cause*] The 'Good Old Cause', referring to the republican constitution of the years immediately following the execution. The phrase was much used at the time of Richard's abdication: see Masson, V, pp. 444–5.   1. Harry] Sir Henry Vane Jr.   Martin] Henry Marten (1602–80), regicide and republican MP; see *For A Treaty* p. 221, l. 4 n.   3. what . . . Thee] 'Ole, quid ad te?' is a refrain in Martial.   7–8] Cf. the reference to the Lamberts in *Upon Lamb*[*er*]*ts repo*[*rted*] *to be Gen*[*eral*], p. 244, ll. 5–6.

Acrosti[*ch*]   1–6 *Initial letters*] James Butler, Marquis and first Duke of Ormond (1610–88), Lord-lieutenant of Ireland in the 1640s, in exile with Charles in the 1650s. Active in negotiations for the Restoration, he accompanied the King to Calais to await the August 1659 rising, and on his eventual return the following May.   6.1 *Sapiens . . . Astris*] *'The wise man will dominate the stars'.* Cf. poem of this title, p. 321.

To The countess of Ruttland upon Her New reedefying of Belvoir   Title. *countess of Ruttland*] Frances (1613–71), daughter of Lord Montagu of Boughton, married John Manners, eighth Earl of Rutland, 1628. He, a distant relative of Fane's, was a Parliamentarian peer, and with the Earl of Stamford, another friend, tendered the covenant to Fane in February 1644 (*Lords' Journals* VI, p. 427a).   *reedefying . . . warr.*] Belvoir Castle, Leicestershire, was twice captured by Royalists, twice surrendered (1646–47), and dismantled with Rutland's consent 1649. For details of the 'reedifying' (rebuilding), which was at the Countess's wish, see Fowler, p. 257. Cf. *A Buck-hunting Jorny to Belvoyr*, p. 108.   *Iam . . . erit*] '*Now there is a cornfield where once was Troy. Belvoyr, previously destroyed by war, shall now be renewed.*' Based on Ovid, *Heroides* I. 1. 53.   Margin] Fane's accounts record the journey: '8 [May] To Ernam, Fullbeck, & Belvoir & back 05.10. 06' (W(A) Misc. 4, p. 179). At this date the rebuilding becomes a powerful symbol for the imminent recovery of Royalist fortunes.   6. Union] Both 'unity' of structure ('Frame') and a large, well formed pearl (Fowler, p. 258).   15] 'All who claim to be architects' (Fowler, p. 258).   17. Skoard out] Fowler suggests scratched, but Fane uses 'score' for a pen in *Upon the Heroike Lady the Markiones of Newcastle*, p. 316, l. 40.   18. Wootten . . . Element] Henry Wotton, *Elements of Architecture* (1624). Wotton's secretary as ambassador to Venice, Rowland Woodward, had become secretary to Fane's father, bringing with him the 'Westmoreland Manuscript' of Donne. He is buried at Apethorpe. Cf. Fane's transcription of a Latin poem by him (Appendix 2: *N*, f. 12v).   19. Quaint Contriver] The architect was John Webb, pupil of Inigo Jones. His ambitious designs were not fully realised.   21. Rayseth] Begun 1655, it was not finished until 1668.   24. Frontespice] Porch, entrance.   25. Scuttchions] Escutcheons, family arms. Placing them above the entrance was 'increasingly popular' (Fowler, p. 258).

Le Monde Renversè / Jordanus Retrorsum   Title] '*The world turned upside down / The Jordan turned back*'. Cf. Psalm 114. 3, 'Jordan was driven back'.   14. Design] Probably the planned rising of 1 August 1659.   21–2] ?Return absolutism to the Continent: Mazarin and Louis XIV had been allies of Cromwell.   23–7] Referring ironically to Waller's elegy on Cromwell, *Upon the late storm*: 'So Romulus was lost! / New Rome in such a tempest missed her king, / And from obeying fell to worshipping. / On Œta's top thus Hercules lay dead' (*Poems*, p. 163, ll. 6–9; cf. Norbrook, p. 386, and *To the People of England*, p. 328, ll. 27–8, where Charles is Remus, murdered by Romulus).

For a Gentleman whose Mistresses name was Ara-bella   1. Fair-Altar] Translating Latin *ara* (altar) and *bella* (fair).   8. Expiat] Purify (in a religious ceremony).   11. Salt and Hayre] Components of black magic ritual.   13. Goat or Kid] Associated with lust.   21.1. *Persarum . . . Beatior*] '*That I might truly be more happy than the King of Persia.*'

Sapit qui sibi sa-pit   Title] '*He is wise who is wise for himself*'. Proverbial, usually in negative form as 'Nequicquam sapit, qui sibi non sapit'; cf. Tilley, W532.   1. Kinton] Kineton, nearest village to Edgehill where the first major battle of the Civil War was fought.

The Cutt-Purses Faier   Title. *November-1658*] Though Cromwell died 3 September 1659, his state funeral took place on 23 November. Fane went to London on that day (W(A) Misc. 4, p. 167) but, even though the procession took seven hours to reach the Abbey, could not have arrived in time to see it.   16. prick up Ears] 'Prick-ear' was a nickname for Roundheads: cf. *A Ballet 3: September 1658*, p. 249, l. 4.

Nec Sicca morte Tyranni   Title] '*Nor unbloody* [*is the usual*] *death of tyrants.*' Juvenal X, 112–13.   5–6] There were predictably many such stories of Cromwell's death.   5. Garth Golia] 'Goliath, of Gath', I Samuel 17. 4.

Fullbeck   Title] Fulbeck Hall, Lincolnshire. Bought from Sir George Manners by his second cousin, Sir Francis Fane (Mildmay's father) 1622. Manners remained there till he became Earl of Rutland, 1632, when Francis Fane the younger (Mildmay's brother) inherited, and apparently rebuilt it. His building was mostly burnt in 1731, only a seventeenth-century wing now remaining. The present house was rebuilt in the eighteenth century, and three of Fane's manuscripts, along with several of his books, were brought there by William Dashwood Fane in the 1890s (see p. 27). *Sic . . . parva*] '*Thus to compare small things with great ones.*' Quoting from memory Virgil, *Georgics* IV, 176: 'si parva licet componere magnis'. The comparison intended may be between Fulbeck and larger houses, rather than between house and patron, as Fowler (p. 248) assumes.   4. Patron's] In the sense of 'Lord, Master'. For Francis Fane, see *The like in Medly for F.F*, p. 99, *Title* n.   Adonis] Cf. *Thorp Pallace a Miracle*, p. 341, l. 9.   15. Twinny] Separate, as in 'atwin', apart (Fowler, p. 248).   20. *Frontespeece*] Entrance, here apparently a gatehouse. Cf. '*To The countess of Ruttland upon Her New reedefying of Belvoir*, p. 330, l. 24.   21. strike saile] Give precedence to.   26. Pyramids] Church spires: 'The Egyptian pyramids were then imagined as very steep' (Fowler, p. 248).   27. Graves] John Greaves (1602–52), antiquarian, mathematician and astronomer, author (l. 28) of *Pyramidologia: Or a Description of the Pyramids of Egypt* (1646).   30. Grand-Cayr] Cairo.   43. Watt] Hare.   Clotty] Cloddy, earthy.   48. *Grotten] Grotto.   51. stoops and Trusses] Swoops and seizes.   Canceleer] *OED* quotes definition of 1704: 'when a light flown Hawk, in her stooping, turns two or three times upon the Wing, to recover herself before she seizes'.

Upon 29th of may Di[*es*] *nat*[*ivitatis*] *Carol*[*i*]   Title. *Di* [*es*] . . . *Carol* [*i*]] '*The birthday of Charles*'. Cf. *Ad Geo: Fane*, p. 248.

Upon the Death of Oliver Crumwell   1. Rose and Thistle] Of England and Scotland.   4. Lillies] Of France, with whom Cromwell made an alliance in 1655.

Unto his Sonn the Lord Richard Crumwell   Title] Parliament agreed Cromwell should nominate his successor: he was said to have nominated Richard just before he died.   2. Skoals] Schools.

Upon immoderat Rayne falling   Title. a little . . . 58] It was in fact to be over six weeks before the funeral.   10. C:] Charles.

Upon the Death of our late famous English Orator and Poet   Title] Cleveland died 29 April 1658. 4. Atroposes] The Fate who cuts the 'Threed': see '*He who such strong lines wont compose*', p. 62, l. 2 n.   5–6, Margin. *Nec . . . Hor:*] '*Nor rich Tullus and Ancus*' (kings of Rome); see *Optimus Thesaurus Cælestis*, p. 301, l. 10 n.   22. Orion] Confusing Orion with Arion, as in *Sapiens Dominabitur Astris*, p. 321, l. 23.

The yong Protector unprotectd   Title. May 1659] See *To the People of England—June-5-1659*, p. 328, *Title* n.   Forraign . . . Foe] The restored Rump withdrew from all foreign commitments made by Oliver and Richard: see Masson, V, p. 467.   6. Contentment's . . . gain] Proverbial: 'Contentment is great riches', Tilley, C629.

Upon the Immoderat Use of Pastime   Title. or . . . abuse] Added later, in a different ink.   27. Triffle out] Trifle out, fritter away, esp. of time.   28. Imping . . . Plume] Adding feathers to the wing (of time).

To Mr Anthony Hungerford   Title] Of Black Bourton, Oxfordshire. The family had a house in the Strand, near the Fanes' property there. Anthony is twice referred to in Fane's accounts, July and December 1658: 'Payd Mr Anthony Hungerford for him ["my sonn" of previous entry] 11. 00. 00' (W(A) Misc. 4, p. 169, 27 December 1658).   5. *Biumvirat] Duumvirate, rule of two (Mars and Venus, l. 6) rather than of the three in the triumvirate of which Mark Antony was one.

Upon taking up of Severall Persons of Honer   Title] Referring to a series of arrests of Royalists suspected of plotting a rising, in preparation for which Ormond (see *Acrosti*[*ch*], p. 329, n.) had been in London in March. One of those 'taken up' in Northampton was Fane's friend Lord Brudenell, who remained under restraint for two to three months. Fane wrote to him on 7 June 1658 (asking to borrow £500) and ending: 'I shall add noe more lines to your trouble & confinement but the sence of trouble I undergoe for the same myself.' (Brudenell I. x. 5). Brudenell was free by late July, when Fane's steward Arney wrote to him at 'his house in Lincoln's Inn Fields' (I. x. 16, 26 July 1658).   Maior] Mayor: see l. 32.   22. Calenture] Fever.   23. Ague] At this date usually a European form of malaria.   23–4] A small number of conspirators were executed in

London, but none in the provinces. 32. Maiors] Exploiting the common etymology of *mayor* and *major*, differentiated in modern but not seventeenth-century century spelling.

Upon Owld Char[les] Cotton   *Title*] 'Old' because father of the poet, also Charles. He died 1658, having obtained large estates in Derbyshire and Staffordshire through marriage, estates he subsequently 'greatly endangered' (*DNB*) through lawsuits. He was a friend of Herrick (297.1, 'that man of men'), Jonson, Donne, Selden, Wotton, Walton and Clarendon, who praised him in his *Life* (1827 ed., I, p. 36). 1. Cottens] Prospers, gets on: thus here 'How does it go?' 12. Hone] Whetstone. 15. two-hedded-Hill] Parnassus. 16. Castalion Fountain] Castalian spring, at foot of Parnassus, sacred to Apollo and the Muses. 18. Predominized] See *In Natalem—1643*, p. 152, l. 4.

Upon the Extream winters Cowld   *Title*] The Latin version is dated 'February:-15-1657' (i.e. 1658). Evelyn wrote that 'This had ben the severest Winter, that man alive had knowne in *England:* the Crowes feete were frozen to their prey: Ilands of Ice inclosd both fish & fowl frozen, & some persons in their boats' (III, p. 211). 2. Candide] Both 'candied', crystallised, congealed, and 'candid', white, pure. 9. *Brears] Briers; *OED* suggests never pronounced to rhyme 'with *bier, tier*, but with *dyer, crier*', but this rhyme proves otherwise. 12. Uthfull] Youthful. 17. Melilot] A leguminous wild flower.

In Niuem profundam et Gelu Frigidum   *Title*] 'On the deep snow and icy cold'. 10. stupid] numbed.

Dum Spiro Spero   *Title*] 'While there's life there's hope'. Latin version dated 'January: 24. 1657 [i.e. 1658] Aeta: 56'. 3. Lowly Cell] Since Apethorpe was one of the largest and grandest of Jacobean houses, this phrase in a birthday poem stretches the tension between *persona* and historical personage well beyond breaking point. 9. woaff] woof, the thread of life.

In Domum Parlementi Alteram sive Novam a Protectore Editam   *Title*] 'On the second or new House of Parliament created by the Protector'. *20° January: 1657*] Cromwell's new House of Lords sat for the first time on this date (see *Wrot the 5ᵗ of November-1657*, p. 281, ll. 27-8 n.) There is no evidence to suggest that Fane was ever considered, though it is possible that he was sounded out. 2. Could's asswag'd] For the cold of 1657-58, see *Upon the Extream winters Cowld*, p. 338, Title n. 4. fadg to] Get on with, accommodate to.

Philomelæac Citharædi Concertatio   *Title*] 'The dispute between Philomela (the nightingale) and the lute-player'. *Margin*. Famian: Strad:] Famianus Strada (1572-1649), Jesuit, whose Latin poem on the musical duel was translated or paraphrased by many seventeenth-century writers, including Crashaw, *Musicks Duell*, Ford, *The Lovers Melancholy* 1.1, Strode, *Academy of Pleasure* (1656, p. 123), and Vilvain, *Enchiridion*, p. 177. Strada's poem appeared in his *Prolusiones Academicæ, Oratoriæ, Historicæ, Poeticæ . . . Coloniæ Agrippinæ* (1617), on p. 351. Fane follows the original fairly closely. 1-2. *Margin*. Claudiani: Stylus] 'The pen (or style) of Claudian', Strada's note. 30. Gammuth] Scale. 45. yeild up Bucklers] admit defeat. 50. Diapason] Here, a resonant chord or melody.

Upon the Lord Gray of Grooby yellow haired   Title. Gray of Grooby] Thomas, Lord Grey of Groby (1623-57), son of the Earl of Stamford (see *To my very noble Cosen the Earl of Stanford*, p. 109), became commander of the Midland Counties Association 1643, and fought subsequently at Preston and Worcester. An enthusiastic regicide (he was the second, perhaps because of rank, to sign the death warrant), he became a Fifth Monarchist, and was arrested on Cromwell's orders in 1655 because of suspected involvement in a Leveller plot against the government. 1. Sorrell] Chestnut colour. 4. *Margin*] William, Earl of Craven, follower and perhaps lover of Elizabeth, Queen of Bohemia. His estates were sold in 1652 by order of Parliament; Grey, who though a member of the Council of State was granted land by the council to help him out of financial problems, was one of those who voted for and profited from this sale. 8.1. Satiatus . . . sitijt] 'He who thirsted for blood was glutted with it.'

'To which his wiser Lady sayd'   1. Lady] Grey's wife was Dorothy, daughter of Edward Bourchier, fourth Earl of Bath. 4. Guss:] Gustavus Markworth, *c.* 1633-59, son of Sir Henry, of Normanton, Rutland, m. Dorothy, widow of Lord Grey of Groby (John Nicholls, *Rutland* I. ii, p. 128), but was killed soon after (August 1659) in a duel with Sir George Booth, perhaps related to Booth's leadership of the rising that month (see *Upon a Rumor of a Generall rising*, p. 328).

Thorp Pallace a Miracle   *Title. Thorp Pallace*] Thorpe or Longthorpe Hall, near Peterborough, built 1653–56 for Oliver St John (see *For A Treaty*, p. 221, l. 4 n.) Fane visited Longthorpe on 23 April 1658 (W(A) Misc. 4, p. 153). Evelyn, 30 August, 1654, noted it was 'a stately Palace of St John's (one deepe in the bloud of our good King) build out of the ruines of the Bishops Palace & Cloyster' (III, p. 134).   3. Impt the wings] See *Upon the Immoderat Use of Pastime*, p. 336, l. 28 n.   9–12. Huntsman . . . Oake] Statues were placed with shrubs and trees that complemented their mythological associations. Some may have come from the dispersal of the royal collection (cf. Fowler, p. 222).   13. Cratippus] Probably the minor philosopher from Mytilene who taught Cicero's son in Athens, rather than the earlier Cratippus of Athens (*c.* 400 BC), historian and probable author of *Hellenica Oxyrynchia*, a continuation of Thucydides' *History*.   15. Paripatetikon] Peripatetic philosopher, a follower of Aristotle; literally one who walks about.   16. Roomes Fencer] A gladiator, probably as Fowler (p. 222) suggests a copy of the Borghese Gladiator.   19. Livia] Apparently a seated figure, rather than one of the three Livia busts in the royal collection.   22–3] Hercules slew the dragon Ladon, guarding the golden apples of the Hesperides.   35. *Encomiomes] Usually encomiums, panegyrics (though this spelling not in *OED*), but the context implies physical enrichment of the rooms. ?Enrichment deserving praise.   36. peece] masterpiece.   37. Roman Circus, Ampitheater] ?Differentiating between the Circus Maximus (not usually on lists of the Seven Wonders of the Ancient or Medieval World) and the Coliseum.   38. even] Both in the sense of an eighth wonder and in the sense of balance, justice.

Octavo Huic Miro Septem Miracula Cedent   *Title*] 'The seven wonders give way to this eighth one', referring to Longthorpe.

Upon the State of England at Present   *Title. July-12-1659*] For the general context, see *To the People of England*, p. 328, *Title* n. In July there was much discussion of a possible constitution. A petition, written or influenced by Harrington (and therefore urging a republic) had been presented to Parliament on 6 July (Masson, V, pp. 483–4). Harrington published pamphlets on 28 July and 31 August, and started the Rota (see *Upon George Munks routing the Rump*, ll. 24–5) in September.   16. Ass . . . Mule] Types of foolishness and obstinacy respectively.

Epitaph of Sir Foulk Hunkes   *Title*] Called a '*Noble Owld Captain*' in the version in *H*, he was a Royalist commander, colonel in Lord Byron's army defeated at Nantwich 1644, then 'commanded a thousand volunteer foot from Ireland and a hundred and twenty musketeers' under Rupert at Newark (Dorothea Townshend, *Life and Letters of Mr. Endymion Porter*, 1897, pp. 214–15). Fane supported him to some extent, e.g. 'Lent Sr F. H. 5.00.00', 18 August 1655 (W(A) Misc. 4, p. 95). In a letter probably written a month before Hunkes's death, Fane tells Lord Brudenell that his servant just caught him 'on horseback at my manege [riding school] . . . I am to performe a work of Charety & visite a sick frend that sent to see me it is Sir Foulk Hunkes . . .' (Brudenell, I. x. 7, 12 October, no year).   5. word] The word of God, the Bible.

To Robin Brudnell Keeper of the Red Deer Park   *Title. Robin Brudnell*] See *To a P.K: that sent to me for 2 Peeces*, p. 316, *Title* n.   *Mall Exon*] Mary Exon: the family are named many times in Fane's accounts, as tenants and servants.   10. standing] A hiding place from which to shoot game.

To Mistress Mary Fair fax   *Title*] See *Upon Buck[ingham']s and his Duch[ess']s Visiting Apthorpe*, p. 271, *Title* n., and *Upon a hunting match defeated by wett weather*, p. 348, for an earlier projected match with John Manners, Lord Roos, in October 1656.   *Fair fax*] While Fane usually plays on the Latin *fax*, torch, firebrand or meteor, when punning on Fairfax's name, here he uses the alternative meaning of 'star': cf. l. 1, and Marvell, *Upon Appleton House* ll. 683–4, comparing Mary to a 'new-born *Comet* . . . Star new-slain'; for the Latin, see Horace, *Odes* IV. 6, l. 38. In ll. 11–14 *fax* becomes 'sun' (cf. Seneca, *Thyestes*, l. 835).   *Margin*. The marriage had taken place at Bolton Percy, Yorkshire (the parish of Fairfax's Nunappleton) on 15 September, with Abraham Cowley (who wrote *To the Duke of Buckingham, upon his Marriage with the Lord Fairfax his Daughter*, *Works* I, p. 462) as best man.   5–6. As T'leese . . . againe] Not merely empty compliment: through the marriage Buckingham regained his estates, which had been confiscated and part of them granted to Fairfax in lieu of a pension. Fairfax returned these as a gift through the marriage, plus the settlement of his own estates on the couple.

To the Noble paier of kinsmen the two Edward Mountaques   *Title*] The Latin version is dated 'Juli-18. 1657'.   *the One Admirall*] Edward Montagu (1625–72), first Earl of Sandwich, fought for Parliament at Marston Moor and Naseby. Took no part in the King's trial, but served on the Council of State from 1653. Friendly with Cromwell, who appointed him conjoint general at sea with Blake (1656). On 26 June 1657, just before the date of this poem, he carried a sword at the second installation of Cromwell as Protector, as later he carried the sceptre at Charles II's coronation. He committed the navy to the Restoration, and was second only to Monck as its agent. He brought Charles to England on his flagship, the *Naseby*, renamed the *Royal Charles* as soon as Charles boarded.   redy . . . sea] After Cromwell's second installation, Montagu took command of the fleet in the Downs.   the Other . . . Travaile] Edward Montagu (1635–65), son of the Parliamentarian peer, the second Baron Montagu of Boughton, and cousin of the admiral, who 'had a particular friendship' with him; Clarendon credits him with persuading Sandwich to support the King in 1659 (*History* XVI. 154). He was admitted to Sidney Sussex 1651, and therefore probably travelling just before July 1657.   Diana Rich] ?One of the daughters of the Earl of Warwick or of Holland. 3. Paphian Queen] Venus: Paphos, Cyprus, was sacred to her. 19. Cynthias] Diana. 23. Sea-borne-Venus] Venus/Aphrodite was often represented (e.g. by Apelles and Botticelli) as born from the foam of the sea (Greek *aphrodite*, 'foam-born'). 34.1. W: M:] Probably abbreviating a Latinised form, such as 'Westmorlandiæ Mildmaius'; a signature, not an attribution to another author with these initials.

A Sonnet upon the same Subject   11. sharp mountain] Translating 'Montacute'. 18. Sylvanus] The god of woods: cf. Horace, *Odes* III. 29, l. 23. 19. *Margin. magnes amoris Amor*] *'Love* [is] *love's magnet.'* Cf. *Sola Bella che piace*, p. 193, ll. 11–12.

To a frend in the City   15. towles] tolls, coverts. 17. Pomonaes] Pomona was the goddess of fruit and fruit trees: Ovid, *Met.* XIV, 623–5.

De Quator magnum importantibus pacem   Based on Thomas à Kempis, *Imitation of Christ* III. 23, 1–2, which itself utilises the New Testament passages cited below   Title] 'On the four bringers of great peace'. 1] Cf. Matthew 26. 39; John 5.30, 6. 38. 2] Cf. I Corinthians 10. 24. 3] Cf. Luke 14. 10.   roome] Post, function. 4] Cf. Matthew 6. 10. 5] Cf. à Kempis, III. 23, 1: 'Behold, such a man entereth within the borders of rest and peace.' 7–8] Cf. Matthew 5. 8 and à Kempis, III. 23, 2: 'O Lord, this short discourse of Thine containeth within itself much perfection. It is little to be spoken, but full of meaning, and abundant in fruit.'

To Julius Martiall   Translating Martial X, 47, which Fane has transcribed without alteration on the facing page. 3. free left means] income left free of incumbrances.

Of an Owld Hagg that desired Verses   34. Macedonian well] Perhaps Fane's most recondite allusion, a hidden Latin/English pun: Pimpla was a spring ('well') in Pieria (Macedonia) sacred to the Muses: the English 'pimple' is not related to the Latin. 36. Phebus] The sun. 37–8. fixt . . . Capricorn] Always at the midwinter solstice. 48. O-wrions] Punning on 'wry' in 'wrymouthed' etc.

To Leucone inviting to cherish pleasure   1–2. Margin] A close, slightly expanded version of Horace's *carpe diem* ode.

Upon a Very fayer Lass   The Latin version has marginal note 'Hor: L.1: Ode: 24:'. Fane is citing from memory, and is in fact echoing the opening of *Odes* III. 24, though after the first word, *Intactis*, both his English and Latin versions have no further connection with Horace. 13. Bereneeces hayer] See *Sapiens Dominabitur Astris*, p. 321, l. 52 n. 18. Segovian] Segovia, in Spain, was famous for its wool.

Upon a hunting match defeated by wett weather   Title. Lord Ros] See *Rosseus Vaticinus*, p. 267, Title n.   Mary Fair-Fax] See *Upon Buck*[*ingham*]*'s and his Duch*[*ess*]*s Visiting Apthorpe*, p. 271, Title n.   Alij . . . Lepôres] Title. 'Let others pursue hares; I [pursue] charms.' Punning on *lepus* (hare) and *lepor* (charm). 6. *Margin. *Ros*] Latin 'dew'. 7. Fair . . . North] Echoing Heywood's title, *Fair Maid of the West*; Mary Fairfax was from Yorkshire. 9. Jhon] Supporting the identification with John Manners, Lord Roos. 14. *Margin. Amantium Iræ&c*] 'Amantium iræ amoris integratiosi', Terence, *Andria* l. 555: 'The quarrels of lovers lead to the renewal of love.' 16–17. *Margin. Contraria inxtase &c:*] 'Contraria inter se opposita magis elucesunt . . . Contraries being set the one against the other, appear more evident,' quoted by Thomas Wilson, *The Art of Rhetorique* (1567), p. 125, as 'a saying in *Logique*'. 17–18. Lame . . . wet] ?Referring to the fire of Vulcan's ardour being quickened by jealousy rather than to the fire of his forge. 32.1. *quod fac sit &c:*] 'Quod facis, fac citius,' 'What you do, do quickly,' John 13. 27 (Vulgate).

To my Sonn Charles in prayse of Horsemanship   The Latin version is dated 8 December 1656. 1–2. *Margin*] As often, Fane only imitates (and that only in his Latin version) the opening words of Horace, whose *Ode* I. 7 is a poem of praise to the Tiber. The English version departs still further from Horace, the whole process showing how loosely classical *imitatio* can work in early modern poetry.   7–11] Cf. *Vita*, p. 37: 'of all the accomplishments of War and the Court, . . . I always held that of horsemanship the first'.   14. Spring of Pegasus] Hippocrene ('the spring of the horse'), like the Castalian spring (see *Upon Owld Char[les] Cotton*, p. 337, l. 16) sacred to the Muses. Pegasus, the winged horse, produced the spring on Mount Helicon by striking the ground with his hoof (Ovid, *Met.* V, 256–7).   17. prove] Attempt (by flying too near the sun, 'Junoes Throne'), though not, as this implies, on a horse.   18–19. Phaeton . . . Destruction] See *The Cosmography of this County*, p. 219, l. 9 n.   20] Chained to a rock for the benefit of a sea monster sent by Poseidon, Andromeda was rescued by Perseus (Ovid, *Met.* IV, 670–764). According to Ovid, however, he was not riding Pegasus at the time.   21–2] Alexander's first evidence of greatness came in riding the 'vicious and unmanageable' horse Bucephalus when others had failed to tame it (Plutarch, *Life of Alexander*, 6).   23. Diversities . . . agree] Proverbial, 'Contraria se mutuo commendant' (cf. Tilley, C630, B435).

'This life when at the best'   9–10. Margin. non . . . vita] See *In Prayse of a Cuntry Life*, p. 319, l. 16.1 n.   19–20. Margin. ut . . . sano] '[pray] for a sound mind in a sound body' (Juvenal X, 356).

Lessianum Title] Léonard Leys or Lessius (1554–1623), Jesuit theologian, wrote *Hygiasticon, seu vera ratio valetudinis bonæ et vitæ* (Antwerp, 1613), trans. T. S. or Nicholas Ferrar as *Hygiasticon: Or, The right course of preserving Life and Health unto extream old Age* (Cambridge, 1634). Cf. Crashaw, *In praise of Lessius his rule of health* (*Poetical Works*, ed. L. C. Martin, p. 156, orig. prefixed to the 1634 translation).   9. Heliogablus] Elagabulus, Roman emperor (as M. Aurelius Antoninus), AD 218–22. Notorious for the extravagance (and obscenity) of the ceremonies he conducted for the sun god of Emessa after whom he was named, he became a type of stupidity, vice, superstition and excess.   Cornarus] Luigi Cornaro, author of *Trattato della vita sobria* (Padua, 1558), abbreviated by Lessius and published with his *Hygiasticon*, from which it was translated (further shortened) as *A Discourse . . . that a Spare Diet is better then a Splendid and Sumptuous* by George Herbert (1634, published as part of the 1634 translation of Lessius, above).

To my sonn Bill upon his Entertainment at Cane-wood   Title] John Bill (1614–80) of Canewood (modern Kenwood House, Hampstead), admitted to Christ's May 1639, aged sixteen, and Inner Temple (also 1639). He married Fane's daughter Diana after the death of Edward Pelham in 1657 (see *On Collonel Ed[ward] Pellam[s] death*, p. 301, *Title* n.). Bill held half the office of King's Printer before the Civil War (his father was one of the backers of the Authorised Version, 1611), and he was restored to the office in 1660. In 1646 his presses and type were seized, and bought by Egglesfield, the probable printer (as well as bookseller) of *Hesperides*. Bill served under Hopton as 'master of a regiment of horse', compounded 1646 following Hopton's surrender (see *Upon Sir Thomas Fayer-Fax*, p. 200), but his estate was again sequestered in October 1648, after he was 'engaged in the late Insurrection in Surrey with the late Earl of Holland against the Parliament'. It was in 'Caen Wood' that Venner's Fifth Monarchists were attacked by Monk's soldiers, January 1661, a few months before this poem was written.

'Sir: That to You I never fayle'   1. Sir:] Not identified; though Fane's nephew Edward (c. 1643–79), fifth son of Sir Francis, of Fulbeck, travelled widely, and was a volunteer in the Four Days' Fight against the Dutch in 1666 (Barron, p. 104), he is unlikely to have commanded a 'Man of War' (l. 4) in his early twenties.   6. Thwart Hazer] Hawser which is athwart (obstructing) the weighing of anchors.   7. in a Trimm] Well rigged, ready for sailing.   13. Ride a *Trip] Make a run, journey; 'trip' was originally a nautical term, as here, but first use recorded by *OED* (s.v. *trip* n1, 3) is 1691.   16. Back-Stay] Long rope helping support mast when under sail.   Lanere] Lanyard (French *lanière*).   18. Trebble Tires] ?Ranks of cannon (see *OED* s.v. *tire* n3), playing on the ancient trireme.   22. Making his usual confusion of Orion with Arion: cf. *Sapiens Dominabitur Astris*, p. 321, l. 23 n.   23–4. Disastrous Brood . . . Storme] Birds, such as the petrel and those in ll. 28–9, which are harbingers of storms.   25. Sea-Swine] Porpoise.   28. Augur Hern . . . Cormorants] All birds associated with bad weather. 'Hern': heron.   35. Antient] Ensign.   40. wast cloaths] Waist-cloths, coloured cloths hung on the ship which hid the men when going into

action. 42. Deadmans eyes] Pulley blocks, here with lanyards attached to the foremast. 47. Roavers] Reivers, pirates. 53. Yare] Sensitive: cf. *My Dream the 8 of September 1637*, p. 228, l. 42. 55. Crank-Keeld] ?Leaning over in sailing; but one meaning of 'crank' was 'vigorous, in good condition ... lively' (*OED* s.v. *crank* a1, 1–2). 56. Last Cabins] ?Applied to 'hammackoes' as the least or 'hanging cabins'. 63. waftage] Sea voyage, passage; cf. *Com. Err.* 4. 1. 95, 'A ship you sent me to, to hire waftage.' 64. Spooning] Scudding, running before the wind. 67. Cadg ... Strem] Kedge anchor, a small anchor used in calm weather; sheet anchor, the heaviest anchor, used in emergencies; stream anchor, an intermediate between sheet and kedge. 68. Cock-bell] Small bell. 74. Voats] Prayers. 76–80. *Margin*] All sailors of the 1650s and 1660s. Pen.] Admiral William Penn (1621–70) became vice-admiral under Blake 1652, and commander-in-chief of the fleet sent to the West Indies in 1654–55, with Venables in command of the troops. The expedition incurred serious losses, partly because of dissension between the two commanders, and both were imprisoned briefly on their return, despite the capture of Jamaica. At the Restoration Penn became a commissioner of the navy and thus subject of much abuse in Pepys's *Diary*. Venables] Sir Robert Venables (?1612–87), Parliamentarian commander, served under Cromwell in Ireland, then appointed general of the land forces sent under Penn's naval and overall command to attack Spanish possessions in the West Indies (see *'For Hispagniola it is gon'* below). Committed to the Tower with Penn, he was relieved of all commands, but released after a month. Buller] ?Sir Richard, b. *c.* 1610, of High Offley, Staffordshire. Blague] ?Colonel Thomas, Gentleman of the King's Bedchamber, Royalist governor of Wallingford in 1640s. Askwe] Sir George Ascue (*c.* 1615–72), admiral in Parliamentarian navy, but without a command from 1652, perhaps because his loyalty was in doubt. Flag officer of White squadron in Four Days' Fight (1666): when his ship ran aground he became (and remains) the only flag officer in the Royal Navy ever to have surrendered in battle.

'For Hispagniola it is gon' 1] Hispaniola was attacked in April 1654, Venables's large force being repulsed with heavy losses, the only serious failure suffered by the Commonwealth forces. 2] Jamaica was taken by Venables in May 1654, but about half his surviving force of 7,000 died in the weeks that followed. 4. Coat Rawly] Quote Raleigh. Oranoak] Oronoco river, first explored by Raleigh in 1595 in search of El Dorado. The reference here is to his second expedition in 1617, which led to his son's death and his own execution. 8.1. *Finis coronat opus*] 'The end crowns the work'. Proverbial: Tilley, E116.

'Whither for th'Strayts or else Un-furld' 1. Strayts] Usually at this date the Straits of Gibraltar, but 'Hazard' (l. 5) suggests the Straits of Malacca, between Java and Sumatra: if so, this would be first recorded use (cf. *OED*, 1686 or 1689). 2. t'other world] The Americas. 4. Synonimaes] Synonyms. 8.1. *Qua pulchra difficillima*] '*What is beautiful is most difficult to get*' (cf. l. 6); Latin proverb, usually as '*Difficilia, quæ pulchra*'.

A Sonnet to my Mistress 1. May-erne] Punning on the name of Sir Theodore Turquette de Mayerne (1573–1655) chief physician to James I and Charles I. Fane employed him at various times in the 1640s: see e.g. W(A) Misc. 7, f. 7r, 29 April 1644: 'To Mal: for Docr Mayern 3-0-0'. 17. Labans will] Jacob worked for seven years for his uncle Laban in order that he could marry Rachel, Laban's daughter (Genesis 29). 19. wages] Genesis 30. 28: 'And he [Jacob] said, Appoint me thy wages, and I will give it.' 23. twice seavn] After the first seven years, Laban cheated Jacob by giving him his 'tender-eyed' elder daughter Leah in Rachel's place; he had to work another seven years for Rachel (Genesis 29. 23–30). 24.3. Cha[rles]: Le-de-Spe[nser] Fane's eldest son: both poem and signature are in Fane's hand, however, and the poem resembles others by him, not least in its puns. It seems likely that the poem is by him and not his son, who is not known to have written poetry. Mayerne had only one daughter who survived him, Elizabeth, who was engaged in 1649 to Lord Hastings (see *Upon the Death of the Lord Hastings*, p. 203). Hastings died (June 1649) on the eve of the wedding, and she married the 'Buffle headed Marquis' de Cugnac in 1652, but died in July 1653 (see *Letters of Dorothy Osborne*, ed. G. C. Moore Smith, 1928, p. 67; *DNB*). The idea of a match with Elizabeth must therefore belong to the period July 1649–52, when Charles was aged fourteen to seventeen, this poem being written by his father as part of the courtship. Charles did in fact wait 'twice seavn' years, marrying Elizabeth Nodes in 1665.

To my Mistres. La Debonaire *Title. La Debonaire*] 'Gracious', as opposed to *La Cruelle* of the companion poem. It is probable that these two poems were also addressed to Elizabeth Mayerne, the recipient of *A Sonnet to my Mistress*. 3. Currall] Coral.
'Candida perspicuo numerantur Lilia vitro' *Title*] '*White lilies are counted under clear glass*'. The Latin quatrain of which this is a translation is a modified version of Martial viii, 68, ll. 5–8.
To Her again *Title. Her*] Referring back to *To my Mistres. La Debonaire*, which originally came immediately before this poem in *F3*, the four lines of Martial and their translation being added later.
On Judg Ask *Title. Ask*] Richard Aske, judge of the Upper Bench (as the King's Bench was called 1649–60), first sat at Maidstone assizes 1652. The assizes of 1655 over which he presided opened two days after the date of this poem: see *Calendar of Assize Records: Kent Indictments 1649–59*, ed. J. S. Cockburn (1989), pp. 111, 194–214. *Margin*] Fane left Apethorpe for London and Mereworth on 8 March (W(A) Misc. 4, p. 103). 5. Profession . . . relates] 'The law is a ass' does not seem to have existed before *Oliver Twist*. 'K' probably refers to the law, maybe for 'King's Bench', precisely because it was not used, or for KC (King's Counsel), 'As[s]' to his nature.
Taken with Love of Adriana 9–11. Sun . . . over] Cf. *1H4*, 1. 2. 197–203. 28] Cf. John 4. 15: 'Sir, give me this water, that I thirst not, neither come hither to draw.'

N: MS Westmorland (A) 6.vi.3/26

Charles Darbyes Coppy taught English *Title. Charles Darbyes*] Charles Stanley, Earl of Derby (1628–72), son of Charlotte Stanley (see *Upon the Death of the Most Heroick and thrice Noble Princes*, p. 311), succeeded when his father was executed, 1651. A leading figure in Booth's rising (1659), he became Lord-lieutenant of Lancaster and Chester, 1660–72. Bearer of third sword at coronation 1661. He married (1650) Dorothea Helena, maid of honour to the Queen of Bohemia (his mother had been cousin of Frederick of Bohemia). *Coppy*] A poem, in this case presumably in Latin, by Derby: cf. *OED* s.v. *copy*, 7. taught English] Translated; a formula used by Fane when translating many of his own Latin verses. 6. Brittans Queen] Catharine of Braganza; see *Queen Katherine Landed at Portmouth in Hampshire*, p. 320, *Title* n. 10. Ioes] Greek and Latin 'Io!', cheer, shout of joy. 26. Gale] Regale, 'feast on the seas'. 48. Cretan Gierle] Diana, sister of Apollo (see l. 50). 49. Idea] Ida, mountain in the centre of Crete. 55. Dryopes] Tree nymphs, from Greek δρῦς, oak tree. 64. *Katern] 'Cathern' was a common seventeenth-century corruption of 'Catherine', but 'Katern', perhaps recalling medieval Latin *Katerina*, is not in *OED*. 68. Puttock] A kind of sail. 76. faun] As a verb, to fawn: give birth. 80. goulden sands] For Tagus's fabled gold, see *To the Suns accosting our Troppick*, p. 286, l. 13 n. 91. Titan] Helios, the sun.

Saxton's Atlas: Yale Center for British Art, Paul Mellon Collection: Christopher Saxton, Atlas of the Counties of England and Wales (1579)

'I am but Saxton and soe toule the Bell' *Title. Saxton*] Christopher Saxton (*c*. 1542–1611), mapmaker. This and the following poem are written by Fane into his copy of Saxton's pioneering *Atlas of the counties of England and Wales* (1579), now in the Yale Center for British Art, Paul Mellon Collection. 'Sexton' was often spelt 'saxton' in the Seventeenth Century. Cambden] William Camden, whose *Britannia* appeared in 1586; cf. *A Pepper-corn or small rent sent to my Lord Campden*, p. 277, l. 11. 4–6] In the 1607 edition of *Britannia*, which included county maps for the first time, Camden acknowledges his debt to Saxton. 8. Mercators] Gerard Mercator (Kramer), Flemish cartographer (1512–94), whose atlas, collecting his earlier maps, and surveying the known world rather than England and Wales, was published in the year of his death. An English edition appeared as *Historia Mundi, or Mercator's Atlas* in 1635.

The Soft and Just Support of Brittans Crown *Title*] Behold . . . *downe*] The poem refers to the portrait of Elizabeth which is the frontispiece to the collection of 35 maps of the English and Welsh counties. It is a close translation of the Latin verses set in two compartments at the bottom of the engraving, apparently utilising the couplet in the first compartment as a title. For nostalgia for the reign of 'Blest Elizabeth' in the mid-Seventeenth Century, cf. *By-Ward to some Cittisens entring the Tower* p. 121, ll. 35–44. . . . 6. bears the Bell] Comes first, leads the way.

Appendix 1

An Epitaph wrot by Sir William Davenant Long Since *Title*] Not in Davenant's *Shorter Poems*, nor found in other manuscript collections. Davenant wrote *c.* 1630 two cantos of a mock epic, *Jeffereidos, Or the Captivitie of Jeffery*, and promised 'a Third part' which was probably never written (*Shorter Poems*, pp. 37–43). Hudson (1619–82) was a dwarf presented by Buckingham to Henrietta Maria 'in a cold baked Pye' (Fuller, *Worthies* II, p. 244).   *Long Since*] The epitaph is obviously related to Davenant's longer mock-epic treatment of Hudson, and probably belongs to the same date.   7. Dunkerk Turky] Hudson had been captured, along with the Queen's midwife and dancing master, by Dunkirk pirates. Davenant elaborated this already unheroic episode by adding a fight between Hudson and a turkey, 'A Foule of spatious wing' (*Canto the second*, l. 50).

Jeffreides or Jeffery the Dwarfs answer   4] Davenant had lost his nose through syphilis.   8] Fuller says Hudson 'was, though a *Dwarf* no *Dastard*, a Captain of horse in the Kings Army in these late civil wars', and that in exile in France he killed 'Mr. Crofts' in a duel (*Worthies* II, p. 244).

Appendix 2

In Dom: D'Holl   Robert Rich (1590–1649) became Earl of Holland in September 1624. He was in Paris from February 1624 conducting negotiations for the marriage of Prince Charles and Henrietta Maria.

In H. M.   Probably Henry Marten, the regicide: see *For A Treaty*, p. 221, l. 4n, and p. 51.

De Comitessa Oxonien   Diana, daughter of William Cecil, second Earl of Exeter, and widow of Henry de Vere, eighteenth Earl of Oxford, who died 1625. She was a noted beauty, who brought de Vere (a bitter enemy of Buckingham) £30,000. She married 1629 Thomas Bruce, first Earl of Elgin.

Unto Sr. Thomas Roe chancellor of the guarter   Thomas Roe: see *A Pepper-corn or small rent sent to my Lord Campden*, p. 227, l. 98 n.

Ad Comiten de Clare Fratrem suum   John Holles (1595–1666), second Earl of Clare, Fane's brother-in-law.

Quid perficiet Homini. . . . Obedia Sedgwicks   Obadiah Sedgwick (*c.* 1600–58), Presbyterian chaplain to the Vere family. Accompanied Horatio Lord Vere to Netherlands, then lecturer at St Mildred's, Bread Street, Vicar of Coggeshall, Essex (presented by Earl of Warwick), and chaplain to Sir Denzil Holles (brother of the Earl of Clare). Became Vicar of St Paul's, Covent Garden, 1646 (?February 1645 O.S.).

Michelbourni Heptades ad Crispum   Edward Michelborne (1565–1626), fellow commoner of Gloucester Hall, Oxford. A Catholic from a Hampshire family, well known Oxford Latin poet in the early seventeenth century. See Appendix 1.

Ad P Pettum   Either Commissioner Peter Pett (1610–72) or his half-cousin Captain Phineas (1635–94). Cf. *Upon Prince Charles riding in the Downes*, p. 225, *Title*, n.

TEXTUAL COMMENTARY

Fulbeck Hall MS 1. Poems, 1621–35

An ode To N.B. an angler To N. B. an Angler. *OS.*   3. for] thus *F2*; so *OS.*   8. didst] did *F2*; 21–41] Not in *F2, OS.*   ***TheoD. Bezæ—Epigramma—In pontem Gardi***   2. bosted] bosteth *Vita.*   9. what's done admiration] admiration what's done] *Vita.*   ***A lecture to be mild in love***   21] *F1* does not have a verse break here.   ***La resverie or Loves Winter Seege***   5. single] flijng *F2.*   6. All quitt] All Usd to quitt *F2.*   20. darts] fiery darts *F2.*   23–30] *F1*; not in *F2.* In *F1 ll.* 1–22 are on *f. 79r, ll.* 23–30 on *f. 79v.* Fane may have failed to turn over the page while copying into *F2.* Although the catchword 'Sharp' is clear at the foot of *f. 79r,* he has made a diagonal cross after *l.* 22, his usual practice in *F1* to mark the end of a poem.

Fulbeck Hall MS 2. Poems, 1623–50

Brook House Bay trees   Occasioned by seeing a Walk of Bay-trees. *OS.*   4. Unleavd] Un'eav'd *OS.*   5] but though the winter's sharpe and keen *H.*   6. keep Green] keep him green *H.*   8.1] Comp. intermt&c Lon. / December 13. 1643 *H.*   ***Upon the Clock going too fast***   Upon a Clock. *OS.*   ***A Valentine for my Lord Savage***   This ed.; A Valentine for my Lo: S. *F2.*   For my Lo: Savage upon his conceipt of the rose & Lilly Crownd for Richmond & Lenox who was his Valentine. *F1,* dated London—1627.   12] To add a Luster to your Valentine *F1.*   ***A Hart Enamelld white to Nel. G***   Fama mendax *F1,* dated London—1627.   5. all] the *F1.*   ***De Imperatorum Julianorum***   2. like to] most like *OS.*   3. seekes] sought *OS.*   5. that] so *OS.*   ***The Tragecomedy of Mans Life***   Dated April: 1633 *F1.*   11. in] with *OS.*   12. doe] doth *OS.*   ***Vita Humana quid?***   12. ere] This ed; e're *F2.*   ***Horace: Ode: 10: Lib*** 2.   9. higher] This ed.; higer *F2.*   ***Horace: Ode: 9: Lib: 1:***   Horr: Ode—9   Lib—1 To My Lord Gerrard my Brother. *F1.*   10. lett] Led *F1.*   24. walk] This ed.; walk. *F2.*   ***Martial: Lib: 5: Epigram: 18***   To Quintianus. *OS.*   5. ill] fond *OS.*   7. would] doth *OS.*   9. Giveth] sendeth *OS.*   10. frend] friends *OS.*   proveth] seems more *OS.*   ***Martial: Lib: 10: Epigram: 47***   A happy Life. *OS.*   1. happy] *OS.* happ *F2.*   2. Are riches] Is substance *OS.*   4. that is never] always free from *OS.*   9. that's not] nothing *OS.*   14. sepulchred] buried   19. whatsoêre] whate're *OS.*   ***Pastor fido:***   Title covers the following two translations, and a Latin version. Italian text transcribed by Fane in left-hand column, facing the translations.   ***Martiall Lib—7. Epigram—38***   Upon Celius. *OS.*   6. gout] Gouty *OS.*   7. truth] falshood *OS.*   8. bands] swathes *OS.*   12. Celius's] *OS.*; Celiu's *F2.*   ***Horace Epod. 2***   This poem faintly crossed out in the same ink used to insert the following two poems at foot of this page (*MS p. 29*).   ***In adventum meum ad antiquos Lares Abthorpienses***   In readventum meum ad Antiquos Lares. *OS.*   1. Earth] the Earth *OS.*   4. day] Light *OS.*   hath] had *OS.*   5. soe] thus *OS.*   ***To Sir Jhon Wentworth upon his Curioseties***   40. Embrace and] Embracing *OS.*   49. Lifeguards] Lifeguard *OS.*   55. would] doth *OS.*   58. Meander-like] This ed.; Meander-like- *F2;* like Serpents are, *OS.*   60. ther] here   62. the] this *OS.*   76. that Looking-glas] each object new. *OS.*   84. were ... ten] more then nine, were ten *OS.*   88. Til] That *OS.*   91. Arras and] Arras, or *OS.*   98. with] in *OS.*   108. of] by *OS.*   ***De sene Veronense***   Of an Old Man. *OS.*   5. his] a *OS.*   8. lonely] homely *OS.*   11. that] man *OS.*   12. soldad] Souldier *OS.*   13. that ... horse] neither strife nor force, *OS.*   14] Of brabling Law-suits ever made him hoarse: *OS.*   16. declare] resolve *OS.*   18. Freer] free *OS.*   ***Epigram: Upon one Beal a minister***   Upon Beale a Minister. *H.*   ***Upon the King and Queens happy meeting again after an absence***   Upon the King and Queens meeting after long absence. *OS.*

14. Frute] Fruits *OS*. 16. Season] *OS omits*. 18. absence] parted *OS*. **Cloris Complaint—July-25.-1644.** *Chloris Complaint. OS*. 1. how-somere] howsoere *OS*. 5. Are] Seem *OS*. 12. his Assotiats] her associate *OS*. 20. 'ts] t's *OS*. 25. though] as *OS*. **Over the Chimny in the great Chamber at Merworth** *Virtus vera Nobilitas. OS*. **An Epitaph for Wimarke** *An Epitaph on E.W. OS*. 4. Wherof] Of which *F1*. chiefest] greatest *F1, OS*. 8.1 *OS adds Defessus est ambulando*. **In Histrionem quendam** *On a Player. OS*. *Dated 1626 London F1*. 4. Exit, bad] exite *F1*. 5. art] act'st *OS*. 8. a Lovers] the lovers *F1*. **In Obitum Ben: Jhons[on]** *Upon Ben. Jhons. death. F1*; In Obitum Ben. Johns. Poetæ eximii. *OS*. 11. Yet] Then *OS*. **He is not dead yet: but Dull** 4. truer] better *F1*. **A Letter sent to E.B. from Apthorpe to Howb[ury]** *To E.B. F1, dated April 1632*. 48. Fann.)] *This ed*.; Fann. *F2*. **A woollen night cap sent to the same** *A new years guift sent to the same—viz—a woollen night cap. F1, dated April 1632*. 18.1 *Le vostre &c:*] Your true frend / W. *F1*. **In praise of my Fidelia** *In praise of Fidelia*] *OS*. 2] With store of ordnance mand to fight *F1*. 9. prize] Price *OS*. 12. In my Fidelia I'le find more] I in Fidelia find much more *F1*. **Her Lading** 8. of] though *F1*. **My Fidelia with whom I had been cross the Street at Devotion** *My Ms: with whom I had lately been over the way in devotion opening her window & finding me reading in on opposite to it begins & I reply. F1, dated at London—1626*. **Amor non patitur Moras.** *Good counsaile to my backward Ms: F1, dated at London 1626*. 7. the] your *F1*. 8. faire] your *F1*. 11. fall'n ... ground's] once on th' earth's *F1*. **Sonnet Comparing Fid[elia] to the 4: Seasons** *Of my Ms: F1*. 5. its] her *F1*. 8. chirping] singing *F1*. 11. Now] & *F1*. 14. cause] make *F1*. **Sonnet: She is Fair and Verteous** 2. smutch't] smutch *F1*. 10. Brests make] neck makes *F1*. 13. bides] dwels *F1*. 15. is] bides *F1*. **Having suffered an absence from my Fidelia I am returnd** *An example by the 4 Elements upon a short absence from ones love—. F1, dated London—1626*. 10. been] *This ed*.; bee *F2*. 12. the] a *F1*. **Upon Fidelia only to be admired not drawn** *Untitled, dated Apth—1632 F1*. 20. limmets] end *overwritten*; toombe can *F1*. **Sonnet** *Untitled F1, dated 1626*. 2. Phebe's] Phæpe's *F1*. **Fidelias Title to the Empire of the World** *My Mses: title to the Empire of the world. F1, dated at Paris 1625* 17. Rich] Faire *deleted*; Faire *F1*. 17-18] *Lines supplied from F1; Fane has begun to revise the fair copy in F2, writing* The purple Violet for smell *for l. 17 but has left a space for l. 18*. 29. noe quier] noething *F1*. **To the County of Kent upon its condition at present—June-1-1644** *Upon the Country of Kent on it's condition at present June the 1 1644. H*. 2. Freequarter] Freequart *H*. 3–4] *Lines transposed in H*. 6. Welldon] weell don *H*. **Upon the Lady of my second adventure Verania** *An allay in love upon sticking at portiä. F1, dated at Mereworth—1626*. 16. bright] clear *F1*. **Upon the fairest Webb that Nature ever Spun** *Upon Ms: Webb. jnr F1*. 24.1] *Signed* W *F1, indicating a date after March 1629*. **Upon a fall which Ms. F: C: had from her horse hunting in my park** *Upon a fall which Ms: F. C had in the parke a hunting—. F1, dated 1632 at Apthorp*. 2. confidence] priviledg *F1*. 22. some] a *F1*. 26. whilst 'tis] yett a *F1*. 30. Coppies] shaddowes *F1*. *Poem followed by short version of La resverie or Loves Winter Seege: see p. 65*. **Epithal[amium] in Nup[ti]as: Sororum** *Epithal: Valen: F1, dated London 1631*. **The like in Medly for F.F.** *Poem followed in F2 by short version of An Ode to N.B. an Angler. See p. 59*. **A Caracter of Newmarket** *Dated 1633 in F1*. 10. White-] the *F1*. 11. some] they *F1*. 12. they] he *F1*. 13. Thus] And *F1*. 14. briny] boyling *F1*. 17. Calmes] Calme *F1*. **A Fishing Sea-Voyage from Lin to Boston** *So F1,which adds:* To myBro[the]rs the Lords Gerrard and Cope *dating the poem: 1633 at Sea*. 3. dark] darks *F1*. 7. Who] And *F1*. 33. might] did *F1*. 37. Which ... on] Casting a mourning weed upon *F1*. 41. rise] break *F1*. 42. some] a *F1*. 48. verse]—*F1*. **The Peake. ode** *My return out of the Peak forrest with incitement thither again. F1*. 6. t'think] *F1; illegible in F2*. **My Fox-hunting** *Dated Apthorp 1632 in F1*. 5. Fortune with a smile] smiling Fortune me *F1*. 10. all other birds] each other bird *F1*. 15. splendor] bewty *deleted*. bewty *F1*. 23. yet] but *F1*. 25. If we] Yet but *F1*. 33. Heer] Thear *F1*. 35. Phoebus (night-capt] *F1*. (Phoebus night-capt *F2*. **Upon his Majesties late jorny into Scotland** *Upon a Journey of His Majesty's into Scotland, and His safe Return. OS*. 11. themselves and] and seem *OS*. 16. in exile] as Exil'd *OS*. 18. through] o'r *OS*. 20] *OS adds two lines:* And so he doth enrich again our Sky, / Bringing those hopes unto maturity,'. 31. skye] world *OS*. 32. A ... Tyranny] Into a Winters Tyrannie t'be hurld *OS*. **The Basse** 26. Lord] *This ed*.; Lerd *F2*. **A Buck-hunting Jorny to Belvoyr** 30. Bull] *This ed*.; Bull *F2*. **To N.B. at Thorp** *To N B. for his Company. OS*. 0.1 Ned] Friend *OS*. **An Ode to N.B** 20. And] *This ed*.; An *F2*. 50. my Lyrick] the Mear *deleted*.

TEXTUAL COMMENTARY ❦ 451

51. [*Wittellsy*]] Wittellsy *deleted F2.*   53. I'le] i'le *F2.*   63. (A Place] A (Place *F1.*   *A sonnet upon a pretty Gierl her mothers darling*   Poem *originally followed by* Did I not deem't presumption in the haight (*see p. 95*) *later deleted.*   *Upon his Majesties return out of Scottland in November 1641* Upon King Charles return out of Scotland in November, 1641. *OS.*   12. With] Pleas'd with *OS.* *Epigram   Inter Acus et Aculeos pugna*   5. uncontrowlable] uncontrowlably *OS.*   11. tilt to] tilt: so *OS.*   *Upon newes of the first beating up the quarters at Leeds and Wakefield*   *Whole poem deleted in F2.*   *Upon the Suddain rise of my Cuntry Men and their defeat*   16. K.] Kent H.   17. note] Not in H.   *Anglia Hortus   Also in OS.   Epigram   Also in H.   The Scottish Pedlers turnd Merchants*   *Marg. notes not in H.*   *My Far-well to the Court—March-25-1644* My Farewell to the Court. *OS.*   24. faint] fond *OS.*   28–9. and . . . rude] or what ere / May stile it rude, because noe Cavalleer *deleted in F2.*   32. Her] its *OS.*   46. Purse] life *OS.*   *Upon the Babes of Grace*   19. 'tis] this 'ts *H.*   *In unitate Trinitas   OS has emblem above title: a triangle in a circle and across both the letters E S T.*   2 Be] For *OS.*   5. providence] prescience *OS.*   7. must] should *OS.*   9. that] our *OS.*   *Cæli enarrant Gloriam Dei—psal: 19*   2. Bartheme] Bartholome *F1;* *Bartime*? *OS.*   4. into a] in a could *F1;* into some *OS.*   9. thy] a *F1.*   14. that] which *OS.*   the Earths] on earth *OS.*   26. o' th' true] of the *F1.*   29. in] int' *OS.*   44. 'S Constraind] Is forc'd *OS.*   48. and] then *OS.*   *Following l. 48. OS adds:* For whilst the Face looks one way, and the Mind / Another, 'tis like Rain brought against the Wind.   49. Soe] Then *OS.*   *The Fallacy of the outward Man*   *OS; untitled in F2.*   2. with'] with th' *OS.*   4. He] it *OS.*   24. by His] let its *OS;*   Him] give *OS.*   25. His] this *OS.*   45. nor noe] grief nor *OS.*   49. make] mak'st *OS.*   *Contemplatio Diurna*   2. with'] ith' *OS.*   *Ut sit et cogitationibus Verbisque*   18. Soe] As *OS.*   20. The] My *OS.*   21. Chanoin] Canon *F1* (Postlike *deleted*); omitted in *OS.*   24. ever send forth] charged be *F1.*   27. fro' th] from th' *OS.*   29. let't] let *OS.*   *Annus annulus ex Diminutione Largimur*   Annus annulus &c. Diminutione Largimur. *OS.*   1. If] As *OS.*   3. w'anew] anew w' *OS.*   4. and] Old *OS.*   5. doe] doth *OS.*   9. was] came *OS.*   32. Betassel] Betasseling *OS.*   36. Fathers] Parents *OS.*   42. patient] bearing *OS.*   their] *omitted OS.*   *Cui in calamitatibus solo sit fidendum*   15–16. as't . . . die] as contrives / A nearness unto Death, yet with reprives. *OS.*   21. Yes if] Unless *OS.*   23. And rise] Rising *OS.*   25. powres at life] Power at life's *OS*   27–8. when . . . ground] then again, when Nature on't doth enter, / It is permitted for to wash the Center. *OS.*   29. they troubled that] such troubled as *OS.*   30. unto either] from side to *OS.*   *A Dedication to my Sonn Charles to Him that made him*   A Dedication of my first Son. *OS.*   4. frutes] fruit *OS.*   22. Nor] No *OS.*   25. thing is lacking] Blessing's wanting *OS.* *A Christmass Karroll sung—an—1634*   A Carroll. *OS.*   2. what . . . to] the blessed Tydings of the *OS.*   9. a] the *OS.*   17. Fin] Fiend *OS.*   21marg. Nicepharas] *Nicepho. OS.*   27. is't,] *OS;* ist? *F2.*   33. these] such *OS.*   34. make . . . a] dress thee up more stately *OS.*   39. thus] more *OS.*   48. or] and *OS.*   54. the] that *OS.*   55. shallt] maist *OS.*   *El Sembrador*   El Sembrador, or, the Sower. *OS.*   29. doth] can *OS.*   33. tag] end *OS.*   *Trium Gratiarum maxima charitas*   19. through] whose *OS.*   *Love begetts Fear*   1. I had] at first I had *OS.*   2. what] and what was *OS.*   3. blind] become blinde *OS.*   5. Soe] By which *OS.*   6. free] Mercy, free *OS.*   8. And soe eschew] That so I might avoid *OS.*   9. awakend] then row'sd up and wak'ned *OS.*   *My Penthouse against the storm of greif*   *OS adds: occasioned upon the Death of a dear Friend.*   8. And] Break clouds and *OS.*   10. sure] Confident *OS.*   11. Thou stil] My Gratious God *OS.*   12. I behould the] I the *OS.*   to] see *OS.*   13. With this assurance] Thus *OS.*   15. A Calm of] Th'assurance of a *OS.*   16. And that these] Wherein such *OS;*   all shall *omitted OS.*   17. I ride out them:] Patience-born; that *OS.*   *My Hand-kerchef to dry my eyes*   My handkerchief to dry my eyes after the loss of a most dear Friend. *OS.*   9. 'Tis . . . mercy] That *OS.*   11. Yet . . . what] 'Tis of meer Mercy, when for all *OS.*   *My Carroll sung upon Christmas Day—1637*   A Carroll. *OS.* 21. raise] t'raise *OS.*   *Easter Dayes Resurrexit composd 1640*   Easter Dayes Resurrexit. *OS.*   25. him] Man *OS*   42. nor] or *OS.*   48. Free again] Set as two lines in *OS.*   *My Charroll—1640* A Carroll. *OS.*   35. guard] guards *OS.*   29. H'] 'T *OS.*   39. And] Then *OS.*   *Upon St Stephens day—the same year*   On the Proto-Martyrs Death. *OS.*   1. b'] be *OS.*   *This is a true saijng and by all means worthy to be received*   This is a true saying, That Christ came, &c. *OS.*   *My reveille-Matin—to my wife*   A Reveille Mattin to my best Friend. *OS.*   29. for t'] to *OS.*   *My Carroll sunge upon Christmas day—1639*   A Carroll. *OS.*   4. thear] where *OS.*   20. Their] Its *OS.*   21. through] with *OS.*   22. Wee'r taught] We learn *OS.*   24. this] Him *OS.*   *A morning*

Fancy upon the Berth of my Sonn Mildmay A morning Fancy upon recovery from sickness, and the birth of a Son at the same time. *OS*. 7. distincticall] distinctiall *OS*. 11. is] was *OS*. 12. and] but *OS*. 27. I seek] it seeks *OS*. 28. through] by *OS*. ***My Figg Tree*** Sham'd by the Creature. *OS*. 11. comes] falls *OS*. 12. seed-time] Season *OS*. 15. Nature . . . soe] pregnant Nature doth so rule and *OS*. 16. truer] better *OS*. 21. before my frutes] for My Fruits, ere *OS*. 22. its] They *OS*. ***My Looking-Glass*** 4. and] or *OS*. 6. come] comes *OS*. 9. ugly*] horrid *OS*. 10. guilts] guilt- *OS*. ***My Charroll Sung—1641*** My Carroll. *OS*. **The attributes of true love** 11. That soe] As thus *OS*. 14. to] sit in *OS*; over] o're *OS*. ***My Reformation*** 7. in] for *OS*. 70. doe] so *OS*. ***My Invocation*** 6. the] again the *OS*. 7. What] Small *OS*. 11. in] of *OS*. 12. spring] fruitfull Spring *OS*. ***My Closs Committe*** 24. cause] t'cause *OS*;. t'march] March *OS*. ***In Natal:—1643.*** A Carroll. *OS*. ***They that sow in Tears shall reap in joy*** 2. the] by *OS*. 4. others, and] other grain; *OS*. ***Ascensus Gratiarum descensus Gratiarum.*** 21. And] Then *OS*. 22. Treasures] Bounties *OS*. ***Upon Easter day—1644: at Stifky*** Upon Easter day. *OS*. 12. serve] serves *OS*. 16. Requird] Requires *OS*. ***An Ode to Mr Waple a great Faulkner upon Prince Ruperts defeat*** Upon a Thanksgiving day for a Victory. *OS*. 20. die] go *OS*. 32. counts] deems *OS*. ***In Sanctam Cœnam Domini*** *OS* lacks marginalia. ***An Ode—upon the times*** Upon the Times. *OS*. 5. we] in words we *OS*. 15. that] who *OS*. ***The True Bread of Life*** 15. that from Ceres] *Ceres* from her *OS*. 23. on the] once on *OS*. 25. They'r] Those *OS*. 30. but] save *OS*. 33. one's] our *OS*. 34. to trust is] seems to trust *OS*. ***For Mr Conyers Darcy Quid Amabilius.*** *OS*. 14. Crave] seek *OS*. 16. the] that *OS*. ***A reveille-Matin Ode*** A Reveille Mattin, or Good morrow to a friend. *OS*. 19. that] then *OS*. 37. 'twer] if *OS*. 44. be destetute Himself] Himself be destitute *OS*. ***In Quadragesimam—1645*** In Quadragesimam. *OS*. 5. is] with's *OS*. 6. we . . . 'tis] why then we deem it *OS*. 12. Gesseron] *Iessuron*, 14. Baltashasser] *Balttashazzer's OS*. 21. 'less] unless *OS*. ***To Easter Day—1646: Ode*** To Easter Day. *OS*. 23. back on our selves] reflect, and back *OS*. 24. in each lamp one hath] either hath in's Lamp *OS*. ***Upon The great Mercy of God in the Deliverance from the Gunpowder Trason*** The Fift of November, being in Kent a stony Countrey. *OS*. 17. its . . . its] my . . . my *OS*. 18. its] my *OS*. 21. the . . . that] that . . . which *OS*. 23. Hatcht . . . Hel] Which Hatch'd below, *OS*. 29. every-one] all of them *OS*. ***Upon Mans Frailty*** To Man, on his frail Condition. *OS*. ***After a weekes sea voyage for pleasure*** My Observation at Sea. *OS*. 22. both] omitted *OS*. 26. of] of Mighty *OS*. 36. that] the *OS*. 44. Afore and Aff] Fore and abaff *OS*. 45. fix] fixt *OS*. ***The 5. Porches to Bethesda*** 3. needfull] sought for *OS*. ***Man Levens the Batch*** *OS* lacks marginalia. 1. makes] made *OS*. 5. nor] no *OS*. 11. He] man *OS*. 12. Man] He *OS*. ***Ode Occationed upon my sonn Veres sicknes*** To Kisse Gods Rod; occasioned upon a Childs Sickness. *OS*, which lacks marginal note. ***Occationd upon the Communion when it was a snowe*** A Hymm occasioned upon going to receive the blessed Sacrament when it was a snow. *OS*. 27. prove] *OS*; prove: F2. ***Upon Dives and Lazarus*** Upon the Rich Glutton, and Poor Begger. Parable. *OS*. 6. did] could *OS*. ***The contempt of this world raises the esteem of the other***] The Contempt of this World raises the Others Esteem. *OS*. 5. doe] should *OS*. our] the *OS*. ***Upon the Berth of my Sonn Henry*** Upon the birth of a Childe. *OS*. 3. Standing] Who stood *OS*. 8. stampt] stamp *OS*. ***Cordium Concordia vera*** Title. *OS*; untitled but headed by illustration in F2. ***To Mall*** To Improve Afflictions. *OS*. 2. should I learn that] would it teach Me *OS*. 3. Afflictions] th'Afflictions *OS*. ***Emblem Two Turtles billing and Death standing over them with a sithe redy to sever them*** Two Turtles billing and death with his Sithe over them, ready to make separation; *OS*. Fane has left a space of 1½ inches below the title, but has not drawn the emblem, nor does it appear in *OS*. 6. Her] Deaths *OS*. ***Amoris Sigillum*** 6. face and mind] Looks and Mindes *OS*. ***A quid retribuam*** 4. In] I'th' *OS*. 5. opned] open *OS*. 8. To] Int' *OS*. 13. praise] t'praise *OS*. 17. that] who *OS*. 20. o'recome] o'r-turn'd *OS*. 27. slack] short *OS*. 28. earth] here *OS*. ***Humiliation without Reformation*** Humiliation without Reformation, a foundation without a Building; Reformation without Humiliation, a Building without a foundation. *OS*. 3. therby] hereby *OS*. 8. whatsomever . . . they] whatsoever there those *OS*. 9. those] They *OS*. 11. they should] for to *OS*. 13. are . . . upon] seemingly cast on *OS*. ***Translation*** Used as a running title for this and succeeding versions of Psalms, with individual titles placed in the margins. ***Unus quisque sanctus Altare Domini*** To Man. Epig. *OS*. 4. promises squeesd] Promise once sent *OS*. 7–8] (A broaken . . . despise) not in *OS*. ***Poemata Quaedam Postnata*** used as running title ('Postnata' *alone on some pages) from p. 202 to p. 214.* **Mundus Vanitas** 2. unto] in of *F3.* 3. be Guilded nothings] Fond Guilded nothing *F3* (Fond *deleted F2*). 18. beware] be wary *F3.* 20. They . . . fall] Those rayse for greater fall *F3.* 22. shall reap Joy; first] reap Joy shall; here *F3.* **Upon occa[sion] of Mr Sharpes text in Great St Bartholmes** *Hoe evry one that Thirsteth &c: F3.* Mr. Sharp St Barth: 1649 *marginal note to title, F3.* 2] Comes heer] cometh *F3.* 13. chaffer] Barter *F3.* 24. that] who *F3* 26. may be] are full *F3.* **To My Cosen Mistress F.F.** 36. Frends] *This ed.* Frens *F2.* **Sola Bella che piace** 6. Improves] Improve *OS.* 7. And] For *OS.* 11–12] *Magnes amoris amor. OS, marginal n.* 14. Sphere] *OS.* Sher *F2.* 19. and] or *OS.*

NRO MS Westmorland (A) 6.vi.1. Poems and prose, 1643–51

In novi anni—1644 To New-years Day *OS*; 3–4. serpents . . . t'beginn] And if't be true, that every change of Skin / To th'creeping brood, doth a new age begin: *OS.* **Upon Sir Thomas Fayer-Fax** 13. Clowdes and] *This ed.*; Clowdes-& *N.* **Out of Martiall Ep.-21-Li-5** 3. vacant] *This ed.*; vacat *N.* 13. wench] *deleted in N.* **His answære to the Caroll** 23. Kettles] Basketts *deleted* 32. down] and *deleted.*

Houghton Library, Harvard: fMS Eng. 645. Poems, 1637–61

To Sir A W Clerk of the Kitt[chen] to K J Upon his well cookt Dish 3–4. which in . . . Kitchin] *Written as two abbreviations* w:^{ch} *and* Kitt ch: *with* in *common to both placed between the two lines.* **My Lottery** 9. t'other] *This ed.*; tother *H.* 74. 'thout] *This ed.*; thout *H.* **Upon New-Lights** 25. bends] *This ed.*; benns ?*H.* **16—December 1641** 12. mimicke] *This ed.*; minicke *H*; 13. Coppefide] *corr. H.*; Coppieide *H originally.* **To Northampton** 22. sphere] *This ed.*; shere *H.* **To Hugh Peters** 11. Sarmants] *This ed.*; ?Armatts *H.* **Upon Madam Severa** *Poem followed in H by* 'Upon the Country of Kent on it's condition at present June the 1 1644.' (see p. 97) *and* 'Upon the Sodaine rise of my Country men and their defeat by Colonel Mannering and Browne the woodmonger Juli-24-1643 at Tunbridge.' (see p. 126). **Upon the Petitionall rising in Kent June-1648** 10. a warrant] *This ed.*; aw arrant *H.* 12. King] Kent *overwritten H.* **To Captaine Minous after his returne the 9th time from the East Indes** *Title.* Minous] Minours *H. originally* 1. Minor] us *written above* or *as alternative ending. H.* 14. Minus] Minors *overwritten. Poem followed in H by* 'Upon the Babes of Grace or the Saints that seek for their portions in this world' (see p. 128). **A Summons to Frank Beumonts Gost upon reviving one of his owld playes** *Poem followed in H. by Epigram* 'The Jealous state with more then Argus eyes', *see p. 127.* **On the Mayor of Evsham** *Title.* Mayor] *This ed.*; Maior *H.* **Upon the Perfume Pembrooke left** 36. Chancelour] *This ed.*; Chacelour *H.* **Cambridge and Oxford** 11. least] *This ed.*; ceast *H.* **Upon Gutt A Greate Glutton** 24.1. out of Christendom] *added in F's hand.* **My Dream the 8 of September 1637** 15. whelps] *This ed.*; wheps *H.* 50. interpreters] *This ed.*; interpters *H, originally* interrupters 58. Joygn on.] *This ed.* Joygn on.* *H, but no revision related to asterisk.* 65. appeard.] *This ed.*; appeard.* *H, Fane's asterisk marking later insertion of* They loost ofe *in Fane's hand.* **Writ at the Campe at Birkes** *Title.* Birkes] Birikes *H. originally.* **To Capt Fra[nk] Court[u]p** 45. oft] *This ed.*; of't *H.* **To my Lady Kat[herine] Scot** 8. Scott, *This ed.*; Scott,: *H.* **Ad P.C.** 0.1.*when one*] *This ed.*; when, one *H.* 13. imply] *This ed.*; imploy *H.* **Upon my reaping Day the 28th of August 1648** *Title.* August] *This ed.*; Augusts *H.* 8. Since] *This ed.*; sine *H.* **A Letter to L.L. at Co. after A yeares absence from each other** 18. its] *This ed.*; it *H.* **Invited to exceed Limits** *Poem followed in H. by* 'Brook house bay trees' (see p. 70). **To the Countess of Exeter upon her brach Lemons whelping** 35. Doft] *This ed.*; D'oft *H.* **An Invitation to R.H: to change the Citty Life** 91. ho-mul-ho] *This ed.*; ho-mul ho- *H.* **To the same after return upon receipt of a second token of Toba[cco]** 4–7] *Inserted in margins.* **Upon Buck[ingham']s and his Duch[ess']s Visiting Apththorpe** 1. seven] ten whole *deleted H.* **A Pepper-corn or small rent sent to my Lord Campden** 65. what] w^t *H; Fowler reads* with, *but this is Fane's usual abbr. of* what.   122. He] He: *H, perhaps to indicate ellipsis.*   **In Rempublicam—1652**   2. become] *This ed.*; beome *H.*   **In partem Capitis vicessimi primi S[anc]ti Mathæi**   *Poem followed in H. by 'Upon that Noble Owld Captain Sir Foulk Hunkes his departure this life the 6.' of 9r 1657' (see p. 342).*   **To Will Martin after a Mischance by a fall**   *Followed in H. by four-page 'Index Libelli', pp. 183–6. The final three poems in the MS are copied on pp. 187–8.*

Fulbeck Hall MS 3. Poems, 1649–65

Sursum corda.   *Followed in F3 by: Mundus Vanitas. See p. 183.*   **Psal:108—Awake Lute and Harp I my self &c**   *Followed in F3 by: Hoe evry one that Thirsteth &c: see p. ••.*   **The best Meditation is that of Death**   5. Coast] Shore *deleted.*   **Coritanum Regio Vel Comitatus et Agris Darbiensis Descriptio**   *Title Agris . . . Descriptio] Ager Darbiensis Saxton's Atlas.*   2. Sowes Piggs] Great Sowes Saxton's *Atlas.*   4. Kindred] Genders Saxton's *Atlas.*   5. through] with Saxton's *Atlas.*   7. Inmost] Inward Saxton's *Atlas.*   **Post Script to the Voyage**   8. not] *This ed.*; no *F3.*   **To Prince Maurice**   17. *sung. wido's*] been a Querister w'in her *deleted.*   **To the Royall Fleet sent out of the Downes into Portugall**]   *Title. our Royal] our most Gratious & Royall   Vita Authoris.*   **Fullbeck**   51. *'thout*] 'th'out *F3.*   **The yong Protector unprotectd. May 1659**   3. When] W^ch *F3.*   **'To which his wiser Lady sayd'**   *Followed in F3 by A Flye that flew into his Mistresses Eye (see Appendix 1, p. 366).*   **Thorp Pallace a Miracle**   13. Cratippus represented] *added in margin in F3*; Heer as a Great Philosopher *F3 originally.*   35. such] *Written above* brave. *The latter is underlined, not deleted, but the deletion of* Soe *(for* As*) in l. 36 indicates that the final reading is* such.   **Of an Owld Hagg that desired Verses**   33. fell] *This ed.*; sell *F3.*   **'Sir: That to You I never fayle'.**   23. All] *This ed.*; (All *F3.*

NRO MS Westmorland (A) 6.vi.3/26

Charles Darbyes Coppy taught English   1, 17, 21, 22, 24. *Letters in square brackets. This ed., conjectural for letters where MS torn or water-damaged.*   79. Bandes] *this ed.*; Banes ?*MS.*

INDEX OF TITLES AND FIRST LINES

A Ballet 3: September 1658 249
A Ballet of Dedication of the new Academy 258
A Ballet To x.x.x. upon his pond on wittring heath 254
A Buck-hunting Jorny to Belvoyr 108
A Caracter of Newmarkt 102
A Carroll—in 47 180
A Carroll in 1648 182
A Christmas Carroll—1655 299
[A Christmas Carroll to the Earle of WestmoreLand] 202
A Christmass Karroll 136
A Crop of honor tis he reaps 225
A cursing the Civel warr waged in the flesh by the Divel 303
A Dedication to my Sonn Charles to Him that made him 135
A Dialogue between a Hunting Swayn and a Shepardes 274
A Dierge For Hasty Ginny 109
A Farcy 186
A Fishing Sea-Voyage from Lin to Boston 103
A game at Tables 214
A Garison? what else: dost thou not heere 218
A Good like man some did presage 309
A good morrow fancy. to E.H. 183
A Groat a day some one May-erne 353
A Hart Enamelld white to Nel. G. 71
A Holy-Day Thou wast, and art soe still 157
A Jorney into Norfolk 116
A lecture to be mild in love 64
A Letter sent to E.B. from Apthorpe to Howb[ury] 89
A Letter to L.L. at Co 239
A morning Fancy upon the Berth of my Sonn 146
A Morning Thought—may 10-1645 165
A Pepper-corn or small rent sent to my Lord Campden 277
A Posy upon a weeks absence from her 100
A quid retribuam 170
A reveille Matin Ode to C.E.H. 159
A Reveille Matin wrot at Copt Hall 298
A Riddle upon Tobacco 244
A Sonnet Pastorall between Coridon and Phillis 276
A Sonnet to my Mistress 353
A sonnet upon a pretty Gierl her mothers darling 115
A Sonnet upon the same Subject 344
A Sorrell Gray which you might guess a Bull 340
A Summons to Frank Beumonts Gost 224

A tinder-box for Ned: Beech[er] chafing at play 62
A Turner's raysd in Counsailes Rumps 245
A Valentine for my Lord Savage 70
A Voyage to Heavnly Canaan: 308
A woollen night cap sent to the same pour Les estresnes 90
A Yong Man that sought Heaven to Christ came 300
About a Government ther is much strife 342
Acrosti[ch] 329
Ad Geo: Fane: in commemorationem natalitij Reg. Car: 2^{di} 248
Ad P.C. 237
Ad Protectorem 272
Ad Quendam tam Potentia quam Intelligentia 169
Ad RemPubl[licam] Bel[lum] Civil[em] reparantem 243
Ad Scoto Brittannum 78
After a Dark and Dismall Night 326
After a weekes sea voyage for pleasure 163
All are solicitous who grounds possess 137
All night it raynes, but in the morn 58
All present good seems smal 77
All's common now since Comonwealths bere sway 291
All that is Commet like amongst the rout 120
Am I in Kent? and can I be noe more 162
Am I with any thoughts opprest 354
Amor non patitur Moras: Sonnet 93
Amoris Sigillum 170
An Answer to it 294
An Epigram upon His Highnes entertainment in the City 273
An Epitaph for Wimarke 88
An Epitaph on Sir Thomas Nicolson Knight 196
An Independents Coate Blazond 214
An invective against Gould 219
An invitation to my Askanius a true Trojan ifayth 257
An Invitation to R.H 58
An Invitation to R.H: to change the Citty Life for this in the Cuntry 261
An Oad sent into Scotland to a Frend by sea 121
An Ode sent into Scotland to a frend 119
An Ode to Mr Waple a great Faulkner upon Prince Ruperts defeat 156
An ode To N.B. an angler 59
An Ode to N.B. 113
An Ode—upon the times—February-20-1644 157
An Others will before thine owne commend 345
An owld man married a yong lass 62

456 ❧ INDEX

Anagram PROTECTOR 295
Anglia Hortus 126
Annus annulus ex Diminutione Largimur 133
A-Peace A-Peace whilst every one doth seeke 220
Are not the Spicy Indies whence all store 101
Are we asleep or doe we see 129
Are we awake, or doe our eyes 130
Arise Arise 148
Arts all will pine now honours must goe downe 214
As dark as pitch 207
As Frend to Death all byepast Merth and Jests 302
As I passt by the Downes 228
As in the Cuntry Parable it's found 153
As many men, soe many minds 260
As opposite as are the Poles 247
As Pricket ore the Course did trip 247
As the Black Curtain of the Night 159
As through Newmarket I passed of late 288
As two great fleets of potent neighbours strive 284
[*Ascend 3 Thrones Great Captain and Divine*] 293
Ascensus Gratiarum descensus Gratiarum 154
Astroites Lapides Belvi-Oris Inveniantur 315
Astronomers for to be easd 108
At Dover the   of June-1652 286
At Jameses putny theirs a hole to start in 239
At Kinton fight I sawe a pit 332
At Newmarket horse race 294
At Rising Chase not far from Lin 328
At the first Glimmering Dawn the morn sends forth 183
Awake dull Soule and from thy fowlde of Clay 136
Awake Lute and Harp I my Self &c\: 299
Awake mine eyes 180
Awake Thou best of sence 157

Be a thing true or false our Nature lies 144
Beal coming wher the Covenant was a guiving 82
Beaumont arise slumber no more in Clay 224
Before we hunt, what weather is't 348
Ben Jhonson Drunk 78
Best Architects whither in brick or ston 171
Be-vile as is thy Name now I have sworne 230
Bishop for up goes soe that game is done 216
Blest Privacy, Happy retreat, wherin 171
Born on the Twenty Ninth of may 334
Both Creame O'th'Poets and of Clergy He 293
Brave Captain though thine honor gaind increase 272
Bread is the Staff of Life, and Life's the Scoap 158
Bred in the Schoole of Mars he did appeer 342
Broad as thy Gates thy hart is Gray and 'twer 109
Brook House Bay trees 70
Brown bread a white neck would inferr 318

But fower teeth Elia had which Caughing shee 235
But just it is, Nature should coynes use 100
But must Frends part awhile? 265
But seek ye first the Kingdome of God 307
By-Ward to some Cittisens entring the Tower 121

Cæli enarrant Gloriam Dei—psal: 19 129
Call in your balletts all yea that reherse 98
Cambridge and Oxford 226
Can I be at home, and you the same 112
Candida perspicuo numerantur Lilia vitro 354
Carroll—1656 301
Cast crosse or Pile draw cutts that wee may see 212
Cast up in Letters 93 120
Catena Causarum ad Salutem pertinentium 166
'Cause these Sullen Spheres 121
Charles Darbyes Coppy taught English 358
Cheaters thy true name, cousnedg christend thee 62
Christ is the way and Heavn the Place of Bliss 298
Cloris Complaint—July-25-1644 87
Cogit amare Jecur 247
Come my Cordelia let's not Leese 267
Commissioners for the Irish affaires 232
Concordia Res Parvae Crescunt Discordiâ Maxima Dilabuntur 310
Contemplatio Diurna 132
Cope loves a Monke, Monke loves a Cope again 296
Cor mihi Carnale est Saxoso durius, adsit 154
Cor Mundum crea Mihi Deus 300
Cordis renovatio 154
Cordium Concordia vera 170
Coritanum Regio Vel Comitatus et Agris Darbiensis Descriptio 309
Corporis Anima Tutela 284
Could Chaucer Die and Spencer be forgott 315
Counsail and advice to a Frend how to make Could weather appeer warme 314
Courage my Lord: let not your fancy skan 211
Cui in calamitatibus solo sit fidendum 134
Cupid although a Child's 240
Cuss—Shall I tel with whom and wher 189

De Fœdere Nationale, February 1643 196
De Imperatorum Julianorum lineæ ultimo 71
De Maria Magdalena 168
De Quator magnam importantibus pacem 345
De Regulo 274
De sene Veronense 81
December once to May was married 62
Did I not deem't presumption in the haight 95
Did I proclaime thee dead before the time 88
Did that Chast Grecian Dame soe long to see 89
Dispos'd to merth and seasond by that time 116
Doe not the Planets (how-somere 87
Doe the fresh streams pay tribute to the Seas 284
Dos't thou not see how in one night 75

Doth Charles return to make our Climat shine 120
Drop down Thy Power 326
Dum Spiro Spero 339

Ease and Luxurious Appetite 190
Easter Dayes Resurrexit 141
Ebsom Well to Cuer sicknes—July-24-1645 190
El Sembrador 137
Emblem Two Turtles billing and Death standing over them 170
Epigram. 127
Epigram In Idem 217
Epigram on the Rump 245
Epigram on the times 220
Epigram Senes bis pueri 247
Epigram: Upon one Beal a minister that took the Covenant 82
Epilogue to the Dream 230
Epitaph of Sir Foulk Hunkes 342
Epithal[amium] in Nup[ti]as Sororu[m] uno eodemque tempore 99
Epithallamy 197
Erect thy nose, gape, shew thy teeth and this 77
Eucaristia 298
Eucharistia 299
Excuses all but bootless are 211

F. The L. M 242
Fair-Altar from whose Fabrick doth arise 331
Fair Shepardes why dost thou weep 274
Fallere fallentem non est Operosa Puellam 77
Far North if Fables lie not thear's a land 107
Farewell Deer ofspring of the lusty vine 91
Father why Innocent? when most men know 291
Fayre Mistress, lett's rejoyce and sing 77
Fayrer She is by much 348
Fayth I beleeve, and tis noe sin at all 211
Fear not my Soule. He that ordaind this food 299
Fear wayts on those who doe Loves stings approve 267
Fidelias Title to the Empire of the World 96
Fill me an Astrolabe with radiant sack 104
Foe to ill faces for thy truth, be free 148
For a Child born the Custom was to bring 307
For a Gentleman whose Mistresses name was Arabella 331
For A Treaty 221
For Hispaniola it is gon 353
For Mr Conyers Darcy 159
Fortunæ 313
Frank I Returne thy hounds with thanks 235
Frends, pray forbear: why Croude yea with such hast 121
Frendships Salamander to x. x. x. 272
Fullbeck 333

Get thee a Ship weel riggd and tight 92
Glasses Transparent Lillies white disclose 354
God both of Seas and Land 286

God made all thinges for good 166
God would his Saints should be bemond 161
Goe (fond deluder of our sences) find 127
Goe to the signe o'th'Hen and Cock 63
Grace before meat and after 210
Gratia 210
Great, and Good God of Justice, Love 151
Great Alexander makes the World appeer 200
Great God in whom all Justice raignes 132
Great master of the Roving Youth of toun 200
Greate Henderson the Scot is gon 217
Greece sung of Hills on Hills that heaped were 63

Had I Appelles pencell and Could Draw 234
Had not the Lord declard Himself for us 147
Happy is He who on his own fields stage 81
Happy is He whom from the right wayes Lawe 172
Hard harted man what canst thou say 173
Harry was Sick and Martin Lame 329
Ha'st th'e're markt the joyfull Spring 94
Have you observd the poysoning breath 226
Having suffered an absence from my Fidelia I am returnd 95
Hayle to that Floating wood 320
Hayle to that sylver hand 238
He a spare diet keeps and doth despise 350
He is not dead yet: but Dull: 88
He that made man without man will not now 157
He that would build, soe prove an Architect 185
He was not his Crafts Master that would bring 324
He who began from brick and lime 88
He who such strong lines wont compose 62
Hee beares partly per pale Atheisme and Turcisme 214
Hee is him selfe a beast or worsse 225
Hee is not out: but howlds up still one eye 227
Heer lies he was dide in Grain 252
Heer one is born, and thear an other dies 72
Hence warrs Beleaguer me, whilst Envy stands 175
Her Lading 93
Her lips to me are far more pretious 93
He's gon he's gon 301
High as the Sphere 298
His answære to the Caroll 202
Homo Vanitas 184
Honos alit Artes 214
Horace: Ode: 7: Lib: 4 74
Horace: Ode: 9: Lib: 1: 75
Horace: Ode: 10: Lib 2 73
Horace: Ode: 13: Lib: 3 73
Horace: Ode: 38: Lib: 1: 73
Horace Epod. 2 78
How are we tost in minde 304
How art disposd of Widdow say 101
How busied's man 152
How com'st about when Sisters are coheirs 226

How Cottens it now Charles is dead? 337
How doe the winds 276
How dull are They 104
How many Chances meet to dress 178
How miserable Men are 302
How shall we pass the Time away 336
How Time turnes up-side down and Fortune failes 126
How we fare if you would know 251
Hug Gross: Epigram to J. Douse of the Woad of Holland 209
Hugh 'twas a grosse mistake when men did call 220
Humiliation without Reformation is a foundation without a building 171

I am but Saxton and soe toule the Bell 362
I am not now soe much engag'd 339
I flow to make some Ebb and Ebb to fill 192
I hate the princely Sumptuousness 73
I hate the vulgar dietyes 242
I hope y'are Constant and not Gibe by Change 328
I must heere tell Sr. Robert Nanton 186
I shall not spare when I severa praise 221
I tooke for compagnion 61
I'le bring noe foreign Voyage on this stage 206
If all the span 149
If any one to reckon ore's Enclind 194
If David found it good He'd been in trouble 170
If Eagles shifting but their Bills have made 196
If I must needs discover 159
If it be a feathers praise 63
If nothing else 152
If one but anoint the sword 61
If Papist for their Ember fastinges merrit 61
If Piety to witt be put to schoole 291
If that this Rose had blown alone 70
If the year Serpent-like doth cast its skin 133
If ther be any Vertue left that can 154
In adventum meum ad antiquos Lares Abthorpienses 78
In Cardinalem Wolsæum 291
In Davidem Lapideum 70
In Diem Natalem etiam et Jejunalem—1644 157
In Domum Parlementi Alteram sive Novam 339
in eandem 63
In Effigiem Caroli 2di 194
In Effigiem Innocentij Decimi nunc Papæ—1652 291
In Effigiem Urbani Octavi Papæ præterit 291
In eundem Euro sufflante 78
In Eundem supra maneriam suam De want-age 232
In Fallacem Leguleium Epigramma 204
In Historiem quendam 88
In Jesuiticum Ordinem 319
In nasutum 77
In Natalem—1643 152
In Natalem—1649 153
In Nivem profundam et Gelu Frigidum 338

In novi anni—1644. Diem primum 196
In Obitum and transportationem per Wainsford Corporis 265
In Obitum Ben: Jhons[on] 88
In partem Capitis vicessimi primi S[anc]ti Mathæi 291
In Pascam 1652 285
In Peace, at home, in bed to die 332
In praise of my Fidelia 92
In Prayse of a Cuntry Life 319
In Quadragessimam—1645 160
In Rem publicam. Epigram 212
In Rempublicam—1652 291
In Sanctam Cænam Domini 157
In the first place when Day 298
In Time of Owld when smiling Fate 277
In Tricessimum Januarij Diem 312
In unitate Trinitas 129
Ingratetude's the worst of ill 277
Inter Acus et Aculeos pugna 120
Invited now to supp with Thee my God 167
Invited to exceed Limits 240
Is Cleveland dead? Could noe Rich Fancies Spell 335
Is it not fitt the mould and frame 135
Is Kent orercome? their enterprize dispatcht? 222
Is ther a Bright starr fallen from our Sphere 203
It alwaies in former times stood 219
It doth comend the stampe of every coyne 220
It is decreed, nor shall thy Fate O-Crom 295
It is not meant that three in One should be 170
It well becomes the glory of the press 240
It's allwayes held a signe of chang in weather 294

Jack would live Batchelour yet neds must wive 221
Jack Prick marcht in Northamton Toun 324
Janus 179

La resverie or Loves Winter Seege 65
Landed a shore: what follows now 'save Praiers 320
Laws-Sonn? I am mistaken: ther appeers 318
Le Monde Renversè 330
Least ther should want a Hallowed Tear 334
Lemon has whelpt O Joyfull newes 252
Lessianum 350
Let all rude Triumphs seace of Cesars Roome 273
Let Burley Sluggish Deities ore whom 115
Let Hollands Fleet no more be Feard 310
Let Men drink wine; for other living things 74
Let the Castalian well be overflown 312
Let us noe Longer now goe on 232
Lett not Arachnes Loome be namd 98
Levite Thou art aswell by Name 295
Like as the pregnant Morn distills its dew 301
Like Lillies when untouch they grow 71
Like medlers lockt up safe when they are gotten 222
Like Sestos to Abydos wher my faire 60

Like Ships by th'same wind favoured, yet can stear 82
Like streams that blend their currant silver, such 237
Like to that Tower whose Light the Seamen guides 196
Long whilst we pray and doubtfully would [brin]g 358
Lord in whose hand it is 305
Lord When the Casements of mine eyes 144
Lord:) sithence the best 140
Love begetts Fear 139
Loves Affirmative 241
Loves Negative 241

Madam: if All the Rhetorick were gon 318
Madam, if to your name you'ld add more land 102
Man is Bethesda and's five sences be 165
Man Levens the Batch 166
Man like a little world opens a pack 120
Man like a Ship by wind and weather tost 308
Mans hart lockt up within his secret Brest 170
Man's hart's soe linkt to sin wedded to vice 166
Mark but the Sluggerds shame, the Change 146
Mark heer what Sympothy is hatcht 292
Mark how each Apprehentions on the rack 283
Martial: Lib: 5: Epigram: 18 76
Martial: Lib: 10: Epigram: 47 76
Martialis Prophetizans 329
Martiall Lib—7. Epigram—38 77
Martiall. Lib. Epig: 77
Maurice coulst thou but Joygn 312
Me nive Cadente petijt mea Julia 58
Me nive cadente petijt mea Julia rebar 230
Meet we heer with cares and crosses 284
Might I enjoy my time with thee 200
Mine eyes Ember weekes fast 61
Minime dum parcant; Parcæ 99
Minor thy name alone goes lesse 223
Most Mercifull and Gratious Lord 306
Ms Urselye—alius Arslys Triumphs 192
Mun I that am thine, and thine all 211
Mundus Vanitas 183
Must Jewes come in 299
My adventure, or a new discovery under the Bear 104
My Carroll sung upon Christmas Day—1637 141
My Carroll sunge upon Christmas day—1639 146
My Charroll—1640 143
My Charroll sung—1641 148
My Closs Committe 152
My Cuntry Audit 171
My Dedicatory at the end of Beaumont and fletchers playes 240
My Dream the 8 of September 1637 228
My Far-well to the Court—March-25-1644 127
My Fidelia with whom I had been cross the Street at Devotion 93
My Figg Tree 147
My Fox-huntinge 105

My George were not the tie 257
My hand-kerchef to dry my eyes 140
My Invocation 151
My Looking-Glass 148
My Lottery 212
My neighbour though to satisfie desire 217
My Noble Holl 208
My Parler window doth descry 323
My Penthouse against the storm of greif 140
My Poole of Bethesda 164
My Reformation 149
My reveille-Matin—to my wife 144
My taking Phisick to cuer my lamenes 211
My tryall and araignment at loves second barr 111

Nature hath ore Affection soe much won 170
Nature lent time, soe He grew owld 88
Nec Sicca morte Tyranni 332
Ned Hide, how can I hide thy Offerings 317
Ned—might I sit 201
Newmarket is the scene wher evry on 102
Nights Curtain ope 103
No one might plead til he first swore to th' Crown 204
Noe Thunder Blasts Joves Plant, nor can 70
Noe tis not beauty must Confine 241
Noe wonder 'tis that man loves fights 250
Noe wonder 'twer though Schooles went doun 292
Nola the Bow Fair France the Arrow guave 319
Not at those Groves chast Cynthias worshipt in 105
Not drunk yet Drunk by People tain yet not 244
Not like the bird whose bewteous train 256
Not like the Gentler Spring whose purle-like dew 337
Nothing can Paralell that prizd delight 173
[Now Christmas comes] 202

O cruell Nimph fayre Adriana, how 355
O how the blasts 140
O how unconstand are thy wayes 313
O Lord thou art my Portion &c. 302
O sacred Fountaine, clearer farre 73
O the deceipt 176
O—ver This World He Conqueror is 329
Occationd upon the Communion when it was a snowe 167
Octavo Huic Miro Septem Miracula Cedent 342
Ode Occationed upon my sonn Veres sicknes 166
Ode: My Valedice to x x xr going to London may .5. 265
Ode—To a frend in Imitation of these 201
Of all the Divels wichcrafts ther is none 183
Of all the meate doth fatt increace 227
Of All the weapons I have read 316
Of an Owld Hagg that desired Verses 346
Of Man to W[illiam] Ar[mine] 250
On Broaken harted Altars Saints express 306
On Collonel Ed[ward] Pellam[s] death 301
On Good Friday—1659 304

On Hunting some, on Fowling Others muse 349
On Judg Ask 355
On King Cromwell 220
On Pembrokes Languishing Diseas 227
On the Mayor of Evsham 225
On the Philsopher who not apprehending 176
Optimus Thesaurus Cælestis 301
Our Husbandry must needs goe on 327
Our Life's a span 72
Out of Martiall 235
Out of Martiall Ep.-21-Li-5 200
Over the Chimny in the great Chamber at Merworth 87
Owld Olivers Gon Owld Olivers gon 249

Pass not bye but read and see 92
Peep but abroad when as the East wind's bowld 78
Phanaticks what are yea that thus swarme 313
Phillis fayr, and why soe Coy? 276
Philomelæ ac Citharædi Concertatio 339
Phylosophy may This averr 176
Poor-Sin-bound-Naked-Creature-Man nere knowes 170
Post Script to the Voyage 310
Post Tenebras Lux 326
Preces et LachrimæSanctorum Oblationes 306
Psal—1. Buchan[ani] Paraphra[sis] 172
Psal 114. Buchan[ani] Paraphra[sis] 173
Psal—120. Buchan[ani] Paraphra[sis] 175
Psal. 124 turnd into meeter 147
Psal—133. Buchan[ani] Paraphra[sis] 173
Psal—134. Buchan[ani] Paraphra[sis] 174
Psal 137. Buchan[ani] Paraphra[sis] 174
Pullin and Tompson spare your paines 274

Queen Katherine Landed at Portmouth in Hampshire the 14 day of May 1662: 320
Qui te fecit sine te non te salvabit sine te 157

Reader behold what past times did afford 210
Res is a harlot Publique's Common 212
Rides Charles i'th'Downes and doe wee warpe and wend 225
Ripe now for Man Mall yeilds to Loves fair charmes 343
Ripe now for man 115
Rivlett of Glass whose liquid Crystall can 199
Robd of my vessell by that PiRat fate 228
Robin for Poesy to a wedding ring 240
Robin if thou but kiss or sip 261
Robin—Like Copper guilded ore 202
Robin sithence I saw thee last 58
Robin two Peeces did request of Me 316
Rosseus Vaticinus 267

Sapiens Dominabitur Astris 321
Sapit qui sibi sa-pit 332
Seav'n wonders to this eight guive way 342
Senec[a] Agamem[non] 1. Chor[us] 176
Senec[a]: Hippolitus—4 Chor[us] 178

Sent to W. Cope when Monke came into England 296
Set the Cliff higher 141
Set up under the Gen[eral's] Picture at the Chang 293
Shall a new tyde of differences 243
Shall freindship wayn becaus the world goes less 239
Shall I commend a Rose 354
Shall we Leese Exiter and with Her all 264
Shall's treat what else for there in may be found 221
Sharp witted Will to occupy some land 287
She is sick 60
She wearieth the Starrs with Her sad Theam 168
Shrove Teusday—1654. when Fra[ncis] Palmes came 294
Sin-buried soule awake and rise 155
Since Lesser things with Greater may compare 333
Since Thou'rt come ofe an Other is Comd on 312
Since Truth breeds Hate Thou must not tak't amiss 274
Sir: That to You I never fayle 351
Sithence all endeavours to advancement move 127
Sithence faithless man 234
Sithence it is guiven 165
Sithence on Earth it is a Fate 93
Sithence that the Rebells now are ther 231
Sithence 'tis decreed, the path of death 109
Sithence 'tis the time when all alive 99
16—December, 1641 216
Skales fower times 3 ascend Arch Traitor Thou 294
Sleep no more, sleep no more 299
Snow falling Julia Me did press 230
Snow falling Julia some at me did throw 58
Snowes now are fled, and fields are deckt with flowers 74
Sola Bella che piace 193
Solatur se etsi Naturaliter Miserum 302
Some for their sport 269
Some Frends to make themselves and Others merry 192
Some Hunger after Riches, Honers some 336
Some may Aspire to sit in State, and ther 339
Some to the Lucrine Lake bequeath 254
Sonnet 95
Sonnet 269
Sonnet Comparing Fid[elia] to the 4: Seasons 94
Sonnet February: 1659 245
Sonnet: She is Fair and Verteous 94
Sonnet upon second amorous thoughts 110
Squier Palms to Apthorp Threshowlds welcome came 294
Stand foot stand my foot, least slipping thou'rt misled 78
Startled awake as if bespoak 197
Strike up the Horn-pipes play some Giggs 309

Sturbridg Fayer 308
Surely the God of love did him inspire 240
Sursum corda 298

*Taken with Love of Adriana His misfortune thus
    He bewailes* 355
Tel me fond Boy 110
Text:/ A new Commandment I guive unto you 305
Text:/ Labour not for the meat that Perisheth 305
That I some miracles may rowse 209
That in December, when guifts fly 76
That in Observance of the new-born year 90
That my Lord B. is yong who can't deny 232
That Number 'bove the rest 129
That the unhappy Nero might be said 71
That 'tis Well-don who is't that dares deny 199
That which creates a hapy life 76
The 5 Porches to Bethesda 165
The attributes of true love 149
The Basse 107
The best Meditation is that of Death 302
*The contempt of this world raises the esteem of the
    other* 169
The Cosmography of this County 219
The Covetous seek Riches, To that Man 301
The Cutt-Purses Faier 332
The English, Scottish Irish knit; increase 196
The Faire's Proclaimd, and evry Bulks Devise 308
The Fallacy of the outward Man 130
The Feilds, and Meads, and fleesy woods all three
    338
The Fox is dead, if subtilty with him 273
*The Genius and houshold Gods salute the little
    stream* 199
The Glory of a Forrest and Joves Tree 316
The guarden of the world wherin the Rose 126
The Heathen Poets in the dark could cry 113
The Heavens countles twinkling Eyes 95
The Humors of This Ile turnd Topsy-Turvy 330
The Invitiation's kind 307
The Ivy—twine 267
The Jealous State with more then Argus eyes 127
The kirk's a horse, the preacher sayd 68
The like in Medly for F.F 99
The Mart is Ope, the Prophet is The Crier 185
The Martiall Swed, with Lap, and Finland joyne
    65
The Martiall Turk, Grim Tartar both agree 310
The Merchant flyes ore Neptunes Plain 303
The newes from north blowes very rife 251
The North-West Passage 101
The North Wind 251
The Parliment sat soe long without head 209
The Peake. ode 104
The Pedegree of Bay Wastnes 231
The Planets whilst they move in severall Sphears
    106
The Princely Prophet statued heer doth stand 70
The Prologue to the Dream 228
The Rose and Thistle overcome 334
The Rump 252

The Savoy—Excetter house 1626 60
The Scepter Shall not depart from Juda 299
The Scepters gon the Law's fullfilld 299
The Scottish Pedlers turnd Merchants 127
The second part to the same tune 270
The Spring tide thus doth Earth repaier 78
The Sun declin'd and taking leav of Day 339
The Swifter lying wheel ore-runs the day 70
The thankfull Soyle manurd and winter-drest
    147
The Times Steerage 82
The Tragecomedy of Mans Life 72
The True Bread of Life—Jhon-6-48: 158
The Various Canes from Severall parts are
    brought 351
The wellcome Showers of Aprills morning dew
    86
The Western Skye 101
The winter fierce with Could doth rage and
    blowe 338
The woods and seas at odds 344
The word of Kindnes: how I doe 345
The Yong man and Christ 300
The yong Protector unprotectd 335
TheoD Bezæ—Epigramma—In pontem Gardi 63
Ther was a certain mighty Rich man had 168
These Astroite Stones, on Belvoyr Coasts appeer
    315
These Hills are Pregnant, and when brought a
    bed 309
These seven dayes I last did pass 271
They are true kisses where with mutuall gaine 77
They that sow in Tears shall reap in joy 153
They w'r of Dewcalions race could b'of noe other
    144
Things that would frame a Life to pleas 346
This fiv't of November 281
*This is a true saying and by all means worthy to be
    received* 144
This life when at the best 350
This may suffize 270
This sonn of Amram soon as born did find 168
This Tarrace turnd to Rubbedge doth express
    274
Thorp Pallace a Miracle 341
Those Labour more for Plentious bords 305
Thou art a witty Man, nor's every one 169
Thou feedst on Bakon I admire 318
Thou may'st live happy, if thy minde 73
Thou Rich-art t'whom Succession brings 334
Thou soon takst fier poor Ned 62
Thou that dost cast into the silver brooke 59
Thou that soe oft in jest wast wont to die 88
Though Childing women may oft long for this
    256
Though Every thing we see or heer may raise 163
Though Munks assume what Powers They will
    245
Though thy pretences may for fair stand 221
3. Graces 211
Thrice as the antient Roma'n stories skoar 182

Thrice happy he who voyd of Care 78
Thrice wet in Greef, how coms't about 311
Thrift, how applid I leave to Judge 233
Thus have I seen the Earth when the rude plowgh 95
Time hath its Seasons. Soe hath Love 266
'Tis but a folly to be nice 193
'Tis happily resolvd (Faier Star) to cast 343
'Tis noe hard Task to cheat a Cosning Lass 77
To a frend from Apthorp in a great Snow 251
To a frend in the City 345
To a Frend upon my Pallace and habitation 325
To a Glass of wine set before one 175
To a P.K: that sent to me for 2 Peeces 316
To Capt Fra[nk] Court[u]p A Huntsman 232
To Captaine Minous 223
To Cleveland before the first interview at maneby 256
To David Earle of Exeter 115
To Docter Brown a Phisitian maried to Mistress South 318
To Easter Day—1646: Ode 161
To Fayre Mrs Doll Peckam 234
To Fran[k] Coortup 235
To H.T. into Nor[folk] 208
To Her again. La Cruelle 354
To Him again in return for a letter he wrot upon the former 256
To his Mistress 58
To Hugh Peters 220
To invite my Lord to walke in the Tower 225
To Julius Martiall 346
To Justefy themselves three wisemen came 183
To Leucone inviting to cherish pleasure and omitt care for the future 347
To Mall 170
To man an Epigram 173
To Mistress Mary Fair fax sayd to be married to the Duke of Buckingham 343
To Morice Upon Sir Francis Comptons marrying 312
To Mr Anthony Hungerford 336
To Mr Levite of Ashwell of that Tribe too 295
To Mr T.T 236
To My Cosen Mistress F.F 189
To my Cosen T.F. 318
To my Frend Mun: gon to London to play at Tennice 211
To my frend Sir William Davenant upon his Opera called the Seege of Roads 315
To my Lady Kat[herine] Scot 234
To my Lord of Portland for a nights Lodging 277
To my Mistres. La Debonaire 354
To my Neph[ew] Gerr[ard] 328
To my sonn Bill upon his Entertainment at Canewood 351
To my Sonn Charles in prayse of Horsemanship 349
To my Tutors Ghost Doctor Travers: 322
To my very noble Cosen the Earl of Stanford 109
To N.B. at Thorp 112
To Northampton 218
To Phi: Wood upon my Lady x x x going To London 264
To Phil: Wood at London 266
To Prince Maurice 312
To Quintillian 200
To R.H. with some Venison 61
To Rob[in] Oliver after his coming ofe from his troubles 237
To Robin Brudnell Keeper of the Red Deer Park 343
To Sir A W Clerk of the Kitt[chen] to K J 210
To Sir Abram Williams upon his Barge Call'd the unthrift 233
To Sir F.F: neer Darby Shire upon Prince Rupert 309
To Sir Jhon Wentworth upon his Curioseties 79
To Sir Thomas Fairfax 221
To the Countess of Exeter upon her brach Lemons whelping 252
To The countess of Ruttland upon Her New reedefying of Belvoir 330
To the County of Kent upon its condition 97
To the Highly approved Statesman . . . Sir Edward Hide now Earle of Clarington 317
To the Impudency of Monsieur de Militiere 294
To the Markiones of Newcastle upon her book of Orations 318
To the Noble paier of kinsmen the two Edward Mountaques 343
To the People of England—June-5-1659 328
To the Royall Fleet sent out of the Downes into Portugall to fetch home our Royall Queen Katherin 320
To the same after return upon receipt of a second token of Toba[cco] 267
To the Society of Phanaticks or more truly Jesuits 313
To the Suns accosting our Troppick 286
To welcome home Veronia 245
To which his wiser Lady sayd 341
To Will Martin after a Mischance by a fall 295
Tom C: hath been in Italy and swears 252
Trium Gratiarum maxima charitas 138
Triumphant Passover Divine 285
True Victory on Fames winges taught 156
Trust not too much thy flattring Bland but know 204
'Twas not in vaine the Antients all 244
'Twas of thy goodnes (Lord) I had 139
Two Daughters' Portians gon, and spent 71
Two Seafaring men invoak the Springs return 276
Two Tees may poynt Tawtology 236
Two various factions of the present time 231

Unconquered Coast: whilst all thy neighbours be 97
Under what Planet in what clime 248
Unto a Lady: that refus'd her amorous Knight his Aproaches for him 230
Unto his Sonn the Lord Richard Crumwell chosen Protector 334

INDEX 463

Upon 29th of may Di[es] nat[ivitatis] Carol[i] 334
Upon a blessed shower from heaven after a drowth 284
Upon a chip of the Royall Oak sent me by a frend 316
Upon a course in the padock 247
Upon a Coyne Stamp't at Newarke 192
Upon a fall which Ms. F:C: had 98
Upon a fine Shower that fel on the 16th of Aprill-1660 326
Upon a Gent: calld F.F. and his Kittling 292
Upon a hunting match defeated by wett weather 348
Upon a mischance or fall 207
Upon a Rumor of a Generall rising 328
Upon a small occation of 10,000£s disburcementraptim 71
Upon a time it did befall 293
Upon a Very fayer Lass 348
Upon a very wett St Stephens day 1647 161
Upon account it's understood 247
Upon an Eclips of the Sun the 29th of march-1652 283
Upon an Escheater a Knave that bought the place 62
Upon Ben Jonsons Playes calld his workes 240
Upon Breaking the Seals 223
Upon Buck[ingham']s and his Duch[ess']s Visiting Apthorpe 271
Upon Candlemas day or the Purification—1664: 307
Upon Dabbling or Fishing 260
Upon Dives and Lazarus 168
Upon Doctor Crafts his Sermon at Court the 24th of June-1660 324
Upon Easter day—1644: at Stifky 155
Upon Fidelia only to be admired not drawn 95
Upon George Munks routing the Rump &c 327
Upon Good Friday 284
Upon Gutt A Greate Glutton 227
Upon his Majesties late jorny into Scotland 106
Upon His Majesties resolution to Dissolve the Parlement 320
Upon his Majesties return out of Scottland in November 1641 120
Upon immoderat Rayne falling a little before the Funerall day of O: 334
Upon Jack Prick at North[ampton] 324
Upon Jack, Tom, Will, and Dick 221
Upon James Martins house at puttny being robd 239
Upon Lamb[er]ts repo[rted] to be Gen[eral] 244
Upon Madam Severa 221
Upon Madam Severa and her Gierle Friskin 222
Upon Mans Frailty 163
Upon Master Alexander Henderson's Death 217
Upon min Hostes Bland at Tousester 204
Upon Moses put yong to sea 168
Upon Ms. B West Widdow to the Lord Darceay 102
Upon my falling Lame under suspition of the Gout 211
Upon my Fidelias Toomb 92
Upon my reaping Day the 28th of August 1648 238
Upon my Sonn Charles return 284
Upon newes of the first beating up the quarters at Leeds and Wakefield 120
Upon New-Lights 215
Upon occa[sion] of Mr Sharpes text 185
Upon occation of a Sermon 185
Upon our Lady's Day or The Anuntiation—1652 282
Upon Owld Char[les] Cotton who died in December 58 337
Upon Prince Charles riding in the Downes 225
Upon Sir Anthonies incomparable peece 199
Upon Sir Jhon Lawsons Eminent Services in the Levant 318
Upon Sir Jhon Prettimans Change in Fortunes 309
Upon Sir Thomas Fayer-Fax 200
Upon St Stephens day—the same year 144
Upon suspition of the Gout to Doctor Bowles 292
Upon taking up of Severall Persons of Honer and quallety 337
Upon the Babes of Grace or the Saints 128
Upon the Berth of my Sonn Henry 169
Upon the Castle in the Ayer and Bower of Bliss 268
Upon the Chimny Act 316
Upon the Clock going too fast 70
Upon the Death of his Excellency Thomas Earle of Cardigan 314
Upon the Death of Mr Jhon Selden the great Antiquary—1654 293
Upon the Death of My Fidelia 91
Upon the death of my Good nag: Fox 273
Upon the Death of Oliver Crumwell Lord Protector 334
Upon the Death of our late famous English Orator and Poet Jhon Cleveland 335
Upon the Death of the Lord Hastings 203
Upon the Death of the Most Heroick and thrice Noble Princes the Owld Countess of Darby 311
Upon the Extream winters Cowld and hopes of a future Spring 338
Upon the fairest Webb that Nature ever Spun 98
Upon the Generall the Lord Fairfaxes resigning 247
Upon The great Mercy of God in the Deliverance from the Gunpowder Trason 162
Upon the Heroike Lady the Markiones of Newcastle 316
Upon the History of Great Brittan by Willson 293
Upon the horse race at Newmarket 288
Upon the Immoderat Use of Pastime 336
Upon the King and Queens happy meeting again 86
Upon the Lady Margaret Marchioness of Newcastle 292
Upon the Lady of my second adventure Verania 97
Upon the little parler Garden at Merewoth 323
Upon the Lord Gray of Grooby 340
Upon the names of her various sutors 101
Upon the Perfume Pembrooke left 226
Upon the Petitionall rising in Kent June-1648 222

Upon the Rebells assault upon the Cass of Lough Gear 231
Upon the rumor of his departure though faigned 252
Upon the Scotch Sermon 68
Upon the Scotsh business—1638 230
Upon the speakers of either houses leveing their charges 209
Upon the State of England at Present—July-12-1659 342
Upon the Strange adventure and memorable voyage of Prince Tomaso 206
Upon the Suddain rise of my Cuntry Men 126
Upon William Sharp a Colliers' ploughing the Moulhill 287
Use and Memory Parents to Wisedome 161
Use out of date and to Remember 161
Ut sit et cogitationibus Verbisque 132

Veritas Odium parit 274
Vina bibant homines, animantia cætera fontes 74
Vita Humana quid? 72

Was all the world by Cesar taxt to know 146
Wash and be clean, Eat, Drink This, and 'twill save 157
Waygh: and lett wind ore Cloth prevaile 237
We call that patience, when provoakt we can 149
We sayd when Symon Dews subscribd to Fate 293
Welcome faier Season that dost bless 245
Well mayst thou be Crum; but Crum-Well 335
Well you wound, and sick you Kill 60
Wellcome Blest day wheron 161
Wellcome wellcome Glorious light 286
Were We some Owld Precept Enjoygnd 305
What at your prayrs again? B: It is most true 93
What breath the dampe 100
What doe we call those silent Howers which 97
What doth He gett whoe're preferrs 87
What doth she seek? a verse of prayse? 346
What doth the red and doughtfull sett portend 101
What ever Cole or wood afford 316
What ever Gods Divine 166
What ist thou wonderst at soe much? to see 265
What Permanence to Earth or Clay is due 163
What pride of humor doth my feet command 292
What Profiteth it a Man to Gain the whol world 303
What shall I say? when Each String Jarrs 321
What thou shouldst doe whilst Phebus hides his Rayes 314
What though't be Could and freez 143
What truths expectable truth to expound 215
What various stories men invent 258
What wonder ist the King to th'Scots is fled 78
What would the Season now inferr 179
When a great Kings Court doth recorded stand 293
When all perfections prove 138
When all the Dayes w'have borrowd are mispent 160
When all the Vertue we can Heer put on 169
When Children would goe, or Cripples stand 164
When first the towring Hills the Loftier Pine 134
When first upon my East-star I did looke 230
When I (O Lord) Thy mercies skan 169
When Infants first into the world doe come 247
When Israells lookes all homeward bent did stand 173
When Neptune's ploughd and Earths turnd Liquid 186
When our white Linnen's staind with bloud 300
When Phebus quitts his watry Bed 96
When Skillfull Gunners ayme a Mark to hit 322
When the eternall hand of love 284
When This world seems to court me with a smile 184
When thou the choise of natures welth hast scand 79
When towrds Jerusalem our Saviour went 291
When we a Gemm or pretious ston have lost 141
When we behowld the Morning Dewe 132
When wonder struck, Amazement ceasd 153
Wher I abide, or whither Fled 325
Wher Troy once stood (some say) now Corne doth growe 330
Whilst all the world is on a flame 272
Whilst all those Lords and Commons heads ere round 232
Whilst Celius can noe longer hear 77
Whilst far from home with sadnes overprest 174
Whilst I desier your frendships understood 267
Whilst Laicks glory in descent of Blood 291
Whilst many a True man felt the Fate 332
Whilst Nature doubts which sex thou'rt best to wear 77
Whilst 'neath sad warr All Nations wearied Lie 362
Whilst Newarke lay beseig'd twas nothing strange 192
Whilst policy doth thus provide 223
Whilst some delight 268
Whilst that in bleating flocks of snow 64
Whilst Thou dost fright the Sea God with thy Armes 343
Whilst Thou'rt my Portion, what's all this worlds pleasure 302
Whilst wee play Rebells all at Levelcoyle 214
Whither amend you wicked Lust 303
Whither for th'Strayts or else Un-furld 353
Whither O wicked Brood do'yea run 328
Who ist that Rides our Circuit? Ask 355
Who so desiers, that, earnestly to see 341
Who so Enjoyes the Cuntry Ayer 319
Why art thou set heer to surprise 175
Why did not some when first I undertook 111
Why do we stile Those workes which wer but Playes 240

Why doe wee Lay the blame to that or this 219
Why is sleaved Silk soe hard 94
Why ist we seek from Room to roav soe far 128
Why should thy Triumphs flourish which are vayn 294
Will-though Mischance hath made thee lame 295
William Martin Anagram 274
Wisedom is Justefied of her Children 183
With what Laborious Care and studied Paines 282
Without an interposing Sea or wall 230
Wouldst thou informed be 347

Woulst thou enquir heer passing bye 314
Writ at the Campe at Birkes 231
Wrot at Mereworth June-9-1661 306
Wrot at Raynam June-23-1659 305
Wrot the 5ᵗ of November-1657 281

Yea servants of the Lord that can enstile 174
Yes, wher less Virtue shines 241
Yong Puppie sonne to owld 231
You see your Senate on their Insteps stand 320
You that Ar-mine 119

Χαλεπα τα καλα ἐστιυ 100

EU authorised representative for GPSR:
Easy Access System Europe, Mustamäe tee 50,
10621 Tallinn, Estonia
gpsr.requests@easproject.com

www.ingramcontent.com/pod-product-compliance
Ingram Content Group UK Ltd.
Pitfield, Milton Keynes, MK11 3LW, UK
UKHW021839210426
5322IPUK00021B/367